Introduction to Waste Management

Introduction to Waste Management

A Textbook

Syed E. Hasan
University of Missouri-Kansas City, Kansas City, Missouri, USA

This edition first published 2022
© 2022 John Wiley & Sons Ltd

Registered Offices
John Wiley & Sons, Inc., 111 River Street, Hoboken, NJ 07030, USA
John Wiley & Sons Ltd, The Atrium, Southern Gate, Chichester, West Sussex, PO19 8SQ, UK

Editorial Office
9600 Garsington Road, Oxford, OX4 2DQ, UK

For details of our global editorial offices, customer services, and more information about Wiley products visit us at www.wiley.com.

Wiley also publishes its books in a variety of electronic formats and by print-on-demand. Some content that appears in standard print versions of this book may not be available in other formats.

Library of Congress Cataloging-in-Publication Data

Names: Hasan, Syed E.- author.
Title: Introduction to waste management : a textbook / Syed E. Hasan.
Description: First edition. | Hoboken, NJ : Wiley, 2022. |
    Includes bibliographical references and index.
Identifiers: LCCN 2021062790 (print) | LCCN 2021062791 (ebook) | ISBN
    9781119433934 (paperback) | ISBN 9781119433958 (adobe pdf) | ISBN
    9781119433972 (epub)
Subjects: LCSH: Refuse and refuse disposal–Textbooks.
Classification: LCC TD791 .H375 2022 (print) | LCC TD791 (ebook) | DDC
    363.72/8–dc23/eng/20220330
LC record available at https://lccn.loc.gov/2021062790
LC ebook record available at https://lccn.loc.gov/2021062791

Cover Design: Wiley
Cover Image: © Lightspring/Shutterstock

Set in 9.5/12.5pt STIXTwoText by SPi Global, Pondicherry, India

SKY10035491_072822

In loving memory of my parents who instilled in me the value of honesty, integrity, and hard work.

—Syed E. Hasan

Contents

Foreword

The seventeen Sustainable Development Goals (SDGs) established by the United Nations Environmental Program in 2015, were bold, visionary, and aimed at achieving a sustainable future for humanity, underpinned by environmental preservation. To translate the 17 SDGs into measurable actions, 25 performance indicators were developed that aimed at eliminating hunger, reducing inequalities, and building sustainable communities across the globe. These indicators cover topics related to resource management and protection of biological, marine, and terrestrial ecosystems; circular economy, and environmentally sound management of chemicals and waste, with the latter being the key element in all. Given the increase in the magnitude and frequency of natural disasters exacerbated by climate change, it is imperative that these goals be incorporated into all sectors of human endeavors. For the academia, it means restructuring the traditional curriculum–utilizing appropriate materials spanning several disciplines–to develop a balanced program, with sustainability at its core, to prepare the future work force.

At the University of Missouri-Kansas City (UMKC), we have taken a bold step to integrate key disciplines having a direct bearing on environmental issues. A single functional unit, named Natural & Built Environment, brings the faculty of architecture, urban planning, civil engineering, and earth and environmental sciences under one administrative and academic unit. These disciplines are closely tied to infrastructure, environment, and sustainability and have a direct influence on the workforce needed to implement the United Nations 17 SDGs. This combination provides unique, broad and deep, multidisciplinary educational, research, and civic (social) learning experiences; thereby creating a new type of sustainability-engaged and focused workforce and researchers. Consolidation of these disciplines that have traditionally conducted individualized research and teaching in a variety of environmental topics, will enable us, as educators, mentors, and researchers, to maximize the synergy of creative minds, academicians and students, leading to the development of new ideas and advanced technologies, supported by solid science and engineering; thereby offering novel and cost-effective solutions to environmental problems.

Introduction to Waste Management is authored by Dr. Syed E. Hasan, an acclaimed expert in the field of waste management. His comprehensive grasp of conventional and emerging waste issues has resulted not only in a masterful treatment of solid, hazardous, medical, nuclear, and electronic wastes, but also the rarely discussed airplane and ship wastes. The ship breaking industry, which is mainly concentrated in the developing south Asian countries, has been threatening the marine ecosystems and adversely impacting workers' health for many years. The author has drawn attention to these issues in this book and emphasized the need for strict and forceful implementation of the international and national laws. In addition, the inclusion of COVID-19 related medical waste is very timely as the lessons learned will serve in better management of medical waste due to the anticipated upsurge in occurrences of zoonosis, causing marked increase in both the severity and duration of future epidemics/pandemics. The aging human population in developed countries along with provision of better healthcare in developing countries, will result in complex medical therapies and larger quantities of medical waste that would require safe and efficient waste management technologies. The chapter on pharmaceuticals and personal care products addresses this critical issue.

The book is a solid contribution to waste management literature with the distinction of being the first textbook to include emerging types of wastes that have received little or no attention so far. *Introduction to Waste Management* will serve as a valuable initiation to students and practioners to the field of waste management.

Kevin Z. Truman, PhD; F.ASCE
Dean, School of Science & Engineering
University of Missouri-Kansas City
1 July 2022

Preface

Waste is a universal issue that transcends the boundary of space and time. It concerns people all over the world in all countries, both poor and rich. Concern for proper waste management goes as far back as 500 BCE when the city of Athens, Greece, issued a decree prohibiting garbage dumping on the street and required its citizens to dispose of their waste at least one mile away from the city walls. In modern time, waste management has evolved from being a dirty business to an essential service in a civic society and is considered an indispensable component of a community's infrastructure. Just as reliable water and electric supplies, functional schools, hospitals, roads, and communication systems are essential to a thriving and healthy community, so is a sound waste management system. Indeed, in recent decades, we have witnessed a change in waste management philosophy: *waste* management is now referred to as *resource* management, emphasizing the use and reuse of materials in the most productive and sustainable ways throughout their entire life cycle. The United Nations Human Settlements Program in 2010 reviewed municipal solid waste (MSW) management practices in 20 cities located in rich and poor countries across 6 continents and concluded: "Managing solid waste well and affordably is one of the key challenges of the 21st century, and one of the key responsibilities of a city government" (UN-Habitat 2010, p. xix). It is imperative that our current way of production of goods and consumption of resources and energy undergoes a major transformation to achieve a sustainable future.

Waste will continue to remain an inevitable product of society that would challenge the ingenuity of future generations to manage it in a safe and sustainable manner. While smart technologies and devices are being increasingly incorporated in smart cities' operations, it is yet to be fully integrated into the waste management industry. Radio frequency identification (RFID), load cell sensors, and advanced weighing technology can be used to improve efficiency of the waste management system. Machine learning, barcode reading device, imaging, and web-based cloud computing, combined with Geographical Information System (GIS) technology can facilitate real-time tracking of waste from its points of origin to final treatment and disposal. It is predicted that waste management in future would move toward using smart technologies along with the Internet of Things (IoT) for a more efficient, less labor-intensive, and sustainable system.

The concept of zero waste (ZW) has been gaining attention globally because of its emphasis on elimination of the waste so that nothing (ZW) ends up in the landfill. The large-scale urbanization, coupled with impacts of globalization, call for a bold vision to manage urban growth and development. Adoption of ZW principle in MSW management policies of local and regional governments is essential in view of the fact that cities of the world use 75% of world's natural resource and generate over 70% of the waste. As our world continues to move toward greater urbanization, city growth must incorporate the three vital elements of sustainable development: environmental preservation, social equity, and economic growth. Waste management must be given high priority in formulating development policies to avoid the triple threat of pollution, wasted resources, and ailing ecosystem. Waste management sector faces problems that can be solved through collaboration with environmental, social, and behavioral scientists, and economists on one hand, and politicians, decision-makers, policy enforcers on the other.

During the past few decades, several books on waste management have been published; some of which, including my award-winning textbook *Geology and Hazardous Waste Management* (Prentice Hall, 1996), were used as a textbook for students enrolled in environmental sciences/studies and environmental engineering degree programs. These texts either covered a specific waste type, e.g. hazardous waste, or the three common types of wastes: MSW, hazardous waste, and medical waste. No existing book covers the entire universe of waste generated in modern societies. When I introduced the course *Introduction to waste management* for our environmental science/studies majors in the late 1990s, I realized the need of an introductory textbook dealing with all types of wastes, designed to meet the need of a diverse group of students with different levels of academic preparation. This book is written to fulfil that need. Recognizing that all students may not have taken courses in college mathematics, I have used mathematical treatment to a minimum, making it simple for students who had taken math courses in high school only.

Introduction to Waste Management is based on my 25 years of teaching waste management at the University of Missouri-Kansas City, where I had designed and taught four courses in waste management from introductory to graduate levels. I have written this book with students as my primary audience and have included materials that I found helpful to students while teaching the course. So, this book has been classroom-tested and represents a most up-to-date treatment of the subject. I believe the addition of a chapter on pharmaceuticals and personal care products (PPCPs) along with thorough discussion of nuclear, electronic or e-waste, airplane, and ship wastes will be very useful for all readers of this book. And, while COVID-19 has impacted everyone in one way or the other, I can claim this book to be the first to discuss its impacts in the waste management field.

Unlike other books, *Introduction to Waste Management* offers a comprehensive coverage of all types of waste. In addition to the commonly discussed MSW, hazardous waste, and medical waste, this book includes detailed coverage of nuclear waste, waste containing PPCPs, and airplane and ship wastes. The last three have not been included in waste management textbooks, and nuclear waste has been dealt with in a cursory manner, if at all. With the current emphasis on sustainability, and increasing volume of discarded airplanes and ships, inclusion of these types of wastes is a timely necessity. *Introduction to Waste Management* is the first textbook to discuss these emerging waste types.

A Word to Students...

Introduction to Waste Management will enable you to grasp the relevance of waste management to modern society, gain in-depth knowledge of problems facing the world caused by mismanagement of solid, hazardous, medical, electronic, and nuclear wastes. You will understand the importance of promising concepts of green remediation, circular economy, and ZW in waste minimization efforts; and will be able to perform waste audits. You will also comprehend the potential ecological and human health issues associated with consumption and use of PPCPs and other wastes.

As you will go through the book, you will notice the tremendous need for skilled professionals to work in the waste management field. I would add this additional note: regardless of what you chose as your major, jobs will be there for you because of two reasons: (i) waste management is one of the fastest expanding sectors in a nation's economy – growing at an annualized rate of 6% worldwide, and (ii) waste management is an interdisciplinary field that needs people with background in business, finance, social and behavioral sciences, engineering and health sciences, and of course environmental sciences/studies. My advice to you is: instead of focusing on a "hot field" put your energy into excelling in whatever major you choose – a good career awaits people who excel in what they do.

To Instructors...

Most chapters have been designed to be covered in one week's lectures, except Chapter 2 on essentials of geology, geotechnics, and toxicology. Condensing even the basics of these three disciplines in a limited space has been a daunting task. But based on my teaching experience and feedback from students, I feel that the coverage provided in *Introduction to Waste Management* is adequate and will not overwhelm the students. Instructors may choose to cover the material in Chapter 2 in two to three weeks.

Acknowledgments

A major undertaking, like writing a college textbook, relies heavily on support from many individuals and organizations. I take this opportunity to offer my sincere thanks to Dr. Ajim Ali, Aligarh, India, for sharing his photographs (Chapter 8). To Dr. Arsalan A. Othman, Iraq Geological Survey, I owe special thanks for his untiring help in preparation of illustrations for this book. Without his cooperation and support, the high-quality illustrations would not have been possible. My long-time college friend, Dr. Lokesh Chaturvedi, Deputy Director (retired), New Mexico Environmental Evaluation Group, Albuquerque, who passed away in July 2020, had reviewed the draft of Chapter 7 (nuclear waste) and offered valuable insights into transuranic waste disposal at the WIPP site in his home state of New Mexico. I pay tribute and offer my heartfelt gratitude to Lokesh for a life-long friendship and professional association, extending over 55 years. I thank Robert Sanchez, Senior Analyst, Natural Resources and Environment, U.S. Government Accountability Office, Denver, Colorado, for providing material for Chapter 7. I am grateful to Dr. S. Shahid Hasan and Irfan Gilani for their assistance in arranging visits and accompanying me to the Ghazipur Landfill in Delhi, India. I thank Scott Martin, Burns and McDonnell, Kansas City, Missouri, for his help in landfill cost estimation and to Dr. David Drake, retired Section Chief, Superfund Division, United States Environmental Protection Agency, Region 7, Lenexa, Kansas, for his help with materials for the Tri-State Mining District. I owe special thanks to Scott Curtis, Teaching and Learning Librarian, Miller Nichols Library, University of Missouri-Kansas City, for sharing his expertise in identifying and obtaining hundreds of journal articles and reports that I have consulted while writing this book. I thank Robert L. Berry, Vice President, International Shipbreaking Limited, Brownsville, Texas, for his insightful tips on ship recycling and permission to use the photograph of the ship recycling facility in Texas (Chapter 9). I offer thanks to the chair and staff, Department of Earth and Environmental Sciences, University of Missouri-Kansas City, for help and use of equipment and facilities during the course of preparation of this book. Finally, I would like to express my deep gratitude to Dr. Frank Weinreich, Publisher, Books and Reference Works, Wiley, whose personal interest in the design of the book cover and production has resulted in a magnificent publication. I will be amiss if I fail to record the support of the entire Wiley team, particularly Umar Saleem, Content Refinement Specialist, whose editorial support and prompt response to my questions made my job pleasant and less arduous.

Department of Earth and Environmental Sciences
University of Missouri-Kansas City
27 May 2022

Reference

UN-Habitat (United Nations Human Settlement Program) (2010). *Solid Waste Management in the World's Cities: Water and Sanitation in World's Cities 2010*, 257 p. London: Earthscan.

1

Introduction

LEARNING OBJECTIVES

After studying this chapter, you will be able to:

- Outline the universe of waste and associated issues.
- Identify human and ecological health consequences of improper waste management.
- Describe the significance of waste management in environmental sustainability and climate change mitigation.
- Summarize future prospects of waste management.

1.1 The Beginning

Humans have been relatively new occupants of the life-sustaining, 4.54-billion-year-old planet Earth, where life in the form of halobacteria is thought to have first appeared about 3.8 billion years ago (Dodd et al. 2017). While the appearance, growth, abundance, and ultimate extinction of species have been part of the natural process, humans have significantly altered this process. We have developed capabilities to level a hill in a matter of hours and razing a mountain to the ground in weeks; our sophisticated technologies can decimate all life in a matter of seconds with powerful nuclear bombs; we can land humans on other planets and take them to the abyssal depths of oceans; we can fight wars without setting foot on battlegrounds, yet we have not been able to treat the Earth in the way it deserves. In fact, we have mistreated and abused it and have exploited its resources in the most careless manner, inflicting great harm to its ecosystem. It is an irony that the Earth, which has been the source of our sustenance, should be so ill-treated and mismanaged: instead of being its *caretaker*, we assumed the role of an arrogant and selfish *master*.

Climate change has come to the tipping point and if humanity does not collectively rise to reduce CO_2 levels to around 300 ppm, future generations will face a tough time to survive. No matter whether we look at the atmosphere, biosphere, hydrosphere, or lithosphere, human activities have degraded the quality and value of all of these natural life support systems through unwarranted pollution. It is time – perhaps the last and only time – that we, the most intelligent, resourceful, and capable species among the millions that have appeared on the Earth, heed nature's warning and come together as world citizens to solve the problems facing us. Doing it on a national, political, or any other basis would not help us get out of this predicament.

Waste is far from a glamourous subject, but it can't be avoided. Depending on lifestyle and consumption patterns, each of us can generate tons of waste over our lifetimes, from long-standing sources such as table scraps, old newspapers, and bottles and cans to the ever-growing stream of consumer electronics that nowadays approach obsolescence mere months after purchase. The total really skyrockets if you include the farm, mine, and industrial wastes generated to produce food, power, and products in the first place.

—*Nick Wigginton et al. (2012, p. 663).*

1.1.1 Historical Perspectives

It was not too long ago, about two generations back, that people could throw their waste on the ground and it would biodegrade and become harmless. Not so anymore because of the huge quantity of plastics and harmful chemicals that have become ubiquitous in modern life. Open dumping of waste is still common among one-half of the world's population of over seven billion, causing the plastics to clog drainage ways leading to flooding (Chapter 4) and killing animals upon ingestion. Chemicals seep out of the dumps, polluting streams and rivers, threatening aquatic lives, and contaminating groundwater, causing diseases and deaths (Chapter 5).

Looking from a historical perspective, we find that concern and need for environmentally safe management of waste has been an evolving challenge for human societies. Starting soon after the 1950s, safe management of municipal solid waste (MSW) in the United States and some other developed countries held the attention of scientists, policymakers, and other stakeholders for over 20 years until the sanitary landfill as a safe method of garbage disposal was developed. Soon afterwards, beginning in the 1970s, we were confronted with hazardous wastes and its horrible impacts on human and ecological health (Case Study 5.1). Next, an increasing quantity of nuclear or radioactive waste and its safe management kept us engaged during the 1960s–1980s. Then, the fast-growing quantities of electronic or e-waste, and the resulting impairment of environmental quality caused by its informal recycling in China, India, and other developing countries brought to fore the need for implementing regulations for its safe management. Recently, pharmaceuticals and personal care products (PPCPs) and per- and polyfluoroalkyl substances (PFASs) are being studied for their impacts on human health and the environment to determine ways for the safe management of waste containing these substances.

In 2015, the United Nations Environment Programme (UNEP) identified the global waste problem as one of the major environmental issues of the twenty-first century, describing it as: "Waste is a global issue. If not properly dealt with, waste poses a threat to public health and the environment. It is a growing issue linked directly to the way society produces and consumes. It concerns everyone" (UNEP 2015). The waste problem will become more challenging due to the increasing global population and urbanization with the resulting increase in MSW and e-waste quantities, along with a substantial increase in medical waste (MW) caused by aging populations in developed countries and their greater dependence on medication and other health care products. In addition, a significant increase in MW quantities caused by an outbreak of epidemics and pandemics that are likely to become more frequent due to climate change and loss of forest ecosystem under the pressure of urbanization and agriculture will demand rapid and safe management of MW. The positive aspect is that we can control major impacts by safely managing our waste and taking suitable measures to mitigate climate change threats, thereby achieving a balance between our needs and environmental preservation to change our role as *caretakers* instead of *masters* of the Earth.

All evidence point to the troubling reality that climate change and human alteration of natural habitats would exacerbate zoonosis, and outbreaks of the COVID-19-like pandemics will become more frequent and intense. Advance planning and adequate preparation to deal with such situations should be given top priority by policymakers the world over. Adequate workforce of personnel in the health care and waste management sectors must be trained and stand on call to deal with such disastrous events.

COVID-19 has reaffirmed Dr. Martin Luther King's prophetic words that he had spoken at the Memphis Sanitation Workers' Strike on 19 March 1968, barely three weeks before he was assassinated as he was getting to address the crowd that had gathered outside his hotel in Memphis: "One day our society will come to respect the sanitation worker if it is to survive, for the person who picks up our garbage is . . . just as significant as a physician. For if he does not do this, disease is rampant."

Waste management is one of the essential utility services underpinning societies in the twenty-first century, particularly in urban areas. Waste management is a basic human need, which can also be regarded as a basic human right. Ensuring proper sanitation and environmentally safe waste management is no less important than the provision of safe drinking water, shelter, food, energy, transportation, and communications to citizens. Despite this, the public and political profiles of waste management are often lower than other utility services.

Modern societies generate a variety of wastes that must be managed in an environmentally sustainable way – a need that was grossly neglected in the past. Developed countries started to remedy the problem in the latter part of the twentieth century and have, to a great extent, been managing most, but not all, types of wastes, in a sound manner. The situation in developing and undeveloped countries, on the other hand, is very different. Waste mismanagement is still prevalent and continues to add high levels of polluting chemicals to the environment, threatening human and ecological health.

Improper waste management has resulted in the release of harmful pollutants that have impacted the Earth's environment and disturbed its ecological balance. Two notables among these impacts are: (i) global warming and ensuing climate change, and (ii) serious and often irreversible impacts on human and ecological health. It is surmised that lack of safe management of wastes is the primary cause of all environmental problems and its solution lies in eliminating the release of harmful chemicals embedded in the waste into the air, water, and land.

Polluting chemicals, generated primarily from industrial sources, are one of the most serious environmental problems that we are facing in the twenty-first century. While the harmful effects of dumping waste materials containing hazardous chemicals on land and water are easy to comprehend, similar impacts on the air may not be very obvious. In fact, one of the long-lasting approaches in managing societal waste was "out of sight, out of mind." As normally expected, the more visible land and water pollution became the focus of remediation efforts but the less visible air pollution remained unnoticed, allowing large amounts of toxic gases, particulate matters (PMs), and other pollutants to accumulate in the atmosphere. The slow but steady buildup of greenhouse gases (GHGs) finally tipped the balance, resulting in global warming.

Despite the fact that we produce enough food to feed the entire human population, globally 811 million people remain hungry every day. While poverty, conflicts, access to food supply, climate variability, and economic slowdown are some of the main causes, the staggering quantities of wasted food (about 1.3 billion t annually) are sobering. In developed countries, 931 million t of food worth \$600 billion was wasted in 2019. For the past few decades, the UN and other organizations have taken several measures to alleviate hunger and food scarcity, including minimizing food waste, but the gains achieved in the past few years have been offset due to extreme climate events and the 2020–2021 COVID-19 pandemic. Food waste reduction offers multifaceted solutions for people and the planet by improving food security, addressing climate change, saving money, and reducing pressures on land, water, biodiversity, and waste management systems. Yet this potential has not been utilized until now.

Food waste, as a class of waste, was overlooked until recently because the true scale of food waste and its impacts have not been well understood. Global estimates of food waste have relied on the extrapolation of data from a relatively small number of countries. Few governments have robust data on food waste to make the case to act and prioritize their efforts. The 2021 publication titled *Food Waste Index Report*, commissioned by the UNEP presents the most comprehensive food waste data to date, generating a reliable estimate of global food waste. The report provides country-level food waste estimates that offer new insight into the scale of the problem and prevention strategies for low-, middle- and high-income countries (UNEP 2021). In addition, the UN Sustainable Development Goal, SDG 12, has set an ambitious target to "halve per capita global food waste at the retail and consumer levels and reduce food losses along production and supply chains, including post-harvest losses" by 2030 (UN 2021).

The presence of PPCPs in rivers, streams, lakes, and also in groundwater in several countries led to detailed investigations in the United States, Europe, China, and other countries during the past 30 years. Use of expired and discarded prescription medicines, and over-the-counter drugs, veterinary medicines, along with the myriad of personal care products, and their non-entrapment through the wastewater (sewer) treatment plants, cause the medicinal products and their metabolites to enter the aquatic environment producing adverse health impacts on fish, amphibians, and other species. Effects on humans are not yet known.

1.2 Importance of Waste Management in Sustainability, Ecological Health, and Climate Change

Waste is a natural product of human existence – just as we cannot survive without air, water, and food, we cannot live without generating any waste. Ever since humans occupied the Earth when they were hunters and gatherers, they were producing waste from unused food (bones, eggshells, wild fruit peels, rinds, seeds, inedible plant stalks, wood, and ash, along with the excreta) that were thrown all around. As their life changed from "on the move" or mobile phase to settlements in villages, and following the discovery of agriculture, some 8000 years before the current era (BCE), waste began to be confined in the limited space of settlements, rather than dispersed over wide areas. Still, the nature and quantity of waste did not pose any problem because of: (i) small human population, and (ii) complete biodegradability of the waste. However, as human civilization advanced and we mastered the use of iron, copper, and other metals to initially fashion tools and equipment and later to make complex machineries and weapons, the quantity of waste soared, becoming increasingly hazardous. As illustrated in Figure 1.1, the advancement of human civilization can be characterized by three major revolutions or landmarks in our history: (i) the agricultural revolution, about 8000 years ago; (ii) the mechanical revolution, commonly known as the industrial revolution (IR), around 1760; and (iii) the digital revolution of 1970 (Hasan 2017). The human population also kept on increasing, acquiring an exponential growth pattern about two generations after the IR, touching the 1-billion mark in 1804, and climbing steeply to 1.65 billion in 1900, 2.57 billion in 1950, and reaching 7.9 billion in 2021 (Figure 1.1).

The second half of the twentieth century has been a remarkable period in human history marked by improved quality of life, space exploration, and instant communication that have made life easier. On the negative side, we have used many of our discoveries and inventions for harmful purposes – nuclear energy for making powerful bombs that can annihilate hundreds of thousands of people instantly; hazardous and deadly chemicals in toxic wastes that cause serious illness and fatal diseases to people and destroy the ecosystems. The main difference between the pre- and

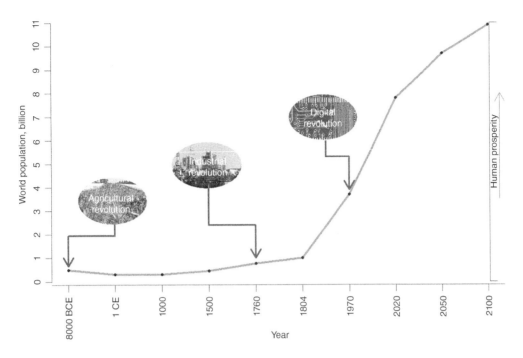

Figure 1.1   Major revolutions and human population.

postindustrial societies is the generation and mismanagement of large quantities of hazardous and toxic wastes that effectively overwhelmed the self-cleansing ability of the natural systems that regulate and maintain the balance of the Earth's ecosystem. Sadly enough, this state of affairs has been the result of our deliberate choice of prioritizing economic gains over environmental protection.

Yet one other factor that has created the grave problem of uncontrolled waste generation is related to manufacturers embracing the planned obsolescence (PO) approach in product design and industrial engineering. In a simple way, PO is a production strategy that relies on designing consumer goods in such a way that it will stop working after a predetermined period of time, or work less efficiently than before, or become outdated, requiring the user to replace it much sooner than if the product were designed to last through its normal life span. Manufacturers of personal electronic devices have the distinction of being the leaders in thoroughly integrating PO philosophy in their product design and marketing. Think of your smartphone and laptop and how aggressively you are pushed by the manufacturers to *upgrade* these devices just a year or two after purchase. You will find a detailed discussion of PO in Chapter 8, but for now, it would suffice to state that manufacturers must divest from the century-old practice of manufacturing products based on linear economy, and adopt the circular economy by redesigning their products for repair, reuse, and assuring a steady supply of replacement parts. You, as the future stewards of humanity's home, have the responsibility to force this change. You must use all available tools at your disposal: telling Apple, GM, Samsung, Toyota, and other manufacturers whose products you use every day to adopt circular economy; become an activist to educate people about the harm the liner economy has inflicted for generations; and demand your elected representatives to enact legislations to ban short-lived, disposable products. The Right to Repair legislation is under consideration in 25 states, and if your state is not among these, contact your elected representatives to promote it.

1.2.1 Waste Management and Environmental Sustainability

The word *sustainable* was first used during the 1610s to mean *bearable*. In 1845, it was adapted for legal use to mean *defensible*; after 1965, it was used to connote processes or patterns that could be continued at a certain level. For example, *sustainable agricultural growth* was used to assure an adequate supply of food. Sustainability is believed to have been used in the general sense of its current meaning in 1972. Later, in response to increasing concerns about ozone depletion, global warming, and other environmental problems, the UN Secretary-General in 1983, invited Dr. Brundtland, then prime minister of Norway, to establish and chair the World Commission on Environment and Development (WCED). In the same year, the UN General Assembly convened a meeting of international experts to develop proposals for long-term global sustainable development in concert with environmental preservation. The commission's report published in 1987, titled *Report of the World Commission on Environment and Development: Our Common Future*, authored by Gro Harlem Brundtland (1987), widely known as *The Brundtland Report*, defined sustainable development as "development that meets the needs of the present without compromising the ability of future generations to meet their own needs." Hasan and Johnston (2016) elaborated on this definition by defining environmental sustainability to include ". . .development plans that consider economic, environmental, and social factors to ensure that it would not take away the right of future generations to these resources."

The Brundtland Report laid the foundation for the Rio Summit that resulted in the creation of the UN Commission on Sustainable Development in 1992. In 2015, the UN set up 17 Sustainable Development Goals (SDGs) that have been adopted by a majority of world countries. Waste management can contribute both directly and indirectly to achieving all 17 of the SDGs (UN 2021). Table 1.1 lists the various SDGs and how the waste management sector can contribute to achieving them.

Table 1.1 Waste management share in achieving the UN Sustainable Development Goals (SDGs).

SDG	Waste management sector contribution in goals' attainment	Remarks
SDG 1 Poverty alleviation	Waste management (WM) is a growing industry. The global WM market was valued at $2080 billion in 2020 and is poised to grow to $2389.9 billion by 2027. The 5% annualized growth rate holds great potential for both skilled and non-skilled jobs.	Indirect
SDG 2 Zero hunger	Developed countries waste millions of tons of edible food. Preventing this loss will feed nearly 900 million people who go hungry each day.	Indirect
SDG 3 Good health	Proper waste management will reduce the release of toxic substances into the air, water, and soil, preventing diseases and illness and assuring well-being of a large number of individuals.	
SDG 4 Quality education	The projected growth of the waste management industry will need thousands of skilled and unskilled workers. It will require preparing the future workforce by imparting them education and training at all levels of education from vocational to college and professional degrees in accounting, IT, engineering, geosciences, economics, social sciences, math and statistical sciences, etc.	Direct
SDG 5 Gender equality	A large number of persons engaged in the waste management field include both men and women. The trend will continue with a larger number of women working in recycling and waste transportation areas.	Indirect
SDG 6 Clean water and sanitation	Proper waste management will prevent polluting substances from entering air, water, and soil, thus eliminating most of the major sources causing degradation of the Earth's environmental quality.	Direct

Table 1.1 (Continued)

SDG	Waste management sector contribution in goals' attainment	Remarks
SDG 7 Affordable and clean energy	Increasing global trend on using MSW and other wastes for energy generation will reduce dependence on fossil fuels and will cut down GHG emissions, notably CH_4, by capturing and utilizing it to produce clean energy. Inedible remains of food waste can be converted into biogas and clean renewable energy.	Direct
SDG 8 Decent work and economic growth	Globally, 1% of the urban population in developing countries earns its livelihood from recovering recyclable materials from waste dumps. The waste management industry is one of the fastest growing in the world. In 2019, it employed over 270 000 people working for 11 000 companies and generating about $82.1 billion in revenue. The industry is poised to grow at an annual rate of 5.5%, with its global market share jumping from $2441.7 in 2017 to $2747.7 by 2027. A large number of millennials with degrees in science, engineering, technology, humanities, and business will be needed that will serve as a powerful catalyst for economic growth.	Direct
SDG 9 Industrial innovation and infrastructure	Waste management industry has been a leader in promoting recycling and waste-to-energy (WtE) conversion, driving industrial innovation in automated waste-sorting machines, waste-collection equipment, and efficient WtE plant design, using geographical information system (GIS), radio frequency identification device (RFID), sensors, and weighing and artificial intelligence (AI) technologies.	Direct
SDG 10 Reduction of inequity	The large number of semiskilled and unskilled workforce needed for the growing WM industry, along with fair wages and basic employment rights for all waste workers will go a long way in reducing inequities.	Indirect
SDG 11 Sustainable cities and communities	Waste collection and disposal is an essential public service, just like water supply, electricity, transportation, etc., that a local town, city, or country must provide to its citizens. Cities and communities thrive when these services are offered to the public uninterrupted, at a reasonable cost, and meet the standards of quality, safety, and reliability. Decent wages and fair employment rights for waste workers are essential for inclusive and sustainable communities.	Direct
SDG 12 Responsible consumption and production	Recycling and resource conservation is the key element of waste management. Waste minimization must become the norm and should be done everywhere, home, office, business, factories, educational and other institutions, etc. Public participation in waste minimization programs leads to avoiding waste and responsible consumption, and controls wasteful production.	Direct
SDG 13 Climate change mitigation	Increasing replacement of fossil fuel-driven vehicles and machineries by those using electric or renewable energy and large-scale implementation of the landfill methane outreach program (LMOP) championed by the US EPA and other international agencies will contribute to the reduction in GHGs.	Direct
SDG 14 and 15 Life below water and life on land	Large quantities of hazardous chemicals from waste dumps seep downward polluting the groundwater. Surface runoff from land also carries significant amounts of harmful chemicals that pollute lakes, rivers, and oceans resulting in devastation of critical aquatic and marine ecosystems. Proper waste management will assure thriving lives in the vital ecosystems.	Direct
SDG 16 Peace, justice, and strong institutions	Substantial benefits and gains in pollution prevention, gender equality in jobs, social and environmental justice, and education and training potential accruing from environmentally sound waste management would contribute to creation of just, peaceful, and strong institutions.	Indirect
SDG 17 Global partnerships	Pioneering international efforts toward environmentally sound management of all kinds of waste have already led to international cooperation among the world nations. Online workers training programs in waste management offered by the UN and other organizations are destined to increase global partnerships between the high-, middle-, and low-income countries of the world.	Direct

1.2.2 Waste Management and Human and Ecological Health

Ask any person "what is the cause of environmental degradation?" and the answer would invariably be: pollution. This may be partly true but in reality, pollution is the *effect* and not the cause. The fact is that pollution is *caused* by improper management of waste generated in our societies. Pollution of the environment caused by careless dumping and unsafe waste management has severely degraded the Earth's environment and adversely impacted human and ecological health. Ecological health in this context refers to the purity and pristine quality of all elements of the Earth's ecosystem that include both its living and nonliving components: animals, plants, soil, sediment, rocks, air, and water. The most familiar example of impairment of ecological health is the warming of the Earth that has led to climate change. Other examples include the formation of "dead zones" in the coastal waters at many locations across the globe, where marine life is unable to survive due to a massive influx of agricultural chemicals, notably nitrate fertilizer, washing down from the land.

Concern about potential problems with garbage and human health has been around for a long time. Recorded history tells us that ancient civilizations were aware of the dangers of careless dumping of waste and had established some kind of control to keep the waste away from where people lived. In fact, the first municipal dump site was established in the City of Athens, Greece about 2500 years ago, and the citizens were required to dispose of their waste at least 1 mile from city walls.

One of the well-documented cases of health problems relates to the Black Death, a lethal variety of bubonic plague that wiped out half of the mid-fourteenth-century European population. This epidemic is believed to be caused by uncontrolled waste dumping (Tchobanoglous et al. 1993). In recent times, Love Canal in New York State stands out as one of the most infamous examples of health problems caused by dumping industrial waste.

A large number of people in developing countries earn their living by scavenging any usable material from waste dumps that comprise a heterogeneous mix of MSW, hazardous, medical, and e-wastes. These *waste pickers* include children, women, and older people, who earn their living by spending long hours at waste dumps to salvage any recyclable material. The long hours spent in heat, cold, and rain, without any protection, cause a wide range of health problems ranging from fatigue, injuries, and joint problems from constant bending and lifting heavyweights, to respiratory tract diseases from inhalation of toxic gases and PMs, and skin cuts and puncture from sharps and hazardous chemicals in the MW. Although not common, cases of vehicular accidents involving young people competing with others to get the best pick of recyclables by jumping onto the moving trucks and bulldozers, result in serious injuries, amputation, and occasional death. Cases of several acute and chronic diseases including typhoid, cholera, respiratory infections, and cancer, and premature deaths among the waste pickers and nearby dump site residents are summarized in Table 1.2.

The solution to health problems associated with waste management requires a multidisciplinary approach by involving Earth and environmental scientists, health care professionals, social and behavioral experts, administrators, politicians, and legal professionals. Some measures that should be taken to alleviate waste-induced health problems include: (i) preparing inventory of all dump sites, i.e. locations where all kinds of waste are disposed of in an uncontrolled way; (ii) strictly enforcing environmental regulations and imposing stiff penalties on the violators, both civil and criminal; and (iii) working with waste pickers for fair compensation and benefits to ensure that any plan for environmentally safe waste disposal would not result in loss of income due to closure of dumps and would guarantee their future economic security.

Table 1.2 Health risks to waste pickers.

Hazards	Health risks
Organic and inorganic compounds	CO_2 and CH_4 are asphyxiants, cause dizziness, confusion, elevated blood pressure, and breathing difficulty. At a CO_2 concentration of >10% humans lose consciousness. CH_4 is flammable, and at a concentration of 5–15% forms an explosive mixture with air; causes nausea, vomiting, headache, lost coordination, coma, and death at higher concentrations.
Heavy metals	Cr^6 is a known carcinogen. Prolonged exposure to As, Pb, Hg, and Cd causes neurological impairments, kidney failure, musculoskeletal diseases, liver cancer, and cardiovascular diseases.
Polycyclic aromatic hydrocarbons (PAHs)	PAHs are harmful compounds; some of them, such as benzo[*a*]pyrene and benz[*a*]anthracene, etc., are known carcinogens.
Volatile organic compounds (VOCs)	VOCs can damage liver, kidney, and the central nervous system. Cause eye, nose, and throat irritation; headache; nausea; etc., at low concentration.
Hazardous compounds	Classified as corrosive, flammable, reactive, or toxic; can cause serious health problems upon chronic exposure; and air, water, and soil pollution.
Medical waste	Pathogens, contaminated syringes, needles, and broken glass pose serious health hazards, including infection and disease.
e-Waste	Informal recovery of valuable metals by acid leaching and open plastic burning releases toxic fumes, PMs, and harmful residues, leading to adverse birth outcomes, DNA damage; affects the immune, cardiovascular, respiratory, and thyroid functions; impaired neurodevelopment and behavior.

1.2.3 Waste Management and Climate Change

Improper waste management leading to the release of harmful substances causes degradation of land, water, and air. Unlike the effects on land and water that can be noticed quickly, adverse impacts on the air quality take much more time to be observed. For example, depletion of O_3 and increase in CO_2 concentration took nearly 200 years before adverse effects began to be noted. Once apparent, the ozone problem was addressed by the developed nations – heavy users of chloro-fluorocarbons (CFCs) and other ozone-depleting chemicals – who came together quickly to devise a solution culminating with the enforcement of the Stockholm Treaty in January 1989 that effectively controlled the level of O_3 in the atmosphere. On the other hand, global warming and ensuing climate change are posing great challenges and the global community is still struggling to implement the 2016 Paris Agreement.

The gradual accumulation of CO_2 from a low of about 280 ppm around the beginning of the IR, climbing to 369 ppm in January 2000 to over 410 ppm in mid-2021 has been a direct consequence of using fossil fuels and releasing the GHGs unceasingly into the atmosphere. It is now well established that landfills emit CO_2, CH_4, and N_2O, all of which contribute to global warming. The amount of GHGs emitted from landfills ranges from 2 to 7% depending on the relative amount of organic materials in the waste, the amount of recyclable materials taken out from the MSW, and provision to capture CH_4 in the landfills.

The Intergovernmental Panel on Climate Change (IPCC), since 1990, has been drawing attention to serious problems associated with uncontrolled CO_2 emissions and suggesting ways to lower GHG emissions. The latest IPCC report (first part of the Sixth Assessment Report), released on 9 August 2021, in a most unequivocal term concluded that human action is responsible for climate change and for the widespread impacts on the Earth's atmosphere, biosphere, and cryosphere (IPCC 2021). The report issued a dire warning stating that GHG concentrations have reached the tipping point, but added an optimistic note that global temperature could stabilize and the air quality can improve in the next 20–30 years, provided measures are taken now for sustained reduction of CO_2 and other GHG emissions.

It should be pointed out that implementation of recommendations made under the provisions of the UN treaties depend upon ratification by the individual nations and do not become enforceable until they are approved by legislatures at all levels of a government. In the case of the United States, it must be approved by majority votes in Congress and the Senate before the president can sign it into law. National politics, finances involved in implementation, and several other considerations often derail the treaties. As an example, despite signing the Paris Agreement on 22 April 2016 (Earth Day) at the UN headquarters in New York along with 188 other countries, the United States on 4 November 2020 withdrew its agreement to be a signatory but rejoined on 20 January 2021.

1.3 Overview of Waste Generation in the United States and Other Countries

Studies have shown that waste generation is related to the GDP and living standard of a country. For example, the United States and other developed countries produce an average of 1.57 kg of waste per person on a daily basis (p/d), whereas the rate for the low- and lower-middle-income countries is 0.43 and 0.61 kg/p/d, respectively (Figure 1.2). However, it should be noted that developed countries have stricter enforcement of environmental laws, which is not the case in developing countries, which release significant quantities of GHGs and other pollutants into the environment.

The IR and the subsequent global environmental impacts it produced were the results of extensive mechanization using coal to power steam engines and other machines, later supplemented by petroleum (oil and gas), primarily by the developed countries, until about the last quarter of the twentieth century. Since then, the emerging economies started to put out large quantities of GHGs in the atmosphere as well. Large-scale use of fossil fuels to run their industries led to the buildup of high levels of GHGs in the atmosphere that resulted in global warming and triggered climate change. Increasing use of hazardous and toxic chemicals to maintain the industrial output of all kinds of products from consumer goods to food, electronics, transportation vehicles, and weapons during the second half of the twentieth century, without proper management of the resulting wastes, led to serious degradation of the environmental quality in the United States and Europe. Fortunately, and to their credit, the developed countries also recognized the severity of problems caused by mismanagement of waste and enacted laws to regulate further release of harmful waste materials. They were the first to develop and enforce rules and regulations to stop uncontrolled waste disposal starting in the last quarter of the twentieth century that made a significant improvement in the environmental quality as far as land and water pollution are concerned. Air pollution, however, presents an entirely different scenario because air pollution knows no national boundaries, is mostly invisible, and GHGs and other pollutants rapidly diffuse and disperse all over the globe by the prevailing atmospheric circulation systems.

While reliable data on CO_2 and GHG emissions and other statistical information on the world economy, demography, etc., are readily available, there is a dearth of resources on statistical information on waste generation at a global scale. Some publications by the UN, EU, and other agencies provide selective data on a few types of waste, but a comprehensive source of information for all waste types is not yet available. Table 1.3 summarizes the partial data on global waste generation, culled from various sources.

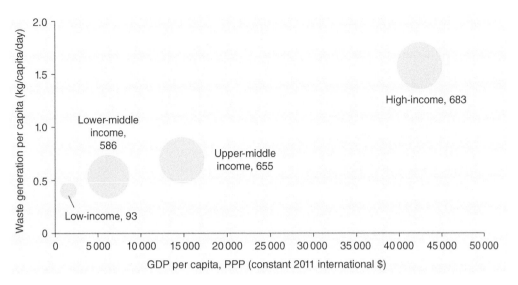

Figure 1.2 Relationship between per capita GDP (in 2011 US$) and MSW quantity. Bubble size represents annual amount of waste in million tons. Waste generation rate in kilogram per person per day for low-income countries is 0.43, lower-middle-income countries is 0.61, upper-middle-income countries is 0.69, and high-income countries is 1.57. Data is for 2016. *Source:* Graphic and data credit: Kaza et al. (2018).

Table 1.3 Global quantities of various wastes (compiled from various sources).

Waste type	Global quantity (year)	Source	Notes
Municipal solid waste (MSW)	2010×10^6 t (2010) estimated to increase to 2590×10^6 t by 2030	Hoornweg, D; Perinaz, B-T[1]	Data used in this report are mostly for the year 2002–2005; some countries reported data for 2017–2018.
Hazardous waste	200–939 200 t (2005)	UN[2]	Based on data from 88 low to high income countries from 2003 to 2009
Medical waste	0.5–8.4 kg/b/d (2001–2015)	Minoglou et al.[3]	Data are for 42 low to high income countries and cover the period 2001–2015. Lowest rate is for Nepal and the highest is for the United States.
Nuclear waste	367 600 MtHM (2013)	IAEA[4]	Estimated quantity of spent nuclear fuels (SNFs) generated from all nuclear power plants (NPPs) worldwide from 1954 till 31 December 2013.
	3193 MtHM (2013)		High level waste (HLW) from research reactors worldwide.
Electronic or e-waste	53.6×10^6 t (2009) will increase to 74×10^6 t by 2030	United Nations (2020)[5]	One of the fastest growing waste types. Highest quantity generated in China: 10.13×10^6 t, followed by the United States: 6.92×10^6 t and India: 3.23×10^6 t
PPCPs	—	—	No data is available
Food waste	1.6×10^9 Mt	FAO[6]	Represents wasted edible food in 2020.

Sources:

1) https://openknowledge.worldbank.org/handle/10986/17388

2) https://unstats.un.org/unsd/environment/hazardous.htm

3) Minoglou (2017). https://doi.org/10.3390/su9020220

4) IAEA (2018). P1799_web.pdf (iaea.org)

5) https://www.itu.int/en/ITU-D/Environment/Documents/Toolbox/GEM_2020_def.pdf

6) FAO – News Article: Food wastage: Key facts and figures.

Mt, million metric tons; MtHM, million metric tons of heavy metals; PPCPs, pharmaceuticals and personal care products; t, metric tons.

As indicated in the table, reliable information is only available for some types of waste and is scanty or missing for other types. In general, developed countries maintain and submit reliable national data to appropriate international organizations, but information and data from many developing countries are generally incomplete or missing altogether. In addition, the data quality is often questionable.

1.4   Future Perspectives on Waste Management

Increasing world population, aided by improved living conditions, and growing urbanization, all point to a corresponding increase in waste quantities. Technological innovations will add to the use of newer and more complex chemicals for manufacturing products to meet the need of future populations. The predicted growth in solid and e-waste sectors, in particular, calls for stricter controls by all countries to ensure environmentally safe management of wastes. While MSW, hazardous waste, and MW are being managed in a proper way in developed countries, nuclear waste has lagged behind. No disposal facility for the high-level nuclear waste has yet become operational anywhere in the developed countries. Environmental problems with consequent health issues occurring at temporary sites where high-level nuclear wastes (HLNWs) are stored pose serious risks that need to be addressed urgently.

The United States, in 2009, shelved its Yucca Mountain nuclear waste repository project after two decades of detailed investigations costing about $13.5 billion. There is no doubt that soon this issue will be re-examined and construction of a deep geological repository will start.

Many countries are switching to renewable energy sources to meet GHG reduction goals and supplementing their energy needs from nuclear power. While this will lower the GHG emissions, management of nuclear waste would continue to pose serious challenges. As of August 2021, 51 nuclear power reactors were under construction in 19 countries with an installed capacity of 53.91 gigawatts (GW) of electricity. Except for Finland, where the world's first deep geological repository for HLNW is expected to start operations in 2023, the remaining 30 countries will need to build their own repository or store their HLNW safely for a long time.

Electronic or e-waste is one of the fastest-growing waste streams in the world. Unlike other types of wastes discussed in this book, e-waste represents a unique type of waste because of the potential to recover valuable and rare metals, such as gold, copper, palladium, platinum, etc., from discarded high-tech equipment and personal IT devices, some of which, like smartphones, are used in billions and discarded after two to three years of use.

Over the past decade, our approach to dealing with societal waste has evolved from considering waste as a useless material to a valued resource that led the United States Environmental Protection Agency (EPA) and other organizations to change their waste management philosophy from *waste* management to *resource* management. Waste is no longer considered a product of no value, but a resource that can yield valuable materials. New concepts of *urban ore* and *urban mining* offer tantalizing options to recover valuable metallic resources from abandoned landfills and urban waste streams. The concentration of metals like Au and Pt in the discarded electronic devices greatly exceeds that found in natural ores. Additionally, the near-surface presence of this urban ore in the anthroposphere, as opposed to that of the natural ores deep in the lithosphere, makes its extraction easy and less expensive, eliminating large quantities of hazardous waste that are generated during mining, processing, and refining these metals from natural ores.

Innovative methods to recycle materials are being developed at all levels: wide-ranging initiatives from low- or no-cost school projects to bring awareness of a clean and healthy environment to young children by engaging them in simple waste-minimization activities, to training college students to conduct waste audits of campus facilities and business establishments, to microfactories (Chapter 9) are excellent examples of innovations in recycling and waste minimization. Many college graduates and young entrepreneurs have successfully created businesses in the waste minimization areas, such as repurposing surplus stocks of usable products that otherwise would end up in landfills. On the more complex levels, the use of ligands and polymers to economically extract minute quantities of valuable and scarce elements used in IT devices and other high-tech products illustrate the unlimited possibilities for innovation in the field of waste minimization (Chapter 8).

Application of new technologies, such as using solid waste to produce green hydrogen – hydrogen that is produced without any fossil fuel input – to generate electricity or heat for industrial manufacturing, is a promising alternative to eliminate fossil fuels to limit CO_2 emissions to 280 ppm. In addition, there is growing interest in using MSW for energy generation. The projected annualized growth in the waste-to-energy (WtE) industry of about 6% from 2020 to 2025 would divert significant amounts of MSW from going to landfills. Global WtE industry leaders include the Emery Company, Everbright Industries, Hitachi, Mitsubishi, Veolia Environment, Waste Management, etc.

College graduates contemplating a career in waste management would find numerous opportunities to be creative and successful by applying their knowledge, irrespective of the major area of their degree education – business, communication, Earth and environmental sciences, economics, engineering, financing, IT, psychology, etc. – to the growing field of waste management.

On the political level, governing authorities must recognize the importance of proper waste management and give it the same level of priority as other essential services for the public. Reluctance, due to lack of awareness or political considerations, should not be the reason to ignore proper and environmentally safe management of societal wastes because the consequences of doing nothing or very little to address the waste problem will impose heavy economic and social costs, coupled with increased morbidity and mortality, and worsening the severe climate change impacts.

1.5 Summary

Humans have been generating waste ever since their presence on the Earth, but its quantity and complexity have increased after the IR. Heavy use of synthetic chemicals in industrial production, increasing population, growing urbanization, consumers' demand for high-tech devices, and aging populations in developed countries have raised global concern for safe management of MSW, hazardous, medical, nuclear, and electronic wastes, besides finding an environmentally safe way to manage PPCPs.

Large-scale adoption of PO in consumer products has been largely responsible for the growing quantity of societal waste and environmental degradation. The linear economy must be replaced by a circular economy by designing consumer products for repair and reuse. The Right to Repair legislation must be enacted at state, federal, and global levels to avert the impending disasters linked to climate change.

We surmise that mismanagement of waste is the primary cause of degradation of the Earth's environmental quality and disposing of the wastes in a controlled and safe manner can help maintain the delicate ecosystem. Waste mismanagement places a severe burden on human and ecological health that results in heavy economic and social costs. The UN SDGs, which call for economic development to work in unison with environmental preservation, can be achieved by dealing with waste in an environmentally safe manner in combination with other measures. The COVID-19 pandemic has demonstrated that waste workers play a vital role, just like the health care workers, in delivering the needed relief and service to the affected population in a timely and effective way.

Available global information points to increasing quantities of wastes, with MSW and e-waste being the two fastest-growing categories of waste. Using appropriate waste minimization methods would help recover valuable materials from waste streams and conserve scarce natural resources. The opportunities for discovering new methods for waste minimization are unlimited and offer an excellent prospect for innovation.

The multidisciplinary nature of waste management and the future increase in waste quantities call for a large workforce with trained people from nearly all fields of learning, which is sure to provide good jobs and career opportunities for young professionals.

Study Questions

1   Discuss the role of humans on the Earth. Do you agree or disagree with the statement "humans should be the caretakers and not the masters of the Earth"? Provide supporting arguments for your viewpoint.

2   List and differentiate the various types of wastes that are generated in modern societies. Why is reliable information on global waste quantities hard to find?

3   Why should waste management be considered as important as other utilities provided to the public by the local government?

4   List the three major revolutions in human history and comment upon the landmark event that has created serious environmental problems that we have to deal with. How could we ensure preserving the environment and ensuring a safe and healthy planet for future generations?

5   Define environmental sustainability. How can waste management contribute to the UN SDGs? Describe the role of waste management in accomplishing at least three SDGs.

6   Explain how waste workers' services during the COVID-19-like pandemics are vital for saving lives and minimizing economic loss.

7   What is planned obsolescence (PO)? What steps should you take to ensure that manufacturers switch to a circular economy, rather than carrying on with the current practice of linear economy?

8   How is the quantity and nature of waste related to lifestyle of people in a country? Are all types of waste generated in each and every country of the world? Which single waste is not generated in underdeveloped countries? Why?

9   What are the problems in implementing the recommendations of the UN treaties, such as the Paris Agreement? Would you recommend that major treaties should be binding on all countries? Why or why not?

10   How do you view the future of waste management? Do you expect that it will offer you a rewarding career opportunity? Explain why or why not.

References

Dodd, M., Papineau, D., Grenne, T. et al. (2017). Evidence for early life in Earth's oldest hydrothermal vent precipitates. *Nature* **543**: 60–64. https://doi.org/10.1038/nature21377.

Hasan, S.E. (2017). *Total Health Initiative and Medical Geology: Need for a Fresh Perspective*, Conference Materials, 7th International Conference on Medical Geology (MEDGEO '17), 38. Moscow: Publishing House of I.M. Sechenov, First MMSU.M.

Hasan, S.E. and Johnston, R.K. (2016). Recycling at a higher education institution: case study of a successful program at the University of Missouri-Kansas City. In: *Geoscience for the Public Good and Global Development: Toward a Sustainable Future*, Geological Society of America Special Papers, SP 520 (ed. G.R. Wessel and J.K. Greenberg), 407–414. Boulder, CO: Geological Society of America.

IPCC (2021). *Climate Change 2021: The Physical Science Basis*, the Working Group I contribution to the Sixth Assessment Report of the Intergovernmental Panel on Climate Change, Press Release 2021/17/PR, 9 August 2021, 6 p. Press_release_wgi_ar6_website-final (ipcc.ch) (accessed 17 August 2021).

Kazak, S., Yao, L., Bhava-Tata, P., and Van Warden, F. (2018). *What a Waste 2.0: A Global Snapshot of Solid Waste Management to 2050*, Urban Development Series. Washington, DC: World Bank, 296 p. https://doi.org/10.1596/978-1-4648-1329-0. https://openknowledge.worldbank.org/bitstream/handle/10986/30317/9781464813290.pdf (accessed 5 November 2018).

Tchobanoglous, G., These, H., and Vigil, S. (1993). *Integrated Solid Waste Management: Engineering Principles and Management Issues*. New York: McGraw-Hill, 978 p.

UN (2021). Goal 12: ensure sustainable consumption and production patterns, Target 12.3. Department of Economic and Social Affairs. un.org (accessed 2 August 2021).

United Nations, Department of Economic and Social Affairs (2021). The 17 goals. Sustainable Development. un.org (accessed 24 August 2021).

UNEP (United Nations Environment Programme) (2015). *Global Waste Management Outlook*. Washington, DC: United Nations Environment Programme, 332 p.

UNEP (United Nations Environment Programme) (2021). *Food Waste Index Report*. Nairobi: United Nations Environment Programme, 99 p.

Supplementary Readings

FAO (Food and Agricultural Organization of the United Nations) (2021). *The State of Food Security and Nutrition in the World 2021. Transforming Food Systems for Food Security, Improved Nutrition and Affordable Healthy Diets for All*. Rome: FAO, 211 p. https://doi.org/10.4060/cb4474en.

Wigginton, N., Yeston, J., and Malakoff, D. (2012). Working with waste. *Science* 337 (6095): 662–663. Science/AAAS|Special Issue: Working with Waste (sciencemag.org). This 80-page special edition of 10 articles discusses various types of waste, and offers a good overview of the subject.

Web Resources

OECD (Organisation for Economic Co-operation and Development). Statistical data (1990–current) on waste in Europe and other countries are posted on its website: Municipal waste, Generation and Treatment (oecd.org).

US EPA. Useful information and links to important data and statistics on various types of wastes are available on its website: Wastes|US EPA.

Acronyms/Symbols

BCE	before common era
CFCs	chlorofluorocarbons
CH_4	methane
CO_2	carbon dioxide
COVID-19	coronavirus infectious disease-2019
Mt	million metric ton
MSW	municipal solid waste
MW	medical waste
N_2O	nitrous oxide
O_3	ozone
t	metric ton

2

Essentials of Geology, Geotechnics, and Toxicology

LEARNING OBJECTIVES

After studying this chapter, you should be able to:

- Describe the essentials of geology and its relevance to waste management.
- Understand various geotechnical aspects of earth materials and their significance in the selection of waste disposal facilities and remediation of contaminated sites.
- Explain the principles of toxicology and relate them to human and ecological health issues caused by waste mismanagement.

2.1   Introduction

> Indeed, in the creation of heavens and the earth, and the alternation of the night and the day; and in the ships that sail through the sea with what benefits the people; and in the waters which God sends down from the sky, giving life thereby to the earth, after it had died, and dispersing all creatures thereon; and in controlling the winds and the clouds that run their appointed courses between the sky and the earth (in all this) there are signs for people who use their intellect.
>
> —*The Qur'an 2:164*

Human beings are the latest species to appear on the earth. We do not know with certainty when the first human being appeared on earth. Early studies estimated it to be about 200 000 years ago. But after the 1962 discovery of five human remains along with their tools in Jebel Irhoud, 100 km west of Marrakesh in Morocco, and subsequent excavation at an abandoned barite mine in early 2002, Hublin and his colleagues concluded that these remains are at least 315 000 years old. Because the tools the ancestral humans used were made of rock not found where the fossilized remains were discovered, but 50 km south of Jebel Irhoud. So, it is very likely that the ancestral humans had traveled carrying their tools along to hunt gazelles, suggesting that modern humans appeared around half a million years ago (Jean-Hublin et al. 2017). Regardless of exactly when humans appeared on the earth, this planet is our home and, just as we like to take care and maintain our home with its plumbing, heating, cooling, electrical, and other components working optimally, we also need to assure that all components of the system earth are working in proper order to assure its long-term survival. Unfortunately, our recent history tells us otherwise.

Introduction to Waste Management: A Textbook, First Edition. Syed E. Hasan.
© 2022 John Wiley & Sons Ltd. Published 2022 by John Wiley & Sons Ltd.

Fortunately, we have now developed a better understanding of what went wrong and what we need to do to correct the situation. Since this book is about waste and how its mismanagement has impacted the earth and its environment, it is essential that we first understand how humanity's home, the earth, works to be able to determine the right solutions. This chapter is an overview of fundamental principles of the fields of geology, hydrogeology, and toxicology to enable the readers to acquire the necessary background to comprehend the interdisciplinary nature of waste management.

2.2 Basic Concepts

We first discuss seven key concepts to introduce the readers to the key ideas that comprise the core of environmental sciences.

> *Concept 1: Environmental science is an applied science that integrates fundamental principles from a number of disciplines to find solutions to environmental problems facing humanity.*

Unlike mathematics, physics, or chemistry, which are considered pure science, environmental science represents an applied field of knowledge. It incorporates important principles of many fields of knowledge, including chemistry, earth, life, and health sciences; mathematics, physics, social and behavioral sciences, and other relevant disciplines. A general comprehension of fundamental principles of relevant disciplines is essential to develop a sound understanding of environmental science. The case study, *Box 5.2 Tri-State Mining District Superfund Site, Cherokee County, Kansas,* is an excellent example highlighting the complex nature, health and environmental impacts, remediation options, plan implementation, and related issues at an abandoned metal-mining operation. Large-scale metal mining and refining operations last for several decades during which a large number of toxic substances are generated that are embedded in mine tailings, milling, processing, and refinery waste. Percolating rain and snowmelt dissolve toxic elements from exposed mine waste, and groundwater inside the mines leach toxic metals, forming acid mine drainage (AMD) that finds its way into surface water bodies and also seeps down to contaminate groundwater aquifers. The prevailing wind scatters airborne toxic metal particles far and wide.

The Tri-State Mega Superfund site involved experts from several disciplines working together to develop and implement the remediation plan that cost tens of millions of dollars and took 3–5 decades. Experts were drawn from geology, engineering, management and financing, economics, psychology, biology, veterinary and health sciences, hydrology, public relations and communication sciences, sociology, and others. Table 2.1 lists the experts, their role, and length of involvement for remediation of contaminated areas resulting from large mining and metal production operations.

> *Concept 2: Geology is integral to understanding and solving environmental problems.*

Geology, the science of earth (geo = earth, logia = science/study) is integral to environmental science. The earth and its inhabitants mutually influence each other: Humans draw all life-sustaining resources from the earth and, in doing so, impact the earth's environment, causing air, water, and soil pollution. Some natural earth's processes, such as river flooding,

Table 2.1   Experts, their roles, and duration of involvement in characterization and remediation of contaminated mining sites.

Expert	Role	Involvement period
Geologist	Assess the occurrence and exploitation of mineral commodities. Review mining history, ore extraction, processing, and refining; prepare detailed maps of contaminated areas; plan and obtain surface and subsurface samples of soil, sediment, surface water and groundwater. Characterize the full nature and extent of contamination, inclusive of air monitoring, if necessary.	Continuous, long-term; project inception to final cleanup; 20–30 years.
Chemist	Perform chemical analyses of media samples and report the concentration of organic and inorganic contaminants. Ensure validity of the chemical data.	Short-term, as needed; few months.
Toxicologist	Interpret chemical analyses results for potential impacts on human and ecological health. Recommend safe levels of harmful contaminants for cleanup goal.	Short- to medium-term may join public meetings; months-year.
Engineer, Civil/ Environmental	Complete engineering design for implementation of the selected remedy. Plan and conduct design investigations as necessary. Assist in overseeing construction of the remedy in accordance with the design.	Medium-term; later project phase after remedy selection; months–years.
Project Manager	Overall project management; control and review of finances; cost over-runs, etc.	Continuous after project starts; long-term; 20–30 years.
Attorney	Evaluate the liability of responsible parties and their ability to fund or participate in the characterization and remediation of the site. Monitor all aspects of the project for legal sufficiency.	Continuous, long-term; project inception to final cleanup; 20–30 years.
Economist/Cost Engineer Media and Communication	Economic analysis of project cost; comparative economic evaluation of alternatives, especially the no-action alternative. Information dissemination to the public using available media; liaison between media and project authority; web portal management and facilitation of in-person meetings for input.	Medium-term; months-years. Continuous after project startup; long-term; years.
Sociologist	Review and analyze demographic data, population characteristics; native people values and concerns; potential social impacts of short- and long-term relocation.	Medium-term; as needed; months-years.
Psychologist	Analyze impacted community's attitudes and behavior toward remediation program; ways to overcome opposition, etc.	Short-medium term, and as needed; months-year.
Hydrologist/ Hydrogeologist	Evaluate contamination of water bodies, including the drinking water aquifer; sampling, analyses, and modeling of contamination spread and effectiveness of remediation measures; availability of alternative drinking water source.	Medium-long-term but noncontinuous; years-decades.

(Continued)

Table 2.1   (Continued)

Expert	Role	Involvement period
Biologist	Survey and analysis of flora and fauna in the area; advise on protected or endangered species; sampling of plants and animals for potential contamination.	Short-medium term; months to years.
Veterinarian	Assessment of impacts on domestic and wild animals from potential contamination: treatment of affected animals.	Medium-term; and as needed; few-several years.
Healthcare	Evaluation of human health issues from possible contamination; treatment measures and long-term health monitoring.	Medium-long term; years to decades.

earthquake, landslide, volcanic eruption, etc., produce adverse impacts on humans and other life forms. The release of large quantities of toxic gases and chemical compounds during volcanic eruptions and mobilization of earth materials following landslides and mudflows adversely impact air and water qualities. Knowledge of geology provides a strong foundation to minimize impacts of hazardous earth processes to humans while enabling us to develop solutions to effectively remediate pollution levels and return the polluted air, water, and land to their clean condition.

Although we generally do not recognize it, geology plays a central role in our lives. Ever since our birth and until we die, we consume a large amount of earth's resources. It is not only food and water, but a variety of minerals and energy resources that we use in large quantities to sustain our lives. Just looking at what you may be carrying on your person today – smartphone, laptop, digital watch, etc. – we find that all are made from metals, nonmetals, plastics, and other substances that are derived from earth materials: minerals, rocks, petroleum, etc. You might have heard about the rare earth elements (REEs) and the platinum group metals (PGMs) that are key components of modern electronic equipment. The REEs are used in many high-tech equipment like space vehicles, windmills, sophisticated military weapons, high-tech sports gear, and many more. REEs are unevenly distributed on the earth, are not very abundant, and have created international tensions among supplying and importing nations. Geology underpins the occurrence and availability of essential metals and offers alternatives when supply runs short or is exhausted. (Chapter 8 discusses the critical role of REEs in electronic devices and the geopolitical concerns).

> *Concept 3: The earth is a system comprising five components that are interdependent, such that a change in one brings about change in the other components.*

A complex system, such as an automobile, comprises several components or subsystems, all of which operate in close coordination with each other to allow the system to perform at an optimum level. If the heating/cooling mechanism of the automobile does not work well and fails to cool the engine, the car won't perform satisfactorily; or, if the transmission component fails, it would affect the overall performance, and so on. In a similar way, we can think of the earth as a system that is made up of several components that operate at optimum levels to maintain the unique ecological balance of the earth. However, if the normal function/pattern of one of the components is disrupted, all other components are affected, causing serious and damaging impacts to the earth. The five interdependent components of the system earth include:

1) The atmosphere
2) The lithosphere
3) The hydrosphere
4) The biosphere
5) The anthroposphere

The atmosphere is an envelope of gases that surrounds the earth from its surface to about 500 km above (NASA 2021). It contains life-supporting O_2, and N_2 – approximately 21 and 78%, respectively – along with minor quantities of water vapor (H_2O), CO_2, O_3, CH_4, and noble gases, such as Ar, Kr, etc., collectively adding up to 1%. These minor gases protect the life on the earth from harmful UV radiations emanating from space and also regulate the earth's temperature. For example, without the 0.03% (300 ppm) of CO_2 in the atmosphere, the earth would be a lifeless and frigid planet. A disproportionate mixture of minor gases, such as CO_2 and O_3 would disrupt the function, and upset the balance causing, for instance, global warming and ozone depletion.

The lithosphere is the outermost layer of the earth and is the critical zone that supports all life forms. It is also the storehouse of all geologic materials, rocks, minerals, soil, and water that are essential for life and provide raw materials for meeting our needs of food, fiber, and shelter. Careless and casual disposal of small amounts of less toxic waste might produce minor harm to soil biota, and affect its fertility, but in larger quantities, or highly toxic waste would poison the soil and water, killing the biota, destroying the food chain, and to those ingesting food products grown on such soil, seriously acute and chronic diseases.

The hydrosphere includes water in all its three states – solid (ice), liquid (ordinary water in streams, lakes, etc.), gas (water vapor in the atmosphere) – and controls its occurrence and movement across the land, oceans, and the atmosphere. Uncontrolled release of toxic vapors and/or fine solid particles and aerosols can degrade the air quality severely, causing both short- and long-term health problems. Unlike land and freshwater contamination that do not spread worldwide, air pollution can reach all corners of the earth in a relatively short period of time, causing a variety of medical, social, and economic problems. The rapid spread of the SARS-CoV-2 virus across the globe within days is a classic example of toxins' transmission through the atmosphere.

The biosphere is where all living forms reside, from the biologically most complex forms (humans) to the simplest (microbes). Under normal conditions and with the proper functioning of each species, the biosphere maintains its ability to support all lives. However, even a slight imbalance in one of the several components threatens the long-term sustainability of all life forms. The increasing acidity of water in the oceans threatening the marine ecosystem, if not controlled, can lead to the potential destruction of all forms of lives, is one of the many examples of such imbalance.

The anthroposphere was not recognized as a component of the system earth until recently. This was needed because of the immense impacts humans can and have produced on the earth, surpassing what natural processes do. For example, humans using powerful equipment and machineries are generating sediments many times greater than the combined erosion and deposition by running water, ice, and wind (Wilkinson and McElroy 2007).

In addition, human activities have caused depletion of stratospheric ozone from excessive use of chlorofluorocarbons (in air conditioning); burning fossil fuels for electricity generation, transportation, etc.; which have led to global warming and destabilization of the climate and is posing a serious challenge to humanity.

The mutual dependency of the earth's five components can be lucidly explained from climate change which is one of the greatest environmental threats of modern times facing humanity. Climate change is the effect of the earth's warming that has occurred in the atmosphere. The natural level of CO_2 in the atmosphere before the Industrial Revolution (IR) was a meager 0.028% or 280 ppm, which has gone up to over 400 ppm in about 200 years. Looking at Figure 2.1, it is easy to see that the change that started in the anthroposphere affected the atmosphere, which impacted the temperature regime on the land (lithosphere) and oceans (hydrosphere), which, in turn, affected vegetation, along with heat-related deaths to humans and other living forms (biosphere).

The mutual dependency of the five components of the system earth constitutes a fundamental principle of ecology which can be stated as: Nothing is independent in nature and everything affects everything else.

Concept 4: Geologic processes, operating in cycles, are continuously modifying the landscape and materials of the earth; but unlike humans who can force changes rapidly and dramatically, geological processes operate at a slower pace.

Figure 2.1   The system earth and its five components.

Most geologic processes take hundreds of thousands to million years. For example, the average tectonic cycle operates for about 250 million years. Yet there is nothing permanent, and the earth is constantly undergoing changes, but the rate of change is highly variable; from sudden and dramatic, such as the eruption of a volcano or occurrence of an earthquake, to extremely slow and imperceptible, such as progressive downslope movement of a mass of earth material, or the gradual breakdown of large rock mass into its individual constituent mineral grains. The important point is: The earth is a dynamic system undergoing changes all the time.

In terms of size and space, geologic features cover a wide range. For example, a fault, a common geologic structural feature, could range from microscopic – a fraction of a millimeter – discernible only under high-power magnification, to extremely large, several hundred km long, such as the San Andreas Fault in California. Despite this variation in scale, geologic processes are continuous and ongoing.

Depending on the location whether at or near, or inside or below the earth's surface, geological processes can be grouped under exogenic (external from Greek *exo* meaning "outside" or "outer part") or endogenic (internal from Greek *endon* meaning "in" or "within"). Collectively, these two processes are responsible for rock weathering, soil formation, and the occurrence of earthquakes and volcanic activities, shaping the earth's topography and landscape. Examples of common exogenic and endogenic earth processes and their features are given in Table 2.2.

> *Concept 5: Solutions to environmental problems require shifting our time scale from human to geologic.*

The earth is 4.6 billion years old. This long period of earth history has been divided into major eras and further subdivided into periods and epochs. Table 2.3 shows the main divisions of geologic time, including the Anthropocene.

An interesting way to relate the enormity of geologic time to human time scale would be to compress the entire 4.6 billion years (Ga) of earth's age into one year of human time, which would mean: 1 geologic month = 383 million human years; 1 day = 12.6 million human years; 1 hour = 525 114 years; 1 minute = 8752 years; and 1 second = 146 years (i.e. one earth second would witness three generations of human activities). If we overlay earth's history over a 24-hour clock, we can comprehend the key events on earth, including the appearance of human beings.

Table 2.2   Exogenic and endogenic earth processes and their characteristics.

Exogenic Processes	Endogenic Processes
Weathering and soil formation, landscape evolution, river flooding, glaciation, hurricanes, and tornadoes	Formation of rocks, continents, oceans, and mountain ranges; occurrence of earthquakes, volcanic activities
Operate externally, i.e. at or near earth's surface, powered by solar energy	Operate internally, i.e. inside or below the earth's surface, powered by heat derived from the decay of radioactive elements
The combined action of air, ice, water, aided by gravity carve, shape, and modify the landscape	Drive the earth's tectonic plates, producing large-scale features of the earth, e.g. oceans, continents, mountain chains; and causing earthquakes and volcanic activities.

Table 2.3 Geologic time scale.

Eon	Era	Period	Epoch	Interval started (my[a])	Interval duration (my)	Percent of time
Proterozoic	CENOZOIC	Quaternary	Anthropocene	1950 CE	—	—
			Holocene	0.012	0.012	—
			Pleistocene	2.58	2.58	0.56
		Neogene	Pliocene	5.33	2.75	0.597
		Paleogene	Miocene	23.03	17.7	0.38
			Oligocene	33.9	10.87	0.24
			Eocene	56.0	22.1	0.48
			Paleocene	66.0	10.0	0.22
	MESOZOIC	Cretaceous	Age of reptiles	145	79.0	1.72
		Jurassic		201.3	56.3	1.22
		Triassic		251.9	50.6	1.10
	PALEOZOIC	Permian	Age of amphibians	298.9	47.0	1.02
		Carboniferous		358.9	60	1.30
		Devonian	Age of fish	419.2	60.3	1.31
		Silurian		443.8	24.6	0.54
		Ordovician	Age of invertebrates	485.4	41.6	0.90
		Cambrian		541.0	55.6	1.21
Pre-Cambrian	PROTEROZOIC	First multicellular life appears		2500	1959	42.58
	ARCHEAN	First unicellular life appears		4000	1500	32.61
	HADEAN	Earth forms		4600	600	13.04

[a] my = million years.

Note: As of September 2021, Anthropocene was not officially recognized by the International Commission on Stratigraphy of the International Union of Geological Congress, although the Anthropocene Working Group in 2016 had recommended adding Anthropocene to the Geological Time Scale with 1950 as its beginning.
In the USA, Carboniferous Period is subdivided into Pennsylvanian Period (began 332.3 my) and the Mississippian Period (358.9 my).

Midnight 12:00 AM	Earth is born
4:00 AM	Simple unicellular life appears on the earth
5:30 AM	Multicellular life starts
9:00 PM	Explosion of life, dominated by invertebrates
9:29 PM	Land plants appear
10:07 PM	Amphibians dominate
10:26 PM	Reptiles appear
10:41 PM	Dinosaurs arrive
11:14 PM	Extinction of dinosaurs
11:49 PM	Mammals appear
11:58 PM	Humans appear

Despite having appeared on the earth in the most recent moment of its enormous life, humans have inflicted heavy damage to the earth's environment and ecosystem.

Environmental problems that we are now facing have taken a long time to manifest. Climate change, for instance, did not happen in years or decades. It took over 200 years for the slow but continuous output of greenhouse gases (GHGs) dominated by CO_2, to exceed the threshold levels to cause serious shifts in a climatic pattern. The toxic chemicals that were dumped 100–150 years ago are still polluting water bodies and soils all over the world. The Tri-State Mega Superfund site in the US Midwest became a dumping ground of toxic waste from mining and processing of lead and zinc ores beginning in 1872. The resulting water and soil pollution, along with adverse health impacts on humans, animals, and plants are still continuing and the cleanup operations that began in 1982, are yet to be completed. Death, acute and chronic illnesses, disruption of the community's social fabric and economy represent a heavy price that we are paying for lack of foresight in managing toxic waste safely. I had my students who began their professional career in the 1980s working at Superfund sites, have now retired and the job is not yet finished. The key point is that while preparing the Environmental Impact Statement (EIS) for new developmental projects, we must expand our time frame by not limiting it to 1–2 generations but to seven generations at a minimum. The elapsed time since the IR and buildup of atmospheric CO_2 to dangerous level is equivalent to seven generations. Ancient cultures knew the importance of this long-term vision and took it into consideration even for minor alteration of the land, for example, digging a narrow trench from the stream bank to divert water for crop irrigation. Modern humans, driven by greed and imprudence, have tossed this wisdom aside. Fortunately, signs of positive change are appearing and the current generation is more conscious about environmental protection than the earlier ones.

Concept 6: Hazardous earth processes must be given due considerations in planning development projects to minimize their adverse impacts.

River flooding, extreme weather events, drought, wildfires, landslides, earthquakes, and volcanic activities are natural processes that pose a certain degree of hazard to people. The magnitude and intensity of these hazards are subject to natural and man-induced changes. Land-use planning must take into account the nature and severity of these hazards and suitable engineering design safeguards must be provided to eliminate or minimize adverse impacts from the natural hazards. Human alteration of land and the natural environment, combined with construction in hazard-prone areas, results in huge loss of lives and economic damage. While the occurrence of natural hazards cannot be eliminated, loss of lives can be minimized by building more resilient infrastructures, using advanced warning systems, adequate emergency preparedness, and efficient response systems. Higher deaths occur in low-income countries with low economic loss, while greater economic loss and lower deaths are common in high-income countries. Figure 2.2 represents the economic cost of all global hazards that include droughts, floods, earthquakes, volcanic activities, landslides and mass movements, hurricanes, heat stress from heat waves, and wildfires for the past 40 years, and Figure 2.3 shows global economic loss for the same period from all hazards (Ritchie and Roser 2014).

An important characteristic of natural hazards is that they vary widely in magnitude and frequency, with larger magnitude (causing most deaths and losses) being less frequent, while those of lower magnitude occurring more frequently.

In terms of deaths, earthquakes have been the most destructive among the natural hazards. On an annual basis, there may not be any large-magnitude earthquake anywhere in the world, but on a decadal basis, the trend becomes very clear as depicted in Figure 2.2.

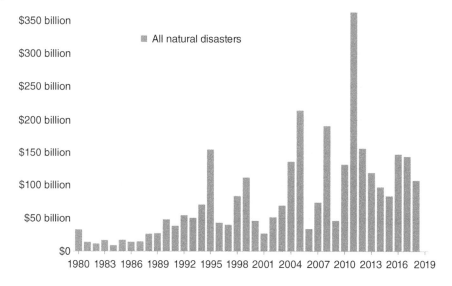

Figure 2.2   Economic loss from all-natural hazards worldwide, 1980–2019. *Source:* Data from Ritchie and Roser, 2014.

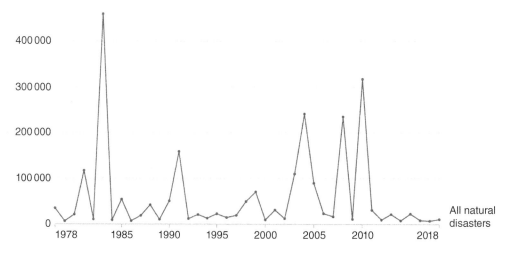

Figure 2.3   Deaths from all-natural hazards worldwide, 1978–2018. *Source:* Data from Ritchie and Roser 2014.

Concept 7: Nature is a great recycler and nothing is ever wasted.

Everything in nature has a purpose and nothing is wasted. Even the apparent abundance of leaves and fruits in trees serves an important ecological need. Using the example of the wild cherry tree, we know that as it blossoms, it is filled with flowers, many of which turn into fruit, which provide food and nutrients to birds and insects and of those that fall on the ground, some germinate to grow into new cherry trees. As the season advances, the flowers, leaves, and barks drop down on the forest floor, which serve as sources of food for detritivores, who break them down into essential soil nutrients, enabling it to remain productive years after years. In nature, there is no such thing as overabundance: despite the countless flowers and fruits that a cherry tree produces, each and every one fulfills the specific needs of the ecosystem where everything used for the growth and survival of the tree is returned to where it came from. There is no waste. In addition, while sustaining itself, the cherry tree enriches the ecosystem by providing additional benefits like removing carbon and producing oxygen through photosynthesis, thereby cleaning the air and water, and promoting a diverse flora and fauna. Even after its death, the cherry tree continues its useful role by releasing nutrients that feed the healthy new growth at the same spot.

The example of the cherry tree as an element of nature's growth presents a stark contrast with the industrial growth that uses an enormous amount of natural resources but returns polluted waste products into nature that destroys the ecosystems and its components, degrades the quality of soil, water, and air. If only we could apply nature's example of production, reuse and recycling, we can not only fulfill all our needs, but also manage the wastes in an environmentally safe manner. Proper waste management, the key to a safe environment, is the underlying theme of this book.

2.3 Geologic Cycles

Earth is a dynamic system where changes are happening all time. Geological processes occur in a cyclic manner. Most take millions of years to go through the various events/steps in the cycle from start to finish (the tectonic cycle takes an average of about 250 million years). The water cycle is shorter and may take hundreds to thousands of years.

The geologic cycle is a broad earth science concept that explains the formation of mountains, transfer of their materials through erosion and sedimentation into oceans, to their reincorporation into newly formed mountains through the tectonic cycle. The geologic cycle is nature's way of recycling earth materials; it includes a set of sub-cycles that are responsible for the formation, occurrence, and distribution of earth materials; evolution and transformation of landforms, and climatic aspects of the earth. The major earth cycles comprise:

- Rock cycle
- Water (hydrologic) cycle
- Tectonic cycle
- Geochemical cycle
- Climate cycle

2.3.1 Rock Cycle

The Rock Cycle is one of the earth's major cycles that results in the creation, destruction, and maintenance of the earth's materials. It is a good example of the recycling of materials in nature. All three major classes of rocks – igneous, sedimentary, and metamorphic – and their numerous varieties owe their origin to the rock cycle. In addition, earth materials that are the source of metals, non-metals, coal, petroleum, and minerals that fuel nuclear power reactors, are all products of the rock cycle. Different types of sediments, including such common materials as sand and gravel, represent a particular stage in the rock cycle. Figure 2.4 shows various pathways in the rock cycle and the resulting products.

Any rock exposed to the surface undergoes a series of physical, chemical, and biological actions that cause it to break down and decompose into its constituent minerals over a long period of time. This natural process of rock disintegration and decomposition is called weathering. The loose

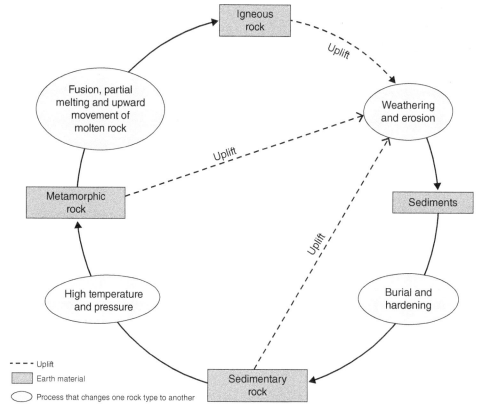

Figure 2.4 The rock cycle.

mineral grains or rock fragments, called sediments, are removed from their original location through the action of wind, water, and/or ice, aided by gravity. After a long period of transportation, the sediments are ultimately laid down on the ocean floor, where they later get covered with fresh loads of sediment continuously deposited into the ocean by rivers. Deep burial, aided by biogeochemical reactions in the ocean results in the formation of sedimentary rocks, through a process called *lithification*. The earth's tectonic process may cause the oceanic floor to be pulled downward into the deeper part of the earth's interior where higher temperature and pressure may cause the rocks to change their appearance (metamorphosis) resulting in the formation of *metamorphic* rocks. If subjected to additional tectonic forces, the newly formed rock can be pulled deeper down inside the earth where high temperature and pressure cause the solid rock to melt, creating a magma reservoir. Ongoing tectonic stresses may squeeze the molten rock (magma) to move upward and either stop some distance below the surface, where after a long period of cooling, the magma may solidify to form *intrusive* igneous rocks. In other cases, the magma may keep moving upward to erupt like a volcano or quietly move down the land slope as a lava flow. When the lava cools and solidifies above the earth's surface, the resulting rock is called volcanic or *extrusive* igneous rock.

What is described earlier is an ideal rock cycle that will go from start to finish as shown in Figure 2.4. More commonly though, the cycle may be cut short and the buried rock may be pushed up to the surface where the processes of weathering will restart the cycle. These shortcuts in the rock cycle are shown by dashed arrows marked "uplift."

2.3.2 Water (Hydrologic) Cycle

The water (also called hydrologic) cycle relates to the occurrence and movement of water through the lithosphere, anthroposphere, biosphere, and atmosphere. As depicted in Figure 2.5, solar heat causes the water in the ocean to evaporate as water vapor, and move around through the atmosphere by prevailing wind. At the right altitude, where the atmospheric conditions are right for phase change, water vapor changes into the liquid phase and, depending upon the altitude and atmospheric conditions of temperature and pressure at a given location, falls on the ground in the form of rain or snow. Precipitation includes both rain and snow that falls on the land. Rain water moving on the land, called runoff, gets channelized in minor streams and tributaries that join the main river which ultimately enters the ocean with its load of sediments (Figure 2.5). However, not all of the runoff enters the oceans and lakes, but a part seeps down (infiltration) through the openings (pores) in soil and rocks to replenish the layers of soil/rock where all pores are saturated with water. The water that occurs in the open spaces in rock or soil materials is called groundwater, and the uppermost surface of groundwater is called groundwater table. The saturated layer of rock/soil is called an aquifer if it can yield an adequate quantity of water to meet the water supply need of the user.

Groundwater moves underground from points of higher elevation to lower elevation along the groundwater slope. The groundwater may discharge at locations where the groundwater table intersects the land surface into a stream or river, or it may emerge as spring. Alternatively, the groundwater could keep flowing down gradient to discharge into the ocean, completing the water cycle. It must be noted that unlike surface water (rivers, streams) groundwater moves extremely

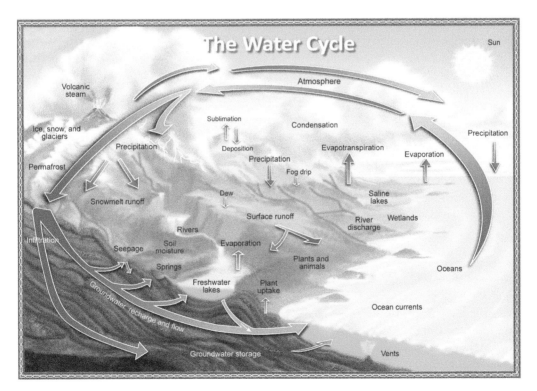

Figure 2.5   The water cycle. *Source:* Public Domain.

slowly. For example, the average rate of groundwater flow ranges between 6- and 10 m/y, whereas the average rate of water flow in stream/river could range from a few km/hr to 10s of km/hr (note the difference in the time unit). This substantial difference in the flow rate is important in the dispersion of contaminants, which are dispersed and diluted quickly in streams/rivers but remain in the groundwater for a very long time due to its slow rate of movement. Hence, once the groundwater gets contaminated, it will remain so for a long time. This intrinsic characteristic of groundwater flow, along with the fact that groundwater is a major source of drinking water supply to about 50% of the US population, calls for taking all possible measures to protect it from contamination.

The total quantity of water that occurs at or near the surface of the earth, within a geographic area, is a function of four factors, expressed by the equation:

$$P = R + I + E \tag{2.1}$$

where,

P = Precipitation (total amount of rainfall and snowfall in the area)

R = Runoff (quantity of water that flows off the land surface after a precipitation event)

I = Infiltration (quantity of water that goes below the surface; recharges groundwater)

E = Evapotranspiration (water used by vegetation for its growth and metabolic function, as well as lost through evaporation from exposed parts of the vegetation).

Equation 2.1 is known as the Universal Hydrologic Equation and is used to estimate the water budget of an area. For example, in the 48 conterminous states in the USA, the average daily precipitation is 15 897 billion liters (4200 billion gallons), of which runoff accounts for 5117 billion liters (1352 billion gallons) and infiltration for 231 billion liters (61 billion gallons). Putting these numbers in the universal hydrologic equation, one can easily determine the amount of evapotranspiration, E, which is 10 549 billion liters (2787 billion gallons)/day.

$$E = P - (R + I)$$
$$= 15897 - (5117 + 231) = 10549 \, \text{billion} \, L / d$$

The total quantity of water available in the world is estimated at 1.39 billion km^3, of which 96.5% is salty and not suitable for drinking. Freshwater accounts for the remaining 2.5%, of which about 69% occurs in glaciers, icecaps and permafrost and is not readily available for use. Water in rivers and freshwater lakes account for only 0.0072% or 176 520 km^3 of the total water on the earth, while groundwater comprises 0.76% or 10.53 million km^3 of freshwater. Figure 2.6 illustrates the occurrence and distribution of water on the earth.

2.3.3 Tectonic Cycle

The tectonic cycle represents a major earth process responsible for the formation of large scale features of the earth, such as mountain ranges, oceans, and continents. The tectonic cycle also controls the occurrence of earthquakes, volcanic activities, and drives the rock cycle. Tectonic forces cause rocks to deform and develop geologic structures, such as folding, faulting, jointing, etc. The tectonic cycle is powered by heat energy liberated from the disintegration of radioactive elements in the earth.

Not much was known about the dynamics of the lithosphere and its makeup below the ocean floor and continents before 1960. However, since the 1950s, through the long and ongoing exploration of ocean floors, earth scientists have developed a clear understanding of the nature of the

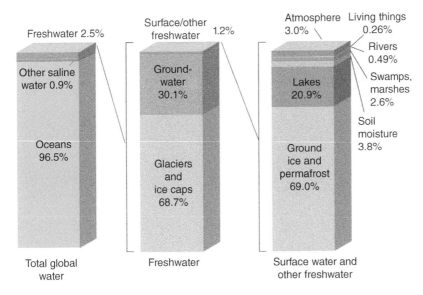

Figure 2.6 Occurrence and distribution of water on the earth. *Source:* Public Domain.

lithosphere and the type of movements associated with it. Meticulous analyses and synthesis of a huge volume of core samples, and geophysical data led to the formulation of the *Theory of Plate Tectonics* in the late 1960s. The plate tectonics theory has emerged as the most important concept in earth sciences and has unified a diverse group of ideas. The theory successfully explains the distribution of oceans and continents; the present positions and similarity in the margins of the continents and their geologic features; the disposition of mountain ranges; past climatic conditions; and the occurrence of various types of faunal, mineral, and rock assemblages in continents that are now separated by oceans. It also explains why some locations, such as California in the United States and parts of the Middle East and Japan, are far more susceptible to earthquake activities than other places on the earth. The occurrence of volcanoes, both present and past, is also satisfactorily explained by the theory of plate tectonics. Although a detailed discussion of the theory is beyond the scope of this book, some of its salient features are listed next:

- Plates are part of the outermost layer of the earth, called the lithosphere. Unlike a continuous sphere, these are broken up into several hard, brittle segments.
- The earth's plates are three-dimensional segments of the lithosphere, with very large length and width but relatively small thickness (like the dinner plate), and are in a state of perpetual motion. The plates are thicker under the continents, about 225 km and thinner, about 70 km, under the oceans. The rate of plate movement is variable, and ranges from 1.3 cm/y to 18.3 cm/y.
- Fifteen large and several small plates have been mapped. Ongoing ocean floor exploration may reveal smaller plates or help refine the existing plate boundaries. Figure 2.7 shows major plates of the earth and their direction of movement.
- The three types of plate boundaries are characterized by compressive (collision), tensile (pulling apart), and shear (sliding past) stresses. These margins, called convergent, divergent, and transform plate boundary, respectively produce different features, such as mountain chains, oceanic trenches, volcanic activities, earthquakes, etc. (Figure 2.8).

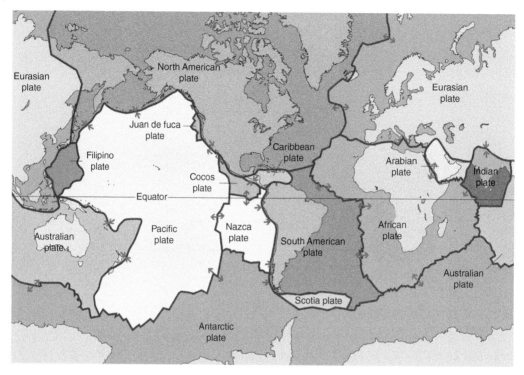

Figure 2.7 Major plates of the earth and their direction of movement. *Source:* Public Domain.

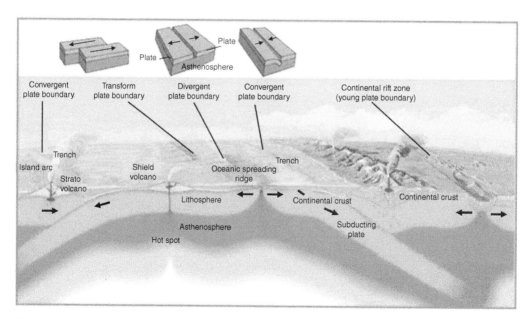

Figure 2.8 Earth's tectonics and features associated with different plate boundaries. *Source:* Public Domain.

2.3.3.1 Significance of Plate Movement

Plate movement affects everything on the earth; most of the changes are subtle and can only be detected by sensitive instruments and occur over a long period of time (thousands to millions of years). Plate movements also result in the formation of new mineral deposits, including coal and petroleum, causing earthquakes and volcanic activities, impacting human lives.

Over periods of millions of years, plate movement may modify the flow pattern of oceanic waters, heralding climatic changes. This may result in some areas receiving higher precipitation, and others becoming drier. The occurrence of certain fauna and flora exclusively in a continent is related to the breakup and isolation of the continents, such as the marsupials in Australia. On the other hand, land bridges between continents facilitate species migration from one continent to the other.

2.3.4 Geochemical Cycle

The geochemical cycle is responsible for the movement and interaction of chemical elements and compounds through various paths in the lithosphere, hydrosphere, biosphere, and atmosphere. It is nature's way of causing the concentration of chemical elements and compounds at one location or their deficiency (removal) at other locations. Pollution of soil, water, and air is largely a result of human activities. Pollution represents an excess of materials that may be harmful to life and the environment. Improper waste management and industrial release of toxic substances into the environment have caused serious environmental pollution.

2.3.5 Climate Cycle

The geologic record, revealed by a meticulous study of rocks, fossils, pollens, and sediments, has proved that the earth's climate has fluctuated through geologic time. Records left in ancient rocks and sediments have revealed major episodes of climatic swings over a given region. For example, deposits of glacial origin are found in places like the tropics, where the present climate is warm and humid and not conducive to formation and growth of glaciers. Yet some 300 million years ago, during the Mississippian and Pennsylvanian periods (the Carboniferous), many places in Africa, South and Central India, South America, and Australia were blanketed by a thick ice sheet. Subsequent climatic changes resulted in the melting and disappearance of the ice sheet, but the glacial deposits were preserved in the rock records, which have revealed the presence of past ice ages in the region.

The younger period of the earth's history, the Quaternary Period (began about 2 million years ago), witnessed at least four major episodes of warming and cooling of the earth. During the Pleistocene Epoch (began 1.6 Ma), the earth's climate alternately ranged from cold (glacial) to warm (interglacial). The duration of these glacial and interglacial periods was variable. During the past one million years, each glacial–interglacial cycle lasted about 100 000 years, but earlier cycles were about 40 000 years long. Some scientists believe that climatic changes that are being experienced now are related to these warming–cooling cycles of the earth's climate, but detailed investigations, supported by modelling studies affirm that the current climate change is largely the result of human activities.

2.4 Earth Materials

The earth materials comprising air, water, soil, and rock, are used for a variety of purposes, including producing food and building structures. While air and water are essential for life, soils are especially significant for humans. As long as they are "clean," they serve to support life.

However, upon pollution, the same life-supporting earth materials may become life-threatening.

A clear understanding of the origin, geologic nature, occurrence, and properties of the earth materials is therefore essential for proper management of various types of waste, particularly the aspects related to the evaluation of contamination of the media and subsequent remediation. A discussion of physical and engineering properties of rocks and soils, important in waste management, is presented in the following sections.

2.4.1 Rocks as Earth Materials

2.4.1.1 Igneous Rocks

When the molten earth material, *magma*, cools and solidifies at some depth below the earth's surface, the resulting rocks are called *intrusive* igneous rocks. When the molten material makes its way to the surface of the earth, it is known as *lava;* the rocks formed by cooling and solidification of lava are called *extrusive* igneous (or *volcanic*) rocks. Chemically, both the intrusive and extrusive rocks from the same magma source will have a similar chemical composition with different sizes of individual minerals – larger in the intrusive and smaller in the extrusive igneous rocks.

2.4.1.2 Sedimentary Rocks

The loose mineral grains, and rock fragments, after being transported by wind, ice, and water, are ultimately deposited on the ocean floor, where they are buried under the column of water and the continuous incoming load of sediments. The pressure of the overburden material, including water, aided by chemical and biochemical reactions that occur in oceans, initiate the process of lithification which is the conversion of sediments into hard layers of rocks, known as sedimentary rocks. Local conditions of water currents, microorganisms, salinity, temperature, and pressure control the formation of various types of sedimentary rocks.

2.4.1.3 Metamorphic Rocks

When the preexisting sedimentary, igneous, or even metamorphic rocks are subjected to the high temperature and high-pressure environment inside the earth, changes in mineral assemblage and texture of the preexisting rocks take place. The new rocks formed as a result of these changes are called metamorphic rocks. All changes occur in the solid state, meaning there is no melting of the preexisting rocks.

2.4.1.4 Engineering Properties and Behavior of Rock Materials

In terms of their strength and performance, non-foliated metamorphic and intrusive igneous rocks are more suitable for engineering construction. Extrusive igneous rocks, because of their susceptibility to weathering and the presence of a large number of discontinuities, are weaker and generally less suitable. At uncontrolled municipal solid waste (MSW) landfills and hazardous waste sites, foliated metamorphic and extrusive igneous rocks are more likely to cause serious problems in contaminant transport because of high permeability.

Engineering use and performance of sedimentary rocks are highly variable. In general, coarse-grained clastic rocks and limestone are suitable for most engineering construction, except when water retention is the main concern, as in dams and reservoirs. Limestone, because of its susceptibility to dissolution in rainwater, tends to develop voids and other solution features, resulting in *karst topography*. Sinkholes and subsurface openings are potential pathways of contaminant movement and require careful investigation. Contaminated surface and groundwater may travel rapidly over large distances through the network of solution openings in limestones.

From an engineering standpoint, metamorphic rocks, in general, are suitable for most construction projects. They have served as a disposal medium for deep well injection of liquid hazardous waste. Surplus chemicals from World War II were disposed of at a depth of 3.6 km, in metamorphic rocks, at the Rocky Mountain Arsenal Site near Denver, Colorado, between 1962 and 1965.

The physical and engineering properties of rocks are greatly influenced by weathering and discontinuities present in them. A strong rock, like granite, possessing high strength, when subjected to a high degree of weathering will be reduced to a loose aggregate of minerals comprised of the original and unaltered quartz and highly decomposed silicate minerals that chemically alter into clay minerals. These weathered materials possess strength that may be a few orders of magnitude lower than that of the unweathered rock. Weathering, in general, also causes an increase in the porosity and permeability of rocks. This aspect is of critical importance in waste management. It is, therefore, very important that a complete evaluation of rocks be done to assess the degree of weathering before any remediation plan is formulated.

The lack of a universal and quantitative weathering index makes it very difficult to distinguish the various intermediate products that fall in between rock and soil – the two extremes. In some situations, sandstone may be weathered to the point that all cementing materials holding the mineral grains together have been leached away, leaving behind a mass of loose grains (sediments). These sediments are completely different from the original rock in the sense that they are unconsolidated, have lower strength, and are disaggregated. On the other extreme, one may find a layer of clay that has been cemented by mineralized water to form a layer of hard, rock-like mass, known as *claypan*. Because of this complexity, a highly weathered rock may be considered a soil material, while a hard, cemented soil layer may be taken to be a rock material. Classifications based on these qualitative factors often result in confusion and litigation at construction projects. For example, a foundation material classified as "earth" (soil) for excavation (because of the absence of any bedrock) may turn out to be a layer of hard claypan or caliche possessing high strength, which requires drilling and blasting for excavation. On the other hand, a foundation material considered rock may turn out to be a highly weathered, soft material, that can be excavated by common earthmoving equipment. With the cost of rock excavation being 4–10 times greater than that for soil excavation, the problems created by such classifications are obvious. It is therefore very important to classify the earth materials as soil or rock on the basis of their strength, and not on their geologic origin. A convenient classification for engineering contract purposes designates soil excavation as one that can be done by using conventional earthmoving equipment. Rocks cannot be excavated in a similar manner and require drilling and blasting. A more accurate distinction between rock and soil can be made on the basis of the unconfined compressive strength (q_u) of the earth material, which can be used to classify it as rock excavation if its q_u is >1380 kN/m^2 (100 psi), or soil excavation, if its q_u is <1380 kN/m^2 (100 psi).

2.4.2 Soils as Earth Material

The term *soil* means different things to different people. To a layperson, soil is dirt but to a soil scientist/agronomist, soil represents the top 1–2 m of the earth's surface that contains organic and inorganic materials and living organisms, which is capable of supporting plant life. To a geologist, soil represents an end product in the weathering continuum. In a broad geologic sense, soils include all loose (unconsolidated) materials, collectively referred to as sediments. A simple way to differentiate soil and sediment is that soils are biotic, i.e. they contain life, while sediments are abiotic, i.e. they are nonliving. These unconsolidated materials occur at the earth's surface, mask the bedrock, and are called overburden. Civil and geotechnical engineers include all unconsolidated materials, including man-made fills, in their definition of soil. Geotechnically, soil represents a three-phase system that comprises discrete solids (the mineral grains), both organic and inorganic, with liquids and gases in between. The most common liquid in conventional geotechnical situations is water, and the most common gas is air. However, in the context of waste management, the pore fluids could be any type of organic or inorganic chemicals. For the purpose of this book, the geotechnical definition of soil is most relevant and henceforth the term *soil* will be used in the context of this definition.

2.4.3 Soil Formation

Soil represents the end product of rock weathering. When a parent material – rock or sediment – is exposed to the atmosphere for a long period of time, it is physically and chemically altered to form soil. In many cases, alteration of the original parent material is aided by biological agents, including humans. Because the process of weathering is primarily responsible for the conversion of parent material into soil, the factors that control weathering also control soil formation. The following five factors control the process of soil formation:

- Parent material
- Climate
- Topography
- Biology
- Time

The original earth material that undergoes weathering to form soil is called the parent material. It could be a rock, sediment, or even older soil. In addition, the chemical composition of the rock also influences the resulting soil. For example, weathering of carbonate rocks would produce fine-grained soils enriched in soluble minerals, like calcite that could form a hard, rock-like layer in semiarid climatic environments. On the other hand, weathering of granites in a warm and humid climate would result in sandy soil dominated by silicate minerals. The same granite in a cold climate would not form any soil layer, other than an assemblage of frost-shattered angular fragments of the rock.

Wet and warm climates are more conducive to soil formation than dry and cold climates. This is because the rate of chemical reactions is faster at elevated temperatures and in the presence of water. This is the reason why soil cover is nonexistent or very thin in dry and hot desert climatic environments.

Generally, the soil formation process is accelerated in the bottomland and depression areas of a region's topography. This is because groundwater is close to the surface in low-lying areas, providing an adequate supply of water to promote the chemical decomposition of the parent material and to sustain life forms that aid in soil formation. The upland part of the landscape is generally deficient in moisture because of accelerated erosion, faster runoff, and deeper groundwater, all of which impede soil formation.

Biologic factors include both animal and plant activities, all of which promote soil formation. Animals cause mixing of materials (burrowing animals), disintegration of parent material and nutrients' recycling (trees and plant roots), and organic matter enrichment (decaying microorganisms).

It may take anywhere from a hundred years to several hundred thousand years for the formation of a particular type of soil. Soils developed from sediments, such as loess, may take as little as a few hundred years to form, whereas soils developed on a crystalline bedrock, such as granite, may take more than several hundred thousand years to develop.

2.4.3.1 Soil Profile

In order to study the nature of soil in the third dimension (depth), shallow pits and trenches are excavated. A soil profile is the view of the entire soil thickness as seen on the wall of the pit or trench. Most soils are characterized by two or more layers of different colors, having different mineralogical compositions. These individual layers are called *soil horizon;* and the entire thickness is called the *soil profile*. A soil profile that shows full development of the prominent horizons is called mature soil. Figure 2.9 shows a typical soil profile in a warm and humid climate.

2.4.3.2 Soil Texture

The term *soil texture* refers to the size of mineral grains that make up the soil solids. Size is measured by using the nominal diameter of soil grains. Three common textural classes are used: sand, silt, and clay. The most frequently used size ranges for sand, silt, and clay size particles are: sand: 4.76 mm to 0.074 mm; silt: 0.074 mm to 0.002 mm; and clay: <0.002 mm.

Various grain-size classification schemes are used by soil scientists, geologists, engineers, and other experts, each with its own size range for clay, silt, sand, granules, pebbles, and gravel. As can be noted from Table 2.4, a different size range (nominal particle diameter) is used to classify soil particles into 5–7 categories. This is yet another reason why clear and unambiguous communication is critical among the various experts working together on waste management projects.

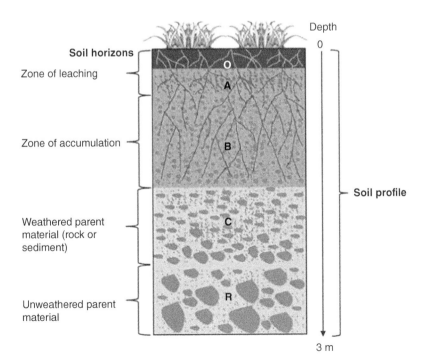

Figure 2.9   A mature soil profile in a warm and moist climatic environment with well-developed horizons.

Table 2.4 Grain-size classification of soil solids (mm) used by various experts.

Expert	Clay	Silt	Sand	Gravel	Pebble	Cobble	Boulder
Geologist	<0.0039	0.0039–0.0625	0.025–2.00	2.00–4.00	4.00–64.00	64–256	>256
Agronomist (USDA)	<0.002	0.002–0.05	0.05–2.00	>2	–	–	–
ASTM	0.001–0.005 <0.001: colloids	0.005–0.075	0.075–4.75	4.75–75	–	75–300	>300
AASHTO	0.001–0.005 <0.001: colloids	0.005–0.075	0.075–2	2–75	–	–	>75
USCS	–	–	0.075–4.75	4.75–76.2	–	76.2–300	–
(Civil/geotechnical engineers)	(all particles <0.075 are classified as fines (silt and clay))						

Another point to note is that the terms *sand* and *clay* are commonly used for the size (texture) of mineral grains, but sometimes they are also used to designate the mineralogy of soil solids, regardless of the grain size. For example, soil comprising the mineral quartz, irrespective of its grain size, is often referred to as sand or sandy. Similarly, the term *clay* is used for soil dominated by clay minerals, regardless of the fact that the mineral particles may be larger than 0.002 mm in diameter.

Soil texture can be estimated from the feel by pinching the soil between the thumb and index finger. Sandy soil feels gritty, silt feels like flour and clay would feel slippery and greasy when moist. In terms of size, sand particles are clearly visible, but a microscope must be used to see silt, and clay particles can be seen under the high-power electron microscope. In scientific work, an American Society for Testing and Materials (ASTM) laboratory procedure is used to identify soil separates by conducting the test called mechanical analysis, using a nest of sieves with different mesh sizes, stacked on top of each other with the largest mesh sieve placed on the top and the smallest at the bottom of the stack, and shaking it under the sieve shaker for about five minutes and recoding weight of each fraction and calculating its percentage relative to the original quantity of soil that was placed in the topmost sieve. The mechanical test is suitable for coarse-grained soils, sand size and larger. For fine-grained soils, silt and clay, the hydrometer test, based on Stoke's Law, is used. This process records the time it takes a specific weight of soil particles to fall to the bottom of a tall cylinder filled with water.

2.5 Index Properties of Soils

The ASTM has standardized various tests to determine the main engineering properties of soil. The ASTM volume 04.08 covers standard test procedure, equipment needed, data analysis and reporting for soil sampling, compaction, field investigation, soil texture, plasticity, density, hydrological properties, etc. Volume 04.09 includes standards on surface and subsurface characterization, erosion and sediment control technology, frozen soils and rock, geotechnics of waste management, and information retrieval and data automation (ASTM 2021).

Soil texture, grain size distribution, degree of saturation, density, porosity, void ratio, and Atterberg limits are called soil index properties. These basic properties are good indicators of the engineering behavior of soil and are used to estimate their suitability and performance for various construction projects.

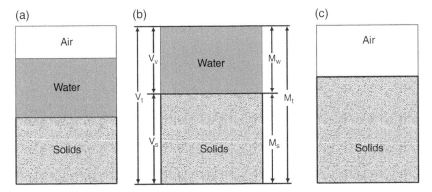

Figure 2.10   Three variations of soil phase (a) three-phase, and (b, c) two-phase.

Because soils are made up of solid, liquid, and gaseous phases, the engineering behavior of soils is heavily dependent on the relative percentages of these phases. Figure 2.10 illustrates the three soil phases, showing the mass–volume relationship. Usually, the mass (M) is shown on the right and volume (V) on the left side of the soil phase diagram.

M_t = total mass of the soil, M_w = mass of water, and M_s = mass of soil solids

$\therefore M_t = M_w + M_w$ (mass of air, M_a, is negligible and assumed zero in such calculations).

Similarly, V_t = total volume of the soil, which includes volume of air (V_a), volume of water (V_w), and volume of solids (V_s), i.e. $V_t = V_s + V_a + V_w$ Or, $V_t = V_s + V_v$ (since the voids, $V_v = V_a + V_w$).

Figure 2.10a represents the most common mode of occurrence of soil, where all three phases: solid, liquid (water), and gas (air) are present. Figure 2.10b represents soil that is fully saturated where water has displaced the air to fill all voids, and the soil comprises two phases only. All submerged soils and those occurring below the groundwater table fall in this type. Figure 2.10c also has two phases where water is totally absent and only solid and air make up the soil phases. Such soils are common in hot and dry climatic environments.

2.5.1   Void Ratio, Porosity, and Degree of Saturation

Three relationships involving the volume of air, water, and solid can be determined from the phase diagram (Figure 2.10).

The void ratio (e) is the ratio of the volume of voids, V_v, to that of soil solids, V_s, and is reported as a decimal. It is expressed by:

$$e = V_v / V_s \tag{2.2}$$

The void ratio for granular soils ranges from about 0.3 to about 1.0, and for cohesive soils, the range is between 0.4 and 1.5. Some organic clays could have e values of up to 5.0. Soils with higher void ratios have lower strength and are highly compressible.

Porosity (n) describes the ratio of the volume of voids to the total volume of the soil, and is reported as a percent. Porosity is expressed by:

$$n = \left(V_v / V_t \right) \times 100 \tag{2.3}$$

Soil porosity ranges from 10 to about 90%. Clays and organic soils, being more porous than granular soils, possess higher porosity.

The degree of (water) saturation, S, of soil is given by the ratio of the volume of water, V_w, to the volume voids, V_v, and is expressed by:

$$S = \left(V_w / V_v\right) \times 100 \tag{2.4}$$

The degree of saturation tells how much volume of the soil voids is taken up by water and how much by air. A fully saturated soil, with no air and $S = 100\%$ is represented in Figure 2.10b, a dry soil, with no water and $S = 0\%$ by (c), and a typical soil with some air and some water in soil voids is shown by (a).

The following relationships involving e and n are useful in geotechnical calculations:

$$e = n / 1 - n \tag{2.5}$$

and,

$$n = e / 1 + e \tag{2.6}$$

2.5.2 Density

Density is defined as the ratio of mass to volume of a substance (M/V). As can be seen in Figure 2.10, soil density will be maximum under fully saturated conditions represented by B, minimum in C, and intermediate in A. The three densities of the soil are called saturated density, total (or moist) density, and dry density, and are usually represented by the symbols, ρ_{sat}, ρ_t, and ρ_d, respectively. The density of soil solids, ρ_d, is related to specific gravity, Gs, of the minerals making up the solids and density of water, ρ_w, and expressed as:

$$Gs = \rho_d / \rho_w \tag{2.7}$$

where, $\rho_w = 1000$ kg/ m^3. Values of Gs can range from 2.0 to 3.0 for common soil solids, but generally lies between 2.65 and 2.80.

ρ_d can also be calculated from:

$$\rho_d = \rho_t / \left(1 + w\right) \tag{2.8}$$

Sometimes, unit weight, γ, is used for soil density; however, since weight involves gravitational force, g, multiplying M by g will give a unit weight of the soil as shown in Equation 2.9.

$$\gamma_t = M_t . g / V_t, \gamma_{sat} = M_{sat} . g / V_t, \text{ and } \gamma_d = M_s . g / V_t \text{ corresponding to } \left(A\right), \left(B\right), \text{ and } \left(C\right) \tag{2.9}$$

2.5.3 Moisture (Water) Content

Water plays a detrimental role in the engineering behavior of soils. For this reason, determination of the moisture (water) content of the soil is routinely carried out. Moisture content, w, is defined as the ratio of the mass (or weight) of water to that of the solids present in the soil. In Figure 2.10b, w can be expressed as

$$w = \left(Mw / Ms\right) \times 100 \left(\text{to express the result in percent}\right) \tag{2.10}$$

where,
   Mw is the mass of water in the soil, and
   Ms is the mass of solids in the soil

Values of *w* range from zero (completely dry soil) to 300% (for marine soils).

Test procedure and related details for the determination of soil moisture content have been standardized by the ASTM under its Test Designation D2216.

2.5.4 Grain-Size Distribution

Soils comprise solids of varying sizes and shapes. Soil that consists of solids falling within *one* size range is extremely rare. The size of soil particles is determined from the average diameter of individual soil minerals. Simple tests, standardized by ASTM, are used to determine the grain-size distribution of soil solids. Two methods are available, depending on the grain size of the soil: (i) the mechanical method, for coarse-grained soils, such as sandy and gravelly, soils, and (ii) the hydrometer method, for fine-grained, silty, and clayey soils. Details of test procedures, equipment needed, and data presentation are given in ASTM Test Designation D421 (sample preparation) and D422 (test procedures).

2.5.5 Atterberg Limits

These properties, originally proposed in 1911 by Albert Atterberg, a soil scientist from Sweden, are good indicators of soil consistency. Atterberg limits apply to fine-grained soils only. They tell us whether the soil is likely to behave as a solid, semisolid, or viscous fluid (slurry-like mass) at a given moisture content. Of the five original limits proposed by Atterberg, three are commonly used in geotechnical engineering: the shrinkage limit (*SL*), plastic limit (*PL*), and liquid limit (*LL*). Shrinkage limit is defined as the water content below which the soil behaves as a hard solid. *The plastic limit* is defined as the lowest water content at which soil will behave as a plastic material. *The liquid limit,* on the other hand, corresponds to the lowest water content at which soil behaves as a viscous liquid; conversely, the liquid limit can also be defined as the moisture content above which the soil will behave like a viscous fluid. The value of soil LL can range from 0 to >600, but most soils have LL of <100. The PL shows a range from 0 to about 125, with most soil having a PL of 40 or less.

Figure 2.11 shows the Atterberg limits in relation to soil water content and strength. With increasing water content, soil behavior changes from that of a solid to viscous liquid with a corresponding decrease in strength, corresponding to SL, PL, and LL, respectively.

The numerical difference between the values of LL and PL is called the *plasticity index* (PI), determined by Equation 2.11.

$$PI = LL - PL \qquad (2.11)$$

where,

PI is the plasticity index, LL liquid limit, and PL plastic limit of the soil.

The plasticity index represents the range in water content over which soil stays in a plastic state. PI is also used to classify fine-grained soils into six types, ML, CL, OL, MH, CH, and OH as shown in Table 2.6.

ASTM Test Designation D4318 provides the detailed procedure and equipment for the determination of the LL and PL of the soil.

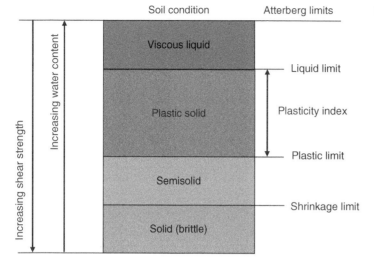

Figure 2.11 Atterberg limits.

Example Problem 2.1 Involving Mass–Volume Relationships of Soil

1) A sample of clayey soil in the vicinity of a hazardous waste site was found to weigh 276 g in its natural state. The same soil, upon oven drying, weighed 192 g. What is its moisture content?

   Solution: First calculate the weight of water in the soil from Mt = Mw + Ms (dry mass is the same as the mass of soil solids).

   $$Ww = 276 \text{ g} - 192 \text{ g} = 84 \text{ g}$$
   From Equation 7.10. $w = Ww / Ws$
   $$= (84 / 192) \times 100 = 43.75 \text{ or } \mathbf{43.8\%}$$

2) The total mass of a soil sample from under a lakebed was found to be 650 g, and its volume was found to be 225 mL. Determine its saturated density.

   $$Density = Mt / Vt$$
   $$= 650 \text{g} / 225 \text{mL} = \mathbf{2.89 \text{g} / \text{mL}}$$

3) The dry weight of soil in Example 2 was found to be 300 g. Calculate its water content. Which of the three phases of the soil, shown in Figure 2.10, is represented by this soil? and why?

   $$Wt = Ww + Ws + Wa = Ww + Ws \left(\text{weight of air, Wa is negligible and can be omitted}\right)$$
   $$650 \text{g} = Ww + 300 \text{g}$$
   $$Or \, Ww = 650 - 350 = 300 \text{g}$$
   $$w = Ww / Ws = (350 \text{g} / 300 \text{g}) \times 100 = \mathbf{116.7\%}. \rightarrow OK \text{ for a water saturated soil.}$$

4) A moist sample of sandy soil had a mass of 65.5 g; upon drying, its mass was found to be 50.3 g; its volume was 42.5 mL. The specific gravity of solids was 2.68. Calculate its (i) void ratio, (ii) porosity, and (c) degree of saturation. Draw a block diagram with values of various parameters.

Figure 2.12 Phase diagram for
Problem 4.

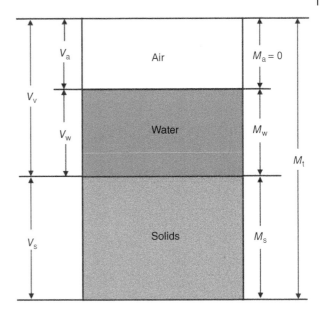

It is always a good idea to draw a phase diagram for such problems, fill in the known values, then use equations to calculate values of the missing components (Figure 2.12).

Since the soil is moist, it has all three phases – air, water, and solid.

Since Mt = Mw + Ms (Wa = 0),

Mw = Mt − Ms = 65.5 g – 50.3 g = 15.2 g. Write this number for W_w in the phase diagram. All data for the right side of the diagram are complete.

From Equation 2.7, calculate ρ_d

$$\rho_d = Gs.\rho_w = 2.68 \times 1\,g/mL\left(\text{standard value}\right) = 2.68\,g/mL$$

Since, $\rho_d = M_s/Vs$, we have,

$$2.68 = 50.3\,g/Vs$$
$$\therefore Vs = 50.3/2.68 = 18.77\,mL$$

Also, since Vt = Vv + Vs,

$$Vv = Vt - Vs$$
$$= 42.5\,mL - 18.77\,mL = 23.73\,mL; \text{ enter values of Vs and Vv in the left side of the diagram.}$$

All volumes are now complete on the left side; use Equations 2.2, 2.3, and 2.4 to calculate *e*, *n*, and *S*, respectively:

a) $e = Vv/Vs = 23.73$ mL/18.77 mL = **1.26** (OK, could be up to 1.50 for noncohesive soil)
b) $n = Vv/Vt \times 100 = (23.73$ mL/42.5 mL$) \times 100 = $ **55.8%**
c) $S = Vw/Vv \times 100 = (15.2$ mL/23.73 mL$) \times 100 = 64.13$ or **64%**

5) Upon performing the Atterberg limits test on the previously mentioned soil, its LL and PL were found to be 69 and 38, respectively. Calculate its PI.

Using Equation 2.11, PI = LL − PL
$$= 69 - 38 = \mathbf{31}$$

2.5.6 Permeability

Permeability is an important soil property that relates to the flow of water (or any fluid) through the void spaces in the earth material. Although it is not included in the Index Properties, it is of much significance in leachate management in landfills, and groundwater remediation.

The relative ease (or difficulty) with which a fluid can move through soil or rock mass is a measure of its permeability. In general, coarse-grained soils and fractured and solutioned rocks have higher permeability than fine-grained clayey soils and massive rocks. Table 2.5 shows the permeability values of various geologic materials.

Permeability of the geologic medium is very important in hazardous waste disposal, as earth materials with very low or negligible permeability are more desirable to serve as landfill liners. The design of a remediation system for contaminated groundwater is based on, among other factors, the permeability of the aquifer to determine the pumping rate, etc.

In the laboratory, the permeability of granular soil can be measured using the test procedures given in ASTM Test Designation ASTM D2434. Caution must be exercised when applying values of hydraulic conductivity obtained from laboratory tests on clayey soils to field conditions. Generally, the field conductivity values are orders of magnitude greater than those obtained from laboratory tests. This is because the effects of macropores, fine root holes, and other openings in clayey soil as it exists in the field are not present in test samples.

Table 2.5   Hydraulic conductivity and porosity of geologic materials.

Geologic material	Porosity, %	Hydraulic conductivity, cm/s
Soils		
Clay	45	10^{-7}–10^{-9}
Silty clay	42–45	10^{-3}–10^{-5}
Sand, clean	35	10^{-3}–1
Sand, fine	43	10^{-2}–10^{-3}
Sand, very fine to fine	40–43	10^{-4}–10^{-3}
Sand, medium to coarse	39	10^{-2}–10^{-1}
Sand, silty	40–43	10^{-5}–10^{-3}
Sand, clayey	45–50	10^{-6}–10^{-9}
Gravel	25–30	1–5
Rocks		
Sandstone	5–20	10^{-8}–10^{-4}
Limestone, dense	5	10^{-7}–10^{-4}
Fractured igneous and metamorphic rocks	30–50	10^{-6}–10^{-2}
Unfractured igneous and metamorphic rocks	0.5–5	10^{-14}–10^{-10}

2.6 Soil Classification Systems

A good classification aims at organizing the wide variety among the individuals in a natural system into a manageable number of convenient classes or groups on the basis of their common features. For example, with over 1000 varieties of rocks, those that owe their origin to solidification of the magma (liquid rock melt) are classified as igneous rocks; those formed under water are grouped under sedimentary rocks class, and so on. The same is true for soils where the wide range of engineering soil types are grouped into 15 classes. The agricultural classification similarly groups all soils occurring the world over into 12 broad classes, called Orders (excludes shifting sands, rocky lands, and ice/glaciers).

2.6.1 Soil Classification

After the moisture content, grain-size distribution, and the Atterberg limits of soil have been determined, it is a simple matter to classify the soil in terms of the USCS. Details of the procedure to be used for classifying the soil are given under ASTM Test Designation D2487. The classification also enables one to estimate other geotechnical properties of the soil. For example, dominant percentages of sand and gravel, and low moisture content, would generally mean that soil has high shear strength, good permeability, and negligible compressibility – all positive attributes that make such soil suitable for most geotechnical projects. On the other hand, fine-grained, clayey soil, with a high liquid limit, would imply low shear strength, extremely low permeability, and high compressibility – all undesirable properties in most geotechnical situations. However, it must be emphasized that this generalization is intended for a preliminary evaluation of engineering soils. In the ultimate analysis, soil properties must be evaluated in relation to the proposed use because an apparently undesirable characteristic, such as very low permeability, may make the soil preferable for a construction project where liquid retention is a major concern. Such situations occur in a landfill, where leachate containment is a primary objective.

Two soil classification systems are in common use – the Agricultural Classification system, also known as the 7th Approximation or Soil Taxonomy. It is used by the US Department of Agriculture (USDA) and is also referred to as the USDA Classification. This classification groups soils based on their physical and chemical properties into Order, Suborder, Great Group, Subgroup, Family, Series, and Species – from most general to very specific. This classification is for agricultural purposes and classifies soils based on their texture, origin, and agricultural productivity; and groups soils into 12 textural classes. These classes are determined by the relative proportion of sand, silt, and clay in a soil mass. Figure 2.13 shows the Triangular Diagram used by the USDA for the classification of soil into one of the 12 types.

The base of the isosceles triangle represents the percent of sand size particles in the unknown soil (values increasing from right to left of the triangle base, as shown in the figure; percent clay is represented on the left side of the triangle and percent silt of its right side. After the relative percentages of sand, clay, and silt in soil are determined from a laboratory test, the percentages of each are plotted on the diagram. The common intersection point determines the textural class of the soil.

For example, a soil sample taken from a cornfield was found to comprise: 30% clay, 45% silt, and 25% sand-size particles. Using Figure 2.13 and following the lines corresponding to 45% silt and 25% sand, we determine that they intersect within the "Clay loam" trapezoidal area marked by the red inverted triangle, which also happens to be the 30% clay line. Note that the point formed by the intersection of two of the soil particle percentages does not change when the percentage of the third is plotted.

The other classification, the Unified Soil Classification System (USCS), is an engineering classification, which is directly applicable in waste management. This classification system is based on grain

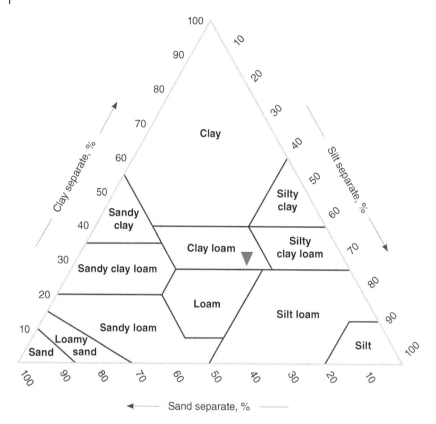

Figure 2.13 USDA triangular diagram of soil texture. *Source:* Public Domain.

size determination and performing the Atterberg limits test to determine the values of the PL and LL of the soil. Both tests are simple to perform, the equipment required is inexpensive, and no specialized skills are needed to run the test and interpret the results. It is for this reason that the USCS has been adopted worldwide. Table 2.6 shows the 15 soil types and their engineering characteristics.

Table 2.6 The unified soil classification system.

Major divisions		Symbol name		Selected engineering properties		
COARSE GRAINED SOILS (Over half of the soil particles are larger than 0.074 mm)	Gravels >50% retained on #4 sieve (4.75 mm)			Compressibility	Permeability	Strength
		Clean gravel	GW	Well-graded gravel	Negligible	High	Very high
		<5% fines	GP	Poorly graded gravel	Negligible	Very high	High
		Dirty gravel	GM	Silty gravel	Negligible	Low	High
		>12% fines	GC	Clayey gravel	Very low	Very low	High-medium

Table 2.6   (Continued)

Major divisions		Symbol name			Selected engineering properties			
	Sands >50% passes the #4 sieve (4.75 mm)	Clean sand	SW	Well graded sand	Negligible	High	Very high	
		<5% fines	SP	Poorly graded sand	Very low	High	High	
		Dirty sand	SM	Silty sand	Low	Low	High	
		>12% fines	SC	Clayey sand	Low	Very low	High-medium	
FINE GRAINED SOIL (Over half of the soil particles are smaller than 0.074 mm)	Silts Non plastic	Liquid	ML	Silt	Medium	Low	Medium	
		Limit	CL	Silty clay	High	Very low	Medium	
		50% or less	OL	Organic silt	Medium	Low	Low	
	Clays Plastic	Liquid	MH	High plasticity silt	High	Low	Medium-low	
		Limit	CH	High plasticity clay	High	Very low	Low	
		>50%	OH	Organic clay	High	Low	Very low	
	Predominantly organic soils		PT	Peat and muck	Very high	Low	Very low	

2.7 Hydrogeology

Hydrogeology is the branch of geology that deals with the occurrence, movement, distribution, and exploitation of groundwater. Of the 2.5% of all freshwater available on earth (Figure 2.6), groundwater is the most commonly used source of drinking water supply due to its relative purity and ready availability. The bulk of freshwater (about 68%) cannot be used as it occurs in solid form, ice, on the ice caps and glaciers; and the remaining 1% freshwater in streams and rivers is generally polluted. Groundwater therefore is the best resource to meet humanity's drinking water needs and priority should be given to prevent its pollution. According to UNESCO, at least 50% of the world's population received its drinking water supply from groundwater, which also provided 43% of all the water used for irrigation (UNESCO 2010).

According to the US Geological Survey, about 280 300 billion gallons per day (bgpd) of fresh water was used in the US in 2015, of which groundwater provided 82 300 bgpd and surface water 198 000 bgpd to meet various needs. About 57 200 bgpd or 48.4% was used for crop irrigation (surface water providing the remaining 51.6%). Livestock farming (livestock watering, feedlots, dairy operations, and related on-farm needs) used 62% of groundwater. City and county water departments used 39% of groundwater (61% surface water) for public uses at homes, businesses, and industries (USGS 2015). About 95% of the country's rural population relies on groundwater to meet its drinking water needs. Industrialization along with the growing human population have resulted in an estimated 20% of the world's aquifers being overexploited (Gleeson et al. 2012), leading to land subsidence and saltwater intrusion. In addition, thousands of wells are closed each year because of contamination from hazardous and other types of wastes. The basic knowledge of hydrogeology is therefore essential to minimize aquifer contamination by using safe waste disposal methods. This section presents a discussion of the fundamental concepts and definitions in hydrogeology relevant to waste management.

2.7.1 Groundwater Occurrence

Groundwater is the water that occurs below the land surface and is "invisible." As discussed in Section 2.3.2, a part of precipitation moves down below the land surface, which is the infiltration component of the Water Cycle. Figure 2.14 shows the occurrence of subsurface water. Two main zones of water occurrences are (i) the unsaturated zone; and (ii) the saturated zone. Terms like vadose zone and phreatic zone were used in older literature for (i) and (ii), respectively.

The uppermost surface of the zone of saturation is called the *groundwater table* (GWT), which can be defined as the elevation of the water surface with reference to a standard datum, usually the mean sea level (MSL), below which all openings in the rock or soil are full of water with no air. A statement like "the GWT at location X is 345 m" would mean that all openings in the earth material below the elevation of 345 m at X are full of water, i.e. saturated with water. Sometimes, the GWT may be reported in relation to the depth below the surface at which the GWT occurs. For example, "groundwater occurs 15 m below the surface" would mean that the openings in the earth materials at a depth of 15 m below the surface, *at that location*, are saturated with water. A layer of impermeable earth material that serves as the confining layer to hold the groundwater in the layer above it called aquitard, underlies the zone of saturation. Water (hydraulic) pressure at the GWT equals the atmospheric pressure and increases with increasing depth in the zone of saturation.

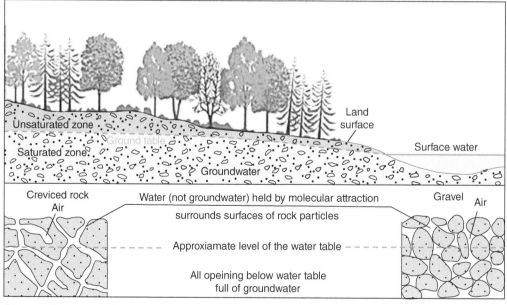

Low groudwater occurs in rocks.

Figure 2.14   Occurrence of groundwater. *Source:* Public Domain.

In terms of soil phases, in the unsaturated zone, the earth material contains all three – soil solids, liquids, and air; while in the saturated zone (below the GWT), only two phases are present: solid and liquid (water). A narrow water-bearing zone above the GWT extends upward into the unsaturated zone due to capillary forces. This zone is called the *capillary fringe* that could range from a fraction of a meter to several meters, depending upon the soil texture: higher in fine-grained clayey soils (up to 23 m), and lower in coarse-grained sandy soil (~0.15 m).

2.7.2 Types of Aquifers

Various geologic materials, depending on the porosity and permeability, are termed aquifer, aquiclude, and aquitard.

Aquifers represent water-saturated bodies of geologic materials that can provide water supply. Aquifers have high porosity and high permeability, such as beds of sand and gravel or sandstone and limestone. Fractured crystalline rocks, such as granite and basalt, can also supply limited quantities of groundwater. Geologic materials of very low permeability despite having high porosity, such as clay and shale cannot yield an adequate quantity of water and are called aquitards.

Hydraulic gradient (discussed in Section 2.7.3) is the most critical parameter influencing groundwater movement. Under the same hydraulic gradient, clay with twofold greater porosity than sand, but with drastically lower permeability, results in extremely low groundwater velocity.

Aquifers, whose upper surface is exposed to the atmosphere are called unconfined or water table aquifers. An aquifer with its upper surface below the ground that is underlain by a confining layer, is called a confined aquifer, which has high hydrostatic pressure, exceeding atmospheric. As shown in Figure 2.15, when a confined aquifer is penetrated by a drill hole, water rises above the regional groundwater table to its maximum elevation called the *potentiometric surface*.

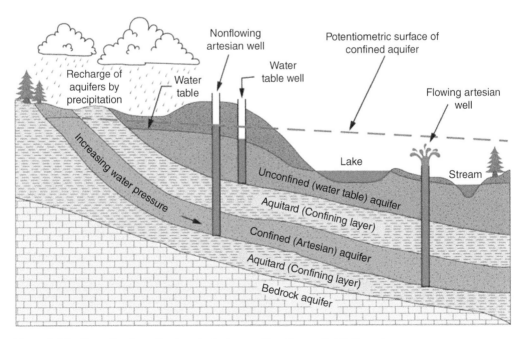

Figure 2.15   Unconfined, confined, and artesian aquifers. *Source:* Public Domain.

The height of groundwater rise is a function of the pressure in the confining aquifer. Generally, it is sufficiently high to allow the water to flow freely at the well head. In rare cases, extremely high water pressure results in the groundwater erupting out as a fountain as soon as the aquiclude cover is broken. In both cases, with time, the pressure dissipates and the flow rate subsides.

2.7.3 Groundwater Movement

As mentioned in earlier paragraphs, groundwater moves from higher elevation to lower elevation, following *Darcy's Law* of fluid flow. The following definitions, relating to Darcy's Law, are explained next:

Hydraulic head (h) is the height of the water column or elevation of the water surface above a reference plane (MSL). In a water well, h can be calculated by subtracting the elevation of the depth to the GWT from that of the surface where the well is located, i.e.

$$h = \text{elevation of the ground surface} - \text{depth to the GWT}$$

(2.12)

For example, in Figure 2.16, the elevation of the well at X is 578 m, and the GWT occurs at a depth of 25 m below the surface; therefore,

$$\text{Elevation of the GWT} = 578 - 25 = 553 \text{m} = h, \text{ the hydraulic head in well at X.}$$

Similarly, for well at Y,

$$h = 400 - 10 = 390 \text{m}.$$

The hydraulic gradient is the rate of change of hydraulic head over a unit distance; it is also the head loss between two wells over the horizontal distance between them. For example, in Figure 2.16, the hydraulic head in well X is 553 m, and in well Y, 390 m; and the two wells are separated by a horizontal distance of 1990 m. So, the hydraulic gradient between locations X and Y is given by:

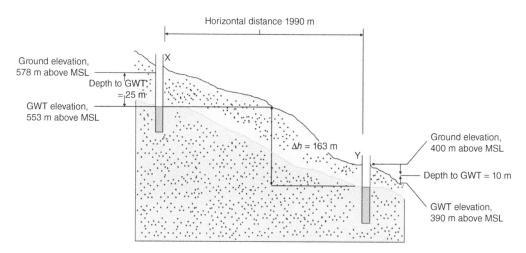

Figure 2.16 Hydraulic conductivity and hydraulic gradient.

$$i = \Delta h / L \qquad (2.13)$$

Where, Δh = the head difference between the wells at A and B, and L = the horizontal (map) distance between them. Therefore,

$$i = 553 - 390\,\text{m} / 1990\,\text{m}$$
$$= 163\,\text{m} / 1990\,\text{m} = 0.082 \; (\text{dimensionless parameter})$$

Darcy's Law relates to the flow of water through porous media. The law states that the flow velocity of water through a porous medium is proportional to the hydraulic gradient. Mathematically, this is expressed as:

$$V \propto i \; \text{or,}$$
$$V = K.i \qquad (2.14)$$

Where V = velocity of water, i = hydraulic gradient, and K is a constant, called coefficient of permeability.

Water discharge, Q, is related to flow velocity, V, and the cross-sectional area of the porous medium, A, by

$$Q = VA$$
$$\text{or,}\; V = Q / A \qquad (2.15)$$

Substituting the value of V in Equation 21.5 from Equation 2.14, we have

$$Ki = Q / A$$
$$\text{or,}\; Q = K.i.A \qquad (2.16)$$

Equation 2.16 is valid for water flow in open channels (such as canals), which gives a superficial (lower) value of groundwater flow velocity. This is because groundwater flow occurs only between the pores and other openings in the earth material and not through the solids that collectively comprise the entire porous medium. Therefore, Equation 2.15 needs to be modified to calculate the actual groundwater flow velocity, Va. Referring to Figure 2.17, if the total cross sectional area of the aquifer material is At, and that of pores and solids Ap and As, respectively, then

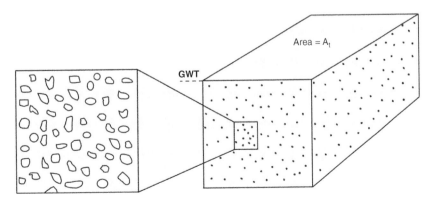

Figure 2.17 Effective porosity of earth material.

$$At = Ap + As$$

Groundwater movement, unlike flow in an open channel, occurs only through voids in the soil. So, its actual flow velocity, Va, is

$$Va = Q / Ap \tag{2.17}$$

Also, assuming a unit volume of the aquifer material, its porosity, n, can be expressed as

$$n = Ap / As = Vv / Vt \tag{2.18}$$
$$or, n = Vv \left(Vt \text{ assumed unit} \right)$$

Example Problem 2.2 Involving Groundwater Flow
1) For a sandy aquifer having a cross sectional area, At = 100 m², pore area = 25 m², and Q = 1000 m³/s, determine the Darcy velocity, Vd, and groundwater flow velocity, Va.

From Equation 2.15, $Vd = Q / A$
$$= 1000\,m^3 / s / 100\,m^2$$
$$= 10\,m / s$$

And, Va $\left(\text{from Equation 2.18} \right) = Q / Ap,$
$$= 1000\,m^3 / s \div 25\,m^2$$
$$= \mathbf{40\,m / s}$$

This shows that Va > Vd, and Va is related to Vd and n by the following equation:

$$Va = Vd / n \tag{2.19}$$

Therefore, knowing Darcy velocity, Vd and the aquifer porosity, n, Va can be calculated using Equation 2.19.
2) The Darcy velocity for aquifer sand with a porosity of 25% was found to be 10 m/s. What would be the actual groundwater flow velocity in this aquifer?
Using Equation 2.19, we have

$$Va = \left(10\,m / s \right) \div 0.25$$
$$= \mathbf{40\,m / s}$$

Essentials of Toxicology

2.8 Introduction

Toxicology is the science that deals with the adverse effects of poisons or toxins on living organisms. Exactly when and what kinds of adverse effects are produced is a function of:

- The quantity or dose of poisonous substances
- The receptor, whether mice, rats, rabbits, dogs, or humans – their age, sex, and physical condition
- Exposure pathways
- Duration of exposure

All other factors remaining the same, dose (the quantity ingested or inhaled) is the most critical factor for producing the toxic effect, which may be therapeutic or harmful. For example, if one drinks a bottle of pure iodine, one may die, but applying a drop of diluted iodine on a cut produces a healing effect. Caffeine in small doses is tolerable by most people, but large quantities produce harmful effects. The key in both examples is the quantity of the substance or the *dose*. A substance may be safe at low levels of dose but may become poisonous at high levels. This fact was recognized by the German physician Theophrastus Bombastus von Hohenheim (1493–1541), otherwise known as Paracelsus. He stated, "If you want to explain each poison correctly, what is there that is not poison – all things are poison and nothing without poison. Solely, the dose determines that a thing is not poison." (Doull et al. 1980, p. 12).

In a strict sense, toxicology is not the science of identification of poisons, but the science that quantifies the levels at which substances become toxic. A poison or toxicant is a substance that, *above* a certain level of exposure or dose, produces detrimental effects on tissues, organs, biological processes, or human health. The majority of industrial chemicals are of concern because of their effects on living organisms. The study of the adverse effects of such substances on life processes constitutes the basis of toxicology. Hazardous substances may occur in:

- The work environment – occupational hazards. The first production of a synthetic dye, aniline, took place in 1860. People working in dye-manufacturing factories developed cancer of the bladder. Chimney sweepers in the United Kingdom developed scrotal cancer, which is associated with coal tar and soot deposits in chimneys.
- The ambient environment itself – air, water, or soil – may have a high concentration of toxic substances, either naturally or from human activities. Examples of natural occurrences include elevated levels of radon (causes lung cancer) in homes and high levels of UV radiation at high altitudes (causes skin cancer). Emissions of vapors and effluents containing toxic substances are examples of human-induced (anthropogenic) factors. Burning high-sulfur coal in power plants releases SOx and NOx, which cause the formation of sulfuric and nitric acids, which are toxic substances.
- The food chain, where hazardous substances may take one of several paths, and ultimately enter bodies of living forms, causing: (i) the substance to either be detoxified by the body's immune system activities and excreted, or (ii) may accumulate in the body and cause chronic effects.

2.8.1 Toxicity and Toxicity Rating

Toxicity is the *capacity* of a substance to produce adverse effects on living forms; it is not the *effect* of poison or a chemical. Toxicity is usually expressed in milligram/kg (mg/kg) of body weight. For air and water, mg/L (ppm) or µg/L (ppb) is the commonly used unit.

Chemicals have a wide range of doses at which they can produce detrimental effects, including death, in living organisms. Some chemicals will cause death when administered even in minute quantities (micrograms); such substances are extremely poisonous. Other chemicals can be tolerated in larger quantities (a few grams); these are less toxic. Table 2.7 shows the probable lethal doses of various chemicals on humans and their relative toxicity class.

2.8.2 Types of Toxic Effects

Depending on the organism's response to toxic substances, one of the following four different toxic effects may be produced:

Table 2.7   Toxicity rating chart.

Probable oral lethal dose for humans

Toxicity rating	Dose	For average adult (68 kg/150 lb)	Example
Practically nontoxic	>15 g/kg	More than 0.94 L (>1 quart)	Bis (2-ethylhexyl) phthalate
Slightly toxic	5–15 g/kg	Between 0.47 L and 0.94 L (1 pint–1 quart)	Ethanol
Moderately toxic	0.5–5 g/kg	Between 29.6 mL and 0.47 L (1 ounce–1 pint)	Malathion
Very toxic	50–500 mg/kg	Between 4.9 mL and 29.6 mL (1 teaspoon-1 ounce)	Heptachlor
Extremely toxic	5–50 mg/kg	Between seven drops and one teaspoonful	Parathion
Super toxic	<5 mg/kg	A taste (less than seven drops)	Sarin

Source: Modified from Doull et al. (1980).

1) *Reversible Toxicity*: Reversible toxicity occurs when a toxicant enters the body but does not cause any permanent effects, either due to the organism's natural defense mechanisms or due to the administration of substances to counteract the action of the toxicants – antidotes. Reversible toxicity generally occurs in rapidly multiplying cells, such as those in the liver, bone marrow, and intestines. For instance, the toxic effects of CO poisoning can be reversed by administering fresh air or O_2 to the victim. Damaged cells are quickly replaced by new cells. For instance, even if 50% of the liver is lost, it can regenerate itself in about six months.

2) *Irreversible Toxicity*: Irreversible toxicity includes effects that last after the toxicant causing the adverse effect has been eliminated. This type of toxicity is common in cells that do not multiply rapidly. For example, when skin is burned with sulfuric acid, the immediate effects are pain and burn, which can be eliminated by using a neutralizing agent or washing with water. But there is still a permanent effect on the skin, which is the scar produced by the acid. Carcinogenic effects of some chemicals are also examples of irreversible toxic effects.

3) *Acute Toxicity*: Acute toxicity involves a short response time (mostly seconds to minutes). Acute toxicity results in responses that are observed soon after exposure to a toxic substance. Acute effects normally result from brief exposures to relatively high levels of a toxicant. Such effects are comparatively easy to observe and can be attributed to a particular toxicant because of the pronounced symptoms displayed. For example, the accidental release of methyl isocyanate at a chemical plant at Bhopal in India on 3 December 1984 caused blindness and eye injuries to 100 000 people who were exposed to the chemical for a brief interval of time.

4) *Chronic Toxicity*: This involves effects that take a long time to manifest. Chronic toxicity results from low exposures to a toxicant over long periods of time. Chronic responses to toxicants may have latency periods as long as several decades in humans. For example, persons working in nuclear weapons' production plants during the 1940s and 1950s were exposed to nuclear radiation, but cancer was not detected until decades after the exposure.

Chronic effects are obscured by normal background symptoms. So, it is very difficult to establish the cause-and-effect relationship with certainty. Nevertheless, chronic effects are useful in understanding the long-term effects of toxic substances.

2.9 Dose–Response Relationship

Toxic effects of a substance are usually determined by conducting a series of laboratory experiments exposing selected organisms to varying doses of the toxicant and carefully monitoring its effect on their health. The experimental results are presented in the form of a graph called the *dose–response curve*. Dose represents the concentration of the toxicant that an organism was exposed to, and response is the observed effect of the toxicant on the organism.

The dose can be defined as the ratio of the mass of the toxicant to the bodyweight of the organism over the period of time for which it was administered. Dose is expressed in units of mass of toxicant/unit body weight, e.g. 0.5 g/kg or 10 mg/kg, etc.

The dose–response curve is a plot of the organism's response to a toxicant as a function of the dose. The horizontal (X) axis is a log scale on which dose is plotted, and the percent response is plotted on an arithmetic scale on the Y axis. Figure 2.18 shows a generalized dose–response curve which shows the response of the organism (% deaths) to a specific dose of a toxicant.

Two distinctive features can be noted in the dose–response curve:

1) It is usually an S-shaped plot, which means that for incremental doses, the response does not increase in a linearly proportional manner.
2) It does not pass through the origin, which may be interpreted to mean that (i) the real response (effects) at low levels of the dose is unknown (the black dashed line), (ii) the response is zero (no effect) for low doses (the blue dashed line), or there is some adverse effect even at zero dose (the red dashed line).

The reasons for these ambiguities are related to the ways in which the dose–response tests are carried out. Since tests involving an organism's response to varying doses of a toxicant are very expensive, as few tests as possible are conducted, and nearly all of them are at higher dose levels. This leads to extrapolation between the test data points. And, because tests are done at higher doses, the curve is extrapolated down for lower dosage.

Figure 2.18 Generalized dose–response curve.

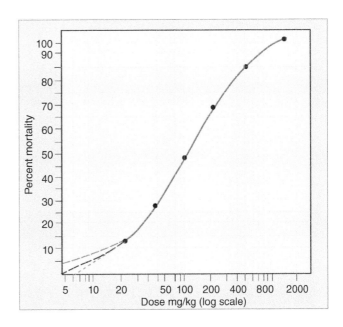

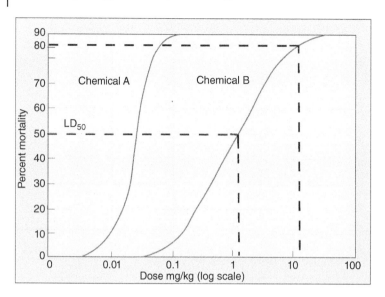

Figure 2.19 The dose–response curves for two chemicals with different toxicity ratings.

LD_{50} on the Y axis in Figure 2.19 represents a statistical estimate of the dose that will cause death in 50% of the subjects; this is also called the *median lethal dose*. Depending upon the nature of the slope of the curve, the dose corresponding to LD_{50} will be different for different organisms, and also different toxicants will produce different effects on the same organism. Therefore, the nature of the toxicant and the organism on which the tests were conducted must be specified.

Figure 2.19 shows the dose–response curve for two chemicals, A and B, on the organism. A is more toxic because a dose of 0.07 mg/kg results in the death of 50% (LD_{50}) of the organism. Chemical B, on the other hand, produces the same mortality rate, LD_{50}, at a much higher dose of 2 mg/kg. The slope of the two curves is another indicator of the relative toxicity of the two chemicals. The steeper slope of Chemical A means that a relatively small increase in the dose – from 0.07 to 0.093 mg/kg (33%) – will result in 85% mortality. But for chemical B, the dose must increase from 2 to 34 mg/kg, or 1700%, to cause the same mortality rate of 85%. Curve A is typical of highly toxic substances, while B represents substances of low toxicity.

The dose–response relationships are based on laboratory experiments done on animals – typically mice or rats. The results are then extrapolated for higher life forms, including humans. This is done by using a factor of safety that ranges from 10^3 to 10^5 for humans. For example, if a 1000 ppm level of dose of a certain toxicant did not produce any adverse response in rats and is accepted as a safe dose for rats, then the safe dose for humans will be:

$$1000\,\text{ppm} / 10^4 = 0.1\,\text{ppm}.$$

This conservative value reflects limitations and uncertainty in the dose–response experimental results. Other factors that control the nature of the dose–response curve include:

- Species habitat (aquatic or terrestrial)
- Sex
- Genetic traits
- Nutrition level

- Age
- Exposure route
- Exposure duration

Even in closely related animals, such as mice and rats, one chemical may prove carcinogenic to, say, mice, but not to rats. Ames et al. (1987) tested 226 chemicals on both rats and mice and found that 96 were toxic to mice but not to rats.

The interspecies difference is by far the most serious problem in the interpretation of test data. For example, aspirin is safe for people but is a teratogen for rabbits and causes birth defects in their offspring. Dioxin is 5000 times more toxic to hamsters than it is to guinea pigs. Effects on humans are not well known.

Exposure path also plays a role; for example, nickel fumes are carcinogenic to humans if inhaled, but are noncarcinogenic if ingested. Another example is that very fine particles of asbestos are carcinogenic because they can easily enter the lungs by inhalation, but larger particles may be ingested and excreted without causing any adverse effects.

The best way to determine the human toxicity of a chemical would be to subject human beings to the dose–response test. But this is not allowed by law, and rightly so. The next best option is to study the effects of chemicals on people working in chemical-manufacturing plants. This too is limited, and not particularly effective because of the latency effect. These limitations have forced toxicologists to rely on laboratory data from tests conducted on animals such as zebrafish and roundworms, etc. However, combining the new technologies of supercomputers, AI, and robotics has led to the launching of the Tox21 program. The Tox21 high-speed robot screening system was established in 2008 and is located at the National Chemical Genomics Center (NCGC) of the National Institutes of Health in Rockville, Maryland. The program aims at developing reliable methods for rapidly and efficiently evaluating the safety of commercial chemicals, pesticides, food additives, contaminants, and pharmaceutical products, by using cells and molecular materials instead of laboratory animals.

TOX21 system can test chemical compounds at multiple concentrations rapidly. Through automated robotic screening, the technology integrates the pharmacologic dose–response relationship with the speed and accuracy of the automated system. Some of the features of the system include:

- Automated robotic screening: about 40 plates per hour and about 1.5 million compounds per day
- Compounds assayed at 15 concentrations ranging over 4 logs (up to 100 μM)
- Miniaturization of assay volumes from 2 to 6 μL in 1536-well plate
- Rapid data processing, curve-fitting, and classification using advanced informatics.

Results obtained so far have been validated with existing conventional toxicity testing data and some of the results have been accepted by the USEPA in its endocrine-disrupting compounds toxicity, and by the World Health Organization as supporting evidence for chemical carcinogenesis (EPA 2020). Continued improvements of TOX21 technology promise the elimination of test animals and drastically reduce time and cost of determining the toxicity of thousands of chemicals that are in commercial use.

2.9.1 Hypersensitivity and Hyposensitivity

When an organism develops adverse effects at a very low dose level of a toxicant, it is called *hypersensitive*. When it takes extremely high doses to produce a response, the organism is called *hyposensitive*. Most organisms, though, respond to toxicants at doses in the mid-range of the dose–response curve, such subjects are called *normals*.

2.10   Exposure Paths of Toxicants to Humans

Toxic chemicals in hazardous wastes or in emissions from industrial plants can enter into the environment through the following pathways:

- Ingestion
- Inhalation
- Dermal contract
- Injection (rare)

In an industrial setting, inhalation has been found to be the primary route of exposure, followed by skin or eye contact, ingestion, and injection.

2.10.1   Ingestion

Toxic substances may be swallowed with food or drink, or alone. The substance then passes directly into the digestive tract, where it may eventually be absorbed into the blood. The most common ways through which we ingest toxicants are by eating or drinking in a contaminated area, or by consuming contaminated food or water.

2.10.2   Inhalation

Inhalation is absorbing toxic substances through breathing. Gases, vapor, fumes, or mist (all suspensions of fine solids/liquids/ gas in one another), and virus, when inhaled, get into the respiratory system, where they are absorbed into the blood in the lung through alveoli (small air sac clusters) and may spread into other organs.

2.10.3   Dermal Contact

Dermal contact involves direct contact of hazardous substances with the skin. Dermal exposure may affect only the contact point, or it may cause the toxicant to be absorbed into the skin and subsequently into the bloodstream.

Sometimes certain hazardous materials may come in direct contact with the eyes (ocular exposure), causing eye damage.

2.10.4   Injection

In injection, hazardous substances enter the bloodstream directly via breakage of skin or tissue-cuts and abrasions, such as from sharps in medical waste.

2.11   Teratogenesis, Mutagenesis, and Carcinogenesis

Adverse effects of highly toxic substances manifest in birth defects to offspring, DNA alteration, and uncontrolled cell replications.

2.11.1   Teratogenesis

Teratogenesis (birth defects) affects offspring while they are still in the fetal stage of development. Teratogenesis usually results from damage to embryonic or fetal cells, inhibiting their normal development. The first 8–12 weeks of pregnancy are the most critical in humans because most defects occur in this period. Chemicals that cause birth defects are called *teratogens*. Teratogenesis is caused by enzyme inhibition, deprivation of vitamins to the fetus, alterations of energy supply, or alteration of the permeability of the placental membrane.

2.11.2 Mutagenesis

Mutagenesis is the process of alteration of DNA, which causes genetic damage to reproductive cells. Birth defects are a common manifestation of mutagens. Such effects are usually felt in the next generation (e.g. mutagenesis due to radiation exposure.)

2.11.3 Carcinogenesis

Carcinogenesis is the process of uncontrolled cell replication (cancer) due to the presence of a toxicant, called *carcinogen*, in the body. Environmental contamination is the primary cause of cancer in humans. It is estimated that only 15% of cancer cases are related to genetic effects and 85% to environmental effects.

Many hazardous substances are potentially carcinogenic. The problem is the determination of the carcinogenic effects of a large number of chemicals. The disturbing fact is that in the EPA's list of 48 500 chemicals, only about one-fifth (<10 000) have been tested for acute effects, and fewer than one-tenth (4850) have been tested for chronic effects (carcinogenesis, teratogenesis, or mutagenesis). This means that no information on the toxic effects of 38 300 chemicals (79%) is available (Postel 1988). The situation has greatly improved with the bioassay results of 10 000 chemicals organized into the online *TOX21 10K Compound Library* that can be used to predict toxicological effects of thousands of chemicals in industrial and commercial use.

2.12 Assessment of Health Risks of Hazardous Waste

In terms of the severity of the risk to human health, hazardous waste is most serious because it contains all kinds of chemicals, many are highly toxic to humans. The first task in the assessment of health risks is to find out what kind of hazardous substances are present in the waste. If accurate records of chemicals in the waste have been maintained, it is helpful. Even then complications may arise because of the chemical and biological transformation of wastes, selective migration of waste, and mutual interaction between the various waste materials that generate other products. Toxicologists know that when two toxic substances combine, the resulting toxicity of the product is not a simple function of the toxicity of the individual components. Terms like *synergism*, *antagonism*, and *potentiation* are used to describe the combined effects of two or more toxic substances.

Synergism relates to the situation in which the combined effect of two chemicals is much greater than the toxic effect of each chemical alone; stated another way, $2 + 3 = 8$. For example, both carbon tetrachloride and ethanol are hepatotoxic agents, but together they produce much greater damage to the liver than the mathematical sum of their individual effects on the liver would suggest.

Antagonism can be described as the situation in which two chemicals, when given together, negate each other's actions, producing an effect that is less than the combined effect of the individual chemicals (for example, $4 + 3 = 5$ or $4 + 0 = 1$). Antagonism is of special interest in toxicology because it constitutes the basis of antidotes. The toxic effect of heavy metals, such as lead, mercury, and arsenic, can be reduced by using dimercaprol.

Potentiation is the situation where a substance does not produce a toxic effect on a certain organ or system, but, when added to another chemical, makes the latter more toxic (for example, $0 + 2 = 5$). Isopropanol, for instance, is not hepatotoxic by itself, but if added to carbon tetrachloride, the hepatotoxicity of carbon tetrachloride becomes much greater than when it is not administered with isopropanol.

2.13 Summary

Among the various disciplines relevant to environmental science, geology plays a central role because it deals with the study of the earth. Waste management impacts the physical and biological environment of the earth besides producing adverse effects on human and ecological health. Humans are relatively newcomers to the earth, but during their short tenure, they have surpassed nature in their ability to transform the earth.

The system earth comprises five mutually interdependent components such that a change in one brings about change in other components. Environmental degradation has largely been the result of massive industrialization along with the mismanagement of waste. While admirable progress has been made in the safe management of waste, a large portion of the human population still dumps its waste in open spaces.

Of the various earth materials, water and soil have been worse impacted due to unsafe waste disposal. Along with air, they represent the worst contaminated environmental media that require taking a holistic approach to System Earth for developing a solution to mitigate and minimize further environmental degradation.

Groundwater, the major reservoir of freshwater supply, must be protected from environmental pollution. Hydrogeology provides insights into the occurrence, movement, and contamination of groundwater, which can be used to preserve groundwater quality.

Soils are vital for human existence. Soil scientists and geotechnical professionals study soils in relation to their fertility and capacity to produce crops; while geotechnical professionals study soils in terms of their suitability for engineering construction. Both aspects are important in waste management for the location of waste disposal facilities and developing remediation plans for contaminated sites.

Toxic effects of thousands of chemicals in common use are not well known due to the costly and time-consuming conventional toxicological testing using lab animals. With the advent of the TOX21 system and the remarkable progress made in the past 12 years, and the online availability of the *TOX21 10K Compound Library*, it will become possible to develop the toxicological profile of a large number of chemicals at minimum cost and avoid animals.

Study Questions

1   Explain how geology is central to environmental science with reference to waste management.

2   What are the five components of the system earth? Why should the anthroposphere be considered one of the components? Substantiate your answer with examples.

3   List the major geological cycles of the earth. Why could the cycles be considered nature's examples of recycling materials? Explain with reference to the rock and tectonic cycle.

4 Discuss the importance of the Holocene period. The IR of the late eighteenth century has been considered both a boon and a bane to humanity. What is your position in this debate? Explain in the context of environmental issues.

5 List four earth materials. What is the difference between: (i) soil and sediment, and (ii) sediment and sedimentary rock?

6 What is the difference between the exogenetic and endogenetic earth processes? Is weathering an example of an endogenetic process? Why or why not?

7 List the natural substances that comprise earth materials. How are rocks different from soils? Discuss at least three main differences.

8 What are the three major groups of rocks? Would a foliated metamorphic rock serve as a good foundation for a landfill? What about extrusive igneous rock? Which of the other type of these two major groups would be more suitable? Explain why.

9 A sample of clayey soil from a proposed hazardous waste disposal site had a volume of 95 mL and weighed 138 g in its natural state. Upon oven drying, its weight was found to be 96 g. If the specific gravity of the solids is 2.68, calculate: (a) void ratio, (b) porosity, (c) degree of saturation, and (d) water content of the soil. Draw a phase diagram to illustrate your calculations and report the values to one significant number.
Answer: (a) **1.7**, (b) **62.3**%, (c) **70.9**%, and (d) **43.8**%.

10 What are the three main Atterberg limits? Draw a sketch to show the three limits in relation to their water contents and strength. What would be the PL of soil that had PI = 45 and LL = 57?
Answer: **12**.

11 Using the USDA triangular diagram, determine the class of soil that had (a) sand 50%, silt 10%, and clay 40%, and (b) sand 10%, silt 70%, and clay 20%.

12 Of the 15 types of engineering soils, which soil types have (a) the highest compressibility, and (very low permeability? Among the four soils of very low permeability, which is the most suitable soil to serve as a landfill liner? Why?

13 What is the difference between a confined and unconfined aquifer? What makes a confined aquifer flow above the land surface?

14 The total monthly precipitation in a certain geographic area is 14 987 million liters (ML), runoff is 5200 ML, and infiltration is 4500 ML. Calculate the amount of evapotranspiration, E.
Answer: **5287 ML**

15 Two water wells were drilled in a sand and gravel aquifer, located 0.5 km apart. The GWT in the two wells was encountered at depths of 43.0 m and 39.5 m. The hydraulic conductivity of the aquifer material was determined to be 9.4×10^{-2} cm/s, and its porosity 40%. Calculate the actual groundwater flow velocity, Va, in cm/s and m/d.
Answer: Va = **0.00165 cm/s or 1.43 m/d**.

16 Define toxicology. Why is knowledge of toxicity helpful in waste management?

17 Explain the difference between: (i) reversible and irreversible toxicity, and (ii) acute and chronic toxic effects. Many soldiers exposed to Agent Orange that was widely used during the Vietnam War were found to develop cancer. Is this an example of acute or chronic effect? Why?

18 What are the three main exposure pathways for toxic substances to enter the human body? Which of these is the mode of infection of the SARS-CoV-2 (COVID-19)?

19 In general, more than one toxic substance is found at contaminated sites. Why is it important to evaluate the toxic effect of all of them?

20 If a poisonous snake bites a person, an antidote is administered to the victim that cures the adverse effect of the poison. Is this an example of synergism or antagonism?

References

Ames, B.N., Magaw, R., and Gold, L.S. (1987). Ranking possible carcinogenic hazards. *Science* 236: 271–280.

ASTM (2021). Soil and Rock (I): D420 - ASTM International – Standards. https://www.astm.org/BOOKSTORE/BOS/0408.htm (accessed 19 September 2021).

Doull, J., Klassen, C.D., and Amdur, M.O. (ed.) (1980). *Casarett and Doull's Toxicology*, 2e, 778. McMillan Publishing Company: New York.

EPA (2020). Toxicology in the 21st century, Tox21 fact Sheet. Tox21_FactSheet_Dec2020.pdf

Gleeson, T., Wada, Y., Bierkens, M.P., and van Beek, L.P.H. (2012). Water balance of global aquifers revealed by groundwater footprint. *Nature* 488: 197–200. https://doi.org/10.1038/nature11295.

Jean-Hublin, J.J., Ben-Ncer, A., Bailey, S.E. et al. (2017). New fossils from Jebel Irhoud, Morocco and the pan-African origin of Homo sapiens. *Nature* 546: 289–292. https://doi.org/10.1038/nature22336.

NASA (2021). *About the Atmosphere*: Background Information, About the Atmosphere: Background Information | MyNASAData

Postel, S. (1988). Controlling toxic chemicals. In: *State of the World* (ed. L.R. Brown, C. Flavin and H. French), 120. New York: W.W. Norton & Company.

Ritchie, H., and Roser, M. (2014) Natural Disasters. Published online at *OurWorldInData.org*. https://ourworldindata.org/natural-disasters (accessed 29 October 2021).

UNESCO (2010). Water for a sustainable world, Facts and Figures. 12 p. WWDR2015Facts_Figures_ENG_web.pdf (unesco.org) (accessed 29 November 2021).

USGS (2015). Groundwater use in the United States. Groundwater Use in the United States (usgs.gov) (accessed 30 November 2021).

Utah Geological Survey (2021). *Groundwater & Aquifers*. Groundwater & Aquifers – Utah Geological Survey.

Wilkinson, B.H. and McElroy, B.J. (2007). Impact of humans on continental erosion and sedimentation. *GSA Bulletin* 119 (1/2): 140–156. https://doi.org/10.1130/B25899.1.

Supplemental Readings

McDonough, W. and Braungart, M. (2002). *Cradle to cradle*, 193. New York, NY: Northpoint Press.
Sample, I. (2017). Oldest Homo sapiens bones ever found shake foundations of the human story. *The Guardian*. From Oldest Homo sapiens bones ever found shake foundations of the human story (accessed 28 August 2017).

Web Resources

ATSDR/CDC. Agency for Toxic Substances and Disease Registry, Centers for Disease Control. Agency for Toxic Substances and Disease Registry (cdc.gov). Valuable source of toxicity profile of hundreds of chemicals and their potential health effects.
National Institutes of Health. Information on the rapid toxicological assessment of hazardous substances using robotics and advanced computation technologies is available at: Toxicology in the twenty-first Century (Tox21) | National Center for Advancing Translational Sciences (nih.gov).
USDA/NRCS. US Department of Agriculture through its Natural Resources Conservation Service offers useful information on agricultural soil, its classification, loss, and productivity, in addition to groundwater resources. Home | NRCS Soils (usda.gov).
USGS. The United States Geological Survey is the premier agency to collect and disseminate data and information on nation's geologic and biologic resources. Valuable information on geologic hazards, mineral resources, and water resources (both surface and groundwater) and its contamination, besides educational materials on basics of geology are available on its website. USGS also provides satellite imageries for scientific research. USGS.gov | Science for a changing world.

Acronyms/Symbols

bgpd	billion gallons per day
d	day
hr.	hour
Ga	Giga (10^9) annum; billion years
Ma	Mega (10^6) annum; million years
Ka	kilo (10^3) annum; thousand years
L	liter
USDA	United States Department of Agriculture
USGS	United States Geological Survey
y	year
μM	micromolar (10^{-6} molar)

3

Environmental Laws

LEARNING OBJECTIVES

After studying this chapter, you will be able to:

- Know the history and evolution of environmental laws in the United States.
- Describe major environmental laws.
- Explain laws dealing with waste management and pollution control.

3.1 History and Evolution of Environmental Laws in the United States

Modern society strives for a balance between economic development and environmental protection, finding a threshold that reconciles the inevitable production of waste with a commitment to ecological sustainability. The depletion of natural resources that may not be renewable, and the (often-related) by-production of hazardous waste, is an increasingly important focus of long-running debates regarding the conflict between state regulation and market forces, between individual action and collective consequences, and between the practical and the ethical impact of new or newly mass-consumed technologies.

—Mitchum, *Encyclopedia of Science, Technology, and Ethics*, 2005

Silent Spring by Rachel Carson, soon after its publication in 1962, became the *New York Times Best Seller* (sold 50 000 copies), and awakened the nation's conscience to the colossal harm that was being inflicted to the environment by the widespread use of insecticides in agriculture. At the same time, unprecedented incidents, like the Cuyahoga River in Ohio catching fire (June 1969) and massive oil spill off the Santa Barbara coast in California (January–February 1969), galvanized the citizens and lawmakers to take measures for preventing environmental degradation. Senator Gaylord Nelson from Wisconsin was already worried about increasing air and water pollution and decided to organize nationwide sit-ins at college campuses to infuse environmental awareness, which led to the creation of Earth Day. The first Earth Day was observed on 22 April 1970, and on the same day since. Twenty million Americans came together on Earth Day to rally around these shared values. They demonstrated against the environmental deterioration from 150 years of industrial development that had devastated human and ecological health. Protests were organized at 1000s of colleges and universities and demonstrations were held all across the country.

Introduction to Waste Management: A Textbook, First Edition. Syed E. Hasan.
© 2022 John Wiley & Sons Ltd. Published 2022 by John Wiley & Sons Ltd.

The movement led the lawmakers to enact a series of legislations in quick succession, starting with the creation of the Environmental Protection Agency (EPA) (2 December 1970), the Occupational Safety and Health Act (29 December 1970), and the Clean Air Amendments Act (31 December 1970). The Ohio River fire and Santa Barbara oil spill forced the amendment of the 1948 Federal Water Pollution Control Act (FWPCA) in 1972 that was renamed the Water Quality Act. A series of major environmental laws were enacted during the decades of the 1970s (Figure 3.1) and the subsequent two decades, addressing key environmental issues. This chapter includes a description of major environmental laws with a detailed discussion of laws related to waste management.

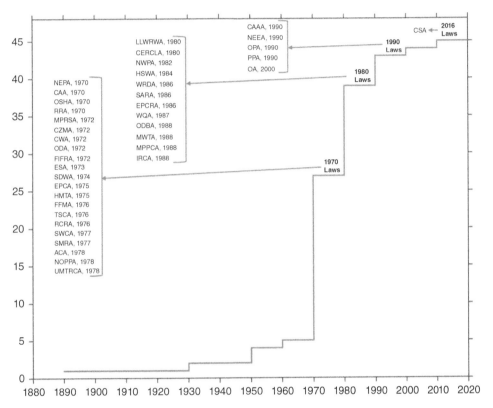

Figure 3.1   Important US environmental laws and years enacted. ACA, Antarctic Conservation Act; CAA, Clean Air Act; CAAA, Clean Air Act Amendments; CERCLA, Comprehensive Environmental Response Compensation and Liability Act; CSA, Chemical Safety Act of the 21st Century; CWA, Clean Water Act; CZMA, Coastal Zone Management Act; EPCA, Energy Policy and Conservation Act; ESA, Endangered Species Act; EPCRA, Emergency Planning and Community Right-to-Know Act; FFMA, Federal Forest Management Act; FIFRA, Federal Insecticide, Fungicide, and Rodenticide Act; HSWA, Hazardous and Solid Waste Amendments Act; HMTA, Hazardous Materials Transportation Act; IRCA, Indoor Radon Control Act; LLRWPA, Low-Level Radioactive Waste Policy Act; MPPCA, Marine Plastic Pollution Control Act; MPRSA, Marine Protection, Research, and Sanctuaries Act; MWTA, Medical Waste Tracking Act; NEEA, National Environmental Education Act; NEPA, National Environmental Policy Act; NOPPA, National Ocean Pollution Planning Act; NWPA, Nuclear Waste Policy Act; OBDA, Ocean Dumping Ban Act; OA, Oceans Act; ODA, Ocean Dumping Act; OPA, Oil Pollution Act; OSHA, Occupational Safety and Health Act; PPA, Pollution Prevention Act; RCRA, Resource Conservation and Recovery Act; RRA, Resource Recovery Act; SARA, Superfund Amendments and Reauthorization Act; SMRA, Surface Mining Reclamation Act; SWRCA, Soil and Water Resources Conservation Act; SDWA, Safe Drinking Water Act; TSCA, Toxic Substances Control Act; UMTRCA, Uranium Mill Tailings and Radiation Control Act; USTA, Underground Storage Tank Act; WRDA, Water Resources Development Act; WQA, Water Quality Act.

3.1.1 Foundation and Strength of US Environmental Laws

Among the world's nations, the US was the first country to pass and enforce laws directed toward the protection of the environment. The series of environmental laws enacted over the past five decades have significantly improved the ecological health and environmental quality of the country, and have reduced citizens' exposure to hazardous chemicals while allowing the public to participate in the decision-making process.

Some of the notable features of US environmental laws include the use of science-based standards to frame laws, transparency, a democratic approach allowing states to adapt to national standards with the ability to modify it in ways that suit the state's unique environment, strict enforcement, and provision of adequate funding mechanisms.

Law-making and enforcement is a complex and challenging task that frequently becomes the focus of public controversy and debate. Political interests sometimes lead to actions that prove harmful. Safeguards must be provided by lawmakers to not alter the fundamental principles enshrined in the environmental laws.

It is a testimony to the strength of US environmental law that many other countries have developed their own environmental laws following the US model. Its first major policy act, the National Environmental Policy Act (NEPA), has been adopted by at least 100 countries.

3.2 Important Environmental Laws

The decades of 1970s stand out as the period when the majority of key environmental laws were passed in the United States. The trend continued during the 1980s and 1990s when a substantial set of legislation had been enacted to address major environmental concerns during the 30-year period. The process of monitoring the nation's environmental quality is continuing and appropriate laws are being enacted as and when necessary. Table 3.1 lists about 30 major environmental laws that had been enacted during the past 50 years; a few passed before 1970 have also been included due to their relevance to environmental protection.

Table 3.1 Important environmental laws, years enacted and purpose.

Federal regulation and year enacted	Purpose/Scope
National Environmental Policy Act, 1970	The 1969 Act signed into law on 1 January 1970 established a broad national framework for protecting the nation's environment. It directed all branches of government to give due consideration to the environment prior to undertaking any major federal action that significantly affects the environment. Over 100 countries have adopted laws similar to NEPA.
Clean Air Act, 1970	Amended the 1967 Air Quality Act, setting goals to comply with the air quality standards.
Comprehensive Environmental Response Compensation and Liability Act, 1980	Covers solid and hazardous waste management; authorized EPA for rulemaking and enforcement. Amended the SWDA of 1965. Also called Superfund.
Chemical Safety Act, 2016	Short form of the Frank R. Lautenberg Chemical Safety for the 21st Century Act. It amends the ineffective Toxic Substances Control Act of 1976.

Table 3.1   (Continued)

Federal regulation and year enacted	Purpose/Scope
Clean Water Act, 1972	Aimed at eliminating water pollution. The official title of the Act is the Federal Water Pollution Control Act (FWPCA). The first Act was enacted in 1948 but was completely rewritten in 1972 in an Act titled the FWPCA Amendments, commonly known as the Clean Water Act.
Coastal Zone Management Act, 1972	Provides for the management of the nation's coastal resources, including the Great Lakes. Aims at preservation, protection, development, and restoration, or enhancement of the nation's coastal zone. The Act is administered by National Oceanic and Atmospheric Administration (NOAA).
Energy Policy and Conservation Act, 1975	The primary goals of the Act are to increase energy production and supply, reduce energy demand, and provide energy efficiency. The Strategic Petroleum Reserve, and Corporate Average Fuel Economy regulations were established under this Act.
Endangered Species Act, 1973	The Act aims at the protection and preservation of endangered plant and animal species and their habitats.
Emergency Planning and Community Right-to-Know Act, 1986	This Act is organized under Title III of the Superfund Amendment and Reauthorization Act of 1986. It is intended to encourage and support emergency planning efforts at the state and local levels and provide residents and local governments with information concerning potential chemical hazards present in their communities. The emergency planning requirements of this Act provide for the establishment and maintenance of contingency plans for responding to chemical accidents which can inflict health and environmental damage as well as cause significant disruption within a community.
Federal Insecticide, Fungicide, and Rodenticide Act	The Federal Insecticide Act was the first pesticide legislation that was passed in 1910. Widespread manufacturing and use of pesticides after World War II led the US Congress to pass the Federal Insecticide, Fungicide, and Rodenticide Act in 1947 to address some of the shortcomings of the Federal Insecticide Act, and assigned the US Department of Agriculture to regulate pesticides. In 1972, the Act was amended and EPA was assigned the authority to oversee the sale and use of pesticides with emphasis on the preservation of human health and protection of the environment by shifting the burden of proof to the chemical manufacturer, enforcing compliance against banned and unregistered products.
Hazardous and Solid Waste Amendments Act, 1984	The Hazardous and Solid Waste Amendments Act represents the 1984 amendments to RCRA, and focuses on waste minimization and phasing-out land disposal of hazardous waste as well as corrective action for releases. Some of the other mandates of this law include increased enforcement authority for EPA, more stringent hazardous waste management standards, and a comprehensive UST program.
Hazardous Materials Transportation Act, 1975	The primary objective of this law is to provide adequate protection against the risks to life and property inherent in the transportation of hazardous material in commerce by improving the regulatory and enforcement authority of the Secretary of Transportation. A hazardous material, as defined by the Secretary of Transportation, is any "particular quantity or form" of a material that "may pose an unreasonable risk to health and safety or property."
Indoor Radon Control Act, 1988	The Indoor Radon Control Act, 1988 established a long-term goal of indoor air to be as radon-free as the ambient outside air, i.e. ~0.4 pCi/L. EPA recommends homes be remediated if the radon level is 4 pCi/L (action level) or more. Because there is no known safe level of exposure to radon, EPA also recommends home radon levels to be between 2 and 4 pCi/L. It is estimated that lowering home radon concentrations to below EPA's action level of 4 pCi/L would avoid nearly one-third of radon-induced lung cancer.

(Continued)

Table 3.1 (Continued)

Federal regulation and year enacted	Purpose/Scope
Low-Level Radioactive Waste Policy Act, 1980	The Act made each state responsible for management including disposal of its Low-Level Radioactive Waste (LLRW) generated within its borders, in cooperation with neighboring states to avoid a proliferation of too many LLRW sites. The Act does not address low-level defense waste, which is the responsibility of the DOE.
Marine Protection, Research, and Sanctuaries Act, 1972	The Marine Protection, Research, and Sanctuaries Act (MPRSA), also referred to as the Ocean Dumping Act, generally prohibits: transportation of material from the United States for the purpose of ocean dumping; transportation of material from anywhere for the purpose of ocean dumping by the US agencies or US-flagged vessels; and dumping of material transported from outside the United States into the US territorial sea. A permit is required from the EPA to deviate from these prohibitions, after determining whether the dumping will "unreasonably degrade or endanger" human health, welfare, or the marine environment.
Medical Waste Tracking Act, 1988	Medical waste management is regulated by state environmental and health departments. EPA has not had authority for medical waste after the expiration of the Act in 1991.
Nuclear Waste Policy Act, 1982	During the first 40 years that nuclear waste was being created in the United States, no legislation was enacted to manage its disposal. The Nuclear Waste Policy Act recommended the use of deep geologic repositories for the safe storage and/or disposal of radioactive waste. The Act established procedures for DOE to evaluate and select sites for geologic repositories in partnership with state governments.
Occupational Safety and Health Act, 1970	The Act aims at ensuring the workers' and workplace safety. Employers are expected to provide their workers with a work environment free from recognized hazards to safety and health, such as exposure to toxic chemicals, excessive noise levels, mechanical dangers, heat or cold stress, or unsanitary conditions. The law is enforced by the federal Occupational Safety and Health Administration.
Superfund Amendments and Reauthorization Act, 1986	The Superfund Amendments and Reauthorization Act amended the Comprehensive Environmental Response, Compensation, and Liability Act in October 1986. The Act provided EPA with new enforcement authorities and settlement tools; increased state involvement in every phase of the Superfund program, increased the focus on human health problems, encouraged greater citizen participation in making decisions on site clean up, and increased the size of the trust fund to $8.5 billion.
Resource Conservation and Recovery Act, 1976	The Act required EPA to establish and enforce regulations for safe disposal of solid and hazardous waste. EPA developed a list and criteria for the classification of waste as hazardous and non-hazardous (ordinary solid waste). A system of tracking hazardous waste from its time of generation to ultimate disposal, called the Manifest System, was created by EPA to track the hazardous waste at every stage of its existence (cradle to grave).
Pollution Prevention Act, 1990	The Pollution Prevention (P2) Act is the second national policy declaration to prevent pollution as the nation's goal. The Act requires pollution to be prevented or minimized at the source, *before* it is produced, rather than controlling it *after* it is generated. P2 includes practices that increase efficiency in the use of energy, water, or other natural resources, and protect the nation's resources through conservation.

Table 3.1 (Continued)

Federal regulation and year enacted	Purpose/Scope
Surface Mining Reclamation and Control Act, 1977	The Surface Mining Control and Reclamation Act (SMCRA) of 1977 is the primary federal law that regulates the environmental effects of coal mining in the United States. SMCRA created two programs: one for regulating active coal mines and a second for reclaiming abandoned mine lands. SMCRA also created the Office of Surface Mining, an agency within the Department of the Interior, to promulgate regulations, to fund state regulatory and reclamation efforts, and to ensure consistency among state regulatory programs.
Soil and Water Resources Conservation Act, 1977	The Act provides for a continuing appraisal of soil, water, and related resources, including fish and wildlife habitats, and established a soil and water conservation program to assist landowners and land users in advancing soil and water conservation.
Safe Drinking Water Act, 1974	The Safe Drinking Water Act is intended to ensure safe drinking water for the public. The Act required EPA to set standards for drinking water quality and oversee all states, localities, and water suppliers to implement the standards. EPA has established protective drinking water standards for more than 90 contaminants, including drinking water regulations issued since the 1996 amendments to the Safe Drinking Water Act that strengthen public health protection. Over 92% of the US population supplied by community water systems receives drinking water that meets all health-based standards.
Toxic Substances Control Act, 1976	The Toxic Substances Control Act of 1976 provided EPA with authority to require reporting, record-keeping, testing, and restrictions relating to chemical substances and/or mixtures. Certain substances are generally excluded from TSCA, including, among others, food, drugs, cosmetics, and pesticides. TSCA addresses the production, importation, use, and disposal of specific chemicals.
Uranium Mill Tailings and Radiation Control Act, 1978	The goal of the Act is to provide for the disposal, long-term stabilization, and control of uranium mill tailings in a safe and environmentally sound manner and to minimize or eliminate radiation health hazards to the public.
Underground Storage Tank Act, 1984	The Act is intended to control leakage of petroleum or other hazardous substances from USTs and the resulting contamination of groundwater and soil. The law requires owners/operators of the USTs to monitor, control, and remediate any contaminations from the tanks.
Water Quality Act, 1987	The purpose is to renew and maintain water quality in the nation's lakes, rivers, and streams. To control water pollution, a permit system, called the National Pollutants Discharge Elimination System (NPDES), was established and states were given the authority to implement it.

3.2.1 The Rivers and Harbors Act

The Rivers and Harbors Act of 1899 is also referred to as the Refuse Act. The Act stated that it is unlawful to throw, discharge, or deposit any type of refuse from any source, except that flowing from streets and sewers, into any *navigable water* or its tributaries, except with the permission of the Secretary of the Army. This law may be considered the first attempt to restrict water pollution; however, the emphasis at that time was not on preserving the environmental quality of waters but on their navigational capabilities. In 1970, the Act was resurrected to effectively begin the process of elimination of indiscriminate dumping of waste materials into streams and rivers.

3.2.2 The Atomic Energy Act

The Atomic Energy Act (1954) was developed to regulate nuclear materials and to manage nuclear wastes. The Atomic Energy Commission (AEC) was established to license the processing and use of nuclear materials in the defense and public sectors. Through an act, known as the Energy Reorganization Act (1974), the AEC was divided into two agencies: (i) The Department of Energy (DOE), and (ii) The Nuclear Regulatory Commission (NRC). The DOE was made responsible for the development of nuclear energy and production of nuclear devices in the defense establishments, and the NRC was assigned licensing and oversight authority for civilian nuclear energy production (nuclear power plants).

3.2.3 Solid Waste Disposal Act

The Solid Waste Disposal Act (SWDA) of 1965 aimed at regulating municipal solid waste and making improvements in solid waste disposal technology. The purpose was to protect human health and the environment and to reduce the volume of waste. The law also authorized funds for the management of solid waste at the state level.

3.2.4 Resource Recovery Act

The SWDA was amended in 1970 and came to be known as the Resource Recovery Act (RRA). The Act encouraged waste reduction and resource recovery, and created a system of national disposal sites for hazardous wastes. This legislation was the forerunner of the Resource Conservation and Recovery Act (RCRA) (1976).

3.2.5 National Environmental Policy Act

The NEPA was passed by the US Congress and Senate in 1969 and signed into law on 1 January 1970 by President Nixon. The NEPA is landmark legislation that affirmed US commitment as a nation toward the protection and maintenance of its environmental quality. NEPA's passage led to the formation of the Presidential Council on Environmental Quality and the EPA. Also, the requirements for preparation of an Environmental Impact Statement (EIS) became mandatory for all projects that are funded, even in part, by the federal government. The EIS addresses environmental impacts of the proposed activity; evaluates unavoidable adverse impacts, alternatives to the proposed activity, and irretrievable commitments of resources. An EIS in effect forces the developer or owner of a project to fully evaluate the environmental consequences of the project before the first clod of soil is turned for construction.

The Council on Environmental Quality comprises well-known experts appointed by the President, who are charged with review and assessment of the nation's environmental quality, and present its report to the President every year. The President may agree with the recommendations and issues orders to control potential environmental problems.

3.2.6 Occupational Safety and Health Act

The Occupational Safety and Health Act of 1970 is the most important law dealing with the protection of the health and safety of employees at the workplace. The Occupational Safety and Health Administration (OSHA) was created to enforce the regulations. OSHA, though not an environmental agency per se, has developed guidelines, in consultation with the EPA, to regulate the health and safety of personnel involved in hazardous waste investigation and cleanup operations. One of the provisions of the Act is the requirement for maintaining up-to-date health records for all employees who are exposed to chemical substances.

3.2.7 Federal Water Pollution Control (Renamed Clean Water) Act

The FWPCA of 1948 was the first major US law to address water pollution. Growing public awareness and concern for controlling water pollution led to sweeping amendments in 1972. Following the 1972 amendments, the law came to be known as the Clean Water Act (CWA). The legislation was enacted with the main purpose of restoring and maintaining the chemical, physical, and biological integrity of the waters of the United States. The Act also gave authority to the EPA and states to take appropriate measures to control water pollution. Before the passage of the act, many of the nation's streams and lakes had been polluted to excessive levels. One of the goals of the CWA was to restore the nation's waters to fishable and swimmable conditions. Under the act, the EPA sets limits on the quantities of pollutants that may be discharged into surface waters by industries and municipalities, which are required to obtain a discharge permit either from the EPA or the state authorities. This permit is part of the National Pollution Discharge Elimination System (NPDES). The Act was amended in 1977 and 1981.

The CWA classifies wastes as (i) toxic, (ii) conventional, and (iii) nonconventional. Water containing toxic materials must be treated before being released into water bodies (stricter standards have been imposed on this category under the RCRA). Conventional pollutants include those found in municipal wastes; for such water, existing technology has to be employed to control the pollutants before they are released into water bodies. Unconventional pollutants should be removed using the Best Available Technology (BAT). The CWA has resulted in a significant improvement in the water quality of the nation's rivers and lakes, many of which have been returned to fishable and swimmable conditions.

3.2.8 Clean Air Act

The Clean Air Act (CAA), enacted in 1963 and amended in 1970, 1977, and 1990, aims at controlling sources of air pollution and improving air quality. The CAA and its amendments govern the emission of pollutants into the atmosphere from industrial and commercial activities. Air-quality standards and requirements to control pollutant release have been set forth in the regulations. The maximum levels of six pollutants – CO, NO_2, O_3, SO_2, Pb, and $PM_{2.5}$ that affect air quality and pose a significant threat to human health were established to set the National Ambient Air Quality Standard (NAAQS). The standards represent the limits on the atmospheric concentration of the six pollutants that cause smog, acid rain, and other health hazards, and apply to outdoor air throughout the country. Table 3.2 shows the pollutants and their limits as established under NAAQS. The CCA allows the EPA to review and revise the standards every five years. For instance, based on the review of scientific evidence by experts, EPA in 1997 changed the maximum concentration level of ozone from 0.12 to 0.8 ppm/h, and lowered the PM's limit to 2.5 μ or smaller from the existing 10 μ. This implies that whereas particles ≤10 μ were allowed to be released in the air, under the new rule, all PMs ranging in size from 10 to 2.5 μ must be captured by the emission control system in the plant, allowing only PMs ≤2.5 μ to be released in the air. The author had attended one of the public meetings in the 1980s and remembers representatives from General Motors and other industries objecting vehemently to the proposed new standards arguing that it will mean major retrofitting of their industrial plants and

Table 3.2 National ambient primary and secondary air quality standards.

Pollutant	Primary/Secondary	Average time	Concentration	Note
Carbon monoxide (CO)	Primary	8 hours	9 ppm	Not to exceed more than once per year
	Primary	1 hour	35 ppm	Not to exceed more than once per year
Lead (Pb)	Primary and secondary	Rolling average of 3 months	$0.15\,\mu g/m^3$	Not to exceed the limit
Nitrogen dioxide (NO_2)	Primary	1 hour	100 ppb	98th percentile of one-hour daily maximum concentrations, averaged over three years
	Primary and secondary	1 year	53 ppb	Annual mean
Ozone (O_3)	Primary and secondary	8 hours	0.070 ppm	Annual fourth highest daily maximum eight-hour concentration, averaged over three years
Particle pollution (PM) – $PM_{2.5}$	Primary	1 year	$12.0\,\mu g/m^3$	Annual mean, averaged over three years
	Secondary	1 year	$15.0\,\mu g/m^3$	Annual mean, averaged over three years
	Primary and secondary	24 hours	$35\,\mu g/m^3$	98th percentile, averaged over three years
Particle pollution (PM) – PM_{10}	Primary and secondary	24 hours	$150\,\mu g/m^3$	Not to be exceeded more than once per year on average over three years
Sulfur dioxide (SO_2)	Primary	1 hour	75 ppb	99th percentile of one-hour daily maximum concentrations, averaged over three years
	Secondary	3 hours	0.5 ppm	Not to be exceeded more than once per year

PM, particulate matters. *Source:* After EPA (2021b).

lead to an increase in the prices of automobiles (similar to the argument before seat belts were made a required safety feature in automobiles) and losing their lead in automobile manufacturing to the Japanese. Of course, EPA dismissed the argument and the new standards became the law in 1990.

The 1990 CAA amendments gave greater enforcement powers to the EPA, enabling the agency to use new civil enforcement (fines up to $25 000 per day for each violation) and enhanced criminal proceedings ($25 000–1 000 000 fines and up to 15-year prison terms) against the violator. If the person or company has a prior conviction for the same violation, the maximum penalty for any subsequent conviction will be doubled. Under the law, individuals as well as companies can be found liable for criminal penalties. The 1990 amendments also authorized the EPA to pay a reward (up to $10 000) to any person who provides information or services that will lead to a criminal conviction or payment of a civil penalty by violators. This is known as the *whistleblower/bounty provision.*

3.2.9 Marine Protection, Research, and Sanctuary Act

The Marine Protection, Research, and Sanctuaries Act (MPRSA) of 1972, also known as the Ocean Dumping Act, relates to the protection of the marine environment. Specifically, the Act prevents or limits the dumping of any waste into the oceans that would adversely affect human health or the marine environment. Some types of wastes are altogether prohibited from ocean dumping, such as high-level nuclear waste (HLNW); biological, chemical, or radiological warfare materials; uncharacterized waste; and floatable natural or synthetic materials. All other wastes to be dumped at sea must have a permit.

3.2.10 Federal Insecticide, Fungicide, and Rodenticide Act

The Federal Insecticide Act was the first pesticide legislation that was passed in 1910. Widespread manufacturing and use of pesticides after World War II led the US Congress to pass the Federal Insecticide, Fungicide, and Rodenticide Act (FIFRA) in 1947 to address some of the shortcomings of the Federal Insecticide Act, and authorized the US Department of Agriculture to regulate pesticides. In 1972, the Act was amended and EPA was assigned the authority to regulate pesticides' distribution, sale, and use, and all parties were required to register (licensed) with EPA. Prior to receiving a license for introducing a pesticide in the market, the applicant must show, among other things, that using the pesticide "will not generally cause unreasonable adverse effects on the environment." FIFRA defines the term "unreasonable adverse effects on the environment" to mean: "(1) any unreasonable risk to man or the environment, taking into account the economic, social, and environmental costs and benefits of the use of any pesticide, or (2) a human dietary risk from residues that result from a use of a pesticide in or on any food inconsistent with the standard under Section 408 of the Federal Food, Drug, and Cosmetic Act."

Pesticides are classified as for *general use* or *restricted use*. Restricted-use pesticides require user certification. Restriction on the use of a certain pesticide can be imposed in areas where there has been a case of groundwater contamination or where a potential for such contamination exists. FIFRA requires premarket clearance of pesticides to prevent potential hazards to people and the environment. The EPA has been collecting information on various pesticides, and those suspected of causing serious problems have been withdrawn from the market. Ethylene dibromide (EDB) and dibromochloropropane (DBCP) are some examples.

3.2.11 Safe Drinking Water Act

The Safe Drinking Water Act (SDWA), first passed in 1974, has been amended twice – in 1977 and 1986. This Act and its 1977 amendments set minimum standards for safe drinking water in the United States. The SDWA also aims at the protection of "sole source" aquifers and other aquifers from contamination resulting from underground injection of waste. All aquifers, including current or potential drinking-water aquifers with a total dissolved solids (TDS)' concentration of less than 10 000 mg/L (cf. freshwater: 0–1000 mg/L) are to be protected from possible contamination from the deep-well injection of liquid waste. The Act was further amended in 1986 (the Gonzales Amendment), authorizing the EPA to designate aquifers that are especially valuable because they are the only source of drinking water in an area. The amendment directed the states to take measures to protect the surface area around public water supply wells from potential contamination from hazardous wastes, pesticides, and leaking underground storage tanks (LUSTs). Underground injection of hazardous wastes and other materials is also regulated under the SDWA.

All drinking (potable) water, including bottled water, contains a number of chemical elements, compounds, and other substances but do not pose any health risk as long as their concentration is within the acceptable limit. The SDWA required the EPA to establish a national drinking water standard for the protection of public health. Initially, EPA regulated only 22 chemicals and pathogens, using the terms "Maximum Contaminant Level (MCL)" and "Treatment Technique (TT)" to represent a concentration of the contaminants. EPA developed two sets of regulations, primary and secondary. The former includes substances that could be toxic in minor quantities, such as Hg, As, Pd, U, atrazine, etc., while aesthetic and cosmetic water characteristics of color, taste, odor, and appearance along with other less toxic substances were grouped in the latter (Tables 3.3 and 3.4).

The MCLs listed under primary standards are enforceable. Fines and penalties could be imposed by the EPA for non-compliance. The TT is used for pathogens in water that must be sanitized using the standardized EPA protocol. Any water supply company that provides drinking water to 25 or more customers must comply with the primary water quality standards. It should be noted that these standards do not apply to private water wells or bottled water suppliers.

Table 3.3 National primary drinking water quality standards.

Contaminant	MCL mg/L (ppm)	Potential health effects from long-term exposure	Contaminant source
A. Inorganic contaminants			
Antimony	0.006	Increase in blood cholesterol; decrease in blood sugar	Petroleum refineries; fire retardants; ceramics; electronics; solders
Arsenic	0.010 PHG = 0	Skin damage; risk of cancer	Air exposure of buried sediments of alluvial aquifers; runoff from glass and electronics manufacturing waste
Asbestos (fibers >10 μm)	7×10^6 fibers per liter (MFL)	Increased risk of developing benign intestinal polyps	Decay of asbestos cement in water mains; erosion of natural deposits
Barium	2	Blood pressure increase	Discharge of drilling waste, and from metal refineries; erosion of natural deposits
Beryllium	0.004	Intestinal lesions	Discharge from metal refiners, coal-burning factories; and from electrical, aerospace, and defense industries
Cadmium	0.005	Kidney damage	Corrosion of galvanized pipes; erosion of natural deposits; discharge from metal refineries; runoff from waste batteries and paints
Chromium (total)	0.1	Allergic dermatitis; cancer risk	Steel and paper pulp mills; erosion of natural deposits
Copper	TT AL = 1.3	Liver or kidney damage	Copper plumbing corrosion, erosion of natural deposits
Cyanide (as free cyanide)	0.2	Nerve damage or thyroid problems	Discharge from steel/metal factories

Table 3.3   (Continued)

Contaminant	MCL mg/L (ppm)	Potential health effects from long-term exposure	Contaminant source
Fluoride	4.0	Teeth mottling; bone diseases	Water additive; erosion of natural deposits; discharge from aluminum and fertilizer factories
Lead	TT AL = 0.15 PHG = 0	Neurotoxic to children: delayed mental and physical development; learning deficiency. Adults: high blood pressure; kidney problems	Corrosion of household plumbing systems; erosion of natural deposits
Nitrate (as N)	10	Blue-baby syndrome, infants less than six months may die if not treated	Runoff from fertilizer use; septic tanks, sewage; erosion of natural deposits
Nitrite (as N)	1	Same as for nitrate	Same as for nitrate
Selenium	0.05	Circulatory system problems; hair or fingernail loss	Petroleum and metal refineries; mines; erosion of natural deposits
Thallium	0.002 PHG = 0.0005	Hair loss; blood changes; kidney, intestine or liver problems	Leaching from ore-processing sites discharge from electronics, glass, and drug factories
B. Organic chemicals			
Acrylamide	TT PHG = 0	Nervous system, blood problems; increased cancer risk	Wastewater and sewage treatment
Alachlor	0.002 PHG = 0	Eye, liver, kidney, or spleen problems; anemia; increased risk of cancer	Runoff from herbicide used on row crops
Atrazine	0.003	Cardiovascular system or reproductive problems	Runoff from herbicide used on row crops
Benzene	0.005 PHG = 0	Anemia; decrease in blood platelets; increased risk of cancer	Discharge from factories; leaching from gas storage tanks and landfills
Benzo(*a*)pyrene (PAHs)	0.0002 PHG = 0	Reproductive difficulties; increased risk of cancer	Leaching from linings of water storage tanks and distribution lines
Carbofuran	0.04	Problems with blood, nervous system, or reproductive system	Leaching of soil fumigant used on rice and alfalfa
Carbon tetrachloride	0.005 PHG = 0	Liver problems; increased risk of cancer	Discharge from chemical plants and other industrial activities
Chlordane	0.002 PHG = 0	Liver or nervous system problems; increased risk of cancer	Residue of banned termiticide
Chlorobenzene	0.1	Liver or kidney problems	Discharge from chemical and agricultural chemical factories

(Continued)

Table 3.3 (Continued)

Contaminant	MCL mg/L (ppm)	Potential health effects from long-term exposure	Contaminant source
2,4-D	0.07	Kidney, liver, or adrenal gland problems	Runoff from herbicide used on row crops
Dalapon	0.2	Minor kidney changes	Runoff from herbicide used on rights of way
1,2-Dibromo-3-chloropropane (DBCP)	0.0002 PHG = 0	Reproductive difficulties; increased risk of cancer	Runoff/leaching from soil fumigant used on soybeans, cotton, pineapples, and orchards
o-Dichlorobenzene	0.6	Liver, kidney, or circulatory system problems	Discharge from industrial chemical factories
p-Dichlorobenzene	0.075	Anemia; liver, kidney, or spleen damage; changes in blood	Discharge from industrial chemical factories
1,2-Dichloroethane	0.005 PHG = 0	Increased risk of cancer	Discharge from industrial chemical factories
1,1-Dichloroethylene	0.007	Liver problems	Discharge from industrial chemical factories
cis-1,2-Dichloroethylene	0.07	Liver problems	Discharge from industrial chemical factories
trans-1,2-Dichloroethylene	0.1	Liver problems	Discharge from industrial chemical factories
Dichloromethane	0.005 PHG = 0	Liver problems; increased risk of cancer	Discharge from industrial chemical factories
1,2-Dichloropropane	0.005 PHG = 0	Increased risk of cancer	Discharge from industrial chemical factories
Di(2-ethylhexyl) adipate	0.4	Weight loss, liver problems, or possible reproductive difficulties	Discharge from industrial chemical factories
Di(2-ethylhexyl) phthalate	0.006 PHG = 0	Reproductive difficulties; liver problems; increased risk of cancer	Discharge from rubber and chemical factories
Dinoseb	0.007	Reproductive difficulties	Runoff from herbicide used on soybeans and vegetables
Dioxin (2,3,7,8-TCDD)	0.000 000 03 PHG = 0	Reproductive difficulties; increased cancer risk	Emissions from waste incineration; and other waste combustion; discharge from chemical factories
Diquat	0.02	Cataracts	Runoff from herbicide use
Endothall	0.1	Stomach and intestinal problems	Runoff from herbicide use
Endrin	0.002	Liver problems	Residue of banned insecticide
Epichlorohydrin	TT PHG = 0	Increased cancer risk; stomach problems	Discharge from industrial chemical factories; an impurity of water treatment chemicals

Table 3.3 (Continued)

Contaminant	MCL mg/L (ppm)	Potential health effects from long-term exposure	Contaminant source
Ethylbenzene	0.7	Liver or kidney problems	Discharge from petroleum refineries
Ethylene dibromide	0.00005 PHG = 0	Problems with liver, stomach, reproductive system, or kidneys increased risk of cancer	Discharge from petroleum refineries
Glyphosate	0.7	Kidney problems; reproductive difficulties	Runoff from herbicide use
Heptachlor	0.0004 PHG = 0	Liver damage; increased risk of cancer	Residue of banned termiticide
Heptachlor epoxide	0.0002 PHG = 0	Liver damage; increased risk of cancer	Breakdown of heptachlor
Hexachlorobenzene	0.001 PHG = 0	Liver damage; increased risk of cancer	Discharge from metal refineries and agricultural chemical factories
Hexachloro-cyclopentadiene	0.05	Kidney or stomach problems	Discharge from chemical factories
Lindane	0.0002	Liver or kidney problems	Runoff/leaching form insecticide, used on cattle, lumbar, and gardens
Methoxychlor	0.04	Reproductive difficulties	Runoff/leaching from insecticide, used on fruits, vegetables, alfalfa, and livestock
Oxamyl (Vydate)	0.2	Slight nervous system effects	Runoff/leaching from insecticide used on apples, potatoes, and tomatoes
Pentachlorophenol	0.001 PHG = 0	Liver or kidney problems; increased cancer risk	Discharge from wood-preserving factories
Picloram	0.5	Liver problems	Herbicide runoff
Polychlorinated biphenyls (PCBs)	0.0005 PGH = 0	Skin changes; thymus gland problems; immune deficiencies; reproductive or nervous system difficulties, increased risk of cancer	Runoff from landfills, discharge of waste chemicals
Simazine	0.004	Problems with blood	Herbicide runoff
Styrene	0.1	Liver, kidney, or circulatory system problems	Discharge from rubber and plastic factories; leaching from landfills
Tetrachloroethylene	0.005 PHG = 0	Liver problems; increased risk of cancer	Discharge from factories and dry cleaning shops
Toluene	1	Nervous system, kidney, or liver problems	Discharge from petroleum factories
Toxaphene	0.003 PHG = 0	Kidney, liver, or thyroid problems; increased risk of cancer	Runoff/leaching from insecticide used on cotton and cattle

(*Continued*)

Table 3.3 (Continued)

Contaminant	MCL mg/L (ppm)	Potential health effects from long-term exposure	Contaminant source
2,4,5-TP (Silvex)	0.05 PHG = 0	Liver problems	Residue of banned herbicide
1,2,4-Trichlorobenzene	0.07	Changes in adrenal glands	Discharge from textile finishing factories
1,1,1-Trichloroethane	0.2	Liver, nervous system, or circulatory problems	Discharge from metal degreasing sites and other factories
1,1,2-Trichloroethylene	0.005	Liver problems, increased risk of cancer	Discharge from industrial chemical factories
Trichloroethylene	0.005 PHG = 0	Liver problems; increased risk of cancer	Discharge from metal degreasing sites and other factories
Vinyl chloride	0.002 PHG = 0	Increased risk of cancer	Leaching from PVC pipes; discharge from plastic factories
Xylenes (total)	10	Nervous system damage	Discharge from petroleum and chemical factories
C. Disinfectants/Disinfection by-products			
Bromate	0.010 PHG = 0	Increased cancer risk	Byproduct of drinking water disinfection
Chloramines (as Cl_2)	MRDL = 4.0	Eye or nose irritation; stomach discomfort	Water additive to control microbes
Chlorine (as Cl_2)	MRDL = 4.0	Same as chloramines	Water additive to control microbes
Chlorine dioxide (as ClO_2)	MRDL = 0.8	Anemia; neurological problems in fetuses and young children	Water additive to control microbes
Chlorite	1.0 PHG = 0.8	Anemia; neurological problems in fetuses	By-product of drinking water disinfection
Haloacetic acids (HAAs)	0.060	Increased cancer risk	By-product of drinking water disinfection
Total trihalomethanes (TTHMs)	0.080	Liver, kidney, or CNS problems; increased cancer risk	By-product of drinking water disinfection
D. Microbiological contaminants			
Cryptosporidium	TT PHG = 0	Gastrointestinal problems	Human and animal fecal waste
Fecal coliform and *Escherichia coli*	Negative for both PHG = 0	Diarrhea, cramps, nausea, headaches, etc.	Human and animal fecal waste
Giardia lamblia	TT PHG = 0	Diarrhea, cramps, vomiting	Human and animal fecal waste
Heterotrophic plate count (HPC)	TT	No health effect, but good indicator of harmful bacteria	Measures range of bacteria present in the environment
Legionella	TT	Legionnaires' disease, a type of pneumonia	Naturally occurs in water, multiplies in heating systems

Table 3.3 (Continued)

Contaminant	MCL mg/L (ppm)	Potential health effects from long-term exposure	Contaminant source
Total coliforms	5.0% PHG = 0	Indicator of the presence of other harmful bacteria	Naturally occur in the environment
Turbidity	TT	Measures water cloudiness that indicates water quality and filtration efficiency; high turbidity means presence of microbes	Soil runoff
Viruses (enteric)	TT PHG = 0	Gastrointestinal problems upon	Human and animal fecal waste short-term exposure
E. Radiological contaminants			
Alpha/photon emitters	15 pCi/L PHG = 0	Increased risk of cancer	Erosion of natural radioactive mineral deposits
Beta photon emitters	4 millirem/y	Increased risk of cancer	Decay of natural and man-made radioactive minerals/elements
^{226}Radium and ^{228}Radium (combined)	5 pCi/L PHG = 0	Increased risk of cancer	Erosion of natural deposits
Uranium	30 μg/L PHG = 0	Increased risk of cancer, kidney toxicity	Erosion of natural deposits

AL, action level; water treatment facilities must use appropriate treatment methods to bring the concentration below the MCL; CNS, central nervous system; MFL, microfibers per liter; MRDL, maximum level of a residual disinfectant allowed; μg, microgram; PAHs, polycyclic aromatic hydrocarbons; PHG, public health goal; TT, treatment technique. *Source:* After EPA (2009).

Table 3.4 National secondary drinking water quality standards.

Contaminant	MCL, mg/L (ppm)
Aluminum	0.05–0.2
Chloride	250
Color	15 color units
Copper	1.0
Corrosivity	Noncorrosive
Fluoride	2.0
Foaming agents	0.5
Iron	0.3
Manganese	0.05
Odor	3 threshold odor number
pH	6.5–8.5
Silver	0.10
Sulfate	250
Total dissolved solids (TDS)	500
Zinc	5

Source: After EPA (2009).

Unlike tap water, bottled water is regulated by the Food and Drug Administration (FDA) which uses EPA's drinking water quality standards for bottled water, except for the amount of lead which is limited to 0.005 ppm instead of 0.015 ppm because, unlike Pb that might be present in pipes used for transferring water from utilities to home faucets, lead pipes are not used in bottled water production. Additionally, bottled water manufacturers are required to follow FDA's "current good manufacturing practice" (CGMP) regulations that require sampling, analyses, and record keeping to ensure that bottled water is safe and produced under sanitary conditions.

3.2.12 Resource Conservation and Recovery Act

The SWDA of 1965 and the RRA of 1970 were amended in 1976 under the RCRA. RCRA authorized the EPA to regulate hazardous waste at every stage of its life: from its generation, transportation, treatment, storage, to disposal i.e. from cradle to grave.

RCRA has three major components: subtitles C, D, and I. Subtitle C regulates hazardous waste, subtitle D regulates solid (nonhazardous) wastes, and subtitle I regulates underground storage tanks (USTs) that hold petroleum and other hazardous substances. RCRA aims at regulating hazardous wastes generated since the passage of the law (1976) and into the future, thereby excluding the hazardous wastes generated prior to 1976. RCRA mandates a permit-and-manifest system for all generators, transporters, and treatment, storage, and disposal (TSD) facility owners/operators. It requires new land disposal facilities to provide for a groundwater monitoring system, and old facilities to be retrofitted for groundwater monitoring. Hazardous waste landfills and lagoons are required to have a double-liner system for leachate management. Land disposal of liquid hazardous wastes and certain other hazardous wastes is prohibited. Details are discussed in Chapters 4 and 5.

3.2.13 Surface Mining Control and Reclamation Act

The Surface Mining Control and Reclamation Act (SMCRA) of 1977 was enacted to address environmental problems caused by surface mining of coal and reclamation of abandoned coal mines. The Act established a nationwide program to prevent adverse effects to the environment from surface coal mining. The Act authorized the establishment of the Office of Surface Mining Reclamation and Enforcement in the Department of Interior with a director appointed by the President. This office was designated an independent federal regulatory body with the power to administer the programs required by this Act and assist the states in the development of state programs for surface coal mining and reclamation. The Act created the Abandoned Mine Reclamation Fund in the Treasury and authorized appropriations of adequate funds to the Secretary of the Interior for allocation to each participating state. It requires operators of coal mines to pay into the fund quarterly fees of $0.35/ton of coal produced by surface mining and $0.15/ton of coal produced by underground mining, or 10% of the value of the coal in the mine, whichever is less. It sets forth requirements for the reporting of quarterly coal production, penalties for misreporting, and requirements for the collection of reclamation fees.

The Act requires surface mining operators to design and use impoundment structures to dispose of an underground mine, surface mine, and coal-processing plant waste; restore the original topography of the mined-out area; return the land to the same land use as the original or better (e.g. an original forested land must be revegetated for forest growth or it can be upgraded for agricultural use); segregate and preserve topsoil during surface mining operations and use it as final cover after the reclamation of the mined-out area; and protection of the hydrologic balance.

3.2.14 Uranium Mill Tailings and Radiation Control Act

The Uranium Mill Tailings and Radiation Control Act (UMTRCA) of 1978 provides for the safe and environmentally sound disposal, long-term stabilization, and control of uranium mill tailings in a manner that minimizes or eliminates radiation health hazards to the public. The EPA has set a soil concentration limit of 5 pCi/g in the top 15 cm of soil and 15 pCi/g in deeper soil for ^{226}Ra in uranium and thorium mill tailings.

Title I of UMTRCA designated 22 inactive uranium-ore processing sites for remediation. The US DOE has remediated 22 inactive uranium-ore-processing sites under the Uranium Mill Tailings Remedial Action Project in accordance with standards promulgated by the EPA. The radioactive materials were encapsulated in disposal cells approved by the US NRC.

Title II of UMTRCA included sites that were active when the Act was passed in 1978. These sites were commercially owned and regulated under an NRC license. For license termination, the owner conducts an NRC-approved reclamation of any onsite radioactive waste remaining from uranium-ore-processing operations. After remediation work performed at a site is complete and approved by the NRC, DOE assumes responsibility for each UMTRCA disposal site under a general NRC license for custody and long-term care. Separate general licenses are established for Title I and Title II sites. UMTRCA disposal sites are managed by the DOE Office of Legacy Management (LM). Figure 3.2 shows uranium mill tailing sites. All except two sites are located in the western United States.

3.2.15 Comprehensive Environmental Response, Compensation, and Liability Act

The Comprehensive Environmental Response, Compensation, and Liability Act (CERCLA) of 1980 is commonly known as the *Superfund*. Its primary goal is to clean up hazardous waste sites that were in existence prior to the passage of RCRA, i.e. before 1976. For this reason, all sites where hazardous waste was deposited before 1976 are called "historic" or "legacy" sites. CERCLA also contains a provision for an emergency response to hazardous material spills and cleanup. The law includes a provision known as *joint and several liability*, which permits the EPA to recover the full cost of cleanup from *any* of the responsible parties, even if the party was responsible for only part of the waste. The law requires the EPA to establish a National Priority List (NPL) of the worst contaminated hazardous waste sites for remedial action on a priority basis. As of September 2021, there were 1322 sites on the NPL. See Chapter 5 for various provisions of CERCLA and a detailed discussion of NPL.

3.2.16 Superfund Amendments and Reauthorization Act

The Superfund Amendments and Reauthorization Act (SARA) of 1986 reauthorized CERCLA to continue cleanup activities around the country. Several site-specific amendments and technical requirements were added to the legislation, including additional enforcement power. SARA addresses financial liability for hazardous waste cleanup. The *strict liability* provision means that the current owner of a property where hazardous waste may be found could still be liable even though that owner was not responsible for the problem. Accordingly, a current owner of a piece of real estate may be held liable for cleanup costs even if the contamination was the result of an earlier owner's action. Another provision of the law makes the liability *retroactive*, meaning that the past owner of a site may be charged with current liability even if that individual had complied with all regulations existing at the time of ownership of the property.

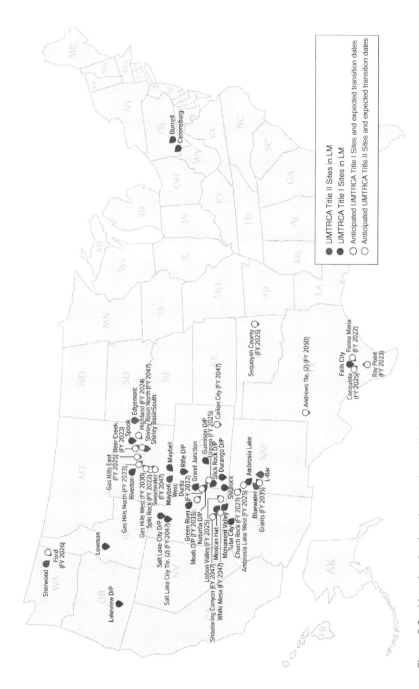

Figure 3.2 Map showing locations and remediation status of UMTRCA sites, as of July 2021. *Source:* DOE (2021). Legacy Management (LM) is an office within DOE that manages UMTRCA sites.

The liability burden under the law led to conducting environmental audits for the transfer of commercial, and even residential, properties. This works to the advantage of both the lender/seller and the owner of the property by alerting them to the potential liability associated with a contaminated site. An environmental audit does not guarantee removal of liability for cleanup but proves that the buyer used *due diligence* to avoid the liability.

3.2.17 Hazardous and Solid Waste Amendments Act

The Hazardous and Solid Waste Amendments Act (HSWA) of 1984 broadened the scope of RCRA and included provisions to protect the quality of groundwater. This led to the restriction of land disposal of hazardous waste by landfilling or surface impoundments. It established the requirement for double liners, leachate management systems, and groundwater monitoring programs at disposal sites. Technical standards for landfill design, leak detection systems, and underground storage of petroleum products and related hazardous substances were developed in pursuance of the act.

HSWA also set new requirements for the management and treatment of small quantities of hazardous waste, such as those generated by automotive shops or dry-cleaning businesses. It also established new regulations for underground tanks that store petroleum or other chemicals. Details are discussed in Chapter 5.

3.2.18 Underground Storage Tanks Act

The Underground Storage Tanks Act (USTA) was added to Subtitle I of RCRA in 1984. USTA aims at preventing leaks and spills, and their detection and remediation when they occur. It also ensures that the owners and operators of UST facilities will have the financial capability to correct any problems arising from leaking tanks. From a historical point of view, the law has set different requirements for "new" and "existing" owners and operators of USTs: Any UST installed after December 1986 is considered new, and those installed earlier are considered existing. Existing owners were allowed to upgrade and retrofit their USTs within a 12-year period ending 22 December 1998 to comply or close their operation. A fine of $11 000/day beyond the deadline was set for noncompliance, which forced many individual gas station owners to go out of business (cost of cleanup of leaking USTs was around $100 000 in the 1980s).

Responsibility for enforcement has been delegated to the states. As of 2020, 37 states had closed over 90% of LUSTs across the US; and the number of LUST sites were reduced from 162 600 in 2000 to 62 500 in 2020.

Approximately, 544 000 USTs nationwide store petroleum or hazardous substances. The greatest potential threat from a leaking UST is the contamination of groundwater, the source of drinking water for nearly half of all Americans.

3.2.19 Toxic Substance Control Act

The Toxic Substance Control Act (TSCA) of 1976 aims at regulating chemicals. Any new chemical manufactured or imported must be registered with EPA in the *TSCA Registry*. Information on the environmental fate of a chemical and associated health effects was to be furnished. Requirements for periodic reporting on production, or import, and any investigations related to alleged health effects, were established under TSCA.

The major flaw of TSCA relates to grandfathering 65 000 chemicals out of about 80 000 that were in industrial use at the time of its passage. In addition, due to the provision of "trade secret" in the law, EPA was ineffective in controlling the use of toxic chemicals. However, the passage of the Frank R. Lautenberg Chemical Safety for the 21st Century Act (the Lautenberg Chemical Safety Act) of 2016 has removed the loophole. See Chapter 5 for details.

3.2.20 Low-Level Radioactive Waste Policy Act

The Low-Level Radioactive Waste Policy Act (LLRWPA) was passed in 1980 and amended in 1985. The law provided a definition for low-level nuclear waste (LLNW), making the states responsible for managing LLNW instead of the NRC, and encouraged LLNW-generating states to form alliances with neighboring states to establish LLNW Compacts. The idea was to encourage states to use an agreed-upon site for disposal of their LLNW and after the site would become full, the second site will be selected in the other state in the compact, thus allowing all states in one compact to take a turn in its LLNW disposal. See Chapter 7 for details of the law and list of various compacts and participating states (Table 7.8). Most states did not pursue the idea of a compact and the 1985 amendment allowed more time by extending the deadline to 31 December 1992. Not much has happened by way of follow-up action and only a few states have moved forward.

3.2.21 Nuclear Waste Policy Act

The Nuclear Waste Policy Act (NWPA) was passed in 1982, requiring HLNW to be deposited in a geologic medium. The Act set the criteria for siting, design, operation, and monitoring of geological repositories. The Yucca Mountain Site was chosen for the repository, and responsibility for the operation of the repository was given to the DOE. The circumstances under which the laws were enacted is a good illustration of power politics and how the vested interests of influential politicians may be used to bypass impartial, balanced, and open debate to force decisions that may not be in the best interest of the nation. This law is discussed in detail in Chapter 7 including a discussion of the politics behind the passage of NWPA.

3.2.22 Emergency Planning and Community Right-to-Know Act

The Emergency Planning and Community Right-to-Know Act (EPCRA) was passed in 1986 in response to concerns about environmental and safety hazards associated with the storage and handling of toxic chemicals, which was triggered by a serious industrial accident at Bhopal, India in December 1984. The Bhopal disaster was one of the world's worst industrial catastrophes. A massive release of methyl isocyanide gas from the Union Carbide Pesticide Plant in Bhopal, India, killed >20 000 people and made 100 000 chronically ill (Amnesty International 2004). The accident raised widespread public concern about toxic chemical storage, releases, and emergency response leading to the passage of EPCRA.

The law required major US industries to report the release of toxic chemicals from their plants and how the release was managed, along with a written plan on minimizing or eliminating the use of hazardous substances in their manufacturing process. Industries are required to submit their report on toxic release annually to the EPA by the 1 July deadline, failing which a stiff fine has to be paid for each day's delay. The EPA compiles and analyzes the data and publishes an annual report titled *Toxic Release Inventory* (TRI).

The 35-year-old TRI is the first information collection and disclosure program of its kind in the world. The EPA, through its TRI program, collects information from about 2100 facilities on the

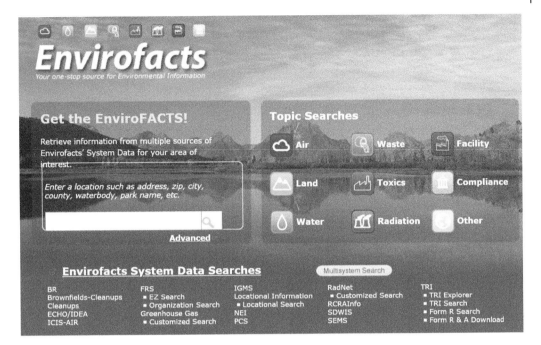

Figure 3.3   Screenshot of USEPA Envirofacts website for access to TRI data. *Source:* EPA.

use of about 760 toxic chemicals and their release into the environment. The annual TRI report provides valuable information to the public on industrial pollution in their communities, its source, and potential health and ecological effects. Many communities use this information to notify polluting industries to take action for the protection of residents' health and the environment. Making these data publicly available also gives companies an incentive to reduce pollution, and to learn from each other's experiences in pollution abatement.

The TRI report helps increase the public's knowledge and access to information on the nature, safe exposure levels, and toxicity of chemicals used at individual facilities, along with the quantity of each chemical released, and their management. The TRI online portal, *Envirofacts* (Envirofacts|US EPA) enables a user to access information on the release of toxic chemicals at any location – state, country, city, town, or by zip code (EPA 2021a). One can even find out which industries are located near one's home by typing in the address in the "MyProperty" button at the bottom (Figure 3.3).

A link for each chemical found for the particular location directs the user to *ToxFAQs* website (maintained by the Agency for Toxic Substances and Disease Registry, ATSDR) that shows a complete toxicological profile of the chemical(s), exposure limits, potential health problems, and clinical method of its detection and presence in the human body. TRI is an effective way to inform the public about the worst polluter in their area, which prompts them to take measures to control or eliminate the toxic release to improve its public image.

During the past 15 years, many industries have been implementing a wide array of modifications in their manufacturing processes. For example, over a 13-year period (2002–2014), pharmaceutical manufacturing facilities have reduced the quantities of toxic chemicals by 58%. Auto industries during the same period were able to achieve a 56% reduction in the release of toxic chemicals despite the fact that autos' production increased sharply during this time.

TRI Explorer (Release Chemical Report|TRI Explorer|US EPA) and TRI Search (TRI Search|US EPA) also provide toxic release data at various levels of detail.

3.2.23 Medical Waste Tracking Act

The Medical Waste Tracking Act (MWTA), added to Subtitle J of RCRA, was passed in 1988, following the panic that resulted from the medical waste that had washed up on the beaches in New Jersey and New York states during 1987–1988. EPA was charged to investigate the incidence and report the findings to the US Congress. The ATSDR was contracted by EPA to conduct the study, which found no serious threats to public health or the environment. Based on this, the EPA set up guidelines for managing medical waste but delegated rulemaking and enforcement responsibilities to individual states to develop their own rules to regulate medical waste. Details of MWTA are discussed in Chapter 6.

3.2.24 Indoor Radon Abatement Act

The Indoor Radon Abatement Act (IRAA), passed in 1988, aims at ensuring that the indoor air is as free from radon as the ambient air outside the building. The law authorized $45 million over three years for radon-related activities at the state and federal levels. IRAA directed EPA to survey the nation's schools to determine radon levels and undertake an effort to mitigate radon hazards.

Since 1988, EPA has administered a voluntary program to reduce exposure to indoor radon by promoting awareness, testing, installation of radon mitigation systems in existing homes, and use of radon-resistant new construction techniques. Still, building codes in some areas do not require new homes to be built with radon-resistant new construction. Much of the progress made in reducing exposure has occurred as a result of real estate transactions. In these cases, a buyer, seller, mortgage lender, and/or real estate agent requests testing a home for radon. Some states and localities do not require testing or the disclosure of test results during real estate transactions.

3.2.25 Pollution Prevention Act

The Pollution Prevention Act, also called P2 Act, was passed in 1990, declaring pollution prevention as the national policy. It emphasized pollution elimination as the top priority, followed by recycling, treatment, and disposal of waste as the last resort. Pollution prevention has been incorporated as one of the key provisions in major US environmental laws, which include CAA, CWA, EPCRA, RCRA, FIFRA, and NEPA. Details of the P2 Act are discussed in Chapter 9.

3.3 Summary

Earth Day, 22 April 1970, which was the brainchild of Senator Gaylord Nelson from Wisconsin, galvanized millions of Americans who came together to express their concerns about the widespread air and water pollution in the country. The demonstration that took place all across the country, prompted lawmakers to enact a series of major environmental laws during the last four decades of the twentieth century, topped by the creation of the EPA on 2 December 1970. From the broad policy statement of the NEPA to the specific IRAA, all laws aim at preserving the environment and protecting human and ecological health.

Nearly two dozen laws specifically relate to the safe management of societal waste. Notable ones include: The CAA and CWA; RCRA, CERCLA and its several amendments, the NWPA; EPCRA,

P2 Act, etc. Maximum concentrations of harmful contaminants in air and drinking water were established under the CAA and the CWA in 1971, and 1975, respectively.

The TRI, required under the EPCRA, is an annual report prepared by EPA that contains information on source of pollution in a geographic area, the generator, quantity, health effects, etc., of toxic substances released into the environment. Handy interactive tools, available on the TRI website, contain valuable information that can be used by the public to notify polluting industry owners to reduce toxic discharges.

The nuclear waste policy has been a controversial issue and has suffered from the vested interest of influential politicians in the US legislature, with the result that even after over 65 years since the first atomic bomb was made, there is no permanent facility for disposal of HLNW in the country. Finland that built its first nuclear power reactor 33 years after the United States, has moved forward with the construction of the deep geological repository for its nuclear waste disposal, which is scheduled to become operational by 2023. On the other hand, the fate of the planned Yucca Mountain repository hangs in balance.

TRI and P2 acts, along with several others, have been quite effective in reducing the quantities of harmful pollutants in the environment, saving lives and preventing serious diseases.

Study Questions

1   Which book made the Americans aware of the harm inflicted on the wildlife and humans, and is considered to have started the environmental movement in the United States? Who was the author?

2   Name the two major environmental disasters that led to the creation of Earth Day. Who was the politician behind the idea? When is Earth Day observed? Has it achieved any positive result? Discuss two of the results.

3   Which of the last four decades of the twentieth century had the largest number of environmental laws enacted? List five major laws and briefly discuss their main features.

4   List three laws that regulate wastes. Provide a brief summary of each.

5   Which of the two laws passed during the 1970s deal with hazardous waste? Which one applies to sites where hazardous waste was dumped prior to 1976? What is the common name of this law?

6   What are some of the special provisions of the Superfund Amendments and Reauthorization Act (SARA) that make the rules seem unfair in terms of putting the cleanup responsibility on someone who had not caused the problem in the first place? Why do you think EPA imposed this requirement?

7   Discuss the requirements under the Surface Mining Control and Reclamation Act (SMCRA) regarding the restoration of the mined-out land?

8   Who is responsible for regulating medical waste in the United States? What has been EPA's role in medical waste management?

9 How has the TRI reporting helped industries in reducing the quantities of toxic substances in the environment? Look up the latest TRI report at the EPA website and prepare a list of five industries within 10 miles of your college/university that might be releasing toxic substances; prepare a table to list these industries, their location, types of chemicals released, their quantities, and potential health effects.

10 Comment on the US policy on nuclear waste management; why has the United States been left behind among other nuclear power-producing countries for disposing of its high-level nuclear waste (HLNW)? Which country has moved ahead and when it is likely to start emplacement of its HLNW in the deep geological repository?

References

Amnesty International (2004). *Clouds of Injustice: Bhopal Disaster 20 Years On*, An Amnesty International Report ASA 20/015/2004. London: Amnesty International, 7 p. India: Summary of Clouds of Injustice - Bhopal Disaster 20 years on (amnesty.org).

DOE (2021). Fact sheet, UMTRCA Title I & II, 3 p. https://www.energy.gov/sites/default/files/2021-07/UMTRCATitleIandIIProgrammaticFactSheet.pdf (accessed 6 July 2021).

EPA (2021a). Envirofacts: your one-stop source for environmental information. Envirofacts|US EPA.

EPA (2021b). NAAQS table. *US EPA* (10 February 2021).

EPA (2009). National Primary Drinking Water Regulations, EPA 816-F-09-004; also available at: National Primary Drinking Water Regulations|US EPA.

Mitchum, C. (ed.) (2005). *Encyclopedia of Science, Technology, and Ethics*, 250. Detroit, MI: Macmillan.

Web Resources

The Nature Conservancy. Environmental Conservation Laws. Available at: Environmental Conservation Laws (nature.org).

US EPA. Laws and Regulations. Available at: Laws & Regulations|US EPA.

Acronyms/Symbols

ATSDR	agency for toxic substances and disease registry
BAT	best available technology
g/L	gram per liter (ppm)
LM	legacy management (of UMTRCA sites)
μm	micrometer (1×10^{-6} m)
NOAA	National Oceanic and Atmospheric Administration
TDS	total dissolved solids
TRI	toxic release inventory
USDA	United States Department of Agriculture

4

Municipal Solid Waste

LEARNING OBJECTIVES

After studying this chapter, you will be able to:

- Summarize the historical perspective on municipal solid waste (MSW) management in the United States.
- Identify health issues caused by the mismanagement of MSW.
- Describe the source, composition, and variability of MSW.
- Explain the US laws regulating MSW.
- Gain thorough knowledge on the landfill (LF) site selection, design, operation, and maintenance.
- Understand the biogeochemical processes that result in the formation of leachate and landfill gas (LFG).
- Differentiate between conventional MSW LF and bioreactor LF.

4.1   Historical Perspective

> One day our society will come to respect the sanitation worker if it is to survive, for the person who picks up our garbage is . . . just as significant as a physician. For if he does not do this, disease is rampant.
>
> *—Dr. Martin Luther King, 19 March 1968 at the Memphis Sanitation Workers Strike that morphed into civil rights movement and resulted in his assassination on 4 April 1968, on the 53rd day of the strike.*

The 1968 Memphis Sanitation Workers' Strike (also known as the Memphis Garbage Strike) offers a snapshot of how solid waste was managed by city governments in the early decades of the twentieth century, and "how our society viewed, in much of the US, black people and 'garbage workers' " (Hickman 2003, p. 506).

In 1968, the city of Memphis, Tennessee, employed 1100 sanitation workers – all were black men. They were made to work under the worst conditions: minimum wage, no pay on rainy days, no sick leave, no vacation, and no job protection. They had to drag 55-gallon drums, or carry on their head metal washtubs (20 gallon/64 L capacity), packed with about 50 kg of garbage, to the truck. Sanitation workers had presented their grievances to the city of Memphis several times but it was ignored. What triggered the strike was the accidental entrapment of two sanitation workers in the garbage truck who were crushed to death in the compactor due to the lack of any safety device to disable the compactor. This galvanized labor unions and other national organizations. What began as a local labor dispute turned into a national civil rights movement, involving Dr. Martin Luther King, NAACP, SCLC, AFSCME, and AFL-CIO. Dr. King led the march on 26 March 1968 that had to be called off because of acts of vandalism around the Main Street where the marchers were walking, and riots erupting on nearby streets. This did not deter the strikers who planned another massive march for 8 April. Dr. King arrived in Memphis on 3 April to join the strikers, and stayed at the Lorraine Motel. On 4 April evening, he got ready to address a huge crowd that had gathered on the street, and stepped out of his first-floor room to greet the crowd. Right at that moment, at 6:01 pm, he was shot at by an assassin from across the motel. He fell unconscious and was rushed to the St. Joseph Hospital where he died at 7:05 pm. After more than two months since the strike began on 12 February 1968, and intervention by President Lyndon Johnson on 5 April, a settlement was reached on 16 April between the Labor Union and the City of Memphis that agreed to meet most of the workers' demands.

Despite major changes to improve the working condition of sanitation workers, the irony is that even in the twenty-first century, the working conditions of waste management workers (as they are called now) have not improved much. Waste Management, Inc., one of the major current waste management companies in the United States, whose workforce is dominated by Latinos and African Americans, refused to accept workers' plea for improved working conditions that forced the workers to strike in 2008.

Conditions in developing countries are even worse: workers carry out their jobs under dangerous conditions, without adequate training and protective equipment, resulting in a high death rate and serious permanent injuries and disease.

4.1.1 The United States Public Health Service and the American Public Works Association

Any discussion on solid waste management in the United States would not be complete without acknowledging the sustained efforts, dedication, and commitment of the United States Public Health Service (USPHS) to find a safe method for the disposal of solid waste. The pioneering work done by USPHS, in collaboration with the American Public Works Association (APWA) between the late 1930s and 1970, not only brought about awareness of the need to manage the nation's solid waste in a safe manner to protect public health and the environment, but also laid the foundation of the field of solid waste management. These two organizations – one in the public and the other in the private sector – have made lasting contributions and rendered valuable services that were based on extensive research, and scientific study of waste disposal problems relating to disease and public health, sanitation, and environmental preservation. The two organizations had a long history of close collaboration in solid waste research, publication, and dissemination of research results that established "best practices" and "standards" for landfill siting, design, operation, and management. In addition, USPHS worked closely with major universities, funding research projects in solid waste management, and with state and local governments, surveying national solid waste disposal practices in large cities across the country, and promoting the sanitary landfill (SLF) method of solid waste disposal. The two organizations were instrumental in the passage of the first national law addressing solid waste – the Solid Waste Disposal Act (SWDA) – in 1965. Until the formation of the United States Environmental Protection Agency (USEPA) in 1970, USPHS had the responsibility to administer the Federal Water Pollution Control Act of 1948, which was substantially expanded and replaced by the Clean Water Act in 1972.

The origin of the USPHS goes back to 1798 when following a severe outbreak of yellow fever, President John Adams signed an act for the care of sick and disabled merchant seamen. A number of hospitals were established, mainly in port cities and were placed under the newly created Marine Hospital Service (MHS). During the nineteenth century, the United States was confronted with frequent outbreaks of some infectious diseases, such as cholera, smallpox, and yellow fever. MHS was given the added responsibility to quarantine and inspect the incoming ships, besides taking care of sick seamen. The MHS built a small bacteriology laboratory on Staten Island, New York in 1887 to diagnose infectious disease cases on the incoming ships. This laboratory later became the famous National Institute of Health (NIH). In 1902, Congress passed the US Public Health and Marine Hospital Service Act to consolidate various functions of the MHS and to conduct health-related research. The name was changed again in 1912 to Public Health Service (PHS). In 1953, PHS was placed under the newly created Federal Security Agency that also included education and welfare departments. Finally, in 1979, PHS was separated from education and welfare and was placed under the US Department of Health and Human Services (USHHS). Its work scope was expanded to sanitation, wastewater treatment, water quality issues, radiological health, air pollution, and solid waste management, besides medical and health issues. The environmental program of PHS was transferred to the USEPA when it was created in 1970.

Unlike PHS, the EPA has legislative power to implement the law. Unfortunately, whereas at the USPHS, health and environmental problems were addressed on the basis of solid scientific studies in a culture led by scientists, medical doctors, and engineers, the USEPA has been led by legal professionals (lawyers and politicians), resulting in a change in work philosophy from science and persuasion to command and control (Hickman 2003).

4.2 Introduction

Solid waste management can be defined as a planned undertaking to control the generation, collection, storage, transportation, processing, and separation of the waste for full resource recovery and disposal of the leftover residue in an environmentally safe manner. Waste management is intimately tied to administrative, financial, and legal functions. Resource recovery here includes recovering metals, glass, etc., that can be reprocessed for use as input materials in the manufacturing process; converting organic and other combustible components of the waste to generate energy, and/or composting; and disposal of the residual waste, all aiming to attain the zero waste goal.

Although the terms "solid waste" and "municipal solid waste (MSW)" have often been used interchangeably, there is a difference, based on the source. The term "solid waste" is used for wastes that are nonhazardous, generated anywhere from human activities that are managed by owners of the facilities and *not* by local government. Residues from crop and food and agricultural production, or dredging and mining operations, are examples of solid waste. Municipal solid waste is generated by people living in an established community, such as villages, towns, or cities, where the responsibility for its management rests with the local municipality, or city government, hence the word "municipal." From a legal perspective, the term "solid waste," as used by the US EPA, represents both these types, with MSW being a subcategory of the broader domain of solid waste. Of all the solid waste generated in the first decade of the twenty-first century, MSW accounted for a tiny fraction – 3 to 5% of the world's waste stream. The global quantity of MSW generated in the first decade of the present century was about 490 Mt as opposed to 8.6 billion t for other types of solid wastes generated by mining, agriculture, industrial, and construction activities, etc. The corresponding figures for the United States were 318 Mt and 10.9 billion t (Mervis 2012).

Humans have been generating and dealing with waste ever since they gave up their nomadic way of life and began to live at stationary locations, marking the beginning of "collective waste." Human "settlement" is believed to have occurred sometimes during the Neolithic period, about 12 000 years ago. But the small population and abundant unpolluted pristine environment averted any adverse impact coming from the meager amount of biodegradable waste, generated by the small population. However, the situation changed as human civilization advanced, population grew to millions of people, hitting the 1 billion mark within 50 years of the Industrial Revolution (IR). For the past 250 years since the IR, human society has become very complex, characterized by large-scale industrialization, urbanization, and environmental degradation. With the estimated human population having reached 7.9 billion people in September 2021, and over 800 000 chemicals in use worldwide, the quantity and nature of waste that we are generating are far beyond nature's capacity to handle. The natural biodegradation process that effectively cleaned up the waste several centuries ago could no longer work because of the large volume and highly toxic nature of the waste that are being generated.

Today, we confront a daunting challenge of managing the world's MSW in an environmentally safe manner. A report by the United Nations Environment Programme (UNEP) highlighted the problem thus: "Waste is a global issue. If not properly dealt with, waste poses a threat to public health and the environment. It is a growing issue linked directly to the way society produces and consumes. It concerns everyone." (UNEP 2015). Urbanization has resulted in a much greater quantity of MSW in recent years than ever before. It is estimated that in 2012, 161 cities of the world with a total urban population of 2.98 billion people had generated 1.3 billion t or 1.19 kilogram per person per day (kg/p/d) of MSW. The quantity is expected to increase to 2.2 billion t or 1.42 kg/p/d in 2025 that would be generated by 4.4 billion urban residents. The corresponding waste management cost is estimated to increase from $205.4 billion in 2010 to $375 billion in 2025 (Hoornweg and Perinaz 2012); this amount is greater than the 2016–2017 national budget of the majority (220) of world countries, with the exception of 12 economically strong countries of the world (US; China, Japan, Germany, France, UK; Italy, Canada, Brazil, India, Spain, and Australia). No doubt, growing world population, with people congregating to established urban centers, would result in ever-increasing quantities of MSW requiring innovative and efficient ways for its proper management.

Waste management is an expensive but essential service; it accounts for a big chunk of municipal budgets – about 20–25%. Adopting a multipronged approach involving energy recovery, reuse and recycling, composting and zero-waste strategy would make waste management economically sustainable. The old attitude of NIMBY must be set aside and landfill and related waste management facilities should be viewed as required services and an essential component of a city's infrastructure, with a duly recognized public and political profile. Waste management, in the twenty-first century, needs to be viewed as one of the essential utilities serving an urban area – similar to drinking water, electricity, gas, storm water, sewage collection and management, communication, and transportation systems – indispensable to society and the economy. In fact, the term "waste management" should be replaced by "resource management" to underscore its economic value and environmental significance. The US EPA embraced this paradigm shift by adopting a new name for its annual MSW report, now titled *Advancing Sustainable Materials Management* (replacing the old title *Municipal Solid Waste in the United States*) to signify its emphasis on sustainability, resource conservation, reuse and recycling, minimizing climate impacts, and protecting ecological health. According to the US EPA ". . .sustainable management of natural capital is increasingly at the forefront of an international dialogue about how to achieve economic growth without compromising human health and the environment. By looking across the life cycle, businesses can find opportunities that enhance and sustain their value proposition and reduce risk through sustainably managing materials." (EPA 2013).

4.2.1   Environmental and Health Impacts from Mismanagement of Municipal Solid Waste

Most of the environmental and health problems associated with wastes are caused by their mismanagement that results from carelessly depositing the waste anywhere and everywhere in an uncontrolled manner. Waste dumps refer to such accumulation of discarded materials. Being uncontrolled, actual contents, quantities, and source of materials in waste dumps cannot be accurately quantified. Landfills, on the other hand, are engineered structures designed to ensure that the waste is contained at the disposal site, has adequate provisions for leachate and landfill gas (LFG) management, and protection of surface and groundwater resources.

One of the well-documented cases of health problems relates to the Black Death – a lethal variety of bubonic plague – that wiped out half of the mid-fourteenth century European population was caused by uncontrolled waste dumping (Tchobanoglous et al. 1993). In recent times, Love Canal in New York State stands out as one of the best-known examples of health problems caused by dumping industrial waste. While strict compliance with laws has essentially eliminated the uncontrolled disposal of wastes in developed countries, uncontrolled waste dumping is very common in developing countries even today.

In unlined landfills, common in many developing countries, like China, India, Nigeria, etc., the release of leachate poses a serious threat to both human and ecological health. Proper design and efficient functioning of the LFG and leachate management systems is therefore critical. Details of design requirements for leachate and gas collection systems are discussed in Sections 4.7.3 and 4.7.4.

Dumping, or uncontrolled disposal of refuse in open areas, land, or water bodies, is a most undesirable practice and must be stopped. The hidden but grave dangers associated with uncontrolled waste dumping not only cause harmful impacts on air, water, land, and the biota; trigger fires and initiate *dumpslides* (landslides involving downhill movement of unstable waste materials deposited on sloping ground), but also pose serious threats to human and ecological health. The sad reality is that despite open waste dumping having been made illegal in a majority of the countries, it is still prevalent globally – specially in developing countries, due to lack or lax enforcement of the law. A recent report indicates that in 2016, up to 93% of the waste ended up at dumpsites in low-income countries, mostly in Asia and Africa (Kaza et al. 2018).

In developing countries, waste pickers and others engaged in refuse collection, are exposed to a number of health hazards that include: acute and chronic illness from daily exposure to harmful materials in the dump; diseases carried by rats, mosquitoes, and other carriers that thrive in dumps; fire hazards, and landslide risk (Case Study 4.1).

Case Study 4.1   Landslide Hazards at Uncontrolled Dumpsite

Three disastrous ground failures that occurred in recent years in China, Ethiopia, and India – all near major population centers – illustrate the hazards associated with uncontrolled dumping of MSW and its toll on life and property. In all three cases, heterogeneous waste materials, piled high on top of each other, became unstable resulting in their rapid movement triggering ground failures. These debris slides and ground collapse are good examples of: (i) hazards of uncontrolled waste dumping without due consideration of safety and lack of proper oversight by authorities.

4.1.1   The Shenzhen, China Slide

This slide, involving construction waste (CW) disposed of at a dumpsite, located at the Hong'ao Village, about 12 km northwest of the industrial megacity of Shenzhen (population 20 million), also known as Silicon Valley of China, occurred on 20 December 2015. CW comprising concrete,

Table B4.1 Top three fatal dumpslides of the twenty-first century in the world.

Rank	Deaths	Date	Volume (×10⁶ m)	Location
1	278	10 July 2000	0.016	Payatas MSW dumpsite, Manila, the Philippines
2	147	21 February 2005	2.70	Leuwigajah MSW dumpsite, Bandung, Indonesia
3	77	20 December 2015	2.73	Construction waste landfill, Guangming, Shenzhen, China

Source: Modified after Yin et al. (2016).

steel, baked clay, and concrete bricks; and mixed with gravel, sand, and clay size materials, derived from completely decomposed granitic bedrock, was deposited in an abandoned quarry on the northern slope of the 307 m-high Dayan Mountain. CW began to be dumped in the terraced quarry around March 2014 and within about 22 months more than 5.83 million m³ of CW was deposited on the quarried hill slope. Ponded water in the quarry along with percolating rainwater made the CW highly saturated causing a buildup of excessive pore water pressure, resulting in the landslide. With a volume of 2.73 million m³, the Shenzhen landslide ranks as the largest solid waste landslide of the twenty-first century (Yin et al. 2016). Table B4.1 lists the top three major landfill slides of the twenty-first century in the world.

The massive landslide extended over a distance of 1.1 km with an average depth of about 16 m. The slide destroyed 33 buildings in three industrial parks, burying one of them completely (Figure B4.1) and ruptured a gas pipeline, causing an explosion. The landslide moved very fast, causing 77 deaths and extensive property damage.

4.1.2 Ghazipur Landfill, India

The Ghazipur landfill, spread over 73 ha, and located near the Indian capital city of New Delhi (2021 population: 31 million), has been in operation since 1984. This uncontrolled dumpsite, like most others across India and other developing countries, does not have any leachate or LFG management system which causes movement of the leachate into groundwater that enters adjacent waterways. The disposal site receives about 10 000 t of garbage that the city generates every day. Waste comprises garbage, hazardous, medical, and C and D wastes, along with animal wastes from poultry, fish markets, and a slaughterhouse. Nearly 500 waste pickers work at the dumpsite, about half of them children, and nearly 3 million people live within 10 km of the site, and some residences are barely 200 m away.

Water in the adjacent drainage canal has turned black due to the high concentration of leachate, and fires from ignition of copious amount of methane – in the 29-year-old, organic-rich dump – is a frequent occurrence. The air and water quality have been seriously impaired causing adverse health problems to the nearby residents. Fetid air, smoke belching from the disposal area (Figure B4.2), and harmful air pollutants have forced the residents to keep the windows and doors closed all the time. A large majority of waste pickers suffer from asthma, tuberculosis, skin diseases, and fire burns. Contamination of the Yamuna River, about 7 km from the Ghazipur dumpsite has been reported (Zafar and Alappat 2004).

The law restricts the height of the landfills to 20 m; but the Ghazipur site is now 65 m tall (about 16-storey) with steep side slopes. The permitted height was attained in 2002 but due to problems in allotment of land for a new landfill and related political and legal issues, waste dumping continued at the site. According to a newspaper report "Commissioned in 1984,

(a)

(b)

Figure B4.1 Shenzhen landslide, 20 December 2015: (a) Aerial view of the landslide engulfing buildings; and (b) Buildings damaged by rapidly moving, water-saturated slide material. *Source:* STR/Stringer/Getty Images.

overflowing since 2002, and operating without certification since 2006 – the deaths at the Ghazipur landfill were perhaps foreshadowed." (Indian Express 2017). Minor fires and slips have been a common occurrence but a major slide that occurred on 1 September 2017 mobilized a large volume of waste materials that moved down at a fast speed, entered the Hindon Canal, creating a large water wave that destroyed part of the road, concrete barriers, and metal fences

Figure B4.2   Smoke emanating from smoldering Ghazipur landfill, India. *Source:* S.E. Hasan (author).

Figure B4.3   MSW dumpslide of 1 September 2017, Ghazipur Landfill, India. *Source:* S.E. Hasan (author).

on the canal banks; and swept away several vehicles (Figure B4.3). Two persons were killed and dozens injured. City authorities ordered the closure of the landfill but it opened two days later.

4.1.3   The Koshe/Rappie, Ethiopia Collapse

The municipal solid waste generated in the capital city of Addis Ababa, Ethiopia, was dumped outside the city at an uncontrolled garbage dump, covering an area of about 37 ha, for over 50 years. An estimated 300 000 t of waste were dumped at the site. In the early years with a smaller population, it was considered to be far and away from the city. But, like many cities, Addis Ababa has also experienced significant urbanization in the past three decades (estimated 2019 population: about 5 million) resulting in frequent expansion of city boundary, and greater MSW volume.

   The city had planned to close the dumpsite and divert the waste to a new landfill but the project stalled due to farmers' opposition. A WtE electric power plant, burning 1400 t of waste/ day to generate 50 MW of electricity, enough to supply power to 30% of households in Addis Ababa, was completed in 2018.

A large collapse involving the mountain of the garbage dump, occurred on 11 March 2017 that killed 116 people, injured 28, and buried 49 shanty dwellings that were made from mud and sticks. Koshe (meaning dirty in local language) has had many small ground failure events in the past but the death toll was small, 2 – 3. In 2010, city officials had warned that the site was running out of space, which stopped dumping, but was resumed 2 – 3 months prior to the disaster.

Koshe LF presents an interesting case study because:

1) It is located in a low-income country (2019 per capita income: $856) and scavenging any useable material from the waste provides living to a large segment of the society. While no estimate is available about the percent of the waste that is salvaged by the *scratchers* – as they are called locally because of using a metal rod with a hook to scratch the dump to find useful material – it enables nearly 500 of them to make a living by selling it directly to recyclers.

2) Poverty and unemployment have forced young people to take huge risks by being the first ones to collect the most valuable materials from the moving trucks as they enter the site every morning. In order to get the most valued recyclable materials, these young people, usually in a group of 5 or 6, jump onto the back of the still moving garbage truck and ride to the tipping point where it would discharge the load. Accidents involving someone caught in heavy equipment, bulldozers, compactors, etc., have resulted in serious injuries, loss of limbs, and even death (Knowles 2014).

3) It illustrates the hazards associated with uncontrolled dumping, in this case, a large ground failure, killing 116 people and destroying numerous shanty dwellings.

4.1.4 Summary and Conclusion

Uncontrolled dumpsite, referred to as landfills in many developing countries, pose a serious threat to the life and safety of people living in their vicinity. Some of the major physical hazards of landslides and fires have been discussed in these selected case studies. But the long-term effects of polluted air, contaminated waters, combined with high population densities in slum-like dwellings and lack of proper sanitation, resulting in chronic health problems causing death and morbidity, need to be addressed to initiate remedial measures.

Lack of awareness of the earlier problems, political wrangling, corruption, or blame-shifting are some of the factors that led to problems and disasters described in this case study. The remedy lies in: administration's transparency; sustained efforts to educate the public on the benefits of proper waste management, their participation in waste minimization efforts, and fair and equitable settlement with waste pickers to improve their working conditions and assure economic well-being.

References

Indian Express (2017). Garbage dump crossed danger mark in 2002 but EDMC, DDA kept shifting blame. https://indianexpress.com/article/cities/delhi/garbage-dump-crossed-danger-mark-in-2002-but-edmc-dda-kept-shifting-blame-4824660 (accessed 2 April 2019).

Knowles, C. (2014). *Flip-Flop: A Journey through Globalisation's Backroads*, 217. London: Pluto Press.

U.S. Department of Labor, Bureau of Labor Statistics (2017). National census of fatal occupational injuries, News Release, No. USDL-17-1667, 10 p; December 19, 2017. https://www.bls.gov/news.release/archives/cfoi_12192017.pdf (accessed 24 September 2018).

Yin, Y., Li, B., Wang, W. et al. (2016). Mechanism of the December 2015 catastrophic landslide at the Shenzhen landfill and controlling geotechnical risks of urbanization. *Engineering* 2: 230–249.

Zafar, M. and Alappat, B.J. (2004). Environmental mapping of water quality of the River Yamuna in Delhi with landfill locations. *Management of Environmental Quality An International Journal* 15 (6): 608–621.

Generally, people living closer to waste dumps are more susceptible to disease and poor health as are garbage pickers who spend long hours at garbage piles. However, other factors, such as wind speed and windstorm frequency, runoff volume and frequency, can also produce adverse health impacts on the population living away from dumpsites. A study conducted at Los Laureles Canyon, a poor neighborhood in Tijuana, Mexico, 32 km from San Diego, CA in the USA, with over 50 illegal dumps, found that people living farther away from the dumps reported higher incidences of extreme fatigue, eye and skin irritations, stomach discomfort, lack of ability to concentrate, and confusion, than people living closer to the dumpsites (Al-Delaimy et al. 2014) due to frequent windstorms and runoffs. Any investigation involving potential health impacts from uncontrolled waste disposal, therefore, should also take into account meteorological factors, such as wind velocity and frequency; precipitation patterns and runoff volume and frequency; and toxicity of hazardous materials in the dump.

It is very common in developing countries for scavengers to spend long hours amidst the waste piles, without any protection, to sort and pick any useful discard that would fetch them some money (Figure 4.1).

It is interesting to note that while fatalities to waste and recycling material handlers in the US and other developed countries are mainly related to accidents and injuries from machineries and equipment, chronic disease and deaths in developing countries for scavengers and residents living near landfills are associated with constant exposure to harmful toxicants through inhalation, ingestion, and dermal contact.

(a)

(b)

Figure 4.1 Waste pickers at the Dhapa Landfill, Kolkata, India: (a) Waste pickers gathered for the best discards as soon as the waste is unloaded; and (b) scavenging through the dumped waste. *Source:* Ajim Ali.

Occupational risk to waste service workers in the US is ranked number 5 among the top 10 occupational risks – greater than drivers, roofers, and electric line workers. Table 4.1 shows an average number of deaths per 100 000 workers for various occupations in the United States (US Dept. of Labor 2017).

Combustible materials in uncontrolled dumps often ignite spontaneous fires that smolder for long periods of time, belching fumes loaded with PMs and other toxins. One recent incident occurred in 2016 at the Deonar Landfill in Mumbai, India, which is the world's eighth largest waste dump, covering an area of 130 ha and attaining a height of up to 50 m (Case Study 4.2). The fire that started on 27 January burned for four days before it was contained. Huge quantities of PMs, VOCs, and other toxins got released into the air, causing a thick smog that hung in the densely populated area for several days and forced the closing of over 70 schools. The fire intensity and smoke plume were so large and conspicuous that they were captured by NASA satellites (Figure 4.2).

The Deonar dumpsite that was opened in 1927 currently receives 10 000 t of garbage/day, generated by 12 million people in Mumbai. It is estimated to have accumulated over 16 Mt of garbage over its 86-year life, making it an ideal site for the continuous formation of combustible gases, resulting in frequent fires. A second major fire occurred two months later on 20 March 2016, pushing the AQI to over 180 (Good: 0–50; >150 unhealthy for sensitive people; US EPA).

Landfill fires are of two types: surface and subsurface. The former is caused when a combustible substance gets ignited. The latter occurs about 4–5 m below the surface where the old organic waste undergoes biochemical decomposition, producing methane and other gases that have a strong potential to catch fire in presence of oxygen. Landfill fires are rather common, and thousands are reported every year in the US. Fortunately, regular surveillance and monitoring of emissions enable putting out the fires without causing much of the problems; but this is not the case in the developing countries where open dumps are abundant and lack proper monitoring.

Throwing out garbage in ditches and drains chokes the drainage ways, causing flooding during heavy rainfall events. Floods not only kill people and cause injuries but also result in the outbreak of diseases. A 2011 flood in Accra, Ghana, caused by blocked drains filled with plastics and other

Table 4.1 Occupational risk for US workers.

Occupation	Rank	Annual fatal injury rate/100 000 workers
Loggers	1	135.9
Fishers and related fishing workers	2	86.0
Aircraft pilots and flight engineers	3	55.5
Roofers	4	48.6
Refuse and recyclable material collectors	**5**	**34.1**
Structural iron and steel workers	6	25.1
Drivers and truck drivers	7	24.7
Farmers and ranchers	8	23.1
Construction and extraction workers	9	18.0
Ground maintenance workers	10	17.4

Source: Data from the US Department of Labor 2017.

Case Study 4.2   Deonar, India: Fires at an Uncontrolled Landfill

Deonar dump, the world's 8th largest uncontrolled landfill, is located in India's largest city of Mumbai (formerly Bombay), the 5th largest metropolitan region in the world. With an estimated population of 20.4 million in 2020 and an area of 4355 km^2, greater Mumbai has one of the largest population densities among the world's metro areas. The city is located in the western part of India, on the eastern coast of the Arabian Sea. Land reclamation from the sea and adjoining low-lying areas have been practiced for a long time to accommodate the ever-growing urbanizing population. The climate in the region is tropical and wet, and falls under the Aw type according to the Köppen and Geiger classification. The region experiences a humid season from March through October and a dry season from November through February. The annual average temperature is 27 °C, and the annual average rainfall is about 244 cm. Flooding from monsoon rains is common during the wet season.

The Deonar Landfill (Figure 4.2) is an unlined dumpsite that has been used as an MSW disposal site since 1927. The site is owned and operated by the Greater Mumbai Municipal Corporation, and contains more than 12 million t of mixed waste that includes garbage, hazardous, and medical waste. The landfill does not have any LFG or leachate collection system.

The current waste disposal areas range in depth from a few meters up to about 30 m. Most of the existing landfill surface is flat or gently sloping, which results in the accumulation of leachate, and ponding of runoff in low-lying areas during heavy rains.

More than 6000 t of waste, comprising 5500 t of garbage, 600 t of silt, and 25 t of medical waste, is deposited each day in the landfill, which is compacted by bulldozers, attaining an in-place density of between 900 kg/m^3 and 1000 kg/m^3. The source of the silt is the city's drainage ditches and canals.

This 95-year dumpsite, with its huge quantity of waste, is a perfect example of a site where biodegradation has progressed to phase IV of landfill gas formation, dominated by methane, a highly combustible gas, that can ignite fires easily. The Deonar landfill has had a history of fires but the one in 2016 was the largest and longest that caused one of the worst episodes of air pollution that lasted several days (Figure 4.2), and resulted in serious health problems to 5 million people living in its vicinity. The cause of the 2016 fire is not known, but any careless activity, such as tossing a cigarette butt, or a spark from mechanical equipment could easily ignite the readily available methane.

A study commissioned by the US EPA in 2007 summer found that adequate quantities of methane are available to generate electric power up to 6.3 MW that will last 15 or more years. Revenues from sale of electric power and savings from potential GHG emission control would offset the capital, operation, and maintenance costs of the project (SCS Engineers 2007).

References

SCS Engineers (2007). Report on the Pump Test and Pre-feasibility Study for Landfill Gas Recovery and Utilization at the Deonar Landfill Mumbai, India. Report prepared for U.S. EPA, Washington, DC; under its Landfill Methane Outreach Program, unpaginated. SCS File No. 02205511.00.

(a)

(b)

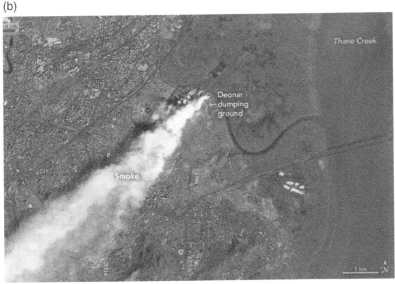

Figure 4.2   Smoke plume from the 27 January 2016 fire at the Deonar dumpsite, Mumbai, India. The 8-km long smoke plume over a densely populated area degraded the AQI to 180. (a) Natural color image, and (b) False color IR image highlighting the fire. Both images captured by NASA Landsat-8 on 28 January 2016. *Source:* NASA.

garbage, caused an outbreak of cholera that killed 14 persons and affected 100 people (UNEP, 2015, p. 3). Earlier, in 1994, heavy rains in western India had caused flooding in the city of Surat, where uncontrolled dumping of waste blocked the drainage ways, causing an outbreak of plague-like disease, affecting about 700 people and causing 56 deaths. The local government ordered the closure of all schools, colleges, public parks, banks, offices, and movie theaters. The economic loss was estimated at $260 million for the city of Surat alone (Pallipparambil, n.d.).

4.3 US Laws Regulating Solid Waste Management

Two laws, the SWDA and the Resource Conservation and Recovery Act (RCRA), govern solid waste management in the United States. SWDA was enacted in October 1965 and its amendments, known as the RCRA, were passed in October 1976.

Globally, all developed countries have enacted laws on environmental protection including rules for waste management. One of the most comprehensive sets of rules, called Directives, have been established by the European Union (EU). Various laws relating to the environment are discussed in Chapter 3. Directive No. 1999/31/EC passed on 26 April 1999 established rules for waste disposal in landfills (EU 1999) for adoption, implementation, enforcement, and reporting by member countries. Amendments are issued periodically to address emerging concerns. The situation in developing countries, on the other hand, is very unsatisfactory despite the fact that the majority of them have enacted laws to regulate waste, which are not strictly enforced.

4.3.1 The Solid Waste Disposal Act

The SWDA, enacted in 1965, represents the first federal effort to improve solid waste disposal for the purpose of protection of human health and the environment; and to control pollution of the nation's land and waterways. The Act was prompted by: (i) a significant increase in the nature and quantities of wastes resulting from advances in manufacturing technology and relative affluence of the American people, and (ii) rapid growth in the number and population of urban areas that were facing major management, financial, and technical problems associated with waste disposal. The act established a framework for states to better control solid waste disposal and set minimum safety requirements for landfills. Provisions were made in the law, and funds were appropriated for research, demonstration, and training for the development and implementation of better disposal methods, resource recovery, and conversion of waste into energy. However, the generalized nature and limited scope of SWDA was not adequate to comprehensively address the ever-increasing waste quantities and associated waste disposal issues. As a result, significant amendments were made to SWDA in 1976, leading to the passage of RCRA in 1976.

4.3.2 The Resource Conservation and Recovery Act

The RCRA is a comprehensive piece of legislation that regulates the disposal of: (i) solid waste, (ii) hazardous waste; and provides guidelines for disposal of medical waste; and underground petroleum- and chemical-storage tanks. The goal was to address the worsening environmental problems the nation was facing from the increasing volume of municipal and industrial wastes, and leaking underground storage tanks (USTs). RCRA, which amended the SWDA of 1965, set national goals for:

- Protecting human health and the environment from potential hazards of waste disposal
- Conserving energy and natural resources
- Reducing the quantity of waste generated
- Ensuring that wastes are managed in an environmentally sound manner.

RCRA established three distinct programs, called Subtitles, to achieve the earlier mentioned goals:

1) The solid waste program, under RCRA Subtitle D, encouraging states to develop comprehensive plans to manage nonhazardous industrial solid waste and municipal solid waste, sets criteria

for municipal solid waste landfills and other solid waste disposal facilities, and prohibits open dumping of solid waste.

2) The hazardous waste program, under RCRA Subtitle C, establishing a system for controlling hazardous waste from the time it is generated until its ultimate disposal, i.e. from "cradle to grave."

3) The UST program, under RCRA Subtitle I, regulating USTs containing hazardous substances and petroleum products.

A fourth program, Subtitle J – the Medical Waste Tracking Act (MWTA) – was added to RCRA in 1988.

Details of Subtitle C are discussed in Chapter 5, and relevant aspects of Subtitle D are included in Section 4.7 of this chapter. Subtitle J is discussed in Chapter 6.

4.4   Source, Composition, and Quantity of MSW

As pointed out before, MSW is a subset of the broader category of solid waste. Households and commercial facilities are common sources of MSW and comprise about 3–5% of the world's solid waste stream. But, agricultural sector, including animal farms, food production and processing operations; mining sector; wastes from health care facilities; and practically every other production and service facility, generates varying quantities of solid waste.

Before attempting to define MSW, we need to first clarify that solid waste – as the term might suggest – does not consist of solids only. It could be in the liquid or gas form or a mixture of all three. Aqueous effluents from manufacturing sites, gaseous emissions from power plants and other industries are good examples of nonsolid forms of waste. While the word "waste" is used to convey different meanings in different countries and cultures, the US professionals have used words like garbage, refuse, rubbish, and trash for various types of MSW: Garbage for wet MSW; trash for dry; refuse for a combination of both dry and wet waste; and rubbish – a "catch-all" term that includes refuse along with construction and demolition debris (C & D). A general definition of waste would be anything that has been discarded, thrown away, abandoned, or is no longer of any use. The technical term, MSW, is used for everyday items that we use and then throw away, such as packaging materials, paper, plastics, furniture, yard waste, clothing, bottles and cans, food scraps, newspapers, magazines, appliances, paint, and batteries. This comes from our homes, educational and research institutions, offices, hospitals, commercial establishments, and public facilities, such as parks, stadiums, etc. As stated before, solid waste also includes the nonhazardous fraction of the waste generated during the production and processing of agricultural products; mineral extraction, dredging, and disaster relief and rehabilitation operations.

4.4.1   MSW Composition

Common discards, such as paper, plastics, food, organics, metals, and yard wastes, are everyday materials that are generated on a routine basis from residential and commercial sources that are collected on a regular basis from residences and businesses. In addition, there are other materials, like furniture, mattresses and other bulky items; electronic- or e-waste, and white goods that are generated from the same sources, but are collected separately on specified dates, or dropped off at a designated collection facility.

Bulky waste comprises used or unwanted items such as furniture, mattresses, bookcases, filing cabinets and other large or bulky items. *White goods* include large appliances, like refrigerators, cloth washers and dryers, dishwashers, stoves, etc. These are usually dismantled for metal recovery before landfilling. These are not considered e-waste in the US, but in Europe and other countries, they are (See Chapter 8 for a detailed discussion of e-waste).

Considerable variation exists in the type of materials that are thrown as waste which can be broadly grouped into various categories, such as: dry, wet; organic, inorganic; infectious, non-infectious, hazardous, radioactive; solid, liquid, or a mixture, like sludge; etc. An uncontrolled waste, the one that commonly ends up as dump, contains most, and sometimes all, of these – a typical occurrence in most developing counties, but rare or nonexistent in developed countries.

Despite wide variations in MSW composition on a worldwide basis, food and organic materials comprise about 44% of MSW, followed by paper and paper products (17%) and plastics (12%). Relative quantities of these materials depend on the economy, and the overall affluence level of the population. For example, food and organic fractions are generally higher in low-income countries, about 56%, compared to high-income countries, about 32% (World Bank 2018). The interesting difference, however, is that while in the former, the organics comprise food waste that is not edible and has to be discarded, in the latter, it is the prepared food that could have been eaten (UNEP 2015). A similar trend can be noted in relation to paper, plastics, metals, and glass discards (Figure 4.3).

In addition, regardless of the income level, the types and quantities of various waste components also vary with technological innovations and public awareness of environmental issues. For example, in the US, coal was commonly used for space heating until about the mid-twentieth century, but was replaced by natural gas and electricity around the1960s. Ash comprised nearly 80% of the waste in New York City in 1905, decreased to 43.0% in 1939, and about 3% in 1971

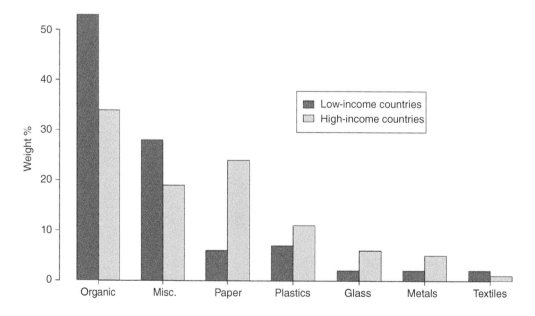

Figure 4.3   Variation in MSW composition among the high- and low-income countries. *Source:* Data from Kaza et al. (2018).

(Walsh 2002). Similarly, food refrigeration and availability of in-sink garbage disposal units led to a marked decline in garbage quantities in the US after WW II. A 1955 study, comparing waste quantities over a 10-year period found that the average annual quantity decreased from 147 Mt in 1946 to 122.5 Mt in 1954 (The American City 1955). The invention, and large-scale use of plastics, on the other hand, is another good example of new materials entering the waste stream and how they add to the total MSW quantities: Plastics that comprised 0.35 Mt or 0.44% of the total quantity of MSW generated in the US in 1960, increased to about 31.3 Mt and accounting for 13.1% of the total 238 Mt of MSW generated in 2015. A similar trend can be noted for e-waste, which became a significant portion of MSW in the US starting from the late 1990s. EPA started including e-waste in its annual MSW report beginning 2000. The data shows that e-waste quantity increased from 1.7 Mt in 2000 to 2.8 Mt in 2015 – an increase of about 65% in 15 years. Figure 4.4 shows a change in the relative amounts of various materials in the MSW generated in the US over a 55-year period.

In the US, environmental awareness of the 1970s led to more people adopting recycling as a way of life. Recycling caught on during the mid-1980s resulting in a marked increase in the recycling rate beginning 1985. National MSW recycling rate that averaged 7.7% in 1985 jumped to 27.1% during the next 25 years, 1985–2010.

The amount of MSW generated depends on the population of the country. Figure 4.5 shows the direct correlation between the average MSW quantities generated, recycling rate, and population size in the US for the period 1960–2010.

As the population increases, so does the MSW quantity. However, it should be noted that while the population is a major indicator, it is not the sole pointer of a country's total MSW volume because a concerted effort on part of the citizens to reuse and recycle materials can result in reduced MSW quantity requiring disposal. Several global initiatives, such as sustainability, zero-waste, and greenhouse gas (GHG) reductions, are all steps directed toward reducing MSW quantity.

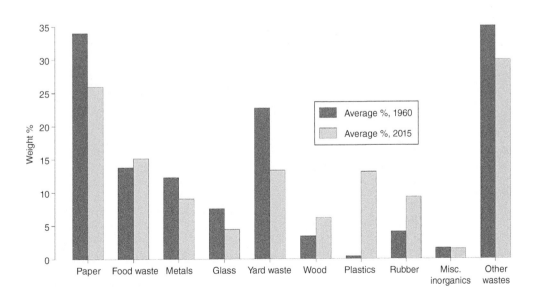

Figure 4.4   Change in composition and quantity of MSW in the USA for the period 1960–2015.

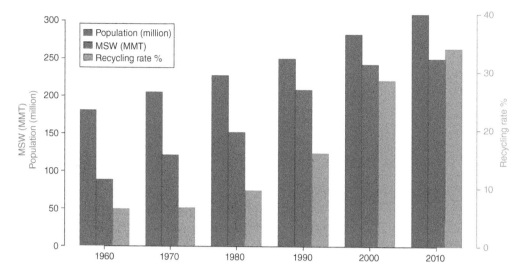

Figure 4.5   U.S. population, MSW generation, and recycling rate for the period 1960–2017.

4.4.1.1   Special Wastes

Special waste includes wastes produced in large quantities, and despite being hazardous, are exempted from the list of hazardous waste under Tittle C of RCRA. They include: fossil fuel combustion waste; crude oil and gas waste; waste from the extraction, beneficiation, and processing of ores and minerals (including phosphate rock and overburden from uranium ore mining); and cement kiln dust (CKD). Common examples of special waste include: CKD which is a fine-grained solid by-product of cement manufacturing; production water, and other waste generated during oil and gas exploration and production; fly ash, bottom ash, boiler slags, and particulate matters (PMs) from coal-fired power plants; and a variety of wastes generated during mineral extraction, processing, and beneficiation.

4.4.2   Quantity of MSW

In a broad sense, MSW includes all nonhazardous waste, such as paper, plastics, metals, glass, organic wastes, textiles, furniture, etc. However, for reporting purposes, the USEPA, following Subtitle D of RCRA rules, excludes construction and demolition debris, biosolids (sewage sludge), and some industrial nonhazardous wastes. The waste types included in RCRA are listed in Table 4.2.

Total quantity of MSW generated in the US has increased from 79.9 Mt in 1960 to 265.3 Mt in 2018; or from 1.22 kg/p/d (2.68 lb./p/d) in 1960 to 2.22 kg/p/d (4.90 lb./p/d) in 2018. Globally, the per capita MSW rate shows a wide range, generally lower for developing countries and higher for developed countries. The average per capita rate in 2016 for developed countries was 1.57 kg/p/d and 0.43 kg/p/d developing countries. The total quantity of MSW in 2010 was estimated at 354 Mt for developing countries and 602 Mt for developed countries, with projected rates for 2025 at 1529 Mt and 686 Mt respectively (UNEP 2015). These numbers reflect larger population growth, higher income levels, degree of urbanization, and improving economic conditions in developing countries.

Table 4.2   RCRA Subtitle D wastes.

Subtitle D Waste included in EPA's MSW reports
- Containers and packaging, such as soft drink bottles and corrugated boxes
- Durable goods such as furniture and appliances
- Nondurable goods such as newspapers, trash bags, and clothing
- Other wastes such as food scraps and yard trimmings.

Subtitle D Wastes not included in EPA's reports
- Municipal (sewage) sludge
- Agricultural wastes
- Industrial nonhazardous wastes
- Oil and gas wastes
- Construction and demolition debris
- Mining wastes

4.5   Collection and Disposal of MSW

A successful MSW management program requires awareness and participation from citizens. Experience in the United States and other countries has shown that public education to bring awareness of the importance of proper waste management is the first, and often the most challenging and time-consuming, step. It may take several months to years of public education, using all media formats, before they would become ready for active participation in the waste management program. Hasan (2004) provides a discussion of how public engagement and involvement at various steps of a waste management program can lead to its success. Figure 4.6 illustrates various steps of a successful waste management program.

Manual waste sorting at the source has been, or is being, phased out in most developed countries due to automation of the collection and sorting processes, but the practice is common in places where automated systems are not available or where labor is inexpensive and manual sorting proves economical. The use of mechanized systems has obviated the need for waste sorting at the point of generation, and all waste are comingled and placed in a single bin or trash bag that is loaded and compacted on a trash truck (Figure 4.7), transferred, and emptied at an enclosed area, then moved to the Material Recycling Facility (MRF), usually located close to the landfill for machine sorting of the various components (Figure 4.8).

Developed countries (annual per capita income: >$12 615) have achieved an almost 100% MSW collection rate, but it is lower in developing countries. The collection rate in low- and middle-income countries ($1036–12 614) that comprise the developing nations ranges between 30 and 60% (UNEP 2015).

4.5.1   MSW Disposal

Disposal of MSW in landfills is the most common method in developed countries and some selected cities in developing countries. Globally, about 36% of MSW is disposed of in landfills, about 19% is recycled and composted, 11% is incinerated, and about 33% ends up as dumps. Figure 4.9 shows the overall management of MSW on a worldwide basis.

In the United States, data on the quantity of MSW and its management have been complied with and maintained by federal agencies since the 1940s, and by some major cities, like New York, since

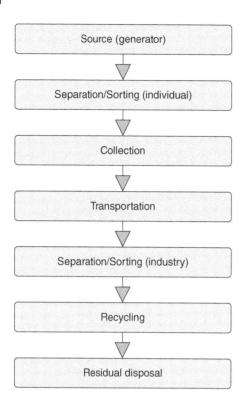

Figure 4.6 Steps in the successful waste management program.

Source (generator)

Separation/Sorting (individual)

Collection

Transportation

Separation/Sorting (industry)

Recycling

Residual disposal

Figure 4.7 Mechanized collection and emptying of a residential waste bin onto the trash truck. *Source:* S.E. Hasan (author).

the early twentieth century. EPA has been publishing an annual report on the MSW generated in the US for over 30 years. These reports are valuable in analyzing the historical trend of the nature and quantities of MSW, recovery, recycling, and overall management of waste materials. The latest report, released by the US EPA, in November 2020, which contains data for the year 2018, stated

Figure 4.8   Automated waste-sorting machine. *Source:* S.E. Hasan (author).

Figure 4.9   Management of MSW in 2018 (global average).

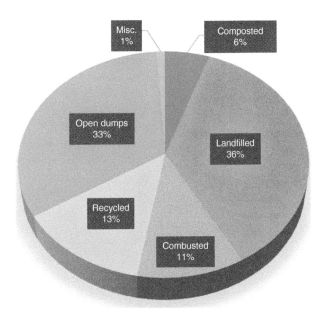

that a total of about 264 Mt of MSW were generated in the US of which about 63 Mt were recycled, and 23 Mt were composted. In addition, about 31 Mt of MSW were combusted for energy recovery, and about 132 Mt were landfilled (Figure 4.10).

4.5.2   Land Disposal

Depositing the waste on land and water was an accepted and widely practiced method of getting rid of the household waste. In the very early history of human civilization, it is believed that the Mayans (8000–10 000 years BP) disposed of their organic waste by mixing it with soil and placing it in large pits. Egyptian, Indian (about 4000 years BP) and Chinese (2000 BP) cultures practiced some kind of waste collection and disposal system where waste collected from built-in trash bins in dwellings was moved away to distant locations. The city of Athens, Greece, is known to have

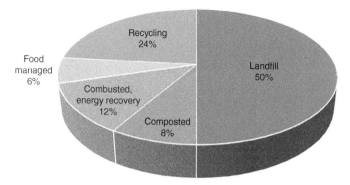

Figure 4.10 Management of MSW in the USA in 2018. *Source:* Data source: EPA, 2020b. Food waste was managed in various ways: edible food donation, animal feed, composting, land application, etc.

established a municipal dumpsite about 2500 years BP, requiring the citizens to dispose of their waste at least 1.6 km (1 mi) away from city walls; and prohibiting dumping waste on streets.

Throwing garbage on the streets was prevalent in Europe and the USA as late as 100 years ago. Garbage was still being dumped on streets in Washington, DC up until the 1860s. Benjamin Franklin, in 1792, attempted to address the problems caused by pests and the occasional outbreak of disease by establishing a street cleaning service in Philadelphia. Following the construction of the first municipal incinerator in Nottingham, UK, some cities in the US – Allegheny (1885) and Pittsburgh in PA; Des Moines, IA (1887), Yonkers, NY; Elmwood, IN, and Washington, DC (all in 1893) also built incinerators to dispose of garbage. Other major US cities, such as Baltimore, Boston, Chicago, and St. Louis used municipal services to collect and haul the garbage to open dumps during the 1880s and 1890s.

According to a survey by the Massachusetts Institute of Technology, by 1902, 79% (127 out of 161) of all US cities offered regular garbage collection service; by 1915, 89% of the cities were served, and by the 1930s, all large cities had a collection and disposal system. Wetlands near cities were favored locations for garbage disposal where they were covered with ash and dirt.

The SLF method for refuse disposal was first adopted in 1916 in England where the method was called "controlled tipping" (Black 1963, p. 120). In the United States, the SLF method was first used in 1942 by the US Army, at Ft. Riley, Kansas, following an order by the Army authorities to use "sanitary fill method" of refuse disposal, as a substitute for waste disposal by incineration. By the end of 1943, this method was being practiced at 111 army posts (Engineering News-Record 1943). This practice was quickly adopted in the civilian sector and, by the end of 1945, nearly 100 cities in the US were using SLFs (Hickman 2003). The Fresno Municipal Sanitary Landfill in California that became operational in 1937 is considered to be the first modern municipal landfill in the US that used trenching, compacting, and covering the waste. To mark its importance, the US Government in August 2001 placed it on the list of *National Historic Landmarks* for its outstanding historical significance.

4.5.3 Incineration and Waste-to-Energy Conversion

MSW disposal by incineration has certain advantages over a landfill, such as small land area requirement, flexibility in location, even portability of the plant, along with some limitations, as shown in Table 4.3.

Table 4.3 Comparison of MSW disposal by incineration and landfilling.

Incineration	Landfill
High capital and operational cost	Lower equipment and operational cost
Highly skilled staff for operation	Minimum training of operators
Location not constrained by site geology	Location controlled by site geology
Small land area (few blocks)	Large land area, 10s of hectares
Flexibility of location anywhere	No flexibility in location
Significant MSW volume reduction: 80–95%	No substantial volume reduction
Air emission: harmful gases and PMs cause serious air pollution, unless captured and treated	Minimum air pollution, CH_4 can be captured for energy generation

In the US, the first trash-to-energy incinerator was built in 1885 on the Governors Island in New York. By the 1960s, hundreds of incinerators were in operation in the United States, discharging ashes and other non-combusted solid wastes on land and water, and releasing toxic gases and PMs in the air. The Clean Air Act (CAA) of 1970 banned the uncontrolled burning of MSW and restricted PMs' emissions. Facilities that did not install pollution control technology to comply with CAA were closed.

By the 1990s, the majority of the operating incinerators had installed pollution control equipment and were also using the waste for energy recovery. Such Waste-to-Energy (WtE) power plants are also referred to as trash-to-energy, energy recovery, or thermal treatment. In the US about 12% of all MSW was being burned for energy recovery in 2018, and 75 WtE plants were in operation in 21 states, the majority in the northeast, with an installed capacity of 2534 MW of electric power, designed to burn 85 496 t of waste/day. The largest plant, the Palm Beach Renewable Energy Facility, is located in W. Palm Beach, FL. The plant came online in 2015, burns 1646 t of solid waste/day, and generates 95.0 MW of electricity. Connecticut, burning 69% of its MSW for energy recovery, 23% recycled/composted, and 8% landfilled, was the top state among the 21 with the highest percentage of its MSW diverted to WtE plants. Globally, Japan is the world leader, burning about 78% of its solid waste for WtE and the remaining 22% recycled/composted (Michaels and Krishnan 2018).

Burning MSW to recover energy can be done in two ways: (i) by directly feeding the combustible fraction of MSW into the incinerator, and (ii) using the LFG, mainly CH_4, to produce energy. The terms Waste-to-Energy (WtE) and Landfill-Gas-to-Energy (LFGTE) are used for the former and latter processes respectively. A modeling study to compare criteria pollutants and GHG emissions, energy recovery, and related economic analysis of the two methods was conducted by Kaplan, et al. (2009), who demonstrated that WtE had distinct advantages over LFGTE in all key considerations. They showed that emission of harmful pollutants, such as GHGs, SOx, and NOx was significantly lower in WtE systems and electricity output for each (short) ton of MSW was over 10 times more as compared to LFGTE plants (Kaplan et al. 2009). Table 4.4 summarizes the key differences.

With continuing technological innovations and improved efficiency of WtE plants, a marked surge in construction has occurred during the current decade. Currently, 2200 WtE plants were operating globally, diverting 300 Mt of MSW from landfills; another 600 new plants were to be added by 2025.

Table 4.4   Air pollutant emission and electric power output in WtE and LFGTE energy recovery systems.

Parameter	Unit	WtE		LFGTE		
		Range	Average	Range	Average	Difference, %
NOx	g/MWh	810–1800	1305	2100–3000	2550	96
SOx	g/MWh	140–730	435	430–900	665	53
GHGs	MTCO$_2$e/MWh	0.4–1.5	0.9	2.3	2.3	156
Electricity	kWh/ton of MSW	470–930	700	41–84	63	101

Source: Data from Kaplan et al. (2009).

Two large WtE plants, under construction at Shenzhen in China and Dubai in the UAE, are expected to become operational in the early 2020s. The Chinese plant will use 5000 t of solid waste/day to generate 168 MW of electricity. The Dubai WtE plant is designed to initially use 5700 t of its MSW to generate 200 MW of electricity, enough to power 135 000 residential units. The Dubai plant, estimated to cost $1.1 billion, is targeted to become operational in 2023 (UAE Barq 2020).

4.5.4   Composting

Food waste and other organic fractions in MSW are amenable to composting – a practice that is becoming increasingly popular. This, along with recycling, is a preferred way to reduce the volume of waste that will otherwise end up in the landfill. The final product of composting is a nutrient-rich, humus-like material that can be used in lawns, home gardens, commercial landscaping, and other agricultural applications, thereby minimizing or eliminating the need for harmful chemical fertilizers, a substantial amount of which washes down into streams and other water bodies, degrading the water quality and adversely impacting aquatic life forms. The quantity of MSW composted has been steadily increasing in recent years: from 3.81 Mt of organic waste composted in 1990 to 22.6 Mt in 2018 (EPA 2020a), representing an increase of over 493%.

4.6   Physical and Chemical Properties of MSW

The modern practice of MSW management involves reusing, recycling, composting, WtE conversion, and controlled disposal in secure landfills using mechanized equipment, along with satisfactory design provisions to manage leachate and LFGs, all of which require reliable data on the physical, chemical, and biological properties of MSW, besides accurate information on the geological and hydrological features at the disposal site. The determination of MSW properties has been a topic of research since the late 1880s. A comprehensive investigation on refuse collection started in 1887 by the Garbage Committee of the American Public Health Association which published a series of reports with basic data, which first appeared in the association's *Transactions* in 1897. These efforts prompted about a dozen major US cities to evaluate their refuse management practices. Results of the physical and chemical properties of garbage in New York City were published as early as 1907 (Hering and Greeley 1921).

Sanitation departments in New York, San Francisco, Washington, DC; Boston, Chicago, Trenton, NJ; and other major cities have maintained a record of garbage quantities since the late 1880s;

physical analyses were performed on weights and volumes of various components. Investigations were also carried out to determine the chemical composition of the refuse, along with physical tests to determine its moisture content, density (unit weight), compaction characteristics, and calorific (heat) values. Later, the USPHS and the APWA conducted national and regional surveys and investigations to gather MSW data and set guidelines for measurements of MSW properties and reporting requirements, along with design, construction, and operation of SLFs (APWA 1966).

Physical, chemical, and biochemical characteristics of MSW are important in engineering calculations of landfill area, and for leachate and gas management systems; MSW collection, transportation, and disposal equipment; and WtE facilities. Studies have continued until now and detailed discussions on these properties are available in Shah (2000) and Oweis and Khera (1998). Some of the important physical properties of MSW that include density, compaction, moisture (or water) content, permeability, calorific (heat) value, and FC, are discussed next.

4.6.1 Moisture Content

Moisture content, m, or the amount of water in a sample of MSW can be expressed on: (i) wet (or natural) weight basis, Equation 4.1, or (ii) dry weight basis, Equation 4.2; (i) is common in the waste management industry, while (ii) is used in geotechnical engineering for soil moisture content.

$$m = \left[\left[Wt - Wd \right] \div Wt \right] \times 100 \tag{4.1}$$

$$\text{and,} \quad m = \left[\left[Wt - Wd \right] \div Wd \right] \times 100 \tag{4.2}$$

where,
  m is the moisture content,
  Wt is the weight of MSW, as delivered
  Wd is the MSW weight after drying (at 105 °C for 6–8 hours in an oven)

Values of moisture content are expressed as a percent. Moisture content is important in the determination of density, heat value, and leachate quantity of MSW. The moisture content of MSW depends upon MSW composition, weather conditions, the season of sampling, and ranges from 15 to 40%. Table 4.5 lists typical moisture content values of MSW components.

Table 4.5 Typical values of moisture content, density, and energy (heat) content of MSW components.

Material	Moisture content, %	Density, kg/m^3	Energy content (range), MJ/kg
Agricultural waste	5.4–7.1	—	14.4
(wheat and rice residues)		723	
Cardboard	5	44–64	13.4–16.8
Chemical sludge, wet	80	1288	—
Composite (CFRP)	—	1500–2000	30
Composite (GFRP)[a]	2 (by vol)	830 at 15 °C	33.6
Dirt, ash	8	620	2.2–11.2
Food waste	70	290	3.3–6.7

(Continued)

Table 4.5   (Continued)

Material	Moisture content, %	Density, kg/m^3	Energy content (range), MJ/kg
Glass	2	200	0.01–1.23
Infectious waste	—	—	7.91
Leather	10	206	14.5–19.0
Manure, wet	94	1288	17.4
Medical (health care) waste	15 (by weight)	100–200	15
MSW	20–25	60–750[b]	10.0–13.4
Paper	5	65–76	11.2–18.0
Plastics	2	60–89	26.8–37.8
Rubber	2	168	20.13–26.8
Textiles	10	60	14.5–17.9
Vegetable waste, mixed	75	463	—
Walnut shells	5	—	18.8
Wood	3	100	16.8–19.0
Yard waste	20	148–380[a]	2.3–17.9

Lower value: uncompacted; higher values: compacted.
[a] CFRP: carbon fiber reinforced polymers; GFRP: glass fiber reinforced polymers.
[b] Data from: Cunliffe and Williams (2003), and others.
Values given here are for example only.

4.6.2   Density

Density (ρ), also referred to as unit weight, specific weight, or bulk density, is the ratio of weight to volume of bulk MSW sample, as shown below.

$$\rho = \text{Wt. of MSW} \div \text{Vol. of MSW.} \tag{4.3}$$

Density is expressed in kN/m^3 or kg/m^3 in SI units, and as lb./ft^3 or lb./yd^3 in the British Engineering unit. Density is a function of the degree of compaction of MSW and is useful in calculating the volume reduction and determination of the capacities of waste containers, MSW hauling equipment such as trash trucks and compactors, used at the disposal site.

Density of MSW ranges from a low of 90–740 kg/m^3 (152–1247 lb./yd^3) for loose uncompacted to well compacted MSW in landfill without cover. Moisture in MSW increases its density: in general, the higher the amount of water, the higher is the density. Dry density (ρ_d) of uncompacted MSW is lowest (about 82 kg/m^3), while the maximum density occurs when it is totally saturated with water and could be more than 550 kg/m^3. Most commonly, typical MSW samples represent the condition in between these two extremes. The symbol ρ (mass/volume) or, γ (for unit weight; weight/volume) is used for the common condition when MSW contains some moisture; ρ_d or γ_d for dry (zero moisture), or ρ_{sat} or γ_{sat} for saturated (100% moisture) conditions. Densities of common components of MSW are listed in Table 4.5.

4.6.3   Volume Reduction

Volume reduction, Vr, is the ratio of the difference in the initial volume, Vi, and final volume, Vf, of the waste to the initial volume, and is expressed as a percentage, as in Equation 4.4.

$$Vr = \left[\left(Vi - Vf \right) \div Vi \right] \times 100. \tag{4.4}$$

4.6.4 Compaction Ratio

Compaction ratio, Cr, is another property that relates to MSW volume change before and after compaction, and is expressed as:

$$Cr = Vi \div Vf. \tag{4.5}$$

Cr is a dimensionless parameter. Cr for mixed, uncompacted MSW from generation point to well-compacted state at a landfill, ranges from 4.8 to 5.7.

Vr and Cr are used to evaluate the performance of baling and compaction equipment.

4.6.5 Permeability

Permeability is a measure of the relative ease (or difficulty) of movement of a fluid through the mass of a material, such as soil, rock, or MSW. Permeability, in a strict sense, is a *qualitative* descriptor of movement of fluid through solids; terms such as highly permeable, good permeability, or poor permeability are commonly used to describe the relative ease or difficulty of water movement through solids. However, for a numerical (*quantitative*) value of permeability, the term hydraulic conductivity is appropriate. For example, clean sand and gravel have good permeability and their hydraulic conductivities (k) range between 1×10^2 cm/s (about 864 km/d) and 1×10^{-3} cm/s (0.9 m/d), whereas silt and silt-clay mixtures have low permeability with their k values ranging between 1×10^{-3} cm/s and 1×10^{-6} cm/s (0.09 cm/d, or <1 mm/d – negligible). Uncompacted residential waste has high permeability with a k value of about 15×10^{-3} cm/s; and dense, baled waste has a k value of 7×10^{-4} cm/s. Permeability is an important property that is used in the design of the foundation of landfills; leachate and gas collection systems, and final cover for a closed landfill. It is also used in the calculation of infiltration rate through landfill cover soil for designing the leachate collection and removal systems of an LF. Hydraulic conductivity, k, can be calculated using Equation 4.6.

$$k = Q \div iA, \tag{4.6}$$

where,
  Q is the quantity of water passing through the porous medium
  i is the hydraulic gradient between measurement points
  A is the cross sectional area of the porous material.

4.6.6 Energy (Heat) Content

The heat generated by various MSW components upon burning is a key factor in the design of WtE systems and for controlling the feed rate of MSW in an incineration plant. In general, dry organic components of MSW have higher heat energy than wet components. Similarly, organic components in the MSW (paper, plastics, food, rubber, textiles, and yard wastes) have higher energy values than inorganics; of these, paper and plastics account for 50–70% of MSW energy content. Table 4.5 shows the energy content of various MSW components.

Heat content, also called calorific value, can be determined by using: (i) Modified Dulong Equation (MDE), or (ii) calorimetry. The former requires elaborate calculations to convert the percent weight of paper, plastics, and other organics in MSW into percentages of elemental C, H, O, and S. The latter requires the use of the bomb calorimeter to determine the quantity of heat released by combusting a dry MSW sample. Both methods are time-consuming. A simple formula, Equation 4.7, for rapid determination of energy content of MSW was proposed by Khan and Abu-Ghararah (1991), which gives energy value with an accuracy of 1–10%.

$$E = 0.051(F + 3.6\text{CP})(0.352\text{PR}) \tag{4.7}$$

where,

E = energy content, MJ/kg
F = weight of food in MSW, %
CP = weight of cardboard and paper, %
PR = weight of plastics and rubber, %

4.6.7 Field Capacity

FC is the amount of moisture that solids in MSW can hold in their voids without releasing it under the pull of gravity. In other words, when the FC value is exceeded, water will begin to flow out of the solid waste under the influence of gravity. FC of comingled, uncompacted MSW from residential and commercial sources, ranges between 50 and 60%. FC is another key property of MSW because aerobic microbial activities occur at an optimum level, at or slightly below its FC. In addition, most efficient composting occurs at or near the FC value of the organic waste; FC value is also used to estimate the amount of leachate in an LF because it is the water in excess of FC that will be available for leachate formation. FC can be determined using Equation 4.8:

$$\text{FC} = 0.6 - 0.55\left[W \div (4500 + W)\right] \tag{4.8}$$

where,

W = Overburden weight of MSW in kg, calculated at mid-height
FC = Field capacity of dry MSW. Amount of water held in MSW at FC is given by the product of dry weight , Wd, and FC.

4.6.8 Particle Size Distribution

The term particle size distribution is used in sedimentology and geotechnics specialties where it is used for the study of soil particles and sediments of geological origin. In both fields, the grain or particle size is assumed to represent a sphere that includes both rounded and elongated particles, which are measured by allowing the material to pass through a set of sieves of varying aperture openings, ranging from a low of 0.02 mm to high of 125 mm. The particle size of heterogeneous components in a typical MSW, unlike the nominal sphere size of sediment and soil, is measured in terms of the three dimensions of solid materials.

The particle size is important in controlling the rate of chemical reactions – the smaller the particle size, the faster is the rate of a chemical reaction. Smaller particle size also promotes faster microbial decomposition of the compost pile, and more rapid combustion in an incinerator. The particle size of MSW components can be determined by directly measuring its diameter (for small fractions), or by dividing the sum of the three dimensions, length, width, and height (or thickness) by 3, i.e. (L + W + H)/3 for large pieces; or for paper or thin objects, adding its length and width and dividing it by 2, i.e. (L + W)/2. The particle size of common MSW components, such as food, paper and cardboard, plastics, glass, textiles, and metals could range from <1 mm to 500 mm; the average being about 140 mm.

Example Problem 4.1

1) A sample of organic fraction of MSW weighed 4900 g in the natural state; upon drying, its weight was found to be 3540 g. What is its moisture content (m)?

    Given: Wt = 4900 g; Wd = 3540 g, find, m

    Substitute these values in Equation 4.1, $m = (Wt - Wd) \div Wt$.

    i.e. $m = (4900 \text{ g} - 3540 \text{ g}) / 4900 \text{ g} = 0.2775$

    or, **27.8%** (m is reported as percentage; rounded off to one decimal place).

2) A sample of MSW weighed 200 kg in natural state (Wt.); its moisture content was found to be 20%. Find its dry weight (Wd).

    Given: Wt = 200 kg, $m = 0.2$; Wd =?

    Equation 4.1 can be rewritten as: $(m)(Wt) = (Wt - Wd)$

    Then, $(0.2)(200 \text{ kg}) = 200 \text{ kg} - Wd$

$$\therefore Wd = 200 \text{ kg} - (0.2)(200 \text{ kg}) = \textbf{160 kg}$$

3) If the volume (V) of the sample in Q. 1 is 0.01 m³, calculate its density.

    Using Equation 4.3, we have:

$$\rho = 4900 \text{ g} / 0.01 \text{ m}^3$$

$= 4.9 \text{ kg} / 0.01 \text{ m}^3 = \textbf{490 kg/m}^3$ (represents a well-compacted sample, Table 4.5).

4) The volume of a loose sample of MSW was found to be 20 m³; upon compaction, its volume was 5 m³; what are its: (i) Vr, and (ii) Cr?

    a) From Equation 4.4,

$$Vr = (Vi - Vf) / Vi$$
$$= \left[(20 \text{ m}^3 - 5 \text{ m}^3) / 20 \text{ m}^3 \right] \times 100 = \textbf{75\%}$$

    b) Cr from Equation 4.5,

$$Cr = Vi / Vf$$
$$= 20 \text{ m}^3 / 5 \text{ m}^3 = \textbf{4}$$

5) List of various components in a sample of MSW along with their wt.% is given below:

Paper and paper products	40
Plastics	17
Glass	6
Metals	5
Food waste	23
Bricks and stones	3
Misc.	6
Total	100

Determine its energy content, E.

Plugging the wt. % of food, paper, and plastics in Equation 4.7, we get,

$$E = 0.051\left(23+3.6\times40\right)\times\left(0.352\times17\right)$$
$$= 0.051\left(167\right)\left(5.984\right)$$
$$= \textbf{50.96 MJ / kg}$$

Which equals 14.2 kWh of power (1 MJ = 0.28 kWh) → enough power for four students to watch their own plasma TV sets for 1 hour; or for a computer lab to run 280 laptops for 1 hour.

6) At an MSWLF, the overburden weight (W) at mid-height of a compacted cell was 550 kg; its moisture content (m) was determined to be 25%. Calculate the FC of MSW, and the dry weight, Wd. Using Equation 4.8, we have:

$$\text{FC factor} = 0.6 - 0.55\left[W/\left(4500+W\right)\right]$$
$$= 0.6 - 0.55\left[550/\left(4500+550\right)\right]$$
$$\text{FC} = \textbf{0.54}$$

To calculate Wd, use Equation 4.1 as follows:

First convert % m to decimal, i.e. m = 25/100 = 0.25
$m = [(W - Wd) \div W]$
or, 0.25 = (550 − Wd) ÷W
or, Wd = 550 − 0.25 ÷W
Wd = **412.5 kg**

And the amount of water held in the MSW at FC = Wd × FC = 412.5 × 0.54 = 223 kg. That is, the MSW will hold up to 223 kg or 223 L of water. Any quantity exceeding this volume will drain out under the influence of gravity.

7) Determine the leachate quantity, Q, that will move through a layer of MSW having a cross sectional area, A, of 2500 cm^2 and hydraulic conductivity, k, of 5 × 10^{-3} cm/s; the hydraulic gradient, i, was 0.01
Using Equation 4.6: Q = kAi, we have:

$$Q = \left(5\times10^{-3}\text{ cm/s}\right)\left(2500\text{ cm}^2\right)\left(0.01\right)$$
$$= \textbf{0.125 cm}^3\textbf{ /s or 0.011 m}^3\textbf{ /d}$$

4.7 Landfill

A landfill is an engineered structure designed for controlled disposal of MSW and other wastes on the land. The purpose is to confine the waste and minimize the release of harmful substances into the environment. The American Society of Civil Engineers (ASCE) defined an SLF as "...a method of disposing of refuse on land without creating nuisances or hazards to public health or safety, by utilizing the principles of engineering to confine the refuse to the smallest practical area, to reduce it to the smallest practical volume, and to cover it with a layer of earth at the conclusion of each day's operation or at such more frequent intervals as may be necessary." (ASCE, n.d.). So, the key elements of SLF include: (i) confining the waste to a designated area, (ii) compacting the waste to the smallest possible volume, and (iii) covering it at the end of day's work. This practice came to be known as the Rule of 3Cs (confine, compact, and cover), which is discussed in Section 4.7.2.

Table 4.6   Main features of different types of landfills.

Landfill type	Features	Applicable law
Municipal solid waste landfill (MSWLF)	Designed for disposal of household and some other types of nonhazardous wastes	RCRA: Title D
Bioreactor landfill (BRLF)	A type of MSWLF designed for rapid degradation of organic waste	
Industrial waste landfill	Designed to collect industrial wastes from commercial sources, bulk of which may be MSW but not acceptable at MSWLF	
Construction and demolition (C and D) debris landfill	Designed to receive construction and demolition materials generated during the construction, renovation, and demolition of buildings, roads, and bridges. Generally, comprise large, bulky items, such as concrete, wood, metals, glass, and salvaged building materials.	
Coal combustion residuals (CCR) landfill	A type of industrial waste landfill for disposal of coal ash and other products of coal combustion.	
Hazardous waste landfill	Designed specifically to receive hazardous waste.	RCRA: Title C
Polychlorinated biphenyl (PCB) landfill	Receives waste products from PCB decontamination	TSCA

EPA classifies LFs on the basis of their capacity to hold MSW as: (i) Large LF, having a total waste capacity greater than 130 000 t (200 000 m^3), (ii) Medium LF: waste capacity between 26 000 t and 130 000 t (52 000 m^3 and 200 000 m^3), and (iii) Small LF: waste capacity less than 26 000 t (52 000 m^3). Landfills can also be classified based on the nature of waste, such as: MSW landfill, coal combustion waste landfill, and others, as listed in Table 4.6.

4.7.1   Types of Landfills

During the early years (decades of the1960s and 1970s) of acceptance of SLF as a preferred method of MSW disposal, three variations of landfill designs were common: (i) area type, (ii) trench type, and (iii) ramp type. Each had some advantages and limitations. For example, area type, because of flat ground, affords easy movement of heavy equipment and machineries, but requires greater land area. Trench type involves an excavated trench or an existing mined-out quarry into which MSW is spread, compacted, and covered. Excavating the earth material for the trench method is best suited for nearly level land where the water table is deeper than the floor of the trench. In the ramp type of landfills, MSW is spread on an existing slope, compacted, and covered. Trench and ramp LFs have problems with machinery movement. Trench type additionally requires carefully designed roadways to assure stability of the slopes. Steeper grades in trench and ramp-type landfills result in increased potential for slope failure, less efficient operation of heavy machineries and higher fuel costs. The last two types have essentially been phased out and a majority of the modern landfills are of the area type.

Landfills are sited, designed, operated, and monitored to comply with federal, state, and local regulations. For example, landfills cannot be built in environmentally sensitive areas; they must have monitoring systems to check for any sign of groundwater contamination and for the presence of LFGs; and designed and operated to ensure preservation of the environmental quality of the area.

All MSWs are regulated under RCRA, with the exception of polychlorinated biphenyl (PCB) landfills that are regulated under the Toxic Substances Control Act (TSCA).

Disposal of solid waste in landfills is the most common method all over the world. SLF became the preferred method of MSW disposal in the late 1950s in the US. Until that time, MSW was disposed of in open dumps across the country, in most cases, without any cover soil. Problems of rodents, flies, and other vectors, in addition to strong odors and nuisance from flies, birds, and contamination of surface and groundwater, were causing concerns that brought to fore the need for comprehensive research in the safe management of solid waste. The APWA, in its 1962 report identified several research areas that justified an annual investment of a minimum of $7.5 million ($67.8 million in 2021 dollars) in solid waste research (Bugher 1962, p. 5). The USPHS carried out some landmark in-house research studies and also awarded research grants to universities across the country to study a variety of projects in the field of solid waste. One of the USPHS projects involved conducting field tests by burying waste in the ground and covering it up with a layer of soil to study fly larvae growth. Based on entomological consideration, it was found that a 6.7 cm (2.62 in)-thick layer of compacted soil would prevent the emergence of flies from the waste pile but on practical considerations, a 15 cm (6 in) compacted soil layer to cover the compacted waste at the end of each day's work was recommended (Black and Barnes 1958). Based on this and several other studies, it was recommended that in addition to institutional control, the following factors must be included in the design of SLFs:

- Site geology should be studied as it is an important factor in construction, water pollution, and lateral gas movement
- Refuse should not be allowed to come into contact with surface water or groundwater; and should be spread and compacted in 2 ft. (0.61 m)-thick layers, and compacted into 8 ft. (2.44 m) lifts, and a daily cover of at least 6 in. (0.15 m) of compacted soil should be applied at the end of the day's work
- The final cover and the closed landfill should be monitored and managed after closure.

These recommendations led to establishing standards for SLF operations that were later modified and expanded by the EPA to become part of the code of practice as outlined in 40CFR Part 258 (CFR 2011).

4.7.2 Daily Operation of a Sanitary Landfill

SLFs, being one of the essential municipal services provided by the city, operate year-round. After the trash truck hauls the garbage to the landfill, the truck first stops at the weighing station (to record the garbage weight), then to the Materials Recycling Facility (MRF) where the recyclables are separated from the comingled MSW. The residue left after all useful materials have been separated, either manually or by using an automatic sorting machine, is moved to the active area of the landfill for disposal. Tractors, compactors, and other machines are commonly used to move the waste around, spread, and compact it. Modern landfills operate on the principle of three Cs. Once all three steps have been completed – typically by the end of the working day – the waste is considered isolated in the "cell" or sanitized. Theoretically, clayey soil, because of its very low permeability, should be the most desirable soil type to prevent water entry through the daily cover. However, its poor workability makes it impractical to use because upon getting wet, it sticks to metal, causing problems in equipment movement, loading and unloading, spreading, and compacting. Silty clays, despite their higher hydraulic conductivity (1×10^{-6} cm/s) as compared to clay (1×10^{-7} cm/s to 1×10^{-9} cm/s), but because of better workability, are preferred for use as daily

Figure 4.11 View of an operating MSW landfill showing various stages of waste disposal and isolation. *Source:* S.E. Hasan (author).

cover soil. Other materials, such as crushed rubble, clay-shale rocks, etc., can be substituted for the daily cover, provided they meet the hydraulic conductivity requirement.

Individual compacted cell ranges in thickness from about 2–7 m; the latter in large landfills. The most common cell thickness for a medium-size landfill is about 2.5 m. After the waste has been compacted, each completed cell has to be covered with suitable soil and a ratio of 4 : 1 for the compacted waste to the cover soil, i.e. for every 4 ft. (1.22 m) of compacted waste, 1 ft. (0.31 m), or a minimum of 0.5 ft. (0.15 m) of the cover soil, whichever is greater, has to be maintained. When the landfill becomes full and must be closed, the final cover has to be a minimum of 2 ft. (0.61 m) thick. Figure 4.11 illustrates various features of a large operating landfill.

4.7.3 Landfill Leachate

Despite the care taken to prevent surface water or snowmelt from entering the landfill, some of it always makes its way inside the waste cells. The percolating water reacts with a heterogeneous mixture of materials containing toxic metals, nonmetals, and other harmful organic and inorganic substances that are present in the landfill, and undergoes complex physical, chemical, and biochemical reactions that result in the dissolution of many of these substances in the percolating water. *Leachate* is a term used for the highly mineralized water-based solution, usually of a dark brown or rust color, with a strong obnoxious odor, and containing a high concentration of harmful substances. This toxic "soup" of contaminants has been responsible for degrading the quality of many of the aquifers all over the world, besides impacting surface waters. The chemical nature of leachate varies with the nature of materials deposited in the landfill and its age. Analyses of leachate from MSW and nonhazardous industrial landfills have revealed the presence of a number of contaminants that can be broadly grouped into: (i) dissolved organic matter, e.g. alcohols, acids, aldehydes, short-chain sugars, etc. (ii) inorganic components (common cations and anions including sulfate, chloride, iron, aluminum, zinc, and ammonia), (iii) heavy metals, such as Pb, Ni, Cu, and Hg, (iv) xenobiotic organic compounds (man-made chemicals that do not have any natural analogues), such as halogenated organics, like PCBs, dioxins, etc., and (v) pharmaceuticals and personal care products (PPCPs) and their metabolites (drugs, such as antibiotics, analgesics, synthetic hormones, etc.). Table 4.7 shows the generalized composition of leachate from landfills, 25 years or less in age (Kjeldsen et al. 2002).

Besides toxic heavy metals, pesticides, and other harmful inorganic and organic chemicals, a new set of contaminants, called contaminates of concern (CECs), that include plasticizers, PPCPs, and steroid hormones, have also been found in landfill leachate. A study involving analyses of fresh leachate samples from 19 landfills in 16 states, located across the USA; by Masoner and his coworkers,

Table 4.7 Leachate composition of MSW landfills.

Parameter	Range
Conductivity $(mScm^{-1})$	2500–35 000
pH	4.5–9
Solids (residual)	2000–60 000
Organic C (TOC)	30–29 000
BOD_5	20–57 000
COD	140–152 000
Organic N	14–2500
Total P	0.1–23
Chlorides	150–4500
Sulfates	8–7750
Bicarbonate	610–7320
Na	70–7700
K	50–3700
Ammonium (N)	50–2200
Ca	10–7200
Mg	30–15 000
Fe	3–5500
Mn	0.03–1400
Si	4–70
As	0.01–1
Cd	0.0001–0.4
Cu	0.005–10
Cr	0.02–1.5
Co	0.005–1.5
Hg	0.00005–0.16
Pb	0.001–5
Ni	0.015–13
Zn	0.03–1000

All unspecified values are in mg/g (ppm) except for conductivity and pH.
Source: After Kjeldsen et al. (2002).

found 129 CECs in one or more leachate samples. The CECs included 62 prescription pharmaceuticals, 23 industrial chemicals, 18 nonprescription (over the counter) drugs, 16 household chemicals (with two pesticides), six steroid hormones, and four animal/plant sterols. The frequency of detection and concentration were higher in samples from areas with an annual average precipitation of >100 cm compared to areas where precipitation was <50 cm (Masoner et al. 2014), indicating the influence of moisture in the volume of leachate formation and greater amounts of contaminants therein.

4.7.4 Landfill Gases

LFGs are produced as a result of aerobic and anaerobic decomposition of organic constituents by microorganisms. Once formed, LFGs can migrate either laterally or vertically through the surrounding soil under a pressure gradient or a concentration gradient (i.e. by diffusion). LFG usually contains 45 to 60% CH_4 and 40 to 60% CO_2 (by volume). Methane is odorless and nontoxic, but becomes explosive in the presence of air at concentrations of between 5 and 15%. At higher concentrations in air, methane is flammable.

LFG also includes small amounts of N, O, NH_3, SOx, H_2, CO, and nonmethane organic compounds (NMOCs) such as trichloroethylene, benzene, and vinyl chloride. Various LFGs, their characteristics and approximate volume, are listed in Table 4.8.

4.7.4.1 Landfill Gas Formation

In conventional landfills, where the waste is buried under a cover of soil, available oxygen in the air, entombed with the waste, leads to waste biodegradation by aerobic microorganisms. However, the aerobic process ceases with the exhaustion of available oxygen within a short period of several days to a few weeks. From this time onward, anaerobic conditions set in and the process of biochemical degradation continues for decades, with most of the reactions occurring under anaerobic conditions.

Table 4.8 Volume and properties of landfill gases (adapted from ATSDR and EPA).

Compound	Characteristics	Volume %
Methane	Colorless and odorless. Landfills are the largest anthropogenic sources of methane	45–60
Carbon dioxide	Colorless, odorless, and slightly acidic in reaction	40–60
Nitrogen	Colorless, tasteless, and odorless; comprises ~79% of the atmosphere	2–5
Oxygen	Colorless, tasteless, and odorless; comprises ~21% of the atmosphere	0.1–1
Ammonia	Colorless with a strong pungent odor	0.1–1
Water vapor	Whitish, odorless	1–10
Non-methane organic compounds	Include acrylonitrile, benzene, 1,1-dichloroethane, 1,2-cis dichloroethylene, dichloromethane, carbonyl sulfide, ethyl-benzene, hexane, methyl ethyl ketone, tetrachloroethylene, toluene, trichloroethylene, vinyl chloride, and xylenes	0.01–0.6
Sulfides	Hydrogen sulfide, dimethyl sulfide (mercaptans), make LFG smell like rotten eggs	0–1
Hydrogen	Colorless, odorless gas	0–0.2
Carbon monoxide	Colorless, odorless gas	0-0.2

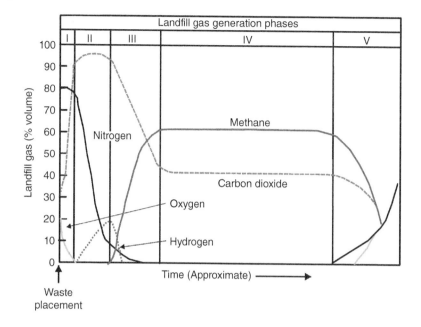

Figure 4.12 Phases of landfill gas formation.

The entire process of LFG formation can be divided into five phases: Phase I to Phase V, as shown in Figure 4.12.

The duration, physical and biochemical conditions, degradation products, and quantities of LFGs produced depend on the composition of MSW and its moisture content. Moisture in LFs comes from two sources: (i) from the materials in MSW, moisture that is chemically bonded to the various substances can contribute 10–20% of water, and (ii) percolation from rain and snowmelt, irrigation, or leachate recirculation. This moisture, aided by microorganisms, causes biodegradation of MSW that can be represented by the following empirical relationship:

$$MSW + Moisture \rightarrow LFGs + Lecahate + Heat$$

This exothermic reaction can generate a temperature up to 66 °C, along with a number of gases, some in large quantities, others in trace quantities. Based on their volumes, LFGs are grouped into:

1) Major LFGs, accounting for >99% of the total LFGs' volume, comprise:

CH_4 and CO_2	40–60% each
N_2	2–5%
O_2, SOx	<1%
NH_3	0.1–1.0%
H_2 and CO	0–0.2%

2) Minor LFGs, <1% in volume:
   Butane, hexane, benzene, terpenes, etc.; their volume ranges from ppm range to 0.6%.

Physical and chemical conditions, along with various LFGs generated during the five phases, as shown in Figure 4.12, are explained below.

Phase I: Initial Adjustment Phase. This phase has the shortest duration and lasts from hours to a few weeks. Aerobic microorganisms carry out MSW degradation, deriving their oxygen supply from the air trapped in the layer of cover soil. Phase I is characterized by the highest temperature range (54–71 °C) and the highest pH (~8–10). N_2 and O_2 are the main gases produced, accounting for ~78 and 21% volume, respectively (same composition as air).

Phase II: Transition Phase. As the oxygen trapped in the cover soil gets exhausted, the aerobic process ceases and the anaerobic degradation process sets in. Physical condition changes from alkaline to acidic as the pH increases to ~5 due to CO_2 generation; and temperature ranges between 37.8 and 54.4 °C. O_2 goes down to near zero and the volume of H_2 begins to increase, peaking at about 18% toward the end of Phase II. CO_2 increases to about 95% and the quantity of N_2 decreases rapidly to <10% at the end of Phase II. Volatile fatty acids (VFAs) begin to form acetic, butyric, and propionic acids in this phase that lasts anywhere from 1 mo to 6 mo.

Phase III: Acid Phase. Conditions become more acidic with pH dropping to below 5; higher acidity causes dissolution of heavy metals that become part of landfill leachate. This phase is characterized by increased microbial activities, resulting in the formation of greater quantities of VFAs; CO_2 declines sharply to about 35%; H_2 decreases to zero; and CH_4 begins to form with a rapid rise in its volume from 0% to about 60% at the end of Phase III, which lasts from about 3 months to about 8 years.

Phase IV: Methane Phase. This phase has the longest duration and lasts from about 8 y to > 40 y. Strict methanogenic microorganisms proliferate, continuously converting VFAs into CH_4 and CO_2, both of which are generated in nearly constant volumes of 60 and 35% respectively. pH increases to between 6.8 and 8, which, in turn, slows down the rate of heavy metal dissolution. The rate of VFAs' formation begins to decrease toward the end of Phase IV, causing a corresponding decrease in the volume of CH_4.

Phase V: Maturation Phase. This phase marks the end of the LFG formation with a significant decline in CH_4 volume; CO_2 also decreases substantially, and N_2 increases to about 80% at the end of Phase V.

The long period of methane generation (several decades) and in large quantities (average ~50%) offers economic and environmental benefits for capturing the gas for power generation. Thereby turning a product of discarded waste into a source of energy, and preventing the escape of methane – the third-largest human-induced source of GHGs in the US – into the atmosphere, eliminating its contribution to global warming.

4.7.5 Landfill Design

A landfill is an engineered structure built to confine MSW and minimize the release of leachate and LFGs into the surrounding areas, with the overall goal of protecting human and ecological health and preserving the environment. A secure landfill – all modern landfills built after the enactment of RCRA (1976) are secure landfills – includes a composite liner and leachate and gas management systems, besides air and water monitoring systems, as its essential components.

Being complex engineered structures, landfill design requires careful considerations of scientific, technical, legal, and economic factors in addition to public attitude. Modern landfills should be designed for a minimum working life of 30 years, longer if land for expansion is available. In addition, because the law requires monitoring of closed landfills for a period of 30 years, and methane gas production may continue several decades after closure, it is important that all short- and long-term aspects, including potential reuse of the land be given due consideration in the planning and design stage.

Design and construction of MSWLF is a time-consuming and expensive process, and depending upon the size of the landfill, it may take anywhere from 3 y to 10 y for siting, design, and construction. Also, depending upon its location and size, landfill construction costs would vary over a wide range. For example, a rough estimate puts the cost of construction of a medium-sized landfill to serve a population of one million at about $10 million (Kaza et al. 2018), which represents the average global cost. Operational costs that include personnel, equipment purchase and service, utilities, fuel, and labor, running into millions of dollars per year, should also be taken into consideration. A more accurate cost for a modern landfill in the US; occupying an area of 40.5 ha (100 ac), and complying with all regulations, is about $29 million for construction, $10 million per year for operation, and an additional $19.5 million for final closure and post-closure monitoring for 30 years; excluding the cost of land and reserve fund for custodial care and maintenance after post-closure (S. Martin, personal communication). Capital costs for individual cell expansions and closures are incurred incrementally from the time the LF becomes operational and until its final closure. Cell expansions and closures are typically funded from the revenues generated from tipping fees, etc. Example 4.1 illustrates the cost breakdown for constructing a landfill in the US.

Example 4.1 Cost breakdown of a 40.5-ha (100 ac) landfill (in 2020 $).

A. Predevelopment cost (feasibility and site selection studies, land survey, hydrogeologic investigation, legal and permitting fee, excluding the cost of land)	700 000
B. Landfill construction (buildings, excavation and stockpiling, soil and FML, leachate and gas collections system, access roads, drainage control, scale and scale house).	27 660 000
C. Construction engineering cost.	750 000
D. Landfill closure cost (clay cap, FML, drainage net, vegetative layer, seed, fertilizer, and engineering).	12 501 000
E. Landfill post-closure cost (30-year monitoring and maintenance).	4 500 000
F. Reserve funds for custodial care and contingency expenses after post-closure	2 250 000
Total cost (LF development, construction, and 30 years post-closure maintenance; excludes annual operation cost of $10 000 000).	$48 361 000

Preconstruction geological and engineering investigations are essential to obtain a clear picture of the regional and local geology of the area to provide input data into the design of an SLF. Any attempt to cut the geological and site investigation budget results in either incomplete information or inaccurate data – both of which lead to future problems and costly corrective measures.

4.7.5.1 Landfill Siting Restrictions

While geological and engineering considerations are important in locating a landfill, certain restrictions that RCRA has imposed, mainly to protect human health and the environment, have to be complied with. Part 258 of the US Code of Federal Regulations, Title 40, in its Subpart B, provides details of restrictions for landfill siting that are summarized next:

Landfill Siting Restrictions:

a) Airports: Landfills cannot be located within 3048 m (10 000 ft.) of the end of airport runway used by turbojet aircraft, or 1524 m (5000 ft.) of airport runway end used by piston-type aircraft so as not to pose a bird hazard to the aircraft. Bird hazard means an increase in the likelihood of bird-aircraft collisions that may cause damage to the aircraft or injury to its occupants.

Owners or operators proposing to site new MSWLF units and lateral expansions within 5 mi (8 km) radius of any airport runway end used by a turbojet or piston-type aircraft must notify the affected airport and the Federal Aviation Administration (FAA).

b) Floodplains: An MSWLF cannot be located in a 100-year floodplain of an inland, coastal, or offshore island water body. An exception can be granted when the owner can demonstrate that the LF will not restrict the flow of the 100-year flood, reduce the temporary water storage capacity of the floodplain, or result in washout of solid waste, posing a hazard to human health and the environment.

c) Wetlands: No MSWLF can be built on a wetland. Exceptions can be granted if the owner can demonstrate that locating it on the wetland would comply with provisions of the Clean Water Act, Endangered Species Act, Marine Protection Research and Sanctuaries Act and other applicable State water quality standards, to safeguard marine life and human health and environment.

d) Fault zones: No MSWLF can be located within 60 m of an active fault (one along which at least one earth movement has occurred in the past 10 000 y). An exception can be granted if the owner demonstrates that locating it <60 m from an active fault would not compromise the structural integrity of the LF and will still ensure the protection of human health and the environment.

e) Seismic impact zones: MSWLF cannot be located in seismic impact zones where there is a 10% or better possibility that the maximum horizontal displacement in solid rocks will exceed 0.1 g in 250 years. An exception can be granted if it can be demonstrated that designed reinforcements would maintain the structural integrity of the LF and all other associated structures, when there is a 90% or better probability that a seismic event would cause a displacement >0.1 g in 250 years.

f) Unstable areas: MSWLF cannot be located in unstable areas, such as: poor foundation conditions, areas susceptible to mass movements, and karst terranes. An exception can be granted if the owners demonstrate that engineering measures have been incorporated into the MSWLF design to ensure that the integrity of the structural components of the MSWLF unit will not be disrupted.

4.7.6 Landfill Design Criteria

The design of MSWLF must incorporate the restrictions as outlined above and should comply with all federal, state, and local regulations. Any departure from the standards must be clearly stated and provisions to ensure the safe operation of the LF along with the protection of human health and the environment must be adequately demonstrated. Federal law requires that owners seeking exceptions must file all relevant documentation with the State and keep a copy in its facility's operating records.

The RCRA, Subtitle D, regulates the construction, operation, and maintenance of landfills. States are responsible for ensuring that federal criteria for operating municipal solid waste and industrial waste landfill regulations are met. States are allowed by the EPA to set more stringent requirements. However, in the absence of an approved state program, the following seven requirements must be satisfied for landfill construction and operation:

1) Location restrictions, to ensure that landfills are built at favorable geological locations, away from faults, wetlands, flood plains, or other restricted areas.

2) Composite liner requirement to include a flexible membrane (i.e. geo-membrane), at least 0.61 m (2 ft.) thick, placed above compacted clayey soil, and lining the bottom and sides of the landfill, to protect groundwater and the underlying soil from leachate.

3) Leachate collection and removal systems located above the composite liner to remove leachate from within the confines of the landfill for treatment and disposal.

4) Operating practices involving compacting and covering waste frequently with suitable soil to reduce odor, minimize moisture infiltration, control litter, insects, and rodents, and protect public health.
5) Groundwater monitoring at and near the landfill involving periodic sampling and testing of groundwater to detect any release of waste materials from the landfill.
6) Closure and post-closure requirements to provide long-term care of closed landfills.
7) Corrective action provisions to ensure control and cleaning up any landfill releases to comply with groundwater protection standards.

The criteria laid out in RCRA provides for two design options: (i) states that do not have an EPA-approved program must include a composite liner and leachate collection system in the LF design; and (ii) EPA-approved states should provide adequate design safeguard to ensure that the Maximum contaminant levels (MCLs), given in Table 4.9, will not exceed in the uppermost aquifer at a "relevant point of compliance" to protect aquifers used for drinking water supply.

Table 4.9 Maximum contaminant levels for MSWLF effluents (CFR 2011).

Chemical	Maximum allowable concentration, mg/L (ppm)
Arsenic	0.05
Barium	1.0
Benzene	0.005
Cadmium	0.01
Carbon tetrachloride	0.005
Chromium (hexavalent)	0.05
2,4-Dichlorophenoxy acetic acid	0.1
1,4-Dichlorobenzene	0.075
1,2-Dichloroethane	0.005
1,1-Dichloroethylene	0.007
Endrin	0.0002
Fluoride	4.0
Lindane	0.004
Lead	0.05
Mercury	0.002
Methoxychlor	0.1
Nitrate	10
Selenium	0.01
Silver	0.05
Toxaphene	0.005
1,1,1-Trichloromethane	0.2
Trichloroethylene	0.005
2,4,5-Trichlorophenoxy acetic acid	0.01
Vinyl chloride	0.002

The key elements of MSWLF design are the provision to prevent the escape of leachate from the landfill to protect drinking water resources; and management of LFGs to prevent fire hazards and air quality degradation. Emphasis is placed on the prevention of drinking water aquifers because of the complex and tedious process of evaluation of the nature and extent of groundwater contamination and high cost and very long time (few years to decades) needed for cleaning up contaminated aquifers. The design requirements for liner, outlined in CFR 40, Part 258, §258.40, specify use of a composite liner system with the upper component comprising a synthetic plastic liner, called flexible membrane liner (FML), at least 30 -mil (0.76 mm) thick; or 60 mil (1.52 mm) thick if made of high-density polyethylene (HDPE). The FML should be placed above a compacted layer of soil having a hydraulic conductivity of 1×10^{-7} cm/s or less. The FML serves two purposes: (i) retards leachate movement, and (ii) minimizes potential degradation of the compacted clay liner. Hasan and Hoyt (1992), in an elaborate laboratory experiment to simulate the effect of leachate on clayey soil, had reported physical and chemical deterioration of the soil upon prolonged exposure to alternating cycles of wetting and drying.

Additional requirements include efficient leachate and gas collection and extraction systems. Details of the leachate collection and LFG management systems are discussed in the following sections.

4.7.6.1 Leachate Collection and Removal System

EPA specifications require two drainage-cum-liner systems for MSWLF. The primary (or upper) leachate collection and removal system is designed to ensure that the depth of leachate that would collect above the liner will not exceed 0.30 m (1 ft.). The secondary (or lower) leachate collection and removal system is designed to detect, collect, and remove any leachate that might percolate through the upper liner.

The design of the primary leachate collection and removal system (PLCRS) incorporates the installation of filters. The conventional filter is made of selected soil materials that are installed underneath or adjacent to structures where seepage of water or other liquids is anticipated. Proper drainage of such soils is essential for preventing the buildup of excessive pore-water pressure that may cause instability of the structure. A filter must satisfy two requirements: (i) allow adequate drainage of water or other liquid, and (ii) prevent fine particles from clogging the voids. Filters made of natural soil materials are common in dams and other hydraulic structures, but geosynthetic fabrics are finding greater use as filters because of the ease of installation and cost considerations. Unlike soil materials, a very small thickness, about 2 cm (<1 in.) of the synthetic drainage material, fulfills the same hydraulic design requirements as a large thickness (0.3 m or 1 ft.) of soil material. Their use in landfills increases their capacity to hold additional quantities of waste. This additional capacity is preferred by landfill owners because of the increased revenue.

Whether the drainage material is a synthetic geonet or natural soil, it must have a high hydraulic conductivity of 1 cm/s. A 0.30 m (1 ft.)-thick gravel layer, without fines and with individual particles in the size range of 6–12 mm (0.25–0.5 in.), serves as the required drainage material to allow for the unimpeded flow of liquid into perforated drain pipes. However, in order to prevent clogging of the void spaces, the upper surface of this drainage medium has to be covered with suitable filter material.

The top of the secondary (or lower) leachate collection and removal system (SLCRS) is covered with an FML at least 0.76 mm (30 mil) thick. Underlying the PLCRS, and above the composite bottom liner, is the secondary leachate detection, collection, and removal system. It has the same type of drainage material as the PLCRS, except that an FML covers its upper surface. In addition, one or more sumps with submersible pumps for leachate removal are installed in the SLCRS. (See Figure 5.3, Chapter 5 for details of the leachate collection system.)

4.7.6.2 Landfill Gas Collection and Extraction System

A secure landfill should have the provision for the collection and venting of LFGs. LFGs from landfills may be vented directly into the air, collected and flared, or used for energy generation. A typical LFG collection system is shown in Figure 4.13: A 30 cm (12 in.)-thick layer of gravel overlies the compacted waste; upward-sloping perforated PVC pipes laid in the gravel layer are connected to vertical riser pipes with a vent at the surface. The layer of gravel is covered with a geonet. Overlying this filter is a layer of compacted soil, with low hydraulic conductivity (1×10^{-7} cm/s) and at least 61 cm (2 ft.) in thickness. This, in turn, is overlain by a minimum 0.5 mm (20-mil)-thick FML. The FML is covered with a layer of coarse soil 30 cm (12 in.)-thick with a hydraulic conductivity of 1×10^{-2} cm/s or greater to facilitate easy runoff of rain or snowmelt water. The coarse soil material may be replaced by a geosynthetic material having the same hydraulic conductivity.

The purpose of the drainage layer is to intercept the water and move it away from the waste. This is achieved by providing a minimum of 3% slope, which causes the percolating water to move rapidly by gravity to a toe drain, away from the perimeter of the waste cells. A geosynthetic filter layer is placed above the drainage layer. Instead of being vented into the air, the LFG can also be extracted by installing a gas extraction system. Such systems use exhaust blowers. Full evaluation of settlement and subsidence potentials, and the maximum depth of frost penetration, are other factors that must be considered in the design of a gas control system.

One of the hazards associated with methane and other LFGs is its uncontrolled release from the landfill. The emission of methane from landfills is not only the greatest source of anthropogenic contribution to GHGs, but its entry into nearby homes and other buildings has resulted in fires and explosions. Depending upon the age and nature of materials in the landfill, site geology, moisture content, pressure, etc., LFGs can travel up to 500 m from a landfill; although the travel distance more commonly is under 75 m. A study at 38 landfills by the

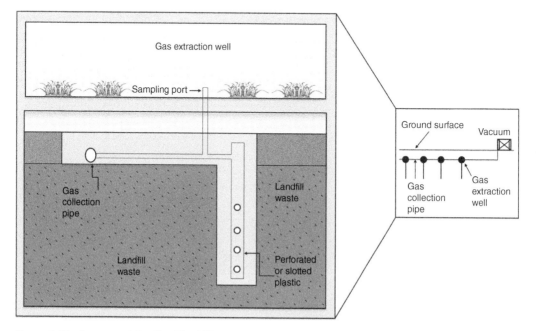

Figure 4.13 Layout and details of landfill gas collection system. *Source:* EPA.

New York State Department of Health found that LFGs migrated about 300 m from one land-fill, about 150 m from four landfills, and about 75 m from 33 landfills (ATSDR 1998). LFG can enter homes and other buildings through cracks in the concrete foundation slab or walls and other openings.

4.7.7 Landfill Area Requirement

One of the main considerations for an owner or developer of an MSWLF is the land area required for the construction of the landfill. An old rule-of-thumb that was suggested during the 1950s was: 1 ac (0.41 ha) of land/10 000 people/year for a 7 ft. (2.1 m)-deep (or high) LF (APWA 1966, p. 96). Since modern MSWLFs have to comply with many regulations, this rule is no more applicable. In order to meet all requirements, modern landfills need space not only for disposal of the waste but also for: (i) machinery storage, service, and repair, (ii) haul roads, (iii) sampling and monitoring wells, (iv) LFG purification plant, (v) LF leachate collection and management structures, (vi) storage of cover soil, and (vii) service buildings that typically include field office, refuse truck weighing station, and guardhouse. All these structures/facilities add up to between 20 and 30% of the actual land area needed for the LF alone, which should be included in the total area required for the construction and operation of the landfill. Example 4.7.1 illustrates how to calculate the total area for the landfill.

Example 4.7.1 Landfill Area Calculation
   The following is a list of key data/information that must be included in the determination of the LF area:

- i) Current and future population of the community
- ii) Per capita rate of the solid waste generated
- iii) Waste volume to be landfilled (after removing all recyclables and compostable fractions)
- iv) Compaction ratio of the waste
- v) Density (or unit weight) of the waste
- vi) Final height of the landfill
- vii) Planned life of the landfill

Example Problem 4.2   Landfill Land Requirement
   Determine the total area, A_T, for an MSW landfill to serve an environmentally committed community comprising 100 000 people, using the following data:

- **a)** Quantity of MSW generated, $Q = 1$ kg/p/d (after diversion of recyclables, compostable, and combustible fractions)
- **b)** LF designed life, $L = 25$ y
- **c)** Population growth rate, P: assume no change (in-migration + birth rate = out-migration + death rate)
- **d)** Density, ρ, of compacted waste at the LF = 500 kg/m^3
- **e)** Final height, H, of the landfill 30 m, including daily cover soil.

Solution:

Recall:

(1) Area (A) is a two-dimensional quantity, while volume (V) represents three dimensions;
(2) Waste is measured as weight (W), not volume (V). So, we need to convert W to V.

Density, ρ = W/V, which is 500 kg/m^3, means that 500 kg of compacted MSW will require 1 m^3 of space (V).

Then, V for 1 kg = 1/500 kg/m^3 = 0.002 m^3, i.e. this is the volume of waste generated by each person/day (since Q=1kg/p/d).

So, waste volume generated in one year, V = 365 × 0.002 = 0.73 m^3/person; and for the community of 100 000 MSW quantity in 1 year = 100 000 × 0.73 m^3 or 73 000 m^3 in 1 year; and, the volume generated in 25 years = 73 000 m^3 × 25 = 1 825 000 m^3

To determine the area, A, of the compacted MSW having a total volume of 1 825 000 m^3, we need to recall (1) so that:

A= V/H = 1 825 000 m^3/30 m = 60 833 m^2 or 0.061 km^2. This is the land area required for the MSW alone.

To calculate the total area, A$_T$, for MSW and ancillary structures, we add 30% to A:

$\therefore$ Total area, A$_T$, = (0.061 km^2 × 0.3) + 0.061 = 0.0183 + 0.061 = 0.0793 km^2 or 7.93 ha (19.6 ac). This can be rounded off to 8 ha or 20 ac.

4.7.8 Landfill Site Selection

Site selection involves evaluation of the physical and biological environment in relation to the proposed project. It is important that *all* relevant features at the proposed site be fully evaluated because each site is unique in terms of its geology and environmental characteristics. The information presented here provides general guidelines for all geologic/geotechnical evaluation, and should always be included in any site-selection process. However, depending on the nature of a particular project, additional factors may have to be evaluated. For example, the site-selection process for an MSWLF must take into account various regulatory details, and public attitude in addition to the required geologic and engineering factors.

Site selection is an organized process that follows a logical sequence, and comprises two main steps: (i) office study and data collection; and (ii) field investigations and laboratory testing.

4.7.8.1 Defining Purpose and Scope

Any geotechnical site investigation must be preceded by careful documentation of the purpose and a clear definition of the scope of the work. This must be done before the first person goes out in the field to commence the investigations. Such documentation helps keep the investigation focused and ensures that all necessary information and data have been gathered. Unfortunately, this simple step is often neglected, resulting in either collection of too much data or missing important data.

4.7.8.2 Office Study and Data Collection

Office study is an important prerequisite of the site-selection process. Valuable information can be acquired by reviewing pertinent reports and documents. During this phase of the study, all available data for the potential site(s) should be gathered and carefully analyzed. Table 4.10 lists common data and information that should be collected during site-selection studies.

It should be noted that this stage of the site-selection process does not require any site visit. In fact, all studies during this phase of site evaluation are carried out in the office, which is far more economical than conducting studies in the field. After the earlier information has been analyzed in relation to the given project, two to three potential sites, called candidate sites, should be tentatively selected and rank-ordered for field investigations. This step enables eliminating all sites with negative attributes, and identifies site or sites that appear(s) to be more promising and possessing features and characteristics that are favorable for the proposed project. This simple and relatively

Table 4.10 Data/information need for landfill site selection.

Data type	Information	Source
Air photos and Remote sensing	Current and historical air photos and satellite data for land use pattern and changes; Digital elevations	USDA; NASA; USGS
Geology	Rock types and sediments; faults	USGS, and state geological surveys
Meteorological	Current and past precipitation data; wind, rain, and ice storm patterns and frequencies	US National Weather Service; NASA
Soils	Occurrence and distribution of soils; rankings for various engineering uses including landfills	USDA
Topography	Lay of the land, elevation, slope, water bodies, wetlands, cultural features: cities, towns, railways, airports, etc.	USGS
Water	Surface and groundwater; discharge, flood stage, and flood zones. Groundwater occurrence, distribution, and quality.	USGS

inexpensive process allows the investigator to conduct detailed field investigations only at the few promising sites having favorable attributes, thus maximizing the effort (Hasan 1994). *Remember:* It is far less expensive to make such decisions in the office than in the field.

4.7.8.3 Field Investigations

Armed with the information gathered during the office study phase, investigators can then visit the site. The goal at this stage of site selection is to study the features as they occur at the site, and to obtain *maximum* information at a *minimum* cost. This presents a challenge to the engineering geologist or the geotechnical engineer because there can never be enough money or time to collect all the information. Budgets for such studies are limited, which means that every aspect of field investigation must be carefully planned and executed. The training and experience of the individual play a very important role in the process and help optimize the time and effort spent on such studies.

During the field visit, information should be gathered from *all* potentially suitable sites, not just the site that appeared most suitable during the office phase of the study. The rationale for this approach is that by focusing on one site to the exclusion of other potential sites, one runs the risk of dropping these sites from further consideration – a move that may later prove expensive. In some cases, the best site may have to be dropped because of problems unrelated to the physical characteristics; such problems may include legal difficulties in the acquisition of the land, unexpected discovery of items of archeological significance, environmental constraints, and the like. In addition, it takes very little extra effort to gather data on other potential sites while out in the field. Mobilization of field crew and equipment is expensive. So, it makes sense to plan site investigations to get as much information in as few a visit as possible to avoid subsequent trips. One of the objectives during the field investigations is to identify potential problems associated with the site and to determine how they may be corrected during later stages of project development.

Collection of soil, rock, and water samples, both from the surface and from the subsurface, should be done during the field visit. Typically, mobile subsurface sampling equipment are used to obtain samples from below the ground level. It is essential that all samples be properly labeled, handled, and stored from the time they are collected in the field to the time they are studied and analyzed in the laboratory. Soil samples (for geotechnical studies) and water samples (for geochemical analyses) are particularly susceptible to changes during storage and transportation; therefore, proper care must be taken to prevent or minimize any alterations.

4.8 Bioreactor Landfill

One of the most serious problems with conventional SLFs is the extremely slow rate of degradation of MSW constituents entombed in the LF. By covering the compacted waste with the soil of low permeability, air supply is cut off, and except for the initial few weeks when the entrapped air promotes aerobic degradation of the waste, the overall rate of biodegradation is extremely slow and LFG formation takes tens of years. As discussed in Section 4.7.4 and illustrated in Figure 4.12, the process of MSW decomposition goes on for several decades, sometimes up to 80 years or longer. Excavations done in old landfills have unearthed newspapers with legible headlines and intact food 30–40 years after burial (Rathje 1989). Such a long period of waste degradation, in turn, results in a longer time for biostabilization of the landfill, which delays its potential reuse.

Municipal solid waste landfills in the United States have conventionally been designed and operated under the containment principles described in Subtitle D of RCRA. Disposal of liquids is not permitted, and low permeability final cover systems are required. This minimizes leachate and LFG production and reduces the risk of groundwater contamination and atmospheric pollution.

It was well known at the time of passage of RCRA (1976), and as early as 1940, that enhanced waste degradation can be effectively achieved by stimulating microbial activity through the controlled addition of moisture to the waste (Eliassen 1942). However, EPA took the position that sufficient information was not available to allow large-scale addition of liquid into MSW landfills for allowing bioreactor landfills (BRLFs) under the regulations. Concerns about the "bathtub" effect (i.e. buildup of hydrostatic head on the liner due to water infiltration and/or liquids' accumulation, outpacing leachate removal) also contributed to Subtitle D emphasizing waste containment.

A BRLF is an MSWLF, or a cell in the LF, where moisture or air is introduced to enhance microbial decomposition and biostabilization of the waste. Moisture content is the single most important factor that promotes accelerated waste decomposition. The addition of moisture in the form of water, leachate, industrial nonhazardous wastewater, or sewage sludge accelerates the natural biodegradation process. Moisture content in bioreactor LFs is maintained in the 35–65% range (about the same as the MSW FC) as compared to 15–25% in conventional MSWLFs.

By controlling the amount of moisture and air, conditions can be created in a BRLF to promote MSW decomposition by aerobic, aerobic, or both aerobic-anaerobic (facultative) microorganisms. Depending upon whether the LF is designed to utilize the aerobic, anaerobic, or a combination of these microorganisms, bioreactor LF could be classified as:

1) Aerobic LF: utilizes the leachate formed at the bottom of the LF and recirculated through the MSW in a controlled manner. Air is injected into the mass using vertical or horizontal wells to promote faster waste decomposition and stabilization
2) Anaerobic LF: maintains optimum moisture levels from recirculated leachate water. Air is excluded to maintain the anaerobic environment for waste degradation
3) Hybrid LF: uses an alternating sequence of aerobic-anaerobic conditions to accelerate waste decomposition; the anaerobic treatment rapidly degrades organics in the upper sections of the LF, with methane collection from the lower sections.

Conventional LFs, built during the past several decades, are designed to minimize water infiltration into the MSW to reduce the quantity of toxic leachate, thereby optimizing the cost of leachate management and environmental pollution. Although this approach serves the intended purpose reasonably well, lack of moisture slows down the rate of decomposition of organic and inorganic constituents of the MSW, delays the formation of methane and other LFGs, and extends the time of methane generation, post-closure monitoring, and site reuse. To overcome these limitations, research in designing an alternative landfill, where moisture can be added, commenced in 1959 (EPA 2007). Laboratory and bench-scale studies (Pohland 1975) had already shown that additional moisture not only accelerates the rate of methane formation but also significantly reduces the stabilization of the LF. Stabilization is defined as the time required for complete decomposition of the MSW to generate CH_4 after all C- and H-supplying substrates have been used up.

A BRLF with the following advantages makes it an attractive option for MSW disposal:

- Decomposition and biological stabilization of the waste in a much shorter time period – years as opposed to decades in conventional LFs
- Greater and quicker yield of LFGs, including methane than conventional LF. Methane extraction in a bioreactor LF can commence within months after waste emplacement, whereas in conventional LF, it occurs after a few decades
- Decrease in long-term environmental risks and landfill-operating and post-closure costs
- Lower waste toxicity and mobility due to both aerobic and anaerobic conditions
- Substantial reduction in leachate disposal costs
- 15–30% gain in landfill space due to increase in density of waste mass – a major economic benefit to LF owners
- Significant increase in LFG generation, earning additional revenue
- Lower post-closure cost.

Since the promulgation of Subtitle D in 1991, a growing number of landfill owners have used leachate recirculation besides the addition of bulk-free liquids, under approval from the EPA for *ad hoc* research and development programs. The purpose was to explore practical means to take advantage of two main benefits of a bioreactor: (i) acceleration of short-term LFG generation, offering economically viable and beneficial utilization of methane as a renewable energy source, and (ii) control of GHGs, such as methane, which is one of the main gases targeted for climate change mitigation. Some of the economic and safety concerns with BRLFs include: (i) increased levels of engineering design, and (ii) operational control, and monitoring. To formally promote innovative landfill technologies, including the adoption of alternative cover systems and bioreactor technology, EPA published the Research, Development, and Demonstration (RD&D) Permit Rule on 22 March 2004. The Rule allows Subtitle D landfills a variance option for adding bulk-free liquids if a demonstration can be made that such a variance will not increase the risk to human health and the environment (CFR 2016). Sixteen out of the 50 states (32%) and one Tribal Agency in Arizona had adopted the RD&D Rule, and an additional seven (14%) were in the process of adoption as of 2016. The main reason cited for not adopting the RD&D Rule was the lack of interest among landfill owners in the state due to additional costs of RD&D permitting needs, costs for operation, data collection, and annual reporting requirements. Interestingly, few technical concerns over site stability, environmental protection, or public safety were raised as issues against RD&D Rule adoption, which was a positive aspect.

To assess the feasibility of BRLF as an approved method of MSW disposal and to formulate appropriate rules, EPA has collaborated with state agencies and private sectors to investigate the advantages and limitations of BRLFs and has selected bioreactor demonstration projects in several states under its Project XL (eXcellence in Leadership) program that was promulgated in 1991, with demonstration projects commenced in 1995 (EPA 2019). Various aspects of design, operation, and maintenance of bioreactor LFs are being studied with particular attention to:

1) Increased gas emissions
2) Increased odors
3) Physical instability of waste mass due to increased moisture and density
4) Instability of liner systems
5) Surface seeps
6) Landfill fires.

   With the breakthrough in sensor and measurement technologies and artificial intelligence, it is likely that cost of BRLFs would become competitive or even lower compared to conventional LF. If the advantages of economic gains from the earlier formation of methane and its recovery in about 10–20 years as compared to several decades in conventional LF, along with the potential for safer redevelopment of closed BRLF sites, and the benefit of climate change mitigation, are factored into return-on-investment considerations, BRLFs may become the preferred way to manage MSW. Waste Management, Inc. has predicted BRLF becoming the accepted method of MSW management in the future (Waste Management, n.d.).

4.9 Waste Audit

Waste audit (WA) is a procedure used to determine the composition and quantity of solid waste generated at a facility. WA provides a quantitative estimate of various components of the MSW and is an important first step in the formulation of a waste minimization plan. WA is frequently conducted at business establishments and academic institutions (Hasan and Johnston 2016) to reduce the solid waste quantity by increasing the recycling and reusing the waste materials.

4.9.1 Waste Audit Methodology

WA is a relatively simple procedure that can be accomplished with a limited budget and time. A typical WA of a small facility can be accomplished within two working days at a small cost.

   Depending on the volume of trash generated at the facility, the number of trash bags/bins containing the waste selected for WA should be representative of the entire waste stream. If the waste quantity generated in a day is about 100 kg, or the entire waste is contained in 20 large (0.2 m^3) trash bags, each holding about 12 kg (30 lb.) of solid waste, all of it should be used for conducting the WA. For larger waste quantities, statistically representative samples can be selected by randomly picking 25% (11–12) of the 55-gallon (0.2 m^3) trash bags (EPA 1993), and recording the total weight of all bags. Next, the contents of each bag are emptied onto a large tarp, sorting them into mixed office paper, corrugated cardboard, paperboard, plastics, glass, aluminum cans, food waste, electronic waste, Styrofoam, and miscellaneous (Figure 4.14). Each type of waste is then placed in a smaller plastic bag, weighed to the nearest tenth of a kg, and their respective weights recorded. Simple calculations are done to determine the relative percentage of each category of the waste. WA should be repeated on two separate days to get a reliable average value. More frequent WA shall be performed if the quantity of waste varies during the days, weeks, or months, to reflect changing nature and quantities of the waste stream.

(a)

(b)

(c)

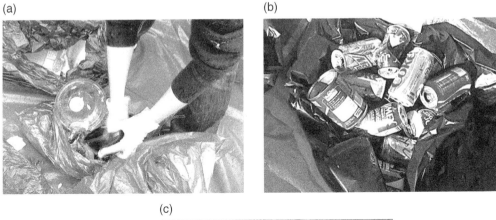

Figure 4.14   (a, b, c): Various types of sorted wastes – food, metals, and plastics, ready for weighing. *Source:* S.E. Hasan (author).

Table 4.11   Safety equipment and supplies for waste assessment.

A. Materials
1) Flat-top (30 cm × 30 cm) electronic balance
2) Tarp (2.5 × 2.5 or 2.5 × 3 m)
3) Plastic bags, 30 gallons (0.1 m^3) capacity with ties
4) Marking pens
5) Masking tape
6) Clipboard

B. Health and safety equipment
1) Disposable nitrile/vinyl gloves
2) Face mask
3) Sanitary wipes
4) First aid kit

It is recommended to take the basic safety measures while conducting WA. Table 4.11 contains a list of safety equipment along with various materials needed for WA, which could be modified for the specific WA project.

A WA report should be prepared to discuss the scope and purpose of the WA, and illustrated with pie/bar charts to show the distribution of various waste components and their relative percentages.

4.10   Summary

Disposal of solid waste has been a vexing problem since early human civilizations. However, it has assumed a serious proportion in modern times due to the ever-increasing human population, and widespread use of thousands of synthetic chemicals containing harmful and toxic substances. In addition, rapid urbanization on a global scale, along with technological innovations, have resulted in much larger quantities of MSW that have been challenging local authorities' capabilities and resources for its safe management.

The USPHS had been addressing problems associated with solid waste management since the early 1900s and some major US cities had been conducting studies, enforcing rules, and adopting better waste management practices since the late nineteenth century.

The composition and quantity of MSW show a wide variation that depends on the geographic location of waste generators, economic and educational levels of the population, their commitment to environmental protection, and use of technology. Regardless of these differences, the global per capita rate of MSW is on the increase, which is forcing decision-makers to consider all available options – reduction, reuse, recycling, composting, and energy recovery – to reduce MSW quantity that will end up at the final disposal facility.

A properly designed landfill has to comply with all local, state, and federal regulations and should include gas and leachate management systems; and surface and groundwater protection measures. Among the various LFGs that form as a result of biochemical degradation of MSW, methane is generated in large quantity over a long period of time, which is now being increasingly captured for use as an energy source.

Landfill site selection is a costly, time-consuming, and challenging task and must be carried out after careful evaluation of site geology, hydrogeology, geological hazards, and with due compliance to all applicable laws and regulations, all of which make LF construction and maintenance very expensive with the cost running between $10 and 50 million.

BRLFs are emerging as a viable alternative to the conventional "dry tomb" LFs. The addition of a copious amount of moisture to accelerate biochemical degradation of MSW reduces the time for the generation of methane, resulting in faster biostabilization of the BRLF. These are attractive economic incentives for BRLF owners as they create additional space for waste disposal and provide a quick return on investment from earlier methane production. These benefits are likely to make BRLFs the preferred option for MSW management in the future.

WA is a simple and inexpensive procedure that can be easily performed for any facility that generates MSW to determine the composition and quantity of various waste components. The data generated from the facility's WA can be used to identify the waste component(s) that can be targeted for waste minimization. On a long-term basis, WA is useful in developing waste minimization and a zero-waste plan for the facility.

Study Questions

1   Discuss the contribution of the US Public Health Service (USPHS) in solid waste management. Which federal agency superseded USPHS? What is the main difference in the work philosophy of the two organizations?

2   How does mismanagement of solid waste result in health problems? Explain with reference to MSW composition, handling, disposal, and leachate and gas generation. Give an example for each.

3   Why did the Solid Waste Disposal Act (SWDA) fail to address problems associated with MSW? Which law replaced SWDA?

4   How is solid waste defined under RCRA? Which solid wastes are included in EPA's "excluded waste" list? Is the exclusion justified? Explain why or why not.

5   What are two common methods for extracting energy from MSW? Compare the advantages and limitations of each.

6   MSW is generated not only from households but other sources as well. List and describe these. What are the main components of various sources?

7   Explain why waste management facilities (landfills, recycling plants, etc.) should be viewed as essential public services in urban areas similar to water and energy supply, roads and highways, communication systems, hospitals, and schools.

8   List and explain possible causes of variation in the composition of MSW. How does climate affect its composition?

9   Discuss the importance of various MSW properties in MSW management.

10 The initial volume of a sample of MSW was determined to be 22 m^3; after compaction, its volume was reduced to 4 m^3. What are the: (a) percentage of volume reduction, and (b) compaction ratio?
    [Ans. **81.8%** and **5.5**]

11 A mass of organic MSW weighed 2.8 kg in natural state and 2.0 kg upon oven drying. What is its moisture content?
    [Ans. **28.6%**]

12 The density of a dry MSW sample was 275 kg/m^3; a natural (moist) sample of the same waste was found to have a moisture content of 20%. Calculate its moist density.
    [Ans. **330 kg/m^3**]

13 The moist weight of a sample at mid-height of an MSW cell was found to be 884 kg; and its moisture content was 20%. Calculate its FC, and the quantity of water that it can hold before it will drain out.
    [Ans. **0.51** and **360.67 or 361 L**]

14 Determine the quantity, Q, of the leachate that will move through a layer of MSW having a cross sectional area, A = 0.25 m^2, hydraulic conductivity, k, of 5×10^{-3} cm^3/s, and hydraulic gradient, i, of .01. Calculate Q in: (a) cm^3/s, (b) m^3/d, and (c) gallons/day.
    [Ans. (a) **0.125 cm^3/s**, (b) **0.10 m^3/d**, and (c) **2.64 g/d**]

15 Calculate the life of an MSWLF for a community that has a population of 1 000 000 people, generates 1.5 kg of solid waste/p/d, and has acquired a 1 km^2 tract of land for the LF. Assume the density of compacted waste at the LF to be 600 kg/m^3, the total height, H, of completed

LF including daily and the final cover to be 30 m, and assuming no population change (in-migration = out-migration and death rate = birth rate). Report the life: (a) without ancillary structures, and (b) with ancillary structures.
[Ans. (a) **32.87y** (b) **21.92y**]

16   A small town with a population of 200 000 people has decided to build a landfill to last 25 years. The per capita waste generation rate is 1.8 kg/d. If the total height of the landfill, including the daily and final covers, is 30 m, and the compacted density of MSW is 620 kg/m^3, how much land will be required for the landfill with ancillary structures?
[Ans. **23.01 ha** or **56.86 ac**]

17   Conventional landfills operate on the principle of 3 Cs. Explain and discuss if the common practice of keeping the MSW as dry as possible in conventional LFs is preferable to BRLFs in terms of leachate and LFG management, settlement, and economics.

18   What are the key factors in the selection of a site for MSWLF? What are the restrictions under RCRA Title D? List and provide brief comments for five of these restrictions.

19   What is a waste audit (WA)? How does it help businesses and institutions in developing a workable waste minimization plan?

References

Al-Delaimy, W.K., Larsen, C.W., and Pezzoli, K. (2014). Differences in health symptoms among residents living near illegal dump sites in Los Laureles Canyon Tijuana Mexico: a cross sectional survey. *International Journal of Environmental Research and Public Health* 11: 9532–9552. https://doi.org/10.3390/ijerph110909532.

APWA (American Public Works Association) (1966). *Municipal Refuse Disposal*, 2e, 528. Chicago, IL: APWA Public Service Administration.

ASCE (American Society of Civil Engineers) (n.d.). Sanitary Landfill, Committee on Sanitary Landfill Practice of the Sanitary Engineering Division of the American Society of Civil Engineers. 61 p.

ATSDR (1998). Agency for Toxic Substances Disease Registry. US Department of Health and Human Services. Investigation of cancer incidences and residence near 38 landfills with soil gas migration conditions. New York State, 1980-1989. Prepared by the New York State Department of Health, Division of Occupational Health and Environmental Epidemiology, Bureau of Environmental and Occupational Epidemiology. PB98-142144. June 1998.

Black, R.J. (1963). Sanitary landfills. *Proceedings: National Conference on Solid Waste Research*, 228 p. American Public Works Association, Special Report No. 29 (2-4 December 1963), Chicago, IL: University of Chicago.

Black, R.J. and Barnes, A.M. (1958). Effect of earth cover on fly emergence from sanitary landfills. *Public Works* 89 (2): 91–94.

Bugher, R. (1962). *Solid Waste Research Needs, APWA Research Foundation Project 113*, 80. Chicago: American Public Works Association.

CFR (Code of Federal Regulations) (2011). 40 CFR 258, Criteria for municipal solid waste landfills. Washington, DC: U.S. Government Publishing Office, p. 428–479. Digital version https://www.gpo.gov/fdsys/granule/CFR-2011-title40-vol25/CFR-2011-title40-vol25-part258 (accessed 7 July 2021).

CFR (2016). Revision to the Research, Development and Demonstration Permits Rule for Municipal Solid Waste Landfills. https://www.federalregister.gov/documents/2016/05/10/2016-10993/ revision-to-the-research-development-and-demonstration-permits-rule-for-municipal-solid-waste (accessed 1 July 2019).

Cunliffe, A.M. and Williams, P.T. (2003). Characterisation of products from the recycling of glass fibre reinforced polyester waste by pyrolysis. *Fuel* 82 (18): 2223–2230. https://doi.org/10.1016/S0016-2361(03)00129-7.

Eliassen, R; 1942. War conditions favor landfill refuse disposal, *Engineering News Record*, Vo. 128, p. 72–74.

Engineering News-Record (1943). Army experience with sanitary fills. *Engineering News-Record* 131 (829): 91–92.

EPA (1993). Business Guide for Reducing Solid Waste. U.S. Environmental Protection Agency Report EPA/530-K-92-004, 82 p.

EPA (2007). Bioreactor Performance. Report No. EPA 530-R-07-007, August 2007, 28 p.

EPA (2013). Advancing Sustainable Materials Management: Facts and Figures 2013, Report No. EPA530-R-15-002, 177 p. https://www.epa.gov/sites/production/files/2015-09/documents/2013_advncng_smm_rpt.pdf (accessed 3 October 2018).

EPA (2019). Bioreactor Landfills. https://www.epa.gov/landfills/bioreactor-landfills (accessed 1 July 2019).

EPA (2020a). Advancing Sustainable Materials Management. 2018 Tables and Figures, 84 p. Advancing Sustainable Materials Management: 2018 Tables and Figures (epa.gov) accessed 8 September 2021.

EPA (2020b). Facts and Figures about Materials, Waste and Recycling. https://www.epa.gov/facts-and-figures-about-materials-waste-and-recycling/durable-goods-product-specific-data#Electronics (accessed 2 February 2022).

EU (European Union) (1999). Council Directive 1999/31/EC on the landfill of waste. https://www.ecolex.org/details/legislation/council-directive-199931ec-on-the-landfill-of-waste-lex-faoc038106 (accessed 29 June 2018).

Hasan, S.E. (1994). Use of soil survey reports in geotechnical projects. *Bulletin of the Association of Engineering Geologists* 31 (4): 367–376.

Hasan, S.E. (2004). Public awareness is key to successful waste management. *Journal of Environmental Science and Health Part A – Toxic/Hazardous Substances Environmental Engineering* 39 (2): 483–492.

Hasan, S. and Johnston, R.K. (2016). Recycling at a higher education institution: case study of a successful program at the University of Missouri-Kansas City. In: *Geoscience for the Public Good and Global Development: Toward a Sustainable Future* (ed. G.R. Wessel and J.K. Greenberg), 407–414. Boulder, Colorado, U.S.A: Geological Society of America Special Papers, SP 520.

Hering, R. and Greeley, S.A. (1921). *Collection and Disposal of Municipal Refuse*, 653. New York, N.Y: McGraw-Hill Book Co; Inc.

Hasan, S.E. and Hoyt, A.J. (1992). Model experiment on Leachate migration through a clayey soil. *Bulletin of the Association of Engineering Geologists* 29 (3): 311–327.

Hickman, H.L. (2003). *American Alchemy: The History of Solid Waste Management in the United States*, 597. Santa Barbara, CA: Forester Press.

Hoornweg, D., and Perinaz, B.-T. (2012). What a waste: a global review of MSW management. Urban Development Series; Knowledge Papers No. 15; 98 p. World Bank, Washington, DC. https://openknowledge.worldbank.org/handle/10986/17388 (accessed 9 September 2018).

Kaplan, P.O., Decarolis, J., and Thorneloe, S. (2009). Is it better to burn or bury waste for clean electricity generation? *Environmental Science & Technology* 43: 1711–1717.

Kaza, S., Yao, L., Bhada-Tata, P., and Van Woerden, F. (2018). *What a Waste 2.0: A Global Snapshot of Solid Waste Management to 2050*, Urban Development Series, 272. Washington, DC: World Bank.

Khan, M.Z.A. and Abu-Ghararah, Z.H. (1991). New approaches for estimating energy content in MSW. *Jr. Environmental Engineering* 117 (3): 376–380.

Kjeldsen, P., Barlaz, M.A., Rooker, A.P. et al. (2002). Present and long-term composition of MSW landfill leachate: a review. *Critical Reviews in Environmental Science and Technology* 32 (4): 297–336. https://doi.org/10.1080/10643380290813462.

Masoner, J.R., Kolpin, D.W., Furlong, E.T. et al. (2014). Contaminants of emerging concern in fresh leachate from landfills in the conterminous Unites States. *Environmental Science Processes & Impacts* https://doi.org/10.1039/c4em00124a.

Mervis, J. (2012). Garbology 101: getting a grip on waste. *Science* 337: 668–672.

Michaels, T., and Krishnan, K. (2018). 2018 Directory of Waste-To-Energy Facilities, 52 p. Energy Recovery Council. http://energyrecoverycouncil.org/wp-content/uploads/2019/01/ERC-2018-directory.pdf (accessed 23 February 2019).

Oweis, I.S. and Khera, R.P. (1998). *Geotechnology of Waste Management*, 472. Boston, MA: PWS Publishing Co.

Pallipparambil, G.R. (n.d.). The Surat Plague and its Aftermath. Montana State University, Entomology Group. http://www.montana.edu/historybug/yersiniaessays/godshen.html (accessed 26 September 2018).

Pohland, F.G. (1975). Accelerated solid waste stabilization and leachate treatment by leachate recycle through sanitary landfills. *Progress in Water Technology* 7: 753–765.

Rathje, W.L. (1989). Rubbish! *The Atlantic Monthly* (December 1989), p. 1–20.

Shah, K.L. (2000). *Basics of Solid and Hazardous Waste Management Technology*, 150–170. Upper Saddle River, New Jersey: Prentice-Hall, Inc.

Tchobanoglous, G., Theisen, H., and Vigil, S. (1993). *Integrated Solid Waste Management: Engineering Principles and Management Issues*, 978. New York: McGraw-Hill, Inc.

The American City (1955). Less Garbage in Kansas City, 70:10. p. 9.

UAE *Barq* (2020). Mohammed bin Rashid reviews Dubai waste to energy project. https://www.uaebarq.ae/en/2020/10/31/mohammed-bin-rashid-reviews-dubai-waste-to-energy-project/ (accessed 31 October 2020).

UNEP (United Nations Environmental Programme) (2015). Global Waste Management Outlook, 332 p.

U.S. Department of Labor, Bureau of Labor Statistics (2017). National census of fatal occupational injuries, News Release. No. USDL-17-1667, 10 p.; (19 December 2017). https://www.bls.gov/news.release/archives/cfoi_12192017.pdf (accessed 24 September 2018).

Walsh, D.C. (2002). Urban residential refuse composition and generation rates for the 20th century. *Environmental Science and Technology* 362: 4936–4942.

Waste Management (2004). Introducing the Bioreactor Landfill, The Next generation of Landfill Technology. http://www.wm.com/thinkgreen/pdfs/bioreactorbrochure.pdf accessed 8 January 2019.

Supplemental Reading

Franklin Associates, Prairie Village, Kansas. A pioneer in U.S. solid waste data collection and analyses, have provided valuable research data and analyses on MSW management in the U.S. since the 1960s. Visit its website for valuable information: http://www.fal.com/solid-waste-management.html

Kaza, S.; Yao, L.; Bhada-Tata, P.; and Van Woerden, F. (2018). *What a Waste 2.0: A Global Snapshot of Solid Waste Management to 2050*. Urban Development Series. Washington, DC: World Bank; 296 p. https://doi.org/10.1596/978-1-4648-1329-0. https://openknowledge.worldbank.org/bitstream/

handle/10986/30317/9781464813290.pdf (accessed November 5 2018). A valuable source for global statistics on MSW.

U.S. EPA. Source of many useful reports and data, going back to 1960, on MSW and other environmental topics. http://www.epa.gov

Web Resources

https://archive.epa.gov/epawaste/nonhaz/municipal/web/html/index.html. US EPA website has useful information and link to related information.

https://www.epa.gov/smm/wastewiswe. This EPA program was launched in 1994 to encourage organizations and businesses to achieve sustainability in their practices and reduce waste. WasteWise is part of EPA's sustainable materials management efforts, which promote the use and reuse of materials more productively over their entire life cycles.

https://www.unenvironment.org/explore-topics/resource-efficiency/what-we-do/cities/solid-waste-management. This United Nations' Environment Programme (UNEP) website is a valuable source of information on global waste management and statistics. Many of its comprehensive reports are available for free download.

https://www.waste.ccacoalition.org/. Maintained by Climate and Clean Air Coalition. Contains information on cities and national governments in their efforts to reduce short-lived climate pollutants from the waste industry, including information from cities that are already taking action to mitigate these pollutants.

https://www.epa.gov/smm/sustainable-materials-management-web-academy. US EPA Solid Waste Academy offers expert's views on a variety of topics, key issues and best management practices on sustainable (waste) materials management presented in webinars. Past webinars are posted and information on upcoming webinars are also available.

https://www.iswa.org/. International Solid waste Association (ISWA) is an excellent resource for all aspects of MSW. Provides information on global waste management situation. Publishes books and reference materials in collaboration with reputed publishers, such as Wiley, covering various topics related to waste management. The section "ISWA Knowledge Base" on the website has a library of reports on various topics relevant to waste issues that can be downloaded free of charge.

https://swana.org/. Official website of the Solid Waste Association of North America (SWANA), one of the largest organizations focusing on solid waste. Provides useful information on solid waste management, and training opportunities. The website contains useful educational materials.

Acronyms/Symbols

ac	acre(s)
AFSCME	American Federation of State, County, and Municipal Employees
AFL-CIO	American Federation of Labor and Congress of Industrial Organizations
BP	Before present (about 2000 years from the beginning of the common era, AD)
BRLF	Bioreactor landfill
ft	foot (feet)
g	gram(s), also for gravitational constant
g/MWh	gram/megawatt-hour
GHGs	Greenhouse gases
ha	hectare(s)

in	inch
kWh	kilowatt/hour
mi	mile(s)
mo	month(s)
MW	Megawatts (electricity)
Mt	million metric tons
MS/m	Megasiemens/m
MSW	Municipal solid waste
$MTCO_2e/MWh$	Metric ton equivalent of CO_2/megawatt-hour
MWh	Megawatt/hour
NAACP	National Association for Advancement of Colored People
n.d.	No date
NIMBY	Not in my backyard
NOx	Various nitrogen gases
SCLC	Southern Christian Leadership Conference
SOx	Various sulfur gases
t	(metric) ton
USPHS	United States Public Health Service
y	year(s)

5

Hazardous Waste

LEARNING OBJECTIVES

After studying this chapter, you will be able to:

- Differentiate between a hazardous substance and a hazardous waste
- Explain health problems caused by hazardous waste mismanagement
- Interpret the US and EU classification of hazardous waste
- Describe sources and generators of hazardous waste
- Acquire sound knowledge on storage, transportation, treatment, and disposal of hazardous waste
- Summarize US laws regulating hazardous waste

5.1 Introduction

The infamous story of an abandoned chemical dump site – Love Canal – near Buffalo, in New York State, caught the media attention in the late 1960s, making hazardous waste a familiar term to the public. In fact, the Love Canal tragedy is not only an excellent case study of how careless dumping of toxic chemical waste could adversely impact the health and well-being of people but also about how sustained and dedicated efforts by ordinary citizens can awaken the conscience of a nation, forcing legislation for the protection of human health and the environment.

> Even more sobering, we spray, eat, wash with, and generally douse our world with thousands of chemicals designed to make a better life for mankind. Are they all safe? How many, like the DDT still made and sold outside the U.S., are quietly poisoning our environment? How many are more deadly than the problems they seek to solve?
> —*William E. Garrett (1985)* National Geographic, *Vol. 167, No. 3.*
> [Editorial in March, 1985 issue of the *National Geographic* on buy-out of the town of Times Beach, a Superfund site near St. Louis, Missouri, following the discovery of dioxin].

The Love Canal movement, spearheaded by ordinary citizens, produced two ground-breaking outcomes: (i) enactment of the Comprehensive Environmental Response, Compensation, and Liability Act (CERCLA), commonly known as the Superfund (discussed in Chapter 3), and (ii) creation of a new federal organization: Agency for Toxic Substances and Disease Registry (ATSDR), charged with the protection of public health from hazardous waste. In addition, the grassroots-level efforts gave birth to modern environmental activism that has inspired numerous communities globally to successfully fight for remediation of toxic waste sites and restoration of their living environments.

Following World War II, industries in the US and many other developed countries began large-scale production of goods and materials, using a wide variety of organic and inorganic chemicals, many of which are highly toxic. Adverse effects of such chemicals were known to scientists but the factory owners did not take any measure to control the harmful impacts on human and ecological health during product-manufacturing and post-manufacturing phases. Workers were routinely exposed to toxic fumes, heavy metal particles, and organic compounds, impairing their health. Wastes coming from the manufacturing processes that almost always contained toxic chemicals were dumped into the nearest available water bodies or land at the convenience of the owner. This was a common and socially acceptable practice that resulted in contamination of about 40 000 sites across the United States, and 342 000 in Europe (EEA 2014), the majority of them containing carcinogenic compounds that contaminated drinking water supplies, and resulted in adverse health impacts to the population. The Resource Conservation and Recovery Act (RCRA) was passed in 1976 to prevent illegal dumping and ensure proper management of waste. RCRA provides strict control by requiring waste generators to manage hazardous waste from *cradle to grave*, i.e. from the time it is generated to its ultimate disposal. Details of the RCRA compliance requirements and other rules are discussed in Section 5.2.

5.1.1 Hazardous Substance and Hazardous Waste

We start with clarifying the difference between hazardous substances and hazardous waste. A hazardous substance is any material, natural or man-made, that is capable of causing harm to humans and/or living organisms. Some naturally occurring elements, such as Cd, Cr, Se, Rn, and others, along with thousands of synthetic organic and inorganic chemicals, are examples of hazardous substances. However, a hazardous *substance*, benzene, for example, is not considered hazardous *waste* as long as it is properly inventoried, labeled, and stored in the laboratory or the factory. But when an empty bottle of benzene, containing even a minute quantity, is thrown into the trash can, not only the empty bottle but all other trash in the bin, even if they are nonhazardous, would be considered hazardous waste. The key point is that when hazardous substances are no longer of any use, discarded, or abandoned, and become part of the waste stream, then and only then do they become hazardous waste, requiring a complex set of legal compliance at every step – from record keeping, reporting, storage, transportation, treatment, to final disposal. On the other hand, a waste containing hazardous substance, awaiting treatment to recover the hazardous substance (for reuse or recycling), is not hazardous waste and would not be subject to similar legal requirements.

5.1.2 Environmental and Health Problems

Mismanagement of hazardous waste, including "no action," can and has adversely impacted human and ecological health. Love Canal (Case Study 5.1) is an excellent example. A wide range of health problems resulting from pollution of surface and groundwater; soil, and air, have been reported from the world over. Minamata disease in Japan; lead poisoning in the US Midwestern states of Kansas, Missouri, and Oklahoma (Case Study 5.2); and cancer cases in the states of Punjab and Haryana in India are a few of the numerous examples. Some popular Hollywood movies, such as *A Civil Action* (1998) and *Erin Brockovich* (2000) have effectively highlighted the human sufferings resulting from hazardous waste mismanagement. The former highlighted the afflictions of

---

Case Study 5.1   Love Canal, Niagara Falls, New York.

5.1.1 Introduction

Love Canal is the name of an abandoned hazardous waste dump in the town of Niagara Fall in New York State. It made history in the 1970s for being the first contaminated site causing cancer and other health problems, including mortality and morbidity from careless dumping of toxic chemicals. Grassroots efforts by Love Canal residents triggered the passage of important environmental laws in the US and gave rise to modern environmental activism worldwide.

5.1.2 Historical Background

Love Canal, located in Niagara Falls, New York state, was named after William Love, who planned a massive economic development in the closing years of the 1890s, consisting of a model city and a long canal to divert Niagara River water for hydroelectric power generation. Groundbreaking for the canal, that came to be known as Love Canal, took place in March 1894; and with a massive contingent of workers, aided by excavators, dredgers, mules, etc., a large section of the canal, about 6-km-long, 24.4-m-wide and ranging in depth from 3–4.5 m was excavated in a little over two years. But soon Love ran into financial problems that led him to abandon the project. The abandoned excavation, partially filled with water, was mainly used for recreational purposes.

By the 1920s, the Niagara Falls region had become a thriving chemical manufacturing center, producing large quantities of industrial-grade chemicals. By the late 1930s, the place became a world leader in the production of organic and inorganic chemicals, such as chlorine, degreasing organic solvents, explosives, plastics, pesticides, and other chemicals. Initially, the Hooker family had established a very successful chemical plant to manufacture two important industrial chemicals: bleaching powder (CaCl) and caustic soda (NaOH). Later, during the 1940s, its business was booming and the Hooker Chemicals & Plastics Corporation (HC&PC) was producing DDT, PVCs, polyester resins, lindane and other pesticides, etc. HC&PC was renamed Occidental Chemical Corporation (OCC) that disposed of about 20 000 Mt of chemical waste comprising many toxic chemicals, including dioxins and pesticides, into the abandoned Love Canal between 1942 and 1953, contaminating soil and groundwater. In April 1953, OCC sold the landfill for a single dollar to the Niagara Falls School Board. One of the clauses in the property deed stated "…that the premises…had been filled, in whole or in part, to the present grade level thereof with waste products resulting from the manufacturing of chemicals by the grantor at its plant in the city of Niagara Falls, New York and the grantee assumes all risks and liability incident to the use thereof" (Newman 2016, p. 88). Afterward, the area near the covered landfill was extensively developed, which included an elementary school and many residential properties.

5.1.3 Environmental Issues and Remediation

Complaints about odors and residues were first reported during the 1960s, which intensified during the 1970s. Local residents noticed foul odors and chemical residues and experienced increased rates of cancer and other health problems. In 1978 and 1980, President Carter declared two federal environmental emergencies for Love Canal, and about 950 families were evacuated from their homes within a 10-square-block area surrounding the landfill. The fenced 28.3-hectare site includes the original 6.5-hectare hazardous waste landfill and a 16.2-hectare cap, as well as a drainage system and leachate collection and treatment system that are in place and operating (EPA 1988).

In September 1983, EPA listed the site on its NPL and initiated clean up actions in collaboration with New York State. Remedial action was carried out in several phases that included: landfill containment, and leachate collection, treatment and disposal; excavation and treatment of the sewer and creek sediment and other wastes; cleanup of the 93rd Street School soils; and purchase, maintenance, and rehabilitation of properties. The New York State Department of Environmental Conservation (NYSDEC) completed all remedial work in 1999, which took 21 years at a cost of $400 million. Currently, an EPA contractor is managing Love Canal operations, which includes oversight of the Treatment Facility, an inspection of the integrity of the landfill cap, and annual monitoring of over 150 groundwater wells, both inside and outside the fenced area. The contractor is required to submit annual reports of its activities that are reviewed by the EPA and NYSDEC. Based on the review of the annual reports along with three five-year performance reports (2003, 2008, and 2013), the agencies have concluded that all systems have been operating as designed.

Cleanup actions, according to EPA, have produced the desired remedy, and Love Canal no longer presents a threat to human health and the environment. In September 2004, the EPA delisted Love Canal from the NPL. As a result of the revitalization efforts of the Love Canal Area Revitalization Agency, new homeowners have moved into the habitable areas of the site. More than 260 formerly abandoned homes in the affected area were rehabilitated and sold to new residents.

Love Canal became a classic example of adverse environmental impact from past industrial activities and the power of grassroots movement by citizens, and gave rise to modern environmental activism. Relentless efforts by ordinary citizens ultimately led to the passage of CERCLA in 1980, and the creation of the ATSDR soon afterward.

References

EPA (2018). Love Canal, Niagara Falls, NY; Cleanup Activities. https://cumulis.epa.gov/supercpad/SiteProfiles/index.cfm?fuseaction=second.Cleanup&id=0201290#bkground (accessed 14 June 2018).

Newman, R.S; 2016. Love Canal: A Toxic History from Colonial Times to the Present, Oxford University Press, New York, NY; 306 p.

Case Study 5.2 Tri-State Mining District Superfund Site, Cherokee County, Kansas

The TSMD is a world-famous mining area noted for its Missouri Valley-type (MVT) deposit of lead and zinc ores. It extends across three states, southeast Kansas, southwest Missouri, and northeast Oklahoma, in the US Midwest, and covers a total area of about $64\,750\,km^2$ (Figure 5.2A). The TSMD was one of the major producers of lead (Pb) and zinc (Zn) in the world for over a century. At one time, about 65 different mining companies were operating in the region, managing 135 mines and 248 mills, and employing more than 11 000 people. However, production declined after World War II and by 1958, most companies had folded their operations.

Galena (PbS) – the main ore of Pb – along with sphalerite (ZnS), occurs in cherty limestone of Mississippian age (350 million years). Mining in the TSMD commenced around 1850 and the last mine closed in 1970. The room-and-pillar method was the most prevalent mining technique used to extract the ores, along with open-pit mining for surficial deposits in the early days. During this 120-year period, about 482 million t of ores were produced, yielding

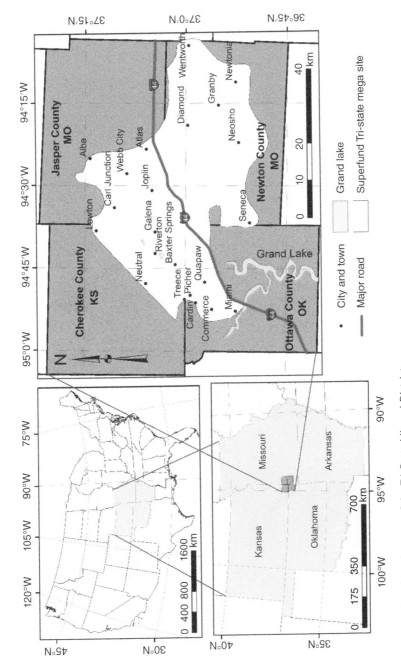

Figure 5.2A Location map of the Tri-State Mineral District.

approximately 25 million t of Pb and Zn concentrates. At the same time mining, processing, and extraction of Pb and Zn left behind over 454 million t of mine waste, processing mills debris, and smelter dust, containing Pb, Zn, Cd, and S that were deposited in the area. As of 2007, about 75% of the waste had been removed (EPA 2007). It is estimated that a total area of about 1700 km^2 was affected by heavy metal contamination (Manders and Aber 2014).

5.4.1 Health and Environmental Problems in Tri-State Mining District

As early as the first decade of the twentieth century, cases of respiratory tract ailments, notably silicosis and tuberculosis, (TB), were common among the miners. In the 1920s, the US Government had taken special measures to reduce the incidence of TB, which was higher than the national average. But the poor air quality in the underground mines and toxic metal dust in the air released from processing and smelting plants, exacerbated the problem so much so that by the 1930s TSMD had the highest rate of TB in the country.

With the decline of large-scale mining operations by the 1950s, and shutting off the pumps to dewater the mines, combined with increased "pillar robbing" to extract the remaining ore, extensive subsidence occurred in the region. One estimate puts the number of collapsed shafts and "sink holes" at about 2600 (Mine Shaft Subcommittee 2000, p. 10). These depressions later became a dumping ground for all kinds of discarded materials (Figure 5.2B).

The network of mine openings, along with the elimination of dewatering operations, led to sulfur and heavy metals-laden waters from the deep aquifers to drain into surface water bodies, resulting in large-scale acid mine drainage (AMD). At the same time, fine metal dust from smelters, and chat (waste rock pieces containing traces of Pb, Zn, and other metals) on

Figure 5.2B Trash dumping near a water-filled subsidence feature over a collapsed mine, Cherokee County Superfund Site, Kansas. *Source:* S.E. Hasan.

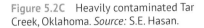

Figure 5.2C Heavily contaminated Tar Creek, Oklahoma. *Source:* S.E. Hasan.

the ground, also added toxic materials to the streams. Tar Creek, one of the streams in the TSMD, was designated by EPA in 1981, as the worst polluted stream in the country (Figure 5.2C).

Domestic animals and wildlife were also adversely impacted by metal contamination. Lead and zinc poisoning was found in wild birds – American robins, northern cardinals, and waterfowl. In addition, the increasing incidence of lead poisoning in children and adults raised serious concerns leading the EPA to place the TSMD on NPL for immediate remedial action.

5.4.2 Tri-State Mining District Remediation Under the Superfund Program

With the unraveling of health and environmental problems in the TSMD, the EPA commenced investigations in the early 1980s to assess the nature and extent of the problem and develop a remediation program. This mega Superfund site – the largest in the United States – was divided into four separate sites: (i) The Cherokee County Superfund Site (CCSS) in Kansas, final listing on NPL: September 1983; impacted area: 298 km^2, (ii) The Tar Creek Superfund Site (TCSS) in Oklahoma, final listing on NPL: September 1983; impacted area: 104 km^2, (iii) The Oronogo-Duenweg Mining Belt in Jasper County Superfund Site (JCSS) in Missouri, final listing on NPL: August 1990; impacted area: 648 km^2 – largest, and (iv) The Newton County Superfund Site (NCSS), also in Missouri, final listing on NPL: July 2000, impacted area: 418 km^2 (includes contaminated groundwater and mine waste). To facilitate remediation operations, and based on technical and administrative considerations, each of four Superfunds sites was divided into subsites that were further subdivided into Operational Units (OUs). For example, CCSS has nine OUs; TCSS and JCSS have five OUs each; and NCSS has two OUs.

Since the protection of public health is the top priority, water supplies drawn from contaminated shallow aquifers were prohibited and bottled water was supplied to the residents until a new water supply system was put in place. Additionally, residential yards and gardens where the level of Pb was found to be 800 ppm or higher were excavated down to 25 cm depth, contaminated soil removed and replaced by clean soil; and the yard was fertilized and seeded. Other remediation works included:

- Removal of metals-contaminated mining and milling wastes, soils, and sediment in streams
- Disposal of the contaminated wastes, soils, and sediment in a central repository
- Capping of the repository with a 0.46-m-thick soil layer
- Recontouring the excavated areas to promote drainage
- Revegetation of the excavated areas and the repository with native vegetation
- Establishing institutional controls to restrict the future use of the disposal area

Monitoring of streams and additional remediation work are still continuing.

References

EPA (2007). Tri-State Mining District-Chat Mine Waste. *Report No. EPA530-F-07-016B (unpaginated)*. https://archive.epa.gov/epawaste/nonhaz/industrial/special/web/pdf/fsr67-607.pdf (accessed 10 September 2018).

Manders, G.G; and Aber, J. S; 2014. Tri-state mining district legacy in Northeastern Oklahoma, *Emporia State Research Studies*, Vol. 49, no. 2, p. 29–51

Mine Shaft Subcommittee (2000). Final Report to Governor Frank Keating's Tar Creek Superfund Task Force, 1 October 2000. Oklahoma Secretary of Environment, Oklahoma City, 23 p. and appendices.

adults and young children in Woburn, Massachusetts, who developed leukemia from drinking groundwater contaminated with trichloroethylene (TCE) – a deadly carcinogen – that was part of the hazardous waste carelessly dumped by WR Grace Company, Beatrice Foods, and UniFirst, in the 1980s (Case Study 5.3). TCE concentrations in shallow wells installed at the Grace facility were found to be in excess of 8000 μg/L and at the Beatrice Foods, over 400 000 μg/L. For comparison, the safe level of TCE concentration in the US drinking water supply, set by EPA, is 5 μg/L (ppm) or 0.005 mg/L (5 ppb), and by the World Health Organization (WHO) 35 μg/L.

Erin Brockovich portrayed the health problems and struggle of the small community of Hinkley in southern California, where residents ingested drinking water contaminated with hexavalent chromium, a known carcinogen, and suffered from a variety of health problems, including cancer. Careless management of hazardous waste by the Pacific Gas and Electric Company from 1952 to 1966 at its Hinkley Gas Compressor Station resulted in aquifer contamination, which was the sole source of drinking water supply for the community.

Case Study 5.3   Drinking Water Well Contamination, Woburn, Massachusetts

Woburn, an industrial city in Massachusetts, U.S.A; is located 21 km (13 mi) northwest of Boston. A small stream, known as the Aberjona River – 15 km (9.3 mi) long, with a 65 km^2 (25 mi^2) basin – flows through Woburn and empties into the Mystic Lakes. The River, now completely urbanized, was used as a dumping area for toxic wastes generated from leather, textiles, paper, pesticides, chemicals, plastics, and uniform cleaning, machine tools, metal parts, and food products manufacturing industries since the early 1900s (Heneghan, 2000).

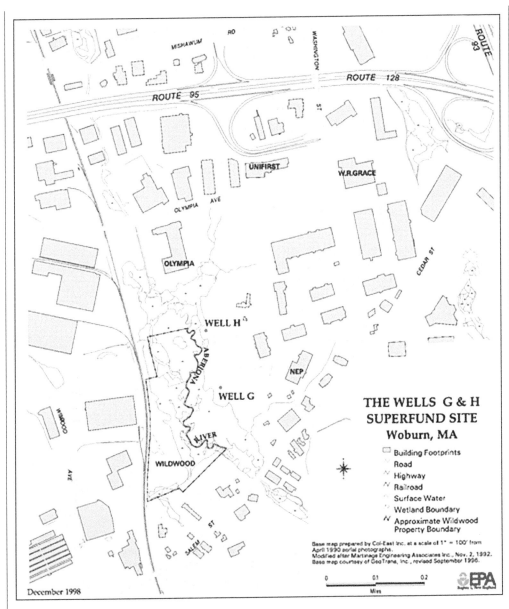

Figure 5.3A   Water supply wells G and H, and other contaminated sites, Woburn, MA. *Source:* EPA 1998.

To meet the growing water supply demand of the residents, the City of Woburn developed Wells G & H in 1964, to supplement the existing municipal water supply, providing 30% of the municipal water supply until 1979 (Fig. 5.3A).

During this period, citizens complained of bad taste and odor of their drinking water. Investigations by city police found about two hundred 55-gallon drums of industrial waste that were abandoned on a vacant lot near the wells. EPA found five properties contributing bulk of the pollutants: (1) a machine tool plant operated by William R. Grace Co; (2) a vacant 15-acre former tannery operations owned by Beatrice Foods Co; (3) industrial dry cleaning facility owned by UniFirst; (4) a vinyl siding manufacturing operation, owned by the New England Plastics Corp; and (5) an undeveloped parcel of land, belonging to the Olympia

Table 5.3A   Contaminants concentration in Wells G and H.

Contaminant	Well G & H concentration, ppb	EPA drinking water MCL, ppb
Trichloroethylene (TCE)	267.4	5
Tetrachloroethylene (PCE)	20.8	5
1,2 Dichloromethane	53	0.1
Arsenic (As)	10	10

Nominee Trust Corp; that had leased it for a truck terminal. Testing by the Massachusetts Department of Environmental Protection revealed high levels of TCE, PCE, chloroform, 1, 2 dichloroethane, As, Pb, pesticides, PCBs, contaminating the groundwater. The wells were shut down in 1979. Many of these chemicals, such as TCE, As, PCBs, have been listed as human carcinogen by EPA, WHO, ATSDR, and the National Toxicology Program (NTP).

Residents' health were adversely impacted from drinking contaminated water. They were exposed to TCE by ingesting the contaminated drinking water and by inhaling the air, mixed with TCE, by using the water for baths, showers, and clothes washing. One child died of leukemia between 1969 and 1973, but five death occurred during 1974-1978. Eighteen adults died from leukemia between 1974 and 1978, when only three deaths were expected due to leukemia. Deaths from kidney and prostrate and urinary tract cancers among adult males doubled from 15 during1969-1973 to 30 from 1974 to 1978. Table 5.3A shows elevated levels of various chemicals in Wells G and H along with their safe levels (MCL set by EPA).

The Woburn site was placed on NPL in 1982, and full-scale investigation commenced at the 330-acre site in 1985. The Olympia Trust site owners were ordered to remove contaminated drums in 1986. Treatment and monitoring wells were installed near G & H sites in 1987. In 1990, EPA negotiated a record-breaking Superfund settlement for cleanup of municipal Wells G & H in Woburn, Massachusetts. EPA and Massachusetts State reached a $69.45 million settlement with W.R. Grace & Company, UniFirst Corporation, New England Plastics, Beatrice Company, Wildwood Conservation Corporation and John J. Riley, Jr. for the cleanup of contaminated properties and additional studies.

Investigation for site remediation began in 1983 that included removal of drums and debris from the site; excavation and removal of contaminated soil and sediment; pump-and-treat and soil vapor extraction (SVE) systems to clean contaminated groundwater and VOCs. Closely spaced treatment wells at the W.R. Grace property used H_2O_2 and UV oxidation to remove VOCs. At the UniFirst site a deep well extending down into the fractured bedrock, uses H_2O_2, UV oxidation, and GAC to treat contaminated groundwater. At the Wildwood and New England Plastics sites, air sparging, SVE, and GAC were used to treat contaminated groundwater and air. Remediation work is continuing at these sites, and at the Olympia Nominee Trust, Whitney Barrel, Murphy Waste Oil, and Aberjona Auto Parts properties.

References

Heneghan, A.K; 2000. The legacy of Woburn, Massachusetts and Trichloroethylene. Research paper, University of Idaho, 23 p. Available at: http://www.webpages.uidaho.edu/etox/resources/case_studies/woburn.pdf ,Accessed August 5, 2018.

EPA, 1993, Superfund at Work: Cleanup Begins at Wells G&H, One Year After Landmark New England Settlement, EPA 520-F-22-015, 6 p. Available at: file:///F:/Book%202%20Wiley/Ch%205%20 Hazwaste/Writing%20Materials/Woburn%20Site.pdf Accessed July 6, 2019.

Numerous cases of adverse impacts from waste mismanagement, such as pollution of water bodies; contamination of land from careless dumping of industrial and mining wastes causing adverse impacts on wildlife and human health; increased incidence of asthma and other respiratory track illnesses related to harmful gases, volatile organic compounds (VOCs), heavy metals, and particulate matters (PMs) released into the air, have been well documented. For example, effluents from industrial plants and manufacturing facilities, discharged into the Cuyahoga River, Ohio, in the Cincinnati area, led to several episodes of the Cuyahoga River catching fire, that were reported in the *Time* magazine (Time 1969). A detailed discussion, including historical fires, and efforts leading to the amendment of the Water Pollution Control Act, now known as the Clean Water Act, is available in Adler (2002). Health and ecological impacts to humans, animals, plants, and water bodies, resulting from century-old mining of lead and zinc in the Tri-State Mining District (TSMD), covering an area of about $65\,000\,km^2$ in southwestern Missouri, southeastern Kansas, and northeastern Oklahoma, in the United States, have been documented by Beyer et al. (2004), and Manders and Aber (2014). Case Study 5.2 discusses health and environmental problems and long-drawn remediation efforts at the Tri-State Superfund site.

Air pollution from uncontrolled waste dumping, still widely practiced in many developing countries, causes a variety of health problems, notably ailments of the respiratory tract. A comprehensive review of health impacts from toxic air pollutants in selected cities in developing countries has been reported by Saliba et al. (2016).

5.2 US Laws Regulating Hazardous Waste

Major environmental disasters of the 1960s along with the tragic tale of Love Canal, and the discovery of other toxic dumps, resulted in the enactment of several environmental laws, during the decades of 1970s and 1980s, to preserve the environment and protect public health. Chapter 3 includes a detailed description of environmental laws; here we present a discussion of US laws that specifically address hazardous waste.

Two laws – the RCRA and the CERCLA – and their amendments, form the backbone of legislation that controls the management of hazardous waste in the United States. These laws along with others that relate to the control of hazardous substances and waste are listed below:

1) Resource Conservation and Recovery Act (RCRA) of 1976
2) Toxic Substances Control Act (TSCA) of 1976
3) Comprehensive Environmental Response Compensation and Liability Act (CERCLA) of 1980
4) Hazardous and Solid Waste Amendments (HSWA) of 1984
5) Underground Storage Tanks Act (USTA) of 1984
6) Superfund Reauthorization and Amendments Act (SARA) of 1986
7) Emergency Planning and Community-Right-to-Know Act (EPCRA) of 1986
8) Frank R. Lautenberg Chemical Safety for the 21st Century Act (the Lautenberg Chemical Safety Act) of 2016.

5.2.1 Resource Conservation and Recovery Act

RCRA, by far, is the most comprehensive law that was passed by the US Congress in 1976. The regulations are codified in the Code of Federal Regulations (CFR) that the EPA developed pursuant to the congressional mandate. RCRA covers every aspect of hazardous waste management – the entire life cycle of the waste: from the time hazardous materials are received at the manufacturing facility, through the various production stages, to its final disposal. Because of its inclusive nature, the law has also been referred to as the *cradle-to-grave* rule.

RCRA regulates all hazardous waste generated since its passage, i.e. from 1976 onward. RCRA is organized into four statutes as follows:

- Subtitle C: regulates hazardous waste
- Subtitle D: regulates solid (nonhazardous) waste
- Subtitle I: regulates underground storage tanks (USTs); added to RCRA in 1994
- Subtitle J: Medical waste tracking act, provides guidelines for the management of medical waste; added in November 1988.

RCRA has provisions to add new subtitles as and when needed.

Subtitles C, I, and J are discussed in Chapter 3 and in Chapters 4 and 6. Here we discuss details of Subtitle C that relates to hazardous waste.

The three primary goals of RCRA are to:

1) Ensure protection of human health and environment through effective waste management
2) Conserve materials and energy resources through waste recycling and recovery, and
3) Reduce or eliminate waste quantities as expeditiously as possible.

A set of detailed rules and regulations have been developed by the EPA to accomplish the goals. These rules apply to all parties – at federal, state, and local levels and Indian tribes – that are involved in the generation, transportation, storage, treatment, and disposal of hazardous waste. All parties are also required to adopt measures to conserve resources and minimize waste quantities.

5.2.2 Toxic Substances Control Act

The Toxic Substances Control Act (TSCA) of 1976 was enacted in the wake of concerns about dichlorodiphenyltrichloroethane (DDT) and polychlorinated biphenyls (PCB) to regulate harmful chemicals. The TSCA Registry contains a list of 83 000 chemicals that were in use to manufacture industrial, consumer, and food products. Any newly manufactured or imported chemical must be entered in the Registry. However, the majority of these chemicals have not been tested for their toxicity. In addition, 64 000 chemicals were allowed to be used without requiring any testing (grandfathered). The law has been ineffective and EPA has banned only two chemicals since the inception of the law: PCB and asbestos (DDT was banned in 1972 prior to the enactment of TSCA). To correct these problems, a new law, known as the Frank R. Lautenberg Chemical Safety for the 21st Century Act, was passed in June 2016.

5.2.3 Comprehensive Environmental Response, Compensation, and Liability Act

As stated before, RCRA regulates hazardous waste generated since 1976 and into the future. However, thousands of sites where hazardous wastes were dumped before 1976 existed in the country, which is not regulated by RCRA. In order to cover such sites, a new law was passed in 1980. CERCLA, came to be known as *Superfund* because of a large amount of money, $1.6 billion, which was appropriated by the US Congress for EPA to clean up the worst contaminated sites. The goals of the Superfund program are fourfold:

1) Protect human health and the environment by cleaning up polluted sites
2) Make responsible parties pay for cleanup work (*polluter pays*)
3) Involve impacted communities in the Superfund process, and
4) Return Superfund sites to productive use

EPA developed the Hazard Ranking System (HRS) to characterize a Superfund site in terms of its severity to cause harm to human health and/or the environment. HRS is used by the EPA or state agencies to calculate a site score (range: 1–100) based on the actual or potential release of hazardous substances from the site through air, surface water, or groundwater. An HRS score of 28.5 qualifies it to be placed on the National Priorities List (NPL) for cleanup action under the Superfund program. As of February 2021, a total of 1327 sites (that includes 157 federal sites) were listed on the NPL. The rate of cleanup and deletion from NPL is subject to budget appropriation from the US Congress which changes on a periodic basis.

CERCLA is based on the concept of *polluter pays* and includes several liability provisions on part of anyone who was involved in the hazardous waste right from the time of its generation to disposal and all stages in between. Three types of liability provisions exist in CERCLA:

1) *Strict liability*, under which the owner of a property contaminated with hazardous waste is responsible for cleanup, even though the contamination was caused by previous owner(s).
2) *Joint and several liability*, under which a party can be liable for the whole cleanup, even though it may have been responsible only for a small part of the overall contamination.
3) *Retroactive liability*, under which a party is responsible for cleanup, even though the contamination may have happened long before CERCLA was enacted.

These provisions were considered draconian, beyond the scope of common laws, and were widely criticized leading EPA to soften it by allowing exceptions in case of inheriting a property that contained hazardous waste, or when the buyer of a contaminated property made due diligence to ascertain its nature by completing an environmental audit of the property.

5.2.4 Hazardous and Solid Waste Amendments

HSWA Act was promulgated in 1984 as an amendment to RCRA to broaden its scope by including provisions to protect the quality of groundwater. This led to restricting land disposal of hazardous waste by landfilling or surface impoundments. It established the requirement for double liners, leachate management systems, and groundwater monitoring programs at disposal sites. Technical standards for landfill design, leak detection systems, and related hazardous substances were developed in pursuance of the Act. HSWA also set new requirements for the management and treatment of small quantities of hazardous waste, such as those generated by automotive shops or dry-cleaning businesses. It also established new regulations for underground tanks that store petroleum or other chemicals. Waste minimization, corrective action for release of hazardous substances, increased enforcement authority for EPA, and more stringent hazardous waste management standards are some of the other provisions of HSWA.

5.2.5 Underground Storage Tanks Act

Responding to public outcry from increasing threat to groundwater caused by leaking underground storage tanks (LUSTs), the US Congress in 1984 added Subtitle I to the Solid Waste Disposal

Act (SWDA) of 1976. The law required preventive measures – such as spill, overfill, and corrosion protection – release detection, corrective action, and demonstration of financial ability to perform corrective actions. HSWA directed EPA to develop a comprehensive regulatory program for USTs that stored petroleum or other hazardous substances, to protect the environment and human health from UST releases. In 1988, EPA issued detailed regulations that set minimum standards for new USTs and required owners of existing tanks to upgrade, replace, or close them. EPA asked owners of LUSTs to upgrade and bring their facility in compliance with new regulations by December 1998 (in 10 years). It imposed a fine of $10 000/day for delay or permanent closure for noncompliance. About 2.1 million USTs were in existence in 1984, of which 1.8 million were closed and 553 000 are in operation at 200 000 sites in the USA. In view of the very large number of USTs, EPA designated states to implement the program. In 1986, Congress amended Subtitle I of SWDA and created the LUST Trust Fund that is financed by a 0.1 cent federal tax on each gallon of motor fuel sold in the country. As of July 2021, the balance in the Fund was approximately $22.7 billion.

5.2.6 Superfund Amendments and Reauthorization Act

The Superfund Amendments and Reauthorization Act (SARA) (enacted 17 October 1986) was an amendment to CERCLA. SARA incorporated EPA's experience in managing the complex Superfund program during its first six years, and made several important changes and additions to the program. SARA:

- stressed the importance of permanent remedies and innovative treatment technologies in cleaning up hazardous waste sites;
- required Superfund actions to consider the standards and requirements found in other State and Federal environmental laws and regulations;
- provided new enforcement authorities and settlement tools;
- increased State involvement in every phase of the Superfund program;
- increased the focus on human health issues from hazardous waste sites;
- encouraged greater citizen participation in making decisions on how sites should be cleaned up;
- increased the size of the trust fund to $8.5 billion, and
- required EPA to revise HRS to accurately assess the relative degree of risk to human health and the environment from uncontrolled hazardous waste sites.

5.2.7 Emergency Planning and Community-Right-to-Know Act

The 2 December 1984 industrial disaster at Bhopal, India, that caused 3800 deaths and also ocular (blindness) and respiratory track injuries to thousands of people as a result of accidental release of highly toxic methyl isocyanate gas from a pesticide-manufacturing plant, owned by Union Carbide, and another accident on 11 August 1985, at a pesticide-manufacturing plant in Institute, W. Virginia, also owned by Union Carbide, led to the passage of EPCRA in 1986. The law aimed at preparing communities to plan for chemical emergencies and establishing reporting requirements for industries on storage, use, and release of hazardous substances. The biennial report, called Toxics Release Inventory (TRI) serves as a useful source of information that can be easily accessed to learn about the use and storage of hazardous and toxic chemicals at various facilities in a community, and their release into the environment. EPA released its latest report in January 2021 for the calendar year 2019.

5.2.8 Frank R. Lautenberg Chemical Safety for the 21st Century Act (Lautenberg Chemical Safety Act)

The TSCA failed to evaluate 64 000 chemicals that were in use prior to 1976 – the enforcement year of TSCA. The law did not make EPA responsible to review the then existing chemicals either. The ineffectiveness of TSCA was raising serious concerns among the public and several failed attempts were made by concerned citizen groups and nongovernmental organizations (NGOs) to change the law but none were successful. Finally, on 22 June 2016, the *Frank Lautenberg Chemical Safety Act for the 21st Century* was enacted and made into law under Public Law, PL 114-182-22 June 2016. The law addresses fundamental flaws in TSCA that for nearly 40 years had limited EPA's ability to protect the public from dangerous chemicals. It is a major victory for chemical safety, public health, and the environment – particularly the mandatory responsibility to evaluate chemicals and risk-based chemical assessments. The salient provisions of the Chemical Safety Act include:

- Mandatory requirement for EPA to evaluate existing chemicals with clear and enforceable deadlines
- Risk-based chemical assessments
- Increased public transparency for chemical information
- A consistent source of funding for EPA to carry out the responsibilities under the new law
- Strict control on the export of toxic mercury compounds.

5.3 Definition and Classification of Hazardous Waste

Simply speaking, hazardous waste is a type of waste that has the potential to produce an adverse impact on human health and/or the environment. However, this simple definition is not adequate from a legal standpoint. Accordingly, to comply with laws dealing with hazardous wastes, the US Congress, in RCRA, defined hazardous waste as "a waste or combination of wastes, which, because of its quantity, concentration, or physical, chemical, or infectious characteristics, may (i) cause or significantly contribute to an increase in mortality or an increase in serious irreversible or incapacitating reversible illness, or (ii) pose a substantial present or potential threat to human health or the environment when improperly treated, stored, transported, or disposed of." Regulatory agencies, such as the United States Environmental Protection Agency (USEPA), and the European Union (EU) have developed detailed rules and tests, along with a special list of chemicals, to identify and manage hazardous waste.

5.3.1 The United States Environmental Protection Agency Criteria

The USEPA considers a waste to be hazardous if: (i) it possesses certain characteristics (ignitibility, corrosivity, reactivity, or toxicity), or (ii) it is on a list of specific wastes or contains chemicals that are determined by the EPA to be hazardous. The former is called characteristic wastes and the latter listed wastes. RCRA regulations, found in CFRs, Part 261 (40 CFR 2012), give the listing of hazardous wastes and also describe hazardous waste characteristics and specify test methods to determine whether or not a waste is hazardous. EPA uses the following three criteria for deciding whether or not to include waste as hazardous:

1) The waste contains toxic chemicals at levels that have the potential to cause adverse effects to humans and/or the environment, if not managed properly. Such wastes are called toxic listed waste.

2) The waste contains such dangerous chemicals that it could pose a threat to human health and the environment even when properly managed. These wastes are fatal to humans and animals even in low doses. Such wastes are known as acute hazardous wastes.

3) The waste typically exhibits one of the four characteristics of hazardous waste: ignitability, corrosivity, reactivity, and toxicity.

According to EPA, waste will be considered hazardous if it meets *any* of the following criteria:

1) It is a *characteristic* waste, i.e. it exhibits any of these four characteristics: (i) ignitibility, (ii) corrosivity, (iii) reactivity, or (iv) toxicity.

2) It is a mixture containing both hazardous and nonhazardous wastes. Exception: The mixture is specifically excluded or no longer exhibits any of the characteristics of hazardous waste.

3) It is *not* excluded from regulation as hazardous waste (a partial list of *excluded* wastes is given in Table 5.1).

4) It contains a "listed" waste, i.e. the waste material is listed as hazardous waste in 40 CFR, Part 261.

5.3.1.1 Listed Waste

A large quantity of waste generated from industrial processes contains harmful chemicals that are included in EPA's lists of hazardous chemicals/wastes. These lists include a wide universe of harmful chemicals, many of which are present in the hazardous waste coming from various sources (some of which are listed in Section 5.4). These wastes are designated by an alphabetic prefix (F, K, P, or U) followed by a three-digit number: for example, F001 includes solvents, such as TCE, etc., that are used as degreasing substances; such chemicals are common bye-products of many industries and are not generated by a specific industry alone. However, unlike the F series, all K series wastes originate from a

Table 5.1 Exempt hazardous waste.

Agricultural waste

Arsenic-treated wood

Cement kiln dust

Fossil fuel combustion waste

Household hazardous waste

Injected groundwater

Landfill leachate or gas condensate derived from certain listed wastes

Mining and mineral processing wastes

Mining overburden

Oil, gas, and geothermal wastes

Petroleum contaminated media and debris from underground storage tanks

Project XL pilot project exclusions

Trivalent chromium wastes

Spent chlorofluorocarbon refrigerants

Used oil distillation bottoms

Used oil filters

specific source. K032, for instance, designates the sludge generated during the production of the pesticide chlordane; K001 represents wastes generated from the wood processing industry that uses creosote or pentachlorophenol for wood preservation. P and U series include pure or commercial grade toxic chemicals. Chemicals are included in the P list if they are acutely hazardous, meaning that they could be fatal to humans in small doses or could cause irreversible or incapacitating illnesses. Wastes containing barium cyanide (P013), dieldrin (P037), phosgene (P095), and other P series substances are examples of acute hazardous wastes. U wastes, because they do not produce similar effects as P series wastes, are considered non-acutely hazardous. P023, for example, includes chloroacetaldehyde; and U002 acetone. 40 CFR Part 261, §261.31, §261.32, and §261.33 contain all four lists along with the four-character alphanumeric codes, name, and CAS reference number for each.

5.3.1.2 Characteristic Waste

EPA has described in detail the terms *ignitibility*, *corrosivity*, *reactivity*, and *toxicity*. The agency has also set specifications and test procedures to determine these characteristics. The rationale is that using these procedures and specifications, it will be easy for waste generators to ascertain if their waste is hazardous because the law puts the responsibility on the waste generators to determine whether their wastes are hazardous or not.

Available test procedures are accurate enough to enable the determination of the four characteristics. Details of test procedures, equipment, data interpretation, and reporting have been standardized in EPA's *Hazardous Waste Test Methods*, commonly known as SW846 (EPA 2018). However, test protocols and data interpretation for measuring carcinogenicity, mutagenicity, phytotoxicity, and potential for bioaccumulation are either poorly developed or are too complex and require high levels of expertise. Because of these limitations, EPA has not included these characteristics in its current definition of hazardous waste. It is likely that with the availability of simpler test procedures and equipment, combined with the desired level of confidence, EPA may, in future, include these characteristics with the four now commonly used to characterize a waste as hazardous. It should be noted that these definitions and tests were developed in the 1980s and experience gained since then, along with new technological developments, may require revision of the standards. For example, EPA was petitioned in September 2011 to change the upper limit of pH range for corrosivity from >12.5 to >11.0. Ammonia, with a pH of 11.5, which is currently a noncorrosive material would be considered corrosive and will expand the universe of waste materials that would need to comply with RCRA hazardous waste regulations. It is known that alkalis can produce more severe damage to the skin than acids, which explains why there was a move for lowering the pH of alkaline waste than the acidic. EPA denied the petition and issued its final ruling in June 2021 (GAO 2021).

- *Corrosivity*: Corrosivity is a measure of the strong chemical reaction of a substance – chemical or waste material – upon contact with an object or another material, to cause irreversible damage by chemical conversion to another material. Hydrogen ion concentration (pH) of the waste is a simple and quick way of determining its corrosivity. Wastes containing materials of very high or very low pH can damage living tissues and produce dangerous reactions with other materials in the waste. A waste is considered corrosive if its representative sample shows either of the following properties:
  1) It is aqueous and has a pH of 2 or less, or greater than or equal to 12.5 (Figure 5.1), as determined by a pH meter, using either an EPA test method or an equivalent test method.
  2) It is a liquid and corrodes steel (SAE 1020) at a rate greater than 6.35 mm (0.25 in.) per year at a test temperature of 55 °C (130 °F), as determined by the test methods specified in the

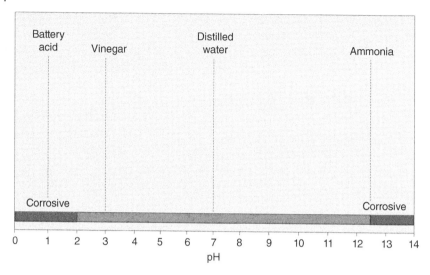

Figure 5.1 pH range for corrosivity characteristic.

National Association of Corrosion Engineers' (NACE) Standard TM016976 (1991), or an equivalent approved test method.

All solid wastes that exhibit corrosivity are assigned EPA Hazardous Waste Code, D002. Acidic wastes (from many industrial processes) and *pickle liquor* (from steel making) are examples of corrosive wastes. Many hazardous wastes contain corrosive materials that can corrode steel drums, resulting in the release of hazardous waste into the environment.

● *Reactivity*: Some hazardous wastes contain materials that may be unstable at ambient conditions of humidity, pressure, and temperature and may have the potential to cause an explosion at any stage of the waste management cycle. Used cyanide solvents and water from TNT operations are examples of reactive wastes.

Solid waste is considered reactive if its representative sample exhibits any of the following properties:

1) It is normally unstable and readily undergoes violent change without detonating
2) It reacts violently with water
3) It forms potentially explosive mixtures with water
4) When mixed with water, it generates toxic gases, vapors, or fumes in a quantity sufficient to present a danger to human health or the environment
5) It is a cylinder of sulfide-bearing waste which, when exposed to pH conditions between 2 and 12.5, can generate toxic gases, vapors, or fumes in a quantity sufficient to present a danger to human health or the environment
6) It is capable of detonation or explosive reaction if it is subjected to a strong initiating source or is heated under confinement
7) It is readily capable of detonation or explosive decomposition or reaction at standard temperature and pressure
8) It is a forbidden explosive as defined in 49 CFR 173.51, a Class A explosive as defined in 49 CFR 173.53, or a Class B explosive as defined in 49 CFR 173.88

All solid wastes that exhibit the characteristic of reactivity are given EPA Hazardous Waste Code D003.

- *Ignitability*: Ignitibility refers to the potential of waste material to cause a fire during storage, disposal, or transport. Ignitable wastes are those that can create fires under certain conditions, are spontaneously combustible, or have a flash point of ⸍60 °C (140 °F). Waste oils and used solvents are good examples of ignitable wastes.

According to the EPA, a representative sample of a waste exhibiting *any* of the following properties will be ruled hazardous if:

1) it is a liquid, other than an aqueous solution containing less than 24% alcohol by volume, and has a flash point of less than 60 °C (140 °F), as determined by a Pensky Martens Closed Cup Tester, using the test method specified in ASTM Standard D93-90 (ASTM 1992), and explained in EPA SW-846 Test Method 1010A; or by a Setaflash Closed Cup Tester, using the test method specified in ASTM Standard 3278-96 (2011);
2) it is not a liquid and is capable, under standard temperature and pressure, of causing fire through friction, absorption of moisture, or spontaneous chemical changes, and when ignited burns so vigorously and persistently that it creates a hazard;
3) it is an ignitable compressed gas as defined in 49 CFR 173.300 and as determined by ASTM Test D323;
4) it is an oxidizer (such as chlorate, permanganate, inorganic peroxides or a mixture that yields O_2 readily) and causes combustion of organic matter.

EPA waste code D001 identifies all flammable wastes. D001 waste could be in liquid, sludge, or solid form.

- *Toxicity*: Toxicity is the ability of a substance to cause death, injury, or impairment to an organism that comes in contact with it. The damaging effects may be systemic, i.e. on the entire body of an organism, such as animal, bacterium, plant; or on an organ or structure of an organism. Examples include: cytotoxicity (toxic effect on a cell); neurotoxicity (toxic effect on the central nervous system); or hepatotoxicity (toxic effect on the liver), etc. Ingestion, inhalation, and dermal contact are common modes of entry of toxic substances into an organism.

The toxicity of waste can be determined by using an EPA test called Toxic Characteristic Leaching Procedure (TCLP), explained in SW846: Hazardous Waste Test Methods, Test # 1311 (EPA 2018). The test identifies the constituents that, when released into the environment, may produce an adverse impact on human health and the environment and can pollute groundwater.

EPA developed the toxicity characteristic test – called TCLP – to identify solid wastes that are likely to leach hazardous constituents into groundwater from improperly managed facilities. The leach test simulates natural leaching action that may occur from a waste disposed of on the land. Solid waste will be considered toxic if, using the test method 1311, the extract from a representative sample of the waste contains any of the contaminants at a concentration equal to or greater than the respective value listed in Table 5.2.

Toxic constituents include organic and inorganic substances, such as benzene, TCE, and many pesticides; or heavy metals, such as arsenic, lead, mercury, etc., they are assigned EPA Hazardous Waste numbers between D004 and D043.

Table 5.2 Maximum concentration of contaminants for toxicity characteristic determination.

EPA HW no.	Contaminant	CAS[a] no.	Regulatory level (mg/L)
D004	Arsenic	7440–38–2	5.0
D005	Barium	7440–39–3	100.0
D018	Benzene	71–43–2	0.5
D006	Cadmium	7440–43–9	1.0
D019	Carbon tetrachloride	56–23–5	0.5
D020	Chlordane	57–74–9	0.03
D021	Chlorobenzene	108–90–7	100.0
D022	Chloroform	67–66–3	6.0
D007	Chromium	7440–47–3	5.0
D023	o-Cresol	95–48–7	200.0
D024	m-Cresol	108–39–4	200.0
D025	p-Cresol	106–44–5	200.0
D026	Cresol	—	200.0
D016	2,4-D	94–75–7	10.0
D027	1,4-Dichlorobenzene	106–46–7	7.5
D028	1,2-Dichloroethane	107–06–2	0.5
D029	1,1-Dichloroethylene	75–35–4	0.7
D030	2,4-Dinitrotoluene	121–14–2	0.13
D012	Endrin	72–20–8	0.02
D031	Heptachlor (and its epoxide)	76–44–8	0.008
D032	Hexachlorobenzene	118–74–1	0.13
D033	Hexachlorobutadiene	87–68–3	0.5
D034	Hexachloroethane	67–72–1	3.0
D008	Lead	7439–92–1	5.0
D013	Lindane	58–89–9	0.4
D009	Mercury	7439–97–6	0.2
D014	Methoxychlor	72–43–5	10.0
D035	Methyl ethyl ketone	78–93–3	200.0
D036	Nitrobenzene	98–95–3	2.0
D037	Pentrachlorophenol	87–86–5	100.0
D038	Pyridine	110–86–1	5.0
D010	Selenium	7782–49–2	1.0
D011	Silver	7440–22–4	5.0
D039	Tetrachloroethylene (TCE)	127–18–4	0.7
D015	Toxaphene	8001–35–2	0.5
D040	Trichloroethylene	79–01–6	0.5
D041	2,4,5-Trichlorophenol	95–95–4	400.0
D042	2,4,6-Trichlorophenol	88–06–2	2.0
D017	2,4,5-TP (Silvex)	93–72–1	1.0
D043	Vinyl chloride	75–01–4	0.2

[a] Chemical abstracts service number.
Source: EPA (2009).

The TCLP test is not required for waste in liquid form because the liquid is considered an extract and analyzed for contaminants listed in Table 5.2.

5.3.2 EU's Classification of Hazardous Waste

The EU has proposed a two-pronged approach to hazardous waste management for use by its member countries. The first is the classification of wastes into different hazard classes, and the second is a code for the entire universe of hazardous waste – called List of Waste (LoW) – for uniform coding and reporting by the member countries; it is intended for accurate statistical record keeping, and data analysis. Table 5.3 shows the various classes of hazardous waste included in of EU's Directive 2008/98/EC (EU 2008).

The directive calls for the revision and addition of new classes of waste to the existing list as and when new information becomes available. For example, wastes from the dismantling and recycling of ships and other transportation vehicles have since been added to the list. The European Union Commission revised the 1994 and 2000 LoWs in 2014 (EU 2014) and developed a comprehensive LoWs that covers all known wastes currently being generated. It is based on a three-tier hierarchical coding system, with a two-digit code for the most general category of waste to six-digit for the

Table 5.3 EU's hazardous waste classes.

Waste code	Waste class	Description
H 1	Explosive	Substances and preparations which may explode under the effect of flame or which are more sensitive to shocks or friction than dinitrobenzene.
H 2	Oxidizing	Substances and preparations which exhibit highly exothermic reactions when in contact with other substances, particularly flammable substances.
H 3-A	Highly flammable	Liquid substances and preparations: having a flash point below 21 °C (including flammable extremely flammable liquids); or that may become hot and finally catch fire in contact with air at ambient temperature without any application of energy; or solid substances and preparations which may readily catch fire after brief contact with a source of ignition and which continue to burn or to be consumed after removal of the source of ignition; or gaseous substances and preparations which are flammable in air at normal pressure; or which upon contact with water or damp air, evolve highly flammable gases in dangerous quantities.
H 3-B	Flammable	Liquid substances and preparations: having a flash point equal to or ≥ 21 and ≤ 55 °C.
H 4	Irritant	Noncorrosive substances and preparations which, through immediate, prolonged or repeated contact with the skin or mucous membrane, can cause inflammation.
H 5	Harmful	Substances and preparations that, when inhaled or ingested or if they penetrate the skin, may involve limited health risks.
H 6	Toxic	Substances and preparations (including very toxic substances and preparations) which upon inhalation or ingestion or if they penetrate the skin, may involve serious, acute, or chronic health risks and even death.

(Continued)

Table 5.3 (Continued)

Waste code	Waste class	Description
H 7	Carcinogenic	Substances and preparations which upon inhalation or ingestion or if they penetrate the skin, may induce cancer or increase its incidence.
H 8	Corrosive	Substances and preparations, which may destroy living tissue on contact.
H 9	Infectious	Substances and preparations containing viable microorganisms or their toxins which are known or reliably believed to cause disease in man or other living organisms.
H 10	Toxic for reproduction	Substances and preparations which, if they are inhaled or ingested, or if they penetrate the skin, may induce nonhereditary congenital malformations or increase their incidence.
H 11	Mutagenic	Substances and preparations which, if they are inhaled or ingested, or if they penetrate the skin, may induce hereditary genetic defects or increase their incidence.
H 12	—	Waste which releases toxic or very toxic gases in contact with water, air or an acid.
H 13	Sensitizing	Substances and preparations which, if they are inhaled, or if they penetrate the skin, can produce a reaction of hypersensitization such that, on further exposure to the substance and preparation, can produce characteristic adverse effects.
H 14	Ecotoxic	Waste which presents or may present immediate or delayed risks for one or more sectors of the environment.
H 15	—	Waste capable by any means, after disposal, of yielding another substance, e.g. a leachate, which produces any of the characteristics listed earlier.

Source: Adapted from EU (2008).

most specific type. For example, waste code 10 includes all wastes generated from thermal processes; those originating from power stations and other thermal plants are identified by the four-digit code 10 01; those from the iron and steel industry by 10 02, and so on. Within each of the various sources, such as waste comprising coal fly ash, is identified by the six-digit code 10 01 01 (most specific), or 10 01 26 wastes from cooling water treatment, etc. Similarly, specific wastes generated in the iron and steel industry are identified as: 10 02 01 for wastes from the processing of slag; 10 02 02 for unprocessed slag; 10 02 10 for mill scales, etc. Details can be found in EU's publication 2014/955/EU (EU 2014). Table 5.4 is a list of two-digit generalized codes for sources generating hazardous waste.

5.4 Sources and Generators of Hazardous Waste

The law defines a generator as any person whose act or process produces hazardous waste, or whose act first causes hazardous waste to become subject to regulation. This places the liability not only on the first producer of the waste but also on those who get involved in its subsequent handling and/or removal. For instance, if the owner of a raw material storage tank hires a contractor

Table 5.4 EU's two-digit codes for wastes from various sources.

Waste code	Waste source
01	Wastes resulting from exploration, mining, quarrying, physical and chemical treatment of minerals
02	Wastes from agriculture, horticulture, aquaculture, forestry, hunting and fishing, food preparation and processing
03	Wastes from wood processing and the production of panels and furniture, pulp, paper and cardboard
04	Wastes from the leather, fur and textile industries
05	Wastes from petroleum refining, natural gas purification and pyrolytic treatment of coal
06	Wastes from inorganic chemical processes
07	Wastes from organic chemical processes
08	Wastes from the manufacture, formulation, supply and use (MFSU) of coatings (paints, varnishes and vitreous enamels), adhesives, sealants and printing inks
09	Wastes from the photographic industry
10	Wastes from thermal processes
11	Wastes from chemical surface treatment and coating of metals and other materials; non-ferrous hydrometallurgy
12	Wastes from shaping and physical and mechanical surface treatment of metals and plastics
13	Oil wastes and wastes of liquid fuels (except edible oils, 05 and 12)
14	Waste organic solvents, refrigerants and propellants (except 07 and 08)
15	Waste packaging; absorbents, wiping cloths, filter materials and protective clothing not otherwise specified
16	Wastes not otherwise specified in the list
17	Construction and demolition wastes (including excavated soil from contaminated sites)
18	Wastes from human or animal health care and/or related research (except kitchen and restaurant wastes not arising from immediate health care)
19	Wastes from waste management facilities, off-site wastewater treatment plants and the preparation of water intended for human consumption and water for industrial use
20	Municipal wastes (household waste and similar commercial, industrial and institutional wastes) including separately collected fractions

Source: Adapted from EU (2014).

to remove waste from the tank, then both the tank cleaner and the tank owner are considered generators according to the EPA definition of generator in 40 CFR, 262.10.

In a strict sense, there is hardly any sector of human activity that does not produce waste that could not be considered hazardous. Besides industrial and manufacturing facilities, common and apparently innocuous establishments, such as beauty salons, dry cleaning shops, automobile repair facilities, and even our homes, produce a certain type of hazardous waste. However, the quantity of hazardous chemicals coming from such sources are far lower than what is generated by major industries; generally, these sources do not contain large quantities of highly toxic substances in their waste streams.

Some of the major generators of hazardous waste include:

- Automobile and transportation vehicle manufacturers
- Batteries manufacturers
- Chemical manufacturers – largest generator in the US., accounts for 55% of all hazardous waste (2019)
- Electrical and electronics industry
- Leather and tanning industry
- Machinery manufacturing
- Metal industry
- Organic chemicals, pesticides, and explosive manufacturers
- Paint and coating manufacturers
- Rubber industry, excluding tire re-treaders
- Paper industry
- Petroleum refining
- Plastics industry
- Textile manufacturing
- Waste oil re-refining

The total quantity of hazardous waste generated by major industries in 2019 was 27.85 Mt (30.7 billion lb.). Figure 5.2 shows the relative contribution of hazardous waste by various industries.

In addition, there are a large number of industries, such as construction, demolition, and renovation industry, printing, photo processing, academic and business laboratories, dry cleaning, educational and vocational shops, and others, that generate hazardous waste. Details of hazardous materials generated by various industrial or manufacturing activities, along with its RCRA waste code, are available at EPA's web post titled "Typical Wastes Generated by Industry Sectors" (https://www.epa.gov/hwgenerators/typical-wastes-generated-industry-sectors).

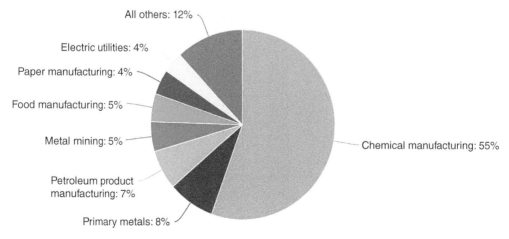

Production-related waste managed by industry, 2019
30.7 billion pounds

All others: 12%
Electric utilities: 4%
Paper manufacturing: 4%
Food manufacturing: 5%
Metal mining: 5%
Petroleum product manufacturing: 7%
Primary metals: 8%
Chemical manufacturing: 55%

Figure 5.2 Hazardous waste generated by major industries in 2019. *Source:* Graphic credit: EPA (2021).

The US EPA collects information from about 22 000 facilities that generate hazardous waste and publishes a biennial report called TRI. The latest report, released in January 2021, contains data for the calendar year 2019. The purpose of the report is to track the release of harmful substances that could result in one or more of the following outcomes:

- Cancer or other chronic human health effects
- Significant adverse acute human health effects
- Significant adverse environmental effects

Using the TRI interactive website, TRI Program|US EPA, one can readily determine the nature and quantity of hazardous substances released at a particular location, along with information about the generator, and their efforts toward pollution prevention and waste minimization. TRI was launched following the passage of the Emergency Planning and Community Right-to-know Act (EPCRA) of 1986, discussed in Chapter 3. The first TRI was published in 1987 and the 31st report came out in January 2021. Over the 30-year period, the quantity of hazardous waste has decreased from 245.85 Mt (271 million tons) in 1985 to12.6 Mt (13.9 million tons) in 2015 – a decrease of about 95% in 30 years.

Military operations also produce substantial quantities of hazardous waste (~8000 contaminated sites in Alaska alone) that are generated from the use of explosives, naval paints and coatings, metal plating, and related processes. In 1986, the US Congress established the Defense Environmental Restoration Act (DERP) to clean up the Department of Defense's contaminated sites. A report by the US Government's General Accounting Office (GAO) lists 5400 contaminated sites at closed military bases; 21 500 at active bases; and over 4700 at formerly used defense sites (FUDS) for a total of 31 600 contaminated sites (as of 2008). While no estimate is available for cleanup cost for all contaminated sites, FUDS sites alone were estimated to cost ~$18 billion and would take more than 50 years (GAO 2010).

5.4.1 Categories of Hazardous Waste Generators

The RCRA of 1976 included two categories of hazardous waste generators: Large Quantity Generators (LQGs) producing ≥1000 kg/month and Small Quantity Generators (SQGs), producing ≤1000 kg/month of hazardous waste. Drawing upon more than 35 years of experience and recognizing the need of the industry, EPA in 2017 (40CFR, V. 28, §262.14) developed the following three-tier classification of hazardous waste generators:

1) Large quantity generators (LQGs), producing 1000 kg or more of hazardous waste per month
2) Medium quantity generators (MQGs), producing between 100 and 1000 kg/month
3) Very small quantity generators (VSQGs), producing <100 kg/month

The new categories allow: (i) a hazardous waste generator to avoid the increased burden of a higher generator status when generating episodic waste, provided the episodic waste is properly managed, and (ii) a VSQG to send its hazardous waste to an LQG under control of the same person or entity. It also added rules for waste generated during cleanup operations.

About 99% of all hazardous waste generated in the US came from LQGs with <1% from SQG and VSQGs combined (EPA 2016). Table 5.5 summarizes various rules and requirements for hazardous waste generators.

Table 5.5   RCRA reporting requirements for hazardous waste generators.

Requirements	Large quantity generator (LQG)/month	Small quantity generator (SQG)/month	Very small quantity generator (VSQG)/ month
Quantity	≥1000 kg, or >1 kg acute hazardous waste	>100 and <1000 kg of acute hazardous waste	≤100, and ≤1 kg of acute hazardous waste
EPA ID	Required	Required	Not required
On-site accumulation	No limit	≤6000 kg	≤1000 or ≤1 kg acute hazardous waste
Accumulation time limits	≤90 days	≤180 days	None
Accumulation standards	Full compliance for management of containers, tanks, drip pads, or containment buildings	Meet technical standards for containers, tanks, drip pads, or containment buildings	None
Personnel training	Required	Basic training	Not required
Emergency procedures	Full plan required	Basic plan required	Not required
Air emissions	Required to control hazardous air emissions from tanks and containers	Not required	Not required
Land disposal restrictions	Meet all requirements	Meet most requirements	Not required
Manifest system	Full tracking required	Full tracking required	Not required
Waste minimization	Full plan required	Good faith effort required	Not required
Pre-transport	Meet packaging, labeling, and transportation requirements to an off-site RCRA facility	Meet packaging, labeling, and transportation requirements to an off-site RCRA facility	Only if required by state or DOT
Biennial report	Required	Not required	Not required
Residue from cleanup of acute hazardous waste	Any quantity	≤100 kg	≤100 kg

5.5   Storage and Transportation of Hazardous Waste

Generators of hazardous waste are required by law to store their waste in a legally compliant manner. The duration for which the waste can be stored at the generating facility and the quantity allowed are specified in RCRA, along with any exemption and reporting requirements.

5.5.1 Hazardous Waste Storage

As stated before, every aspect of hazardous waste from generation to final disposal is regulated under RCRA, and each party involved in any of these steps must possess a license issued by the EPA with an ID number. It is illegal for any hazardous waste generator to engage unlicensed parties for waste storage, transportation, treatment, and/or disposal.

According to EPA, storage of hazardous waste means holding the waste at the point of generation for a temporary period of time before it is treated, disposed of, or stored elsewhere. Storage containers include anything from the typical 55-gallon drum to an entire containment building. Hazardous waste can be stored either at a satellite accumulation area for a brief period or at the designated hazardous waste storage area for a longer time period. The satellite accumulation area or zone is the area at or near the point of the waste generation that is under the control of the operator of the waste process. "At or near" means that the designated area is within the facility near the actual point of generation and not far away at another site or in another building. The main rationale behind this provision was to provide generators with up to three days to move their waste to the main storage area, or to have it removed off-site by a licensed removal company.

Satellite accumulation must comply with the following rules:

- Up to 55 gallons of hazardous waste, or one quart of acutely hazardous waste, can be accumulated here
- Waste containers must display the correct date so that when the 72-hour limit for each is reached, the wastes can be sent off to treatment, storage, and disposal (TSD) facilities or to the main storage area
- Must be labeled with the appropriate identifying markers, e.g. "hazardous waste," "acute hazardous waste," "corrosive," "X-ray waste," "cyanide," and
- Containers must be in a good working condition and sealed, unless removing or adding hazardous waste, and must be compatible with the criteria of the waste itself, that is, able to safely withstand and hold its contents
- Weekly inspections must be conducted and logged in a record book.

5.5.2 Hazardous Waste Transportation

RCRA requires that hazardous waste transportation must be carried out by licensed and registered entities that should carry and produce the required documentation in their carriers. EPA can and has imposed fines for non-authorized transporters. Even transporting a small quantity of hazardous waste in a personal automobile is illegal and subject to civil and criminal penalties by the EPA.

Hazardous waste transporters play a key role in the cradle-to-grave hazardous waste management system by delivering hazardous waste from its point of generation to its destination. Since such transporters carry a controlled substance on public roads, rails, air, and waterways, they are regulated jointly by the US EPA and the US Department of Transportation (DOT). Details of transportation requirements are available in 40 CFR Part 263 (GPO 2018); the main points are summarized below:

- A hazardous waste transporter under Subtitle C is any person engaged in the off-site transportation of hazardous waste within the United States. Offsite transportation of hazardous waste includes shipments from the property of a hazardous waste generator to another facility for treatment, storage, or disposal. Transporter regulations only apply to the off-site transportation of hazardous waste. The transporter regulations do not apply to on-site transportation of hazardous waste within a facility's property or boundary. Examples of such on-site transportation include generators and TSD facilities transporting waste within their facilities, or on their own property.

- The Manifest System is an excellent way to track the fate of hazardous waste at any time between its generation and final disposal. With the exception of water and rail shipments and the transport of certain SQG recycling wastes, a transporter may not accept hazardous waste from a generator unless the waste is accompanied by a properly prepared manifest. Upon receiving the waste, the transporter must sign and date the manifest to acknowledge receipt and return a copy to the generator before leaving the generator's property. A copy of the manifest must accompany the shipment of the waste at all times. Once a transporter has accepted a waste, the transporter is required to deliver the entire quantity of waste to the next designated transporter or to the designated facility. Upon turning the waste over to another transporter or to the designated facility, the transporter is required to have the manifest signed and dated by the recipient. All transporters are required to keep a signed copy of the manifest for three years from the date the initial transporter accepted the waste.
- Transporters accepting hazardous waste from a generator or another transporter may need to hold waste temporarily during the normal course of transportation. A transfer facility is defined as any transportation-related facility, such as loading docks, parking areas, storage areas, and other similar areas where shipments are held during the normal course of transportation. A transporter may hold waste at a transfer facility for up to 10 days.

5.6 Treatment of Hazardous Waste

One of the main requirements of RCRA is proper control of hazardous waste after it is generated. Treatment methods, if selected properly, either eliminate or lower the concentration of hazardous substances to meet compliance standards.

The nature and volume of hazardous waste to be disposed of depend on the manufacturing process, the waste minimization options used in the process, the nature of the feedstock, and the finished product(s). It is therefore very important that the entire waste streams for each process be fully characterized before selecting the most suitable treatment method.

Treatment technologies are evolving at a rapid pace. The EPA, through its Superfund Innovative Technology Evaluation (SITE) program, promoted the development, commercialization, and implementation of innovative hazardous waste treatment technologies for 20 years (1987–2007). During this period EPA provided funds, $20 million each year, to the private sector, universities, and other federal and state agencies for research and demonstration of innovative methods of hazardous waste remediation. The program offered environmental decision-makers relevant data on cost and performance of new remediation technologies advantages as compared to conventional treatment technologies.

Hazardous waste treatment methods can be grouped into physical, chemical, biological, or their combination. Filtration to remove uncontaminated water from hazardous solids is an example of physical treatment. The use of chemicals to precipitate dissolved toxic heavy metals from an aqueous solution is a common chemical treatment method; while using microbes to clean petroleum-contaminated soil, or plants to remove toxic heavy metals from the soil, are examples of biologic treatment methods.

Discussion of treatment of hazardous waste presented in this chapter is intended to provide an overview of the fundamental principles used in these technologies; it does not address engineering and other details. A large volume of the published literature dealing with treatment technologies is available. In addition, proceedings of symposia addressing the subject of hazardous waste treatment, held on a regular basis have been published. *Emerging Technologies in Hazardous Waste Management* (Tedder and Pohland 2002) provides comprehensive coverage of the treatment of contaminated soils, groundwater, and radioactive waste.

Treatment methods effectively reduce the toxicity of hazardous wastes, making them suitable for disposal in a conventional manner. However, because of their unique chemical nature and economic considerations, many other kinds of hazardous wastes are disposed of without subjecting them to treatment, as in deep injection of liquid waste, (see Section 5.7.3.4).

5.6.1 Hazardous Waste Treatment Methods

As stated before, the goal of treatment is to detoxify the hazardous waste such that the concentration of hazardous substances is at or below the permitted levels. Some of the common treatment methods used are discussed below.

5.6.1.1 Neutralization

Acidic or alkaline wastes can be neutralized by treating them with a suitable base (alkali) or acid. A simple chemical reaction to neutralize an acidic liquid to a neutral material (pH range 6–8) is shown in Eq. (5.1), and that for an alkaline solution to neutral in Eq. (5.2).

$$\underset{\text{(sulfuric acid)}}{H_2SO_4} + \underset{\text{(calcite in limestone)}}{CaCO_3} \rightarrow \underset{\text{(gypsum)}}{CaSO_4} + \underset{\text{(carbon dioxide)}}{CO_2} \tag{5.1}$$

$$\underset{\text{(sodium hydroxide)}}{NaOH} + \underset{\text{(hydrochloric acid)}}{HCl} \rightarrow \underset{\text{(salt)}}{NaCl} + \underset{\text{(water)}}{H_2O} \tag{5.2}$$

The final products of a neutralization reaction are neutral solid and water or gas. Neutralization reactions are exothermic. Therefore, adequate safety measures must be taken to control the buildup of high temperatures.

Acidic wastewater can be neutralized with lime (CaO), slaked (hydrated) lime [Ca (OH)$_2$], caustic soda (NaOH), or soda ash (Na$_2$CO$_3$). Slaked lime, because of its low cost, is used more frequently than other bases. Alkaline wastewater can be neutralized with a strong acid, such as H$_2$SO$_4$ or HCl, or with CO$_2$, which forms carbonic acid with water.

Neutralization is an example of a chemical treatment method; other chemical methods used to treat hazardous waste include: coagulation, ion exchange, oxidation-reduction, and precipitation. Details are available in Hasan (1996).

5.6.1.2 Sorption

Sorption is an example of physical treatment and is commonly used to remove a soluble hazardous substance, called sorbate, from aqueous hazardous waste. Sorption involves the adhesion of contaminant molecules to the surface of the solid sorbent. Activated charcoal (AC) is one of the most commonly used sorbents to remove organic and inorganic chemicals in aqueous hazardous waste. Common organic compounds amenable for sorption by activated carbon are shown in Table 5.6.

Different materials are used for making AC either in granular or powder form. Coconut shells, almond shells, wood, bituminous coal, or lignite, is first dehydrated by heating to 170 °C, and

Table 5.6 Organic compounds amenable to sorption treatment by AC.

Type/class of organic compound	Common example
Aliphatic and aromatic acids	Benzoic acids, tar acids
Aromatic and aliphatic amines	Aniline, diamine, toluene
Aromatic solvents	Benzene, toluene, xylene
Chlorinated aromatics	Chlorobenzene, DDT, endrin, PCBs, toxaphene
Chlorinated solvents	Carbon tetrachloride, perchloroethylene
Fuels	Gasoline, kerosene, oil
Pesticides/herbicides	Alachlor, aldicarb, atrazine, carbofuran, simazine, 2,4, D
Phenolics	Alkyl phenols, chlorophenols, cresol, nitrophenols, phenol, resorcinol
Polycyclic aromatics	Biphenyl, naphthalene
Soluble organic dyes	Methylene blue, textile dyes
Surfactants	Alkyl benzene sulfonates

Source: EPA (2000).

gradually raising the temperature to convert it into a charcoal-like product. This is then subjected to treatment with superheated steam – or activation – that causes the pores to expand, removes the ash, and increases the surface area of the charcoal. AC has an extremely high surface area: about $1000–1400\,m^2/g$ (Watts 1998).

5.6.1.3 Precipitation

This is another common method used to remove the soluble hazardous substance from liquid hazardous waste by treating it with a precipitating chemical. The reaction results in the formation of an insoluble compound that can be separated from the waste by filtration, coagulation or flocculation. Equation (5.3) shows how dissolved Cd can precipitate out of a hazardous waste solution with the addition of hydrogen sulfide (HS) gas.

$$Cd_{(dissolved)} + HS \rightarrow CdS_{(solid)} + H \tag{5.3}$$

The efficiency of AC carbon goes down with use. For this reason, spent carbon has to be regenerated or replaced to maintain the peak performance of the treatment system. In large treatment plants, activated carbon is regenerated in situ by heating the bed of spent activated carbon above the boiling point of the adsorbed organic compounds to drive off (desorb) the volatiles. The volatiles can be either burned off in an incinerator or passed through condensers and collected as a usable liquid. Spent carbon that cannot be regenerated in situ can be regenerated by heating in an incinerator.

Precipitation is suitable for removing hazardous metals and other substances from wastewaters produced from electronics, inorganic pigments, metal plating and finishing, mining, steel, and nonferrous metals industries.

5.6.1.4 Reverse Osmosis

Normal osmosis involves the flow of a solvent (e.g. water) from a weaker (dilute) solution to a stronger (concentrated) solution through a semipermeable membrane. This results in the reduction of the concentration of the stronger solution. By applying pressure to the stronger solution greater than the osmotic pressure of the solution (osmotic pressure is the pressure that, when applied to the semipermeable membrane, will prevent the passage of the solvent through the membrane), the solvent can be made to flow from the stronger (concentrated) to the weaker (dilute) solution – hence the term "reverse osmosis" (RO). The process can be used to produce brine concentrate and high-purity water from aqueous salt wastes. RO is commonly used for the desalination of seawater to obtain potable water. Most bottled drinking waters use RO to purify the water.

5.6.1.5 Stripping

Stripping involves the transfer of dissolved molecules from a liquid into a vapor stream or gas flow. Stripping is commonly done by passing air, heated nitrogen gas, or steam through the liquid waste. Stripping causes volatiles to transform into the gas phase. Air stripping is used to remove volatile organic contaminants from water or aqueous waste streams. Groundwater contaminated with benzene, toluene, and TCE has been successfully remediated by air stripping. The process works best when the concentration of VOCs is less than 100 mg/L. It is possible to remove more than 99% of the VOCs from water by using a properly designed and efficiently operating air stripper. Air stripping, in which the flowing gas is air, is most efficiently accomplished in a packed tower where air and contaminated water flow in opposite directions; the air is blown from the bottom of the tower and contaminated water enters from the top.

Air sparging involves the introduction of air into contaminated media to remove the contaminants. Two variations of air sparging are used to clean up contaminated groundwater: physical air sparging and biological air sparging: In physical air sparging, the air is introduced below the groundwater table to clean up groundwater contaminated with VOCs. The introduced air promotes the volatilization of the VOCs present in the groundwater. The vapors purged from groundwater move upward and accumulate in the vadose zone, where a vapor extraction system is installed to remove the VOCs from the vadose zone. In biological air sparging, the air is introduced into the contaminated groundwater to promote microbial growth for biodegradation.

In general, air/gas stripping is more suitable for the removal of hazardous materials with high vapor pressures and low water solubilities, such as chlorinated hydrocarbons and aromatic compounds. Steam stripping is suitable for less volatile materials with low vapor pressures. These include high-boiling-point chlorinated aromatics and hydrocarbons, alcohols, and ketones. Air stripping can be used for the removal of VOCs from geologic materials having a hydraulic conductivity of as low as $10\,\text{cm}^{-5}/\text{s}$.

5.7 Hazardous Waste Treatment and Disposal

Treatment and disposal of hazardous waste constitute a vital link in the cradle-to-grave concept of hazardous waste management. Improved treatment technologies have resulted in the reduction of the volume of hazardous waste that must be disposed of, but hazardous wastes cannot be completely eliminated; there will always be some quantity of residual waste that will need disposal. EPA, following the directives of RCRA, has developed a number of criteria and requirements for hazardous waste landfills, other land disposals, waste incineration, deep well injection, and related disposal options. Common treatment and disposal methods for hazardous waste generally fall into one of the following types:

A) Land disposal methods
    a) Landfill
    b) Land farm
    c) Waste pile
    d) Surface impoundment
    e) Mines, caverns, and other underground openings
    f) Deep well injection (liquid waste)
B) Treatment methods
    a) Thermal methods. Thermal treatment is generally used for hazardous wastes containing highly toxic substances, such as dioxin, PCBs, and other recalcitrant compounds. Thermal methods are more expensive, and include:
        1) Incineration
        2) Pyrolysis
        3) Miscellaneous
    b) Biological methods
        1) Plants
        2) Microorganisms
    c) Miscellaneous
        1) Permeable Reactive Barriers (PRBs)
        2) Vitrification
        3) Wetlands

5.7.1 Land Disposal

Land disposal refers to the disposal of hazardous waste, after proper treatment, on the land – both at the surface and in the subsurface. Land disposal requires prior conversion of hazardous waste into nonhazardous products through the processes of degradation, transformation, or immobilization. Landfills, surface impoundments, waste piles, land farms, and concrete vaults and bunkers are examples of disposal on the land (above ground); deep well injection and disposal in salt domes, bedded salt formations, and mines and caverns are examples of subsurface (underground) disposal.

5.7.1.1 Regulatory Aspects of Land Disposal

In view of the threat to the environment, particularly to the quality of groundwater resulting from improper disposal of hazardous wastes on the land, severe restrictions were imposed for land disposal of hazardous waste under the 1984 HSWA to the 1976 RCRA. All land disposal is regulated under RCRA except deep well injection, which is regulated under the 1986 Amendments to the Safe Drinking Water Act (SDWA).

5.7.2 Land Disposal Restrictions

Although modern landfills are designed to control the leaching of hazardous chemicals into the environment, they cannot completely eliminate entry of rain or snowmelt through the cover to the untreated waste, allowing leachate containing hazardous chemicals to seep into the groundwater. The Land Disposal Restrictions (LDR) program was created by the US Congress in 1984 as part of the HSWA. HSWA prohibits land disposal of untreated hazardous wastes to provide an additional layer of protection to the groundwater. The regulations require EPA to specify either concentration levels or treatment standards for hazardous waste before land disposal. The regulations describing EPA's LDR program can be found in 40 CFR Part 268.

As discussed before, the main goal of RCRA is to protect human health and the environment from the mismanagement of hazardous waste from cradle to grave. The LDR program ensures that properly treated hazardous waste bound for land disposal do not pose a threat to human health and the environment. Thus, making hazardous waste less harmful to groundwater by reducing the potential for leaching of hazardous constituents and by reducing waste toxicity by destroying or immobilizing harmful constituents.

The LDR program applies to both generators of hazardous waste and TSD facilities. LDRs do not apply to hazardous waste from households, or pesticide-container residue disposed of by farmers on their own land.

5.7.2.1 Key Provisions of the LDR Program

Key elements of the LDR program are: (i) disposal prohibition, (ii) dilution prohibition, and (iii) storage prohibition. The disposal prohibition states that before hazardous waste can be land disposed, treatment standards specific to that waste material must be met. A facility may meet such standards by either: (i) treating hazardous chemical constituents in the waste to attain required treatment levels; any treatment method can be used to bring concentrations to the appropriate level except dilution, or (ii) treating hazardous waste using a treatment technology specified by EPA. Once the waste is treated with the technology required under LDR (described in 40 CFR §268.40), it can be disposed of on the land. The dilution prohibition states that waste must be properly treated and not simply diluted by adding large amounts of water, soil, or nonhazardous waste. Dilution does not reduce the toxicity of hazardous constituents. The storage prohibition states that waste must be treated and cannot be stored indefinitely. This prevents generators and TSD facilities from storing hazardous waste for long periods to avoid treatment. Waste may be stored, subject to LDR, in tanks, containers, or containment buildings – but only for the purpose of accumulating quantities necessary to facilitate proper recovery, treatment, or disposal.

5.7.2.2 Land Treatment/Disposal

Terms like land treatment, land farming, land cultivation, land application, and sludge spreading refer to the practice of using the soil (the land) as a medium for simultaneous treatment and disposal of hazardous waste. Land treatment aims at the degradation, transformation, or immobilization of hazardous waste. The natural biodegradation process brought about by the organisms present in the soil, or by chemical reaction, is taken advantage of in rendering the waste nonhazardous. The process can be optimized by tilling the soil for aeration, controlling the soil pH and water content, and fertilization (to provide nutrients for organisms). Land treatment is best suited for listed petroleum wastes (codes K048 to K052), although sewage sludge is also amenable to land treatment. Halogenated organic compounds and hazardous wastes containing heavy metals are not amenable to land treatment; for this reason, sewage sludge containing heavy metals is also not suitable for land treatment and disposal.

The law requires the owner or operator of a land treatment facility to:

- Carry out analyses of the waste prior to its placement on the land to determine the concentrations of hazardous and toxic constituents.
- Conduct a pretreatment demonstration to verify that the hazardous constituents of the waste will be properly treated.
- Monitor the soil and the vadose zone to ensure that no migration of hazardous constituents is occurring. If migration is indicated from monitoring, a permit application has to be filed with

the EPA indicating changes in the operating practice to rectify the problem. Migration is considered to have occurred when the monitoring results show a higher concentration of constituents compared to the background concentrations in untreated soils.

- Carry out proper closure procedures at the facility, which include: maintaining the optimum conditions to maximize degradation, transformation, and immobilization of the wastes; minimization of precipitation and runoff from the treatment zone; and control of wind dispersion. A vegetative cover should be placed over the treated soil to promote plant growth to protect the site from wind or water erosion. Regulations prohibit growing food-chain crops in land-treated areas where the hazardous waste is known to contain arsenic, cadmium, lead, and mercury, unless it is demonstrated that they will not be transferred to the food portion of the crop or occur in concentrations greater than in identical crops grown on untreated land in the same region.

5.7.3 Secure Landfill

The 1984 HSWA requires all new facilities for land disposal of solid hazardous waste – landfills and waste piles – to include a minimum of two liners for containment of leachate, a leachate collection and removal system, a leak detection system; and inspection and monitoring systems to check for possible leaks of leachate on a weekly basis. A landfill that includes all these components is called a secure landfill and has to comply with all legal requirements during its operating life and after it is closed. The law required existing landfills to be retrofitted with these features, or else close down. A secure landfill (Figure 5.3) must meet the following requirements:

- Double liner, upper synthetic geomembrane liner, and a lower composite liner of geomembrane over compacted soil at least 0.91 m (3 ft) thick and hydraulic conductivity no greater than 10^{-7} cm/s.
- Double leachate collection and removal systems
- Leak detection system
- Run-on, runoff, and wind dispersal controls
- Construction quality assurance program

Operators must also comply with inspection, monitoring, and release response requirements. Since landfills are permanent disposal sites and will be closed with the hazardous waste in place, they are subject to closure and post-closure care requirements including:

- Installing and maintaining a final cover, at least 0.6 m (2 ft) thick, with a minimum of 3% slope
- Continuing operation of the leachate collection and removal system until leachate is no longer detected
- Maintaining and monitoring the leak detection system
- Maintaining groundwater monitoring
- Preventing stormwater run-on and runoff
- Installing and protecting surveyed benchmarks

5.7.3.1 Waste Piles

A waste pile is a non-containerized accumulation of non-flowing, solid hazardous waste. Depending on whether the waste pile is used for storage, treatment, or disposal, different requirements have to be satisfied. The owner or operator of a waste pile must meet the following requirements:

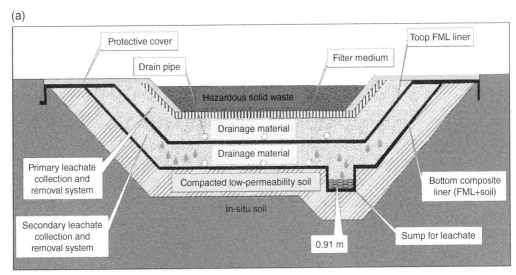

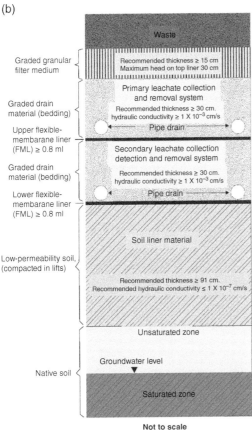

Figure 5.3 Main features of a secure landfill: (a): cross-sectional view; (b) details of various layers. *Source:* Modified after EPA (1989).

- Have a double liner system: top liner, a synthetic geomembrane, to prevent migration of hazardous materials into the liner; and a composite bottom liner consisting of synthetic geomembrane and 0.91 m (3 ft) of compacted soil having a permeability of not more than 1×10^{-7} cm/s on a supporting base or foundation to prevent migration of any waste in vertical and horizontal directions.
- Have a leachate management system installed above the bottom liner to remove all leachate.
- Have a system to control water run-on resulting from a 25-year storm for at least 24 hours.
- Weekly inspection, as well as after every storm.
- Removal or decontamination of all contaminated equipment, structures, liners, and soils, in accordance with the closure plan, to *clean close*. If the facility cannot be clean-closed, it must comply with closure requirements for a landfill.

Waste piles containing nonmagnetic materials (called *fluff*) generated from automobile shredding operations are a good example of hazardous waste piles because they contain concentrations of lead and cadmium above the levels prescribed in the TCLP toxicity test. They also contain synthetic fabrics, rubber, plastic, and insulation material. These are usually saturated with oil and have a tendency to auto-ignite.

5.7.3.2 Surface Impoundments

Surface impoundment is a facility designed to hold an accumulation of liquid wastes or wastes containing free liquids. The impoundment may be in a natural topographic depression, manmade excavation, or diked area (basin). Holding, storage, and aeration pits, ponds, and lagoons are examples of surface impoundments. Surface impoundments are different from tanks in that impoundments cannot maintain their structural integrity without support from the surrounding earth materials, unlike tanks, which maintain their structural integrity upon removal of the surrounding earth materials. A surface impoundment may be used for the storage or disposal of hazardous wastes. The following requirements apply to the owners or operators of surface impoundments:

- Carry out analyses of the waste to be treated or stored.
- Maintain at least 0.61 m (2 ft) of freeboard, which must be inspected daily to ensure compliance. In addition, a weekly inspection must be conducted of the dike, surrounding vegetation, and the impoundment area to detect any leaks, deterioration, or failures in the impoundment.
- Must have two or more liners, along with a leachate collection and removal system.
- Groundwater monitoring system.
- Dikes or berms along the perimeter of the impoundment.
- No ignitable or reactive waste can be placed in a surface impoundment.

The impoundment may be clean-closed by removing or decontaminating all equipment, liners, structures, underlying and surrounding soils and groundwater, if any. If clean closure cannot be achieved, the impoundment must be closed as a landfill.

Except for hazardous waste landfills, other land disposal facilities such as waste piles and surface impoundments may be either clean-closed or closed. For clean-closing, the owners and operators of such units have to ensure that all hazardous wastes and waste residues have been removed from the site, that the facility and equipment have been effectively decontaminated, and that the air, soil, surface water, and groundwater samples have not indicated a level of concentration exceeding the EPA's recommended limits. Upon approval by the EPA, the owners or operators of clean-closed units do not have to carry out post-closure care for the unit.

5.7.3.3 Mine Storage/Disposal

Voids, left behind after extraction of useful mineral commodities, can be used for both storage and disposal. Storage involves waste placement at a suitable location that allows access, retrieval, and removal of hazardous waste. Disposal involves placing the hazardous waste at a suitable location without the ability for retrieval. Mines are used for both storage and disposal of hazardous waste. Various countries in the EU dispose of their hazardous wastes in landfills located underground (Wendenburg 2018).

Extraction of mineral resources creates large volumes of mined-out space in the subsurface. Such spaces offer an attractive alternative for the storage and/or disposal of hazardous waste (Hasan 1990). Existing mined-out spaces are generally more economical for hazardous waste disposal/storage than space specially created by mining. However, if the mined-out earth material can find a ready market then the cost of mining will be offset by the sale of the material, justifying the creation of the space for hazardous waste disposal/storage.

Many rock formations, such as limestone, sandstone, bedded salt and potash, salt domes, and granite, are suitable for the storage/disposal of hazardous wastes. Sandstone, limestone, and granites may be mined by drilling and blasting, which results in the creation of a patterned space in which the void space, called a *room*, is created from the extraction of the geologic material. The excavated areas are supported by columns of geologic material, called *pillars*; this mining technique is known as the *room-and-pillar* method. The ratio of the volume of room to the volume of pillars determines the available space for disposal/storage. Generally, an extraction ratio of 75% or more would mean that a sufficiently large volume of void space is available for storage/disposal. Figure 5.4 shows a limestone mine with rooms being used for storage of merchandise and for roadways, and pillars supporting the overburden above the mine roof.

5.7.3.4 Deep Well Injection

In the United States, the disposal of industrial wastes into underground wells by the oil and chemical industry has been carried out since the 1950s. With the passage of the SDWA of 1974 and the HSWA of 1984, strict requirements have been placed on waste disposal using deep wells.

Figure 5.4 A room-and-pillar mine in limestone being used for storage, light manufacturing, and business in Kansas City, Missouri. Such mines can also be used for storage of hazardous waste. Car on left for scale. *Source:* S.E. Hasan (author).

The purpose is to protect the nation's underground sources of drinking water (USDW) from possible contamination by improper disposal of hazardous waste into subsurface geologic formations. Deep well injection, though permitted by law, should be considered only after source reduction, waste minimization, and other disposal options have been exhausted. Hazardous waste restricted from land disposal cannot be disposed of in underground injection wells unless it has been treated or exemption has been granted by the EPA or the delegated state authority.

5.7.4 Thermal Treatment Methods

Despite its high cost, thermal disposal remains the only option when the toxic chemicals comprising the hazardous waste cannot be destroyed or rendered less toxic by using available treatment methods. In recent years, technological advances have led to a more efficient design of incinerator plants that can also be used for energy recovery, making it a competitive option for disposal.

5.7.4.1 Incineration

Incineration utilizes heat and oxygen (from the air) to destroy the organic fraction of a waste stream. Incineration requires high temperatures, generally 900 °C or more. From a chemical point of view, incineration represents an *exothermic oxidation process* that converts organic compounds into CO_2 and H_2O (steam), with an accompanying release of heat.

Waste streams that are fed into incinerators may not entirely consist of organic compounds; in fact, inorganic materials, including metals and glass, are frequently found in the waste streams. Hazardous metals and nonmetals in the waste stream undergo oxidation as a result of incineration; for example, metallic copper changes into copper oxide, sodium into sodium hydroxide, potassium into potassium hydroxide, fluoride into hydrogen fluoride or fluorine, chloride into hydrogen chloride (HCl), and carbon into carbon dioxide. Other waste constituents either go into the residual ash or into the flue gas after incineration, both requiring special handling, treatment, and disposal.

Performance standards of incinerators for hazardous waste disposal are regulated under RCRA. The key requirements are:

An incinerator must achieve a destruction and removal efficiency (DRE) of 99.99% for each principal organic hazardous constituent (POHC) for each waste feed. DRE has been defined as:

$$DRE = [(W_{in} - W_{out}) \div W_{in}] \times 100 \tag{5.4}$$

where, W_{in} is the mass feed rate of one principal POHC in the waste stream, and W_{out} is the mass emission rate of the same POHC in exhaust emissions prior to release into the atmosphere.

An incinerator burning hazardous waste and producing stack emission of HCl must control its emission to less than 1.8 kg/h (4.0 lb/h), or 1% of HCl in stack gas prior to its entry into any pollution-control equipment.

An incinerator must not emit PM exceeding 180 mg/dscm (day standard cubic meter) corrected for the amount of oxygen in the stack gas, according to the formula:

$$P = P_{cc} \left(\frac{2}{3} - O \right) \tag{5.5}$$

where, P is the measured concentration of particulate matters; P_{cc} is the corrected concentration of particulate matters; and O is the measured concentration of oxygen in the stack gas, as determined by using the Orsat method for oxygen analysis of dry flue gas.

RCRA covers all hazardous wastes except PCBs, which are considered toxic material and are regulated under the Toxic Substances Control Act (TSCA). Rules for the destruction of PCBs using incineration, established under TSCA, require that PCBs be disposed of by incineration unless their concentration is less than 50 ppm. If the concentration is between 50 and 500 ppm, the PCB waste can be used as fuel in high-efficiency boilers. The general requirements of TSCA for incineration of liquid PCBs are:

- Liquids fed into the incinerator must be maintained for a residence time of two seconds at a temperature of 1200 °C (±100 °C) and 3% excess oxygen in the stack gas. Or the liquids must be maintained for a residence time of 1.5 seconds at 1600 °C (±100 °C) and 2% excess oxygen in the stack gas. Using these conditions, a DRE of ≥99.9999% must be achieved for liquid PCBs.
- Combustion efficiency (CE) shall be at least 99.99%, computed by the equation:

$$CE = [(CCO_2) \div (CCO_2 + CCO)] \times 100 \tag{5.6}$$

where, CCO_2 is the concentration of carbon dioxide and CCO that of carbon monoxide.

For nonliquid PCBs, the requirement is that mass air emission from the incinerator must not be >0.001 g of PCB/kg of the PCB introduced into the incinerator; this corresponds to a DRE of ≥99.9999%. In addition, other requirements concerning monitoring of gases in the emissions, incinerator temperature, PCB feed rate, and installation of scrubbers have been set forth for both liquid and nonliquid PCBs.

Both RCRA and TSCA require a trial burn, or test data equivalent to a trial burn, to ensure that the hazardous waste incinerator complies with the performance standards.

5.7.4.2 Pyrolysis

Pyrolysis also utilizes heat for the destruction of hazardous waste constituents at a lower temperature in the absence of oxygen. However, it differs from incineration in that the decomposition process involves an *endothermic* reaction. The general temperature range for pyrolysis is between 425 and 750 °C. Pyrolysis is a two-step process: The first step involves heating the mixed waste at lower temperatures (425–750 °C), which results in the separation of volatile fractions from the nonvolatiles. In the second step, the volatiles are burned in a fume incinerator to achieve a DRE of 99.9999%, leaving behind ash (solid residue). The two-step process allows for the precise control of temperature and requires smaller equipment.

5.7.4.3 Other Thermal Destruction Methods

Other methods of destruction of hazardous waste using high temperature include: molten salt combustion, calcination, wet air oxidation, industrial boilers, and furnaces. Facilities using these methods are regulated under RCRA (40 CFR, Part 270) and are required to perform trial burns or similar tests. Molten salt combustion utilizes simultaneous combustion and sorption to burn organic constituents and sorb the objectionable combustion products from the gas stream, respectively. The hazardous waste, in the presence of air, is mixed together in the combustion chamber, where molten sodium carbonate is maintained at a temperature of 815–1100 °C. Organic constituents, such as hydrocarbons, oxidize to carbon dioxide and water; the inorganic constituents, such as arsenic, halogens, phosphorus, and sulfur, react with sodium carbonate to form salts that are retained in the melt. Sodium carbonate has to be periodically replaced to maintain its efficiency and ability to absorb acidic products.

Another technology, called Low-Temperature Thermal Desorption (LTTD) has been employed for the removal of contaminants from solid media (e.g. soils) by volatilizing them with heat, at temperatures low enough not to cause combustion of the media. LTTD has been widely used to treat a wide range of VOCs, such as highly volatile TCE, to moderately volatile compounds such as chlorinated pesticides, to extremely low volatility compounds, like PCBs, pentachlorophenols, and dioxins. Contaminated solids include soil, sediments, lagoon sludge, process filter cakes, and other man-made debris (ITRC 1997). This technology has been used at many Superfund sites.

5.7.5 Biological Methods

Biological methods involve the use of plants or microorganisms to: convert the hazardous constituents of waste into less hazardous or neutral material (bioremediation, using microbes); or removal of heavy metals or other hazardous substances from contaminated soil and its translocation into plant tissues (phytoremediation).

Microorganisms (bacteria and fungi) utilize organic matter as nutrients for their growth and survival. Existing biological treatment methods work most effectively for organic contaminants present in wastewaters, in groundwater, or when they exist as a separate solid phase.

Ideally, organic waste could be degraded to the point that it either does not leave any residue or leaves only recyclable residues. The term mineralization is often used for this type of biodegradation, which results in the formation of CO_2, H_2O, and other ions. Mineralization can be defined as the process that causes the conversion of complex molecules present in organic compounds into simple chemical forms.

5.7.6 Miscellaneous Disposal Methods

A variety of innovative methods have been and are being developed for the cost-efficient disposal of hazardous wastes. These are briefly discussed in the following sections.

5.7.6.1 Permeable Reactive Barriers

PRBs are a remediation technology that has been evolving since the mid-1990s, and is used for cleaning up contaminated groundwater. The first full-scale PRB was installed in 1994 to treat a TCE plume at the Intersil Site in Sunnyvale, California. More than 200 contaminated groundwater sites have been remediated in the past 20 years.

A PRB is essentially a wall in the ground created by the excavation of the aquifer materials that have been backfilled with a suitable reactant to treat the contaminated groundwater. Construction of a PRB system involves digging a narrow trench in the path of contaminated groundwater to a depth of about 15.2 m (50 ft). The trench is filled with a reactive material, such as zero-valent iron, or iron filings (Fe^0), limestone, AC, or mulch, to clean up the contamination (Figure 5.5a). It is essential that the "fill material" be packed in such a way to make it more permeable than the contaminated groundwater medium to allow it to flow through the barrier and not around it. Adding sand to the reactive material can increase the permeability to the desired level. Sidewalls, by digging trench above the barrier wall and backfilling it with impermeable material, such a clay, help direct the flow toward the reactive wall (Figure 5.5b). Such configuration is known as funnel-and-gate PRB.

(a)

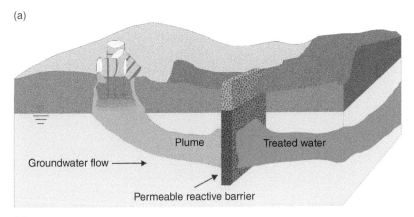

(b)

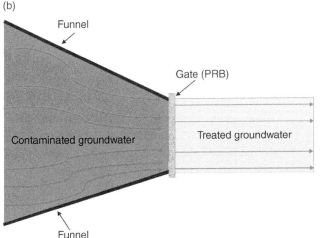

Figure 5.5   Permeable reactive barriers (PRBs): (a) continuous PRB, (b) funnel-and-gate-type PRB.

PRBs remove the contaminants in several ways that include:

- Sorption, which is adhesion (sticking) of contaminants to the reactive material. For example, hydrocarbon compounds sorb onto the surface of activated carbon particles as the contaminated groundwater flows through the barrier.
- Precipitation initiates a chemical reaction between the dissolved metals in groundwater and the reactants to cause metals to precipitate and be trapped at the barrier wall. Powdered limestone or seashells have been used to remove dissolved lead and copper in contaminated groundwater.
- Chemical degradation: Organic contaminants, such as TCE, PCE, and other chlorinated compounds, react with Fe^0 in the barrier wall that transforms it into less toxic or less harmful compounds.
- Biodegradation: Microbes in organic materials can break down toxic compounds into simple materials, such as H_2O or CO_2. Organic mulch, based on plant materials, has been used to clean up groundwater contaminated with toxic organic compounds, such as TCE, chlorinated VOVs, RDX, and HMX (explosives).

PRB has the following advantages:

- Confines the plume (holds it from further migration down gradient) while the source is being remediated
- Lowers the quantity of contaminant, thereby enhancing natural degradation
- Versatile, can be used to treat a range of contaminants
- Eliminates the need for drilling, pumping, and monitoring wells and is unobtrusive
- Low operation and maintenance costs
- Is a green and sustainable remediation (SR) technology; requires less energy compared to pump and treat and other methods.

Some limitations include:

- Suitable when contaminated groundwater occurs at shallow depths, ideally < 15 m; but can be used for up to 30 m depth
- Takes very long time for treatment to complete
- Possibility of clogging of pores in the reactant (iron filings), resulting in decreased efficiency, requiring replacement.

5.7.6.2 Vitrification

Vitrification is the process of conversion of contaminated soil into glass by using heat. Some highly toxic compounds, such as mixed waste containing radionuclides, pesticides, herbicides, or heavy metals, such as arsenic, lead, and mercury, have been remediated by vitrification. The process is expensive and slow but, when no other remediation options are feasible, vitrification is used. Two variations of vitrification are available: (i) in situ, and (ii) ex-site process. The in situ process involves placing electrodes in the contaminated soil, passing high-voltage current (up to 4000 V) that generates a high temperature of 1600–2000 °C (2900–3650 °F), causing the soil to melt, embedding the contaminants in a glassy matrix that solidifies upon cooling and resembles obsidian or basalt (volcanic rocks). Silica and calcium carbonate, or glass scraps, may be used as process additives, and their quantity may vary from 20 to 70% by weight of the total feed. The ex-situ process involves removing and transporting the contaminated soil to a suitable location where it can be heated by using natural gas, coal, or microwave, to raise the temperature in the 1500–2000 °C range to melt the mass which, upon cooling, forms a vitreous inert material. Radionuclides and other heavy metals become a part of the vitrified, non-leachable, inert mass.

5.7.6.3 Wetlands

Constructed or artificial wetlands are manmade wetlands designed to treat contaminants, typically in water, such as streams, that flow through them. They are constructed to function as natural wetlands and are often referred to as "natural kidneys" due to their capacity to remove contaminants from the flowing water. This is because of the rich biota that thrives in wetlands; the combination of plants and microbes facilitates efficient bioremediation of contaminated water. Wetlands are solar-driven with minimum or no energy requirements; offer the potential for habitat restoration, are passive treatment system, and use a natural process to clean up the contamination. Wetlands are an attractive option for the treatment of contaminated water compared to conventional treatment systems because of low operation and maintenance costs, and ready public acceptance as a *green technology*. Figure 5.6 shows a wetland constructed to treat streams contaminated with Pb, Zn, Cd, and other heavy metals at a Superfund site in the Oklahoma portion of the TSMD.

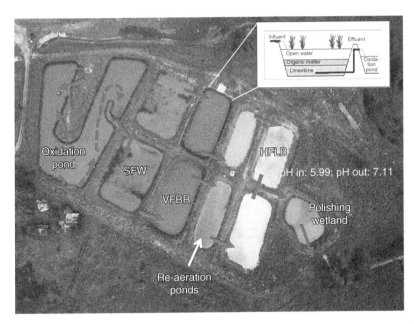

Figure 5.6 Aerial view of a constructed wetland for treatment of acidic waters resulting from Pb and Zn mining in the Tri-State District. SFW: surface flow wetlands; VFBR: vertical flow biochemical reactors; HFLB: horizontal flow limestone beds. Note change in pH from acidic (5.99) at entry point to nearly neutral (7.11) at the wetland exit. *Source:* Courtesy: Center for Restoration of Ecosystems and Watersheds at the University of Oklahoma, Norman, OK.

The use of wetlands to treat contaminated water is not new: wetlands have been used in the US for over 100 years for treating municipal wastewater; but the use of constructed wetland to treat water contaminated with hazardous waste is relatively new, about 25–30 years old. Wetlands have been used to treat municipal and industrial wastewaters, storm runoff, landfill leachate, effluent from agricultural lands, and toxic heavy metals from mine drainage. A number of natural processes promote remediation of contaminated water that can be grouped as: (i) biotic and (ii) abiotic. These processes along with their mechanisms are listed in Table 5.7.

Two variations of constructed wetlands are available: (i) Surface flow wetlands, and (ii) Subsurface flow wetlands.

Surface flow wetlands allow the contaminated water to flow over the soil in a sloping trench excavated to a shallow depth to channelize the contaminated water to utilize the natural biotic and abiotic processes to clean up the contaminants. Since the water is exposed to air, the aerobic degradation mechanism dominates.

Subsurface wetlands are designed to cause the contaminated water to flow below the ground surface through a permeable medium, commonly a sand or gravel bed. Subsurface wetlands are preferred in areas of the long and cold winter season.

5.7.6.4 Combination Methods

It is quite common in remediation work to use a combination of one or more of the earlier mentioned methods. For example, in cleaning up contaminated groundwater, combining two or more methods has been found to be more cost-efficient. One such method that has proved quite successful is the Accelerated Remediation Technology (ART) system. It has been used at many sites in the United States and overseas (www.artinwell.com) to clean up contaminated groundwater. At these sites,

Table 5.7   Cleanup mechanism of constructed wetland.

Process	Mechanism
Abiotic	Settling and sedimentation
	Sorption
	Chemical oxidation and reduction
	Precipitation
	Photooxidation
	Volatalization
Biotic	Aerobic or anerobic
	• Biodegradation
	• Biotransformation
	Phytoaccumulation
	Phytostabilization
	Rhizodegradation
	Phytodegradation
	Phytovolatalization

Source: From ITRC (2007a).

treatment wells, using air sparging, air stripping, etc., had been in operation for up to five years, costing hundreds of thousands of dollars, without successfully lowering the contaminants' concentration to acceptable regulatory levels. After they were retrofitted with the ART system, contaminants' concentration was brought down to regulatory levels within periods of several months to <2 years, leading the site to be certified "cleaned" by the authorities, and allowing the owners to reuse the site. Details of the ART system are discussed in Case Study 5.4.

Case Study 5.4   Accelerated Remediation Technology

ART developed an innovative groundwater remediation system, in the early 2000s, utilizing the well-established remediation concepts. The ART Integrated Remediation System combines in situ air stripping, air sparging, soil vapor extraction (SVE), and enhanced bioremediation/ oxidation, along with subsurface groundwater circulation. The ART system, in most cases, can be adapted to fit existing treatment wells, saving costs of mobilization of drilling equipment and well installation.

The air sparging component results in lifting (mounding) the groundwater table. A submersible pump is placed at the bottom of the well to push the contaminated groundwater toward the top for downward discharge through a spray head (Figure 5.4A). Vacuum pressure – generated by the SVE component – is applied at the top of the well point to extract vapors from the vadose zone along with vapors released by the in-well stripping process. The negative pressure from vacuum extraction creates additional water mounding while boosting the net hydraulic gradient from the periphery to the center of the well; it also removes vapors from the unsaturated zone and well annulus. The SVE and air sparging components, operating synergistically in the same well, enlarge the radius of influence and increase water circulation. The radius of influence, up to ten times the water column, has been achieved by the ART system.

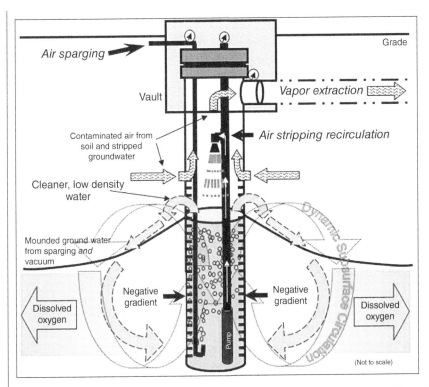

Figure 5.4A Schematic of the ART System. *Source:* ART System description and illustration courtesy Dr. M. Odah, Accelerated Remediation Technologies, Inc.

The ART system can be installed in wells with a minimum diameter of 10 cm (4 in.). Another primary benefit of the system that sets it apart from similar remedial alternatives is its capacity to treat the same mass of contaminated groundwater as many times as necessary by subjecting it to multiple stripping cycles.

The ART system has been successfully used to clean up contaminated groundwater in sediments and rocks to depths of over 100 m. It has been used to clean up groundwater contaminated with TCE, PCE, DCE, chloroform, methylene chloride, 1,4-dioxane, BTEX, MTBE, VC, and VOCs at a reduced cost and shorter time.

The ART system has been used to clean up contaminated groundwater at many locations in the United States and overseas. In most cases, conventional remediation, using air sparging, air stripping, and similar methods, had reached a plateau in lowering the concentration of the contaminants even after years of operation without attaining the desired regulatory level of cleanup. ART system not only brought the levels to within acceptable regulatory standards but achieved it in a matter of months, thereby saving huge costs and bringing the remediation operation to a closure. Details of ART system and case histories are available at its website: http://artinwell.com/Overview.asp?rid=0.

References

Accelerated Remediation Technology (2014). Art Integrated Technologies Overview. https://artinwell. com/Overview.asp?rid=0 (accessed 6 July 2016).

5.7.7 Sustainable (Green) Remediation

Sustainable, or Green, Remediation (SR) aims at *minimizing environmental cost and maximizing environmental benefits* by efficient use of natural resources and energy, reducing negative impacts on the environment, minimizing or eliminating (preferred) pollution at its source, and minimizing waste quantities. Strategies for green remediation rely on sustainable development to ensure that environmental protection does not preclude economic development and that economic development is ecologically viable today and into the future. Green remediation promotes incorporation of state-of-the-art methods for:

1) Conserving water and other resources
2) Improving water quality
3) Increasing energy efficiency
4) Managing and minimizing toxic materials
5) Managing and minimizing waste, and
6) Reducing the emission of criteria air pollutants (O_3, CO, NO_2, SO_2, Pb, and PMs), and greenhouse gases (GHGs)

SR emphasizes:

- Designing treatment systems with optimum efficiency and adaptability to prevailing site conditions
- Using renewable resources such as wind and solar energy to reduce or eliminate power demands of energy-intensive treatment systems or auxiliary equipment
- Using alternate fuels to operate machinery and routine vehicles
- Generating electricity from byproducts such as methane gas or secondary materials, and
- Participating in power generation or purchasing electricity from renewable resources.

Opportunities to implement SR exist throughout the investigation, design, construction, operation, and monitoring phases of site remediation. Several Superfund sites are being remediated using the SR principle, thereby entailing cost-saving and returning contaminated sites to acceptable land use. Details of SR along with case histories are available in the EPA document titled *Green Remediation: Incorporating Sustainable Environmental Practices into Remediation of Contaminated Sites* (EPA 2008).

5.7.7.1 Triad Approach

The Triad approach (TA) represents the best management practice developed from experience in the remediation science to provide the needed tools for making better cleanup decisions at contaminated sites. The TA is built on an accurate conceptual site model (CSM) that supports project decisions about exposure to contaminants, site cleanup and reuse, and long-term monitoring. The TA also incorporates the application of successful work strategies and the use of technology options that can lower project costs while ensuring that the desired levels of environmental protection are achieved. The three components of TA include:

1) Systematic planning that involves the gathering of any and all information related to the cleanup goal. Most importantly, the goal of the remedial effort is determined after consultation with all parties involved in the project, which include the site owner, potential buyer, insurer, regulator, and community spokespersons. Any uncertainties that could cause erroneous

decisions are identified, and a process to communicate, document, and coordinate all project activities are clearly defined.

2) Dynamic work strategies to develop consensus-derived decision logic for prompt, real-time decision making so that fieldwork can be modified as new information becomes available. A highly trained and experienced team is established and given the flexibility to make quick decisions in the field based on the evaluation of new data as they are obtained.

3) Use of real-time measurement technologies including geophysics and other imaging techniques, in situ analytical techniques, and expedited turnaround from mobile and fixed labs., to quickly provide data that can be used to refine the CSM while the project team is still in the field.

TA saves uncertainty in decision making, besides time, and money. Triad focuses on establishing clear project goals and a common understanding of the site in the form of a CSM. Consequently, systematic project planning is the single most important element in TA. Once project goals are understood, uncertainties that stand in the way of achieving those goals can be addressed by the team and stakeholders. Usually, environmental data will be collected to manage decision uncertainty. When data are used to make decisions, the sampling and analytical uncertainties inherent to environmental data generation must be managed to a level commensurate with project needs. Additional information on TA is available in *Triad Implementation Guide* (ITRC 2007b).

5.8 Superfund Program and Cleanup of Hazardous Waste Sites in the United States

Although two laws, the SWDA (1965) and the Resource Recovery Act (1970) were in existence, they were essentially ineffective due to the lack of specific rules and guidelines for proper management of waste. Nonetheless, these legislations were the forerunners of comprehensive laws that were enacted during the late 1970s. The RCRA enacted in 1976, affirming the need for proper management of solid and hazardous wastes with the goal to protect human health and the environment, is a good example of such legislations.

The USEPA, created subsequent to the passage of the National Environmental Policy Act (NEPA, 1970), was charged with translating the intent of the law into workable rules and guidelines. This being the very first instance worldwide for such a task – when environmental science did not exist as an academic discipline, and no trained professional, except epidemiologists and sanitary engineers, were available to carry out the huge task – it naturally took the time (about four years) for EPA to formulate the detailed and complex set of rules and guidance to implement RCRA. That the effort was worthwhile was fittingly recognized by Fortuna (1989, p. 1.7) who wrote: "Together these landmark statutes mark the end of the beginning of the national program by establishing the beginning of the end of unrestricted land disposal. They represent an enduring commitment to the creation of a hazardous waste management system in the United States that we can at last look on with pride and a sense of certainty rather than look back on with chagrin."

Four years after the passage of RCRA, the plight of Love Canal residents became well known nationally and internationally and under pressure from the citizen's group and lawmakers, the

US Government enacted the CERCLA in 1980. The law aims at cleaning up hazardous waste sites that were in existence *prior* to the passage of RCRA. It contains a provision for an emergency response to hazardous materials spills and cleanup, and a provision known as *joint and several liabilities*, which permits the EPA to recover the full cost of cleanup from *any* of the responsible parties, even if the party was responsible for part of the waste mismanagement. The law required the EPA to establish a National Priority List (NPL) of hazardous waste sites for accelerated remedial action with respect to their threat to human health and the environment. Details of CERCLA and its accomplishments over the past 40 years are discussed in Chapter 3. Here we focus on the hazardous waste site remediation process under the provision of RCRA and CERCLA.

According to the EPA in 2016, an estimated 35 million tons of hazardous materials were managed in the United States. Despite the technological know-how for the treatment and disposal of hazardous waste, progress toward cleaning up legacy sites where hazardous waste was produced and improperly disposed of has stalled, due to flat budget allocation at about $1.1 billion for the past 10 years. There are approximately 1300 Superfund sites where cleanup activities are either incomplete or not yet begun (ASCE 2021). Around 60% of all nonfederal Superfund sites are located in areas that may be impacted by flooding, storm surge, wildfires, or sea-level rise related to climate change.

5.8.1 Remedial Actions under RCRA and CERCLA

Two laws, RCRA and CERCLA, regulate the management and cleanup of hazardous waste in the United States. So, in practice, many of the methods used for cleaning up contaminated sites are common to both, the key difference is the year when the hazardous waste was dumped on the ground, i.e. its historical age. Like the majority of laws where the legal applicability begins from the date of its enactment, RCRA addresses hazardous waste generated since 1976 (and into the future). On the other hand, CERCLA addresses hazardous sites that existed prior to the passage of RCRA, i.e. before 1976. Love Canal, along with about 40 000 other contaminated sites, are examples of such historic or legacy sites.

Briefly, the CERCLA process involves the following sequence of actions: upon the report of a suspected dump containing hazardous substances, EPA initiates a preliminary action by sending its contractors to examine the reported occurrence to determine whether or not hazardous substances are indicated at the site. If it does, follow-up actions are initiated to determine the nature and extent of hazardous substances and potential threat to the population in its vicinity and to the environment, including wildlife, vegetation, surface water, and groundwater, especially if the latter is a source of drinking water supply. Media samples (soil, water, and air, if the presence of volatile compounds is indicated) are collected for subsequent analyses. The report of site evaluation and chemical analyses is used to rank the site in terms of its potential threat, using the HRS. Based on the ranking it receives, the site is either earmarked for cleanup action on a priority basis or placed low in the priority list for cleanup action. Table 5.8 contrasts the RCRA and CERCLA process for cleanup action.

As stated elsewhere, RCRA regulates hazardous waste generated since its enactment in 1976; the cleanup process is less complicated than CERCLA, which deals with all hazardous waste sites that existed before 1976 and could go back to hundreds of years which makes it difficult or impossible to find the polluter. Of the approximately 30 000 hazardous waste sites, estimated under CERCLA, 1600 worst-contaminated sites were placed on NPL. These included

Table 5.8 Comparison of CERCLA and RCRA remediation processes.

	CERCLA (owner not known)	RCRA (owner known)
START	Preliminary assessment (abandoned site)	RCRA facility assessment (current site)
	Site investigation	No RCRA equivalent
	Hazard Ranking System (HRS) scoring	No RCRA equivalent
	National Priority List (NPL) placement	No RCRA equivalent
	Remedial Investigation (RI)	RCRA facility investigation
	Feasibility studies	
	Record of Decision (ROD)	Corrective measure(s) study
	Remedial Design (RD)	
	Remedial Action (RI)	Corrective measure(s)
END	NPL deletion	No RCRA equivalent

1170 general (nonfederal) and 157 federal sites, as of February 2021. Since the inception of the Superfund program in 1980 and until June 2019, 413 sites have been cleaned and deleted from NPL.

The CERCLIS Database, containing a list of all Superfund sites in the United States, that was maintained by EPA since 1980 was retired in 2014. The data has been copied into a new database, named the Superfund Enterprise Management System (SEMS), which became operational in January 2016.

5.9 Summary

Uncontrolled dumping of hazardous waste had left a legacy of over 30 000 contaminated sites across the US. RCRA and CERCLA, besides other laws, were enacted in the 1970s and 1980s to prevent illegal waste dumping. While RCRA controls hazardous waste dumped after the passage of the law, i.e. from 1976 onward, CERCLA covers all waste dumped before 1976. EPA developed a comprehensive set of rules and regulations to implement the laws. Large budget allocation (billions of dollars) allowed EPA to begin cleanup work by prioritizing the worst contaminated sites, using the HRS, and placing them on the NPL for cleanup action. A biennial report, called TRI by EPA shows the status of hazardous substances released into the environment by various generators, and the steps undertaken for reducing the waste quantities. Special training and reporting requirements have been set for waste generators who are categorized as: LQGs, MQGs, and VSQGs. Rules have also been established for the storage and transportation of hazardous waste.

Various treatment and disposal methods are used for the safe management of hazardous waste. Physical, chemical, and biological methods can be used singly or in combination to render the hazardous waste neutral or reduce its toxicity to permissible levels. Green or Sustainable remediation is becoming common as it minimizes environmental cost and maximizes environmental benefits. The TA represents the best management practice of SR.

Study Questions

1   What is the difference between acute and non-acute hazardous waste? Give two examples of each.

2   What properties are used for defining RCRA characteristic waste? Discuss each of them.

3   What is the pH range of a noncorrosive waste? Give two examples of such materials.

4   What test method is used for the determination of toxicity of a waste? What waste product does this test simulate?

5   What type(s) of waste materials are included in the F, K, P, and U series wastes? Give one example of each.

6   Name the two major US laws that regulate hazardous waste.

7   Discuss the cradle-to-grave concept for hazardous waste management. What is a hazardous waste manifest?

8   Many of the waste materials from our homes that we throw in the garbage bag contain hazardous substances (such as toxic chemicals in batteries, leftover paints, cleaners, etc.), yet household waste is not classified as hazardous waste in the US. Explain the reasons.

9   List the training, reporting, and other compliance requirements for LQGs. Can the category of waste generators (LQG, MQG, and VSQG) change over time?

10   Who, among the various parties in handling hazardous waste (generator, transporter, and TDS facility owner), is responsible to ensure that the waste containers are properly marked and labelled?

11   Simple treatment of hazardous waste generated at a manufacturing facility is always desirable because it results in separating the nonhazardous portion from the hazardous portion. Explain why, giving suitable examples.

12   What is the destruction and removal efficiency (DRE)? Why does RCRA require a DRE of nearly 100% for the destruction of hazardous waste by incineration?

13   What is LDR? Give three examples. What are the main requirements for land disposal of hazardous waste?

14   Define green remediation and discuss its key elements.

15   What is the Triad process? List its three main features.

16   How does disposal of hazardous waste under RCRA contrast with CERCLA? Which law would govern a hazardous waste dumped on land in 1970?

References

40 CFR (2012). *Code of Federal Regulations, Title 40: Protection of Environment, Part 261: Identification and Listing of Hazardous Waste*. U.S. Government Publishing Office https://www.gpo.gov/fdsys/pkg/CFR-2012-title40-vol27/xml/CFR-2012-title40-vol27-part261.xml#seqnum261.20 (accessed 27 February 2018).

40 CFR (2017). *Code of Federal Regulations, Title 40: Protection of Environment, Part 262, v. 28, §262.14, Generator Category Determination*. https://www.gpo.gov/fdsys/pkg/CFR-2017-title40-vol28/xml/CFR-2017-title40-vol28-sec262-14.xml (accessed 23 May 2018).

Adler, J.H. (2002). *Fables of the Cuyahoga: Reconstructing a History of Environmental Protection*, 89–146. Faculty Publications Paper 191. http://scholarlycommons.law.case.edu/faculty_publications/191 (accessed 24 February 2018).

ASCE (2021). Infrastructure Report Card: Hazardous Waste, 62 p. Hazardous-Waste-2021.pdf (infrastructurereportcard.org) (accessed 29 July 2021).

Beyer, W.N., Dalgarn, J., Dudding, S. et al. (2004). Zinc and lead poisoning in wild birds in the TSMD (Oklahoma, Kansas, and Missouri). *Archives of Environmental Contamination and Toxicology* 48, Springer Science Business Media: 108–117.

EEA (European Environment Agency) (2014). Progress in Management of Contaminated Sites. https://www.eea.europa.eu/data-and-maps/indicators/progress-in-management-of-contaminated-sites-3/assessment (accessed 14 June 2018).

EPA (1989). Seminar Publication: Requirements for Hazardous Waste Landfill Design, Construction, and Closure. *Report No. EPA/625/4-89/022*, 127 p.

EPA (2000). Wastewater Technology Fact Sheet: Granular Activated Carbon Adsorption and Regeneration. *EPA 832-F-00-017*, 7 p, Washington, DC.

EPA (2008). Green Remediation: Incorporating Sustainable Environmental Practices into Remediation of Contaminated Sites. *Office of Solid Waste and Emergency Response Report No. EPA 542-R-08-002*, 56 p.

EPA (2009). Hazardous Waste Characteristics A User-Friendly Reference Document, 30 p. https://www.epa.gov/sites/production/files/2016-01/documents/hw-char.pdf (accessed 5 March 2018).

EPA (2016). Hazardous Waste Generator Improvements Final Rule; CLU-IN Webinar Archives (30 November 2016). https://clu-in.org/conf/tio/hwgenerators_113016/default.cfm#tabs-4 (accessed 19 March 2018).

EPA (2018). Hazardous Waste Test Methods/SW846. https://www.epa.gov/hw-sw846/sw-846-compendium (accessed 8 March 2018).

EPA (2021). Comparing Industry Sectors. Comparing Industry Sectors|US EPA (accessed 30 August 2021).

EU (2008). Directive 2008/98/EC of the European Parliament and of the Council of 19 November 2008 on waste and repealing certain Directives, Annex III; EUR-LEX 32008L0098. http://eur-lex.europa.eu/legal-content/EN/TXT/?uri=CELEX:32008L0098 (accessed 18 March 2018).

EU (2014). Commission Decision of 18 December 2014 amending Decision 2000/532/EC on the list of waste pursuant to Directive 2008/98/EC of the European Parliament and of the Council, Document No. (2014/955/EU), unpaginated. http://eur-lex.europa.eu/legal-content/EN/TXT/PDF/?uri=CELEX:32014D0955&from=EN (accessed 18 March 2018).

Fortuna, R.C. (1989). Hazardous-waste treatment comes of age. In: *Standard Handbook of Hazardous Waste Treatment and Disposal* (ed. H.M. Freeman), 1.7. New York: McGraw-Hill, Inc.

GAO (Govt. Accounting Office) (2021). Corrosive Waste Rulemaking Petition; Denial. Federal Register: Corrosive Waste Rulemaking Petition; Denial (accessed 30 August 2021).

Government Publishing Office (GPO) (2018). Electronic code of federal regulations (e-CFR), Title 40, Part 263. https://www.ecfr.gov/cgi-bin/text-idx?SID=f8dbf7319774464838cb34cd865f2508&mc=true&node=pt40.26.263&rgn=div5 (accessed 29 May 2018).

Hasan, S.E. (1990). *Some Unique Uses of Underground Space in Kansas City, U.S.A.: Proceedings, 6th International Congress, International Association of Engineering Geology, A.A*, vol. 4, 2727–2735. Netherlands: Balkema Publishers.

Hasan, S.E. (1996). *Geology and Hazardous Waste Management*. Upper Saddle River, NJ: Prentice Hall 387 p.

ITRC, 1997. Technical Requirements for On-site Thermal Desorption of Solid Media Contaminated with Hazardous Chlorinated Organics. *Final Report, TD-2*, 52 p. https://clu-in.org/conf/itrc/td-2.pdf (accessed 24 July 2018).

ITRC (2007a). Constructed Treatment Wetlands, Training PowerPoint Slides. file:///D:/BOOK%202/Ch%205%20Hazwaste/ITRC%20Wetland%20PP,%202017.pdf (accessed 5 August 2018).

ITRC. 2007b. Triad Implementation Guide. *SCM-3*, 63 p, Washington, D.C. www.itrcweb.org (accessed 23 May 2018).

Manders, G.C. and Aber, J.S. (2014). Tri-State Mining District legacy in northeastern Oklahoma. *Emporia State Research Studies* 49 (2): 29–51. file:///E:/BOOK%202/Ch%205%20Hazwaste/Manders%20&%20Aber2014%20Tristate%20legacy%20paper.pdf (accessed 24 February 2018).

Saliba, N.A., Nassar, J., Hussein, F. et al. (2016). Chapter five – airborne toxic pollutants: levels, health effects, and suggested policy implementation framework in developing countries. *Advances in Molecular Toxicology* 10: 187–233.

TIME (1969). America's Sewage System and the Price of Optimism. http://content.time.com/time/subscriber/article/0,33009,901182-1,00.html. (accessed 24 February 2018).

Watts, R.J. (1998). *Hazardous Wastes: Sources, Pathways, Receptors*, 764. New York, NY: Wiley.

Wendenburg, H; (2018), Underground disposal – a key element of the German waste management concept. Workshop Volume: Underground Disposal of Hazardous Waste. https://www.grs.de/sites/default/files/kum/Workshop-Volume.pdf (accessed 19 July 2018).

Supplementary Reading

Hasan, S.E. (1996). *Geology and Hazardous Waste Management*. Upper Saddle River, NJ: Prentice Hall 387 p.

Newman, R.S. (2016). *Love Canal: A Toxic History from Colonial Times to the Present*. New York, NY: Oxford University Press 306 p.

Tedder, W.D. and Pohland, F.G. (2002). *Emerging Technologies in Hazardous Waste Management 8*. New York: Kluwer Academic Publishers 256 p.

Web Resources

EPA. Hazardous Waste|US EPA. This site provides comprehensive coverage of all aspects of hazardous waste management: identification of hazardous substances, laws pertaining to hazardous waste, compliance requirements for hazardous waste generators; treatment and disposal; Superfund program, and related information.

EU. Hazardous waste – Environment – European Commission (europa.eu) Useful information on all aspects of hazardous waste management in EU countries.

Acronyms/Symbols

M   million
n.d.   no date
ppb   parts per billion, µg/L (micrograms per liter, µg/L)
ppm   parts per million, mg/L (milligrams per liter, mg/L)
t   ton, metric

6

Medical Waste

LEARNING OBJECTIVES

After studying this chapter, you will be able to:

- Understand the history and need for regulating medical waste (MW) and the Medical Waste Tracking Act (MWTA).
- Interpret various definitions and the difference between USA and WHO's definition.
- Describe various types, sources, and associated hazards of MW and its safe management.
- Explain waste types generated in hospitals, best management practice, and benefits of segregating regular waste from regulated medical waste (RMW).
- Summarize methods of treatment and disposal of RMW.
- Review COVID-19 and other emerging diseases and their impact on MW management.

6.1 Introduction and Historical Context

Medical waste (MW), also called health care or biomedical waste, is a special category of waste that contains infectious agents or hazardous materials that have the potential to cause adverse health impacts to humans and the environment. The term health care waste (HCW) is commonly used in Europe and other countries for waste generated at hospitals, and other health care facilities, while the term medical waste (MW) is common in the USA.

> No epidemiologic evidence suggests that most of the solid or liquid wastes from hospitals, other health care facilities, or clinical/research laboratories is any more infective than residential waste. . . .. Moreover, no epidemiologic evidence suggests that traditional waste disposal practices of healthcare facilities (whereby clinical and microbiological wastes were decontaminated on site before leaving the facility) have caused disease in either the healthcare setting or the general community. This statement excludes, however, sharp injuries sustained during or immediately after the delivery of patient care before sharp is "discarded."
> —CDC (2015b).

Not much attention was given to the management of MW until the 1980s, when the outbreak of HIV/AIDS swept across the USA and the rest of the world, creating fear among the public that was based on false notions. Discovery of MW, comprising syringes that washed up on beaches in

Introduction to Waste Management: A Textbook, First Edition. Syed E. Hasan.
© 2022 John Wiley & Sons Ltd. Published 2022 by John Wiley & Sons Ltd.

New York and New Jersey during 1987–1988, creating scare of HIV/AIDS infection, led to the closure of a 50-mile stretch of beaches in New Jersey State. The scare, termed the *Syringe Tide* by the media, was put to rest when investigations revealed that it came from the *Fresh Kill Landfill* on Staten Island, NY. The Syringe Tide scare prompted the US Congress to amend and pass a new law, called Medical Waste Tracking Act (MWTA), which was added as Subtitle J to RCRA on 24 March 1989. The law required the United States Environmental Protection Agency (US EPA) to create a program to track MW from the source to its final destination/disposal facility (the cradle-to-grave concept) to eliminate the waste fouling up the nation's waterways. EPA developed a set of regulations that were implemented in June 1989 in New York, New Jersey, Connecticut, Rhode Island, and Puerto Rico. The regulations expired on 21 June 1991. At the end of the 2-year period, EPA concluded that the maximum potential for causing disease exits at the point of generation of MW, which tapers off away from the source. EPA also noted that the risk of disease caused by exposure to MW to the general public is much lower than the risk to health care workers (EPA 1990).

The MWTA also directed EPA to study the status of MW management in the country along with preparing a guidance document on MW management for use by officials in the US states and territories. EPA report titled *Medical Waste Management in the United States First Interim Report to Congress* (EPA 1990) provided for the first time comprehensive documentation on the source, quantity, and disposal methods of MW in the USA. The MWTA also mandated EPA to develop guidelines and validation procedures to help the US state and territorial governments formulate MW management policy. To accomplish this task, EPA convened several meetings and published a report titled *Technical Assistance Manual: State Regulatory Oversight of Medical Waste Treatment Technologies* (EPA 1994). Since the report was addressed to the State and Territorial Association on Alternate Treatment Technologies (STAAT), its thermal treatment validation test has been referred to as STAAT and has been quoted as such by many investigators and agencies including the World Health Organization (WHO) in their MW/HCW publications.

It is a well-recognized fact that MW poses risk to patients, health care workers, the community at large, and the environment (EPA 2017; WHO 2017; Windfield and Brooks 2015). Every community, regardless of its population size, should have a safe and reliable MW management system in place because proper handling and disposal of MW will reduce disease burden and entail savings in health care expenditure for the community. Most developed and some developing countries already regulate the hazardous fraction of MW comprising infectious agents, toxic chemicals, and radioactive substances, generated by health care facilities. Many other developing countries, on the other hand, have been lagging behind and to help them, the WHO has been offering successful training programs to establish, operate, and finance MW management programs (WHO 2020). The program has been successful and many countries in Africa and south and south-east Asia have developed an MW management system based on available resources.

The global MW market has been experiencing a rapid increase for the past several years. It is estimated that the global market value of MW management would increase from $13.4 billion in 2019 to $18.9 billion by 2025 end (Research and Markets 2020). The main reasons for the increase include:

- Aging population in developed countries that needs greater medical care. Among the developed countries, the US is the largest consumer of medical products
- Spiraling consumption of medical products
- Improved health care on a global basis results in an increasing number of hospitals and related health care establishments to treat more patients resulting in a larger volume of MW
- Emerging diseases: COVID-19, SARS, Ebola, MERS, W. Nile Virus, etc.

6.1.1 Definition

MWs comprise blood and other body fluids, tissues, and anatomical parts; used syringes, needles, razors, scalpels, bandages, and gauzes that are generally contaminated with hazardous chemicals and/or pathogens. However, the entire quantity of MW generated in a health care facility is not hazardous – bulk of it, between 75 and 90% – is nonhazardous and consists of common solid waste (WHO 2020). The Centers for Disease Control and Prevention (CDC) maintains the position that "No epidemiologic evidence suggests that *most* of the solid or liquid wastes from hospitals, other health care facilities, or clinical/research laboratories is any more infective than residential waste" (CDC 2015b). The statement exempts the minor part (10–25%, more commonly 15%) comprising "sharps" (needles, syringes, broken glass vials, etc.) that may carry potentially harmful substances capable of causing health problems to human beings.

The US EPA, recognizing that the entire MW stream generated in health care facilities, is not hazardous, uses the term "regulated medical waste" (RMW) to identify the small portion of MW that is potentially harmful and therefore subject to regulation. RMW is defined as a subset of MW, which is generated in the diagnosis, treatment, or immunization of human beings or animals, in related research studies, or in the production or testing of biologicals (EPA 1990). It does not consider waste generated by health care providers in private homes and excludes it from regulation (US Government 1989).

The WHO uses the term HCW and defines it as the waste generated by health care establishments, research facilities, and laboratories, and from other sources, home health care, such as dialysis, self-administration of insulin, recuperative care (WHO 2018). A major difference between the EPA and WHO's definition is that EPA does not include home HCW in its definition of MW.

The Occupational Safety and Health Administration (OSHA), of the US Department of Labor, defines "regulated waste as any waste that contains liquid or semiliquid blood or other potentially infectious materials; contaminated items that would release blood or other potentially infectious materials in a liquid or semiliquid state if compressed (blood-soaked bandages); items that are caked with dried blood or other potentially infectious materials that are capable of releasing these materials during handling; contaminated sharps; and pathological and microbiological wastes containing blood or other potentially infectious materials." OSHA also defined blood-borne pathogens as pathogenic microorganisms that are present in human blood and can cause disease in humans (OSHA 1991). Essentially, OSHA definition of RMW includes:

1) Liquid or semiliquid blood
2) Blood-soaked items that would release blood if squeezed
3) Pathological and microbiological waste (cultures and specimens)
4) Contaminated sharps
5) Isolation ward waste

Vomit, urine, feces, and solidified (nonliquid) blood are generally not considered regulated waste in federal or state waste guidelines.

OSHA requires that biohazard label (Figure 6.1) or red bag be used for RMW and visible labels be affixed to containers used for storage, transporting, or shipping. OSHA does not specify treatment and/or disposal method, which is done by states.

The MWTA classified the RMW into several categories as listed below:

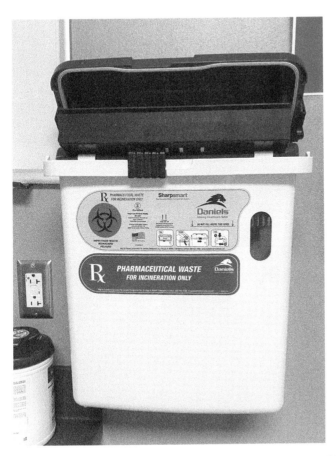

Figure 6.1 Medical waste container with biohazard label. *Source:* S.E. Hasan (author).

1) Cultures and stocks of infectious agents and associated biologicals, including cultures from medical and pathological laboratories, cultures and stocks of infectious agents from research and industrial laboratories, wastes from the production of biologicals, discarded live and attenuated vaccines, and culture dishes and devices used to transfer, inoculate, and mix cultures.
2) Human pathological wastes, including tissues, organs, and body parts that are removed during surgery or autopsy, or other medical procedures; and specimens of body fluids and their containers.
3) Waste human blood and products of blood, including serum, plasma, and other blood components; materials saturated or dripping with blood, that are now caked with dried human blood and their containers that were used or intended for use in patient care, testing and laboratory analysis, or the development of pharmaceuticals.
4) Sharps that have been used in human or animal patient care or in medical, research, or industrial laboratories, including hypodermic needles, syringes (with or without needle), Pasteur pipettes, scalpel blades, blood vails, test tubes, culture dishes (regardless of the presence of infectious agents); all broken or unbroken glassware that came in contact with infectious agents, including slides and coverslips.

5) Contaminated animal carcasses, body parts, and bedding of animals that were exposed to infectious agents during research, production of biological materials, or testing of pharmaceuticals.
6) Wastes from surgery or autopsy that were in contact with infectious agents, including soiled dressings, sponges, drapes, lavage (body part washing) tubes, drainage sets, underpass, and surgical gloves.
7) Isolation waste including all biological waste and discarded materials (PPE) contaminated with blood, excretions, exudates or secretions from the humans who are isolated, to prevent the spread of communicable diseases, or from animals known to be infected with highly communicable diseases (SARS and Ebola are examples of such diseases).
8) Unused or discarded sharps including hypodermic needles, suture needles, syringes, and scalpel blades.
9) Laboratory wastes from medical, pathological, pharmaceutical, or other research, commercial, or industrial laboratories that were in contact with infectious agents, including slides and coverslips, disposable gloves, laboratory coats, and aprons.

Some other types of MW are exempted either because they are covered under other laws, or are impractical to implement. These exempted MWs include:

1) Ash from the incineration of RMWs
2) Hazardous waste, such as toxic chemicals or radioactive materials, identified or listed in 40 CFR Part 261 (discussed in Chapters 5 and 7)
3) Household MWs
4) Human remains intended for cremation or internment

6.2   Nature, Source, and Quantity of Medical Waste

Large modern hospitals are complex establishments comprising many units that include: reception and patient's waiting area, accounting and billing division, food service unit, general and specialized wards, operating rooms, radiological diagnosis and treatment units, pharmacy, store and supplies units, waste segregation areas, besides the usual parking spaces, vehicles and patients loading and unloading areas, and building and ground maintenance units. Smooth functioning and coordination among all units is a complex undertaking and calls for thoughtful planning, careful monitoring, and adequate supervision. Large, multispecialty hospitals and clinics employ trained hospital administrators to accomplish the task. In addition, a trained environmental management person is on the staff to assure compliance with all legal matters as required by local, state, and national health agencies.

6.2.1   Nature of Medical Waste

Safe management of MW calls for thorough planning and implementation of a carefully crafted waste management plan with a goal toward sustainability. The WHO (2020) provides a detailed list and characterization of different types of hazardous MW that should be included in a sound MW management program. Table 6.1 lists various types of MW generated in large hospitals where the bulk of the waste comprises nonhazardous solid waste, with a smaller amount of hazardous chemical (including radioactive) and infectious wastes.

Table 6.1   Medical waste generated at hospitals and other health care facilities.

Department	Sharps	Infectious and pathological waste	Chemical, pharmaceutical and cytotoxic waste	General waste, non-hazardous
From hospitals				
Medical wards	Hypodermic and intravenous needles, broken vials and ampules	Dressings, bandages, gauze, and cotton contaminated with blood and body fluid	Broken thermometers and blood pressure gauges; split medicines; spent disinfectants	Packaging, food scraps, paper, plastics, flowers, empty saline bottles, non-bloody diapers, IV tubing and bags
Operating theater	Needles, IV sets, scalpels, blades, saws	Blood and body fluids; suction canisters, gowns, gloves, masks, gauze; other blood- and body fluids-contaminated wastes; organs, tissues, body parts, fetuses	Spent disinfectants	Packaging, unconta-minated gowns, gowns, masks, gloves, hats, and shoe covers
Laboratories	Needles, broken glass, Petri dishes, slides and cover slips, broken pipettes	Blood and body fluids; microbiological cultures and stocks; infected animal tissues and carcasses; containers and tubes contaminated with blood or body fluid	Fixatives; formalin; toluene, xylene, methanol, methylene chloride, and other solvents; broken lab thermometers	Packaging, paper, and plastic containers
Pharmacy	Broken bottles and thermometers	—	Expired drugs, spilled drugs, empty containers	Packaging, paper, plastics
Radiology	—	—	Silver, fixing and developing solutions, glutaraldehyde, radioisotopes	Packaging, paper, plastics
Chemotherapy	Needles and syringes	—	Chemotherapeutic waste; vials, gloves and other materials contaminated with cytotoxic agents; radioisotopes, contaminated excreta	Packaging, paper, plastics
Vaccination	Needles and syringes	—	Bulk vaccine waste, vials and gloves	Packaging, paper, plastics
Cleaning services	Broken glass	—	Disinfectants, cleaners, spilled mercury, pesticides	Packaging, flowers, plastic and glass containers, yard waste, newspapers, cardboard, and magazines
Engineering	—	—	Cleaning solvents, thinners, oils, lubricants, asbestos, broken mercury devices, batteries	Packaging, C&D waste, metals, wood

(Continued)

Table 6.1 (Continued)

Department	Sharps	Infectious and pathological waste	Chemical, pharmaceutical and cytotoxic waste	General waste, non-hazardous
Food service	—	—	—	Food scraps, paper, plastics, metal and glass containers; packaging.
Other health care facilities				
Physicians' office	Needles, syringes broken ampules, and vials	Cotton, gauze, dressing, gloves, masks, and other materials contaminated with blood or body fluids	Broken thermometers and blood pressure gauges; expired drugs; spent disinfectants	Packaging, office paper, newspapers, magazines; uncontaminated gloves and masks
Dental clinic	Needles, syringes broken ampules	Cotton, gauze, dressing, gloves, masks, and other materials contaminated with blood	Dental amalgam; spent disinfectants	Packaging, office paper, newspapers, magazines; uncontaminated gloves and masks
Home health care	Lancets, injection needles; insulin	Bandages and other materials contaminated with blood or body fluids	Broken thermometers	Domestic waste

Source: After WHO (2018).

6.2.2 Sources of Medical Waste

Any facility that offers health care services is a source of MW. In the US and many other developed countries, health care provided through a number of large and small, government or privately owned, facilities including those providing veterinary services, are all sources of MW. Such facilities include:

a) Ambulatory Health Care Services. The following types of facilities are covered under this category:
  a) Physicians' offices
  b) Dentists' offices
  c) Other health practitioners' offices
  d) Outpatient care centers
  e) Medical and diagnostic laboratories
  f) Home health care services
  g) Other ambulatory health care services. These include chiropractic care, massage, acupuncture, and acupressure
b) Hospitals. A number of health care facilities are covered under this category.
  a) General medical and surgical hospitals
  b) Psychiatric and substance abuse hospitals
  c) Specialty (except psychiatric and substance abuse) hospitals, includes: academic medical center/university-based/teaching hospitals, community hospitals, specialty hospitals, such

as orthopedic or pediatric, and tertiary care facilities, qualified to handle major trauma cases (burns and catastrophic accidents)

c) Nursing and residential care facilities. This category includes the following types of facilities.
  a) Nursing care and assisted living facilities
  b) Residential mental retardation/health and substance abuse facilities
  c) Community care facilities for the elderly
  d) Other residential care facilities. Home nursing, and other residential care facilities
D) Pharmaceutical research and testing establishments
E) Veterinary services. This industry includes licensed veterinary clinics primarily in the practice of veterinary medicine, dentistry, or surgery for animals, and establishments providing testing services for licensed veterinary practitioners
F) Miscellaneous sources: autopsy centers, illicit drug houses, and mortuaries

It should be noted that although all the above establishments generate MW, some of them are not regulated by EPA, such as home nursing care and residential care services. These are regulated by a majority of states in the US. Illicit drug houses also generate RMWs that are regulated by states and EPA.

Proper provision for segregating different types of waste at their point of origin is essential for workers' and patients' safety. Significant savings in disposal cost and potential legal problems caused by exposure to workers can be realized by following a carefully designed waste collection, segregation, and storage plan. Figure 6.2 shows a generalized floor plan for collection, segregation, and storage of various types of wastes for subsequent disposal.

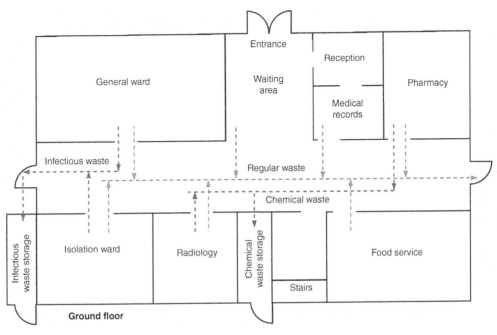

Figure 6.2 Floor plan of a hospital showing collection and segregation of various types of wastes.

6.2.3 Wastes from Major Health Care Establishments

Wastes generated from hospitals and other health care establishments can be grouped into four classes:

1) Infectious waste
2) Hazardous waste including chemical waste
3) Radioactive waste
4) General waste (MSW)

Infectious waste contains agents like bacteria, viruses, parasites, or fungi (pathogens) in a concentration sufficient to cause disease in susceptible hosts. It includes cultures and stocks of infectious agents from laboratory work, and waste from infected patients in isolation wards comprising excreta, dressings from infected or surgical wounds, and clothes heavily soiled with human blood or other body fluids. Waste contaminated with blood or other body fluids include: free-flowing blood, blood components, and other body fluids; dressings, bandages, swabs, gloves, masks, gowns, drapes, and other materials contaminated with blood or other body fluids; and waste that has been in contact with the blood of patients undergoing hemodialysis, including dialysis equipment such as tubing and filters, disposable towels; and personal protective equipment (PPE).

Waste from autopsies, animal bodies, and other waste items that have been inoculated, infected, or in contact with highly infectious agents are all infectious waste. Discarded instruments or materials that have been in contact with persons or animals infected with highly infectious agents are also considered infectious waste. Such waste must be properly packaged in red plastic bags with a clearly marked biohazard label.

Hazardous waste generally comprises chemicals and other substances that are: corrosive, reactive, ignitable, or toxic; or are included in the EPA's list of hazardous substances, as defined in the US Resource Conservation and Recovery Act (RCRA) of 1980 (see Chapter 5 for a detailed discussion of hazardous waste characteristics). This portion of hospital waste must comply with record-keeping, reporting, storage, handling, and other compliance requirements as set forth in RCRA. Chemical waste is a subcategory of hazardous waste and is subject to the same rules for compliance as hazardous waste. Similar requirements also apply to noninfectious pharmaceutical wastes. Table 6.2 lists major groups of hazardous chemicals found in MW generated at health care facilities.

Radioactive wastes represent a special class of hazardous wastes that are contaminated with radionuclides. Various diagnostic and treatment procedures in large hospitals generate radioactive waste. *In vitro* analysis of body tissue and fluid, *in vivo* organ imaging, tumor localization; and various investigative and therapeutic procedures generate radioactive wastes.

Radionuclides used in health care come either as unsealed (open) or sealed sources. Unsealed sources are usually in liquid form that are applied directly, while sealed sources are radioactive substances contained in parts of the device or encapsulated in unbreakable or impervious objects, such as pins, needles, or "seeds" (a tiny radioactive material, such as ^{125}I, ^{103}Pd, ^{192}Ir, or ^{137}Cs; about the size of a rice grain, placed inside the body for treatment of prostate cancer). The majority of radioactive HCW have short half-lives (hours to a few days), but some procedures involve radionuclides with longer half-lives. Waste in the form of sealed sources may have relatively high radioactivity, but is generated in low volumes. Sealed sources are generally returned to the supplier and should never be allowed to enter the waste stream.

Table 6.2 Major groups of hazardous chemicals in medical waste.

Chemical waste	Examples
Halogenated solvents	Chloroform, methylene chloride, perchloroethylene, refrigerants, trichloroethylene
Nonhalogenated solvents	Acetone, acetonitrile, ethanol, ethyl acetate, formaldehyde, isopropanol, methanol, toluene, xylenes
Halogenated disinfectants	Calcium hypochlorite, chlorine dioxide, iodine solutions, iodophors, sodium dichloroisocyanurate, sodium hypochlorite (bleach)
Aldehydes	Formaldehyde, glutaraldehydes, ortho-phthalaldehyde
Alcohols	Ethanol, isopropanol, phenols
Other disinfectants	Hydrogen peroxide, peroxyacetic acid, quarternary amines
Heavy metals	Arsenic, cadmium, chromium, lead, mercury, silver
Acids	Acetic, chromic, hydrochloric, nitric, sulfuric
Bases	Ammonium hydroxide, potassium hydroxide, sodium hydroxide
Oxidizers	Bleach, hydrogen peroxide, potassium dichromate, potassium permanganate
Reducers	Sodium bisulfite, sodium sulfite
Miscellaneous	Anesthetic gases, asbestos, ethylene oxide, herbicides, paints, pesticides, waste oils

One of the ways to attain sustainability in MW management is to perform an audit of the waste stream at the health care facility, using the waste audit form shown in Table 6.3 to determine how much of the total waste comprises RMW that would require special handling, treatment, and disposal. Next, a waste audit of the ordinary MSW, as described in Chapter 4, should be conducted. This will enable the health care facility to implement a waste recycling program for the MSW that will result in significant cost savings.

6.2.4 Quantity of Medical Waste

The type and quantity of MW are related to the size and level of health care services offered by the facility. For example, a primary care clinic in a rural area in a developing country would generate some sharps, pharmaceuticals, bandages, and gauzes but hardly any pathological, anatomical, or radioactive waste. On the other hand, multispecialty hospitals in an urban area in developed countries would generate all types of RMWs in substantial volume, besides large amounts of MSW.

The quantity of MW generated is commonly represented in kg/bed/day (kg/b/d). It is calculated by measuring the total weight of MW generated at the hospital in a day, and then dividing it by the number of occupied beds at the hospital. The total weight includes both ordinary waste that can be disposed of in landfills and RMWs that must be disposed of at licensed facilities in an approved manner. The total amount of MW generated in the US in 2012 was 3.5 million t/y or 10.7 kg/b/d of MW of which 2.79 kg/b/d comprised RMWs (Windfield and Brooks 2015). Like the MSW, the quantity of MW also depends on a number of factors, notably level of economic development, demographic characteristic, and quality of health care in the country. Table 6.4 shows a generalized average of MW generated in 42 selected countries in Africa, Americas, Asia, and Europe for which data were available.

The MW amounts shown in Table 6.4 have been averaged from the values reported by Minoglou et al. (2017), who used a number of papers published between 2001 and 2016. As new and more

Table 6.3   Medical waste audit form.

Date_____		Name of data collector _____		
Name of health care facility _____				
Number of occupied beds _____		Number of outpatients _____		
Department/unit	**Waste type**[a]	**Weight, kg**	**Volume, L (liters)**	**Notes**

[a] Use the following abbreviations for waste types:

A Sharps
B Infectious
C Pathological/anatomical
D Chemical
E Pharmaceutical
F Radioactive
G General (common waste, MSW). Record weights of paper, plastics, food, and other common wastes for developing a recycling program at the facility and to minimize RMD volume.

Table 6.4   Generalized quantity of medical waste in 42 selected countries.

World region	MW quantity (average)	Range, kg/b/d
Africa (8 countries)	0.78 kg/b/d	0.44 (Mauritania)–1.1 (Egypt)
Americas (6 countries)	4.41 kg/b/d	1.85 (El Salvador)–8.4 (United States)
Asia (18 countries)	2.45 kg/b/d	0.50 (Nepal)–5.70 (Lebanon)
Europe (10 countries)	3.1 kg/b/d	1.18 (Latvia)–3.6 (Germany and Greece)

Source: Modified after Minoglou et al. (2017).

detailed research studies have been conducted during the past five years, the reported values are likely to be different. Nonetheless, the information presented in Table 6.4 confirms the fact that, like most other types of wastes, MW too has a direct correlation between the quantity generated and the GDP of the country.

Some researchers have attempted to examine relationships between socioeconomic indicators and the quantity of MW generated in a country to develop a reliable statistical model to predict the MW quantity. Windfield and Brooks (2015) used three indices, gross domestic product (GDP), health care spending, and health care system performance, and quantity of MW generated in the country. They found that two indices, GDP and health care expenditure, showed strong correlations with the MW quantity. Another study by Minoglou et al. (2017) attempted to mathematically predict MW quantity using empirical models. They used 12 socioeconomic and environmental indicators (Table 6.5), and using multiple linear regression modeling, found a good correlation between life expectancy, CO_2 emissions, and MW generation rate. They concluded that the human

Table 6.5 Indicators for predicating medical waste quantity.

Indicator	Description
GDP per capita	This is the gross domestic product (GDP), in US $/capita, using purchasing power parity rates.
Total health expenditure	Health expenditure (HE) or health care spending in US $/capita, is the sum of public and private health expenditures; is a percentage of the GDP.
Human Development Index	Human Development Index (HDI) is a summary measure of average achievement in key measures of human development, i.e. a long and healthy life, knowledgeable citizens, and a decent standard of living. The HDI does not consider inequalities, poverty, human security, empowerment, etc.
Inequality-adjusted Human Development Index (IHDI)	IHDI combines the country's average achievement in health, education and income with how those achievements are distributed among the country's population.
Multidimensional Poverty Index (MPI)	MPI identifies the number of people who are multi-dimensionally poor and the number of deprivations with which poor households typically strive. MPI refers to developing countries only, as there are no relevant data for developed countries.
Life expectancy (LE)	The number of years that a newborn infant could expect to live if prevailing patterns of age-specific mortality rates at the time of birth stay the same throughout the infant's life
Mean years of schooling	Average number of years of education received by people 25 years and older
HIV prevalence, adult	Percentage of the population (ages 15–49) who are living with HIV
Deaths due to tuberculosis	Number of deaths due to tuberculosis from confirmed and probable cases, expressed per 100 000 people
Deaths due to malaria	Number of deaths due to malaria from confirmed and probable cases, expressed per 100 000 people
Under-five mortality rate	Probability of dying between birth and the age of five, expressed per 1000 live birth
CO_2 emissions	Carbon dioxide emissions (in t/capita/y) coming from the burning of fossil fuels and cement manufacturing; includes CO_2 produced during consumption of solid, liquid, and gas fuels and gas flaring

Source: Based on Minoglou (2017).

development index and mean years of schooling can also be used for predicting MW quantity. Among these four indicators, annual CO_2 emissions were found to be the index that affected the MW generation rate the most. This is explained by the fact that the health care sector in developed countries, like the USA, contributes a significant amount of CO_2 emissions, up to 8% (Pichler et al. 2019) to total CO_2 emissions for the country. This may seem odd because the health care sector is essentially a service sector that does not produce any material goods. However, the use of a large number of medical equipment and consumable substances in aging and affluent nations result in greater CO_2 emissions and larger amounts of MW.

The practical application of statistical models is that certain readily available indicators for various countries can be used to mathematically predict MW quantity using such models, thus obviating the need for MW audit that is costly and potentially hazardous.

6.3 Hazards Associated with Regulated Medical Waste

Everyone in the health care facility is at risk of harmful exposure. In a major hospital, physicians, nurses, ward staff, cleaners, and waste handlers are all exposed to needle sticks, blood spatter, pathogenic aerosols, and spills that usually result from unsafe work practices or lack of awareness. Patients too could be exposed to improperly discarded sharps found in linens, or to accidental spills, all of which can be minimized by proper education of the hospital staff in workplace health and safety issues through comprehensive training and annual refreshers. The main sources of infections in a hospital are:

- **Staff:** Staff who are untrained in health and safety issues or do not take proper measures to minimize risks are a major source of infections to patients and others in the hospital.
- **Patients:** During treatment and stay in the hospital, patients release body fluids and other potentially hazardous substances that, if not properly managed, could expose others.
- **Environment:** In the controlled and nearly sealed environment of a hospital, hazardous substances, chemicals, and microorganisms in aerosols (e.g. the virus SAR-CoV2); and tiny bits of PVCs in plastic bags and tubing (microplastics) remain suspended in the air for a long time. Adequate air exchange and use of high-efficiency particulate air (HEPA) filters can eliminate most of the airborne hazardous substances, but not all. The filters are designed to trap 99.7% of particles > 0.3 micron (μ) in size. Viruses are very minute, from <0.1 to $0.004\,\mu$ in diameter, and the SAR-CoV2 that caused COVID-19 has a diameter ranging between 0.06 and $0.14\,\mu$ (average about $0.10\,\mu$). A recent study (Li et al. 2020) found a large quantity of nano plastics, in the 0.3–$0.8\,\mu$ size range, comprising degradation products of polypropylene (PPE) baby feeding bottles. Although the health impact from ingestion of nano plastics by babies is yet to be studied, the use of plastic feeding bottles, bags, and tubing have the potential to cause serious health problems. The education and training of hospital staff should keep up with such scientific findings and appropriate measures taken to minimize their exposure.

The production, segregation, transportation, treatment, and disposal of health care wastes involve the handling of potentially hazardous material. All workers must be given proper training to protect themselves against personal injury. Health and safety training should cover: risk identification and assessment; surveillance of workplace hazards; designing safe workplaces; developing and monitoring workplace health and safety plans including evaluation of safety and potential hazards associated with new equipment; training on occupational health safety and hygiene, and use of PPE; and familiarity with first aid and emergency treatments and surveillance of workers' health. MW management policies should be monitored continuously to enhance workers' safety.

Although RMW comprises only a small fraction of the total volume of MW generated in a hospital, it poses a significant risk to humans and the environment, if not managed properly. Strict regulations and enforcement in developed countries have minimized the risks, but cases of serious health impacts from exposure to RMW in developing countries are quite common. Hazards from RMW are due to the presence of infectious agents, genotoxic or cytotoxic chemicals, toxic or hazardous chemicals, or biologically aggressive pharmaceuticals, radioactive substances, and sharps.

While physical injuries from exposure to syringes, needles, and broken glassware are frequent, even a tiny amount of radioactive waste from discarded containers could result in serious injuries and death. In general, however, such injuries are uncommon and occur from ionizing radiations from unsafe operation of X-ray equipment, improper handling of radiotherapy solutions, or inadequate control of doses of radiation during radiotherapy. One extreme incident in Brazil (Case Study 6.1) illustrates the deadly impact on the population from unintentional exposure to radioactive substances from a health care facility.

By far, the greatest risk from RMW is infection from live pathogens (Table 6.6). Bacteria and viruses are known to cause serious diseases and even death if no medical intervention is available.

Case Study 6.1   Radiological Waste Management Following The 1987 Radiological Accident at Goiania, Brazil.

This case study describes one of the many radiological accidents that are reported to the International Atomic Energy Agency (IAEA) by its member countries. IAEA has a database of all major and minor accidents involving radioactive materials, which is available on its website. The Goiania accident highlights a life-threatening emergency that resulted from mismanagement of lethal radioisotopes used in medical diagnosis and treatment and the challenging task of managing the radioactive waste subsequent to the accident. The Goiania radiological accident of 1987 presents a sobering case study of: (i) deaths and serious irreversible injuries to people when highly radioactive medical substances accidentally end up in wrong hands and at wrong places, and (ii) the daunting task of managing the radioactive waste resulting from unauthorized removal of the deadly radioisotope, and tracking its movement across a wide area.

The case study serves as a good example of how a developing country, without any prior experience of handling such emergency and managing radioactive waste, used available resources, to complete the formidable task in a safe and efficient manner.

Regulated medical waste (RMW) comprises infectious, hazardous, and radiological materials, collectively grouped under RMWs by the US EPA and account for 10–15% of the total volume of MW generated at health care facilities. Of this minor fraction, radiological waste accounts for even a tinier fraction, 1–5%. Yet, despite this small quantity, some of the radioisotopes, like ^{60}Co or ^{137}Cs, have the potential to cause serious injuries, even death to people. Fortunately, such dangerous materials are highly regulated to ensure their safe-keeping and overall security. Generally, the national or local atomic energy authority of a country formulates rules and regulations for safe handling and management of such radioisotopes, placing the responsibility for its safe custody and oversight on the hospital's chief administrator, or the owner of cancer treatment clinics.

6.1.1. Use of Radioisotopes for Treatment of Cancer

Dozens of radioisotopes are routinely used in the diagnosis and treatment of diseases. Radiotherapy is a common method for the treatment of cancer. Depending upon the type and severity of cancer, either brachytherapy or teletherapy can be used. Brachytherapy involves internal radiation where tiny radioisotopes of ^{103}Pd for prostate cancer, or ^{131}I for thyroid cancer, called seeds, are placed inside the patient's body at the site of the cancerous area. The precisely placed radioisotope delivers the required radiation dose onto the cancerous mass and does not affect the surrounding healthy tissues because the radiation drops off inversely as the square of the distance from the source. Such type of treatment is called brachytherapy and has been successfully used to cure various types of cancers all over the world (Mayo Clinic 2020).

Teletherapy is used to treat other types of cancer where the high-energy external radiation source is outside the body. ^{60}Co is one of the commonly used radioisotopes in modern machines to deliver a beam of high-energy radiation from a distant source onto the affected area. Teletherapy is a confusing term because it is also used for other types of teletherapies that are delivered remotely via the Internet, e.g. psychiatric and other medical therapies, which became very popular during the 2020–2021 COVID-19 pandemic. Using the prefix "radiologic" teletherapy should remove this confusion.

During the 1950s to early 1960s, machines manufactured for the treatment of cancer used ^{137}Cs as a radiation source. Many radiation therapy machines using ^{137}Cs were imported in Brazil from the USA and other European countries during the 1950s. One such machine was involved in the Goiania radiological accident.

The radioactive source material, ^{137}Cs, in the form of cesium chloride salt, is supplied by the manufacturer in a small, sealed metallic container to the cancer treatment facility with the provision that after the radioisotope decays over time and loses its radiation, it should be returned in the original sealed container to the manufacturer. In nearly all cases, this protocol is strictly adhered to, but in rare cases, due to human errors or negligence, the sealed containers end up at unsecured places where untrained people tamper with it, exposing themselves and others to harmful doses of radiation, causing severe injuries and death.

6.1.2. Goiania Accident Background

Goiania, a large city (1980 population: 1 million) and capital of Goia State, is located on a plateau, about 1350 km NW of Rio de Janeiro in Brazil. A private cancer therapy clinic, the *Institute Goiano de Radioterapia*, was built in 1971 near a charity hospital in the central city. According to an IAEA report, the Brazilian National Nuclear Energy Commission, CNEN, had approved the import of the machine from Italy in June 1971, which became operational soon afterward (IAEA 1988). Under the terms of the operating license issued by CNEN, a physicist and a physician (one of the partners) were jointly responsible for ensuring that the conditions of the license were complied with. After a few years' use, the machine was phased out and replaced by a newer ^{60}Co machine in 1978. In December 1985, the clinic, along with the ^{60}Co machine, was located elsewhere in Goiânia, but the old machine with cesium was left at the clinic. Some reports indicate that due to litigation with the charity hospital, the clinic owners could not transfer the ^{137}Cs machine (Leite and Roper 1988). The hospital and most of the clinics were demolished but not the radiation treatment rooms due to the litigation, making it easy for the vagrants to enter the unsecured structure.

The radioisotope, ^{137}Cs, was used as the radiation source in the Italian-made 1950s vintage teletherapy machine involved in the Goiania accident. The radioisotope was likely manufactured at the Oak Ridge National Laboratory, USA, and supplied in a small multi-shield, cylindrical capsule, about 5 cm in diameter and 4.75 cm long, containing about 27 g of ^{137}Cs, with an activity level of 50.9 TBq, (1375 Ci). Despite the small quantity of about 19 g of ^{137}Cs (about 8 g had decayed since its manufacture), the total radioactive wastes that were generated from this source amounted to about 3500 m^3 (about 275 truckloads) – almost 150 000 times more than its initial volume – with activity level ranging between 47 and 49.6 TBq, or 1370 and 1340 Ci (Paschoa et al. 1993).

6.1.2.Release of Gamma (Υ) Radiation

On 13 September 1987, two scavengers entered the derelict structure of the former cancer clinic and removed the rotating source assembly from the radiation head of the teletherapy machine to sell as scrap metal, unaware of its contents. They tried to open the assembly by using a hammer, causing the assembly to rupture, and puncturing the capsule containing the radioactive cesium chloride salt, which is a highly dispersive solid and readily dissolves in water. Remnants of the source assembly were sold for scrap to a junkyard owner, who was fascinated to notice that the material glowed blue in the dark (cesium chloride glows blue upon moisture absorption). Word quickly spread around and several persons came to see the phenomenon. The owner distributed rice-size grains of cesium chloride to several families. This went on for five days, by which time a number of people developed gastrointestinal symptoms due to radiation exposure. Some exposed persons traveled by bus to nearby localities, causing radiation contamination to others.

Initially, radiation exposure was not recognized as the cause of the symptoms, but on 28 September, an exposed individual took pieces of the source to the public health department, *Vigilancia Sanitdria* (VS), of the city and gave the bag to a doctor telling him the stuff was killing his family. The physician, suspecting pieces of an X-ray unit, kept the bag outside the office and contacted the Goias State Department of Environment. The next day, a medical physicist arrived with a scintillation counter and was stunned to see the needle going off the scale while he was still some distance away from VS. He was thus able to identify radiation exposure as the cause, and advised the evacuation of all personnel. A few hours later, he took the scintillation counter to the junkyard and nearby houses where the needle again went off the scale. Convinced that there was a major radiation source, he alerted the authorities who ordered all radiation victims to be evacuated.

Four persons died, one person had his forearm amputated, and 249 people suffered injuries from external and internal radiation: 120 persons who received external exposure were treated (decontaminated) using showers, soap, and mild disinfectants. Of the remaining 129 who had received both external and internal radiation, 120 had received a dose of <1.0 Sv/h' and nine received doses ranging between 1 and 7 Sv/h (both on a 70-year basis). Treatment of sick persons continued for some time. In addition, authorities ordered the demolition of a number of contaminated structures, excavation of yard soils, and temporarily stored nearly 3500 m^3 of the radioactive waste in steel drums and containers near the accident site. This operation was completed by 9 December 1987. Pending the selection of the final repository site and two years later, the waste was moved to a temporary location, near the village of Abadia de Goias, about 23 km from Goiania.

6.1.3. *Management of Radioactive Waste*

Demolition of contaminated buildings, excavation and removal of contaminated soils from the $1\,km^2$ affected area yielded a large volume of waste that was grouped into the following three categories (IAEA 1988):

1) Nonradioactive waste: Radiation level <74 kBq/kg (2 nCi/g)
2) Low-level waste: Dose rate <2 mS/h
3) Intermediate-level waste: Dose rate >2 mS/h – <20 mS/h

The Brazilian exemption level for a waste to be considered radioactive is 0.3 mSv/h ($\approx$87 Bq/g). Thus, the worst-contaminated portion of the waste, amounting to about $1850\,m^3$, would become innocuous in a maximum period of 356 years (Paschoa et al. 1993).

Taking into consideration the geology, hydrology, and IAEA requirements for near-surface waste disposal facilities, three candidate sites were identified for the final repository: the first was located at a distance of 400 m from the temporary storage site at Abadia de Goiás, and the other two at small villages, 74 and 100 km from the temporary storage facility, respectively. All three sites had similar safety ratings and the State of Goiás selected the Abadia de Goiás as the final repository site (Magalhães et al. 2005). Site characterization and site selection investigations were commenced in 1991 and completed in 1993.

The waste for final disposal was reclassified based on its level of radioactivity and anticipated decay time to attain safe levels of 87 Bq/g. The entire waste was regrouped into five categories as shown in Table B6.1.

All wastes were disposed of in two near-surface waste repositories built of reinforced concrete. The nonradioactive waste in Group 1 was disposed of in a separate large reinforced concrete structure, measuring 54 m × 14 m × 4 m. Group 1 waste, comprising 40% of the total waste volume contained in steel drums, metal boxes, and shipping containers, was disposed of in this structure and backfilled with local clay. The waste emplacement was completed in May 1995.

Wastes belonging to groups 3–5, comprising about 60% of the total waste volume, including the recovered ^{137}Cs source, were disposed of at another nearby reinforced concrete structure, measuring 60 m × 19.6 m × 6.2 m. Group 2 and Group 3 waste were placed in 90 concrete containers with 15 cm-thick wall; Group 4 and Group 5 waste were repacked in 16 steel cylinders. Placement of the wastes was done with the highest radioactivity level (Group 5) kept in the center and surrounded by progressively lower activity wastes, such that the Group 2 waste was at the periphery of the repository. Both repositories were capped by 50 cm-thick soil and vegetated by grass (Pontediero 2018).

Table B6.1   Waste classification for final disposal.

Group	Radiation level	Approximate volume, m^3	Decay period, years
1	Below exempt level	1500	—
2	Lowest	770	≤90
3	Lower	580	90–150
4	Low	430	150–300
5	Low-medium	50	>300

Source: Data from Magalhães (2005); and Paschoa et al. (1993).

For this facility, engineered barriers were designed to isolate the waste for a period of 300 years, with no retrieval. By providing adequate diversion of surface runoff, no leakage from inside the repositories is likely to occur over the 300-year life. Modeling studies performed recently confirmed that there is no likelihood of any radioactive material reaching the 4–5 m-deep water table during the lifespan of the repository, and people living in the vicinity will not encounter unsafe levels of ^{137}Cs in the groundwater (Pontediero 2018).

References

IAEA (1988). The Radiological Accident in Goiania, 152 p, Vienna, Austria. This and all other accident reports are available at: https://www.iaea.org/topics/accident-reports (accessed 12 December 2020).

Leite, M.A.S; and Roper, L.D. 1988. The Goiania radiation incident: a failure of science and society. Internet Archive: http://arts.bev.net/roperldavid/GRI.htm (accessed 27 December 2020).

Magalhães, M.H., Mezrahi, A., and Xavier, A.M. (2005). Considerations on the licensing of Brazilian waste repository in Goiania. *Proceedings: 2005 International Nuclear Atlantic Conference – INAC 2005*, Santos, SP, Brazil, unpaginated (28 August–2 September 2005).

Mayo Clinic (2020). *Brachytherapy*, Mayo Clinic (accessed 26 December 2020).

Paschoa, A.S; Tranjan Filho, A; and J.J. Rosenthal; 1993. Revisiting Goiania: toward a final repository for radioactive waste, *IAEA Bulletin*, 1993/1, p. 28–31.

Pontediero, E.M.B.D; Heilbron, P.F.L; Perez-Guerrero, J; Sue, J; and Van Genuchten, M.T. 2018. Reassessment of the Goiânia radioactive waste repository in Brazil using HYDRUS-1D; *Journal of Hydrology and Hydromechanics*, 66 (2);202–210 https://doi.org/10.1515/johh-2017-0047.

Table 6.6   Infection risk from exposure to pathogens.

Infection type	Caused by	Transmitted through
Gastronomic infections	Enterobacteria, e.g. *Salmonella Shigella* ssp., *Vibrio cholerae, Clostridium difficilie,* helminths	Feces and/or vomit
Respiratory infections	*Mycobacterium tuberculosis*, measles virus, *Streptococcus pneumoniae*, severe acute respiratory syndrome (including SARS-CoV-2)	Inhaled secretions, saliva
Ocular infections	Herpesvirus	Eye secretions
Genital infections	*Neisseria gonorrhoeae,* herpesvirus	Genital secretions
Skin infections	*Streptococcus* spp.	Pus
Anthrax	*Bacillus anthracis*	Skin secretions
Meningitis	*Neisseria meningitis*	Cerebrospinal fluid
Acquired Immunodeficiency Syndrome (AIDS)	Human Immunodeficiency virus (HIV)	Blood, sexual secretions, body fluids
Hemorrhagic fevers	Junin, Lassa, Ebola and Marburg Viruses	
Septicemia	*Staphylococcus* spp.	Blood
Bacteremia	Coagulase-negative *Staphylococcus* spp. (including methicillian-resistant *S. aureus), Enterobacter, Enterococcus, Klebsiella* and *Streptococcus* spp.	Nasal secretion, skin contact
Candidemia	*Candida ablicans*	Blood
Viral hepatitis A	Hepatitis A virus	Faeces
Viral hepatitis B and C	Hepatitis B and C virus	Blood and body fluids
Avian influenza	H5N1 virus	Blood, feces

Source: Modified after WHO (2014).

Since all live pathogens can be destroyed by subjecting RMW to high temperatures, incineration and autoclaving of such waste are the best way to kill them. Methods of safe treatment and disposal of RMW are discussed below.

6.4 Treatment and Disposal of Medical Waste

The main purpose of the treatment of RMWs is to eliminate or substantially minimize its potential to cause adverse health impacts to humans and the environment. RMWs' treatment is a necessary step before its final disposal.

The nonhazardous portion of the MW, comprising ordinary trash, does not require any pretreatment and can be sent directly to a disposal site, such as a landfill. On the other hand, RMWs, depending upon their nature, need to be pretreated before disposal.

Bulk of the MW, about 85%, is nonhazardous and comprises ordinary MSW containing paper, plastics, food, etc., that can be safely disposed of in landfills. For this reason, it is essential that this fraction of the waste be collected and stored separately from hazardous and infectious wastes to save disposal cost as it costs anywhere between 6 and 10 times more to dispose of RMW as compared to MSW. A 24-month investigation at the Johns Hopkins University's surgical suites in the adult, pediatrics, outpatient, and surgicenter units found that segregating the RMWs from the total MW, resulted in a substantial reduction in the quantity of RMWs, from about 50 to 38% entailing disposal cost saving of over $576 000 (Stonemetz et al. 2011). Although the cost savings represent an overestimate as it excludes the cost of staff time involved in the study. Other studies have shown that some hospitals have brought their RMW quantity down to 6% of the total MW by implementing waste minimization measures (H2E 2020).

There are no federal requirements governing the treatment of RMW in the US. Various US states, but not all 50, have developed and put in place regulations to manage RMWs. Common practice involves segregating, bagging, and biohazard labeling at the point of origin of RMWs before it is collected by a licensed transporter to carry it to a treatment or disposal facility. Many health care establishments have agreements with MW treatment companies that collect and transport RMWs to their treatment facility. Upon arrival at the treatment facility, information on the shipper, weight, etc., of the RMW is recorded before the waste is subjected to treatment. Several large international WM management companies operate in the US and other countries including: Biomedical Waste Solutions, Clean Harbors, Stericycle, Suez Environmental, Viola Environmental Services, US Ecology, Waste Management, and others.

No pretreatment for RMW is required at the generation source, other than sorting, packaging, and labeling. Sharps, biological agents, pathogen-contaminated materials, etc., should be appropriately segregated, properly packed, and clearly labeled at the time and point of generation and safely stored at a designated place before shipment to the treatment facility. Incineration is a common method of RMW disposal but other methods are also used. The choice of a treatment method mainly depends on: (i) nature of RMW, (ii) regulatory compliance, (iii) cost and disinfection efficiency, and (iv) public health and environmental considerations. The last factor is very important as certain disposal options may effectively reduce the infectious hazards of RMWs but, at the same time, may result in other health and environmental problems. For example, without adequate control of emissions, incineration of RMWs could release fine particles of toxic heavy metals and other combustion products such as dioxins, furans, etc., into the atmosphere, causing potential health problems to the nearby populations, particularly those downwind from the incinerator. Land disposal, in poorly designed landfills – common in many developing countries – results in ground and surface water pollution.

6.4.1   Methods of Treatment and Disposal of Regulated Medical Waste

Incineration used to be the preferred method of MW disposal. Before 1997, more than 90% of potentially infectious waste generated in the US hospitals was disposed of by incineration. Many large hospitals in the US and other developed countries had onsite incinerators. The total number of incinerators in the US before 1997 was estimated at around 2400 (EPA 2005). Significant concerns over harmful emissions affecting human health led to promulgation of stringent air emission standards for RMW incinerators by EPA in August 1997. With the new standards, many incinerators were shut down and the number of operating RMW incinerators in the United States steadily declined to about 54 in 2010 (EPA 2010). Stringent emission rules led to an increase in the use of alternative technologies for the treatment of RMW. These alternative treatments are now used to render the MW noninfectious, after which the waste can be disposed of as solid waste in landfills or WtE incinerators. Some of the commonly used RMW treatment methods include:

A) Thermal treatment
   a) Low-heat process
   b) Microwave and frictional heating process
B) Biological treatment
C) Chemical treatment
D) Radiation treatment
E) Encapsulation

6.4.1.1   Thermal Treatment

Thermal treatment of RMW uses heat energy to destroy pathogens. In general, low-heat thermal technologies for waste treatment operate between 100 and 180 °C and the processes take place in either moist or dry heat environments. Moist (or wet) thermal treatment involves the use of steam to disinfect waste and is commonly performed in an autoclave or steam-based treatment system (WHO 2014). High heat processes take place above 180 °C and most operate at temperatures of 850 °C or higher. Incineration is high-temperature combustion that reduces organic and combustible waste to inorganic, incombustible solid residues and gaseous by-products. Pyrolysis is the thermal degradation of materials through the application of heat in the absence of oxygen. Gasification involves the addition of small, controlled amounts of oxygen or steam. Well designed and properly operating incinerators can reduce waste volume by 80–90% and mass by about 75%. The main drawback of incineration is the emission of toxic products, including furans and dioxins, toxic metals, etc., unless they can be captured or neutralized before being released into the air.

6.4.1.1.1   Low-Heat Thermal Processes   Steam-based treatment technologies are widely used to destroy pathogens contained in infectious and sharp wastes by using heat (thermal energy) for a defined period of time, depending on the size of the load and its content. Sterilization, in the health care field, is defined as the process that destroys all forms of life including the dormant ones. Steam has been used for centuries to sterilize surgical tools and other medical equipment for microbial inactivation. Destruction of pathogens in an autoclave or a steambed treatment system is a good example of moist low-heat treatment processes. RMWs containing pathogens in sharps and infectious wastes are subjected to heat for a certain period of time that is predetermined on the basis of the quantity and content of the RMD.

An autoclave consists of a metal vessel designed to withstand high temperature (120–160 °C), and pressure (40–80 psi or 276–552 kPa), with a sealable door, pipes, and valves for entry and exit of steam from the vessel. Air is a key factor in determining the efficiency of steam treatment, and due to its insulating nature, it must be periodically removed from the autoclave to ensure full penetration of heat into the waste. Autoclaves for RMWs' treatment must also treat the withdrawn air to prevent the release of pathogenic aerosols. This is usually done by treating the air with steam or passing it through a specific filter, e.g. HEPA filter, or microbiological filter before release. The resulting condensate must also be decontaminated before discharging it into the wastewater system. Autoclaves have long been used in health care facilities for equipment and material sterilization, such as glassware, steel wares, and microorganisms. Autoclaves are the most common method used to inactivate microorganisms in RMWs. Figure 6.3 shows the essential components of a vacuum autoclave and a self-contained small shredding autoclave.

(a)

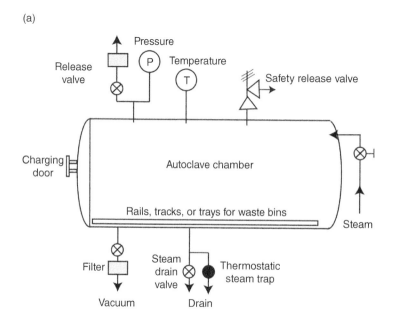

(b)

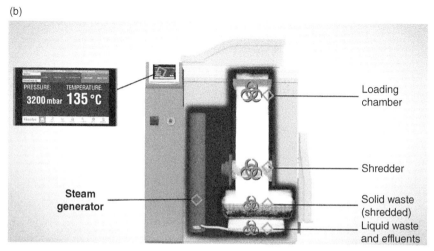

Figure 6.3 Vacuum autoclave: (a) schematic diagram and (b) a portable shredding autoclave. *Source:* Tesalys/Sterishred, France.

To guarantee the full inactivation of RMWs, the treatment process should be validated. The validation process uses biological, chemical, and physical test parameters. This is determined by the ability of the heat to penetrate the RMD load to destroy the pathogens. If a microorganism from the vegetative bacteria, fungi, lipophilic/hydrophilic viruses, parasites, and mycobacteria group is used to test the efficacy of the treatment process, it must achieve a destruction level corresponding to log10 reduction, also known as log_{10} kill. A log_{10} kill of 6 corresponds to 99.9999% reduction, or a one-millionth (0.000 001) survival probability, or a 10^6 kill; in other words, reduction of an initial microbial population of one million to zero or near zero (EPA 1994). A 4 log_{10} kill is equal to a 99.99% reduction, or a one-ten thousandth (0.0001) survival probability, or a 10^4 kill. If *Geobacillus* (formerly called *Bacillus*) *stearothermophilus* spores or *Bacillus atrophaeus* (formerly called *Bacillus subtillis var. niger*) spores are used, reduction levels should be 4 log_{10}, i.e. reduction by 4 orders of magnitude, or 0.0001 (UNDP 2010). Both the US and EU regulations require that the result of waste decontamination efficiency for each cycle of treatment be properly documented. These validation methods can be used to determine the efficacy of thermal, chemical, or irradiation treatments.

Modern RMD autoclaves use a vacuum pump and/or a steam ejector to evacuate the inside air before introducing steam, to ensure safe decontamination of the waste. This is done in one of the two ways: (i) using vacuum to evacuate the air before injecting steam as in high vacuum autoclaves, or (ii) using a pulsed or fractionated vacuum process (FVP) to remove the air. Autoclaves with FVP evacuate inside air and allow steam to enter several times under varying pressures ranging from near zero (vacuum) to about 0.5 bar absolute 3 psi or 20 kPa to ensure maximum removal of air from the chamber. After all air is removed and vacuum condition is attained, steam at about 2 bar absolute pressure (29 psi or 200 kPa) is maintained during the treatment to ensure better steam penetration and temperature uniformity during the inactivation phase. A post-treatment drying phase is added to protect the operator against exposure to hot steam when opening the door. After treatment, the waste is considered nonhazardous and can be disposed of in a landfill or used in WtE plant.

6.4.1.1.2 Microwave and Frictional Heat

Both are examples of moist (about 10% water content) thermal treatment processes because disinfection occurs through the action of moist heat generated by microwave energy or by friction. Generally, small-scale microwave treatment is accomplished in batches by feeding a known quantity of RMWs into the device that generates heat (temperature: > 90 °C) from a microwave source that inactivates the bacteria and viruses in RMWs. For large-scale and industrial treatment, continuous feed microwave systems are used. In a typical industrial microwave system, radio frequency energy at 2450 MHz is absorbed by RMWs, causing frictional heat in water molecules, which kills and inactivates the pathogens. The efficiency of microwave treatment depends on frequency, moisture content, exposure duration, and mixing of the waste. Microwave treatment can effectively inactivate most RMWs except cytotoxic, hazardous, or radioactive wastes.

Frictional treatment uses the heat generated by friction and impact of RMWs by rotor blades. Heat is provided by heaters or generated by a rotor operating at high speeds, usually between 1000 and 2000 rpm. A moist environment is maintained inside the chamber while retaining negative pressure. To decontaminate the waste, it is held between 135 and 150 °C for several minutes. Vapors generated upon heating flow through heat exchangers that convert steam to water. Activated carbon and HEPA filters are used to capture harmful materials before releasing the leftover vapors into the environment. Significant waste volume reduction, unrecognizable and nonhazardous nature of the residue are the main advantages of the frictional heat-treatment process. Some of the disadvantages include high operation and maintenance costs due to damage to rotor blades from the high-speed movement of materials.

Low-heat treatment can be combined with mechanical methods like shredding, grinding, mixing, and compaction to reduce waste volume, but such treatments do not destroy pathogens. Shredders and mixers before treatment improve the rate of heat transfer by increasing the surface area of waste for treatment. Mechanical methods should not be used for infectious and sharp waste before the waste is decontaminated, except if the mechanical process is part of a closed system that decontaminates the chamber of the mechanical process and air before it is released into the surrounding environment. Mechanical methods involve greater operational and maintenance costs but have the advantage of reducing the waste volume to the minimum possible extent.

6.4.1.2 Biological Treatment

Biological treatment mimics natural biodegradation. Composting, vermiculture, biodigestion, and natural decomposition of human and animal remains through burial are examples of biological treatment of RMWs. Placenta and human anatomical parts can be treated by biological processes. Generally, a minimum period of two years should be allowed for the decomposition and inactivation of all pathogens. A tight-fitting solid cover made of concrete or thick steel should be used to prevent the escape of any gas. Care should also be taken to ensure that the burial site is not in hydraulic connection to any surface or groundwater source.

6.4.1.3 Chemical Treatment

RMWs can also be decontaminated with chemicals. Generally, manual methods using chemicals for decontamination of RMWs are not efficient due to lack of precise control of the extent and duration of contact between the waste and the chemical, and difficulty in maintaining the operating temperature, pH, and humidity during the treatment. Generation of toxic liquid waste during treatment requires neutralization before releasing from the system; and potential harmful reaction products require additional safety measures. Due to these limitations, manual chemical inactivation has been replaced by fully automated chemical disinfection processes that monitor the chemical concentration continuously, control the operating conditions, and assure safety for workers and the environment.

Powerful disinfectants, such as sodium hypochlorite (NaClO), chlorine dioxide (ClO$_2$), or a mixture of glutaraldehyde (C$_5$H$_8$O$_2$) and quaternary ammonium salts such as cetrimonium (C$_{19}$H$_{42}$ClN), O$_3$, or alkaline (NaOH) hydrolysis, are used for the inactivation of pathogens. Some highly hazardous HCWs, including microbiological cultures, infected sharps, and certain pharmaceuticals, can also be disinfected chemically.

Fully automated chemical treatment methods using disinfectants are problematic as they produce toxic effluents and increase the risk of exposure of toxins to HCW workers. Two exceptions are ozone treatment and alkaline hydrolysis. Ozone is a strong gaseous disinfectant and can be generated on site, avoiding the need to transport and store it. Alkaline hydrolysis uses sodium or alkaline hydroxide at high temperatures, 100 °C, to destroy tissues. It is also proven to destroy prion-containing RMWs (McDonnell et al. 2013). Prions are infectious proteins that cause devastating neurological diseases, such as transmissible spongiform encephalopathies (TSEs), a group of progressive, invariably fatal conditions that occur in animals (mad cow disease) and humans (Creutzfeldte Jakob disease variant). Alkaline hydrolysis is also capable of destroying cytotoxic pharmaceuticals.

Sodium hypochlorite-based automatic treatment technology. This automated chemical treatment system utilizes the strong oxidation power of sodium hypochlorite (NaClO). Unlike the manual treatment of infectious waste by chemicals, this process is automated and controlled continuously, resulting in effective and safe decontamination of pathogenic tissues, liquid waste such as blood, urine, stools, or hospital sewage. The system is designed to automatically control operating conditions, such as pH, temperature, and conductivity during the oxidation process. Waste is fed into the system by a conveyor belt or directly into the shredder where an oxidizing condition is maintained under negative pressure. The air is filtered by a HEPA filter. During the oxidation process in the reactor, an air-aspiration system conveys the gases into a liquid chemical trap for neutralization, and then through carbon filters, eliminating the release of any hazardous substances into the atmosphere. At the end of the decontamination process, the residual waste is neutralized with sodium thiosulfate to remove free chlorine.

The use of automated sodium hypochlorite treatment has the following advantages and disadvantages: Low environmental impact, no hazardous residues, significant reduction of waste volume, and unrecognizable residue. Some disadvantages include: difficulties in real-time monitoring of chemical concentration, strict occupational safety measures, and higher operational and maintenance costs. NaClO is a strong oxidizer and its reaction products are corrosive.

6.4.1.4 Radiation-based Treatment

Irradiation is the process of using a source of energy to inactivate pathogens. RMWs are commonly treated using electron beams, ^{60}Co, or UV irradiation. These technologies use harmful electromagnetic radiation in the form of high-energy waves or particles and require shielding to prevent occupational exposures. Electron beam irradiation uses a stream of high-energy electrons to destroy microorganisms in the waste by chemical dissociation and rupture of cell walls. The efficacy of the process to destroy pathogens depends on the dose absorbed by the waste, which depends on the level of radiation, which itself is a function of waste density and electron energy. Germicidal ultraviolet radiation (UV-C) has been used as a supplement to other treatment technologies. Irradiation does not alter the waste physically and would require a grinder or shredder to render the waste unrecognizable for final disposal in landfills.

6.5 The COVID-19 Pandemic and Its Impact on Waste Management

The 2019–2022 COVID-19 pandemic that took a toll on millions of lives worldwide was caused by a new form of corona virus that had triggered severe acute respiratory syndrome (SARS) disease some 20 years ago. SARS had first appeared in Guangdong Province in China in November 2002, after it had jumped from animal to human. It later spread to 30 countries, including the United States. A total of 8437 people were infected and 813 died during November 2002–July 2003 (WHO 2003). Its later variant, MERS-CoV, led to Middle East respiratory syndrome (MERS) disease in 2012. From July 2012 to November 2019, it caused 2494 infections and 858 deaths (WHO 2019), majority in Saudi Arabia (2102 cases; 780 deaths). The 2013–2016 Ebola outbreak infected over 27 000 people and caused deaths to over 11 000 globally (CDC 2015a). Compared to these, the pandemic resulting from SARS-CoV-2 caused several million deaths and infected nearly 500 million people throughout the world, dwarfing the mortalities and morbidities from SARS, MERS, and Ebola combined. Recent studies (UNEP & ILRA 2020, UNEP 2020b) have shown that in future such zoonotic diseases are likely to rise in both frequency and intensity, which will require much sophisticated and effective approaches to deal with these not only in terms of saving lives but also for safe management of the large quantities of MW that will be generated.

6.5.1 The Great Pandemic of 2020 and Medical Waste

Lethal nature and rapid transmission capability of the SARS-CoV-2 (Delta variant, B.1.617.2) created a global crisis that galvanized the world to address its horrible impacts on a warlike footing (Daughton 2020). The multi-faceted problems impacted every sector of society, notably health care, economy, food security, and politics. In about two years (March 2020–March 2022), COVID-19 resulted in over 6.2 million deaths and 521 million infections as of 14 May 2022 (Johns Hopkins University 2022). Large-scale use of facial masks, gloves, aprons, gowns, face shields and discarded syringes, needles, and plastic and paper packaging used for vaccine transportation generated a colossal amount of MW. This large-scale increase strained the waste handling and disposal ability of the worst-affected countries, creating serious environmental impacts. Increased quantity of plastics manufactured for packaging and shipping of billions of vaccines across the globe and the resulting waste has caused concerns about its impacts on fresh and marine water ecosystems. Besides the increase in MW quantity, the fact that about 67% of health care facilities worldwide do not have waste segregation and disposal system in place has further exacerbated the problem.

The COVID-19 pandemic caused a record number of deaths and infections worldwide due to its poorly understood biology and unique pandemic onslaught. Wuhan, China, where the first case of COVID-19 was reported on 17 November 2019 and which is believed to be the place where the SARS-CoV-2 virus jumped from animal to human (zoonosis), witnessed a dramatic increase in the amount of MW generated. The average volume of MW in Wuhan before the onset of the pandemic was about 45 t/d, but during the pandemic it increased to 115–150 t/d in mid-February and peaked at 247 t/d on 1 March 2020. Normal volume resumed in early May 2020 (Wei 2020). An interesting aspect of COVID-19-related MW was uncovered in its density change during this time period: While the average density of MW in China is 120 kg/m^3, in Wuhan it was found to drop by nearly 50% to 67 kg/m^3 during January–March 2020, increasing to 77 kg/m^3 in April and 85 kg/m^3 in May. This reduction in MW density was caused by addition of a large volume of lighter weight PPE and single-use plastics that were consumed and discarded in large quantities during the pandemic. Low weight of PPE and lightweight materials, despite greater volume, initially lowered the MW density, during the early months of the pandemic, but gradually increased as the infection intensity began to taper off and regular and heavier MW replaced the lighter PPE. These aspects along with measures taken in Wuhan, China, to combat COVID-19, and lessons learned, are described in Case Study 6.2.

Case Study 6.2   Medical Waste Management in Wuhan, China

With a staggering population of 1.4 billion people and being the first country to be hit by SARS-CoV-2 in November 2020, China dealt with the pandemic in a most expeditious way to keep the death and infection rate under control. Unlike many developed countries, China had learned its lessons on how to combat novel zoonotic diseases, as early as 2003, when it was devastated by SARS. Since 2003, the country has enacted more than 30 laws, regulations, standards, and specifications related to emergency management of medical waste (MW). In 2020, Chinese experts produced an authoritative book, *Handbook of Emergency Disposal and Management of Medical Waste in China* (Chen and Guo 2020) to provide guidance for the safe management of the COVID-19 waste. For the benefit of other users, the authors and publishers offered free copyright of the book for use by any country or region in the world.

It is believed that the first known case of infection occurred in a 55-year-old male in Hubei province on 17 November 2019 when the SARS-CoV-2 virus jumped from bat to humans, possibly via pangolin. By 22 January 2020, 41 confirmed cases of COVID-19 were reported in Wuhan – the worst impacted city (Huang et al. 2020).

The peak of pandemic occurred between 15 February and 15 March 2020 and, as of 21 March 2020, the country's MW disposal capacity had reached 6067 t/d compared to 4903 t/d before the pandemic. In the Hubei province, the capacity increased from 180 t/d before the pandemic to 667 t/d after and in the provincial capital, Wuhan city, the disposal capacity jumped to 247 t/d during the peak – nearly six times greater than before the pandemic (Singh et al. 2020).

Incineration was recommended as the preferred method for emergency disposal of MW. The country strictly observed *Collect all to be collected, leaving no MW of the day till the next morning* rule followed by on-site disposal, off-site transportation, and final disposal. Taking advantage of the technology of the Internet of Things (IoT) involving sensors, global positioning system, scanning devices, and video surveillance, they were able to achieve real-time tracking of MW from processing, collecting, storing, transportation to final disposal, including remote real-time monitoring, data gathering, and analyses.

Nearly all literature on COVID-19 MW in China, instead of quoting the quantities of MW generated, refer to waste disposal capacity, which seems odd. However, considering the massive and urgent task of saving thousands of lives and implementing necessary measures on a war footing, along with the need to retain the army of workers involved in the effort, it seems judicious to use proxy for the quantities of MW generated. A careful record of the disposal capacities of incinerators, microwave systems, furnaces, and kilns was maintained which served as reliable proxies for MW quantities.

6.2.1. Lesson Learned

The staggering number of infections and deaths in a very short time period overwhelmed the MW management infrastructure in Wuhan. The city was put under lockdown from 23 January to 8 March 2020 and although the highest priority was saving lives and flattening the curve, the challenge of managing the huge volumes of MW was never lost sight of. At the outset, it was realized that letting the MW pile up would lead to further infection and would add to the burden of disease. Accordingly, the collection, storage, transportation, and disposal of MW were managed in the most efficient manner. Looking back, it is safe to conclude that the Chinese success story in mitigating COVID-19 resulted from prompt mobilization and effective deployment of the country's health care system for effective management of the COVID-19 waste. It also brings to fore the point that both medical personnel and waste personnel offer essential service to the population and is a resounding authentication of the words of Dr. Martin Luther King that he had spoken over a half-century ago (Chapter 4 opening quotation).

The main lessons learned from the Chinese experience of dealing with the pandemic can be summarized as follows:

1) Pandemics, like COVID-19, generate a large volume of discarded face masks, gloves, and other single-use protective gears, syringes, and needles, all of which are a potential source of the virus and must be treated as RMW.
2) Prompt collection and safe disposal of the waste must be carried out by concerned parties, and to ensure compliance, strict penalties should be imposed on those failing to observe the rules.
3) Resources must be provided to increase storage, collection, and disposal capacities without delay, to manage the mounting quantities of RMW. Mobile incinerators, along with storage facilities should be put into immediate service.

4) Since timely collection and disposal of the COVID-19 waste is of paramount importance in combating the pandemic, possible adjustments must be made to manage the waste safely and promptly. For example, the location of centralized MW storage and collection units in the affected area (particularly for large cities like Wuhan with a population of 11 million) should be changed by supplying many additional decentralized units across the area for efficient and timely collection and disposal of the RMWs.
5) RMWs that are successfully managed in normal times using certain treatment methods, such as incineration, should be expanded to include other methods, such as autoclaving, dry heat destruction, chemical disinfection, and microwave inactivation.
6) All available resources to expedite the collection, treatment, and disposal of pandemic wastes should be placed into service.
7) The entire MW management process should be automated so as to require as few personnel as possible to prevent potential infection.

In all fairness, credit must to given to China for its "rapid and efficient capacity to identify and investigate a newly emerging disease; and second, our continued global vulnerability to epidemics and pandemics. From the date of the first cluster of cases admitted to a local hospital on 27 December 2019, the Chinese scientists identified this disease as a new syndrome, discovered the pathogen as the cause, and reported its genetic sequence to the world in less than 14 days" (Daszak et al. 2020).

All evidence point to the troublesome reality that climate change and human alteration of natural habitats would exacerbate zoonosis and outbreaks of epidemics will be more frequent. Advance planning and adequate preparation to deal with such situations should be given top priority by policymakers in all countries. A reserved workforce of personnel in the health care and waste management sectors must be trained to deal with the emergency. Online MW management training programs developed by WHO (2020) are excellent resources to train interested people at the lowest possible cost. The key to successfully control the onslaught of epidemic/pandemic is advance preparation, using all available means, including disease surveillance, diagnostics, emergency preparedness, fully stocked PPE and medical supplies, infection-control protocols, and dedicated health care and waste management teams to save lives and minimize economic loss.

As of 14 May 2022, global cases of infection and deaths from COVID-19 had reached 520.9 million and 6.3 million, respectively, with the US leading the world at 82.4 million infections and 999 528 deaths (more than the 1918–1919 flu pandemic death toll of 675 000), compared to 95 748 infections and 14 566 deaths in China (Johns Hopkins University 2022). The number is rising but mass vaccination of the populations should help control further spread of COVID-19. Scientific knowledge about the SARS-CoV-2 virus is not yet fully developed and its mutations into newer forms and potential resistance to the vaccines are worrisome. Ongoing research and trials offer the hope that with public willingness to get vaccinated, the pandemic will be brought under control.

References

Chen, Y; and Guo, C; 2020. *Handbook of Emergency Disposal and Management of Medical Waste in China*, (English edition); Montreal: Royal Collins Publishing Company, 162 p.

Daszak, P; Olival, K. J; Hongying Li, H. 2020. A strategy to prevent future epidemics similar to the 2019-nCoV outbreak, *Biosafety and Health*, Volume 2, Issue 1, p. 6–8. https://doi.org/10.1016/j.bsheal.2020.01.003.

Huang, C, Wang Y, Li X et al. 2020. Clinical features of patients infected with 2019 novel coronavirus in Wuhan, China. *Lancet*, 395: p. 497–506. https://doi.org/10.1016/S0140-6736(20)30183-5 Published online 24 January 2020.

Johns Hopkins University (2022). COVID-19 Map - Johns Hopkins Coronavirus Resource Center. Coronavirus Resource Center jhu.edu.

Singh, N; Tang, Y; Zhang, Z; and Zheng, C, 2020. COVID-19 waste management: Effective and successful measures in Wuhan. *Resources, Conservation & Recycling.* 163 105071. https://doi.org/10.1016/j.resconrec.2020.105071.

WHO (2020). Comprehensive coverage of all aspects of biomedical waste management. *Training Modules in Health-Care Waste Management.* https://www.who.int/water_sanitation_health/facilities/waste/training_modules_waste_management/en/ (10 September 2020).

6.5.2 COVID-19 Waste

In the context of waste management, the COVID-19 pandemic has impacted the industry in three significant ways: (i) large increase in volume of MW, (ii) shortage of trained workers to manage COVID-related waste, and (iii) limited disposal options. These factors combined with the contagious nature of SARS-CoV-2 virus, its novelty, lack of experience in dealing with it, misinformation, and suspicion created instability in the waste management industry. Global, national, and local health organizations and governments geared up to deal with the pandemic by mandating use of facial masks, safe distancing, and imposing lockdowns. Required COVID-19 testing necessitated by travel, work, or other reasons led to generation of an enormous volume of MW. Massive vaccination commencing in 2021 resulted in administration of nearly 11 billion doses of COVID-19 vaccine, covering 35% of the global population; billions more were planned (WHO 2022a). All these activities produced an enormous amount of COVID-19-related waste, some of which, like other MW, was hazardous. According to an assessment by UNEP, the amount of hazardous component of the MW arising from COVID-19 increased by 3.4 kg/b/d in five Asian cities – Manila, Jakarta, Kuala Lumpur, Bangkok, and Hanoi (UNEP 2020b). This is approximately 10 times more than the average volume of hazardous MW, which ranges from 0.2 to 0.5 kg/b/d.

Highly contagious nature of COVID-19 combined with misinformation, and heightened concern to control mortality and morbidity, led to a large volume of PPE being used and discarded in the early months of the pandemic outbreak in 2020. Besides the health care professionals who routinely use gloves, masks, and other PPE, the public all over the world was directed to use mask, and many countries treated all COVID-19 waste as hazardous. All of which resulted in a dramatic increase in global MW quantity by 14–425% from February to September 2020 during the peak of COVID-19. For the same period, the global quantity of COVID-19 waste jumped from 200 t/day to 29 000 t/day (Liang et al. 2021). According to Benson et al. (2021), globally up to 3.4 billion single-use masks were discarded each day in 2020.

Rising global demand for masks resulted in a 1200% increase in mask production in 2020. It is projected that after the pandemic subsides the PPE market, which experienced a 300% increase at the peak of the pandemic, will continue to grow, with global demand anticipated to increase by about 6–9% between 2022 and 2025.

6.5.2.1 Determination of the Quantity of COVID-19 Waste

The growing use and demand for medical- and non-medical grade PPE worsened the global waste management system because the majority of PPE products, made from plastics, were

Table 6.7 Weight of various PPE.

Type of PPE	Weight (kg)
Surgical/exam gloves (pair)	0.018
Heavy-duty gloves (pair)	0.2
Hair cover	0.0175
Body bag	1.85
Coveralls	0.11
Gowns (8.5 kg/50 pieces)	0.17
3-ply mask (0.25 kg/50 pieces)	0.005
Respirator	0.02
Shoe cover (0.31 kg/50 pairs)	0.006
Apron protection/plastic	0.18
Disposable face shield	0.0356
Disposable lab coat	0.0554

Source: Modified from WHO (2022a, 2022b).

designed for single use and were not biodegradable. The PPE used by an estimated five billion people added to the waste volume that was disposed of by incineration. Without a better strategy for minimizing PPE waste, the volume of plastic waste is estimated to double in the next 20 years, which will result in a fourfold increase in the amount of plastics ending up in the world's oceans (WHO 2020).

Based on published literature and surveys conducted in selected countries in Asia and the United Kingdom on COVID-19 waste management practice, the WHO complied information to calculate the quantity of COVID-19 waste, shown in Table 6.7.

6.5.2.1.1 Calculation of Medical Waste Quantity
The rate of generation of all MW (solid + regulated) can be calculated from Eq. (6.1).

$$Q = n \times W \tag{6.1}$$

where Q is total quantity of MW in kg, n is the number of patients, and W is the average rate of waste generation in kg/p/y

6.5.2.1.2 Determination of COVID-19 Waste Quantity
The quantity of COVID-19 waste, Wc, can be determined by knowing the number and volume of the bags, assuming that 80% of each bag is filled with COVID-19 waste (20% allowance for bunching the bag top and securing the opening), and average density of COVID-19 waste, using Eq. (6.2).

$$Wc = Vc \times \rho \times f \times n \tag{6.2}$$

where Vc is the volume of COVID waste/bag, ρ is the density of COVID waste, f is the bag filling factor (generally 0.8), and n is the total number of bags filled per unit time (per day, or week).

Example Problems 6.1

1) Example: Determine the average quantity of medical waste in tons generated per month in a community hospital that has 45 beds (assume 90% occupancy) and generates 4 kg of MW/b/d. Using Eq. (6.1), we get

$$Q = 45 \times 4 \text{ kg} / \text{d} \times 0.9 \left(\text{for } 90\% \text{ occupancy} \right)$$
$$= 162 \text{ kg} / \text{d}$$

Total MW generated in one month $= 162 \times 30 = 4860 \text{ kg} = 4860 \text{ kg}/1000 = $ **4.86** or ~**5 t/mo**.

2) At the height of COVID-19 pandemic, a major hospital was filling up 950 bags per day with PPE. Assuming 80% filling of bags, waste density of 125 kg/m³, and volume of each bag to be 170 L, determine the total weight of COVID-19 waste (in tons) generated in one month.

First, make sure that all numbers in the equation are in the same unit of measurement (so, convert either volume of bag from liter to m³ or density from kg/m³ to L/m³).
From conversion tables, $125 \text{ kg/m}^3 = 0.125 \text{ L/m}^3$ and $170 \text{ L} = 0.17 \text{ m}^3$.

Using 0.17 m^3 for volume of each bag and Eq. (6.2), we have

$$Wc = 0.17 \text{ m}^3 \times 125 \text{ kg} / \text{m}^3 \times 0.8 \times 950$$
$$= 16\,150 \text{ kg} / \text{day}$$

Weight of COVID waste in one month $= 16\,150 \text{ kg} \times 30 \text{ days} = 484\,500 \text{ kg}$ in one month $= 484\,500/1000 = $ **484.5 or 485 t/mo**.

6.5.3 Reducing COVID-19 Waste Quantity

Globally, several multinational enterprises and start-ups are developing innovative solutions using biodegradable, compostable, or recycled materials in PPE, while meeting the strict performance standards at a reasonable price. Other innovations include converting the COVID-19 waste into high-quality products such as construction materials or new PPE items.

Many international and national organizations issued specific guidelines and advisories to manage COVID-19-related waste, particularly the regulated waste, by adopting proper segregation, collection, storage, transportation, and treatment of potentially contaminated waste, to control the steep increase in PPE generated during the pandemic. Plastic waste from PPE is being phased out by replacing multi-layer single-use, plastic masks by reusable high-quality, single-layer polymer masks. Biodegradable or renewable materials are also being used in PPE manufacturing. Predicted increase in major disasters will place increasing demand on PPE, which offers an opportunity for new innovations and investments in research and development in the materials industry (WHO 2022a, 2022b).

Rapid innovation is occurring in manufacturing environmentally sustainable masks and other PPE. As of February 2022, manufacturers in 20 countries were producing and selling high-quality, affordable PPE products (WHO 2022a, 2022b). This proves that much of the current supply of unsustainable PPE could be met with more sustainable and safe options, while pointing to the need for ongoing research and innovations.

The COVID-19 pandemic not only inflicted unprecedented deaths but also disrupted health care systems and destabilized the already strained medical waste management systems worldwide. However, it must be noted that the health sector contributed a relatively small proportion of COVID-19-related waste as compared to the large increase generated by the public. The lessons learned provide the opportunity to adopt sustainable MW management practices, especially those arising from massive natural disasters and pandemics, that include waste minimization, green procurement, safe reuse, recycling, and recovery.

Studies carried out during the latter half of 2020 and 2021 have concluded that the amount of pandemic waste could be greatly reduced by adopting a number of waste minimization approaches. These include innovations in PPE design, vaccine packaging, and delivery and no-burn waste treatment. These measures would protect human and ecological health in the event of future climate and health emergencies. The WHO (2022a, 2022b) has recommended the following measures:

- Promote and invest in more environmentally sustainable PPE and circular waste management systems: identify environmental innovations and actions that could save costs and reduce environmental impacts.
- The WHO, CDC, and other agencies should promote and support safe and environmentally sustainable management of MW by recommending more sustainable, safe, and reusable PPE products in their guidelines. Governments should be made aware of the benefits of using sustainable PPE and how it could reduce negative impacts on the ecosystem from overuse of disposables.

6.5.4 Waste Management Industry's Response to COVID-19

All major waste disposal businesses and trade associations, like the International Waste Management Association (IWMA), Solid Waste Association of North America (SWANA), and others, geared up promptly to deal with the increased volume of MW resulting from COVID-19. The former added equipment and personnel to collect and treat the increased quantities, and the latter proactively took steps for recognition of waste management as one of the essential services and issued and urged management of waste companies to follow guidelines from health agencies – local and state health departments, federal government (CDC, NIH, and others), and WHO to protect their workers. In addition, prominent MW treatment companies regularly posted important information about COVID-19 and its impact on the industry on their websites. Stericycle, a major international MW treatment company, presented many lectures and panel discussions on COVID-19-related topics via Zoom for information and education of interested parties (Stericycle 2020).

6.6 Summary

MW, also called biomedical, health care, or hospital waste, did not receive much attention prior to 1986. Discovery of MW, which washed up on beaches in New York and New Jersey, created a scare, termed the *Syringe Tide* by the media. The scare prompted the US Congress to pass a new law in March 1989, called MWTA. The law expired in June 1991 but EPA developed guidelines for MW management and encouraged states to adopt similar laws to manage MD in their respective US states and territories. Most developed countries have comprehensive laws to manage hazardous components comprising about 15–20% of the total MD, but developing nations are lagging behind. WHO has launched a major online initiative to train health care workers.

The hazardous portion of MW, called RMW, comprises infectious waste, hazardous waste, and radioactive waste, and requires special handling and treatment. Hospitals are major sources of MW besides dozens of other sources. On a global basis, the quantity of MW generated varies widely with developed countries generating larger quantities as compared to developing countries.

Health care workers and patients are at the highest level of risk from RMWs, and improper management of MW can cause adverse environmental impacts as well. Incineration that was the most common method of MW treatment before the mid-1990s was gradually phased out in the US due to its negative impact on the environment. Alternative treatment methods, mostly low-temperature thermal treatments, such as autoclaving and microwave inactivation are more common now; biological, chemical, radiation, and encapsulation methods are also used for MW treatment.

COVID-19, the disease caused by SARS-CoV-2 virus that originated in Wuhan, China, in November 2019, engulfed the world like a planetary wildfire and as of 14 May 2022, about 521 million people were infected and 6.3 million had died worldwide. Mass vaccination that began in early December 2020 effectively controlled the infection and deaths from COVID-19. The pandemic resulted in a huge increase in the volume of MW that was handled safely by the waste management industry. There is an urgent need to prepare and plan ahead to combat such outbreaks before they cause heavy morbidity and mortality.

Study Questions

1   Which event in the US led to the enactment of the Medical Waste Tracking Act (MWTA)? What caused the scare and what was the source of MW found in coastal areas? Is the law still in force? Who regulates MW in the US?

2   What was the most common method of MW disposal prior to 1997 in the US? Why were incinerators phased out? What harmful substances are released from poorly designed incinerators? Do modern incinerators prevent these? How?

3   What other terms are used for MW? What is the main difference between the medical MW definition used by the EPA and WHO?

4   What is the difference between infectious waste and MW?

5   What are regulated MW? What other types of materials are present in MW coming from a multispecialty hospital?

6   What are the sources of MW? Name two sources that generate MW but do not provide any health care to people. Of the various sources of MW, which health care facility generates the maximum quantity?

7   What factors affect the quantity of MW generated in a country? Discuss why countries, like the USA generate a greater amount of MW than developing countries? What is the prediction for the future quantity of MW on a global scale? What steps should be taken for its safe management in countries that do not have any law or guidelines for MW management?

8   What are the relative percentages of ordinary waste (MSW) and RMW in a typical MW? Why is it important to segregate MSW from RMW?

9   Discuss the hazards associated with RMWs, at the individual (worker's) level, the community at large, and the environment. What measures can be taken by the health care establishments to minimize the hazard and risk to people?

10   List the methods of treatment and/or disposal of RMWs. Which are the two most common methods?

11   How did COVID-19 impact the waste management industry in general and MW management businesses in particular? Does COVID-19 waste pose a threat to marine life? Explain.

12   The main multispecialty hospital in a large city has 650 beds with an occupancy rate of 85%. The average quantity of MW generated per day is 3.5 kg/bed. Calculate the total quantity of (a) MW generated per month in tons, (b) RMD per month assuming it comprises 15% of all MW, and (c) the quantity of MSW.
      [Ans. **(a) 68.25 t/mo; (b) 10.24 t/mo**].

13   At a COVID-19 vaccination center, 100 medical personnel administered Pfizer vaccine to 1500 persons in one day. The discarded PPE filled 75 bags, each of 150-L capacity and 80% full. The discarded syringes, needles, and empty vaccine vials together with the packaging materials filled 45 biohazard containers, each of 50-L capacity and 75% full. If the density of PPE is 125 kg/m^3 and the biohazard waste is 137 kg/m^3, determine the weight of (a) PPE, (b) biohazard waste generated, and (c) the % weight of MSW.
      [Ans. **(a) 1125 kg, (b) 231.5 kg, (c) 20.6%.**]

14   What useful lessons can be learned from the Chinese example of dealing with COVID-19?

15   "During a pandemic like COVID-19, waste management workers play as important a role as the health care workers, and society should treat them with equity." Explain whether you agree or disagree with this statement.

16   Based on the Goiania radiological accident of 1987, discuss possible problems that might arise when some unauthorized people remove highly radioactive isotopes, such as ^{137}Cs or ^{60}Co. What precautionary measures might be taken to avert such incidence?

References

Benson, N.U., Bassey, D.E., and Palanisami, T. (2021). COVID pollution: impact of COVID-19 pandemic on global plastic waste footprint. *Heliyon* 7 (2): https://doi.org/10.1016/j.heliyon.2021.e06343.

CDC (2015a). Ebola report: Ebola by the numbers. https://www.cdc.gov/about/ebola/ebola-by-the-numbers.html (accessed 21 March 2022).

CDC (2015b). Regulated Medical Waste. https://www.cdc.gov/infectioncontrol/guidelines/environmental/background/medical-waste.html (accessed 26 September 2020).

Daughton, C.G. (2020). Wastewater surveillance for population-wide Covid-19: the present and future. *Science of the Total Environment* 736 (2020): 139631. https://doi.org/10.1016/j.scitotenv.2020.139631.

EPA (1994). Technical Assistance Manual: State Regulatory Oversight of Medical Waste Treatment Technologies. https://archive.epa.gov/epawaste/nonhaz/industrial/medical/web/pdf/1-6.pdf (accessed 1 December 2020).

EPA (2005). Profile of the Healthcare Industry. *Project Report No. EPA/310-R-05-002*, 142 p. https://archive.epa.gov/compliance/resources/publications/assistance/sectors/web/pdf/health.pdf (accessed 9 November 2020).

EPA (2010). Hospital/Medical/Infectious Waste Incinerators: Summary of Requirements for Revised or New Section 111(d)/129 State Plans Following Amendments to the Emission Guidelines. *EPA Publication No. EPA-453/B-10-001*, 258 p. https://nepis.epa.gov/Exe/ZyPDF.cgi/P1009ZW6.PDF?Dockey=P1009ZW6.PDF (accessed 9 November 2020).

EPA (2017). Medical Waste. https://www.epa.gov/rcra/medical-waste#:~:text=Medical%20waste%20is%20primarily%20regulated%20by%20state%20environmental,environmental%20program%20first%20when%20disposing%20of%20medical%20waste (accessed 30 September 2020).

H2E (Hospitals for a Healthy Environment) (2020). Regulated Medical Waste Reduction. Regulated Medical Waste Reduction: 10 Steps to Implementing a Regulated Medical Waste Reduction Plan, 6 p. hospital2020.org (accessed 13 August 2020).

Johns Hopkins University (2022). Coronavirus Resource Center, COVID-19 Map – Johns Hopkins Coronavirus Resource Center. https://coronavirus.jhu.edu/map.html (accessed 14 May 2022).

Li, D., Shi, Y., Yang, L. et al. (2020). Microplastic release from the degradation of polypropylene feeding bottles during infant formula preparation. *Nature Food* 1: 746–754. https://doi.org/10.1038/s43016-020-00171-y.

Liang, Y., Song, Q., Wu, N. et al. (2021). Repercussions of COVID-19 pandemic on solid waste generation and management strategies. *Front. Environ. Sci. Eng.* 15 (6): 115. https://doi.org/10.1007/s11783-021-1407-5.

McDonnell, G., Dehen, C., Perrin, A. et al. (2013). Cleaning, disinfection and sterilization of surface prion contamination. *Journal of Hospital Infection* 85: 268–273. https://doi.org/10.1016/j.jhin.2013.08.003.

Minoglou, M., Gerassimidou, S., and Dimitrios Komilis, D. (2017). Healthcare waste generation worldwide and its dependence on socio-economic and environmental factors. *Sustainability* 9: 220. https://doi.org/10.3390/su9020220.

OSHA (1991). Bloodborne Pathogens. *Standard No 1910.1030*. https://www.osha.gov/laws-regs/regulations/standardnumber/1910/1910.1030 (accessed 24 October 2020).

Pichler, P., Jaccard, I.S., Weisz, U., and Weisz, J. (2019). International comparison of health care carbon footprints. *Environmental Research Letters* 14: 6. https://doi.org/10.1088/1748-9326/ab19e1.

Research and Markets (2020). Medical Waste Management Market Research Report by Type of Waste, by Service, by Treatment Site – Global Forecast to 2025 – Cumulative Impact of COVID-19, June 2020. https://www.researchandmarkets.com/reports/4896474/medical-waste-management-market-research-report.

Singh, N., Tang, Y., Zhang, Z., and Zheng, C. (2020). COVID-19 waste management: Effective and successful measures in Wuhan, China. *Resources, Conservation & Recycling* 163: 105071. 2 p. https://doi.org/10.1016/j.resconrec.2020.105071.

Stonemetz, J., Pham, J.C., Nichochea, A.J., and Mcgreedy, J. (2011). Reduction of regulated medical waste using lean sigma results in financial gains for hospital. *Anesthesiology Clinics* 29 (1): 145–152. https://doi.org/10.1016/j.anclin.2010.11.007.

U.S. Government (1989). *Rules and Regulations, Federal Register*, vol. 54, no. 56, 12337–12344. Washington, DC: U.S. Government Printing Office.

UNDP (2010). Guidance on microbiological challenge testing of health care waste treatment autoclaves, 9 p. Guidance on Microbiological Challenge Testing for Medical Waste Autoclaves November 2010. lvif.gov.lv (accessed 1 December 2020).

UNEP (2020b). Waste management during the COVID-19 pandemic: from response to recovery. Nairobi: United Nations Environment Programme. https://www.unep.org/ietc/resources/report/waste-management-during-covid-19-pandemic-response-recovery (accessed 17 March 2022).

UNEP & ILRI (United Nations Environment Programme and International Livestock Research Institute) (2020). *Preventing the Next Pandemic: Zoonotic Diseases and How to Break the Chain of*

Transmission. Nairobi: Kenya 72 p. https://wedocs.unep.org/bitstream/handle/20.500.11822/32316/ZP.pdf?sequence=1&isAllowed=y.

United Nations Environmental Programme (UNEP) (2020a). Zoonotic Diseases [Fact Sheet]. https://wedocs.unep.org/bitstream/handle/20.500.11822/32285/ZD.pdf?sequence=1&isAllowed=y (accessed 4 May 2021).

Wei, G. (2020). Medical Waste Treatment Lessons from the COVID-19 Outbreak in Wuhan. WMW. https://waste-management-world.com/a/guest-blog-medical-waste-treatment-lessons-from-the-covid-19-outbreak-in-wuhan.

WHO (2003). Cumulative Number of Reported Probable Cases of SARS From: 1 Nov 2002 To: 11 July 2003, 17:00. https://www.who.int/csr/sars/country/2003_07_11/en/.

WHO (2018). *Health-Care Waste.* https://www.who.int/news-room/fact-sheets/detail/health-care-waste (accessed 10 September 2020).

WHO (2019). MERS Situation Update. https://applications.emro.who.int/docs/EMRPUB-CSR-241-2019-EN.pdf?ua=1&ua=1&ua=1.

WHO (2020. Training Modules in Health-Care Waste Management. https://www.who.int/water_sanitation_health/facilities/waste/training_modules_waste_management/en/ (accessed 1 September 2021).

WHO (2022a). WHO Coronavirus (COVID-19) Dashboard | WHO Coronavirus (COVID-19) Dashboard With Vaccination Data. https://covid19.who.int/ (accessed 17 March 2022).

WHO (2022b). *Global Analysis of Healthcare Waste in the Context of COVID-19: Status, Impacts and Recommendations,* 71 p. Geneva: World Health Organization.

Windfield, E.S. and Brooks, M.S. (2015). Medical waste management, a review. *Journal of Environmental Management* 163 (9): 98–108. https://doi.org/10.1016/j.jenvman.2015.08.013.

Supplementary Reading

WHO (2014). *Safe Management of Wastes from Health-Care Activities,* 2e (ed. Y. Chertier, J. Emmanuel, U. Ute Pieper, et al.). Geneva: WHO, 308 p. https://www.euro.who.int/__data/assets/pdf_file/0012/268779/Safe-management-of-wastes-from-health-care-activities-Eng.pdf (accessed 30 September 2020).

WHO (2017). Safe Management of Wastes from Health-Care Activities, A Summary, 24 p, Geneva, Switzerland. Summarizes the main points of the above 308 p. report.

WHO (2019). Overview of Technologies for the Treatment of Infectious and Sharp Waste from Health Care Facilities, 42 p, Geneva, Switzerland.

Web Resources

Daniel Health: https://www.danielshealth.com/state-and-federal-regulations-medical-waste-disposal. Concise summary of various types of medical waste along with a map and link to medical waste legislation in the 50 U.S. states.

EPA. https://archive.epa.gov/epawaste/nonhaz/industrial/medical/web/html/publications.html. Provides details on medical waste management.

Health Care Environmental Resource Center: http://www.hercenter.org/rmw/rmwoverview.php#

Health Care Without Harm (HCWH). https://noharm-uscanada.org/issues/us-canada/waste-management. Issues in medical waste management globally; promotes sustainably and waste minimization in health care facilities. Partners with Green Health (https://practicegreenhealth.org) on these issues. Both have published useful research reports on medical waste incineration and related topics.

Metro Disposal: https://www.medprodisposal.com. Despite being a commercial site Metro has posted comprehensive information on all aspects of MW in a simple way that is a good source for anyone interested to learn basics of medical waste management.

Stericycle (2020). Several webinars in COVID-19. Webinar Recordings – Stericycle.

UNEP (2012). *Compendium of Technologies for the Treatment/Destruction of Healthcare Waste*, 225. Japan: Osaka.

WHO (2020). Training Modules in Health-care Waste Management. https://www.who.int/water_sanitation_health/facilities/waste/training_modules_waste_management/en/. Comprehensive coverage of all aspects of biomedical waste management.

Acronyms/Symbols

b	bed (hospital)
COVID-19	Coronavirus infectious disease-2019 (year indicates first reported case)
d	day
HIV	Human immunodeficiency virus
AIDS	Acquired immunodeficiency syndrome
MERS	Middle East respiratory syndrome
n.d.	No date
SARS	Severe acute respiratory syndrome
t	metric ton(s)
WHO	World Health Organization
y	year

7

Nuclear Waste

LEARNING OBJECTIVES

After studying this chapter, you will be able to:

- Describe the history of radioactivity and nuclear fission.
- Understand the basic concepts of atomic physics and nuclear technology.
- Develop a sound knowledge of nuclear waste management.
- Summarize the global status of high-level waste management.
- Explain the US and international laws on nuclear waste management.

7.1   Introduction

> There is probably no better example of science and engineering being so thoroughly mixed in a cauldron of politics, policy, and regulation than Yucca Mountain.
>
> — *Mcfarlane and Ewing (2006)*

Within a few decades after the discovery of radium and polonium in 1898 by Pierre and Marie Curie, who coined the word "radioactivity", and after the successful fission experiment by Otto Hahn in 1938, scientists in the United States and Europe began to study ways to harness the enormous energy locked up in the nucleus of uranium. Soon after, the race for developing nuclear technology for military purpose between the USA and Germany began in right earnest in 1939. The ensuing five years witnessed an unprecedented commitment on part of the US Government which spent close to two billion dollars (~32 billion in 2022 dollars) to the effort, and employed a workforce of nearly 130 000 people that included three Nobel laureates and a team of brilliant and dedicated scientists and engineers, who came out ahead and produced the first atomic bomb that was field-tested on 16 July 1945 at the "Trinity" site near Alamogordo in the New Mexico desert. A few weeks later, on 6 and 9 August 1945, two atomic bombs were dropped at Hiroshima and Nagasaki in Japan that essentially sealed the fate of World War II. Death from radiation, blast injuries, and heat were enormous and a total of 107 000 people perished – 67 000 died within one day, and 36 000 within four months with thousands suffering from radiation exposure for the rest of their lives (World Nuclear Association 2016a). Over half of the two cities (covering about $15\,km^2$ area) were completely destroyed. The world was awestruck by the enormous power of the atom. For the next several years,

Introduction to Waste Management: A Textbook, First Edition. Syed E. Hasan.
© 2022 John Wiley & Sons Ltd. Published 2022 by John Wiley & Sons Ltd.

research efforts remained focused on developing more powerful bombs; both the USA and former USSR (Union of Soviet Socialist Republics; 1922–1991) kept on making more lethal and destructive nuclear weapons for military use. As of May 2021, an estimated 13 100 nuclear weapons, far more powerful than the ones used in Japan, are in possession of nine countries: China, France, India, Israel, N. Korea, Pakistan, Russia, United Kingdom, and the USA, with Russia and the USA accounting for 11 807 (about 90%) of the total nuclear warheads (Kristensen and Korda 2021). These military programs have generated huge quantities of extremely dangerous nuclear waste that is awaiting permanent disposal.

7.1.1 Nuclear Waste

Nuclear (or radioactive) waste is a special class of waste containing radionuclides (products of nuclear fission), possessing harmful radiation, and which is discarded and currently not of any use. The phrase "not of any use" is a critical part of the definition, as it could characterize it either as a *nuclear waste* or *nuclear material*. For example, the spent nuclear fuels (SNFs), taken out of the nuclear power reactors at the end of their useful life, are classified as nuclear waste in the United States because SNFs are not currently reprocessed to recover U and Pu. However, France, India, Russia, the United Kingdom and other countries consider it a resource to recover U and Pu and not a "nuclear waste." Reprocessing was extensively carried out at US military weapons facilities at the Hanford site in Washington (1944–1988), Savannah River site in South Carolina (1952–2002), and the West Valley site in New York State (1966–1972). The larger of the three facilities – the Hanford site (Figure 7.1) – had nine nuclear reactors, and five reprocessing plants for recovery of ^{239}Pu. The liquid wastes were stored in 177 steel tanks, some of them have leaked. The Hanford facility, covering an area of 1518 km^2, contains two-thirds of all high-level waste (HLW) generated in the USA, which is being remediated by the United States Department of Energy (DOE).

7.1.2 Types of Nuclear Waste

The Nuclear Regulatory Commission (NRC) in the United States classifies nuclear wastes into three main types: low-, intermediate-, and high-level wastes. The International Atomic Energy Agency (IAEA) uses two additional categories – exempt waste (EW), and very low-level waste (LLW).

LLW has a low radiation level, does not produce heat, nor requires any shielding during handling, and transportation, and can be safely disposed of in properly designed shallow pits and trenches. LLW accounts for about 90% of the volume but only 1% of the radioactivity of all nuclear wastes. Intermediate-level waste (ILW) contains radionuclides having elevated levels of radiation, low levels of heat, and requires some shielding. ILW comprises 7% of the volume and 4% of the radioactivity of all nuclear wastes. HLW is highly radioactive with considerable heat and requires cooling and shielding, and extreme caution in handling, transportation, storage, and disposal. Although HLW account for a small volume, it accounts for 95% of the radioactivity of all nuclear wastes (Figure 7.2).

7.1.3 High-Level Wastes: SNF and HLW

Used (or spent) nuclear fuel (SNF) that comes out of the nuclear reactor is an extremely hazardous substance, characterized by high levels of radiation and heat. SNFs after removal from the reactor generate ~2000 kW of heat for each metric ton (t) of the spent fuel. Heat level drops down to 1.47 kW/Mt in 120 y after removal. The radiation level of SNF, one month after discharge from the reactor, is ~10^7 Bq/m^3.

Figure 7.1 Aerial view of the Hanford site by the Columbia River in Washington state (1960); the sprawling complex, covering an area of $1518\,km^2$ (*one-half of Rhode Island*). The site contains two-thirds of America's HLW by volume. A total of nine reactors along with five reprocessing plants to recover ^{239}Pu were operating from 1944 to 1987 that left behind one of the worst contaminated nuclear waste sites. *Source:* US Department of Energy.

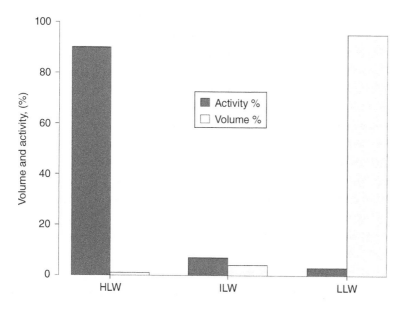

Figure 7.2 Volume and radioactivity of three classes of nuclear waste.

The SNFs, almost all in solid form, earmarked for direct disposal, represent one type of HLW. The other type comprises those resulting from reprocessing of SNFs (mostly liquid with some solids). Both are examples of HLW but different terms are used to distinguish them, based on their origin. Recovery of Pu and U renders the reprocessed waste less radioactive than SNFs.

The US DOE defines SNF as "fuel that has been withdrawn from a nuclear reactor following irradiation, the constituent elements of which have not been separated by reprocessing." HLW, on the other hand, is defined as ". . .the material resulting from the reprocessing of SNF, including liquid waste produced directly in reprocessing and any solid material derived from such liquid waste that contains fission products in sufficient concentrations" (DOE 2004). Both possess a high level of radiation (over 125 billion GBq) and heat (about $2\,kW/m^3$), and must be adequately contained and isolated to prevent the release of harmful radiation into the environment. The uranium fuel cycle disused in Section 7.4.2 and illustrated in Figure 7.11 shows all stages from mining to enrichment, fuel fabrication, generation of SNFs, and final disposal with or without reprocessing. Details of the US and EU classification of nuclear waste are discussed in Section 7.4.5.2.

7.1.4 Nuclear Waste Management

Nuclear Waste Management represents a set of separate but related operations carefully carried out to prevent the release of harmful radiation into the environment to minimize adverse impact on the biosphere. Nuclear waste management involves: segregation, monitoring, transportation, storage, and disposal, with or without reprocessing. Retrieval of SNFs from the reactor core and placing it into a specially designed deep-water tank for temporary storage; its subsequent removal and transportation to either a reprocessing facility or to a dry storage site; and final disposal in a deep geological medium is a good example of various steps involved in nuclear waste management.

7.1.5 Early Years of Nuclear Waste Management in the USA

During the decades of the 1940s and 1950s, issues related to radiation hazards and nuclear waste disposal did not receive due attention because the United States' efforts were focused on developing the atomic bomb. While health professionals quickly addressed the problems associated with radiation exposure, the question on what to do and how to manage the nuclear waste remained in abeyance and no serious thinking emerged until several years later. One of the reasons was the lack of knowledge about the potential hazards of HLW. In fact, as early as 1948 Robert Oppenheimer, chairman (1947–1952) of the newly formed General Advisory Committee of the Atomic Energy Commission (AEC), had dismissed the radioactive waste problem as "unimportant" (Alley and Alley 2013, p. 3). Later, Carroll Wilson, first general manager (1947–1950) of AEC, said: "Chemists and chemical engineers were not interested in dealing with the waste. . ... The central point is that there was no real interest or profit in dealing with the back end of the fuel cycle" (Makhijani and Saleska 1992, p. 37).

It was not until 1954 when the original Atomic Energy Act (AEA) of 1946 was amended, and the Army Manhattan Engineer District, charged with research and production of the atomic bomb, was folded in the civilian sector (in June 1947), that problems of radiation hazards and nuclear waste management began to receive some attention. In 1957, the AEC issued a report titled *Atomic Energy Facts: A Summary of Atomic Activities of Interest to Industry* where the application of nuclear energy in the commercial sector was encouraged and various uses were discussed in detail, but only a passing reference was made to nuclear waste management (AEC 1957, pp. 125–129).

Unlike most other scientific discoveries, the first use of nuclear energy was for destructive purpose, and it was not until the mid-1950s and later that the world saw nuclear energy being used for peaceful purposes such as electric power generation, diagnosis and treatment of disease, scientific research, and other beneficial applications. Regardless of whether nuclear energy is used for military or peaceful purposes, it generates a large amount of dangerous waste that requires careful handling and safe and secure disposal. The irony is that despite 75 y since the development of the atomic bomb, and the generation of tens of thousands of tons of extremely hazardous nuclear waste, we still do not – as of this writing – have a single high-level nuclear waste disposal facility anywhere in the world!

7.2 Basics of Nuclear Science

This section provides a summary of the basic concepts of nuclear physics, chemistry, geology, and their application in nuclear technology as employed in nuclear power generation and other peaceful uses.

7.2.1 Radioactive Elements

While uranium, thorium, and radium are well known for their radioactive properties, there are other naturally occurring elements listed in the Periodic Table that exhibit the phenomenon of spontaneous disintegration with a simultaneous release of heat, charged particles, and radiation. These elements, include astatine (At), actinium (Ac), americium (Am), berkelium (Bk), californium (Cf), curium (Cm), francium (Fr), polonium (Po), promethium (Pm), protactinium (Pa), radon (Rn), neptunium (Np), plutonium (Pu), and technetium (Tc), are shown in Figure 7.3. For a long time, Am, Bk, Cf, Cm, Np, and Pu were not considered naturally occurring but recently they have

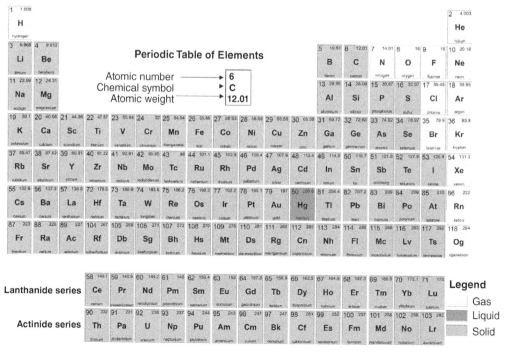

Figure 7.3   Periodic Table of elements.

been discovered in trace quantity in the primary uranium ore, pitchblende. In addition to these naturally occurring elements, many other radioactive elements have been synthesized in the laboratory, with atomic weight ranging between 96 and 118.

7.2.2 Radioactive Minerals

Geologically, minerals are aggregates of two or more elements, with the exception of native elements which almost entirely comprise a single element, such as native iron, native gold, etc. Minerals are the primary source of all naturally occurring radioactive elements. Uraninite (UO_2), previously called pitchblende, and thorianite (ThO_2) are the two most common radioactive minerals found on the earth that are a major source of U and Th. Uraninite occurs as cubic crystals, while pitchblende is the massive (noncrystalline) form of uraninite (Frye 1981, p. 692). They occur in all three types of rocks – igneous, sedimentary, and metamorphic – and also in sediment. Igneous and sedimentary rocks host some of the world's largest uranium deposits, such as the McArthur River uranium deposit in Canada, the Kazakhstan uranium deposits, and the central Australian deposits. Monazite sand deposits, occurring in India and Brazil, represent the two largest sedimentary deposits of Th.

Uranium ores are scarce and unevenly distributed across the globe. Of the 54 224 t of global production of U_3O_8 in 2019, over 98% came from eight countries, with Kazakhstan and Canada accounting for 55%; Australia and Namibia 22%; and Niger, Russia, Uzbekistan, and China accounting for 20%. The remaining 3% was supplied by Ukraine, South Africa, India, and the USA (IAEA 2020). Table 7.1 shows the global uranium production and resource as of 2019.

7.2.3 Nuclear Fission and Electric Power Generation

The force that binds the nuclei of radioactive elements represents an enormous amount of energy. Fission, or splitting of the nucleus, is the process that results in the release of this energy. Figure 7.4 shows how subjecting a fissionable material, for example, ^{235}U, to streams of neutrons in a reactor

Table 7.1 World uranium resource and production, 2019.

Country	U production (t)	U resource (t)	Percentage of world resource
Australia	6 613	1 692 700	28
Canada	6 994	564 900	9
China	1 650	248 900	4
Kazakhstan	22 808	906 800	15
Mongolia	—	143 500	2
Namibia	5 103	448 300	7
Niger	3 053	276 400	4
Russia	2 900	486 000	8
Uzbekistan	3 500	132 300	2
Other	799	3 207 100	31
World total	54 224	6 147 800	100

Source: Data from IAEA (2020).

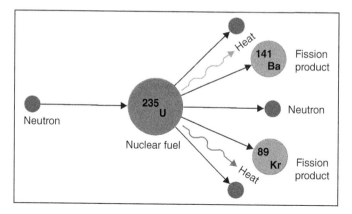

Figure 7.4 Fission of ^{235}U; for each ^{235}U atom, three to four neutrons are generated that, in turn, cause further fission of ^{235}U, resulting in a chain reaction. The containment structure in the nuclear reactor is designed to decrease the fission rate or stop it altogether.

chamber, where physical conditions (temperature, pressure, and density) are controlled to attain a critical level, cause the ^{235}U atom to split, releasing fission products, heat, radiation, and three to four additional neutrons for each incoming one. These neutrons, in turn, cause further fission of the remaining ^{235}U, producing more fission products, additional heat, radiation, and neutrons. This process is self-perpetuating and would continue until all ^{235}U is exhausted. Such reactions are called uncontrolled chain reaction; atomic bombs are a good example of uncontrolled chain reactions. However, in a nuclear power reactor, suitable devices (cadmium or boron rods, graphite, heavy or light water) are put in place to control the rate of fission or stop it altogether. Such reactions are called controlled chain reactions.

Large quantity of heat (~2 kW/m³) is generated during fission which is utilized in a nuclear power reactor to produce electricity. The major difference between a conventional electric power plant and a nuclear plant is the source of heat. As Figure 7.5a and b illustrates, heat is generated by burning coal, oil, or gas, or from the fission of uranium, which is then used to boil water to make steam that is led into turbines that are synchronized to generators to produce electricity. In a geothermal power plant, the earth's natural heat in the form of steam is used to generate electricity. In hydroelectric power plants and windmills, the kinetic energy of falling water or the wind is used directly to turn the turbine.

7.2.4 Energy Potential of Radioactive Elements and Use of Nuclear Energy

The energy liberated during the fission of ^{235}U is generally expressed as:

$$235U + n \rightarrow P_1 + P_2 + 2.5n \left(+200 \text{ MeV} \right) \tag{7.1}$$

where,

n designates neutrons,
P_1, P_2 fission products, and
MeV (mega electron volt) the atomic energy.

Noting that 200 MeV of energy is liberated from fission of a single nucleus of ^{235}U; and that 1 g of ^{235}U contains 2.56×10^{21} atoms of ^{235}U, 1 g of ^{235}U would produce 82 GJ or 22.8 MWh of electric energy – same as contained in 40 tankfuls (40-L capacity) of gasoline. Similarly, 1 kg of ^{235}U

(a)

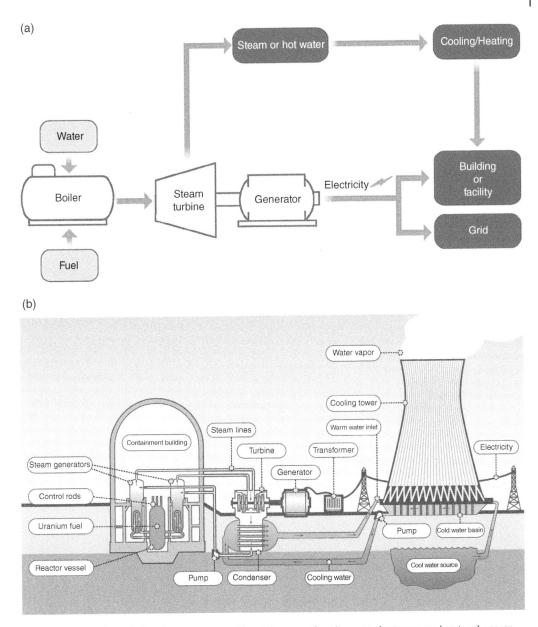

(b)

Figure 7.5 Principle of electric power generation: (a) conventional power plant uses coal, natural gas, or steam emanating from the earth as fuel; and (b) nuclear power plant, that uses ^{235}U as fuel. *Source:* NRC.

produces the same amount of heat energy as would come by burning 16 Mt of coal! In general, about 44 000 MWh of electricity is produced from 1 Mt of natural uranium. Generating the same quantity of electricity would require burning over 20 000 Mt of coal or 8.5 million m^3 of natural gas. In terms of waste, uranium fission generates only 1 g of waste to generate 1 MW of electricity; but to produce the same amount of electricity from coal, the waste produced would be 2.5 t (Murray 2003, p. 43). A single fuel pellet that contains 0.3 g of ^{235}U produces energy equivalent to ~17 000 ft^3 of natural gas, 1 780 lb. of coal, or 149 gallons of gasoline.

Of the various possible uses of nuclear energy for peaceful purposes, the idea of producing electricity using nuclear fission caught on rather rapidly. For several developed countries, including the United States, nuclear fission offered a promising alternative to supplement its ever-growing need for energy. Other countries, that either did not have any fossil fuel resources or had them in short supply, also found nuclear energy very attractive because of the very small quantity of nuclear material needed to produce large quantities of electricity.

7.2.4.1 Nuclear Energy for Electric Power Generation

Nuclear energy is a major source of electric power in many countries. France, for example, obtained about 71% of its energy from nuclear power in 2020. In terms of global electric power generation from 451 nuclear power reactors, the USA was the top producer, accounting for about 31% (789.92 GWh) of the total global output of 2553.21 GWh in 2020 (IAEA 2021a). Figure 7.6 shows the relative share of nuclear energy for 30 countries.

A small experimental breeder reactor (EBR-1), built in Idaho, USA, produced electricity for the first time in December 1951. The former Soviet Union is credited for building the first commercial nuclear power plant (NPP) that came online on 27 June 1954. The AM-1 (*Atom Mirnyi*, meaning peaceful atom) reactor was built by the Soviets at Obninsk, 100 km from Moscow. This 5 MW plant fed electricity to the grid and operated successfully for 48 y. In the USA, the first commercial reactor was built by the AEC at Shippingport, Pennsylvania in 1957 with an installed capacity of 60 MW. Since the 1950s, both the number and capacity of NPPs have increased and globally plants with 1000 MW capacity are very common.

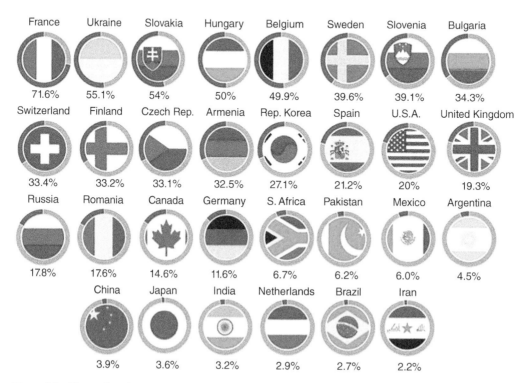

Figure 7.6 Share of nuclear energy in various countries, July 2018. *Source:* NRC.

During the peak of nuclear power, covering the period 1961–1985, 635 reactors were brought online worldwide. However, a marked slowdown in new reactor construction occurred in 1986 that lasted until 2005, with only 83 reactors coming on line in 20 y. A resurgence in construction began in 2006 and, during the period 2006–2020, 103 new nuclear power reactors were under various stages of construction. Table 7.2 represents new power reactor construction worldwide, grouped on a five-year activity basis.

The nuclear hiatus that began around the mid-1980s led to the cancellation or suspension of construction of many reactors in serval countries. A number of factors led to the decline in the construction of new power reactors. Some of the major factors include: (i) overcapacity of existing power plants and overestimation of future energy requirement; (ii) failed promise of the US Government to transfer SNFs from wet storage at NPP sites by 31 January 1998, resulting in gradually diminishing capacity for onsite storage; (iii) the looming possibility of shut down if SNFs can no longer be stored on site; (iv) the ever-increasing cost and complex financing to build NPPs; and (v) the two major nuclear accidents. The first accident occurred on 28 March 1979 at the Three Mile Island NPP near Harrisburg, Pennsylvania, where a combination of equipment malfunction, design flaws, and worker errors, led to a partial meltdown of the reactor core but with the very small off-sites release of radiation. The accident resulted in exposure to about two million people to an average dose of about 1 millirem (mr) of radiation (exposure from a full set of chest X-rays is about 6 mr). The second accident occurred on 26 April 1986 in an NPP at Chernobyl, Ukraine, in the former Soviet Union. Human error led to the failure of the system that supplied cooling water, causing the temperature in the reactor core to rise above 3000°C, melting the uranium fuel that resulted in a massive explosion with attendant release of high levels of radiation. This major accident caused 31 deaths, destroyed the reactor, and led to the evacuation of about 135 000 people.

These accidents raised serious concerns about the safety of nuclear reactors and put a damper on the nuclear power industry to the point that many utility companies in the USA that had already planned or ordered the construction of additional generating units either cancelled their orders or put their plans on indefinite hold. According to Yang (2009, p. 164), orders for 94 reactors were cancelled between 1974 and 1982. Elsewhere in the world, the construction of new NPPs continued, but not at the same pace as prior to 1980. It was not until around 2005 that a revival of nuclear energy took place and as of September 2021, 50 reactors were under construction in 20 countries (Figure 7.7), including two in the United States, with a planned capacity of 52.56 GW of electric power (IAEA 2021b). This trend is likely to continue and additional nuclear power reactors will be coming

Table 7.2   New power reactor construction worldwide from 1954 to 2020.

Years	New reactors construction	Years	New reactors' construction
1954–1955	9	1986–1990	39
1956–1960	42	1991–1995	11
1961–1965	38	1996–2000	20
1966–1970	127	2001–2005	13
1971–1975	152	2006–2010	50
1976–1980	136	2011–2015	31
1981–1985	82	2016–2020	22

Source: Data from IAEA (2020).

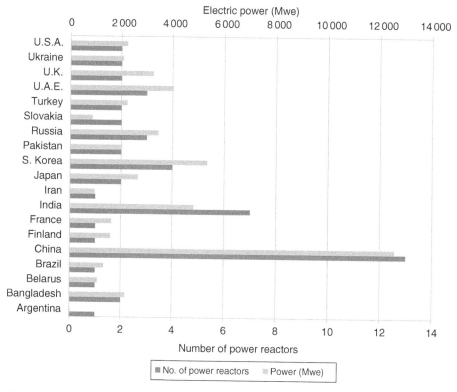

Figure 7.7 Nuclear power reactors under construction, September 2021. *Source:* IAEA.

on line because of the following reasons: (i) elimination of fossil fuel imports for countries that do not have their own deposits or whose deposits are fast depleting, and (ii) cutting down on the emission of CO_2, the dominant gas responsible for global warming. It is estimated that the 441 nuclear reactors operating in 2004 eliminated 2.5 billion tons of CO_2 emission each year out of a total of 5.8 billion tons generated from coal-fired power plants (Abraham 2005); (iii) safer and more efficient design of generation-IV nuclear reactors, including close-loop system, that would allow reprocessing of spent fuel and minimize the proliferation of nuclear materials (Marcus and Levin 2002), and availability of the 50 MW capacity, pressurized water small modular reactor (SMR), being developed by NuScale Power, Portland, Oregon (NuScale 2018). Its design and safety features were reviewed by NRC that issued an approval certification in January 2018. Final Safety Evaluation Report was approved in August 2020 after which NuScale plans to provide SMRs to US customers for licensing, construction, and operation. Lower cost, easy road and rail transportation, scalability (six units can be placed in a single power plant to generate up to 600 MW of electricity), enhanced safety features, smaller number of operators, and self-contained power supply are some of the key features.

In the USA, licensing, construction, and operation of an NPP are regulated by NRC. A typical nuclear reactor, generating 1000 MW of electricity, takes about 10 y (range 3–33 y) for design, licensing, and construction, and costs nearly $10 billion. As of June 2021, there were 93 operating reactors, housed in 55 NPPs in 28 states, providing about 20% of total US energy (NRC 2021). Fifty-eight of the operating NPPs have one power reactor, 32 plants have two, and 3 plants have three reactors, such as the Palo Verde NPP in Arizona, each of the three reactors generating 1127 MW of energy. The Barakah NPP, under construction in the United Arab Emirates, has four reactors, each of 1400 MW capacity. Globally, the USA has the largest number of operating reactors, with 93 operating reactors, providing about 20% of the nation's energy.

7.2.4.2 Other Uses of Nuclear Energy

Although the first use of nuclear energy in 1945 was for military purposes, interest in using it for "peaceful" purposes soon followed. The US Government, subsequent to the passage of the AEA in 1946, declared that ". . . the development and utilization of atomic energy shall, so far as practicable, be directed toward improving the public welfare, increasing the standard of living, strengthening free competition among private enterprise, and promoting world peace" (AEC 1965). In his famous "Atoms for Peace" speech at the United Nations General Assembly on 8 December 1953, President Eisenhower made the plea to shift the emphasis from "atoms for war" to "atoms for peace," heralding the use of nuclear energy for meeting humanity's need for energy, food, health care, industrial applications, and scientific research. In the intervening 65 y, nuclear materials have been used in a wide variety of applications that affect our daily lives, such as assuring the quality of drinking water supply, transportation vehicles, food preservation, health care, space vehicles' power supply, and many more. Some of the common uses of radioisotopes are described below:

- *Electricity Generation*: Nuclear reactors have been used for producing electricity since the early 1950s and as of January 2020, there were 451 operating nuclear reactors in 30 countries generating about 2553.21 GW of electricity (IAEA 2020a). In the wake of global warming and the ensuing climate change, there has been a marked increase in the construction of new NPPs since 2006.
- *Food and Agriculture*: Nuclear and related biotechnologies are being increasingly utilized to improve food production and to assure sustainable agriculture to meet the need of the world's current and future population. One strategy is to prevent food loss: Insects destroy nearly 10% of harvested crops worldwide. Loss of farm animals from Medfly, screwworm, and certain parasites in developing countries cause economic loss to the tune of billions of dollars. Using the Sterile Insect Technique (SIT), which involves sterilizing insect eggs with gamma radiation before hatching and releasing the males in infested areas, and allowing them to mate with females, eliminates any offspring. Repeated release of sterilized males in the infested areas has resulted in a dramatic decrease in insect population (World Nuclear Association, 2014). Similar technology has recently been used for controlling the spread of mosquitoes that carry the Zika virus.
- *Water Resources*: Isotope hydrology techniques are commonly used in groundwater resource management, conservation, and investigations for aquifer decontamination. Radioactive isotopes also provide useful information for assessing leakage through dams and irrigation canals, river flow, discharge measurements, and sedimentation rates. Electricity and heat generated from fossil fuel power plants have been used for desalination in several countries, but nuclear power has been found to be cost-competitive with gas-fired power plants. Recent studies (World Nuclear Association, 2017a) showed that the best economy of scale could be achieved by using small- to medium-sized reactors, in the range of 38–330 MW. Such plants for desalination and cogeneration of electricity are being actively investigated in the Middle East, North Africa, India, Japan, and other countries.
- *Medicine*: Use of radioisotopes and nuclear radiation in the diagnosis and treatment of diseases is the most familiar example of "atoms for peace." More than 10 000 hospitals worldwide use radioisotopes in medicine: over 20 million nuclear medicine procedures are performed annually in the USA and about 10 million in Europe (World Nuclear Association, 2014). Nuclear medicine is perhaps the best success story of the peaceful use of nuclear energy.

- *Dating*: Several radioisotopes are used for dating geologic materials and artifacts in determining the age of rocks and other materials in geological, anthropological, and archeological investigations.
- *Manufacturing*: Numerous common consumer products and specialized devices use one or more radioactive materials. For example, smoke detectors at home and other buildings use ^{241}Am. Some watches and clocks contain a small quantity of ^{3}H (tritium) or ^{147}Pm, which provides light. Older watches and clocks (built before 1970) used ^{226}Ra paint on dials and numerals to make them visible in the dark. Thorium coating is used to make incandescent gas lantern mantles; some camera lenses (thoriated lenses) manufactured during the 1950s–1970s used a coating of ^{232}Th to adjust its refractive index. Various scientific instruments, such as gas chromatograph, employ low-energy radiation sources for the detection and precise measurement of the type and quantities of various organic compounds. Many gauging devices use a variety of radioactive materials, such as the nuclear density meter – a device that is extensively used in geotechnical and construction engineering the world over to measure soil density – which employs ^{137}Cs.

7.3   Radioactivity, Natural and Induced Radiation, and Half-Life

This section discusses key elements of nuclear physics, the difference between natural and induced radiation, and radiation exposure and its health impacts, as they relate to nuclear waste management. Half-life is a key concept that forms the basis for the designed life of a nuclear waste disposal facility.

7.3.1   Radioactivity

The nucleus of an atom of a radioactive element is inherently unstable and undergoes gradual breakdown, accompanied by loss of energy, to assume a more stable configuration. Radioactivity is defined as the process of spontaneous disintegration of the nucleus of an atom causing it to emit energy in the form of electromagnetic radiation. Radiation produced during radioactive disintegration dominantly comprises alpha (α) and beta (β) particles, and gamma (γ) rays that have different properties (Table 7.3). For example, α radiation is the slowest of the three, but most energetic, and has minimum penetrating power, while β radiation moves faster and penetrates deeper. Gamma rays have the highest penetrating power, move with the speed of light, and, unlike the other two radiations, are not deflected by a magnetic field.

In terms of health effects, α particle, when it enters living tissues, either by inhalation or ingestion, or through a wound or cut in the skin, can damage living tissues by releasing all its energy in a few localized cells resulting in serious damage to cell structure and DNA. Alpha radiation, outside the living cell, does not pose any hazard as it is absorbed in the air. Ra, Rn, Th, and U are some of the alpha emitters.

Beta particles can travel up to a few meters in the air, have greater penetrating power than alpha particles, but are less damaging to living tissues and DNA because the ionization they produce is more widely spaced. Beta radiation can penetrate human skin to the germinal layer, where new skin cells are produced. Most β particles can be stopped by thin metal sheets or glass. ^{90}Sr, ^{14}C, ^{3}H, and ^{35}S are some examples of beta emitters.

Gamma radiation, being a form of electromagnetic radiation, is strongly penetrating and produces external damage, as opposed to α and β particles that cause internal damage. They can easily

Table 7.3 Characteristics of ionizing radiations.

Particle/radiation type	Speed	Energy level	Penetrating power	Blocked by
α (charged particle, 2 units)	Slowest	Higher	$3 \times 10^{0.2}$ m (air); $4 \times 10^{0.5}$ m (tissue)	Sheet of paper, clothing, skin
β (charged particle, ±1 unit)	Slower	Lowest	3.0 m (air); $1 \times 10^{0.2}$ m (tissue)	A few mm of thick aluminum sheet, plastic, glass
γ (neutral, no charge)	Fastest 1.07×10^9 km/s	Highest	Very strong	Many centimeters of lead; several meters of concrete

Source: Modified after Rahman (2008).

penetrate barriers, such as skin and clothing, which can stop alpha and beta particles. Gamma rays can be blocked by a 10–20-cm-thick layer of a dense material like lead, or a few m of concrete. Gamma rays can cause ionization that damages living tissues and DNA. Examples of gamma emitters include: ^{131}I, ^{137}Cs, ^{60}Co, ^{226}Ra, and ^{99}Tc.

7.3.2 Radiotoxicity

Radiotoxicity is a measure of the harm to individuals from exposure to radiation. Radiation in the form of α, β, γ, neutron, or other charged particles, carries a certain amount of energy that impacts atoms and molecules of living cells, disrupting their normal functions causing sickness and disease. Radiation sickness is a general term for exposure to a large radiation dose that manifests itself in immediate (or acute) effects, such as nausea, hair loss, bleeding, and fatigue; and delayed (or chronic) effects such as gene mutation (mutagenesis), and teratogenesis (birth defects, such as cleft palate/lip, microcephaly [smaller head size], microphthalmia [small eyes], mental retardation, etc.).

Naturally occurring radioactive elements, particularly U, emit radiation as it disintegrates; however, the energy level is very low and relatively harmless. The natural fission reactor at Oklo in Gabon, W. Africa is an excellent example of a natural fission reaction that began about 2.0 billion years ago and went on and off 17 times when it finally stopped after one million years (Mervine 2011). The radiation generated had modest energy, about 100 kW, enough to power 1000 light bulbs each of 100 W rating for one hour (compared to modern nuclear reactors that produce 1000 MW of energy that can power 10 million, 100 W lightbulbs for an hour).

Depleted SNF rods emit strong radiation with high energy levels and deep penetrating power. SNFs emit radiation level of 10^{17} Bq/t of fuel (a million times more than fresh reactor fuel) that can cause death to an unprotected person in minutes. Since the harm is caused without ingestion or inhalation, it is called external or remote radiation. On the other hand, when the radiation-emitting radionuclides enter the body through ingestion or inhalation, it is called internal or contact radiation. In general, radiotoxicity is severe for short-lived radionuclides as compared to long-lived ones. The current approach in nuclear waste management is to isolate the waste that contains both the medium-lived radionuclides – half-lives of up to 50 y (^{144}Ce: 284.6 d; ^{106}Ru: 1.020 y; ^{147}Pm: 2.62 y; ^{85}Kr: 10.76 y; ^{3}H or Tritium: 12.32 y; ^{241}Pu: 14.4 y; ^{90}Sr: 28.9 y; and ^{137}Cs: 30.1 y) with high thermal energy and radiation, and the long-lived ones, half-lives thousands of years (^{226}Ra: 1600 y; ^{14}C: 5715 y; ^{79}Se: 2.9×10^5 y; ^{99}Tc: 2.13×10^5 y; ^{237}Np: 2.14×10^6 y; ^{135}Cs: 2.3×10^6 y; and ^{129}I: 1.7×10^7 y) – to prevent the release of harmful radiations.

7.3.3 Radiation Exposure and Acceptable Radiation Dose

Radiation from a nuclear reactor is in the form of α and β particles, γ rays, and neutrons. All modern operating reactors in NPPs in the USA and other countries are designed to contain these radiations within the plant's containment structure. So, the possibility of its release into the environment is extremely unlikely. Even if it would escape outside, its intensity will decrease significantly because radiation intensity is an inverse function of the square of the distance from the radiation source (reactor core), expressed as:

$$i = 1/d^2 \tag{7.2}$$

where, i is the intensity of radiation, and d the distance from the source.

In addition, γ radiation does not stick to a surface (is evanescent). It is the γ rays-irradiated fallout dust that would stick to the surface, including skin, but the dust can be easily washed off without causing serious damage. It is only after the fallout dust is ingested or inhaled that it causes serious problems.

Based on experiments exposing rats to the radiation source, it has been determined that man can be exposed to a radiation level of about 1 rem/week or 0.025 r/h without noticeable effects. Using 2000 hr as typical annual work hours, a worker at a nuclear reactor would be exposed to a radiation level of 50 r/y. Using a safety factor of 10, the International Commission on Radiological Protection has recommended the maximum permissible annual exposure (MPAE) of 5 r/y or 50 mSv (= 2.5 mr/h) for a nuclear reactor worker. The US NRC has also set the maximum annual dose for a nuclear worker at 5 r/y. Figure 7.8 shows the radiation doses set by the US regulatory agencies (NRC 2017b).

Radiation shield in a nuclear reactor is designed to ensure that the maximum radiation level does not exceed 2.5 mr/h in areas where personnel may have to work in close proximity to the

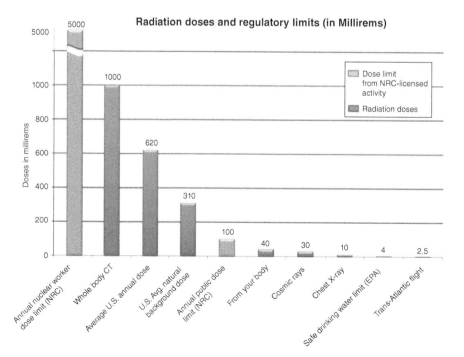

Figure 7.8   US radiation doses. *Source:* NRC.

Table 7.4 Estimated annual radiation exposure, the USA.

Source	Radiation level	Radiation type
Cosmic rays	102 mr/y	Whole body
Chest X-ray	6 mr/y	Whole body
^{40}K	55 mr/y	Whole body
^{14}C	3.6 mr/y	Whole body
Nuclear test fallout, 1950–1960	3 mr/y	Whole body
Three Mile Island accident	1 mr	Whole body
One airplane flight	1–10 mr	—
Coal pile	50–100 mr/y	—
Living in Denver, Colorado	50–100 mr/y	—
Ultraviolet radiation from the sun	115 mr/hr	Average, on a year-round basis

reactor. As shown in Equation (7.2), outside of the reactor building, the intensity of radiation drops off significantly. For example, if the maximum radiation level inside the reactor building is 2.5 mr/h, 10 m away, it would drop off to 0.025 mr/h, and 100 m away to 0.00025 mr/h. In fact, the average annual dose measured at the nuclear plant boundary is 0.6 mr (or 6 mSv). NRC specifies a radiation dose limit of 3 mr/y (0.03 Sv/y) at NPP boundary; and 25 mr/y (0.25 mSv/y) at the site boundary of an LLW disposal facility. The annual radiation dose for an NPP worker is 1.9 mSv/y (or 0.19 r/y), which is extremely low as compared to the background (natural) radiation of 311 mr/y (3.11 mSv) and 300 mr/y (3 mSv) from medical diagnosis and treatment, respectively, that an average person in the USA receives (NCRPM 2008). Table 7.4 lists the estimated amount of radiation and its source that an average American is likely to receive.

Since radiation exposure does not produce equal damage to the entire body, safe radiation limits take into account the organ/body part that may be exposed. Based on this consideration, US EPA recommends that the maximum radiation exposure to protect workers against cancer should be limited to 5 r/y (0.05 Sv); 15 r/y (0.15 Sv) to protect the lens of the eye; and 50 r/y (0.5 Sv) for any other organ, including skin, or extremities of the body (EPA 1988, p. 6). No upper limit has been set for radiation doses for medical use where the principle of "benefit outweighs the risk" applies.

7.3.4 Induced Radioactivity

Radioactivity can be induced in any material by exposing it to specific radiation. Induced radiation was discovered by the husband-and-wife team of Frederick Joliet and Irene Curie, for which they received the 1935 Nobel Prize in chemistry (earlier in 1911, Irene's mother, Marie Curie had received her second Nobel Prize in chemistry for her discovery of radioactivity). Neutron activation – the capture of free neutrons in atomic nuclei – is the most common method of inducing radioactivity in an otherwise nonradioactive (stable) material. Neutron capture can cause natural materials, such as air, water, or soil, to become radioactive. Induced radioactivity is also called artificial or man-made radioactivity. Thousands of such synthesized radioactive materials have been developed and a large number of them are used in various applications, including medical diagnosis and treatment; food preservation, manufacturing, research, etc. Another example of induced radioactivity is the radioisotopes of many metals like Co, Ni, Se, Sn, Zr, and other elements – used in the special alloy, called zircalloy, that forms the metal cladding of the fuel rod, which encases individual fuel pellets – that get irradiated during fission reaction in the reactor core (Bruno and Cera 2006, p. 334, 335), and require careful and safe management.

7.3.5 Naturally Occurring Radioactive Materials and Technologically Enhanced Radioactive Materials

Many naturally occurring geological materials contain radionuclides that emit a low level of radiation, are not significantly higher than normal background levels and, therefore, do not require radiation protection. Geological deposits of coal, petroleum, uranium, thorium, radium, and raw materials for making fertilizers that occur in sedimentary, igneous, and metamorphic rocks, in their undisturbed state are examples of naturally occurring radioactive materials (NORMs). Technologically enhanced radioactive materials (TENORMs), on the other hand, include materials that, upon disturbance, such as during mining and processing, undergo an increase in the concentration of neutrons which, in turn, elevate its radioactivity to levels that may pose a health hazard, requiring proper radiation control measures. The terms NORMs and TENORMs have been used loosely, causing confusion. For example, the World Nuclear Association does not draw a clear distinction between NORM and TENORM and includes disturbed radioactive materials in NORMs (World Nuclear Association, 2016b). The US EPA, on the other hand, differentiates the two and defines NORM as "materials which may contain any of the primordial radionuclides or radioactive elements as they occur in nature, such as radium, uranium, thorium, potassium, and their radioactive decay products, that are undisturbed as a result of human activities." TENORM is defined as "naturally occurring radioactive materials that have been concentrated or exposed to the accessible environment as a result of human activities such as manufacturing, mineral extraction, or water processing" (EPA 2008, p. ES.1). The key point is that a NORM should not be considered *technologically enhanced* unless it is disturbed and subjected to human activities, resulting in an increase in its radioactivity.

Nuclear waste generated by mining and milling of uranium and thorium ores, and also from extraction and processing of other NORM bearing deposits, such as phosphate rocks, e.g. Phosphoria Formations of W. Sahara, India, Morocco, Syria, Togo, Tunisia, and the USA (in Florida); mineral sands, some gold-bearing rocks, coal, hydrocarbons, etc., contain relatively low concentrations of long-lived radionuclides. Sahu et al. (2014) reported radiation levels in phosphate rocks from South India ranging between 0.009 Bq/g (0.243 pCi/g) and 1.34 Bq/g (32.22 pCi/g), emanating from ^{226}Ra, ^{232}Th, and ^{238}U. These levels are low in comparison to similar deposits in Morocco and Florida (1.1 Bq/g or 29.73 pCi/g, and 1.9 Bq/g or 51.35 pCi/g, respectively). Oil and gas production also generates a large volume of TENORMs in the wastewater coproduced during their extraction. These radionuclides precipitate out as sulfate and carbonate deposits, forming scales and sludge on pipes, storage tanks, etc., with radioactivity levels of up to 1000 Bq/g (~27 027 pCi/g). Fracking operations also generate wastewater with high levels of radioactivity, many times greater than the drinking water MCL of 0.186 Bq/L (5.03 pCi/L).

The most serious hazard from TENORM wastes at uranium mining and processing plants comes from radium that decays to radon, emitting α particles; and elevated levels of γ radiation from other radionuclides. Other hazardous substances include toxic heavy metals and contaminated water. Analysis of 58 samples from 17 uranium mines, from across the USA, showed that more than 50% of the samples had ^{226}Ra concentration of > 20 pCi/g or 0.74 Bq/g (EPA 2008, pp. 3–21) – much higher than the EPA's recommended action level of 4 pCi/L for homes. The quantity of waste materials was estimated at 3 billion t from surface mining (range 1–8 billion t), and 67 t (range: 5–100 million t) from underground uranium mining. Millions of hectares of disturbed land at uranium mining, milling, and processing sites in the western USA, that are examples of TENORMS, are estimated to cost $30 000/ha for remediation. A study conducted by DOE in 2000 indicated that the reclamation cost at 54 such locations would be about $2.28 billion (EPA 2008, pp. 4–17). Ion exchange and reverse osmosis; electrodialysis; filtration; permeable reactive barriers (PRBs); and bioremediation are some of the methods that have been suggested for remediation of contaminated water and mining dumps.

The very large volume of TENORM waste – millions of tons at uranium mining and processing plants, phosphate mining, and petroleum production site – makes it impractical, if not impossible, to dispose it of in deep geological repositories, despite the long half-life and associated radiological hazard of some of its associated radionuclides. NORM waste, because it is not regulated by the NRC, is classified as hazardous waste by the US EPA.

7.3.6 Radioactive Decay and Half-life

Radioactive elements exhibit the phenomenon of disintegration of their nuclei, along with the release of radiation and heat. The process known as radioactive decay causes the original radioactive material to gradually lose its radioactivity with time, until it assumes a stable configuration, i.e. becomes nonradioactive. A definite relationship has been observed involving time and radiation loss during radioactive decay. Half-life is defined as the time taken by a radioactive material to lose its radiation level to one-half (50%) of its original value. For the majority of radioactive materials, it has been found that they will lose most of their radiation and become harmless after undergoing 10 half-life cycles. There is a wide range in the half-life of radionuclides: from a fraction of a second to hundreds of thousands of years. In general, the shorter the half-life, the more intense (dangerous) is its radiation intensity, and vice versa. Table 7.5 lists half-lives of some naturally occurring radioactive elements.

Table 7.5 Naturally occurring radioactive elements and their half-lives.

Element (symbol)	Atomic number	Most stable isotope	Half-life of most stable isotope
Technetium (Tc)	43	^{91}Tc	4.21×10^6 y
Iodine (I)	53	^{131}I	8 d
Cesium (Cs)	55	^{131}Cs	30 d
Promethium (Pm)	61	^{145}Pm	17.4 y
Polonium (Po)	84	^{209}Po	102 y
Astatine (At)	85	^{210}At	8.1 hr
Radon (Rn)	86	^{222}Rn	3.82 d
Francium (Fr)	87	^{223}Fr	22 minutes
Radium (Ra)	88	^{226}Ra	1600 y
Actinium (Ac)	89	^{227}Ac	21.77 years
Thorium	90	^{229}Th	7.54×10^4 y
Protactinium (Pa)	91	^{231}Pa	3.28×10^4 y
Uranium (U)	92	^{236}U	2.34×10^7 y

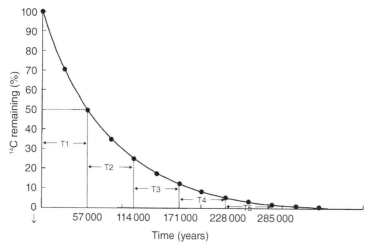

Figure 7.9 Half-life cycles of ^{14}C.

Half-life is an important concept in nuclear waste management, and health and safety considerations. It constitutes the basis for estimating the designed life of a nuclear waste disposal facility and related aspects of monitoring, storage, retrieval, transportation, and disposal. The amount of radioactivity in a material is expressed in units of Becquerel (Bq) or Curie (Ci).

Figure 7.9 illustrates the half-life concept of ^{14}C (half-life: 5715 y). Assuming its radioactivity level to be 100% at the time of its formation (at time T0), it would drop off to one-half (50%) of the original level after 5715 y (time T1); and in the next 5715 y, it would further decrease to one-half of the level at time T1, i.e. it will be left with 25% of the original radioactivity (at T2). Similarly, at time T3, the radiation level will be down to 12.5%, and so on until at T10 (57 150 y since formation), it would be only 0.1% of the original (insignificant).

7.4 Nuclear Waste

Nuclear waste is a special type of waste that is no longer of its original use and contains radionuclides having radioactivity levels that could be harmful. EW class includes all waste with a radioactivity level of under 10 μS (1 mr). Nuclear power reactors in the civil sector and weapons program in the defense sector produce large volumes of long-lived and dangerous HLW that emit harmful radiation. Certain manufacturing processes, medical use, and other industrial and research applications generate ILW and LLW. The terms radioactive waste and nuclear waste are used interchangeably – in the USA, nuclear waste is common, while radioactive waste is commonly used in Europe and some other countries.

Nuclear waste represents a highly hazardous form of waste that requires cautious handling and careful management. But, unlike common hazardous (or industrial) waste, nuclear waste has unique characteristics that include: (i) easy detection and quantification of radioactivity levels in nuclear wastes as compared to expensive and tedious characterization of chemicals and other harmful materials in hazardous waste, (ii) progressive decline of radiation in nuclear wastes over periods of time, eventually becoming harmless, as opposed to some poisonous elements – As, Cd, Cr, Hg, Pb, besides many carcinogenic organic compounds in hazardous waste – that last forever. However, it is the combination of high levels of thermal energy and radioactivity generated during the fission process in a power reactor that make the nuclear waste unique and dangerous. The goal of nuclear waste management, therefore, is to contain both the heat and the radiation from escaping into the biosphere to prevent possible harm to human and ecological systems. Yet another challenging feature of nuclear waste is the large range in the half-lives of radionuclides – from as low as seconds, such as ^{16}N: 7.3 seconds; ^{90}Kr: 33 seconds; ^{97}Kr: 1 second; ^{139}Xe: 41 seconds; ^{140}Xe: 16 seconds to millions of years (Ma), such as ^{99}Tc: 0.211 Ma; ^{93}Zr: 1.53 Ma; ^{135}Cs: 2.3 Ma; ^{107}Pd: 6.5 Ma, and ^{129}I: 15.7 Ma, that call for safe management on both short- and long-term bases.

7.4.1 Sources of Nuclear Waste

Considerable attention has been given to the safe management of nuclear waste, generated from military and civil applications of nuclear materials. High levels of radiation combined with heat and long half-lives of some of the radionuclides present in nuclear waste call for extreme care during its handling, storage, transportation, and disposal. Nuclear waste, generated in weapon fabrication plants, is often mixed with hazardous industrial solvents and other toxic chemicals. Such waste is termed mixed waste and, in the USA, it is regulated jointly by the US EPA, under the provisions of the Resource Conservation and Recovery Act (RCRA), and the NRC, under its AEA authority. Their requirements are generally compatible, but provisions of RCRA take precedence when the requirements are inconsistent. Nuclear wastes come from numerous sources; the more common sources are listed next:

1) NPPs as SNFs
2) Decommissioning (dismantling) of old NPPs
3) Nuclear propulsion vehicles, such as submarines and ice breakers
4) Military weapons program
5) SNF reprocessing plants
6) Medical diagnosis and treatment
7) Manufacturing of commercial and industrial measurements and analytical devices using nuclear materials
8) Pharmaceutical research and manufacturing
9) Agricultural industry
10) Uranium and phosphorus mining, processing, beneficiation; and oil production (TNORMs)
11) Contaminated wastes from nuclear accident sites (Chernobyl, Fukushima, etc.)
12) Research reactors (majority at US land grant universities).

A nuclear power reactor with 1000 MW installed capacity generates about 30 t of HLW and approximately 300 m^3 of LLW and ILW on an annual basis. The bulk of reactor waste comprises LLW; SNFs contain 1.3% HLW by volume but 95% of radioactivity; ILW accounts for 7% volume and 4% radioactivity; and LLW for about 90% volume and 1% radioactivity (Baisden and Choppin 2007) (see Figure 7.2).

According to Murray (2003), SNFs from a typical light water reactor, removed after three-year operation, contain:

- 95.6% UO$_2$ ($< 1\%$ of which is ^{235}U)
- 2.9% stable fission products (^{140}Ce, ^{94}Zr, etc.)
- 0.4% Pu (^{240}Pu, ^{241}Pu, ^{242}Pu)
- 0.3% ^{137}Cs and ^{90}Sr
- 0.1% ^{131}I and ^{99}Tc
- 0.5% other long-lived fission products (^{226}Ra, ^{14}C, ^{79}Se, ^{99}Tc, ^{237}Np, ^{135}Cs, ^{239}Pu, and ^{129}I).

Although comprising < 1%, the very long half-lives (hundreds to millions of years) of these radio-nuclides make SNFs very hazardous, requiring extreme care and isolation from the environment for a very long time – tens to hundreds of thousand years. ^{137}Cs and ^{90}Sr are short-lived and account for most of the initial radiation in the HLW; both decay to a low level in 300–1000 y; but the long-lived ^{99}Tc (half-life: 0.22×10^6 y), ^{129}I (half-life: 17×10^6 y), ^{237}Np (half-life: 2×10^6 y), could continue to emit dangerous levels of radiation for millions of years.

7.4.2 Nuclear (Uranium) Fuel Cycle

Uranium, the most common fuel in nuclear power reactors, occurs in three forms: ^{238}U (half-life 4.47 billion years), ^{235}U (half-life 700 Ma), and ^{234}U (half-life 246 000 y). The former is most abundant and accounts for 99.28% of natural uranium; ^{235}U – the only fissile variety – accounts for 0.72%, while ^{234}U accounts for 0.0054% of all uranium found in nature.

In the nuclear energy industry, various steps from the mining of uranium ore to the generation of nuclear waste in the reactor are grouped into the front end and back end of the fuel cycle (Figure 7.10). This grouping is significant from nuclear waste management standpoint because the volume of waste generated in the front end of the fuel cycle is very large but its radiation levels are relatively low as compared to the back end where the radiation levels are very high but the waste volume is low.

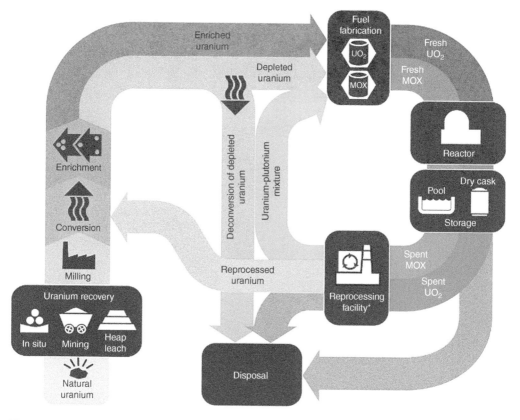

Figure 7.10 The uranium fuel cycle. *Source:* NRC.

Uranium ores are mined in many countries including Australia, the USA, India, Canada, Russia, China, India, Uzbekistan, etc. Uraninite or other uranium ores after mining are crushed and pulverized to a fine powder. This is then subjected to an acidic or alkaline leaching operation that separates uranium from the waste rock. The largest quantities of nuclear waste materials (with low radiation levels) are generated at this stage. Acidic leaching (using sulfuric acid) is generally preferred over alkaline (sodium carbonate and bicarbonate) because of cost considerations. In the heap leaching process, an acidic solution is sprayed over a heap of uranium ore that dissolves uranium as it percolates through the pile of crushed ores. This process concentrates the uranium that forms a yellow solid called yellowcake. Yellowcake is a concentrated form of naturally occurring uranium and contains 99.3% ^{238}U and 0.7% ^{235}U. The yellowcake after drying is placed in 200-L drums and shipped to enrichment plants to enhance ^{235}U concertation. This is done by treating the yellowcake to fluorine that converts U_3O_8 to uranium hexafluoride (UF_6), a solid at room temperature that can be easily converted to gas form at the low temperature of $57^{\circ}C$. Fluoridation raises U_3O_8 concentration to 3% and lowers ^{238}U concentration to 97%, but the two isotopes still remain mixed and need to be separated. The isotope separation is done by using fast-spinning gas centrifuges or gas diffusers. The process separates gaseous uranium hexafluoride into two streams: one being UO_2 containing about 3% ^{235}U, while the other stream gets progressively depleted in ^{235}U and is called depleted uranium (DU). DU comprises the bulk (96%) of enrichment byproduct, which can be used for armor, radiation shielding in medical therapy, and ballast (because of its very high density of 19.1 g/mL). The enriched UO_2 is then sent to a fuel fabrication facility where it is ground, mixed with ceramic materials, heated, and pressed into solid pellets, about 1 cm in diameter and about 1.6 cm long. These pellets are placed in zircalloy cylinders, up to 4 m tall that form fuel assembly for placement in the reactor core. Depending on the design of the reactor, anywhere between 250 and 750 fuel assemblies are used to produce electricity (Figure 7.11). About one-third of the fuel assemblies are replaced every 18 months to ensure continuity of power supply. After retrieval from the reactor core, SNFs are kept under circulating water to allow it to cool down for a period ranging from a minimum of 3 y to about 20 y (NRC 2017a).

Some of the U_3O_8 in the fuel assemblies, due to neutron activation turns into isotopes of Pu, approximately one-half of which is the fissile ^{239}Pu that also undergoes fission, contributing about one-third of the reactor's energy output. SNFs typically comprise about 1.0% ^{235}U and 0.6% fissile ^{239}Pu (out of a total of about 1% total Pu), about 95% U_3O_8, and about 3% fission

Figure 7.11 Fuel pellet, fuel rod, and fuel assembly. *Source:* NRC.

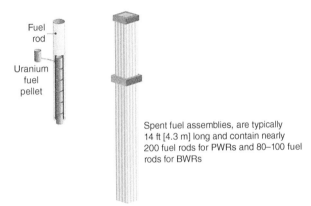

Fuel rod

Uranium fuel pellet

Spent fuel assemblies, are typically 14 ft [4.3 m] long and contain nearly 200 fuel rods for PWRs and 80–100 fuel rods for BWRs

Figure 7.12   Wet storage of spent nuclear fuel. *Source:* US Department of Energy.

products and minor actinides. SNFs removed from the reactor, continue to emit both radiation and heat, and are stored in specially designed, steel-lined, air-circulating water tank at the reactor site (Figure 7.12). Water in the tank serves the dual purpose of shielding the radiation and absorbing the heat. SNFs after being kept in wet storage for about five years can be transferred to a remote, naturally ventilated dry storage facility. In the long term, SNFs must either be reprocessed to recover most of ^{239}Pu, or prepared for permanent disposal in a subsurface geological medium.

7.4.2.1   Spent Fuel Reprocessing

After removing SNFs from the reactor core, it can either be earmarked for final disposal, or reprocessed to recover Pu and U. Currently, Belgium, France, India, Germany, Japan, Russia, Switzerland, and the United Kingdom reprocess SNFs, but Canada, South Korea, Spain, Sweden, and the USA do not.

Reprocessing, except for the disadvantage of recovered Pu falling in hands of unstable countries or terrorists, has several benefits that include: (i) conservation of U and Pu reserves due to high recovery rates (over 90%), (ii) substantially lower quantity of residual waste that requires disposal, and (iii) economically and technologically successful.

PUREX (Plutonium and Uranium Recovery by Extraction) is the most common process used for Pu and U recovery from SNFs and HLW. The basic process involves: shearing SNF rods into smaller pieces, acid dissolution, separating Pu, U, and other fission products from the solvent, and conversion of Pu and U into oxides that are mixed to form mixed oxide (MOX) that can be used as reactor fuel. Figure 7.13 depicts the various stages of the PUREX process.

7.4.3   Waste Forms and Packaging

Nuclear wastes occur in all three forms of matter – solid, liquid, and gas, and are found in a variety of materials that include:

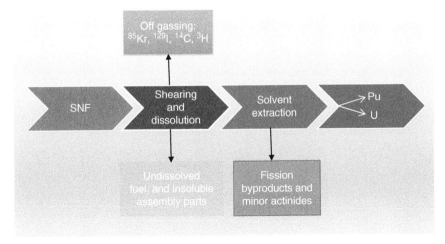

Figure 7.13   Simplified flow diagram of the PUREX process.

a) Gloves, overalls, rags, tools, and solvents contaminated with radioactive substances. They come from NPPs (in relatively small quantities), hospitals and other medical facilities, manufacturing plants, and research establishments. They require sturdy packaging (hard plastic or cardboard containers) for transportation and disposal.
b) SNFs that come out of a nuclear reactor consist of intermediate to long-lived radionuclides, mostly in solid form, which requires careful handling and storage. Packaging standards are much more stringent and require such wastes to be placed in specially designed "casks" with several barriers to prevent accidental release of radiation during transportation and storage.
c) HLW in liquid form, often referred to as defense HLW, comes from reprocessing of U to produce Pu for nuclear weapons. The solvent extraction process used to recover U and Pu produces highly acidic waste that is neutralized using NaOH to minimize corrosion of carbon steel storage tanks. The largest quantity of high-level liquid waste, 208 million liters, generated from defense program in the USA, is stored in 177 tanks at DOE's Hanford Site in Washington State (Figure 7.1); while smaller quantities, 125 million liters, and 5.3 million liters are stored at the Savannah River Site in South Carolina, and the Idaho National Engineering Laboratory, respectively. Total radioactivity at DOE's sites amounts to 460 million Ci (Lutze 2006, p. 354). Figure 7.14 shows common forms of nuclear wastes, comprising TRU and LLNW mixed with hazardous waste. They include clothing, tools, rags, debris, residues, and other discarded items.

7.4.4   Nuclear Waste Management

Safety should be the foremost consideration at every step of nuclear waste management of the entire Uranium Life Cycle, beginning from uranium mining, processing, enrichment, reactor fuel manufacturing, spent fuel generation, interim storage, reprocessing spent fuels, and ending in the disposal of HLW. Safe waste management requires using the best available technologies and resources that meet national and international standards and provide maximum protection to humans and the environment. Guidelines provided by the IAEA, recommendations from the International Nuclear Societies Council and the regulations of the US NRC, all underscore the importance of safety in nuclear waste management.

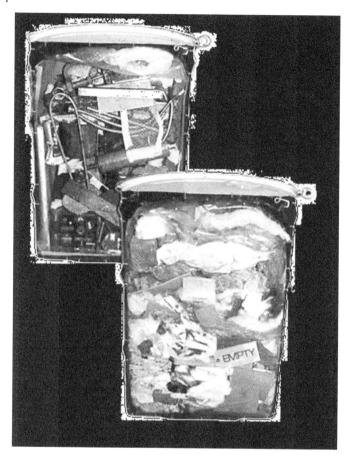

Figure 7.14 Various types of nuclear wastes comprising TRU, LLNW, mixed with radioactive and hazardous. *Source:* U.S.Department of Energy.

7.4.5 Nuclear Waste Classification

Unlike other types of hazardous waste, management of nuclear waste calls for the highest standards of safety due to its potential to ionize living tissues and disastrous health consequences, if not properly isolated. Any classification of nuclear waste must include safety as its foremost considerations. The classification should not be used to recommend a disposal path because its misuse could produce adverse personal and ecological impacts. Accordingly, the main objectives of the classification system should be to: (i) facilitate clear and accurate communication, by providing a good descriptive tool for the exchange of information, and (ii) assure safety during handling, storage, transportation, and disposal.

Two common classification systems are in use worldwide; both are based on waste origin, safety considerations, and/or radioactivity levels. The classification system used in the USA is the one developed by NRC and its forerunner, the AEC, and has legal authority for implementation. The IAEA classification system, on the other hand, provides guidelines for adoption by its member countries. Of the 168 members (as of February 2016), many have developed their own classification system using IAEA guidelines with appropriate modifications. European Union's (EU) radioactive waste classification system is a good example that is based on IAEA's guidelines.

7.4.5.1 The IAEA System

The IAEA classification system is based primarily on considerations of long-term safety associated with the disposal of nuclear waste. Its purpose is to: (i) develop a general scheme for classifying nuclear waste, and (ii) characterize the radiation range for different classes of nuclear waste and provide limiting values for the various classes. Waste can be grouped in one of the following six categories:

1) EW includes all waste from the nuclear industry that has been cleared, exempted, or excluded from regulation. The radiation level is negligible or very low and the annual dose to the public is $< 10\,\mu Sv$ (or 1 mr).

2) Very short-lived waste (VSLW) contains radioactive materials that can be slightly above the exempt level. Disposal facilities for such waste do not need a high level of containment and isolation, and disposal in a landfill is generally suitable. Some examples of VSLW include soil and rubble with a low activity level that do not require shielding.

3) Very low-level waste (VLLW). This class of waste includes nuclear waste containing short half-life radionuclides; a majority of this type comes from research and medical facilities. It can be stored for a limited period (up to a few years) to allow it to lose most of its radioactivity for subsequent clearance for uncontrolled disposal or discharge.

4) Low-level waste (LLW). Waste that contains material with radionuclide content above clearance levels, but with limited duration of long-lived activity. It requires adequate isolation and containment for periods of up to a few hundred years, typically 300. It includes waste materials that emit very high levels of radiation, with a short half-life that requires shielding, along with some long-lived materials with relatively low activity levels.

5) Intermediate-level waste (ILW). Waste which, because of containing large quantities of radionuclides, requires a higher level of containment and isolation than is provided by near-surface disposal. However, ILW needs little or no provision for heat dissipation during its handling, transportation, and disposal. ILW includes long-lived, α-emitting radionuclides that will not decay to an acceptable activity level for several hundreds to thousands of years. Such waste needs to be buried in a geological medium at the depth of hundreds to thousands of meters.

6) High-level waste (HLW). Waste with radioactivity levels intense enough to generate significant quantities of heat from the radioactive decay process or with large amounts of long-lived activity, which need to be considered in the design of the disposal facility. Placement in deep, stable geological formations is the preferred option for the disposal of HLW. This class of waste includes spent reactor fuel which has been declared as waste, vitrified waste from the processing of reactor fuel, and any other waste requiring the degree of containment and isolation provided by geological disposal. Figure 7.15 illustrates waste classes in relation to half-lives of radionuclides.

7.4.5.2 The US System

In the United States, nuclear waste is classified into three categories: (1) high-level nuclear waste or high level waste, (2) intermediate-level or transuranic waste, and (3) low-level radioactivewaste. These categories are based on waste source, safety, handling, transportation, and disposal considerations.

1) High-Level Wastes: HLW includes: (i) SNFs discharged from nuclear power and research reactors, and (ii) wastes resulting from reprocessing of SNFs to recover Pu and U. HLW occurs in solid, liquid, and gas forms and (i) are highly radioactive (some radionuclides have a very long half-life, e.g. ^{239}Pu [half-life: 24 000 y]), (ii) continuously give off heat and radiation as they

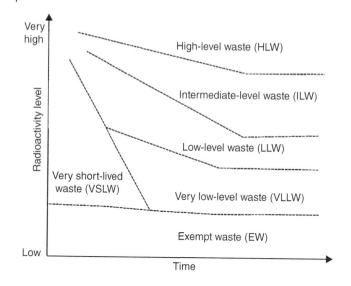

Figure 7.15 IAEA classification of radioactive wastes.

decay, and, therefore, need to be cooled, contained, and isolated from the environment. SNFs that comprise reactor fuel assemblies are the most dominant component of HLW from NPPs and research reactors. HLW from defense facilities are mostly in liquid form and are stored in tanks.

2) Transuranic or Intermediate Level Waste (TU or TRU): EPA defines TU waste as waste materials containing isotopes with atomic numbers greater than 92 and concentrations of α-emitting radionuclides higher than 100 nCi/g (3.7 MBq/kg) and with half-lives greater than 20 y. TU waste is further classified as "contact-handled" (CH) and "remote-handled" (RH), based on the radiation level measured at the container surface. Contact-handled TU has a radiation level of under 200 mr/h (2 mS/h), whereas remote-handled TU can emit radiation dose ranging from > 200 mr/h (2 mS/h) to 1000 r/h (10 S/h). Contact-handled TU neither has high radioactivity nor generates high heat; in contrast, remote-handled TU can be highly radioactive, with high heat.

TU waste comes from NPPs, SNF-reprocessing facilities, and the fabrication of nuclear weapons. Bulk of the TU waste has a low radioactivity level but contains some long-lived radionuclides, such as ^{239}Pu, ^{243}Am, ^{241}Am, ^{244}Cm, and ^{237}Np. It is due to the presence of these long-lived radionuclides – half-life ranging between 433 y (^{241}Am) and 24 000 y (^{239}Pu) – that they are managed separately. Bulk of the TU wastes give off very little heat and do not require remote handling.

Initially, an estimated 497 000 m^3 of TU wastes was disposed of in shallow trenches at DOE facilities, but since 1970, they have been placed in retrievable storage. The volume of CH TU at all DOE facilities is estimated to be 108 927 m^3 and that of RH 2 246 m^3 (Murray 2003). As of March 1999, TU waste, in the USA is being disposed of at the Waste Isolation Pilot Plant (WIPP) in New Mexico (discussed in Section 7.7.2).

TU category is used in the USA only. Wastes with similar characteristics in other countries are classified as long-lived intermediate-level waste (LILW).

3) Low-Level Radioactive Waste (LLW): Low-level waste includes materials that have become contaminated with radioactive substances or have become radioactive through exposure to neutron radiation. It does not include SNF, HLW, TU waste, or NORM. LLWs do not contain TU elements and have low radiation levels. As such, they do not require any shielding and can be handled directly. LLW includes slightly radioactive trash, such as mops, gloves, shoe

covers, clothing, filters, tools, luminous dials, medical tubes, injection needles, syringes, and lab animal tissues. DOE categorizes LLW into four classes – Classes A, B, C, and GTCC (Greater than Class C) – based on its radioactivity levels and radiation dose. Class A waste becomes harmless after 100 y; Class B waste after 300 y; and Class C waste after 500 y. Because of its higher hazard, Class C waste must be buried at least 5 m below the ground surface using an engineered barrier.

GTCC waste is a special category of LLW that either: (i) has radioactivity levels higher than Class C of LLW, and (ii) contains a greater quantity of TRU materials that come from nuclear fuel testing or fuel fabrication plants. GTCC cannot be disposed of in near-surface facilities. DOE has assumed responsibility for its final disposal. Table 7.6 shows various classes of LLW and their activities.

A broad comparison of the IEA and US nuclear waste classification, along with their disposal, is given in Table 7.7.

Mill Tailings that are generated from the mining and processing of uranium ores contain low levels of radiation but are not classified as LLW. The tailings contain small amounts of U and Th and are present in the liquid sludge that comes out of the mills. They are held in pits or tailing dams and allowed to dry. The dry solid needs to be managed properly to prevent its entry into the surface and groundwater reservoirs or into the atmosphere as fine dust.

Table 7.6 Various classes of low-level waste and their activities.

Class	Activity
A	Waste mainly contaminated with radionuclides that have short half-lives; average concentration: $0.1 \, Ci/ft^3$. Radiation level drops down to harmless in about 100 y. Least radioactive of all LLW classes. Accounts for 90% of LLW generated in the USA.
B	Waste contains larger amounts of short-lived radionuclides than Class A; average concentration: $2 \, Ci/ft^3$. Becomes harmless in about 300 y. About 9% of the US LLW falls in this class.
C	Waste contains greater amounts of both long- and short-lived radionuclides than Classes A and B; average concentration: $7 \, Ci/ft^3$. Takes up to 500 y to become harmless; accounts for < 1% of all US LLW.
GTCC	Higher concentration of long-lived radionuclides: $300–2500 \, Ci/ft^3$ (average). No near-surface disposal allowed by DOE and must be treated like HLW for disposal. Most radioactive of all LLW classes. Comprises < 0.2% of all LLW.

Table 7.7 Comparison of IAEA and US nuclear/radioactive waste classification systems.

IAEA	USA	Disposal option
HLW	HLW	Deep geological repository
ILW	TU or GTCC	Intermediate depth; not near-surface
LLW	Class C	Near-surface
	Class B	
	Class A	
VLLW and VSLW	NA	Landfill
EW	NA	Landfill upon receiving clearance

7.5 Laws Regulating Management of Nuclear Waste

Various countries have enacted laws to regulate nuclear waste. While the USA has developed its own sets of laws, most other countries have followed the guidelines provided by the IAEA for formulating their national policies on nuclear waste management. The directives prepared by the EU incorporate the IAEA guidelines and are included in this section, along with a detailed discussion of the US laws.

7.5.1 EU's Nuclear Waste Management Law

The EU in July 2011 released a comprehensive document, providing a detailed framework for responsible and safe management of nuclear waste for adoption by its member countries (EU 2011). All 28 countries generate nuclear waste and have developed regulations, based on the EU Directives. The directive emphasizes safe management of nuclear waste and recommends its containment and isolation from the environment for a long period of time. The main requirements of the Directives are summarized below:

- All member countries should adopt a national policy for nuclear waste management.
- Each country should establish and implement rules and regulations for the management and disposal of all SNFs and other types of nuclear waste generated in the country.
- A comprehensive set of regulations, along with a competent and independent regulatory body, as well as financing mechanisms, should be created for implementing the policy.
- Public participation should be encouraged with complete transparency to allow easy access to information on nuclear waste.
- Each member country should periodically conduct self-evaluation and have their policies reviewed by international experts.
- Export of nuclear waste to countries outside the EU is not permissible except under exceptional cases.

7.5.2 The United States Nuclear Waste Management Laws

Although the AEA was promulgated as far back as 1946, it mainly addressed the use of the newly discovered nuclear energy, and did not include any provision for the management of nuclear waste. Even the subsequent 1954 amendments – that established rules for use of nuclear energy by private enterprises – failed to address nuclear waste management in any detail. However, troubled by the increasing volume of HLW generated from the defense program, the AEC, in 1955, contracted the US National Academy of Sciences (NAS), asking it to evaluate various disposal methods and advice on research programs needed to determine the scientific basis for managing its HLW. NAS appointed eight prominent geoscientists to a committee that released its report in 1957, concluding that: (i) "waste disposal in tanks is at present the safest and possibly the most economical method of containing waste" and (ii) "disposal in salt is the most promising method for the near future. . ." (NAS 1957). The committee did not consider crystalline rocks as a suitable disposal medium at that time but alluded to the "possibility for the more distant future" (NAS 1957, p. 6). AEC subsequently conducted detailed investigations at the Carey salt mine at Lyons, Kansas between 1963 and 1967 to test the effects of elevated temperature and radiation emanating from HLW (see Section 7.7.4.1 for details). Although no substantial structural problems were observed in the salt beds arising out of high thermal and radiologic loading, the project was abandoned in

1972 due to geological uncertainties (OTA 1985, p. 210). Continued setbacks and failure on part of the AEC to locate a disposal site for one decade led to the passage of the Energy Reorganization Act in 1974 that abolished AEC and created: (i) the Energy Research and Development Administration (ERDA), and (ii) the NRC. The former was charged with managing energy research and development, nuclear weapons, and naval reactors programs. The NRC was given the authority for licensing, inspection, and enforcement, involving the use of nuclear materials for electric power generation, medical diagnosis and treatment, manufacturing, etc., ERDA had a short tenure and was dissolved in October 1977; it was replaced by the Department of Energy that assumed all responsibilities of ERDA.

7.5.2.1 Low-Level Radioactive Waste

Low-level radioactive waste (LLRW), due to lack of any legislation, was being carelessly dumped in the oceans or buried in unlined landfills between 1940s and 1950s (ocean disposal ceased in 1970). A law to regulate the disposal of LLW – the Low-Level Radioactive Waste Policy Act (LLRWPA) – was passed by the US Congress in 1980 that made each state responsible for disposing of non-DOE-generated LLW within its boundaries. The law encouraged states to share their land with neighboring states and select a site to receive a license from NRC for LLW disposal to form low-level waste compacts.

The Low-Level Radioactive Waste Policy Amendments Act (LLRWPAA) of 1985 supplemented the 1980 law and provided monetary incentives and deadlines for states to form LLW compacts. Nine interstate compacts were formed and for each, a host state was designated. Six states – NY, NC, MI, NH, ME, and RI – opted to remain unaffiliated while the remaining states agreed to form the compacts. In addition, NRC can authorize a state to license and inspect source or sources of nuclear materials and their byproducts used within their state borders. Such states are designated Agreement State. NRC's requirements for Agreement State can be found in 10 CFR Part 150. Table 7.8 lists various states in each of these compacts.

The idea of compacts did not receive much acceptance and many states pulled out of it that ultimately led to the failure of compacts plan. Public and political opposition, reduced LLW volume due to better treatment methods, access to existing disposal facilities, and high cost of construction and operation of new LLW disposal facility, have been cited as the main reasons.

7.5.2.2 High-Level Nuclear Waste

It was not until 1982, almost 40 y after the nuclear waste began to be generated, first from the production of nuclear weapons and later from the electric power generation and other "peaceful" uses

Table 7.8 Low-level waste compacts and member states.

Appalachian Compact: Delaware, Maryland, Pennsylvania, West Virginia
Atlantic Compact: Connecticut, New Jersey, South Carolina
Central Compact: Arkansas, Kansas, Louisiana, Nebraska, Oklahoma
Central Midwest Compact: Illinois, Kentucky
Midwest Compact: Indiana, Iowa, Minnesota, Missouri, Ohio, Wisconsin
Northwest Compact: Alaska, Hawaii, Idaho, Montana, Oregon, Utah, Washington, Wyoming
Rocky Mountain Compact: Colorado, Nevada, New Mexico
Southeast Compact: Alabama, Florida, Georgia, Mississippi, Tennessee, Virginia
Southwest Compact: Arizona, California, North Dakota, South Dakota
Texas Compact: Maine, Texas, Vermont
Unaffiliated: Maine, Massachusetts, Michigan, New Heaven, New York, North Carolina

Table 7.9 Comparison of various management options for HLW.

Onsite storage	Centralized storage	Deep geological repository
No transportation needed Short-term measure (200–300 y). Least expensive	Transportation risks of moving SNFs from the reactor to the storage facility have to be addressed Assures short-term (hundreds of years) safety; long-term (thousands of years) monitoring questionable. Moderate cost.	Transportation risks need to be managed effectively. Eliminates both long-term and short-term radiation safety hazards. Most expensive, about $5 billion.

of nuclear energy, that a legislation – the Nuclear Waste Policy Act (NWPA) – was enacted to manage the disposal of HLW. However, soon after its enactment, a number of political and legal issues surfaced that resulted in political maneuvering by densely populated (and hence higher representation in federal legislative bodies) and influential states, resulting in the passage of the Nuclear Waste Policy Act Amendments in 1987 that singled out Yucca Mountain in Nevada as the site for the disposal of HLW waste in a geological medium. This was in marked contradiction to the advice of the first NAS committee on waste disposal that had stated: 'The question should not be phrased: "How can we dispose of waste at X site?" but should be: Can or cannot waste be disposed of at X site?' (NAS 1957, p. 6).

HLW is currently being managed in three ways, each having certain advantages and limitations. Table 7.9 provides a comparison of the three disposal options. While global consensus favors deep geological repository (DGR), some countries use an interim storage facility for the management of HLW.

7.5.2.2.1 Nuclear Waste Policy Act The Nuclear Waste Policy Act (NWPA), passed in 1982, was intended to settle several controversial issues, such as the government's preference of salt formations as the most suitable disposal site; construction of large interim retrievable storage facility located away from reactors (AFR); and the 1977 decision by President Carter to ban reprocessing of HLW. The reprocessing ban essentially eliminated "disposal" as an option for HLW and shifted the emphasis on a retrievable storage facility – a repository – that could, in future, be accessed to retrieve the HLW for recovering Pu and U. To settle many of these issues and to assure the nuclear industry about finding a solution to HLW disposal, the 97th US Congress passed the NWPA in December 1982 that was signed into law by President Regan in January 1983. The law settled the growing concerns and provided a timeline for siting, licensing, construction, and operation of a DGR. The law also provided for the collection of a levy on each kilowatt of nuclear power generated to pay for the expenses related to all aspects of nuclear waste management including the "identification, development, licensing, construction, operation, decommissioning, and post-decommissioning maintenance and monitoring of any repository, monitored retrievable storage facility, or test and evaluation facility constructed under this Act" (DOE March 2004, NWPA, p. 100). The main features of NWPA are summarized below:

- Deep geological disposal will be developed for the isolation of nuclear wastes.
- Monitored retrievable storage (MRS) was approved as an SNF management option.
- DOE to study possible locations, nominate five (candidate) sites for DGR, and recommend three of these sites for site characterization.

- Set the process and timelines for:
  - DOE to recommend a site to the President by 31 March 1987.
  - Acceptance by the President and his recommendation to the Congress (site designation to become effective after president's recommendation, subject to objections from the governor of the state or the Native American Tribe where the repository might be located)
  - Submission of construction license application by NRC within 90 d from the effective date of site designation
  - DOE to apply for another license to accept waste by 1998, following the completion of repository construction.

- Limited the quantity of waste for emplacement in the repository at 70 000 t of heavy metal.
- A second repository to be located in the eastern USA.
- Required DOE to take control of SNFs, held in temporary storage at NPPs. Concerned parties signed a contract in 1987 affirming the removal of SNFs.
- Established a Nuclear Waste Fund (NWF) by levying 0.1 cent/kWh fee on the generators of commercial nuclear power. NWF would be used to pay for the cost of developing the repository. Total fees paid, as of 2014: $29.9 billion (when DOE, under court order, stopped collecting the fee in May 2014).
- Softened the requirements of full environmental impact assessment (EIA) by asking DOE to submit an "environmental assessment" instead.
- Established the Office of Civilian Radioactive Waste Management (OCRWM) within DOE.

In 1983, the DOE identified nine sites, seven in salt and two in volcanic formations:

- Volcanic rocks – (1) Hanford site in Washington State. Geology: Columbia River Basalt, maximum thickness: > 3500 m; lava erupted intermittently between 17 and 15.5 Ma ago during the middle Miocene Epoch. (2) Yucca Mountain site in Nevada State. Geology: Topopah Spring Tuff, about 350 m thick at the repository level, is a densely welded tuff, resulting from volcanic eruptions that occurred about 12.8 Ma ago.
- Salt dome – (3) Cypress dome, Mississippi; (4) Richton dome, Mississippi; (5) Vacherie dome, Louisiana. All of Permian age (~250–300 Ma)
- Bedded salt – (6) Davis Canyon, Utah; (7) Deaf Smith County, Texas; (8) Lavender Canyon, Utah; and (9) Swisher County, Texas; also of Permian age.

Yielding to the strong political pressures from Louisiana, Texas, and Utah, DOE dropped all seven sites in salt formations from active consideration.

7.5.2.2.2 *Nuclear Waste Policy Act Amendments*   The NWPA was amended in 1987 to include the following provisions:

- Designated Yucca Mountain as the sole repository site for all HLW and directed DOE to conduct studies to determine its suitability; dropped the idea of a second repository.
- DOE was asked to recommend a site for an above-ground MRS facility. This facility would store a limited amount of SNF temporarily before sending it to the permanent repository.
- SNFs and HLW should be transported in NRC-certified containers.
- DOE should follow NRC's regulations regarding advance notification to states, local governments, and tribal officials prior to transportation.
- DOE should provide technical assistance and funding for safety and emergency response training of state, local, and tribal officials in affected areas.

- Created the Nuclear Waste Technical Review Board (NWTRB), an independent body within the Executive Branch to evaluate the technical and scientific soundness of OCRWM's activities.

7.6   Nuclear Waste Storage and Transportation

As discussed before, safety is of paramount importance in nuclear waste management to prevent any possible release of harmful radiation at every step of the life cycle of the waste – from generation to storage, transportation, and ultimate disposal. Half-life and associated radiation and heat hazards are some of the key characteristics that are evaluated to determine the most appropriate handling, packaging, storage, transportation, and disposal system for nuclear wastes. In general, these requirements are relatively simple for LLW but progressively become more complex for TU and HLW. We will first discuss special packaging and transportation requirements for nuclear wastes followed by disposal methods.

7.6.1   Transportation of Nuclear Waste

As a general rule, the higher the hazard of radiation exposure, the stronger are the packaging and transportation requirements. 10 CFR Part 71 provides US Department of Transportation (DOT) regulations on radioactive material transportation, along with details of container design and construction, record keeping, reporting, and radiation limits (GAO 2017). Requirements for packaging, transportation, and disposal of nuclear wastes have been established by DOE/NRC, EPA, and DOT. DOT has drawn up standards and rules for waste handling and packaging, available in 49 CFR Parts 170–179. NRC regulatory requirements can be found in 10 CFR Parts 19–71.

7.6.2   LLW Transportation

Other than the additional hazard of low radiation, LLW is not much different from hazardous waste insofar as their storage, handling, and packaging for transportation is concerned. No radiation shielding is required during the handling and transportation of LLW. The following is a summary of main requirements: (i) LLW can be stored at the place of origin for a period of time until it decays to harmless levels or accumulates in ample quantities for shipment to a treatment or disposal facility, (ii) the waste generator is not identified by name in the Manifest but is assigned a unique code identifying the state of origin. Some shipments include waste from several states and/or from multiple waste generators; these are delivered via brokers or waste processors, (iii) LLW, generally in solid form, is transported in drums, after being compacted to reduce the volume to a minimum, and (iv) waste is disposed of in secure landfills that are monitored for the potential release of radionuclides in the environment.

7.6.3   TU/ILW Transportation

The presence of long-lived radionuclides in TU waste calls for robust shielding and enhanced care during handling and transportation. TU waste, in solid form, is placed in specially designed containers that are tested to withstand 30 ft vertical drop, $802\,^{\circ}C$ ($1475\,^{\circ}F$) fire heat, and pressure equivalent to 150 kPa (or 50 ft column of water; ~21.7 psi). During transportation, a satellite and ground communication network allows for tracking of the waste through the TRANSCOM System, which

Figure 7.16   Cask for TRU waste transportation. *Source:* S.E. Hasan (author).

is the DOE satellite tracking and communications system used to monitor nuclear material shipments that enable automatic tracking of the truck with five-minute updates, and allows the driver
to be in constant communication with a central monitoring room.

7.6.4   HLW/SNF Transportation

High levels of radiation and heat associated with SNFs require the highest integrity of the packaging system and extreme caution in its transportation. The SNF assemblies are placed in specially
designed, high-integrity shipping containers called casks (Figure 7.16). These casks have been subjected to rigorous design analyses and thorough testing including smashing one cask loaded on an
open 18-wheel trailer against a concrete barrier. Transportation casks are very expensive, costing
between $1.5 million and 3 million (GAO 2014, p. 17).

7.7   Nuclear Waste Disposal

Disposal of HLW has been a vexing issue ever since the 1940s when the United States embarked
upon the complex and massive task of building the atomic bomb. The priority for the Manhattan
Project was to build the bomb as quickly as possible, and the related problems of radiation exposure to workers and waste disposal did not receive the attention they deserved. Although health
physicists and some sanitary engineers had expressed their concerns, it was either ignored or not
considered important (Walker 2009, pp. 1–8). One other reason, besides the urgency to develop the
atomic bomb, was the lack of knowledge and experience about human and ecological impacts
from exposure to radiation, and the complexity, both scientific and politico-legal, associated with
HLW disposal. While we have now been able to understand the effects of radiation on living cells
and formulate safe levels of radiation exposure for human and ecological protection, disposal of
HLW has been an elusive issue that we have not come to grips with yet. Disposal of LL and TU
wastes, on the other hand, has been relatively less challenging and both are being managed
satisfactorily.

Table 7.10 Commercial low-level waste landfills.

Landfill name and location	LLNW class accepted	Status
Waste Control Specialists LLC, Andrews County, Texas	Classes A, B, and C wastes from Texas, federal government facilities, and 34 other states	Operating since 2012
Chem-Nuclear Systems LLC, Barnwell, S. Carolina	Classes A, B, and C wastes from Connecticut, New Jersey and S. Carolina	Operating since 1971
Beatty, Nevada	First LLNW disposal site in the USA; 0.122 million m^3 of LLNW are buried here	Operated 1962–1992
EnergySolutions, formerly Envirocare, Clive, Utah	Accepts Classes A, B, and C waste from all regions in the USA	Operating since 2001
Maxey Flats, Kentucky	About 0.142 million m^3 of LLW from corporations and government agencies were disposed of in 52 unlined trenches.	Operated 1963–1976
US Ecology Richland, Washington	Classes A, B, and C wastes from Washington, Alaska, Hawaii, Idaho, Montana, Oregon, and Wyoming; and Colorado, Nevada and New Mexico	Operating since 1966
Sheffield, Illinois	About 0.085 million m^3 of LLW, containing ^{3}H, ^{14}C, ^{129}I, ^{90}Sr, ^{137}Cs, ^{60}Co, and $^{238-241}$Pu were deposited in 21 trenches.	Operated 1967–1978
West Valley, New York	The only site for HLW reprocessing that never became operational, but received about 0.068 million m^3 of LLW that were deposited in 14 trenches.	Operated 1963–1975

7.7.1 Low-Level Radioactive Waste Disposal

The US NRC has set the following criteria for near-surface disposal of LLW: (i) The external exposure to a member of the public resulting from release of the waste shall not exceed 25 mr/y, and (ii) the dose to a person who inadvertently intrudes into the disposal site after loss of institutional control (100 y) shall not exceed a one-time dose of 500 mr or 100 mr/y for the first 1000 y after emplacement.

By far, the largest volume of nuclear waste comprises LLW. They are packaged in sturdy containers and stored, transported, and disposed of at a secure landfill that is licensed to receive LLW. Accurate records must be maintained at all stages of the waste life, and the site should be monitored during and after the closure for any possible release of radionuclides that may adversely impact the environment. Secured landfill for LLW is similar in design to that used for modern landfills (discussed in Chapter 4), with added monitoring and surveillance. In the USA, LLW facilities have been in operation for decades at several locations; some of them have been closed after becoming full. Table 7.10 lists commercial LLW facilities.

7.7.2 Transuranic Waste Disposal

Transuranic (TU) wastes contain TU elements, those with atomic weight > 92 (U). They are generated from nuclear weapons' production, nuclear research, and power production, and comprise protective gear, tools, residue, and debris. Although the relative quantities of the TU elements are small compared to the bulk of the waste, this waste is not considered LLW but requires isolation from the biosphere, along with special packaging and transportation requirements due to long half-lives of some of the elements contained in TU waste.

DOE began studying sites for the construction of the WIPP near Carlsbad, New Mexico in 1973. After a long period of site investigations (1975–1998), the site was approved for receiving TU waste generated at defense establishments. Although the facility can store all past and future TU waste generated by defense establishments, currently, the WIPP Land Withdrawal Act has put a limit of $175\,500\,m^3$ that can be emplaced at the site.

First, TU waste shipment was received on 26 March 1999. Since then, and as of December 2013, over $90\,900\,m^3$ of defense-related TU and mixed wastes had been received and stored at the WIPP facility. No waste was received in 2015 and 2016 due to a transport vehicle catching fire that occurred on 5 February 2014, and an incident on 14 February 2014, when a continuous air monitor detected a radiological release underground (DOE 2014, p. 13). Waste shipment was put on hold while the facility's equipment and systems were carefully examined during 2014–2016. The DOE and site contractor conducted final operation readiness checks in December 2016 and waste storage was resumed in January 2017.

The WIPP site is located about 655 m below the ground surface in Permian (250–290 Ma) salt beds, known as the Salado Formation. Using a combination of drills and mechanized continuous mining machines, a large number of openings have been excavated in the bedded salt deposit (Figure 7.17). The WIPP site has 56 storage rooms underground, each room approximately 91.4 m (300 ft) long. The plant is estimated to accept TU waste for 25–35 y at an estimated cost of $19 billion.

7.7.3 High-Level Nuclear Waste Disposal

High-level nuclear waste (HLW) can assume all three states of matter, e.g. solid, liquid, and gas. In a nuclear power reactor, bulk of the waste is in solid form contained in the SNFs with some radioactive gases, such as: ^3H, ^{85}Kr, ^{135}Xe, ^{131}I, and ^{222}Rn, with half-lives of 12.3 y, 1.76 y, 9.2 hr, 8.04 d, and 3.82 d, respectively. In the military weapons program and in SNF reprocessing operations, considerable quantities of HLW in liquid form were also generated during Pu and U recovery. The residue left after Pu and U recovery, still containing radionuclides with long half-lives, can be immobilized by vitrification. It involves mixing the residue with glass-forming materials – mainly silica (SiO_2), and boron oxide (B_2O_3), heating it to melting temperature (about $1150\,^{\circ}C$), and pouring the melt into metallic containers. Upon cooling, the melt solidifies to form borosilicate glass, which encapsulates radionuclides. These vitrified masses, resembling logs, are kept in temporary storage for ultimate disposal in a DGR.

After the uranium fuel in the reactor has been used up, SNFs are routinely stored at the reactor site in a 12.2 m (40 ft)-deep water pool (wet storage). These high-integrity pools are made of thick reinforced concrete with steel liners. The water serves both to shield the radiation and cool the rods. Fuel is typically cooled for at least five years in the pool before it is transferred to dry storage in casks. In certain cases, the NRC may authorize transfer as early as three years, but the industry norm is about ten years. NRC also permits off-site storage of SNFs in dry cask at licensed Independent Spent Fuel Storage Facilities (ISFSFs). By the end of 2009, 62 683 MTHM of SNF had accumulated in the United States, of which 78% was stored in wet pools at reactor sites and 22% as dry cask storage. Figure 7.18 shows the location of ISFSFs across the country.

Disposal of HLW has been one of the most challenging problems because of the presence of high levels of radiation and heat in addition to extremely long half-lives of certain radionuclides, requiring its isolation for 10 000–1 million years. Realizing that modern science and engineering cannot

(a)

(b)

(c)

Figure 7.17 Transuranic waste disposal at the WIPP site, New Mexico, USA. Location map of the storage facility in excavated salt bed. *Source:* US Department of Energy; (b) Drift in salt formation for TU waste storage; and (c) TU waste in barrels ready for storage at 655 m depth. *Source:* (b and c) S.E. Hasan (author).

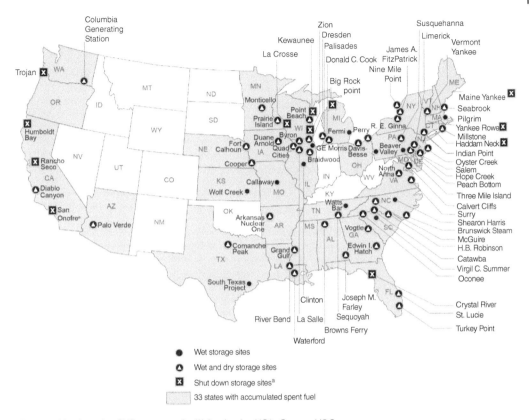

Figure 7.18   Interim SNFs storage facilities in the USA. *Source:* NRC.

assure the integrity of any man-made structure for such a long period of time, various options such as burying HLW in the polar ice sheet, shooting it off into space, or dumping it into deep oceanic trenches were considered but all were determined to be impractical. The consensus is to put it down into deep geological formations, relying on the combined geological (natural) and engineered (man-made) barriers for effective isolation. This principle of multiple barrier isolation is discussed in Section 7.8.2.

Selection of a geological repository for safe disposal of HLW should, at a minimum, meet the following requirements:

- No possibility of release of radiation into the environment for thousands of years
- Stable geologic environment: no significant erosion, or the possibility of major earthquakes, volcanic activities, or flooding for thousands of years
- Ability to remain intact from changed climate conditions in the future
- Fail-safe mechanisms for handling and transportation of HLW
- Sufficiently away from population centers.

The International Atomic Energy Agency (IAEA 1995) has developed a set of broad guidelines to ensure long-term safety aspects, legal issues, and protection of human health and the environment from radiological hazards. These include:

- *Protection of human health and the environment.* HLW should be managed to safeguard human health and the environment.

- *Protection beyond national borders.* HLW management should include consideration of possible effects on human health and the environment beyond national borders.
- *Protection of future generations.* HLW should be managed in such a way that predicted impacts on the health of future generations will not be greater than currently acceptable standards; and no undue burdens should be placed on future generations.
- *Legal framework.* HLW should be managed within an appropriate national legal framework including clear allocation of responsibilities and provisions for independent regulatory functions.
- *Radioactive waste generation.* Waste minimization techniques should be given due consideration to assure minimization of the volume of waste generated.
- *Security.* Radioactive waste management facilities should be appropriately secured and their safety assured during their lifetime.

These requirements have created a set of unique and complex, but not insurmountable, challenges. Geologic and engineering studies that comprise site selection result in a very costly and time-consuming site characterization process. A recent DOE estimate indicates the cost to range between $30 billion (low) and $90 billion (high); (GAO 2017, p. 17).

Among the 30 countries that generate HLW, the USA was the first one to study the feasibility of HLW disposal in a geological medium. Billions of US taxpayers' dollars have been expensed over five decades with the goal of selecting a site to safely isolate the HLW; yet, as of 2021, no site has been approved to receive and store the HLW. This failure should not be construed to mean that the US has neglected this critical aspect because as early as 1949, the AEC had acknowledged that "improvement in control of wastes requires continued research and development work" and was aware of the need to develop "better means of isolating, concentrating, immobilizing, and controlling wastes. . ." (Mazuzan and Walker 1984, p. 348). However, shifting government priorities, lack of a consistent policy coupled with pre-emptive political decisions that resulted in prolonged litigations have blocked HLW waste disposal at the Yucca Mountain site. In its 2012 report, the Blue Ribbon Commission on *America's Nuclear Future*, while commending DOE for its successful completion of the WIPP facility, noted that "The overall record of DOE and of the federal government as a whole, however, has not inspired widespread confidence or trust in our nation's nuclear waste management program" (BRC 2012, p. x).

7.7.4 HLW Management in the United States

Management of HLW involves several separate, but related, steps: Waste isolation and placement in wet and dry storage media; transportation in casks to an interim dry storage facility; final transportation and emplacement in a deep geological facility, with or without the ability to access the waste for maintenance and control to ensure safe isolation. The term "disposal" represents the final stage in HLW management that relies on engineered and natural barrier systems to achieve permanent isolation from the environment, without the ability to retrieve it. Storage, on the other hand, represents an interim stage to isolate the HLW allowing controlled access for maintenance. Stored waste would ultimately need disposal. The term repository represents a combined facility capable of both storage and retrieval of HLW. Because of the uncertainties and lack of prior experience with an HLW disposal facility, the Yucca Mountain project was to allow access for maintenance and retrieval of the HLW should there be evidence of serious problems threatening the safe operation of the facility. However, since the inception of studies at the YM site, in the early 1980s and the knowledge and experience gained from intensive site characterization studies, retrievability of the waste may not be considered important, and future facilities may be designed for disposal only.

It is instructive to review the history of HLW management in the USA as it offers an explanation for why no disposal facility exists despite the passage of 75 y since the first HLW was generated in the 1940s in the defense sector; and in the public sector, since commissioning of the first commercial NPP at Shippingport, PA in 1957. As mentioned before, serious efforts to locate a site for HLW disposal began in the early 1960s and in 2002, the US President recommended it to the Congress, but politics and litigation thwarted further action and repository construction could not begin because the Obama Administration defunded the project in 2009. Major events in United States' nuclear program along with its efforts toward HLW disposal are listed in Table 7.11.

Table 7.11 Major events in the United States' nuclear program.

Date	Event
1934	Enrico Fermi successfully splits uranium atom, achieving world's first nuclear fission in a pilot plant at the University of Chicago.
2 August 1939	Albert Einstein signs Leo Szilard's letter to President Franklin Roosevelt, requesting research funding to study fission process for weapon making as the Nazi Germany may also be conducting similar investigations.
9 October 1941	President Roosevelt authorizes the Manhattan Project.
2 December 1942	First successful controlled, self-sustaining nuclear fission experiment carried out at the University of Chicago under the supervision of Enrico Fermi, heralding the *atomic age*.
January 1943	Hanford, near Richland, Washington, selected for large-scale production of plutonium for use in atomic weapons; nine reactors, widely-spaced, built along the Columbia River.
16 July 1945	First atomic bomb exploded at the *Trinity* site in New Mexico.
6 August 1945	First atomic bomb dropped over Hiroshima in Japan.
9 August 1945	Second atomic bomb dropped over Nagasaki, Japan.
1946	Atomic Energy Act passed, allowing use of nuclear energy for peaceful purposes.
1951	First electric power generated from experimental reactor at the Idaho National Research Laboratory to light four bulbs.
1955	First U.S. commercial nuclear power plant for generating electricity commissioned in Pennsylvania.
1957	The National Academy of Sciences (NAS) releases its first report on geologic disposal of radioactive waste; recommends HLW disposal in salt deposits.
1963–1971	AEC approved *Project Salt Vault* and conducted studies on HLW disposal in bedded salt in an abandoned salt mine (the Carey Mine) near Lyons, Kansas.
1966–1972	First SNFs reprocessing plant, called the West Valley Plant, built in the U.S. at Ashford, near Buffalo, NY. The plant reprocessed SNFs from the defense weapons program, but spent fuel from commercial nuclear power plants was never reprocessed. The plant was shut down in 1972 due to high retrofit cost to meet strict regulatory requirements.
June 1970	AEC designated Carey Mine as a tentative site for HLW storage.
1970	AEC informs Idaho that all wastes stored in the state will be moved to the Lyons facility by 1980.
1971	Congress directs AEC to stop work at the Lyons site until its safety can be assured.

(*Continued*)

Table 7.11 (Continued)

Date	Event
1972	Under intense criticism from the State of Kansas for failure of AEC investigators to identify numerous abandoned drill holes, land use conflicts, and unanswered scientific questions, AEC abandoned the Project Salt Vault.
1974	Congress enacted the Energy Reauthorization Act, abolished AEC, and created two separate organizations: ERDA and NRC.
1976	ERDA began investigation of the Columbia River basalt formations in Washington for HLW waste repository. Project dropped in 1982.
1977	Congress abolished ERDA in October and created DOE that assumed all ERDA's responsibilities.
1978	DOE conducts public hearings on its proposed Waste Isolation Pilot Project in New Mexico.
1980	Low Level Waste Policy Act promulgated.
1982	The Department of Energy announces a major shift in Site selection criteria – from saturated zone to the unsaturated zone of the groundwater system.
1982	The Nuclear Waste Policy Act (NWPA) passed: among its various provisions it identifies several candidate sites for HLW repository.
1983	The President signed the NWPA into law on January 7.
	NRC publishes broad guidelines for high level waste in 10 CFR Part 60.
1984	DOE's publishes detailed site selection guidelines in 10 CFR Part 960, addressing geochemistry, lithology, erosion potential, tectonics, dissolution, meteorology, besides social and human factors.
1985	EPA publishes radiation standards 40 CFR Part 191. The President rejected proposal for a separate repository for defense HLW.
1986	DOE recommends three HLW sites, including Yucca Mountain, for detailed study.
1987	Nuclear Waste Policy Amendments Act (NWPAA) passed: Yucca Mountain selected as the sole site for detailed investigation; work at all other candidate sites stopped.
1988–2002	Extensive site characterization studies conducted at Yucca Mountain by DOE.
1992	Last of the PUREX reprocessing plant at Hanford, WA closed.
1992	Energy Policy Act passed: NAS designated to recommend health and safety standards for Yucca Mountain; EPA asked to develop standards.
1995	NAS releases its report on Technical Bases for Yucca Mountain Standards.
1999	Disposal of defense-generated TRU waste at the WIPP facility begins in March.
2001	EPA publishes standards for Yucca Mountain, 40 CFR Part 197.
2001	NRC finalizes regulation for Yucca Mountain, 10 CFR Part 63
2001	DOE publishes Yucca Mountain suitability criteria, 10 CFR Part 963.
February 2002	President George W. Bush recommends the Yucca Mountain site to Congress.
April 2002	State of Nevada submits notice of disapproval to Congress.
July 2002	President Bush signs joint resolution approving the Yucca Mountain repository.
2004	U.S. Court of Appeals rejects the 10 000-year compliance period selected by EPA.
2008	EPA revises the radiation protection level to 1 mSv/y (100 mr) for 1000–1 million year.
	DOE submits a license application to NRC for construction of the YM repository.

Table 7.11   (Continued)

Date	Event
2009	President Obama defunds the Yucca Mountain Project; DOE suspends activities at the site.
January 2010	Blue Ribbon Commission on America's Nuclear Future appointed by President Obama to examine present and future nuclear waste management in the U.S.A.
January 2012	The Commission submits its report titled *Blue Ribbon Commission (BRC) on America's Nuclear Future* to the DOE, making three key recommendations.
2013	DOE issued a new HLW waste management strategy based on BRC's recommendations.
2014	DOE issued a report on various options for management of defense HLW and commercial SNF.
2015	DOE announces it will pursue a consent-based approach for HLW storage and disposal.
2020	$27.5 million appropriated to DOE for nuclear waste disposal activities, allowing use of $7.5 million from the Nuclear Waste Fund.

7.7.4.1   The Lyons Salt Mine Project

Following up on the 1957 recommendations of the NAS to dispose of the HLW in an underground salt formation, AEC, under the supervision of its Oak Ridge National Laboratory (ORNL) started work on *Project Salt Vault* in 1963 and conducted geological studies at the abandoned Carey salt mine near the town of Lyons in central Kansas. From November 1965 to January 1968, seven sealed canisters containing 14 SNF assemblies from the Engineering Test Reactor in Idaho were transported by truck in a lead-shielded carrier to the project site. The canisters were lowered about 1000 ft below the ground surface onto the mine floor, one at a time, through a 19-inch-diameter shaft, and were placed in 12-ft-deep steel-lined holes drilled down the mine floor. Electric heaters were used to raise the temperature of the salt bed to $350\,^{\circ}$C to study the effect of thermal loading on the salt, with SNFs being replaced every six months. Radiation levels in the surrounding rocks, recorded during the 19-month testing, were found to be as high as 800 million rad (800×10^6 Gy), but the maximum personnel dose recorded to a worker's hand was only 200 mr (Master Resource 2010).

Ignoring requests from the State of Kansas for additional site studies, and based on the results of the preliminary studies, AEC in 1970 made a hasty announcement that the Carey salt mine would be used for TU and HLW disposal (Walker 2009). This announcement was quickly challenged by the State of Kansas on the basis of uncertainties about the effect of heat produced by the decay of radionuclides on salt, waste retrievability, and the presence of numerous abandoned oil and gas boreholes that had been drilled nearby; along with the startling revelation of the loss of 643 520 L (170 000 gallons) of water pumped into an adjacent injection well for solution-mining of salt that never circulated back to a return well at the surface as expected, indicating the presence of pathways for water movement through salt along the cavities. William Hambleton, Director of the Kansas Geological Survey, remarked that "the Lyons site is a bit like a piece of Swiss cheese, and the possibility for entrance and circulation of fluids is great" (Kansas Geological Survey, 1971). Faced with these scientific revelations and strong political opposition from Kansas, AEC after having spent $3.2 million over eight years, cancelled the site in 1972.

A final note about the Lyons site: despite its failure for selecting the Carey salt mine as an HLW disposal site, the Lyons project has the distinction of being the *only one* in the world where genuine SNFs were used for scientific investigations.

7.7.4.2 Other US Repository Sites

The AEC came under criticism due to its hasty decision in announcing the location of the HLW and TU waste repository at Lyons, while ignoring Kansas State's concerns that were based on solid science (Thompson 2008). Soon afterward, attention shifted to a site in New Mexico to locate the HLW repository in salt beds. This project, named WIPP, discussed in Section 7.7.2, was later selected for disposal of TU waste from defense facilities only.

Beginning around the mid-1970s, DOE and its forerunner, ERDA, directed its efforts to locate a repository for HLW in basalt flows of the Columbia River Group, at Hanford, north of the town of Richland in the State of Washington. From 1976 to 1982, DOE conducted extensive site characterization studies at this location, named Basalt Waste Isolation Project (BWIP). Site investigations revealed the presence of high levels of ambient earth stresses in the basalt formation with high potential for rock bursts during excavation. In addition, high hydrostatic head in the deep Columbia aquifer had the potential to flood excavated deep underground openings. Despite these limitations, DOE recommended BWIP as a candidate site, which was approved by President Regan in May 1986. Additional Quality Assurance studies were to be conducted for a complete evaluation of BWIP suitability as an HLW repository. But before DOE could perform the study, the NWPA amendments were passed in December 1987, designating Yucca Mountain as the sole site for detailed studies, asking DOE to terminate all work at the BWIP site.

The 1987 amendments to NWPA directed DOE to focus solely on the YM site for the HLW repository. After spending $13.5 billion over 20 y (BRC 2012), on-site characterization and related investigations, DOE recommended YM as the final repository for HLW disposal. The recommendation was accepted by President Bush in 2002. However, political and legal issues resurfaced, leading to defunding of the YM Project by President Obama in 2009, bringing the project to a standstill.

7.7.4.3 Politics of the Yucca Mountain Project

Legal problems, such as the imprecise definition of low- and high-level and TU wastes by the US legislatures, hasty and pre-emptive passage of the NWPA amendments in 1987, rejection of veto powers of the host states by the US Congress (OTA 1985), and the *decide and announce* policy of AEC and NRC, further complicated the already complex issue of nuclear waste management. Critics have pointed out that because of a smaller population, Nevada was considered a "politically weak" state that was outmaneuvered by representatives from the more populous and influential states of Texas and Louisiana where the presence of thick salt formations (the Palo Duro Basin in TX; and salt domes in LA) qualified them as "candidate sites" for the repository. In December 1982, the Congress and Senate passed nuclear waste bills but the two pieces had significant inconsistencies that needed to be reconciled, which is normally done by a conference committee, but there was not adequate time before the winter recess for conference committee review. So, Senators James McClure (R-ID) and Morris Udall (D-AZ) crafted a legislation and got it passed in 90 minutes during a lame-duck session of the 97th Congress before the Christmas break was about to start. Many members were absent that day. The Bill came to the Senate on 20 December 1982, which approved it after discussing it only for 15 minutes. Many senators did not even know what the bill was about.

Makhijani and Saleska (1992) have provided a critical look at the nuclear waste management program in the USA and concluded that "the entire efforts have failed because of the lack of a sound waste classification system and institutional management policy"; they highlighted the need for waste reclassification based on a combined hazard and longevity approach and health-based criteria. They suggested allowing SNFs to be stored at reactor sites for up to 100 y in dry casks, and recommended that DOE should not manage nuclear waste; instead, an independent nuclear waste management authority should be entrusted with the job. These points have been reiterated after 20 y in the Blue Ribbon Commission Report (BRC 2012).

In July 2004, the US Circuit Court of Appeals for the District of Columbia rejected lawsuits against the YM project that challenged: (i) the site selection criteria used by DOE, (ii) NRC's repository licensing criteria, (iii) constitutionality of the US Congress 1987 decision to designate the YM as the sole site for HLW repository, and (iv) EPA's radiation protection standards. The court rejected the first three claims but cited EPA for failure to observe proper radiation protection standards based on and consistent with the recommendations of the NAS. The EPA in 2008 revised its criteria to extend the radiation protection time frame, setting the exposure limit at 1 mSv/y (100 mr) for 1000–1 million years.

7.8 Global Status of HLW Disposal

A large quantity of HLW has accumulated worldwide, most of which is in temporary wet storage at reactor sites, a small quantity (~10%) has been moved to interim dry storage sites, but there is no permanent disposal facility or repository for HLW anywhere in the world in operation (as of 2021).

Among the 30 countries that are using nuclear material to generate electric power, only three have an active program to construct a DGR. These are: Finland, Sweden, and the USA. Details of three active repository projects are discussed in Sections 7.8.3–7.8.6.

7.8.1 Quantity of HLW

Instead of using volume to describe the HLW quantity, IAEA, NRC, and all other countries use the internationally accepted measure of weight (metric tons of heavy metals; MTHM) to express HLW quantity. MTHM represents the mass of heavy metals (U, Pu, Th, and minor actinides) that are contained in fresh nuclear fuel loaded in a reactor. Both IAEA and US NRC comply and publish reports on various aspects of nuclear energy including the quantities of HLW on a regular basis. According to the United States Government Accountability Office (USGAO), a total of about 155 717 MTHM of HLW generated from commercial and defense sectors are estimated to have accumulated in the USA, of which about 14 359 MTHM (10.1%) was from defense establishments, and 141 423 MTHM from the commercial sector (GAO 2017). USGAO also estimated that on average, about 2200 MTHM is generated each year, with the rate progressively decreasing as the aged reactors shut down. Figure 7.19 shows the projected trend of MTHM through the year 2067. Worldwide about 367 600 MTHM from commercial reactors were estimated to have accumulated between 1954 (since the first commercial NPP came online) and 31 December 2016. An additional 3193 MTHM was generated from research reactors worldwide as of 31 December 2013 (IAEA 2018).

7.8.2 United States

This section provides scientific and technical aspects of the YM repository that was a major US Government undertaking in compliance with the NWPA amendment of 1987 that directed DOE to conduct detailed site characterization studies at the YM site. The proposed site for disposal of HLW is located at YM in Nye County in the State of Nevada (Figure 7.20a), about 150 km NW of Las Vegas (Figure 7.20a map; Figure 7.21b photograph). After over two decades of intense scientific and engineering studies, costing $13.5 billion, President Bush, on 23 July 2002, approved the site for a DGR, but his successor, President Obama defunded the project in 2012. However, in August

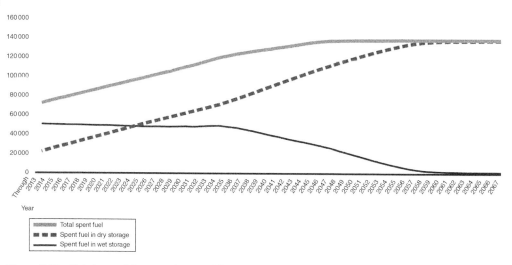

Figure 7.19 Existing and future estimate of SNFs' accumulation in the U.S., in metric tons. *Source:* US Government Accountability Office, Denver, CO. Illustrator: Dan Royer, April 2017.

2013, the federal Appeals Court ordered the NRC to resume its review of the DOE's application for a license to construct and operate the YM repository. Both the EIA and the NRC's experts established that the repository design would prove safe for one million years. The final status of the project as of August 2021 was uncertain.

The Yucca Mountain site has the following favorable conditions: (i) Land acquisition is not a problem as it belongs to the federal government; (ii) no permanent population exists within 22 km of the site; (iii) dry climate: the area receives average annual precipitation of about 19.1 cm, of which approximately 95% either runs off the surface, evaporates, or is taken up by desert vegetation, with only about 1 cm available for infiltration; (iv) very deep groundwater table (GWT) – about 610 m; and (v) insignificant to very low rate of erosion – 0.1–0.5 cm/1000 y in the area. The dry climate is an important factor because the aqueous pathway is the primary mode of radionuclides movement from the repository. The repository will be located about 305 m below the surface. So, any water that does not run off or evaporate at the surface would have to move down nearly 305 m before reaching the repository and then an additional 305 m before it would reach the GWT.

All planned repositories world over are designed to be located below the GWT in the zone of saturation, where reducing conditions prevail in the absence of free O_2. The YM repository, on the other hand, will be located in the unsaturated (vadose or aeration) zone with the minimum, if any, possibility of intrusion of sufficient quantity of water to compromise the integrity of the 15-mm-thick titanium drip shield that will be placed over the waste package. The drip shield would act as a barrier to the waste package from rockfall and deflect any dripping water away from the waste package.

The YM repository design incorporates the principle of multiple barriers that will prevent the HLW from escaping into the biosphere. It relies on both engineered and natural barriers. Spent fuel assemblies will be placed within an open double-shell cylinder; the inner one made of 316 nuclear grade (NG) stainless steel, and the outer one of a corrosion-resistant nickel alloy, Alloy-22. A set of three-piece lids will be used for closing the cylinders at both ends.

In addition to the engineering barriers, the natural geological barriers comprising the surface soil, topography, unsaturated zones above and below the repository, and rock (tuff) above and

(a)

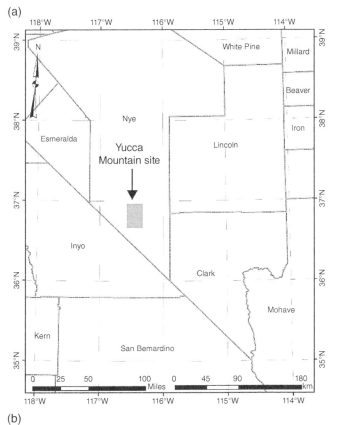

(b)

Figure 7.20   Yucca Mountain. (a) Location map; (b) showing the Yucca Mountain (background), buildings, and other structures during the site investigation period, 2006–2016. *Source:* NRC.

(a)

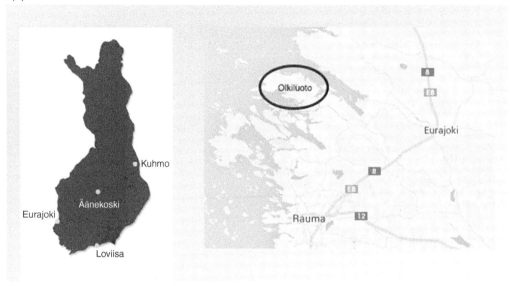

(b)

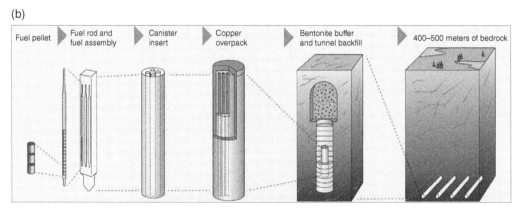

Figure 7.21 Finland deep geological repository: (a) Location map, and (b) multiple barrier system (*Source:* Posiva Oy granted rights to John Wiley & sons).

below, with or without crushed rock backfill surrounding the engineered waste package, would retard any radionuclides movement outside the repository.

DOE, after a thorough investigation of the site, has identified five key features that would assure the long-term performance of the YM facility (DOE 2002):

1) Limited water entering waste emplacement drifts
2) Long-lived waste package and drip shield
3) Limited release of radionuclides from the engineered barriers
4) Delay and dilution of radionuclide concentrations by natural barriers and
5) Low mean annual radiation dose considering potentially disruptive events.

The selection of YM as the final repository site and the science behind it has been a subject of intense debate and controversy. Strong views both for and against have been expressed. However, it must be recognized that the YM project is the very first project that requires integrity of the built structure for hundreds of thousand years – a task for which there has not been any precedence and none of the existing knowledge and technology can guarantee the safety of an engineered structure for half a million to million years. At the same time, we have millions of tons of HLW sitting at the surface, and near-surface facilities, posing serious hazards to human health and the environment. Therefore, a prudent approach would be to use all available resources to arrive at the most suitable option for managing the waste, even if some uncertainties remain unresolved, using the best scientific expertise and technologies. The process of scientific investigation, as required by law, has to continue throughout the entire life of the project, including licensing, waste emplacement, site closure, and post-closure. In terms of national security, storing the HLW over 300 m below the ground surface, inside a mountain, surrounded by some of the highest security facilities, such as the Nevada Test Site and the Nellis Air Force Range, would be far more secure than allowing it to be stored at 131 temporary above-ground sites in 39 states.

7.8.3 Finland HLW Repository

Finland has four nuclear reactors at two NPPs that provide 30% of electric power and generate 70 t of SNF each year. A fifth reactor (1600 MWe capacity) was completed in March 2022 and joined the grid in July. A sixth reactor is under construction and expected to produce electricity by 2029, raising the country's share of nuclear power to 60% of its total energy need. Finland began planning for permanent disposal of HLW as early as the 1970s when its first two NPPs were still under construction. Pursuant to its Nuclear Energy Act, the Finnish Government in 1993 set the target date of 2010 for the construction of the DGR. Finland aggressively moved forward with site characterization and environmental impact studies, and in 2001, selected the final site for the DGR on the island of Olkiluoto in Eurajoki municipality, in the southwestern part of the country on the Baltic Sea coast (Figure 7.21). Pursuing an aggressive policy based on the best scientific knowledge and the Finnish Government's determination to phase out coal by 2030 and achieve carbon neutrality by 2035, Finland's Posiva Oy has emerged as the global leader in DGR design and construction. Following are the key dates for the repository project:

1978	Geological screening for candidate disposal sites started
1983	Site characterization studies began
1993–2000	Detailed site investigations and EIS conducted at Romuvaara in Kuhmo, Kivetty in Äänekoski, Olkiluoto in Eurajoki, and Hästholmen in Loviisa municipalities
2001	Finnish Government approved the Olkiluoto site
2015	License for construction approved by the Finnish Government
2021	Excavation of the first five tunnels for waste emplacement commenced in July 2021
2021	Application for operating license planned for submission to the Government by year-end
2022	Excavation of all five tunnels to be completed by December 2022
2023	HLW waste emplacement begins
Mid-2120s	Repository closure

The geological repository will be located at a depth of 400 m below the sea level in granitic rock, where about 9 km of tunnels and shafts have been excavated to access the final disposal depth. The repository will store up to 6500 t of SNF in copper canisters. The repository is designed to store the waste for 100 000 y and will remain safe against possible geological events like flooding and climate change. The planned date for depositing SNFs is around the mid-2020s. The facility will operate for 100 y. After one year from waste emplacement, the radiation level of 50 000 mS/h (5×10^6 mr/h) at 1 m from SNF, would drop down to 4 mS/h (400 mr/h) in 500 y – the same as an average Finnish person receives in one year. The level would further decrease to 0.3 mS/h (30 mr/h) in 10 000 y (Figure 7.22).

Finland's is a model case study because it illustrates the importance of thorough planning, public engagement, the community's right to reject a site, and the political will of the government in the selection of HLW repository. The Finnish Government in 1983 made the decision that companies generating HLW should also be entrusted with its management. Accordingly, the two owners of NPPs – TVO and Fortum Power and Heat – formed a joint venture, called Posiva Oy, in 1995. After detailed site characterization studies, Posiva submitted its application to the government, which approved it in 2000 that was ratified by the Parliament by a 159-to-3 vote in May 2001. The proposal also had a strong community support, and the local Eurajoki Council – which held the power to veto the decision – voted favorably (20 : 7) for locating the repository at Olkiluoto Island within its jurisdiction. Selection of the Olkiluoto site was based on: (i) geological suitability, (ii) public acceptance, (iii) environmental considerations, and (iv) technical feasibility. Finland's example is instructive because it placed great importance on public acceptance and the owners took appropriate steps to settle this challenging issue very early. The public was fully engaged in the decision-making process from the beginning and the DGR site was selected after the respective municipal councils had voted in favor of the location. This is the most desirable approach as it eliminates costly delays arising out of legal and political challenges.

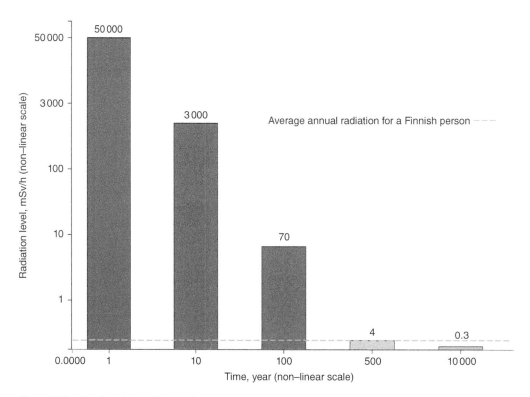

Figure 7.22 Predicted radiation decline over time at the Finland deep geological repository. *Source:* Posiva Oy (n.d.).

Based on site investigations and safety analyses, as well as the EIA, all investigated sites were found suitable for the final disposal of SNF. However, the consent was highest in Eurajoki and Loviisa, but the Olkiluoto Island in Eurajoki had a larger area for the repository. In addition, a significant quantity of SNF was already stored on the island, which has two operating NPPs about 3 km from the repository site, and the other NPP was under construction nearby. The Eurajoki community, as compared to the Loviisa community, was very familiar with nuclear issues that enabled it to volunteer for hosting the site.

Finland has collaborated with Sweden in the design of copper canisters for packaging spent fuel assemblies. Using the multiple barrier approach, fuel assemblies, after 30–40 y of wet storage, will be placed in a canister made of cast iron with a copper overpack layer, each holding between 9 and 12 fuel assemblies and weighing 16.21 t. The canister will be transported to the repository site where it will be placed in the excavated rock, entombed in bentonite before being backfilled by concrete or a similar material. These barriers, combined with 400-m-deep disposal environment, would assure that the waste would remain isolated and pose no danger to humans and/or the environment for a very long period of time (several hundred thousand years).

7.8.4 Sweden

As of May 2021, Sweden had three NPPs comprising six operating reactors, providing about 40% of the country's electricity. No new reactors are currently under construction and eight have been permanently shut down. According to Sweden's law, owners of NPPs are responsible for all costs associated with storage, handling, and disposal of HLW. The law requires payment of a fee by NPP owners into the NWF, which was valued at $7.6 billion in 2016 (SKB 2017). The Radiation Safety Authority of the Swedish Ministry of Environment serves as an independent regulator, while a private corporation – the Swedish Fuel and Waste Management Company (Svensk Kärnbränslehantering or SKB) is responsible for the management of HLW, including disposal. Sweden's HLW management policy includes a three-step process that includes:

1) Placing SNF rods in wet storage for one year at the NPP.
2) Packing the waste in casks and transporting it to Sweden's Central Interim Storage Facility – known as CLAB – at Oskarshamn in northeast Sweden where pools are built in an underground rock cavern to shield the radiation. It is estimated that 30 y of cooling will result in a substantial lowering of temperature and will reduce radioactivity by 90%.
3) Final transfer of the waste, on a specially designed ship, to the DGR.

The nuclear waste disposal facility comprises: construction of an encapsulation plant next to CLAB, and the DGR at Forsmark for final disposal, planned for the 2030s.

After preliminary site screening studies conducted in eight municipalities between 1993 and 2000, two candidate sites were selected for further studies – in the municipalities of Östhammar and Oskarshamn. Detailed investigations commenced in 2002 and by July 2005, three sites were identified as potential HLW repository locations: Forsmark in the former and Simpevarp and Laxemar in the latter. SKB in June 2009 announced its decision to build the repository near Forsmark (Figure 7.23a) in the Östhammar municipality. This was based on thorough geologic site characterization that included hydrogeology of fractured granite, thermal effects from the heat emanating from the SNF, along with system modeling studies.

The repository, designed to store 12 000 t of HLW for 100 000 y, will be located at 500-m depth below the sea level in Precambrian (1.9 billion years old) granite. Final design calls for a 5-km ramp that will connect to 66 km of tunnels (Figure 7.23b), and a multiple barrier system. Spent fuel rods

(a)

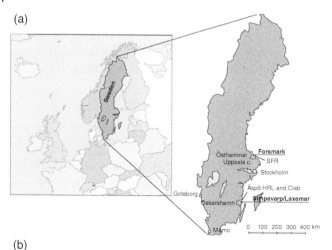

Figure 7.23 Sweden deep geological repository: (a) Location map (*Source:* SKB 2017) and (b) Cut-away view showing access ramps and tunnels (*Source:* Courtesy of SKB, Sweden, Illustrator: Jan Rojmar: SKB, Sweden).

(b)

will be placed in a cast iron-copper canister. The canister will be entombed in a layer of bentonite and overpacked with crushed rock and concrete before being deposited in granitic rocks, similar to Finland (Figure 7.21b).

When fully developed (by 2080s), the repository is estimated to occupy about $4\,km^2$ of underground space, housing 6000 copper-cast iron canisters containing SNFs. Each 25 t canister will hold 2 t of SNF. The canisters are planned to be placed both vertically and horizontally. SKB, after conducting a detailed study of possible release of radiation, backed by model studies, has determined that the radiation will be contained within the repository. Based on these studies, SKB in 2011 submitted its findings along with the application for repository construction to the Swedish Radiation Protection Authority (SRPA) for review and recommendation to build or not build. The application went through a lengthy review by the SRPA which, in January 2018, recommended to the Swedish Government that a license be granted to SKB to proceed with the construction of the repository.

7.8.5 France

As of 2020, France had 56 operating reactors, one under construction and 14 under permanent shutdown. Nuclear energy provides about 71% of the country's total energy, making France Number One in the world in the use of nuclear energy. The National Agency for Radioactive Waste Management, ANDRA – a government-owned public service agency – is responsible for all aspects of nuclear waste management, including disposal. France chose the closed fuel cycle for its nuclear program, involving reprocessing SNFs to recover U, Pu, and other radioactive substances for reuse and to reduce the volume of HLW for disposal. Reprocessing allows 30% more energy to be extracted from the original U.

France started studies on the management of HLW in 1971 to determine: (i) the feasibility of separating and destroying certain radionuclides from the waste, and (ii) disposal of waste in deep geologic formations. Basic principles for nuclear waste management were laid out in the Bataille Act of December 1991. It was subsequently modified in the Planning Act of 2006 that called for sustainable management of radioactive materials and waste. The main provision of the 2006 Act was the decision to build a DGR in the Kimmeridge Clay Formation of Upper Jurassic (~155 Ma) age, near Bure village, in northeastern France. Kimmeridge Clay is a sedimentary deposit comprising argillaceous (clay and shale) rocks with interbedded limestone strata. The planned repository, called CIGEO (*Centre Industriel de Stockage Géologique*) will be located 500 m below the surface in a tight 145-m-thick argillite bed within the Kimmeridge Clay Formation. The repository is designed to hold 10000 m^3 of HLW and 75000 m^3 of long-lived ILW for 100 y; and it is expected to become operational in 2025.

A notable feature of the French program is the emphasis on transparency and stakeholders' opinions. ANDRA conducted a series of public meetings and opinion polls in 2005 and 2013. The results indicated that the public was in favor of the CIGEO project, subject to satisfactory results of the full-scale tests (ANDRA 2016).

7.8.6 HLW Management in Other Countries

The status of management of HLW in other countries ranges widely from a very preliminary plan for deep geological disposal to the actual construction of the facility. Table 7.12 presents a summary of the status of HLW management efforts in these countries as of 2020.

7.8.6.1 Shared Repository Concept

The idea of shared (or regional) repositories for the disposal of HLW has received a favorable reaction from several countries. The concept is based on the fact that for small countries situated in a particular geographic region, such as Eastern Europe, the high cost of building a DGR will be beyond their resources, and it would be far more economical and expedient to construct the repository in one of the countries in the region where each participating country can send its HLW. The concept is especially attractive to countries with unfavorable geologic conditions who will greatly benefit from such regional repository.

There have been several proposals for regional and international repositories for the disposal of HLW, and in 2003, the concept received strong endorsement from the IAEA. After further studies, IAEA prepared a guidance document to provide a framework for institutional and other aspects of developing international repositories. Taking into consideration the technical, institutional, economic, social, and political considerations, IAEA (2004) concluded that:

- The international repository concept does not contradict ethical considerations
- The economy of scale will be achieved due to the high ratio of fixed to variable repository costs

Table 7.12 Status of HLW management in various countries (as of 2020).

Country	Operating reactors	Nuclear energy share (%)	Nuclear Waste Management Authority	Disposal method	Public policy	Siting status	Remarks
Belgium	7	39.17	Underground research laboratory established in 1984 at Mol. Opted for DGR in 1998; repository opening planned by 2080. HLW being stored at a centralized facility near Dessel.				
Canada	19	14.6	Nuclear Waste Management Organization (NWMO): a private corporation of NPP owners	DGR; with an option for shallow underground storage	Inclusive, transparent; willing host community	Early stage; repository likely to be located in one of the four nuclear provinces. No firm date for siting has been set	Final siting decision by the government upon recommendation by the Canadian Nuclear Safety Commission. No central interim storage facility
China	51	4.9	Early stage, DGR likely by 2050.				
Germany	6	11.3	Repository planning started in 1973; the Gorleben site may be operational after 2025. SNFs being stored in salt domes at Ahaus and Gorleben				
India	23	3.3	Vitrified reactor and reprocessing wastes stored at three sites. Research on DGR underway.				
Japan	33	25.1	NWMO: a private organization formed by NPP owners	DGR in granite	Transparent; voluntary acceptance by the host community and local governments	Two underground sites being investigated. No decision about the final location	No schedule for repository opening. SNF storage at Rokkasho.
Russia	38	20.6	A national organization, called "Rosatom" established in 2011 for nuclear waste management	DGR	—	Early stage; site studies underway at the Kola Peninsula	SNFs being stored at reactor sites; has one centralized "wet" storage facility
S. Korea	25	30.3	Early stage; a centralized interim storage facility under study.				
Spain	7	22.2	Government-owned, Spanish National Company	No decision about DGR	—	—	National Safety Council is the independent regulator. The final siting decision rests with the Ministry of Industry, Tourism and Trade
Switzerland	4	32.9	Four candidate sites in opaline clay are under investigation DGR planned for 2060.				
United Kingdom	15	14.5	Nuclear Decommissioning Authority (NDA)	DGR along with an interim disposal facility	Public acceptance; benefit package to host community. W. Cambria has expressed interest	Early stage; no date set for opening	No site has been identified.

DGR, deep geological repository.

• Transport of nuclear materials has been very safe and the long-haul distances to the international repository will not produce any significant impact on public health and safety.

McCombie and Boutellier (2004) have argued in favor of such international collaboration, outlining the following advantages:

• Ensuring common standards for safety, handling, and disposal
• Affordability by economically disadvantaged countries and the possibility of fair compensation if the international repository is located in such a country
• The ethical and political benefit of shared responsibility
• Better security from potential terrorist activities

A strong argument in favor of a shared international repository in Europe, according to McCombie and Boutellier (2004), is that the USA – a single country with a far greater land area than the combined area of HLW-generating countries in Europe – is having serious problems in finalizing its first HLW repository. The problems would be far more complex and time-consuming for the 17 eastern and western European countries if each decides to build its own repository.

The former Soviet Union had been receiving HLW from other communist countries for storage and reprocessing. In 2001, Russia passed a law, permitting the import of SNFs. In 2003, it identified a site for the proposed international repository at Krasnokamensk, a city about 7000 km east of Moscow in the Chita region.

Australia was one of the first countries to consider the possibility of an international HLW repository. As early as 1983, the Government had asked the Australian Science and Technology Commission (ASTEC) to examine the country's role in the uranium fuel cycle. In its 1984 report, ASTEC not only recommended uranium mining but also proposed fuel enrichment and indicated the need for international collaboration in HLW management, including access to the most suitable geological sites.

In the wake of renewed interest in the international repository, the South Australian Nuclear Fuel Cycle Royal Commission, studied the scientific, economic, and legal feasibility and released a report in May 2016. The Commission recommended a site for international high- and intermediate-level waste in South Australia (WNA 2017b).

Vast desert regions in the Middle East and North Africa, because of the absence of any habitations in large sections, are also potential sites for shared international HLW repository, provided suitable transportation routes can be developed.

7.9 Nuclear Waste From Reactor Decommissioning

According to the NRC, decommissioning "involves removing the spent fuel (the fuel that has been in the reactor vessel), dismantling any systems or components containing activation products (such as the reactor vessel and primary loop), and cleaning up or dismantling contaminated materials from the facility. All activated materials generally have to be removed from the site and shipped to a waste-processing, storage, or disposal facility. Contaminated materials may either be cleaned of contamination on site; the contaminated sections may be cut off and removed (leaving most of the components intact in the facility); or they may be removed and shipped to a waste-processing, storage, or disposal facility. The licensee decides how to decontaminate material; the decision is usually based on the amount of contamination, the ease with which it can be removed, and the cost to remove the contamination versus the cost to ship the entire structure or component to a waste disposal site" (NRC 2000, p. 4).

NRC is responsible for rulemaking and oversight for decommissioning of all facilities that use nuclear materials. Several options are available to the owners of the closed reactor, who may choose one or more of the following:

1) The DECON option, indicating that the owner plans immediate dismantling. DECON involves decontamination or removal of all equipment, structures, and parts of the facility containing radioactive contaminants to a level that permits release of the property and termination of the NRC license.
2) The SAFSTOR option allows the owner to defer reactor dismantling after it ceases to produce electric power, provided the facility is maintained and monitored satisfactorily to allow the radionuclides to decay prior to the plant dismantling and decontamination of the property.
3) The ENTOMB option involves permanent encasement of all radioactive contaminants at the reactor site in structurally sound material, such as concrete. The facility must be maintained and monitored until the radionuclides decay to a level permitting restricted release of the property. No NRC-licensed facility has requested this option.

Based on the availability of waste disposal sites, and the rate of radionuclides decay, NRC may allow the owner to use a combination of the first two options, enabling it to dismantle or decontaminate some portions of the facility and leaving the remainder in SAFSTOR. Decommissioning is an expensive process, may take up to 60 y after reactor shutdown for complete decontamination, and release of the site for land reuse. Decommissioning cost is estimated to be between $300 and 400 million (NRC 2018, p. 2). Factors, such as timing and sequence of the various stages of the decommissioning program, type of reactor or facility, location of the facility, radioactive waste disposal costs, and plans for spent fuel storage, affect the total reactor-decommissioning cost. Considering that average life of an operating nuclear power reactor is about 36 y, most of the 99 operating US reactors would close in the next 35–40 y, unless they receive permission to continue operation. This will generate large volumes of nuclear waste that will have to be managed properly.

As of October 2020, 23 power reactors were in various stages of decommissioning in the US (NRC 2020a). Table 7.13 gives a list of the decommissioning status of US nuclear reactors in the commercial sector.

7.10   Summary

The discovery of nuclear fission in the 1930s ushered nuclear technology that was first used for making the most destructive weapons known to human beings; and since the 1950s, for generating electricity, diagnosing and treating diseases, and numerous other peaceful applications as well. While protecting human health from harmful radiations emanating from using nuclear substances has been well addressed, the issue of disposal of HLW has been an unresolved vexing problem that has cost US taxpayers billions of dollars over the past 75 y. Selection of a repository site for HLW has been hindered not so much due to scientific and technical reasons but from legal and political challenges. The result is that the United States does not have any HLW disposal facility despite having investigated three sites in considerable detail. However, credit must be accorded to the US DOE for constructing a disposal facility for TU waste in deep salt formation that has been operating since 1999.

Judging from the progress made by Finland and Sweden, it appears that the former would be the first country in the world to build and successfully operate a DGR for HLW, with Sweden being the next country. Fate of a national HLW storage site in the USA is very uncertain due to the lack of

Table 7.13 U.S. power reactors undergoing decommissioning.

Reactor name	Location	Year started	Shutdown year	Completion date Year	Completion date Status
Crystal River, Unit 3	Crystal River, FL	1976	2013	2074	SAFSTOR
Dresden, Unit 1	Morris, IL	1960	1978	2036	SAFSTOR
Fermi, Unit 1	Newport, MI	1965	1972	2032	SAFSTOR
Fort Calhoun	Fort Calhoun, NE	1973	2016	2026	DECON
General Electric Co., EVESR	Sunol, CA	1963	1970	2025	SAFSTOR
General Electric Co., VBWR	Sunol, CA	1957	1963	2025	SAFSTOR
Humboldt Bay	Eureka, CA	1963	1976	2020	SAFSTOR
Indian Point, Unit 1	Buchanan, NY	1962	1974	2034	SAFSTOR
Indian Point, Unit 2	Buchanan, NY	1974	2020	—	—
Kewaunee	Kewaunee, WI	1973	2013	2073	SAFSTOR
LaCross Boiling Water Reactor	Genoa, WI	1967	1987	2019	DECON
Millstone, Unit 1	Waterford, CT	1970	1998	2056	SAFSTOR
Nuclear Ship Savannah	Baltimore, MD	1962	1971	2031	DECON
Oyster Creek	Forked River, NJ	1969	2018	2035	SAFSTOR
Peach Bottom, Unit 1	Delta, PA	1967	1974	2034	SAFSTOR
Pilgrim Nuclear Power Station	Plymouth, MA	1972	2019	2032?	DECON
San Onofre, Unit 1	San Clemente, CA	1968	1992	2032	SAFSTOR
San Onofre, Units 2 and 3	San Clemente, CA	1968	2013	2051	DECON
Three Mile Island, Unit 2	Middletown, PA	1978	1979	2053	SAFSTOR
Vermont Yankee	Vermont, VT	1972	2014	2030	DECON
Zion, Units 1 and 2	Zion, IL	1974	1998	2024	DECON

—, Unknown.
Source: Data from NRC (2020a).

uniformly agreed log-term policy on part of two major political parties. A recent request to NRC from the private firm HOLTEC International to build and operate an HLW storage facility in Lea County, S.E. New Mexico (NRC 2020b) has added additional uncertainty to the Yucca Mountain project.

Existing systems of nuclear waste classification have certain limitations that have caused controversies. There is a definite need for a better classification system based on radioactivity levels. In addition, finding substitute radioisotopes for medical use that have shorter half-lives and lower radioactivity levels should be given priority in R&D; reprocessing of HLW deserves similar consideration.

The idea of a shared multinational/international repository has received a great deal of attention during the past 15 y with Russia and Australia being strong contenders for hosting it. However, the intricate details of national and international laws, financing, safety, ethical, and related sociopolitical aspects need thorough considerations to ensure that the repository will serve the intended purpose without causing international conflicts and political problems.

Study Questions

1   Scientific discoveries and inventions have the potential for both beneficial and harmful applications. Drawing upon the invention of dynamite and its uses, how would you characterize discovery of the fission science and its technological applications?

2   The US military programs have generated a large volume of HLW that is costing the nation a huge amount of taxpayers' money for its management. At the same time, to maintain our military supremacy, we are still diverting national resources for producing more sophisticated nuclear devices. Should we stop it and use these resources to address pressing environmental and social problems, or do both?

3   Realizing that disposal of HLW is a first-of-its-kind undertaking, the US efforts to solve it have not met with success despite spending billions of dollars over seven decades. Explain if it were inevitable? Or a different approach might have worked?

4   The NRC nuclear waste classification system places greater emphasis on HLW origin and not as much on its radionuclides content. Since the latter determines the radiation levels and time period during which it would remain harmful, should not the classification be based on the radioactivity level alone? Discuss the merits and drawbacks.

5   Is the USA's current policy of direct disposal of HLW without reprocessing it for Pu and U recovery scientifically and politically sound?

6   Judging from the history of locating a site for the HLW repository, it seems the policy of "decide and tell" has failed to work. Why might an open policy based on public involvement be successful? How does the case of Finland add strength to stakeholders' participation argument?

7   Australia has developed a plan for a shared international repository for the disposal of HLW generated in various countries. What are the pros and cons of this concept? Would the uninhabited large deserts in the Middle East and North Africa also serve as suitable locations for similar projects?

References

Abraham, S. (2005). Generation IV International Forum, Remarks of Secretary of Energy to the National Press Club. 14 January 2005. https://www.energy.gov/articles/generation-iv-international-forum (accessed 8 October 2017).

AEC (U.S. Atomic Energy Commission) (1957). *Atomic Energy Facts: A Summary of Atomic Activities of Interest to Industry*. Washington, DC: U.S. Government Printing Office, 216 p. https://digital.library.unt.edu/ark:/67531/metadc783726 (accessed 25 April 2017).

AEC (U.S. Atomic Energy Commission) (1965). Atomic Energy Act of 1946 (Public Law 585, 79th Congress), Vol. 1, 22 p. https://www.osti.gov/atomicenergyact.pdf (accessed 26 April 2017).

Alley, W.M. and Alley, R. (2013). *Too Hot to Touch: The Problem of High-Level Nuclear Waste*, 3. New York, NY: Cambridge University Press.

ANDRA (2016). Cigéo Project: Deep geological disposal facility for radioactive waste in Meuse/ Haute-Marne departments, 22 p. https://www.andra.fr/download/andra-international-en/ document/editions/568bva.pdf (accessed 23 November 2017).

Baisden, P.A. and Choppin, G.R. (2007). Nuclear waste management and the nuclear fuel cycle, in *Radiochemistry and Nuclear Chemistry*. In: *Encyclopedia of Life Support Systems (EOLSS), Developed under the Auspices of the UNESCO* (ed. S. Nagy). Oxford, UK: Eolss Publishers. http://www.eolss.net.

BRC (Blue Ribbon Commission) (2012). Blue Ribbon Commission on America's Nuclear Future: Report to the Secretary of Energy, 189 p. https://energy.gov/sites/prod/files/2013/04/f0/brc_finalreport_ jan2012.pdf (accessed 2 May 2017).

Bruno, J. and Cera, E. (2006). Spent fuel. In: *Uncertainty Underground: Yucca Mountain and the Nation's High-Level Nuclear Waste* (ed. A.M. Mcfarlane and R.C. Ewing). Cambridge, MA: The MIT Press, 431 p.

DOE (U.S. Department of Energy) (2002). Yucca Mountain Science and Engineering Report: Technical Information Supporting Site Recommendation Consideration, Revision 1. Report No. *DOE/ RW-0539-1*, Office of Civilian Radioactive Waste Management, North Las Vegas, Nevada. https:// energy.gov/sites/prod/files/edg/media/SER.PDF (accessed 13 November 2017).

DOE (U.S. Department of Energy) (2014). U.S. Fifth National Report-Joint Convention on the Safety of Spent Fuel Management and on the Safety of Radioactive Waste Management. Report No. *DOE/ EM-0654, Rev. 4*, 180 p. https://energy.gov/sites/prod/files/2014/10/f18/5th_US__National%20 Report_9-18-14.pdf (accessed 13 December 2017).

DOE (U.S. Department of Energy) (2004). *Nuclear Waste Policy Act as Amended with Appropriations*. Washington, DC: U.S. Dept. of Energy, Office of Civilian Radioactive Waste Management, 139 p. https://energy.gov/sites/prod/files/edg/media/nwpa_2004.pdf (accessed 28 October 2017).

EPA (U.S. Environmental Protection Agency) (1988). Limiting Values of Radionuclide Intake and Air Concentration and Dose Conversion Functions for Inhalation, Submergence, and Ingestions. Federal Guidance Report No. 11, *EPA Report No. EPA.520/1.88.020*, 225 p.

EPA (U.S. Environmental Protection Agency) (2008). Technologically Enhanced Naturally Occurring Radioactive Materials from Uranium Mining, Volume 1: Mining and Reclamation Background. Report No. *EPA 402.R.08.005*. https://nepis.epa.gov/Exe/ZyPDF.cgi/P100TBAM.PDF?Dockey=P100TBAM.PDF (accessed 15 February 2018).

EU (European Union) (2011). Council Directives 2011/70/Euratom of 19 July 2011 establishing a Community framework for the responsible and safe management of spent fuel and radioactive waste, 56 p. http://eur-lex.europa.eu/legal-content/EN/TXT/PDF/?uri=CELEX:32011L0070&from=EN (accessed 19 October 2017).

Frye, K. (1981). *The Encyclopedia of Mineralogy (Encyclopedia of Earth Sciences Series, v. 4B)*. Stroudsburg, PA: Hutchinson Ross Publishing Company, 793 p.

GAO (2014). U.S. Govt. Accounting Office. Spent Nuclear Fuel Management: Outreach Needed to Help Gain Public Acceptance for Federal Activities That Address Liability. Report *GAO-15-141*, 56 p. http://www.gao.gov/assets/670/666454.pdf (accessed 12 November 2017).

GAO (2017). U.S. Govt. Accounting Office. Nuclear Waste: Benefits and Costs Should Be Better Understood Before DOE Commits to a Separate Repository for Defense Waste. *GAO-17-174*, 77 p. http://www.gao.gov/assets/690/682385.pdf (accessed 3 April 2017).

IAEA (1995). *Establishing a National System for Radioactive Waste Management*, IAEA Safety Series No. 111-S-l. Vienna: IAEA, 28 p. https://gnssn.iaea.org/Superseded%20Safety%20Standards/ Safety_Series_111-S-1_1995.pdf (accessed 13 December 2017).

IAEA (2004). Developing and Implementing Multinational Repositories: Infrastructural Framework and Scenarios of Co-operation. Report, *TECDOC 1413*, 55 p.

IAEA (2018). *Status and Trends in Spent Fuel and Radioactive Waste Management*, 59 p., IAEA Nuclear Energy Series No. NW-T-1.14. Vienna: International Atomic Energy Agency.

IAEA (2020). Uranium 2020: Resources, Production and Demand, NEA No. 7551, 479 p. iaea.org (accessed 25 August 2021).

IAEA (2021a). Power Reactor Information System (PRIS): nuclear share of energy generation in 2020. PRIS – Miscellaneous reports – Nuclear share. iaea.org (accessed 25 August 2021).

IAEA (2021b). Power Reactor Information System (PRIS): under construction reactors. PRIS – Reactor status reports – Under construction – By Country. iaea.org (accessed 16 September 2021).

Kansas Geological Survey (1971). Records; Hambleton, Selected Speeches. Box 26 (American Salt Corp., AEC), Series I, Subject Files (Salt Vault: Atomic Energy Commission), pp. 140–141.

Kristensen, H.M. and Korda, M. (2021). *Status of World Nuclear Forces*. Federation of American Scientists. fas.org (accessed 25 August 2021).

Lutze, W. (2006). Glass. In: *Uncertainty Underground: Yucca Mountain and the Nation's High-Level Nuclear Waste* (ed. A.M. Mcfarlane and R.C. Ewing), 353–364. Cambridge, MA: The MIT Press, 431 p.

Makhijani, A. and Saleska, S. (1992). *High-Level Dollars, Low Level Sense: A Critique of Present Policy for the Management of Long-Lived Radioactive Wastes and Discussion of an Alternative Approach*, A Report of the Institute for Energy and Environmental Research. New York: Apex Press, 138 p.

Marcus, G.H. and Levin, A.E. (2002). New design for the nuclear renaissance. *Physics Today* 55 (4): 54–58.

Master Resource (2010). U.S. Spent Nuclear Fuel Policy: Road to Nowhere [Part II: Project Salt Vault], https://www.masterresource.org/energy-policy/spent-nuke-fuel-policy-2/ (accessed 9 November 2017).

Mazuzan, G.T. and Walker, J.S. (1984). *Controlling the Atom: The Beginnings of Nuclear Regulation, 1946–1962*. Berkley: University of California Press, 530 p.

McCombie, C. and Boutellier, C. (2004). Problems of an international repository for radioactive waste: political and legal aspects of international repositories. *Internationalisierung des Atomrechts* 2005: 87–97.

Mcfarlane, A.M. and Ewing, R.C. (ed.) (2006). *Uncertainty Underground: Yucca Mountain and the Nation's High-Level Nuclear Waste*. Cambridge, MA: The MIT Press, 431 p.

Mervine, E. (2011). Nature's nuclear reactors: the 2-billion-year-old natural fission reactors in Gabon, Western Africa, Scientific American Guest Blog. https://blogs.scientificamerican.com/guest-blog/natures-nuclear-reactors-the-2-billion-year-old-natural-fission-reactors-in-gabon-western-africa/ (accessed 7 February 2022).

Murray, R.L. (2003). *Understanding Radioactive Waste*, 5e. Columbus, OH: Battelle Press, 231 p.

NAS (National Academy of Sciences) (1957). *The Disposal of Radioactive Waste on Land: Report of the Committee on Waste Disposal of the Division of Earth Sciences*. Washington, DC: National Research Council, 142 p.

NCRPM (National Council on Radiation Protection and Measurements) (2008). *Ionizing Radiation Exposure of the Population of the United States*, Report No. 160. Bethesda, MD: National Council on Radiation Protection and Measurements, 387 p.

NRC (Nuclear Regulatory Commission) (2000). Staff Responses to Frequently Asked Questions Concerning Decommissioning of Nuclear Power Plants Final Report. Report *NUREG-1628*, 68 p. https://www.nrc.gov/docs/ML0037/ML003726190.pdf (accessed 19 December 2017).

NRC (Nuclear Regulatory Commission) (2017a). Spent fuel storage in pools and dry casks, key points and questions & answers. https://www.nrc.gov/waste/spent-fuel-storage/faqs.html (accessed 12 October 2017).

NRC (Nuclear Regulatory Commission) (2017b). Radiation doses and regulatory limits (in millirems). https://www.nrc.gov/images/about-nrc/radiation/factoid2-lrg.gif (accessed 11 November 2017).

NRC (Nuclear Regulatory Commission) (2018). Decommissioning nuclear power plants (backgrounder), 5 p. https://www.nrc.gov/docs/ML0403/ML040340625.pdf (accessed 8 September 2019).

NRC (Nuclear Regulatory Commission) (2020a) Locations of power reactor sites undergoing decommissioning. https://www.nrc.gov/info-finder/decommissioning/power-reactor/ (accessed 5 November, 2021).

NRC (Nuclear Regulatory Commission) (2020b). Environmental Impact Statement for the Holtec International's License Application for a Consolidated Interim Storage Facility for Spent Nuclear Fuel and High Level Waste. Draft Report No. *NUREG-2237*.

NRC (Nuclear Regulatory Commission) (2021). Operating reactors. NRC.gov (accessed 25 August 2021).

NuScale Power (2018). How NuScale technology works. http://www.nuscalepower.com/our-technology/technology-overview (accessed 26 February 2018).

OTA (Office of Technology Assessment) (1985). *Managing the Nation's Commercial High-Level Waste*, U.S. Congress; Report No. OTA-O-171. Washington, DC: U.S. Government Printing Office, 347 p. http://govinfo.library.unt.edu/ota/Ota_4/DATA/1985/8514.PDF (accessed 19 July 2017).

Posiva Oy (n.d.). Pocket guide to final disposal. http://www.posiva.fi/files/4118/Pocket_Guide_to_Final_Disposal.pdf (accessed 11 February 2018).

Sahu, S.K., Ajmal, P.Y., Bhangare, R.C. et al. (2014). Natural radioactivity assessment of a phosphate fertilizer plant area. *Journal of Radiation Research and Applied Sciences* 7 (1): 123–128. https://ac.els-cdn.com/S1687850714000053/1-s2.0-S1687850714000053-main.pdf?_tid=17ea50c4-1265-11e8-9c0d-00000aacb35f&acdnat=1518708784_8f36208444941a7f56421c3583c69dfb (accessed 15 February 2018).

SKB (2017). Our owners finance our expenditure. http://www.skb.com/about-skb/funding/ (accessed 14 February 2018).

Thompson, G.R. (2008). The US effort to dispose of high-level radioactive waste. *Energy & Environment* 19 (3–4): 391–412.

Walker, J.S. (2009). *The Road to Yucca Mountain: The Development of Radioactive Waste Policy in the United States*. Berkeley, CA: The University of California Press, 228 p.

World Nuclear Association (2014). The many uses of nuclear technology. http://www.world-nuclear.org/information-library/non-power-nuclear-applications/overview/the-many-uses-of-nuclear-technology.aspx (accessed 19 May 2017).

World Nuclear Association (2016a). Hiroshima, Nagasaki, and subsequent weapons testing. http://world-nuclear.org/information-library/safety-and-security/radiation-and-health/hiroshima,-nagasaki,-and-subsequent-weapons-testin.aspx (accessed 17 February 2017).

World Nuclear Association (2016b). Naturally-Occurring Radioactive Materials (NORM). http://www.world-nuclear.org/information-library/safety-and-security/radiation-and-health/naturally-occurring-radioactive-materials-norm.aspx (accessed 17 January 2017).

World Nuclear Association (2017a). Desalination. http://www.world-nuclear.org/information-library/non-power-nuclear-applications/industry/nuclear-desalination.aspx (accessed 3 November 2017).

World Nuclear Association (2017b). International nuclear waste disposal concepts. http://www.world-nuclear.org/information-library/nuclear-fuel-cycle/nuclear-wastes/international-nuclear-waste-disposal-concepts.aspx (accessed 17 January 2018).

Yang, C.-J. (2009). *Belief-Based Energy Technology Development in the United States: A Comparative Study of Nuclear Power and Synthetic Fuel Policies*. Amherst, NY: Cambria Press, 255 p.

Supplemental Reading

Ahn, J. and Apted, M.J. (ed.) (2010). *Geological Repository Systems for Safe Disposal of Spent Nuclear Fuels and Radioactive Waste*. Cambridge: CRC/Woodhead Publishing, 762 p.

Alley, W.M. and Alley, R. (2013). *Too Hot to Touch: The Problem of High-Level Nuclear Waste*. New York, NY: Cambridge University Press, 370 p.

Mcfarlane, A.M. and Ewing, R.C. (ed.) (2006). *Uncertainty Underground: Yucca Mountain and the Nation's High-Level Nuclear Waste*. Cambridge, MA: The MIT Press, 431 p.

Murray, R.L. (2003). *Understanding Radioactive Waste*, 5e. Columbus, OH: Battelle Press, 231 p.

OTA (Office of Technology Assessment), U.S. Congress (1985). Managing the Nation's High-Level Radioactive Waste. Report No. *OTA-O-171*, 347 p.

Rahman, A. (2008). *Decommissioning and Radioactive Waste Management*. Dunbeath, Scotland/Boca Raton, FL: Whittles Publishing/CRC Press, 448 p.

Vandenbosch, R. and Vandenbosch, S.E. (2007). *Nuclear Waste Stalemate: Political and Scientific Controversies*. Salt Lake City: The University of Utah Press, 313 p.

Web Resources

Eureka County, Nevada – Nuclear Waste Office: http://www.yuccamountain.org. Valuable source for reports and related documents on the Yucca Mountain Project.

IAEA (International Atomic Energy Agency): https://www.iaea.org. Has comprehensive information on the civil nuclear programs of all countries. Publishes annual reports on status of existing power reactors, electric generation, age, new reactors construction, old reactors decommissioning, along with related information on peaceful use of atomic energy.

Nevada, Sate of–What's New. A regularly updated online resource on latest articles, news reports, federal legislative developments, and related information on nuclear waste: http://www.state.nv.us/nucwaste/whatsnew.htm

Nuclear Energy Institute (NEI). https://www.nei.org/ Promotes peaceful use of nuclear energy. Has useful information, in simple language, on its "Knowledge Center" page.

Posiva Oy (2019). Information about the deep geological repository under construction in Finland with latest update and reports. http://www.posiva.fi/en.

Posiva Oy (2020). Series of short videos explaining nuclear waste management at the Finland deep geological repository. http://www.posiva.fi/en/media/videos#.XziTYuhKg2w

SKB (2019). Information about the deep geological repository in Sweden with latest update and reports. https://www.skb.com/

U.S. DOE (U.S. Department of Energy): https://www.energy.gov/science-innovation/energy-sources/nuclear. Good source of information, statistics, and images on various energy resources, including nuclear, along with various U.S. regulations governing nuclear waste management.

U.S. Energy Information Administration (EIA). https://www.eia.gov/nuclear/. Besides information on all sources of energy, the site also has useful information on nuclear energy specially uranium production, supply, nuclear power plants generating capacity, etc.

U.S. NRC (U.S. Nuclear Regulatory Agency): https://www.nrc.gov. Comprehensive information on nuclear reactor licensing, operation, shut down, and regulations are available at this site.

World Nuclear Association (WNA) website: http://www.world.nuclear.org/information.library.aspx. Hosts an Information Library section that has useful information on various aspects of nuclear energy including nuclear waste management.

Acronyms/Symbols

d	day(s)
m	milli (10^{-3})
GWh	1 billion watts of electricity per hour
hr	hour
Ma	million years
mo	month(s)
MTHM	metric tons of heavy metals
MWe	megawatts electric power
p	pico (10^{-12})
t	tons (metric)
y	year(s)
μ	micro (10^{-6})

Unit Conversions

Energy

Joule (J) $= \text{kgm/s}^2$ (same as the unit of work)

MeV (Mega electron volts) $= 1.602 \times 10^{-13}$ J

High-level waste

1 HLW canister (US) $= 0.5\,\text{m}^3$

Unit weight $(\gamma) = 2800\,\text{kg/m}^3$

Power

$1\,\text{W} = 1\,\text{J/s}$

$1\,\text{kW} = 1000\,\text{W}$

$1\,\text{MW} = 1000\,\text{kW}$

$1\,\text{GW} = 1000\,\text{MW}$

$1\,\text{TW} = 1000\,\text{GW}$ or $1 \times 106\,\text{MWh}$

Radiation

Effective dose

  rem (r) $= 1000$ millirem (mr)

   $1\,\text{Sv} = 100\,\text{mr}$

   $1\,\text{mSv} = 100\,\text{mr}$

   $1\,\mu\text{Sv} = 0.1\,\text{mr}$

Absorbed dose

   $1\,\text{Gy} = 100\,\text{rad}$

   $1\,\text{mGy} = 100\,\text{mrad}$

Activity

   $1\,\text{Bq} = 27\,\text{pCi}$

   $1\,\text{Bq/m}^3 = 0.027\,\text{pCi/L}$

   $1\,\text{MBq} = 0.027\,\text{mCi}$

   $1\,\text{Bq/kg} = 0.027\,\text{pCi/g}$

8

Electronic Waste

8.1   Introduction

We live in a digital world. Our life is engulfed in digital devices that have enabled us to increase our productivity, access information readily, communicate across the globe instantly, and enjoy many other conveniences of life. Each person possesses two to three electronic devices, which, due to their short life span, affordability, negligible resale value, and lack of repair options, become obsolete after a few years of use, adding to the waste stream. In barely five years, the global quantity of electronic or e-waste increased from 44.4 Mt in 2014 to 53.5 Mt in 2019, and is estimated to reach 74.7 Mt by 2030 (Forti et al. 2020). The fast-accumulating quantities of e-waste and lack of its safe management have resulted in the establishment of crude "backyard" recycling industries in developing and underdeveloped countries, notably in South Asia and Africa. The alarming severity of adverse impacts on human and ecological health has been widely reported in the literature (Chen et al. 2011; Grant et al. 2013; Perkins et al. 2014). Regrettably, this practice is still prevalent in low- and middle-income countries of the world (Kwarteng et al. 2020).

> [Electronic] technologies have become critical to our way of life. . . With these technologies, however, comes the increasing challenge of protecting human health and the environment from the harmful effects associated with the unsafe handling and disposal of these products. Meeting this challenge will require a new strategy for electronics stewardship – one that is innovative, flexible, and pragmatic – that allows Americans to manage the electronics we use today more sustainably, and simultaneously promotes the new and innovative technologies of the future.
>
> —*U.S. Environmental Protection Agency (2011).*

Many initiatives and programs are being developed and implemented to manage the rapidly rising quantities of e-waste in a sustainable way. For example, innovative studies on using plastics in discarded e-waste to supplement natural aggregate in concrete (Ullah et al. 2021); and manufacturing high-performance, thermal composite materials from nonmetallic components of printed circuit boards (Yang et al. 2020) have shown promising results. Commercialization of such technologies would reduce the volume of residual e-waste that will require disposal. A multipronged approach that includes recycling to capture valuable metals along with secondary use of less valuable materials, and WtE applications, would be a desirable way to reduce the volume of e-waste that otherwise might end up in landfills.

8.1.1 Metals in e-Waste

The onset of the Digital Revolution has resulted in a dramatic increase in metal consumption in the global economy. From just about half a dozen metals used until about the mid-20th century, it went up to 25 by 1980 and shot up to 40 in 2015, reflecting the increasing demand for high-tech equipment to meet the global need (Hageluken 2014). Mobile phones of the 1980s vintage contained only a few elements but weighed about 800 g, whereas a modern smartphone weighs just about 100 g but contains over 40 elements (Williams 2016).

Unlike other wastes, e-waste represents a unique category of waste because it contains both hazardous materials and valuable rare earth elements (RREs). They represent a scarce but valuable resource of unique metals, and are widely used in computers, and other high-tech equipment, such as windmills, space vehicles, autos, and industrial catalysts, military, and a number of other applications. Because of their rare occurrence and limited supply, precious metals, platinum group elements (PGEs), and REEs have received a great deal of attention during the past 10–15 years and have been included in a special list, called the critical mineral group (CMG). CMG is defined as mineral commodities that have important uses and are vital for the world's major and emerging economies, whose supply may be at risk due to geological scarcity, geopolitical issues, trade policies, or other factors (US Govt. 2018). The US, the EU, and the UK are heavily reliant on imports of CMG elements, the majority of which come from China (Table 8.1). CMG has been a topic of intense study and many developed and developing countries are investigating options to secure uninterrupted supply to sustain their high-tech industries.

It is interesting to note that while the recycling rate of Au, Ag, Co, Ni, and Pt, is >50%, that of technology metals – precious and specialty metals – is <1% (Reck and Graedel 2012). Although mobile phones and IT equipment contain a very small amount of precious and specialty metals, the sheer number of discarded devices represent a promising source of these metals. It is estimated that 1000 kg (1 t) of discarded mobile phones contain 3500 g Ag, 340 g Au, 140 g Pd, and 130 000 g Cu, valued at about $21 000 (in 2020 price). With an average weight of 100 g/smartphone, it will require about 13 000 smartphones – a small fraction of the billions of discarded smartphones, to recover large quantities of valuable metals. Recycling and recovery have been challenging problems in the United States and other developed countries because of high labor cost, low profit, and other economic considerations. This has resulted in unsafe and unauthorized recycling operations, called informal recycling, in developing countries that thrive on the crude deconstruction of e-waste to extract valuable metals for sale in the secondary market. Such unsafe and primitive recycling operations have caused serious damage not only to workers' health and the ecosystem, but also to unborn babies whose mothers get exposed to the harmful chemicals (Chen et al. 2011; Grant et al. 2013).

Table 8.1 Selected critical mineral group elements, largest producer, price, and application (2017 values).

Element	Price $/t	Largest producer	Quantity, t	Percentage of world production	Major applications
Beryllium	170	USA	630 000	74	Aviation industry, guided missiles, space vehicles, satellites
Cadmium	1 700	China	8 200	36	Batteries; control rod in nuclear fission reactors
Gallium	565 000	China	—	—	Renewable energy, electronics
Germanium	1.36×10^6	China	88	66	Infrared devices, fiber optics
Indium	360 000	China	310	43	Renewable energy, electronics, specialty alloys, and touch screens
Iridium	2.9×10^6	S. Africa	—	—	Specialty alloys; space vehicle generators
Lithium	13 900	Australia	18 700	44	Renewable energy, electronics, batteries
Molybdenum	18 000	China	130 000	45	Special alloys, stainless steel
Niobium	18 000	Brazil	57 000	89	Specialty alloys
Palladium	27.7×10^6	Russia	83	40	Automotive and chemical catalyst
Platinum	30.9×10^6	S. Africa	136	73	Specialty alloys
REEs	186 782	China	105 000	81	Renewable energy, electric vehicles, military technologies, electronics, specialty alloys, batteries
Rhenium	1.6×10^6	Chile	27	52	Specialty alloys, chemical catalyst
Rhodium	33.8×10^6	S. Africa	19.2	82	Automobiles catalyst
Ruthenium	1.96×10^6	S. Africa	—	—	Specialty alloys for hard, wear-resistant electrical contacts
Selenium	930	China	23 810	28	Photocells, highly conducting Se–Li batteries
Tantalum	193 000	Rwanda	390	30	Mobile phones, laptops; medical devises: pacemakers; hearing aids, knee and hip implant plates
Tellurium	280	China	36 000	67	Solar panels, semiconductors, rewriteable optical discs (CD, DVD)
Tungsten	24 500	China	79 000	83	Specialty alloys

8.1.2 Definition of Electronic Waste

There is no universally accepted definition of e-waste. In the United States, e-waste includes computers, televisions, VCRs, stereos, copiers, cell phones, entertainment electronics, fax machines, but excludes electrical appliances, such as refrigerators, washing machines, lamps, and toasters, etc. The EU and the majority of other countries, on the other hand, include both large and small appliances in their definition of e-waste.

There has not been a consensus on what should be included in electronic and electrical waste. The term electronic waste has been defined differently in the US, the EU, and the UN. Lack of a standard, universally acceptable definition creates problems in global scale review, and statistical data analyses of e-waste. The following discussion provides a summary of definitions adopted by the USEPA, EU, and UNEP.

8.1.2.1 The United States

There is no legal definition of e-waste in the US; instead, e-waste is considered a subcategory of hazardous waste under the 1976 Resource Conservation and Recovery Act (RCRA) due to the fact that e-waste invariably contains substances that are hazardous. All electronic products contain toxic metals and/or toxic chemicals that meet USEPA's criteria of characteristic or *listed* hazardous substance. So, the discarded e-waste becomes hazardous waste (see Chapter 5 for details). The USEPA defines e-waste as consumer electronic products, such as computers, mobile phones, tablets, fax, copying machines, electronic game devices, and entertainment devices that are nearing the end of their useful life, are discarded, or given to a recycler. Large appliances, refrigerators, washing machines, cooking range, air conditioners, etc., are excluded. However, with the increasing use of microchips, permanent Nd-alloy magnets, and/or sensors in these appliances, and other electronic equipment, they all should be included in the definition of e-waste.

8.1.2.2 European Union

The EU uses the term e-waste for waste electrical and electronic equipment (WEEE) and includes a wide variety of electrical and electronic equipment (EEE) including large and small appliances, lamps, air conditioners, heat pumps, dispensing machines, etc.

8.1.2.3 United Nations

The United Nations uses EEE in its definition of e-waste and, like the EU, includes air conditioners, refrigerators, washing machines, dryers, TVs, computers, mobile phones, and many other household and business equipment with circuitry or electrical components that use electricity or battery to operate. Under the provision of the Basel Convention, e-waste is regulated as hazardous waste for the purpose of controlling its movement across national borders.

Despite the absence of a uniform definition of e-waste, the recent trend has shown that the UN definition has been accepted by a majority of the countries with the exception of the US. In this book, we will use UN's definition to include all EEE, including large appliances, kettles, toasters, etc., as listed in Table 8.2.

It must be pointed out that none of the three organizations includes used batteries in their definition of e-waste.

To avoid inconsistencies in e-waste definition, the independent nongovernmental organization (NGO), StEP (Solving the e-waste Problem) provided a nonlegal, universal definition for e-waste to include all household and business EEE and its parts that have been discarded by the owner as waste without the intention of reuse (StEP 2014).

For the purpose of standardizing data collection, reporting, and analyses of information on various aspects of e-waste worldwide, the United Nations University (UNU) developed a comprehensive classification and provided 4-digit identification keys for various e-waste items (Forti et al. 2018). EEE are classified into 54 major product categories based on a similar function, comparable material composition, average weight, and similar EoL features to improve comparability between countries, enabling integration of all statistical and related data into a normalized e-waste statistic. Table 8.3 provides a partial list of the UN keys for common electrical equipment.

Based on characteristics relevant to e-waste management, the 54 EEE product categories have been grouped into six broad categories: (i) temperature exchange equipment (TEE), (ii) screens

Table 8.2 Items included in e-waste by the USEPA, UN, and EU.

Agency	Electronic/electrical equipment
USEPA	Computers: desktop central processing units (CPUs) and portables; Computer displays: cathode ray tube (CRT) monitors and flat-panel monitors; keyboards and mice; printers, fax machines, scanners, digital copiers, and multifunction devices; TVs: monochrome, CRT, flat-panel, and projection; entertainment electronics; mobile devises: cell phones, personal digital assistants (PDAs), smartphones, and pagers.
UN	TVs, computers, mobile phones, white goods (fridges, washing machines, dryers, etc.), home entertainment and stereo systems, toys, toasters, kettles, and other household and business electrical equipment.
EU[a]	Large and small household appliances; IT and telecommunications equipment; consumer equipment; lighting equipment; electrical and electronic tools; toys, leisure, and sports equipment; monitoring and control instruments; and automatic dispensers.

[a] This list is per EU Directive.

Table 8.3 Partial list of electronic and electrical equipment and their UN Keys (codes).

UN code	Description	EEE category under EU-6
0001	Central heating (household installed)	Large equipment
0002	Photovoltaic panels (including inverters)	Large equipment
0101	Professional heating and ventilation (excluding cooling equipment)	Large equipment
0102	Dishwashers	Large equipment
0103	Kitchen equipment (large furnaces, ovens, and cooking equipment)	Large equipment
0104	Washing machines (including combined dryers)	Large equipment
0105	Dryers (washer-dryers and centrifuges)	Large equipment
0106	Household heating and ventilation (hoods, ventilators, and space heaters)	Large equipment
0108	Fridges (including combination fridges)	Temperature exchange Equipment (TEE)
0109	Freezers	TEE
0111	Air conditioners (household installed and portable)	TEE
0112	Other cooling equipment (dehumidifiers, heat pump dryers)	TEE
0113	Professional cooling equipment (large air conditioners, cooling displays)	TEE
0114	Microwaves (includes combined, excludes grills)	Small equipment
0201	Other small household equipment (small ventilators, irons, clocks, and adapters)	Small equipment
0202	Food preparation equipment (toasters, grills, food processing, frying pans)	Small equipment
0203	Small household equipment for hot water preparation (coffee, tea, and water cookers)	Small equipment
0204	Vacuum cleaners (excludes professional)	Small equipment
0205	Personal care equipment (toothbrushes, hair dryers, and razors)	Small equipment

Table 8.3   (Continued)

UN code	Description	EEE category under EU-6
0301	Small IT equipment (routers, mice, keyboards, external drives, and accessories)	Small IT
0302	Desktop PCs (excludes monitors and accessories)	Small IT
0303	Laptops (includes tablets)	Screens and monitors
0304	Printers (scanners, multifunctionals, and faxes)	Small IT
0305	Telecommunication equipment (cordless phones and answering machines)	Small IT
0306	Mobile phones (smartphones and pagers)	Small IT
0307	Professional IT equipment (servers, routers, data storage and copiers)	Large equipment
0308	Cathode ray tube monitors	Screens and monitors
0309	Flat display panel monitors (LCD and LED)	Screens and monitors
0401	Small consumer electronics (headphones, remote controls)	Small equipment
0402	Portable audio and video (MP3 players, e-readers, and car navigation)	Small equipment
0403	Musical instruments, radio, Hi-Fi (including audio sets)	Small equipment
0404	Video (Video recorders, DVD and Blu-ray players, set-top boxes) and projectors	Small equipment
0405	Speakers	Small equipment
0406	Cameras (camcorders, photo and digital still cameras)	Small equipment
0407	Cathode ray tube TVs	Screens and monitors
0408	Flat display panel TVs (LCD, LED, and Plasma)	Screens and monitors
0501	Small lighting equipment (excludes LED and incandescent)	Small equipment
0502	Compact fluorescent lamps (includes retrofit and non-retrofit)	Lamps
0503	Straight tube fluorescent lamps	Lamps
0504	Special lamps (professional mercury, high- and low-pressure sodium)	Lamps
0505	LED lamps (incudes retrofit LED lamps)	Lamps
0506	Household luminaires (includes household incandescent fittings and household LED luminaires)	Small equipment
0507	Professional luminaires (offices, public space, and industry)	Small equipment
0601	Household tools (drills, saws, high-pressure cleaners, and lawnmowers)	Small equipment
0602	Professional tools (for welding, soldering, and milling)	Large equipment
0701	Toys (car-racing sets, electric trains, music toys, drones, and biking computers)	Small equipment
0702	Game consoles	Small IT
0703	Leisure equipment (sports equipment, electric bikes, and juke boxes)	Large equipment
0801	Household medical equipment (thermometers, and blood pressure meters)	Small equipment
0802	Professional medical equipment (hospital, dentist, and diagnostics)	Large equipment

(Continued)

Table 8.3 (Continued)

UN code	Description	EEE category under EU-6
0901	Household monitoring and control equipment (alarm, heat, and smoke)	Small equipment
0902	Professional monitoring and control equipment (laboratory and control panels)	Large equipment
1001	Non-cooled dispensers (for vending, hot drinks, tickets, and money)	Large equipment
1002	Cooled dispensers (or vending and cold drinks)	TEE

Source: After Forti et al. (2020).

and monitors, (iii) lamps, (iv) large equipment, (v) small equipment, and (vi) small IT and telecommunication equipment.

8.2 Laws Regulating Electronic Waste

The most comprehensive regulations on e-waste or WEEE management have been established in the EU. In addition, the United Nations has developed a classification of various types of e-waste, and provided guidelines that are being used to formulate e-waste regulations in other countries of the world. Globally, there has been a marked increase in the number of countries that have adopted policies to regulate e-waste: from 64 out of 193 countries in 2014, it rose to 67 in 2017 and to 78 in 2019. In terms of population, the policies covered 44% of the global population in 2014, 66% in 2017, and 71% in 2019, mainly because China and India – the two most populous countries – have adopted national legislations to regulate e-waste. However, inadequate funding, lack of political motivation, and poor law enforcement hinder efficient collection and proper management of the e-waste. In addition, in many countries, the scope of the legislation is different from the e-waste classification suggested by the UN that causes problems in normalizing e-waste statistics across countries (Forti et al. 2020).

8.2.1 The United States

There is no specific federal law to regulate e-waste in the United States. In 2011, a bill titled *Responsible Electronics Recycling Act* was introduced during the 112th Congress but was not passed. Responsibility for managing e-waste has been relegated to the states who have developed their own regulations. As of 2014, out of the 50 US states, 26 had enacted laws on e-waste management. They vary in scope: some prohibit landfilling or incineration of e-waste, while others require adding an advance recycling fee in the purchase price of the device that the consumer has to pay upfront, and holding the manufacturer responsible for proper management of the product after it is discarded (known as manufacturer's take-back responsibility). Table 8.4 shows the states that have passed e-waste laws along with their years of enactment.

8.2.2 The United Nations

The United Nations is a global organization that has been investigating problems and issues affecting all aspects of human life. It develops guidelines for rule-making and makes recommendations to individual countries to implement them. Recognizing the severity of environmental issues and

Table 8.4 E-waste laws in various states in the USA and year enacted.

State	Year enacted
California	2003
Maine	2004
Maryland	2005
Washington	2006
Connecticut, Minnesota, Oregon, North Carolina, and Texas	2007
Hawaii, Illinois, Michigan, Missouri, New Jersey, Oklahoma, Rhode Islands, Virginia, West Virginia	2008
Indiana, and Wisconsin	2009
New York, Pennsylvania, South Carolina, and Vermont	2010
Utah	2011
District of Columbia (DC)	2014

the need to address them, it created the United Nations Environment Programme (UNEP) in 1972 following the *United Nations Conference on the Human Environment* in Stockholm, Sweden. UNEP develops a framework for international environmental agreements and provides guidelines for its implementation. However, neither UN nor UNEP has the legal authority to implement them, which is done by the member countries.

The UNEP had been studying e-waste since the 1980s. One of its earliest accomplishments involved restrictions on hazardous substances in printed circuit boards and plastics containing brominated flame retardants (BFRs), along with asbestos, and toxic metals such as Hg, Pb, Cd, and Se, in the 1989 Basel Convention on *Transboundary Movement of Hazardous Waste and their Disposal*. In 1998, e-waste was added in Annex VIII of the Basel Convention at the 4th meeting of the Conference of the Parties (COP). In 2000, e-waste was selected as a focused study area of the United Nations University (UNU) (established, 1972) as part of its activities on strategic approaches toward sustainable development.

For the past 20 years, the UN through its various partners has been addressing e-waste issues. The first comprehensive initiative was the Mobile Phone Partnership Initiative (MPPI) launched in 2002 under the Basel Convention. Later, in 2006, at the 8th COP meeting, held in 2006, the need for environmentally sound management of WEEE was emphasized, which subsequently led to the formal launching of the Partnership for Action on Computing Equipment (PACE) program in 2008. Several reports dealing with testing, refurbishing, and repairs of computing equipment (UNEP 2013a) and material recovery and recycling of discarded computing equipment (UNEP 2013b) were produced that serve as valuable guidelines on sound management of Information and Communications Technology (ICT) waste. UNEP's publications are a valuable resource, providing national and global perspectives on e-waste management, including invaluable statistical analyses on each country's e-waste quantity, management approach, and laws. Its latest report titled *The Global E-waste Monitor 2020* (Forti et al. 2020) is full of useful data and information on the status of global e-waste management.

The United Nations Institute for Training and Research and the UNU are actively engaged in capacity building and training on various aspects of waste management in developing countries. Online certificate programs have been established, and the E-waste Challenge Massive Open

Table 8.5 Regrouping of EU's WEEE categories per Directive 2012/19/EU.

WEEE in 2012 directive (until 14 August 2018)	WEEE in 2012 directive (after 15 August 2018)
1) Large and small household appliances	1) Temperature exchange equipment (TEE)
2) Small household appliances	2) Screen, monitors' equipment, surface screen >100 cm²
3) IT and telecommunications equipment	
4) Consumer electronic equipment	3) Lamps
5) Lighting equipment	4) Large equipment
6) Electrical and electronic tools	5) Small equipment
7) Toys, leisure, and sports equipment	6) Small IT and telecommunication equipment
8) Medical devices	
9) Monitoring and control instruments	
10) Automatic dispensers	

Online Course (MOOC) launched in 2020, offers scientific and technical information that is freely available to everyone. The course comprises five mini-modules, each requiring four to six hours to complete the on- and off-line learning activities and tests to earn a certificate (UNEP 2020). The course aims at capacity building by training local people on the safe management of e-waste to reduce GHG emissions, mitigate climate change, and prevent hazards to human and ecological health.

8.2.3 The EU

The EU's Directive 2002/96/EC on WEEE, together with the *Restriction of Hazardous Substances* or the RoHS Directive 2011/65/EU, became the EU law in February 2003. The intent of the law was to ensure environmentally safe management of e-waste by adopting a comprehensive five-point strategy that included: (i) product design, (ii) e-waste collection, (iii) e-waste recovery, (iv) e-waste treatment and financing, and (v) user awareness.

An interesting provision of the 2003 directive was grouping WEEE into historic (pre-2005) and non-historic categories, based on whether the equipment was placed in the market before or after 2005. For the historic WEEE, the directive placed the responsibility for its recycling on the owner of the equipment; and for the non-historic, the responsibility rests with the producer/distributor of the equipment for its collection and recycling. The 2012 directive grouped WEEE into two lists, based on the cutoff date of 14 August 2018 to facilitate reporting and statistical data management (Table 8.5).

Addressing the problem of e-waste recycling, EU's Directive 2012/19/EU set the goal to recycle at least 85% of WEEE by 2016. The WEEE were grouped on the basis of similar function, comparable material composition, average weight, and similar end-of-life attributes into 54 categories, according to the United Nations University Keys (UNU-KEYS).

8.3 Nature and Composition of Electronic Waste

In a broad sense, all EEE are made from plastics, metals, and nonmetals. So, the resulting e-waste represents a complex mixture of dozens of organic and inorganic chemicals, many of which are hazardous and toxic that can impair air, land, and water quality, and are also capable of causing serious acute and chronic diseases, if not properly managed. At the same time, e-waste also contains precious metals like Au, Pt, Pd, and other REEs, making e-waste a highly valuable resource.

The electronics industry has witnessed unprecedented growth during the past 50 years. Old materials and technologies are rapidly giving way to new breakthroughs that have significantly altered the characteristics and composition of electronic products, and drastically lowered the price. For example, the first commercial mobile phone, introduced in 1983 – the $4000 Motorola DynaTAC 8000X – called "the brick" – measured about $33 \times 9 \times 5$ cm (the size of a brick), and weighed 0.8 kg (1.8 lb), compared to a modern smartphone that weighs only about 0.1 kg ($<$0.25 lb.), measures $15 \times 8 \times 0.8$ cm, and costs 4–8 times less. In addition, the Motorola phone had limited memory and could store only 30 phone numbers, and did not have any other capability, such as text messaging, email, camera, etc., which are standard features of smartphones. The older mobile phones did not use any of the REEs or platinum group metals (PGMs) either, which are essential components of modern smartphones.

Rapid advances in technology have led to changes in the design, material composition, size, weight, and capabilities of EEE. Since the composition and equipment weight are key factors in calculating quantities of discarded e-waste and estimating quantities of useful materials that can be recovered, any discussion on e-waste recycling must take into account the age when the equipment was placed in service.

8.3.1 Planned Obsolescence

The word obsolescence is derived from obsolete which means no longer used, out of date, or no more relevant. Some items become obsolete when a better product becomes available with the same or improved functionality at a reasonable price. Centuries-old slide rule becoming obsolete with the advent of inexpensive and powerful handheld electronic calculators in 1974 is a good example of the natural cycle of obsolescence. Unfortunately, it has now given way to planned obsolescence where consumer products are deliberately designed to become obsolete much sooner than their normal life. This business strategy is best exemplified by one of its proponents, J. Gordon Lippincott, who in his book *Design for Business* unabashedly claimed: "Our custom of trading in our automobiles every year, of having a new refrigerator, vacuum cleaner, or electric iron every three or four years is economically sound. Our willingness to part with something before it is completely worn out is a phenomenon noticeable in no other society in history. It is truly an American habit." (Lippincott 1947).

The concept was first adopted as a business strategy in 1923 by Alfred P. Sloan Jr., President of General Motors (GM), to compete with its rival, Ford Motor Co.; whose Model T had dominated the automobile market during the first two decades of the twentieth century. So, he decided to introduce annual model-year changes in GM cars by adding cosmetic features. This strategy, which he termed dynamic obsolescence, worked well and GM car sales surpassed Ford's in 1931. The idea was quickly adopted by many industries and the leading manufacturers of light bulbs in America and Europe (GE, Osram, Philips, Tungsram, and others) formed the Phoebus Cartel in Switzerland in 1925, and made a decision to limit the useful life of an incandescent bulb to 1000 hours as opposed to 1500–2000 hours that was common in those days. Any manufacturer who produced bulbs lasting over 1000 hours was fined. Thus, the intentional design to produce low-durability products became acceptable across industries, and in the 1930s, Sears Roebuck Co. began to introduce a new refrigerator model every year, despite the fact that there was hardly any functional difference. The auto industry also had great success in inducing its consumers to buy new cars frequently, resulting in the average duration of auto ownership shrinking from five years in 1934 to two in the mid-1950s. In the later decades of the twentieth century, the electronics industry embedded planned obsolescence in its business policy, capitalizing on consumer psychology of owning something newer, better, and sooner than necessary. Planned obsolescence underpins ICT equipment production where high and fast profits are the main objectives. Inefficient design that includes parts failing to work after a fixed period of time, none or very expensive factory authorized repair (often as expensive as buying the new model), incompatible software, etc., became the industry standard. Apple heads the list of manufacturers whose products are designed to wear out, stop working, or slow down in a few years, requiring replacement.

As pointed out in Chapter 1, a new movement against planned obsolescence has emerged, demanding manufacturers to design their products that can be repaired and reused with a steady supply of parts. Europe has taken the lead to restrict planned obsolescence in manufacturing consumer products. In 2015, the French Government made it mandatory for appliance manufacturers to offer a two-year warranty covering free repair or replacement of defective products and to inform buyers about product lifespan, and years of availability of spare parts. The regulations imposed a fine of up to €300 000 ($330 000) and jail term for up to two years for any manufacturer using built-in design for its product to fail. In 2018, French prosecutors charged Apple for intentionally shortening the lifespan of their products, resulting in Apple paying $27 million fine (an amount that they make in just three hours!). In the United States, the court in March 2020 ruled that Apple pay up to $500 million in settlement to owners of its iPhones 6, 7, and 7 Plus whose devices failed to perform properly due to incompatible software updates loaded on customers' smartphones. The Right-to-Repair movement in the United States has gained momentum and, as of September 2021, bills had been introduced in nearly all 50 states, and 25 had already passed the law. The Federal Trade Commission on 21 July 2021, by a unanimous vote of its five members, issued a policy statement against repair restrictions by manufacturers, urging them to allow repair by independent repair facilities and provide parts to facilitate repairs of their products.

It can be surmised that the excessive amount of waste produced in the developed and developing countries during the past 50 years is directly related to planned obsolescence aimed at a profit as the sole motive with complete disregard for environmental protection.

8.3.2 Material Composition of e-Waste

WEEE represent an assortment of large and small appliances and personal use devices with a wide range in size and weight. For example, a side-by-side refrigerator and freezer, on an average, measures $1800 \times 910 \times 750$ cm, and weighs 90 kg, while smartphones measure $15 \times 8 \times 0.8$ cm, and weigh about 0.1 kg. As shown in Table 8.6, WEEE include complex electronic machines of varying size and weight that are made from a wide variety of materials whose composition depends on the type of equipment and the technology used in its production.

The total weight of e-waste has been decreasing over the years because the equipment are getting lighter (but with greater functionality). A major recycling company in Europe reported that the total weight of e-waste collected decreased by 7% in 2018 when compared to the previous year (SWISCO 2019).

Any attempt to provide the quantities of various materials (metals, plastics, etc.) that comprise WEEE has to be a generalized estimate at best. Based on the review of a number of published articles and reports, the UN Economic and Social Commission for Asia and the Pacific (2009) gave the following average composition of WEEE: iron and steel: 50%; plastics: 21%; nonferrous metals: 13%; and other materials (glass, wood, various other metals, etc.): 16% (Figure 8.1).

Table 8.6   Estimated weight of selected electronics and electrical equipment.

Item	Weight, kg/piece	
	2005[a]	2016[b]
Large household appliances		
Washing machine	65–75	72.54
Dryer	35 (tumble)	46.0 (large)
Combination washer-dryer		58 (2022)
Cooking range (stove), electric	60	47.7 (electric/gas)
Cooking range (stove), gas	45	—
Dishwasher	50	43.3
Refrigerator	35	—
Fridge-freezer (single unit)	45	40.8
Freezer, chest	30	40.1
Small household appliances		
Microwave	15	22.9 (large)
Vacuum cleaner	8–12	5.9
Coffee maker, small	—	1.9
Iron	1	—
Kettle	1	1.9
Toaster	1	1.9 (toaster oven)
Fan	10	—
Food mixer/processor	1–5	3.3
Hair dryer	1	0.6
Electric heater, small	5–7	—
Electric heater, large	15	—
Stereo Hi-fi with small speakers	10	—
Videos: DVD, Blue-ray, projectors	—	3.51
Headphone, remote control	—	0.4
Information and communications technology (ICT)		
Desktop computer	9.9	8.8
Laptop computer	3.5	1.3
Tablet	1	1.3
Professional IT servers, routers, and storage	—	40.0
CRT screen	14.1	22.0
LCD screen	4.7	5.50
Mouse	0.05	—
Keyboard	1	0.40
Printer	6.5	10.3
Mobile phone, smartphone, pager	0.1	0.1
Mobile phone charger	0.3	—

(Continued)

Table 8.6   (Continued)

Item	Weight, kg/piece	
	2005[a]	2016[b]
Telephone, cordless	1	0.5 (with answering machine)
Consumer electronics		
Television, plasma	20–30	10.20
Video recorder/DVD player	5	2.14
Hi-Fi system	10	—
Radio	2	—
Electrical and electronic tools		
Electric drill	2	—
Power saw	2	—
Lawn mower	5	—
Miscellaneous		
CFL lamps	—	0.08
Straight tube fluorescent lamp	—	0.08
Hg, high- and low-intensity Na lamps	—	0.08
Household luminaries	—	0.5

[a] Anon (2005).
[b] After Forti et al. (2018).

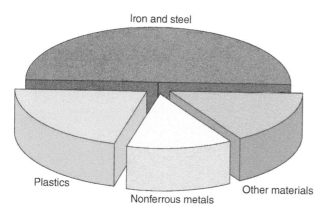

Figure 8.1   Average composition of waste electrical and electronic equipment (WEEE).

8.3.3   Material Composition of Desktop Computers

No other personal electronic device has undergone as much rapid evolution in design, efficiency, user-friendliness, price, and computing power as the personal or desktop computer. The author recalls his graduate years at Purdue University during the mid-1970s when he had to make endless trips to the only Computing Center on the campus to deposit boxes containing several hundred IBM 18.7 cm × 8.3 cm punch cards to be read by the mainframe computers and return next day to collect the output in the form of printed dot-matrix maps in a single shade of grey color – a task that is now accomplished within minutes with amazing graphics and outstanding full-color outputs at a substantially reduced cost.

Personal computers (PCs) were introduced in the mid-1970. Compared to the mainframe computers, they were small enough in size and weight to be placed on the desk or table and were called desktop computers. Desktops are self-contained machines capable of data input (keyboard and mouse), output (printer and screen), and data storage (initially on removable floppy discs), and monitor. Modern PCs have no semblance to the earlier models either in appearance or computing power – dictionary-size machines possessing astounding memory (1 TB, compared to just a few kB of the 1970s model) along with a huge drop in price (from $8000–$10000 to <$1000).

While the use of rare and valuable metals, application of nanotechnology, and lower manufacturing costs have increased affordability, their designed obsolescence within a few years of use is a cause for serious concerns. A short life span is a common feature of all personal devices that become obsolete within a few years. Desktop computers, for instance, have an average life span of about three years after which they become obsolete.

Modern PCs comprise a number of materials dominated by plastics, glass, metals, and nonmetals. The relative amount of each component depends on the model and year of manufacturing. In general, though, most PCs are made from steel, glass, plastics, and metals. The average material composition of a PC is shown in Figure 8.2, and metal content in Table 8.7.

8.3.4 Material Composition of Laptops

Older versions of laptop computers, released in the early 1980s, were more like a bulky briefcase, weighing about 5 kg compared to the thin and sleek laptops of the 2020s, weighing slightly over 1 kg. Computing power, data storage capacity, and functionality have improved tremendously resulting in a laptop's popularity, leading to its sale surpassing that of PCs in 2005: The lead has been maintained since then, and in 2019, 173 million units of laptops were sold worldwide as compared to 94 million PCs. Projected sales for 2020 stood at 218 and 79 million units, respectively (Statista 2021). Laptops have a shorter life span than desktop computers, between two and five years, because of their compact size and greater wear and tear due to portability, among other reasons.

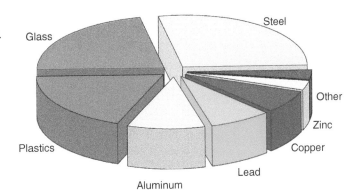

Figure 8.2 Generalized composition of desktop computers.

Table 8.7 Average metal content (g) in laptop, tablet, desktop, smartphone, and plasma TV without battery.

Metal	Laptop	Tablet	Desktop	Smartphone	Plasma TV
Aluminum, Al	30.570	—	—	3.274	720.000
Antimony, Sb	0.770	0.154	—	0–0.084	0.710
Arsenic, As	0.010	0.002	—	—	—
Barium, Ba	2.500	0.490	—	—	—
Beryllium, Be	0.015	—	<0.001	0–0.003	—
Cerium, Ce	<0.001	<0.001	—	—	<0.001
Chromium, Cr	0.070	0.014	—	—	
Cobalt, Co	20.890	0.013	0.017	5.377	0.022
Copper, Cu	125.578	27.000	—	14.164	502.00
Dysprosium, Dy	0.060	0.012	—	—	—
Europium, Eu	<0.001	<0.001	—	—	<0.001
Gallium, Ga	0.004	—	0.003	0–0.061	0.005
Gadolinium, Gd	<0.001	<0.001	—	—	<0.001
Germanium, Ge	—	—	—	0–0.003	—
Gold, Au	0.192	0.044	0.061	0.034	0.193
Indium, In	0.101	0.008	—	0–0.005	0.591
Iron, Fe	407.560	—	—	7.664	77.000
Lead, Pb	5.300	1.100	—	0.600	—
Mercury, Hg	<0.001	<0.001	—	—	—
Lanthanum, La	<0.001	<0.001	—	—	<0.001
Lithium, Li	—	—	—	<0.001	0.022
Molybdenum, Mo	—	0.008	—	—	—
Neodymium, Nd	1.417	0.427	—	0.050	—
Nickel, Ni	3.600	0.722	—	1.500	—
Palladium, Pd	0.065	0.008	0.031	0.053	0.027
Platinum, Pt	0.004	—	—	0–0.004	—
Praseodymium, Pr	0.274	0.055	—	0–0.010	—
Ruthenium, Ru	0.006	—	—	—	—
Silver, Ag	0.428	0.050	0.376	0.213	0.447
Tantalum, Ta	1.607	—	0.073	0–0.166	—
Terbium, Tb	<0.001	<0.001	—	—	0.002
Tellurium, Te	—	—	<0.001	0–0.007	—
Tin, Sn	4.88–14.08	—	—	1.057	18.000
Tungsten, W	0.038	—	0.020	0–0.215	—
Yttrium, Y	—	<0.001	—	—	—
Zinc, Zn	—	<0.001	—	1.000	12.000
Light REEs	2.928–7.808	—	—	0.394	1.311
Heavy REEs	0–0.697	—	—	0–0.034	0–3.933

Source: Data from various sources: Cucchiella et al. (2015), Mao (2020), Zhu et al. (2017), and others.

Increasing use of specialty metals that include REEs, PGEs, and precious metals like Au and Ag, combined with advanced manufacturing technologies have led to the production of newer models with the desired capabilities at an affordable price. Easy acquisition and simultaneous obsolescence of laptops have added to the e-waste problems. In terms of material composition, laptops comprise similar materials as desktops, but their relative percentages are different. For example, on an average, the quantity of Au, Ag, and Pd in laptops was found to be greater by 38, 48, and 33%, respectively, as compared to desktops sold and discarded (in China) between 1997 and 2016 (Mao et al. 2020). Table 8.7 shows the metal composition of laptops.

8.3.5 Material Composition of Tablets

Tablets (also referred to as notebooks in Europe and other countries) are different from laptops in the sense that they do not have a separate keyboard or a touchpad. Although prototypes of modern tablets were produced in the 1980s, they did not get popular due to their limited capabilities, weight, and high price, about $3000. Modern tablets with web capabilities were introduced around the 2000s and gained immediate acceptance and popularity with about 220 million units shipped from factories in 2013, surpassing that of laptops at 181 million. However, tablets' shipment has experienced a decline since 2014 and the trend is predicted to last beyond 2024.

A typical tablet is made up of the following components:

- Printed circuit boards (PCBs) for the motherboard
- LCD screen
- Hard disk drive
- Optical drive for CD, DVD, Blue-ray player
- Cooling elements and fans
- Battery pack

Different manufacturers use varying combinations of plastics and metal to encase the PCB, batteries, and other components of laptops and tablets. Like laptops and mobile phones, about 12–20 precious and REEs are used in various components of a tablet. The average content of metals in tablets is listed in Table 8.7.

8.3.6 Material Composition of Mobile Phones

The use of mobile phones has grown exponentially from the first several hundred users in the early 1980s to an estimated 8.82 billion in 2020. Smartphone use has gone up by 40% in four years (2016–2020), and surpassed conventional mobile phones in 2013 (Gartner 2014). By 2020, 3.5 billion people, representing 48% of the world population, were using smartphones. The number is projected to go up to 7.33 billion by 2023 (Statista 2021). China leads the world with the largest number of smartphone users – 851 million (or 60% of its population) followed by India, 346 mn users (25.2%), and the United States, 260 million users (79%).

Although mobile phone composition varies with the manufacturer and the model, the bulk composition of the newer smartphone includes: plastics (polycarbonate, PC; and acrylonitrile butadiene styrene, ABS): 40%; nonferrous metals: 32%; glass and ceramics: 20%; ferrous metals: 3%; and other materials 5%. Among the nonferrous metals, base metals such as Cu and Sn comprise 40%, and the remaining 60% includes specialty metals such as Co, In, and Sb; precious metals: Au and Ag; and platinum-group metals, such as Ir, Os, Pd, Pt, Rh, and Ru. The material composition of smartphones is given in Table 8.7.

Table 8.8 Total weight of e-waste, metal quantities, and values of discarded mobile phones, laptops, desktops, and Plasma TVs for 2020–2025 in China.

Device	Year	Weight, t	Au, t	Ag, t	Pd, t	Total value^a of Au, Ag, Pd
Mobile phone	2020	252 090.54	143.22	362.82	28.64	$33.34 billion
	2025	420 139.45	238.69	604.69	47.74	NC
Laptop	2020	21 119.03	44.84	78.29	14.24	$6.706 billion
	2025	19 461.97	41.32	72.15	13.12	NC
Desktop	2020	3 825.37	10.87	25.83	6.80	$1.26 billion
	2025	2 889.43	8.21	19.51	5.13	NC
Plasma TV	2020	15 398.54	75.02	150.04	—	$4.90 billion (Au, Ag only)
	2025	20 625.75	100.49	200.98	—	NC

NC = Not calculated due to price fluctuations over the next five years.
^{a} Metals' market value has been calculated based on 31 December 2020 price of Au, Ag, and Pd as found on APMEX (www.apmex.com). *Source:* Modified after Mao (2020).

Despite the miniscule quantities of precious, PGMs and REEs in each smartphone, the high rate of their obsolescence (two to three years in high-income countries, and – three to five years in middle-income countries), amounting to millions of discarded smartphones, makes the potential for recovery of valuable metals very high. A detailed study on the economic value of recovered metals from smartphones by Cucchiella (2015) found that recycling 19 000 t of smartphones would yield a revenue of €348 m (or $421.1 m), based on the 2014 market price of metals. They also estimated the revenue to increase to €746 m ($902.7 m) by 2020 due to an increase in the number of smartphone users to 3.5 billion and an increase in precious metals' prices.

A detailed study was carried out by Mao et al. (2020) to predict quantities of valuable metals that can be recovered from four common personal devices: mobile phones, laptops, desktops, and plasma TVs (MLDP). The study utilized data for these devices sold in China for the period 1997–2016 to estimate quantities of three valuable metals, Au, Ag, and Pd. Using the Grey Theory (Li 2009), they estimated the tonnage of precious metals that could be recovered from the four equipment annually for the period 2017–2025. The goal was to develop a reliable estimate of MLDPs' quantity for the realization of China's circular economy goals. Table 8.8 lists the metal content of discarded MLDPs and the market value of Au, Ag, and Pd. The table also gives the estimated tonnage of MLDPs for 2025 along with the quantities of Ag, Ag, and Pd that could potentially be recovered; however, their market values have not been included due to price volatility, design changes, and production fluctuations. No such study has been done for other countries and since China has emerged as the topmost country in terms of e-waste volume (Blade et al. 2017), the results can offer insights into individual countries for better e-waste management.

8.4 E-Waste Quantity

Electronic waste has become one of the fastest growing waste streams in the world, increasing by 9.5 Mt in just five years between 2014 and 2019. The e-waste quantity is estimated to increase to 65.3 Mt in 2025 and 74.7 Mt by 2030 (Figure 8.3). However, only about 17.4% (19.3 Mt) were recycled in 2019 from which 4 Mt of valuable raw materials, valued at $10 billion, were recovered.

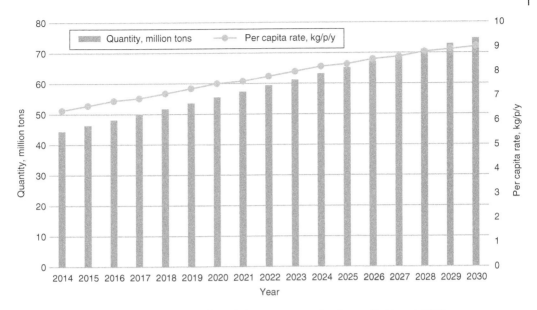

Figure 8.3 Past and predicted increase in global e-waste quantity. *Source:* Forti et al. 2020.

Table 8.9 The world's top five countries in the quantity of e-waste generated, population, and per capita rate for 2019.

Country	WEEE quantity 2019, Mt[a]	Population 2019, million	Per capita rate 2019, kg/p/y
China	10.13	1 407 271 880	7.2
USA	6.92	331 408 069	21.0
India	3.23	1 375 071 375	2.4
Japan	2.56	1 26 010 000	20.4
UK and N. Ireland	1.59	69 783 897	22.8

[a] Million metric tons.

In 2019, a total of 53.6 Mt of e-waste was generated worldwide, which translates to 7.3 kg/p/y. Of course, like municipal solid waste (MSW) and other wastes, there is a wide range in the quantity of e-waste generated in individual countries with the larger quantities coming from high-income countries. According to the latest published statistics on e-waste, in 2019, China with 10.13 Mt led the world in terms of quantity of e-waste, followed by the United States and India with 6.92 and 3.23 Mt, respectively. However, these numbers need to be viewed with caution because the ranking will be different when normalized on a per capita basis. Therefore, as compared to the 2019 world average rate of e-waste at 7.3 kg/p/y, China's rate was 7.2 kg/p/y, the United States was 21.0 kg/p/y, and India's 2.4 kg/p/y, respectively. Table 8.9 shows the top five countries in terms of total e-waste quantity generated, and the per capita annual rate in the country. On a regional (continental) basis, Asia generated the highest quantity of e-waste, 13.1 Mt, with potential value of recovered materials estimated at $26.4 billion (bn), followed by the Americas: 13.1 Mt valued at $ 14.2 bn; and Europe: 12.0 m valued at $12.9 bn. The per capita rate was just the opposite: 5.6, 13.3, and 12.2 kg/p/y, respectively (Forti et al. 2020). The breakdown of e-waste quantities in each of the six major

Table 8.10 Change in waste quantities generated in the five major EEE categories worldwide in 2016 and 2019.

Waste category	Category description	Total e-waste quantity generated, Mt		Percent change
		2016	2019	
Small equipment	Vacuum cleaners, microwaves, ventilation equipment, toasters, electric kettles, electric shavers, scales, calculators, radio sets, video cameras, electrical and electronic toys, small electrical and electronic tools, small medical devices, small monitoring, and control instruments	16.8	17.4	3.6
Large equipment	Washing machines, clothes dryers, dishwashing machines, electric stoves, large printing machines, copying equipment, and photovoltaic panels	9.1	13.1	44
Small IT and telecommunication equipment	Mobile phones, Global Positioning System (GPS) devices, pocket calculators, routers, personal (desk) computers, printers, and telephones	3.9	4.7	20.5
Lamps	Fluorescent lamps, high-intensity discharge lamps, and LED lamps	0.7	0.9	28.6
Screens and monitors	Televisions, monitors, laptops, notebooks, and tablets	6.6	6.7	1.5
Temperature exchange equipment	Refrigerators, freezers, air conditioners, and heat pumps	7.6	10.8	42.1
Total of all six categories		**44.7**	**53.6**	**20**

Source: After Forti et al. (2020) and Blade et al. (2017).

categories is given in Table 8.10. It can be noted that the quantities of various WEEE generated globally in 2019 were dominated by small equipment (17.4 Mt), followed by large equipment (13.1 Mt), and TEE (10.8 Mt), screens and monitors (6.7 Mt), small IT and telecommunication equipment (4.7 Mt), and lamps (0.9 Mt). Comparing these quantities with the 2016 quantities, it can be seen that the largest increase (by weight) occurred in the quantity of large equipment (44%), followed by TEE (42%), lamps (29%), small IT equipment (21%), small equipment (4%), and screens (2%). The trend reflects the improving living standards in developing countries where refrigerators, air conditioners, cloth washers, and dryers are being used in larger numbers. In contrast, small IT and telecommunication equipment have been growing at a lower rate, with the lowest increase (1.5%) for screens and monitors, likely due to replacement of CRT monitors and screens by flat panel displays.

8.4.1 Estimation of e-Waste Quantity

One of the major challenges in estimating the quantity of e-waste generated worldwide has been lack of a universally accepted definition of e-waste, legislation to track items discarded and collected for recycling, and disposed of otherwise (e.g. landfilled, left in drawers, illegally exported, etc.). Owing to the dual nature of recovery of valuable materials, along with adverse environmental impacts, if not managed properly, e-waste quantity estimation has been a subject of intense research in several countries, notably China, the United States, and India (Perez-Belis et al. 2015).

Mathematical equations have been developed for calculating quantity of each item in WEEE. A simple estimate of the quantity of an item entering e-waste stream can be made by using Eq. (8.1).

$$Q = \left(w \cdot n\right)/l \qquad\qquad (8.1)$$

where,
Q = Quantity of the item entering the e-waste stream, kg/y
w = Weight of the item, kg
n = Number of items in service
l = Average life of the item, y

To ensure a reliable method for record keeping, reporting, and uniform statistical analyses of e-waste generated in countries with different system of e-waste management, the Global E-waste Statistics Partnership, formed by the UNU, International Telecommunication Union (ITU), and International Solid Waste Association (ISWA), has recommended use of the UNU keys (codes) to select the most relevant items, based on the following considerations:

- The product comprises a significant share of the total electronics market in terms of weight. Such products include washing machines, refrigerators, and air conditioners, or
- The product contains environmentally toxic components. Such products include refrigerators and air conditioners, PCBs, and plastics containing BFRs.
- The product has the potential for recovery of significant amount of valuable resources, such as IT equipment, mobile phones, and flat panel televisions or monitors, and
- The product is sold in both developing and developed countries.

When applying these criteria, it is recommended to specifically compile e-waste statistics for the following UNU-keys:

- Washing machines (UNU key: 0104)
- Fridge or combined fridge/freezer (UNU key: 0108)
- Household air conditioner (UNU key: 0111)
- CRT monitors and TVs (UNU key: 0307 and 0407)
- Laptop, notebook, tablet (UNU key: 0303)
- Mobile phones (UNU key: 0306)
- Flat panel display for computer (UNU key: 0309)
- Flat panel televisions (UNU key: 0408)

Quantifying e-waste is a key step toward addressing the global e-waste challenge. Uniform system of information gathering and reporting at the international level is essential to monitor e-waste quantities, set standards and guidelines for data collection, and identify policies. This approach would allow reliable comparison of e-waste among countries, and determine best practices for recycling policies. Better e-waste data will also result in minimizing e-waste generation, prevent illegal dumping and trade, promote recycling, and create jobs.

Example Problem 8.1 The average weight of Au in a laptop is about 0.1 g. What would be the quantity and value of Au that can potentially be recovered from 15 000 discarded laptops? And in a single laptop?

Wt. of Au in 15 000 laptops = $0.1 \times 15\,000$ = **1500 g**, or 1.5 kg of Au, assuming 100% recovery.
Gold price (May 2021) = \$60.88/g (fluctuates; current price available at www.apmex.com).
Value of Au in 15 000 laptops = 1500×60.88 = **\$91 320**
Value of Gold in one laptop = $\$60.88 \times 0.1$ = \$6.088 or **\$6.1/laptop**

Example Problem 8.2 People living in an effluent town (population: 1 million) discard 11 000 laptops, 15 000 smartphones, and 9500 desktops each year. Assuming average life of the three devices to be 3, 2.5, and 6.5 years, respectively, and using the weights given in Table 8.6, determine the quantity of WEE that will have to be managed every year.

Using Eq. (8.1), $Q = (w.n)/l$, first calculate weight of each device as follows:
$Q_L = (1.3\,\text{kg} \times 11\,000)/3 = 4767\,\text{kg/y}$ – laptops
$Q_S = (0.1\,\text{kg} \times 15\,000)/2.5 = 600\,\text{kg/y}$ – smartphones
$Q_D = (8.8\,\text{kg} \times 9500)/6.5 = 128\,62\,\text{kg/y}$ – desktops

Total wt. of all devices = $4767 + 600 + 128\,62 = 18229\,\text{kg/y}$, or **18.229 t/y** (~18.23 t/y)

8.5 E-Waste Recycling and Recovery of Valuable Metals

It is not only the large quantity of e-waste that has drawn the attention and interest in its recycling but other factors have also equally contributed to intense study and efforts to recover useful materials, particularly the precious, scarce, and, specialty metals. The major drivers are listed below:

- Large and fast-growing quantity of e-waste being generated globally
- Ecological and human health problems associated with unrecovered toxic materials in the e-waste stream
- Eliminating or minimizing the threats to human health, and to control serious environmental degradation resulting from informal recycling of e-waste in developing countries
- Global emphasis on sustainability, resource conservation, and attainment of sustainable development goals (SDGs) proposed by the UNEP and adopted by many countries
- Augmenting the unreliable supply of specialty metals to maintain the desired production levels of high-tech equipment through controlled e-waste recycling and urban mining.

Highly efficient and successful recovery of some base and precious metals has been carried out for a long time; for example, recovery rates of >95% have been achieved for metals, like Fe, Al, Pb, Au, and Ag. Certain specialty metals, such as Pt, widely used in automobile catalytic converter, have recovery rates of 60–70%, mainly due to easy disassembly of the part, and high yields. On the other hand, recovery rates for specialty metals, such as REEs from e-waste are <1% (Izatt 2016).

Personal communication and computing devices have become an inseparable part of modern life, and individuals living in affluent societies possess two to three devices each, all of which contain over 40 elements, dozens of them with names unfamiliar to most people. Ask a college student about what metal is represented by the chemical symbol of In, Dy, Nd, or Tb, found in his/her smartphone or laptop, and chances are that he/she will pull a blank. Awareness of the value of REEs on part of the general public is negligible. Therefore, it is very important to educate the users to bring awareness of the potential value of the specialty metals found in their devices so they can take appropriate measures to ensure that their discarded equipment are available for recycling and contributing to the national economy through recovery of valuable metals.

It is now widely recognized that e-waste comprising personal communication devices – laptops, tablets, mobile phones – despite containing tiny amounts of valuable metals, represent an untapped resource, termed "urban mine" because of the huge volume of these devices and their easy accessibility. Unlike conventional mineral deposits that occur in the lithosphere – generally at some depth – the urban mines are located in the readily accessible anthroposphere, right at the surface. Urban mines represent important "ores" of Ag, Au, Pt, Pd, Cu, and the REEs, occur in concentrations 40–50 times greater than in natural ores, and can be put to immediate use with minimal or no treatment, thus avoiding the expensive, complex, and ecologically destructive processes of metal mining and refining. A catalytic converter in an automobile, for instance, containing 2 kg of Pt (or 2%) in each ton of the ceramic block, represents 200 times greater concentration than the required natural concentration of <10 g/t (or <0.01) for profitable Pt mining (Izatt 2016).

Urban mining can be defined as extracting valuable metals from discarded personal devices that a typical urbanite replaces after two to three years of use, and from which significant quantities of precious and rare metals can be obtained. In this respect, old landfills have turned out to be a new resource for valuable materials, including metals. A project called enhanced landfill mining (ELFM) was launched in 2016 in Germany to explore the feasibility of mining the waste buried in old landfills, up to 100 years, to recover useful materials. Initial results indicate that e-waste buried in landfills could be a new source of useful materials (Waste Management World 2020).

Urban mines are emerging as an important resource for secondary raw metals for high-tech manufacturing. Innovative methods to recover valuable metals are likely to boast recycling rate of e-waste. This would alleviate the pressure on primary mining of virgin raw materials and lead to easing the demand of specialty metals in a sustainable manner for countries that do not possess adequate supply to meet the demand of their high-tech industries.

A 2020 report published by the UN University (Forti et al. 2020) estimated the potential values of Au, Ag, Bi, Co, Ge, In, Ir, Pt, Pd, Ru, Rh, Ir, Os, and Sb contained in e-waste generated in 2019 at approximately $57 billion. This calculation is based on complete (100%) recycling of e-waste and economic feasibility of doing so, something that is not currently achievable. However, with continued improvement in metal recovery technology, combined with improved e-waste collection and recycling practices on a global scale, it is very likely that valuable metals may be readily available to re-enter the manufacturing sector, thereby contributing to circular economy by conserving limited supplies of natural mineral deposits. Even with the current collection and recycling rate of 17.4%, raw materials valued at $10 billion can be potentially recovered from e-waste, contributing about 4 Mt of secondary raw materials for manufacturing new products. With nearly 83% of the e-waste not formally collected or managed in 2019, the potential for future recovery of metals is astounding as more of the waste would be available for maximum recovery of specialty metals.

8.5.1 Metal Recovery from E-Waste

As discussed before, e-waste represents a significant resource of precious and valuable metals. Despite the low level of interest on part of electronic equipment users and the current low recycling rate, effective recovery of Au, Pt, Pd, and Pb continues to be made. There is no doubt that with heightened awareness of the value of discarded personal devices, combined with increasing rate of e-waste recycling, metal recovery would improve significantly.

Public awareness is a key element in any successful recycling program (Hasan 2004). The public needs to be educated about the specialty metals that are present in their personal electronic devices and the vital role they play in the high-tech industry. Attractive cards and brochure sent in the mail to the community, radio, TV, and social media messages, emphasizing citizen's involvement are proven ways to engage the public. In addition, providing convenient locations and easily accessible collection facilities for depositing their used cell phones, laptops, etc., would result in greater participation. Offering prepaid mailers for smartphones and laptops can also result in greater return rate of discarded personal e-devices. Installing weatherproof drop boxes at popular places, such as shopping centers, supermarkets, college campuses, etc., is yet another way to encourage users to return their discarded items for recycling. Collection of e-waste can be made more cost-efficient by attaching internet-enabled radio frequency (RF) sensors, GIS mapping tools, etc., on drop boxes for efficient collection.

Collected e-waste must be sorted and preconditioned. The latter may include dismantling, mechanical shredding of large appliances, or disassembling the automobile catalytic converter case, etc. Mobile phones, MP3 players, batteries, and circuit boards in a mixed e-waste stream must be sorted and separated from large appliances before mechanical pre-processing. The goal of pre-processing should be to allow maximum recovery of metals from the metallurgical and/or chemical recovery process.

Pyrometallurgy has been extensively employed to separate metals from ores in the mining industry, but the large-scale generation of toxic waste has caused serious environmental problems world over. Newer methods to reduce or eliminate toxic wastes are being investigated and the green chemistry initiative has resulted in some promising metal extraction technologies. Green chemistry – elimination or reduction of hazardous materials in chemical products and processes – is being used to develop new chemicals and chemical processes that reduce or eliminate hazardous products. Molecular Extraction Technology has been successfully used since the 2000s to separate metals by using ligands (from Latin to bind), which are donor ions or molecules that attach to a central atom or ion. Ligands can be anions (e.g. CN^-: cyanide), cations (e.g. NO^+: nitrosamine), or neutral molecules (e.g. NH_3: amino or amine). SuperLig® and AnaLig® are commercial ligand products that have been successfully utilized to extract PMG and REE metals in laboratory settings (Furusho et al. 2016; Izatt et al. 2016).

New technologies for metal recovery from e-waste are being developed at a rapid rate. A recent study by Hong et al. (2020) on recovery of gold in PCBs, using a highly porous, covalent organic polymer, COP-180, led to gold recovery of 94%. The study holds high potential for commercialization because of its cost efficiency – at an estimated cost of $5/g for COP-180 polymer, gold worth $64 can be recovered.

8.5.2 Benefits and Challenges of e-Waste Recycling

Recycling of e-waste to recover specialty metals offers the benefit of avoiding mining natural sulfide ores to obtain these metals. Typically, sulfide ores also contain minor amounts of As, Hg, Cd, Tl, U, and Th which are released in the anthroposphere as waste materials after mining, refining, and extraction of Pb, Zn, Ag, Au, and other metals from the ore. Prior to the 1970s little, if any attention, was given to properly manage these wastes that has left a legacy of thousands of hazardous waste sites across the world. The adverse impacts on human and ecological health from the abandoned toxic mining dumps have been well documented in literature (Chapter 5).

With efficient recycling, specialty metals of high purity can be recovered from e-waste at a much lower cost. This would eliminate use of large volumes of water and energy, and capital-intensive mining operations. For example, a naturally occurring Au ore is considered profitable to mine if it can yield 5g of Au/t (0.005%) of the ore, whereas PCBs in mobile phones can yield 150g Au/t (0.15%) – 30 times more (Izatt 2016).

Different types of plastics, such as PC, ABS, PMMA, and HIPS, mixed with BFRs are commonly used to encase computing equipment and mobile phones. The amount and type of plastics vary with the design of the equipment. Based on analyses of 81 front covers from desktop computer housings, 166 laptop back covers, and 73 tablet housings from post-consumer e-waste collected from a recycling center in Belgium, Wagner et al. (2019) reported that the largest amount of plastics, 97%, was used in laptops, with desktops and tablets each comprising about 70%. In terms of chemical purity of recovered PC/ABS plastics, they reported that laptops offered highest purity of nearly 93% as compared to 70% for desktops and tablets. Purity of recovered material is a function of types of fasteners used to affix the housing to internal components, ease of removal of glued informational labels, and whether or not separation can be accomplished by simple mechanical disassembly process or physical treatment (heat and pressure), or complex chemical process.

Sustainable product manufacturing must aim at long-term reuse, repair, recovery, and recycling of EEs by incorporating simple mechanical disassembly features, using easily removable labels, and completely modular design. Manufacturers should, at the same time, be required to ensure adequate supply of parts to facilitate repair and reuse.

8.6 Health and Environmental Impacts

Electronic waste is unique among the various types of waste, notably in terms of the value, variety, and complex nature of the metals, plastics, and organic chemicals it contains. Most of them are hazardous, many are toxic, and several are known carcinogen; the latter includes As, Br, Cd, Cr, Pb, etc. Plastic housing of computers, mobile phones, and other EEE also contain highly toxic halogenated compounds, such as BFRs which, upon burning form dioxins and furans, both of which are highly toxic and carcinogenic. This characteristic of the e-waste requires safe management soon after the EEE enter the waste stream to prevent adverse human health impacts and minimize ecological damage.

Safe recycling of e-waste complying with environmental regulations involves special facilities and equipment that are very expensive, and due to the minute quantities of metals in discarded pieces, major metal recyclers in the United States avoid it, preferring wastes that contain greater quantities of useful metals. This creates a serious impediment in recovery of REEs from e-waste. For instance, recovery of Nd and Pr from magnets in hard drive is cost-prohibitive due to their minute quantities leading the recyclers to seek e-waste containing large magnets, such as those used in windmills, electric vehicles, and large generators (GAO 2016).

8.6.1 Informal E-Waste Recycling

Informal e-waste recycling involves dismantling e-waste using crude processes and primitive methods. Various steps involved in informal recycling are shown in Figure 8.4.

Open burning and acid baths to recover metals are commonly practiced, with the residual toxic waste from such operations being carelessly discarded, allowing pollutants to seep into the ground and water bodies. All recycling operations are performed without protective equipment, using bare hands to obtain larger quantities of less contaminated valuable metals, increasing occupational injuries. Such practices exacerbate the intrinsic risk of hazardous substances in the original e-waste due to: (i) addition of caustic chemicals during metal recovery, and (ii) new chemical compounds

Figure 8.4 Steps in informal e-waste recycling.

formed during recycling. Although toxicity of original materials in the e-waste is generally known, that of the resulting complex chemical mixtures are unknown, adding another level of risk to workers, residents, and the environment.

Major informal e-waste recycling centers sprung up in developing countries in the late 1990s due to the absence of commercially profitable e-waste recycling facilities in the United States. It is noteworthy that although the United States had signed the Basel Convention on *Transboundary movement of hazardous waste* in 1990, and the Senate had agreed for its ratification in 1992, no legislation has occurred till date to enable the President to sign it into law (EPA 2020). The limited scope and enforcement of existing EPA regulations to restrict export of CRT monitors and TVs, exclude other e-wastes that find their way to South Asia (China, India, the Philippines, Thailand, and Vietnam), and Ghana and Nigeria in Africa. Southern China, specially the Taizhou area in Zhejiang province and Guiyu in Guangdong province, and some cities in India, such as Delhi, Ghazipur, and Bengaluru (formerly Bangalore), became centers for informal recycling.

The main port of entry of e-waste is Hong Kong in China and Mumbai (formerly Bombay) in India. Guiyu receives 70% of world's e-waste (Li and Achal 2020). Guiyu, located in the coastal area of South China Sea, in the early 1990s, was a cluster of four rice-growing villages in Chaoyang district of the Guangdong Province. Since 1995, Guiyu became a major e-waste-recycling center and in 2013, was listed as the world's largest e-waste site in the world in the *Guinness World Records* (2013, p. 37).

Unregulated informal e-waste recycling is generally carried out in workshops of seven to eight employees without any protective equipment at temporary sites, dwellings, and other available public spaces. Such operations are performed by poor, unemployed people who are desperate to earn a living at the cost of their health and safety. These workers use unsafe and risky processing practices without knowledge of potential harm. It is not uncommon to find children working in e-waste-recycling operations as their small hands make them ideal to dismantle equipment (Lancet 2013). Common primitive labor practices include using acid baths, burning cables, breaking apart toxic solders, and dumping the resulting toxic waste anywhere (StEP Initiative 2011). Workers dismantling e-waste may come into direct contact with polychlorinated biphenyls (PCBs) and other persistent organic pollutants (POPs) in fluids, lubricants, and coolants in the e-waste (Grant et al. 2013). Processing cables to recover copper often involves burning the plastic sleeves, which releases harmful PVC, dioxins, furans, BFRs, and polycyclic aromatic hydrocarbons (PAHs) into the environment. While the cables burn, the immediate environment where people work and live is engulfed in thick black toxic smoke. The harmful combustion by-products released while burning e-waste can increase risk of respiratory and skin diseases, eye infections, and even cancer for people nearby (Robinson 2009). Workers and people playing or living in or near informal facilities are chronically exposed to myriad chemical pollutants either directly through contact or inhalation, or indirectly through contamination of the food and water supply (Lancet 2013). Figure 8.5 illustrates crude extraction methods used at the recycling centers in China and India.

Figure 8.5 (a, b) Informal e-waste recycling in India, using crude methods to salvage useful materials. Note absence of PPE. *Source:* Ajim Ali.

(a)

(b)

8.6.2 Health and Environmental Impacts of Informal Recycling

One of the earliest studies that provided a systematic review of health consequences of e-waste was published in the *Lancet Global Health* (Grant et al. 2013). The review involved searching major electronic databases for articles on e-waste exposure and health outcomes. Grant et al. (2013) reported adverse neonatal outcomes, indicated by increases in spontaneous abortions, still- and premature births, reduced birthweights and lengths, besides evidence of greater DNA damage to adults living or working at informal e-waste recycling centers than those in control towns.

Electronic waste contains metals, plastics, and chemical compounds that are toxic and detrimental to human health. Example includes heavy metals, such as Cd, Cr, Hg, Pb; organic chemical compounds, such as chlorofluorocarbons (CFCs), hydrochlorofluorocarbons (HCFCs); and plastic casings containing BFRs, such as polybrominated diphenyl ethers (PBDEs), polybrominated biphenyls (PBBs), PCBs, and other POPs. POPs are bioaccumulative, toxic, and persist in the environment for a long time. Use of PBDEs and PBBs is banned in Europe. Recycling of plastic containing BFR represents a major challenge in e-waste recycling because of the high cost of separating plastics containing PBDEs and PBBs from other plastics. In addition, recycled plastic with PBDE and PBB content greater than 0.1% cannot be used for manufacturing other products, including EEE. Informal and unregulated e-waste recycling also causes altered neurodevelopment, adverse learning outcomes, adverse cardiovascular and respiratory effects, skin diseases, hearing loss, and immune system impacts. Long-term monitoring of occupational exposure to metals, $PM_{2.5}$, POPs, and PAHs, and their environmental concentrations are needed to quantify the full impact of e-waste on human health. While adequate information on health effects from e-waste exposure to small population groups is available, there is a paucity of data on the effects upon larger population suffering from the effects.

Environmental degradation from unsafe recycling of e-waste and illegal dumping in landfills have been reported from all over the world. Informal e-waste recycling in developing countries, as also illegal disposal activities in developed countries, have adversely impacted all environmental media – air, biota, soil, and water. Common modes of media contamination include: atmosphere deposition, both wet and dry; leaching, adsorption–desorption, complexation resulting in formation of secondary heavy metal-organic matter compounds; plant uptake leading to accumulation in food sources; biochemical degradation, and volatilization. Several studies have reported presence of hazardous and toxic substances in and around areas of informal e-waste-recycling facilities, exposing population to serious risks (Chen et al. 2011; Grant et al. 2013; Li and Achal 2020). China and India are major centers of informal e-waste recycling; these two countries account for about 50–70% of all e-waste imported or informally recycled.

Surface and groundwater contamination, including metal contamination of stream sediments have been reported from areas surrounding informal e-waste-recycling towns, notably Guiyu in China. One study found toxic heavy metals in fine dust dispersed across the Pearl River Delta region (about 100 km southeast of Guiyu) by prevailing winds, exposing 45 million people to serious health risks (Robinson 2009). Many toxic compounds, released during informal e-waste recycling such as PCBs and other toxic heavy metals, were found in relatively high concentrations in e-waste recycling areas three decades after informal recycling work was banned. Women living and working near informal e-waste-recycling areas are highly susceptible to exposure that affects them and the fetus. A study involving 634 pregnant women in Guiyu revealed high concentration of Pb, 6.66 µg/dL, in maternal blood, nearly 2 times higher than in the control group (Kim et al. 2019).

Informal recycling releases harmful substances into air, water, and land. Gaseous pollutants, containing dioxins, furans, O_3, HCl, and other caustic vapors, and PMs carrying toxic heavy metals, along with denser chemicals, settle down on the ground causing contamination of soil and water bodies. Consuming food products grown on contaminated soil, or drinking contaminated water leads to acute and chronic health problems, such as respiratory track ailments, neurological impairments, and cancer. Table 8.11 shows common toxic substances in e-waste and their health impacts.

Soil contamination has serious implications for food consumed by people living in the vicinity of e-waste dumps and informal recycling areas. Plants can absorb and accumulate heavy metals and other toxic substances from the contaminated soil through their roots and transfer them to crops and vegetables. For example, soils at an e-waste recycling facility in Bangalore, the 4th most populous city in India (2020 population: 12.6 million), were found to contain up to 2850 ppm Pb, 39 ppm Cd, 4.6 ppm In, 180 ppm Sb, 957 ppm Sn, 49 ppm Hg, and 2.7 ppm Bi (Ngoc et al. 2009). Compared to the control site near the same city, these values were more than 100 times higher.

Table 8.11 Common toxic substances in e-waste and their health impacts.

Substance	Used in	Health impact
Antimony	CRT glass, plastic computer housings, cause stomach pain, vomiting, diarrhea and and solder alloy in cabling	Antimony has been classified as a carcinogen. It can stomach ulcers through inhalation of high antimony levels over a long time period
Arsenic	Gallium arsenide is used in light-emitting diodes (LEDs)	Arsenic causes skin disease and lung cancer and impaired nerve signaling
Barium	Sparkplugs, fluorescent lamps, and CRT gutters in vacuum tubes	Causes brain swelling, muscle weakness, and damage to the heart, liver and spleen through short-term exposure
Beryllium	Power supply boxes, motherboards, relays and finger clips	Exposure to beryllium can lead to berylliosis, lung cancer and skin disease. Beryllium is a carcinogen
Brominated flame retardants	Printed circuit boards and plastic housings, keyboards and cable insulation to reduce flammability	During combustion printed circuit boards and plastic housings emit toxic vapors known to cause hormonal disorders
Cadmium	Rechargeable NiCd batteries, semi-conductor chips, infrared detectors, printer inks and toners	Cadmium compounds pose a risk of irreversible impacts on human health, particularly the kidneys
Chloro-fluorocarbons	Cooling units and insulation foam	Depletes the ozone layer, leading to a greater incidence of skin cancer
Chromium VI	Plastic housing, cabling, hard discs	Chromium VI is extremely toxic, causes DNA damage and permanent eye impairment
Lead	Solder, lead-acid batteries, cathode ray tubes, cabling, printed circuit boards, and fluorescent tubes	Can damage the brain, nervous system, kidney and reproductive system and cause blood disorders. Low concentrations of lead can damage the brain and nervous system in fetuses and young children
Mercury	Batteries, backlight bulbs or lamps, flat panel displays, switches and thermostats	Mercury can damage the brain, kidneys and fetuses
Nickel	Batteries, computer housing, cathode ray tube and printed circuit boards	Nickel can cause allergic reaction, bronchitis and reduced lung function and lung cancers
Polychlorinated biphenyls	Condensers, transformers, and heat transfer fluids	PCBs cause cancer in animals and can lead to liver damage in humans
Polyvinyl chloride (PVC)	Monitors, keyboards, cabling, and plastic computer housing	Incomplete combustion of PVC release huge amounts of hydrogen chloride gas that form hydrochloric acid (HCl). HCl can cause respiratory problems
Selenium	Older photocopy machines	High concentrations cause selenosis

8.7   Sustainable Management of E-Waste

Adverse impacts on human and ecological health resulting from informal e-waste recycling in China, India, and Africa have been investigated in great detail. Guiyu has been the focus of such work as evidenced by two bibliometric studies, one by Perez-Belis et al. (2015) and the other by Gao et al. (2019). China led the world in number of publications, which is not surprising as Guiyu is ranked number one in terms of WEEE recycling.

Perez-Belis reviewed about 300 articles on WEEE published during the 20-year period, 1992–2012, and grouped them into six categories:

1) Generation – estimation of WEEE quantity, and source
2) Characterization – physical and chemical characteristics and material composition of WEEE
3) Social aspects – consumer habits and behavior toward recycling; and health and environmental impacts of WEEE
4) Reuse and repair – feasibility and barriers for repair and reuse of WEEE
5) Design – needs and benefits of sustainable and eco-friendly design of WEEE, and LCA/LCC
6) Economics – economic benefits of WEEE, and cost-benefit analyses

Gao and his colleagues (Gao et al. 2019) covered a longer period (1981–2018) and used the *Web of Science* and the *Science Citation Index* to extract nearly 2800 publications. Their analyses confirmed China as the leading country with 1146 or 41% of all published articles, followed by the United States: 345 or 12%; and India: 190 or 7%. An interesting aspect of this bibliometric analyses was the quality of paper which was measured in terms of citations. The top two authors, among the 10 most cited, were from the United States with over 300 citations each, followed by Chinese and other nationals whose citations ranged from 132 to 270. In terms of number of publications and growth rate of articles dealing with e-waste, it was noted that between 1981 and 2001, only a few articles (1–5) were published each year, rising to 13 in 2003, and increasing to 100 in 2009, and 428 in 2017. The growth pattern reflects the concern and need for safe management of e-waste in a sustainable way to minimize environmental pollution and protect human and ecological health.

8.7.1   United Nations Sustainable Development Goals and E-Waste

In September 2015, the United Nations identified 17 SDGs for assuring equitable human living and environmental preservation, to be achieved by 2030 (Figure 8.6). Of these 17 goals, four are related to e-waste:

SDG 3 on good health; SDG 8 on good jobs and economic growth; SDG 11 on sustainable cities and communities; and SDG 12 on responsible consumption. Specific indicators and targets have been set to monitor e-waste in regard to achieving the SDGs as discussed below.

SDG 3.9 target: Substantially reduce the number of deaths and illnesses from hazardous chemicals, and from air, water, and soil pollution. E-waste contains a number of hazardous components, which when dismantled and processed improperly, can threaten healthy lives by contaminating water, soil, and air. The elimination of hazardous substances during the design and production of EEE, and dismantling and processing of e-waste should be carried out in an environmentally sound manner.

SDG 8.3 target: Promote development-oriented policies that support productive activities, decent job creation, entrepreneurship, creativity and innovation, and encourage growth of micro-, small- and medium-sized enterprises. In developing countries, e-waste recycling is largely carried out in

Figure 8.6   United Nations' 17 sustainable development goals. *Source:* UN.

the informal sector. This sector calls for regulations to ensure workers' right and environmentally safe management of e-waste.

SDG 11.6 target: Reduce the adverse environmental impact in cities by controlling toxic emissions from e-waste. Over half of the world's population now lives in urban areas, consuming 75% of the world's natural resources. E-waste collection rate is very low in urban areas in developed countries due to insufficient separate collection bins for mobile phones, laptops, notebooks, and other items. Open burning and dumping of e-waste near major urban centers in developing countries cause air pollution and degradation of the overall environmental quality that need to stop.

SDG 12.4 target: Achieve environmentally sound management of chemicals and all wastes throughout their life cycle, in accordance with agreed international frameworks, and significantly reduce their release into air, water, and soil in order to minimize their adverse impacts on human health and the environment. Currently, the e-waste management practices most common in developing economies involve open dumping or the use of chemical processes such as acid baths and amalgamation to separate valuable materials.

SDG 12.5 target: Substantially reduce waste generation through prevention, reduction, repair, recycling, and reuse. By designing EEE with nonhazardous components that can be easily separated and manufactured using recycled metals, it would be possible to reduce e-waste. It is important that manufacturers shift from planned and perceived obsolescence design to realistic design based on circular economy to meet consumers' demand for more durable products. Manufacturers should be required to meet extended producer responsibility (EPR) and held accountable for the collection and proper recycling of discarded WEEE at their EoL.

A measure to determine the national recycling rate has been proposed and defined in SDG 12.5.1 as follows:

$$\text{National } e-\text{waste recycling rate} = \left[\text{Total } e-\text{waste collected} / \text{Total } e-\text{waste generated} \right] \times 100$$

Using this measure, the global e-waste recycling rate in 2019 was estimated at 17.4%.

Despite the ambitious goals, SDGs' success depends on how various member countries enact legislation to incorporate the goals in their national policies and, more importantly, how strictly they are enforced. Nonetheless, SDGs offer commendable guidelines that deserve serious consid erations for adoption by all nations.

8.7.2 Other Measures for Sustainable E-Waste Management

A combination of national legislation, the political will to implement it, technology transfer, IT industry support and collaboration, and consumers' involvement is imperative for attaining sustainable management of e-waste on a global scale.

National regulations should focus on eliminating illegal trade and operations in e-waste by imposing stiff fines, followed by a criminal penalty for repeated violators of the law. Developing countries must ban the import of toxic e-waste. If a total ban may not be possible, then custom duties should be increased. New technologies on valuable metal recovery, reuse, and repair should be freely shared between various countries. Electronic and electrical equipment manufacturers should be required by law to design their products for easy disassembly and assure a steady supply of spare parts for repair and replacement. Eco-design should be promoted to substitute toxic metals, such as Pb, and Hg with less hazardous or nonhazardous materials. Easily removable and pilfer-proof labels should be standardized for placement on all EEE and consumers should be encouraged to buy equipment displaying such labels. Consumers should be educated using mass media and social media about e-waste problems and should be made responsible for the safe deposition of discarded WEEEs.

8.8 Summary

Various definitions have been used for e-waste. Most countries include the full range of discarded large and small EEE that need electricity or battery to operate in their definition of e-waste. The United States, on the other hand, excludes discarded large and small electric and electronic equipment, and restricts e-waste to ICT devices, copying and fax machines, electronic games, and entertainment equipment. The all-inclusive definition of EEE has been adopted by the EU countries, UN, and majority of other world countries, and should also be adopted by the United States. A universally acceptable definition of e-waste is necessary for tracking its quantities, recycling rate, and comparative analyses of individual country's status of e-waste management, and for global-level data reporting and statistical analyses.

Planned obsolescence in consumer products' design has been the backbone of American manufacturing since the early twentieth century; it became deeply entrenched in ICT equipment manufacturing during the latter decades of the past century. This wasteful business strategy has resulted in an increased quantity of waste and associated pollution. Recent moves to restrict the deliberate design to limit product durability, etc., are promising developments that need to be adopted the world over.

Electronic waste represents a unique category of waste among the various waste types generated in modern society due to its dual nature of being hazardous and of high economic value at the same time. For example, smartphones, laptops, and notebooks, etc., despite containing miniscule amounts of Au, Ag, Pt, Pd, and other precious metals can yield large quantities of these metals due to the huge volume of discarded devices. In 2019, 17.4% of the e-waste was recycled yielding about 4Mt of raw material valued at $10 billion. The potential to recover valuable metals has resulted in large-scale export of e-waste from Western countries to developing countries in Africa and Asia where a majority of the e-waste is subjected to informal recycling. Loopholes in international and national laws encourage such practices that need to be plugged.

Informal recycling has created a huge industry in southern China, India, Ghana, Nigeria, and some other Southeast Asian countries, with Guiyu in China being the largest and most infamous for causing a serious impact on human and ecological health. Poor people, many of them children, are employed to work using crude and primitive methods, such as acid baths, amalgamation, etc., all of which are performed without any protective equipment. All kinds of health problems have been reported among the workers and population in the vicinity of informal recycling centers. This aspect represents one of the major challenges of e-waste recycling in the informal sector that needs to be carefully addressed.

Safe e-waste management is one of the top items on the agenda of the United Nations. Of its 17 SDGs, four are directly related to e-waste. Eco-design of consumer products, especially ICT devices that would make them repairable, allow easy dismantling, along with readily available replacement parts, and appropriate legislations, would alleviate current problems facing the e-waste-recycling industry.

Study Questions

1   Define e-waste. Explain how the difference between the United States and EU/United Nations definitions causes problems in data normalization and statistical analyses of e-waste on a global basis.

2   What are the two main aspects of e-waste that set it apart from other wastes generated in our society? Explain.

3   The Basel Convention prohibits transboundary movement of waste and its disposal, why, then, do businesses in the United States tend to profitably export e-waste to faraway countries in Africa and Asia?

4   Discuss and explain why informal e-waste recycling is detrimental to human and ecological health? Provide examples. What measures should be taken to stop such practices?

5   The EU and UN have been actively engaged in promoting safe management of e-waste. What is the reason for the lack of serious involvement by the USA?

6   What are PGEs (or PGMs)? Which single PGE has been used as a catalytic converter in the automobile industry for the longest period? What makes its recycling easy?

7   List 10 specialty elements found in smartphones and laptops. In which component(s) of the devices are they used?

8   Why is e-waste considered one of the fastest-growing waste types? What is the estimated annual rate of increase of e-waste quantity? Which country has the highest per capita rate of e-waste generation?

9   Why is China at the forefront of taking proactive measures for the safe management of e-waste than other countries? Where does the United States stand?

10   Of the 17 UN sustainability goals, discuss the four that are related to e-waste. How can the e-waste-recycling rate of a country be calculated?

11   Using the data given for a town of 100 000 people who regularly use and annually discard their devices, determine (i) the quantity of e-waste, in Mt, comprising 3500 plasma TV, 12 500 desktop computers, 10 000 laptops, and 42 200 smartphones, and (b) $ value of Au in smartphones at its market price of $57 790/kg.
     A [Useful lives: Plasma TV, 7 y; desktops, 6 y; laptops, 3.5 y; and smartphones, 2.5 y. Use Table 8.6 for weight (2016 estimates) of the devices]. Ans. (a) **2.883 Mt/y**, (b) **$82 929**.

12   How many used mobile phones and laptops/notebooks/electronic games do you possess? What do you do to the old ones that you have replaced with new models? How can ordinary United States citizens be motivated to participate in the recycling of discarded electronic devices lying around in their homes? What are the reasons for the general lack of interest in recycling? What could be done to change this attitude?

References

Anon (2005). Set of average weights for furniture, appliances and other items. https://democracy.york.gov.uk/documents/s2116/Annex%20C%20REcycling%20Report%20frnweights2005.pdf (accessed 28 March 2021).

Blade, C.P., Forti, V., Gray, V. et al. (2017). *The Global E-waste Monitor – 2017*. Bonn/Geneva/Vienna: United Nations University (UNU), International Telecommunication Union (ITU) & International Solid Waste Association (ISWA) 109 p.

Chen, A., Dietrich, K.N., Huo, X., and Ho, S.-m. (2011). Developmental neurotoxicants in e-waste: an emerging health concern. *Environmental Health Perspectives* 119 (4): 431–438.

Cucchiella, F., D'Adamo, I., Koh, S.C.L., and Rosa, P. (2015). Recycling of WEEEs: an economic assessment of present and future e-waste streams. *Renewable and Sustainable Energy Reviews* 51: 263–272.

EPA. (2020). Frequent Questions on International Agreements on Transboundary Shipments of Waste. https://www.epa.gov/hwgenerators/frequent-questions-international-agreements-transboundary-shipments-waste (accessed 2 May 2021).

EPA (2011). National strategy for electronics stewardship. https://www.epa.gov/sites/default/files/2015-09/documents/national_strategy_for_electronic_stewardship_0.pdf (accessed 9 February 2022).

EU (2012). Directive 2012/19/EU on waste electrical and electronic equipment (WEE), Annex I. Directive 2012/19/EU of the European Parliament and of the Council of 4 July 2012 on Waste Electrical and Electronic Equipment (WEEE) Text with EEA Relevance. europa.eu.

Forti, V., Blade, K., and Kuehr, R. (2018). *E-waste Statistics: Guidelines on Classifications, Reporting and Indicators*, 2e. Bonn: United Nations University 71 p.

Forti, V., Blade, C.P., Kueh, R., and Bel, G. (2020). *The Global E-waste Monitor 2020: Quantities, Flows and the Circular Economy Potential*. United Nations University (UNU)/United Nations Institute for

Training and Research (UNITAR) https://www.itu.int/en/ITU-D/Environment/Documents/Toolbox/GEM_2020_def.pdf.

Furusho, Y., Rahman, I.M.M., Hasegawa, H., and Izatt, N.E. (2016). Application of molecular recognition technology to green chemistry: analytical determinations of metals in metallurgical, environmental, waste and radiochemical samples. In: *Metal Sustainability: Global Challenges, Consequences, and Prospects* (ed. R.M. Izatt). Chichester: Wiley 527 p.

GAO (2016). Electronic Waste: DOD Is Recovering Materials, but Several Factors May Hinder Near-Term Expansion of These Efforts. *Report No. GAO-16-576*, 37 p. https://www.gao.gov/assets/gao-16-576.pdf.

Gao, Y., Ge, L., Shi, S. et al. (2019). Global trends and future prospects of e-waste research: a bibliometric analysis. *Environmental Science and Pollution Research* 26: 17809–17820. https://doi.org/10.1007/s11356-019-05071-8.

Gartner, Press Release (2014). Gartner Says Annual Smartphone Sales Surpassed Sales of Feature Phones for the First Time in 2013. Gartner Says Annual Smartphone Sales Surpassed Sales of Feature Phones for the First Time in 2013.

Grant, K., Goldizen, F., Sly, P.F. et al. (2013). Health consequences of exposure to e-waste: a systematic review. *Lancet Global Health* 1: 350–361.

Guinness World Records (2013).

Hageluken, C. (2014). Recycling of (critical) metals. In: *Critical Metals Handbook* (ed. G. Gunn), 41–69. Oxford: Wiley.

Hasan, S.E. (2004). Public awareness is key to successful waste management. *Journal of Environmental Science & Health* A39 (2): 483–492.

Hong, Y., Thirion, D., Subramanian, S. et al. (2020). Precious metal recovery from electronic waste by a porous porphyrin polymer. *Proceedings of the National Academy of Sciences* 117 (28): 16174–16180. https://doi.org/10.1073/pnas.2000606117.

Izatt, S.R., McKenzie, J.S., Bruening, R.L. et al. (2016). Selective recovery of platinum group metals and rare earth metals from complex matrices using a green chemistry/molecular recognition technology approach. In: *Metal Sustainability: Global Challenges, Consequences, and Prospects* (ed. R.M. Izatt). Chichester: Wiley 527 p.

Kim, S., Xu, X., Zhang, Y. et al. (2019). Metal concentrations in pregnant women and neonates from informal electronic waste recycling. *Journal of Exposure Science & Environmental Epidemiology* 29: 406–415. https://doi.org/10.1038/s41370-018-0054-9.

Kwarteng, L., Braiden, E. A., Foil, J., Arko-Mensah, J., Robins, T., & Batterman, S. (2020). Air quality impacts at an E-waste site in Ghana using flexible, moderate-cost and quality-assured measurements. *GeoHealth*, 4, e2020GH000247. https://doi.org/10.1029/2020GH000247.

Lancet (2013). Electronic waste—time to take stock. *The Lancet* 381 (9885): 2223. https://doi.org/10.1016/S0140-6736(13)61465-8. (editorial).

Li, Q.X. (2009). Grey dynamic input–output analysis. *Journal of Mathematical Analysis and Applications 359* (2): 514–526.

Li, W. and Achal, V. (2020). Environmental and health impacts due to e-waste disposal in China – a review. *Science of the Total Environment* 737: 139745. https://doi.org/10.1016/j.scitotenv.2020.139745.

Lippincott, G.J. (1947). *Design for Business*, 223. Chicago: Paul Theobald.

Mao, S., Kang, Y., Zhang, Y. et al. (2020). Fractional grey model based on non-singular exponential kernel and its application in the prediction of electronic waste precious metal content. *ISA Transactions* 107: 12–26. https://doi.org/10.1016/j.isatra.2020.07.023.

Ngoc, H.N., Agusa, T., Ramu, K. et al. (2009). Contamination by trace elements at e-waste recycling sites in Bangalore. *Chemosphere* 76: 9–15.

Perez-Belis, V., Bovea, M.D., and Ibanez-Fores, V. (2015). An in-depth literature review of the waste electrical and electronic equipment context: trends and evolution. *Waste Management & Research* 33: 3–29. https://doi.org/10.1177/0734242X14557382.

Perkins, D.N., Drisse, B., Nxele, T., and Sly, P.D. (2014). E-waste: a global hazard. *Annals of Global Health* 80 (4): 286–295. https://doi.org/10.1016/j.aogh.2014.10.001.

Reck, B.K. and Graedel, T.E. (2012). Challenges in metal recycling. *Science* 337: 690–695.

Robinson, B.H. (2009). E-waste: an assessment of global production and environmental impact. *Science of the Total Environment* 408 (2): 183–191. https://doi.org/10.1016/j.scitotenv.2009.09.044.

Statista (2021). Shipment forecast of tablets, laptops and desktop PCs worldwide from 2010 to 2024 https://www.statista.com/statistics/272595/global-shipments-forecast-for-tablets-laptops-and-desktop-pcs/ (accessed 14 February 2012).

Step (2014). Solving the E-waste Problem White Paper, One Global Definition of E-waste, 13 p. https://www.step-nitiative.org/files/_documents/whitepapers/StEP_WP_One%20Global%20Definition%20of%20E-waste_20140603_amended.pdf (accessed 11 February 2021)

SWISCO (2019). We are forward thinking, Technical Report 2019, p. 14. https://www.erecycling.ch/dam/jcr:15a3a714-7b11 (accessed 11 February 2022).

U.S. Govt (2018). Final list of critical minerals 2018. *Federal Register* 83 (97): 23295–23296. https://www.federalregister.gov/documents/2018/05/18/2018-10667/final-list-of-critical-minerals-2018 (accessed 2 February 2021).

Ullah, Z; Qureshi, M.I; Ahmad, A; Khan, S.U, and Javaid, F, 2021. An experimental study on the mechanical and durability properties assessment of E-waste concrete, *Journal of Building Engineering*, Vol. 38:102177, https://doi.org/10.1016/j.jobe.2021.102177.

UN Economic and Social Commission for Asia and the Pacific (2009). Waste management (hazardous AND solid wastes). Report No. EDD/2009/RIM.18/4, p. 14.

UNEP (2013a). Guideline on environmentally sound testing, refurbishment and repair of used computing equipment. Report No. UNEP/CHW.11/INF/12/Rev.1, 44 p.

UNEP (2013b). Guideline on environmentally sound material recovery and recycling of end-of-life computing equipment. UNEP.CHW.11/INF/13/Rev.1, 65 p.

Wagner, F., Peeters, J., De Keyzer, J. et al. (2019). Quality Assessment of Plastic Recyclatcs from Waste Electrical and Electronic Equipment (WEEE): A Case Study for Desktop Computers, Laptops, and Tablets. In: *Technologies and Eco-innovation towards Sustainability II* (ed. A. Hu, M. Matsumoto, T. Kuo and S. Smith). Singapore: Springer https://doi.org/10.1007/978-981-13-1196-3_12.

Waste Management World 2020). Depth: Cracking the Conundrum of What To Do with Old Landfill Sites? https://waste-management-world.com/a/in-depth-cracking-the-conundrum-of-what-to-do-with-old-landfill-sites (accessed 16 December 2020).

Williams, I.D. (2016). Global metal reuse, and formal and informal recycling from electronic and other high-tech wastes. In: *Metal Sustainability: Global Challenges, Consequences, and Prospects* (ed. R.M. Izatt), 23–51. Chichester: Wiley.

Yang, S., Jiang, J., and Qi Wang, Q. (2020). The novel application of nonmetals from waste printed circuit board in high-performance thermal management materials. *Composites Part A: Applied Science and Manufacturing* 139: 106096. https://doi.org/10.1016/j.compositesa.2020.106096.

Zhu, X., Lane, R., and Werner, L.L. (2017). Modelling in-use stocks and spatial distributions of household electronic devices and their contained metals based on household survey data. *Resources, Conservation and Recycling* 120: 27–37.

Supplementary Readings

Izatt, R.M. (ed.) (2016). *Metal Sustainability: Global Challenges, Consequences, and Prospects.* Chichester: Wiley 527 p.

UNEP (United Nations Environmental Programme) (2015). *Waste or Wealth? A Photo-Illustrated Book with Facts and Data on Valuable Materials in Mobile Phone.* Geneva: Secretariat of the Basel 56 p. UNEP-CHW-WAST-BROC-MPPI-WasteorWealth.English%20(2).pdf (accessed 16 January 2021).

UNEP, Basel Convention (2020). *The E-waste Challenge Massive Open Online Course (MOOC) [Brochure].* MOOC (basel.int).

Web Resources

EPA (US Environmental Protection Agency): Sustainable Management of Electronics|US EPA. Useful source of information on life cycles of electronics, list of e-waste recyclers, and link to detailed information on e-waste issues.

StEP (Solving the E-waste Problem): https://www.step-initiative.org/organisation-rev.html. Solving the E-waste Problem (StEP), an independent, multi-stakeholder organization was established in 2004 to provide guidance to help find solutions to global e-waste challenges. StEP is headquartered in Vienna, Austria. Its website lists numerous publications that contain valuable information, data, and maps on e-waste on a global basis.

UNEP, Basel Convention (2020). *The E-waste Challenge Massive Open Online Course (MOOC) [Brochure].* MOOC (basel.int). This free online certificate is designed to prepare nations to meet the global challenge of e-waste through a free, on online course, covering the nature and scope of e-waste, its health impact, ways to partner with business and engage policy makers to achieve sustainable e-waste management practices. The five modules require about 2 hours each of screen time (can be spread over several sessions each of 30 minutes duration), and average of 4 hours each off-line time, so that the entire course can be completed in about 30 hours to qualify for the certificate.

Acronyms/Symbols

bn	billion
CRT	cathode ray tube
EoL	End of life
EU	European Union
HIPS	High impact polystyrene
ICT	Information and communications technology
KB	kilobyte, 1×10^3 (computer memory)
LCA	Life cycle analysis
LCC	Life cycle cost
m	million
MLPD	Mobile phones, laptops, personal computers, and plasma TVs
Mt	million metric ton
PMMA	Polymethyl methacrylate; also known as Plexiglas, or acrylic
t	metric ton
TB	terabyte 1×10^{12} (generally used for computer memory)
W	weight
y	year

9

Waste Minimization

LEARNING OBJECTIVES

After studying this chapter, you will be able to:

- Discuss the historical development of waste minimization approaches
- Compare and contrast integrated waste management and source reduction
- Explain the zero-waste concept
- Understand US laws related to waste minimization and recycling
- Describe innovative waste minimization trends
- Summarize the status of airplane and ship waste recycling

9.1 Introduction

Any used or discarded material, destined to the landfill, represents a wasted resource in terms of energy and material. Modern nations, especially developed countries, consume excessive amounts of natural resources and products made from them, and generate huge quantities of waste that leads to environmental pollution and creates adverse impacts on human and ecological health. Unsustainable consumption practices, inefficient waste-centric design, built-in obsolescence in manufacturing processes, and throwaway attitude, are the main reasons for ever-increasing amounts of waste. Waste minimization offers a viable solution to this global problem.

> Zero Waste is an ethical, economical, and eco-efficient goal that offers a road map for people to adopt sustainable behavior and modify their life styles to emulate nature where all discarded materials get used as a resource for others.
>
> —*Zero Waste International Alliance*

Waste minimization can be defined as a method or program to eliminate or minimize the quantity of waste with the goal of conserving resources, preventing pollution, and assuring environmental preservation. Every waste generator needs to be part of this effort: from individuals to businesses and industries. A successful waste minimization program does not comprise a single measure, recycling for example, but all possible measures, such as source reduction, reuse, material substitution, process change, recycling, public education, political support, and ongoing research to find innovative methods for resource conservation and waste minimization. The ultimate goal of a waste minimization program should be to eliminate waste altogether,

Introduction to Waste Management: A Textbook, First Edition. Syed E. Hasan.
© 2022 John Wiley & Sons Ltd. Published 2022 by John Wiley & Sons Ltd.

i.e. achieving zero waste (ZW). However, in a practical sense, attaining the zero-waste goal may not be feasible for everyone because of economic, social, and political constraints. Regardless, every generator should set ZW as its waste minimization goal and strive to get as close to ZW as possible.

9.2   Definitions

A number of terms have been used in the waste minimization and recycling business, often in a loose manner. To avoid confusion and to provide a context for the discussions to follow, we begin with providing a correct definition of various terms.

Pollution Prevention: It is any approach or method that eliminates, reduces, or prevents pollution at the source. Pollution prevention (P2) is also referred to as source reduction.

Recycling: A process of removing products or materials from the waste stream, followed by separation and processing and returning it into the economic mainstream in the form of raw materials, or remelting into new finished goods. Converting waste papers into newsprint, waste plastics into fence, benches; aluminum beverage cans into metal aluminum; scrap steel into new steel beams, etc., are all examples of recycling.

Reuse: Use of a product or material repeatedly for the same purpose, either in its original form or with little enhancement or change, e.g. refilling a returnable bottle with juice or water, a canvas bag for shopping, etc.

Reclamation: The process of collecting and separating wastes to make them suitable for reuse. Converting wastewater into clean water that can be reused for other purposes, such as irrigation, or replenishing surface water, or for groundwater recharge; collecting volatile organic solvent in the waste stream for use as input material for making other products as in waste exchange are some examples of reclamation.

Refurbishing: A process of making superficial or cosmetic changes to update the appearance of waste material, such as cleaning, painting, or refinishing to make it suitable for reuse. This term is often associated with used office furniture, clothes, etc., and differs from remanufacturing in that none of the structural parts of the product is replaced.

Remanufacturing: The process of restoring used durable discarded materials by replacing worn or damaged parts to new condition, making them suitable for use in their original function, e.g. salvaging useable parts from discarded laptops or smartphones to replace broken or nonfunctioning parts in another laptop or phone.

Repurposing: Using industrial byproducts or unwanted materials for a new purpose; giving second life to a discarded material, e.g. using the discarded wooden floor of a basketball court to make furniture, paneling, etc.

Resource recovery: A general term for extracting material from the waste stream to produce energy or products for different uses, e.g. glass from waste for use in road construction, or, shredded rubber from used tires to make mulch, swing and slides, or cushions, in a school playground, etc.

Source reduction: The practice of reducing the amount of materials in the manufacturing process by redesigning the product, modifying the manufacturing process, changing purchasing preferences, and reusing materials, in order to minimize the quantity and/or toxicity of the waste generated. This term is often used synonymously with "waste reduction."

Source separation: Removal of useable material from the waste stream; done by individuals or robots and their separation into metals, cans, plastics, paper, etc.

Waste to energy: Conversion of combustible waste materials into energy by burning them in an incinerator. The heat produced can be used directly for space heating or, most commonly, for making electricity.

9.3 Approaches to Waste Minimization

Concern about reducing the volume, and safe management of waste is not a phenomenon of modern time alone: it is a vexing issue that has been of concern for centuries. Accordingly, our philosophy and approaches to waste management have undergone many changes over time. These changes reflect prevailing societal attitudes, level of economic development, industrialization, and heightened awareness of environmental fragility. Various approaches from *dilute and disperse* practiced in the first century of the Industrial Revolution to *concentrate and contain* during the decades of the 1930s and *conserve and recycle* during the 1970s and early 1980s, to *integrated waste management*, *pollution prevention*, and *zero waste* initiatives of the late 1990s and early 2000s, have been practiced. Each method served the purpose in a limited way, which was consistent with the accepted societal standards of the time, but gave way to better methods that incorporated new scientific knowledge, technological advancements, and increased understanding of the vulnerability of the environment, along with changing nature and composition of wastes.

Up until the 1970s, discussions on waste issues were limited to wastes generated *after* a product was manufactured. Recycling and reclamation were the main emphases for reducing waste volume and capturing useful materials from the waste stream for reuse. This *end-of-the pipeline* approach, despite resulting in a notable reduction in waste quantity and increased recycling rate, ignored the possibility of reducing waste *before* and *during* the manufacturing process. The concept and methods of limiting or eliminating waste before and during the manufacturing process, termed non-waste technology (NWT), was first discussed in 1973 by the committee on Environmental Problems of the Economic Commission for Europe (ECE), which developed the following definition for NWT at its 1974 meeting in Geneva, Switzerland:

> The practical application of knowledge, methods and means, so as within the needs of man, to provide most rational use of natural resources and energy and to protect the environment.
> *(ECE 1978).*

In the USA, the concept of waste minimization in a legal way was first put forth in the 1984 amendments to its Resource Conservation and Recovery Act of 1976. The new act, called Hazardous and Solid Waste Amendments (HSWA), required generators of hazardous waste to certify compliance with waste minimization requirements when preparing the hazardous waste manifest (discussed in Chapter 3). HSWA defined waste minimization as "the use of source reduction and/or environmentally sound recycling methods prior to treating or disposing of hazardous wastes."

Waste minimization was reinforced in the Pollution Prevention Act (commonly referred to as the P2) of 1990 that also led to the creation of a national policy to eliminate or reduce pollution at the source. The law states:

> The Congress hereby declares it to be the national policy of the United States that pollution should be prevented or reduced at the source whenever feasible; pollution that cannot be prevented should be recycled in an environmentally safe manner, whenever feasible; pollution that cannot be prevented or recycled should be treated in an

environmentally safe manner whenever feasible; and disposal or other release into the environment should be employed only as a last resort and should be conducted in an environmentally safe manner.

The P2 Act expanded the scope of waste minimization to include pollution prevention as its key element, and provided a hierarchical guideline for source reduction, reuse, recycling, and treatment of the waste before its final disposal (Figure 9.1). Pollution prevention essentially includes any method that can be used to reduce, eliminate, or prevent pollution at its source. Reducing pollution at the source means less waste to control or dispose of, and in the case of hazardous waste, less waste to treat before disposal along with reduced legal liabilities. In the energy sector, P2 includes: improving efficiency in energy use, and substituting environmentally benign energy sources for fossil fuels. In the agricultural sector, it involves reducing the use of water and chemicals; and using environmentally safe pesticides. In industries, it includes modifying the manufacturing process to produce nonhazardous wastes by using nontoxic or less toxic chemicals as cleaners and degreasers; and implementing water and energy conservation practices. Pollution prevention is intertwined with waste minimization because effective P2 measures invariably result in lower quantities of waste.

Controlling pollution and reducing waste at the source can be achieved by employing a number of techniques. The first step is to take a careful look at the process used for making the product. No matter, whether it is a building, a complex machinery, such as an automobile, or a relatively simple product like a cooking utensil, all of them use certain raw materials (called feedstock) that are subjected to a series of physical (heat, pressure, and mechanical), chemical (treatment with acidic or alkaline, organic or inorganic compounds), and/or biological (using microbes, genetic modifications, etc.) processes to manufacture the final product. A careful review of each step of the manufacturing process – from procurement, and shipment of raw materials by the supplier, to arrival and storage at the factory, and its use in making the finished product – offers opportunities to reduce or eliminate waste. Figure 9.2 summarizes various options to reduce the amount of waste, thereby preventing pollution at the manufacturing facility.

Following the passage of the P2 Act, and incorporating green manufacturing emphasis, the "Recycling" part in Figure 9.2 has been removed and current waste minimization techniques focus

Figure 9.1 Waste minimization hierarchy. *Source:* US EPA.

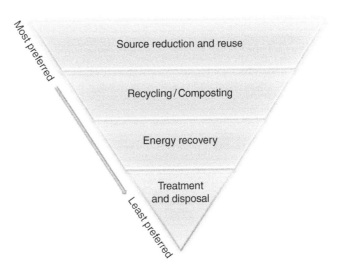

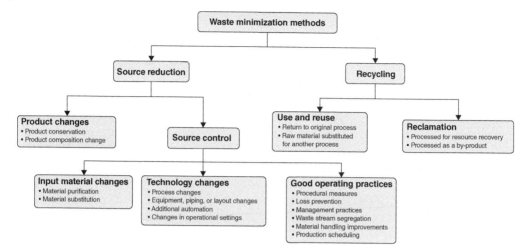

Figure 9.2 Waste minimization methods. *Source:* Modified after US EPA 1988.

solely on "Source Reduction" because recycling and reclamation although desirable, do not reduce pollution that is generated before and during the manufacturing process.

Source reduction includes a number of approaches, such as good operating practices, inventory control, spill and leak prevention, surface preparation and finishing, cleaning and degreasing; and material, or product modifications. These are described below.

Good Operating Practices include improved maintenance scheduling, record keeping, or procedures; adjusting production schedule to minimize equipment and feedstock changeovers; and in-line product quality monitoring or other process analysis system.

Inventory Control involves establishing procedures to ensure that materials do not stay in inventory beyond their shelf life (expiration date); using outdated material if still effective; eliminating shelf-life requirements for stable materials; using better labeling procedures; and setting up a clearinghouse to exchange materials that would otherwise be discarded.

Spill and Leak Prevention includes improved storage or stacking procedures; improved loading and unloading procedures and transfer operations; installing overflow alarms or automatic shut-off valves; installing vapor recovery systems; inspection or monitoring of potential spill or leak sources.

Raw Material Modifications include increased purity of raw materials; substituting raw materials, or reagent with a different material, or with none or less hazardous chemical.

Process Modifications involve optimizing reaction conditions or improving synthesis efficiency; instituting recirculation system within a process; modifying equipment, layout, or piping; using a different catalyst; minimizing throwing away of empty bulk containers; reducing the use of organic solvent; and using biotechnology in the manufacturing process, where appropriate.

Cleaning and Degreasing include modification of stripping and cleaning equipment; replacing solvent cleaning by mechanical stripping or cleaning; substituting solvent cleaners by aqueous cleaners; modification of containment procedures for cleaning units; improving draining procedures; installing or modifying design and operation of rinse system.

Surface Preparation and Finishing include modifying spray systems or equipment; coating materials substitution; improving application techniques; modifying the spray system to desirable improvement in its efficiency.

Product Modifications involve changing product specifications; modifying the design or composition of the product; improving packaging; developing new chemical products to replace a previous (more hazardous) chemical product.

Current approaches to "green manufacturing" and "cleaner production" hold great promise in that both aim at reduction or elimination of pollutants at the source, i.e. at the beginning of the pipeline, and not after they are generated-end of the pipeline. It is very likely that future approaches to waste minimization will be further modified by incorporating new advances in material sciences and technology, making it a more efficient and cost-effective process. Waste minimization should, therefore, be viewed as a dynamic exercise that keeps pace with new knowledge and advances in technology. Sustained efforts to waste minimization is an ongoing process and in recent years, concepts of life cycle analysis (LCA), and products repair and remanufacturing (PRR), are being increasingly incorporated in waste minimization practices.

Building upon RCRA and P2 laws, the US EPA developed a Waste Minimization Program that, besides assuring legal compliance, targeted 31 Priority Chemicals for elimination or substantial reduction from commerce and industries. These chemicals are called persistent bioaccumulative and toxic (PBT) chemicals and include 28 organic compounds, three heavy metals, existing and banned pesticides, and other dangerous chemicals (Table 9.1) that are highly toxic, do not easily biodegrade, persist in the environment for a long time, bioaccumulate in humans and/or wildlife, in food chains, and can travel over large distances.

Table 9.1   The US EPA List of Priority Chemicals (PCs) for elimination/reduction.

Chemical	CAS number
1,2,4-Trichlorobenzene	120-82-1
1,2,4,5-Tetrachlorobenzene	95-94-3
2,4,5-Trichlorophenol	95-95-4
4-Bromophenyl phenyl ether	101-55-3
Acenaphthene	83-32-9
Acenaphthylene	208-96-8
Anthracene	120-12-7
Benzo(g,h,i)perylene	191-24-2
Dibenzofuran	132-64-9
Dioxins/Furans	1746-01-6
Endosulfan, alpha and Endosulfan, beta	959-98-8 and 33213-65-9
Fluorene	86-73-7
Heptachlor and Heptachlor epoxide	76-44-8 and 1024-57-3
Hexachlorobenzene	118-74-1
Hexachlorobutadiene	87-68-3
Hexachlorocyclohexane, gamma- (Lindane)	58-89-9
Hexachloroethane	67-72-1
Methoxychlor	72-43-5
Naphthalene	91-20-3

(Continued)

Table 9.1 (Continued)

Chemical	CAS number
Pendimethalin	40487-42-1
Pentachlorobenzene	608-93-5
Pentachloronitrobenzene (Quintozene)	82-68-8
Pentachlorophenol	87-86-5
Phenanthrene	85-01-8
Polycyclic Aromatic Compounds (PACs) / PAH Group Polychlorinated Biphenyls (PCBs)	1336-36-3
Pyrene	129-00-0
Trifluralin (common herbicide)	1582-09-8
Cadmium	7440-43-9
Lead	7439-92-1
Mercury	7439-97-6

PBTs are generated by industries and end up in the soil, sediment, groundwater, surface water, air, plant, animal, and human tissues. The priority is to first eliminate these chemicals at the source, but if they cannot be eliminated or reduced at the source, then they should be recovered or recycled.

Twenty-one of the 31 PBTs have been included in the list of some 650 chemicals that industries have to report under the requirements of the Emergency Planning and Community Right-to-Know Act (see Chapter 3 for details). The law requires industries to develop and implement a waste minimization plan to reduce or eliminate the release of toxic chemicals including the 21 PBTs, and submit it to the EPA. The data is analyzed and published in an annual report called the *Toxic Release Inventory* (TRI). The waste minimization program has been very effective in reducing the quantities of hundreds of hazardous and toxic chemicals by nearly 54% between 1990 and 2016 (EPA 2020). Implementation of the P2 program has improved the recycling rate from 36% in 2003 to 53% in 2019 (EPA 2021)

A comprehensive study by Ranson et al. (2015), using rigorous analyses of TRI data for the period 1991–2012, and involving 334000 source reduction projects, found that in 22 years the P2 program had resulted in an average reduction of harmful chemicals by about 13% (range 9–16%) and eliminated between 2.27 and 6.35 million MT (5–14 billion lb.) of toxic release (Figure 9.3). Of the several source reduction methods, the raw material modification was found to yield maximum reduction.

Specific examples of various source reduction approaches used by manufacturers are available at EPA website in its Pollution Prevention (P2) and TRI topic under Toxic Release Inventory program Pollution Prevention (P2) and TRI US EPA (https://www.epa.gov/toxics-release-inventory-tri-program/pollution-prevention-p2-and-tri).

The size of the product package is another important element in waste minimization. A recent study by Becerril-Arreola and Bucklin (2021) concluded that changing the packing size of PET water bottles from small <16 oz (473 mL) to medium size (16–100 oz; 0.5–3 L) could reduce PET waste by >10000 t annually in the USA alone.

Globally, waste minimization is being practiced in the EU and many other countries. The United Nations Environmental Program (UNEP) in 1990 developed the idea of *Cleaner Production* and

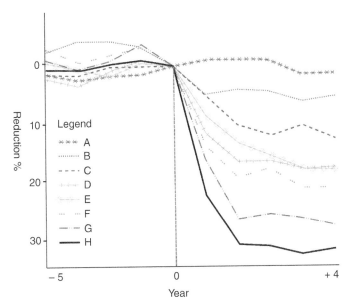

Figure 9.3 Comparison of various source reduction methods (Data from Ranson, et al. 2015, modified for illustration). A-Inventory control; B-Good operating practices; C-Spill and leak prevention; D-Surface preparation and finishing; E-Process modifications; F-Product modifications; G-Cleaning and degreasing; H-Raw materials modifications.

defined it as: "The continuous application of an integrated environmental strategy to processes products and services to increase efficiency and reduce risks to humans and the environment." Later, the concept was broadened to include resource efficiency, called Resource Efficiency and Cleaner Production (RECP) that attempts to: (i) improve production efficiency by optimization creative use of input materials, energy, and water at all stages of the production cycle; (ii) use of sound environmental management principles to minimize adverse impacts of industrial production systems on the environment, and (iii) promote human development by minimization of risks to people and communities while supporting their social and economic development.

The UNEP is actively promoting RECP and offers training programs and financial assistance to developing nations to incorporate it in their sustainable development plans.

9.4 Recycling

Recycling has been practiced from time immemorial. Before the large-scale application of chemical fertilizers in agriculture, it was a common practice to dispose of animal manure and human waste (night soil) in the fields to provide nutrients to plants. Animal excreta, leaves and plant debris, and human waste were applied to agricultural lands for centuries to increase soil productivity. Animal manures are rich in ^{15}N, the isotope of nitrogen particularly beneficial to plants, and are known to have been used to increase crop yield as far back as 6000 years ago (Bogaard et al. 2013). A comprehensive review of the physical, chemical, and biological composition of human excreta (feces and urine) from many developed and developing countries of the world by Rose et al. (2015), found that both urine and feces contain fair amounts of N, P, and K (more in urine than feces), which are essential plant nutrients. They also reported that feces contained several heavy metal micronutrients such Cu, Fe, Mn, Mo, Zn, Ni, and Cd which were absent in urine. An average calorific value of about 62 000 kcal/kg (17.2 MJ/kg), which is nearly the same as wood and more than paper, was also reported for human feces.

In a simple way, recycling can be defined as a process to make used or discarded materials useable again. Examples include converting used beverage cans to make aluminum metal; turning discarded paper products into newsprint, automobile batteries to produce metal lead, etc. A relatively new method involves converting used fats, oil, and grease (FOGs), generated primarily in restaurants, into methane to produce electricity. FOG includes cooking oil, animal fat and lard, grease, butter, tallow, shortening, and margarine, all of which are used in food processing and preparation of food. If not properly trapped, uncaptured FOGs enter sewer lines, causing blockages and sewage spills that pose a threat to public health and safety. When FOG is poured down the drain, it cools and solidifies on the walls of the sewer pipes, restricting or impeding wastewater flow. This can result in a wastewater backup into homes and businesses or discharge into the environment. Diverting and collecting FOGs from entry into the sewer system is an effective way to minimize their accumulation in sewers. Using FOGs to generate electricity is an added benefit that should be included in the city's waste minimization plans.

Figure 9.4 shows a WtE energy plant at the Douglas L. Smith Middle Basin Wastewater Treatment facility in Overland Park, Johnson County, Kansas, where FOGs collected from area restaurants and food processors are fed into anaerobic digesters. Microbial action breaks down FOGs into methane and other compounds. Methane is separated, cleaned, and fed into a generator to produce electricity. The plant generates about 7000 MWh of electricity that meets the electricity need of all buildings and equipment at the wastewater treatment facility, saving $600 000 annually and eliminating about 8800 tons of GHGs.

Figure 9.4   Waste-to-Energy plant, Johnson County Wastewater Treatment facility, Overland Park, Kansas. *Source:* S.E. Hasan (author).

Recycling is market-driven and unless the cost of recycled material is less than what it would cost to produce the same material from virgin sources, it would not be economically viable. Plastics and paper are two main waste materials whose recycling is highly dependent on global market demand. Metal recycling, in general, is not impacted because of its higher market value, but the paper and plastic recycling market fluctuates widely. For example, before 2017, when China stopped importing waste paper from the USA and other developed countries, the paper recycling market was thriving, commanding a price of $75/t that fell to just a few dollars/t in 2018. Plastic prices also fell drastically. Up until the Chinese ban, discarded plastics had a profitable recycling market. A large portion of waste plastics was exported to China from the USA, Europe, Japan, and Australia, commanding an average price of over $2000/t but plummeted to below $100/t after the ban.

Before the ban, 70% of waste plastics collected for recycling in the USA, and 95% in the EU were sent to Chinese processors. Cargo ships – loaded with consumer goods produced in China for delivery in the United States of America and Europe, that otherwise would have returned empty – offered cheap transportation. In addition, low labor cost, and acceptance of contaminated paper and plastics were other factors in making it a profitable venture. This has changed as the new Chinese law prohibits the import of contaminated papers and plastics, imposing a limit of a maximum 5% contamination, (i.e. 95% purity) for the import of waste paper and plastics.

While the 2017 Chinese ban on importing contaminated waste paper, plastics, and textiles hit the Western recycling markets hard, it opened up new destinations for these materials. Some of the inferior grade paper and plastic wastes have been diverted to other south Asian countries, such as India, Indonesia, Malaysia, and South Korea where environmental requirements are less stringent. This is however temporary, as increasing environmental awareness and concern for pollution prevention in developing countries will ultimately put an end to import of poor-quality waste materials for recycling.

The recycling industry in the West took the Chinese ban as an opportunity for new initiatives to improve the quality of waste materials and reduce contamination by upgrading equipment, and adding additional workers to enhance quality control during waste sorting. It also prompted improvement in the design and efficiency of automated sorting machines, using optical sensors, and a variety of detectors to identify and sort metals, mixed color materials, etc. accurately and rapidly. Using advanced robotics and artificial intelligence (AI) technology manufacturers have recently introduced smart and highly efficient automatic sorting machines. For example, the SamurAI™ sorting robot, manufactured by Machinex Corp; Canada, and introduced in the market in July 2020, uses four articulation robots and AI technology to attain precise quality control and accurate identification of various materials in the waste stream. Some other leading automated waste sorting machine manufacturers include CP Manufacturing, the USA; Beston Co., China; and others. Such machines are expected to become quite prevalent in the waste recycling industry in future.

On a long-term basis, source reduction seems to be the most desirable waste minimization option and should be given top priority. Past experience shows that it can be accomplished by prohibiting manufacturing single use consumer items, and imposing taxes on recyclable items that people have tendency to throw away as waste. Such measures have been successfully implemented in several countries: For instance, the European parliament in October 2018 agreed to ban plastic cutlery and plates, cotton buds, straws, drink stirrers, and balloon sticks. Implementation in the EU countries is expected in the 2020s. The United Kingdom is planning to impose a tax on manufacturers of plastic packaging containing less than 30% recycled materials. Norway recently adopted a system where single-use bottle makers pay an environmental levy that declines as the return rate for their products rises. This has resulted in a return rate of over one billion bottles in a short period of four years. In addition, many other countries are diverting their waste paper and plastics to WtE facilities for producing electricity.

9.4.1 Plastic Recycling

Plastics are everywhere: in rivers, lakes, oceans, land, human body, marine animals, and even in the air (Wetherbee et al. 2019). Plastics or resins that belong to the synthetic polymers class of chemicals have become ubiquitous in modern life. The popularity and widespread use of plastics can be gauged from the fact that in 1960 waste plastics accounted for barely 0.1 million tons of the total weight of MSW generated in the USA, but rose to 13.2 million tons in 2017 (EPA 2019).

The huge *plastic ocean garbage patch* made a worldwide headline in the early 2000s. Initially, it was thought to be floating on the ocean surface, but subsequently, it was found that besides larger pieces floating at the surface, microplastics are present in oceans at various depths below the surface. It is estimated that about 10% of the mass of all plastics floating around in the form of a gyre in the world's oceans may be present below the surface at depths of up to 2 km (Egger et al. 2020). The finding adds to the increasing problems of persistence and distribution of fuel-based plastics and highlights the need to replace them with fully biodegradable plastics.

Several unique properties of plastics, such as high tensile strength, lightweight, durability, tear and shatter-resistance, made them material of choice in tubing, packaging, construction, and containers replacing rubber, glass, wood, paper, etc. Packaging products are made from different plastic resins, most of which are derived from petroleum. Soft drink and water bottles made out of polyethylene terephthalate (PET); milk and water jugs from high-density polyethylene (HDPE); film products (including bags and sacks) from low-density polyethylene (LDPE); other containers and packaging (including packing clamshells, trays, cups, lids, egg cartons, loose fill, produce baskets, coatings, and closures) are made from polyvinyl chloride (PVC), polystyrene (PS), polypropylene (PP), and other resins. Plastics are also used in the manufacture of durable goods, such as appliances, furniture, luggage, casings of lead-acid batteries, and other products. Table 9.2 shows the code, applications, recyclability, and properties of various plastics.

Table 9.2 Code, application, and properties of common plastics.

Plastic code chemical name	Packaging Applications	Recycled products	Properties (ρ in g/L^3; MP (melting point) temperature in °C
♷ 1 PETE Polyethylene terephthalate	Soft drink, water bottles, mouthwash bottles; peanut butter and salad dressing containers; juice bottles; vegetable oil bottles	Containers for both food and nonfood products. Fibers for clothing, athletic shoes, luggage, upholstery, furniture, carpet; fiberfill for sleeping bags and winter coats; industrial strapping, sheet, and film; automotive parts, such as luggage racks, grills, headliners, fuse boxes, bumpers, and door panels.	PETE or PET is a polyester; transparent, resealable, shatter-resistant. Most recycled resin in the world. Postconsumer recycled PET yarns are in heavy demand for making carpets and producing fiberfill and geotextiles. Most common food packaging resin. Melting point (MP): 250–260; Density (ρ): 1.35–1.38 g/L^3

Table 9.2   (Continued)

Plastic code chemical name	Packaging Applications	Recycled products	Properties (ρ in g/L^3; MP (melting point) temperature in °C
2 **HDPE** High Density polyethylene	Milk containers, juice and water bottles; bleach, detergent, and shampoo bottles; trash bags, grocery and retail carrying bags; motor oil bottles; butter and margarine tubs; household cleaner bottles, yogurt containers, and cereal box liners.	Drainage pipe; liquid laundry detergent container; oil bottles; pens; benches; doghouses, floor tile, picnic tables, fencing, lumber, and mailbox posts.	HDPE bottles are both pigmented and unpigmented; unpigmented resin is translucent. Has good stiffness and barrier properties, ideal for products with short shelf-life such as milk. Good chemical resistance allows use as containers for household or industrial chemicals. Pigmented resin has higher crack and chemical resistance than unpigmented. MP: 115; ρ: 0.947–0.977 g/L^3
3 **PVC** Polyvinyl chloride	Cooking oil bottles; window cleaner, detergent, and shampoo bottles; clear food packaging; wire and cable jackets; medical tubing; significant usage as siding, piping, and windows.	Binders; decking, paneling, mud flaps, roadway gutters; flooring; cables, speed bumps; and mats.	Vinyl, or polyvinylchloride (PVC) is transparent; possess good toughness and strength; resistant to grease, oil, and chemicals. It has excellent chemical resistance; well-suited for injection molding. ρ: 1.35–1.50 g/L^3. MP: 85
4 **LDPE** Low-density Polyethylene	Squeezable bottles, bread bags, frozen food bags, tote bags, clothing, furniture, dry cleaning bags, and carpet; wire and cable insulation and jackets.	Film and sheet; floor tile; garbage can liners; shipping envelopes; furniture, compost bins, trash cans; paneling; lumber, landscaping ties.	LDPE has good strength and high flexibility; and ease of heat sealing, ease of processing, and barrier to moisture. ρ: 0.92 g/L^3; MP: 101–117
5 **PP** Polypropylene	Yogurt containers, syrup, and ketchup bottles, caps, straws, medicine bottles.	Traffic lights; battery cables; brooms, ice scrapers; brushes; auto battery cases; landscape borders, rakes; bicycle racks, pallets, and trays.	PPE is strong and resistant to chemicals. High strength, resistance to chemicals, and heat; High melting point makes it suitable for use as a hot liquid container. ρ: 0.9 g/L^3 (lowest of all resins). MP: 160–170.
6 **PS** Polystyrene	Hot cups and tubs, trays; to-go food containers; shipping cushion; cartons.	Thermal insulation; light switch plates; egg cartons; picture frames; rulers; foam packing, flower pots; hangers; carry-out containers.	Ease of forming, rigidity; clarity, low heat, good thermal insulation. Polystyrene can be made into rigid or foamed products. ρ: 1.04–1.05 g/L^3; MP: 100–120.
7 **OTHER**	Polycarbonate; bottles; safety glasses; DVDs; eyeglass lenses; auto headlight lens.	Electronics housing; auto parts; plastic lumber; custom-made products	The category of "Other" includes any resin not numbered 1, 2, 3, 4, 5, or 6; e.g. acrylic, nylon, ABS, BPA, PLA plastics; melamine, etc.

ABS: Acrylonitrile butadiene styrene; BPA: Bisphenol A, used to make polycarbonate plastics that are used in containers to store food and beverages, such as water bottles; PLA: (polylactic acid, corn-based plastic).

It must be noted that although the recycling symbol is assigned to all seven types of resins, not all of them are recyclable. Some, like PET, can be easily recycled into new products while PVC, PS, and several in the OTHERS category contain toxic chemicals making them unsuitable for recycling into products that might get into direct contact with people, such a cloth, food containers, etc. Plastics with recycling codes 3 and 7 made from bisphenols or phthalates are harmful (Sierra 2020). Although # 1 PET is relatively safe, it should be kept away from heat to prevent leaching of harmful constituents. In addition, PET is not impermeable, so its low porosity can allow harmful microbes to accumulate since many of them are of nano-size (0.5–5 nm). An empty PET water bottle, therefore, should not be used as a makeshift container.

9.5 Innovative Waste Minimization Technologies

The environmental sustainability movement of the past decades resulted in concerted efforts to find new ways to convert waste materials into useful substances. New technologies have been evolving at a rapid pace, most of them coming from universities and research institutions, but concerned individuals have also been applying novel ideas toward effective waste minimization. A brief discussion of some of these approaches is presented next to illustrate the potentially unlimited possibilities of innovation in the waste minimization field.

9.5.1 Innovation in Plastic Packaging

Extremely slow and minimal degradability of fuel-derived packaging plastics has been a nagging problem, driving focused research to develop plant-derived, easily biodegradable substitutes. A promising development in the Netherlands, now being piloted by Avantium, a Dutch renewable chemical company, based in Amsterdam, uses sugars derived from wheat, beat, and corn to manufacture plastic. Packaging materials and beverage bottles can be made to biodegrade into simple elements and compounds within a year when mixed with compost, and in a few years if left in the open (compared to several decades for conventional bottles). Avantium has developed a new technology that uses polycondensation of the monomers FDCA (2,5-furandicarboxylic acid) and MEG (mono-ethylene glycol) to produce polyethylene furanoate (PEF), claimed to be superior to the widely used petroleum-based packaging plastics. The unique molecular structure of PEF imparts them high strength and low gas permeability – the latter being an advantageous property in beverage packaging where the escape of gas has to be prevented. The CO_2 permeability of PEF is over 10 times lower than PET plastic, making it a very desirable material for carbonated drink packaging that requires a strong barrier against the release of CO_2 gas. Avantium has started producing thin films of PEF that can be bonded on paper packaging cartons for carbonated drinks, eliminating the need for metal cans. Avantium has joined hands with major corporations to create what it calls *PEFerence* consortium, an EU-sponsored project to establish an innovative FDCA and PEF supply chain. A plant to manufacture 5000 tons is under construction with a planned startup in 2023 (Avantium 2020). FDCA will be converted into PEF and will be used in a variety of high-value applications including: specialty films for use in electronics and displays; PEF-enhanced bottles for premium beverages and cosmetics; and recyclable flexible packaging, including bottles for carbonated soft drinks and other beverages. Avantium has also started manufacturing transparent recyclable plastic storage bags that could potentially replace existing plastic bags which are not recyclable and take decades to biodegrade.

Many additives, such as dyes, fillers, or flame retardants substances that are used in conventional plastic packaging to make it tough and flexible are tightly bonded to the monomers that stay in plastic during the recycling process (e.g. chopping into tiny bits, melting), resulting in degradation of its quality and performance. For this reason, a reusable shopping bag made with recycled plastic quickly wears out. It cannot be upcycled or even recycled to make a new product; it is either incinerated to produce heat, electricity, or buried in a landfill. An evolving research investigation involving laboratory formulation of new plastic, called poly diketoenamine or PDK, that can be recycled indefinitely into new products of any shape, or color without degradation in its characteristics, holds the potential to change plastic lifecycle from linear to circular. The recyclable PKD, developed at the US Department of Energy's Lawrence Berkeley National Laboratory in the USA, can be disassembled into its constituent components at the molecular level by treating it with a strong acidic solution, such as H_2SO_4. The acid breaks the bonds between the monomers and separate them from the chemical additives, making it ready for new uses (Christensen et al. 2019). Many common plastic products, such as adhesives, computer cables, smartphone cases, shoes, and other products that are currently not recyclable, can be made by molding hot PDK plastics, which will be repeatedly recycled. The PDK- and PEF-based plastics offer a promising alternative to many fuel-based, nonrecyclable types that are currently in widespread use.

9.5.2 Microfactories

Microfactories represent yet another innovation to transform waste materials into useful products, thus enabling communities to achieve their sustainability goals. Microfactories are small or mini-factories that work on the principle of "economy of purpose." Modular microfactories are small, do not need large space, can operate at sites as small as $50\,m^2$, and can be conveniently located near waste stockpiles. Microfactories offer a viable solution to burning or burying waste materials that can be transformed into useful substances and products, bringing economic benefits to the local community. Microfactories are ideal for remote locations, or in small islands where waste transportation and processing costs are prohibitive.

The world's first microfactory was established in April 2018 at the University of New South Wales (UNSW) at Sydney, Australia, at its Center for Sustainable Materials Research and Technology (SMaRT), after 10 years of extensive research, lab investigations, and bench-scale testing. Results indicate that almost anything in waste streams can be transformed into value-added products. Waste plastics, for example, can be subjected to a series of processes to create plastic filaments for 3D printing. Electronic waste from discarded smartphones and laptops can be converted into a variety of valuable materials for reuse, thereby providing a sustainable solution for sound management of the huge quantities of electronic waste that, when not properly managed, endanger human and ecological health. Microfactories can transform several components of the common waste stream such as plastic, glass, and tires into useful products for new applications, thus contributing to the circular economy (UNSW 2018).

A microfactory consists of a number of small modules, each with a specific function, to transform waste materials into useful products. Discarded electronic devices such as computers, smartphones, and printers are first placed into one module to break them apart, while the next module may use a robot to identify and separate useful parts. Another module may use a small furnace that transforms these parts into valuable materials under a precisely controlled thermal process. The transformed products include metal alloys, such as copper and tin, along with a range of micromaterials. The micromaterials can be used in industrial-grade ceramics, while plastics from computers, printers, and other discarded sources are put through another module that produces filaments suitable for 3D printing. The metal alloys can be used as metal components in new or existing manufacturing processes.

Old tires can be transformed into slag foaming reagents in the electric arc furnace (EAF) process to facilitate a chemical reaction which is crucial to a good-quality product. This process not only reuses a waste material, but improves energy efficiency, and reduces emissions and cuts down on the demand for nonrenewable coking coal.

Waste shells of Australian macadamia nuts were used in the microfactory to transform them into high-value silicon carbide and silicon nitride – super-hard ceramics that can be used for a range of applications in medical devices, drilling tools, and high-temperature engine linings in performance cars.

9.5.3 Repurposing

Repurposing means acquiring an unwanted material from an owner, or removing one from a waste stream, and using it for another purpose. Repurposed materials are unwanted byproducts or waste materials that have value in "as is" form. Anything can be included under this broad definition: chemicals, concrete, glass, metals, woods, and many others. Examples include using bowling alley flooring for making new furniture; discarded flooring materials from gymnasium as new flooring in the hotel meeting room; or, giving a second life to old ski cables by using it as hand railing in a luxury condo building, etc. (Figure 9.5).

While the idea of using a material after it is no longer needed and making it available to another user is very simple and attractive, turning it into a viable business enterprise is a complex undertaking; but the example of a relatively young company called *repurposedMATERIALS*, based in Denver, the USA is very instructive. Started by a college student in 2010, the company purchases waste byproducts or used materials, mainly from industries – that otherwise would have ended up in the landfill – and sells them to buyers who put it to new use. The company started by leasing a warehouse in Denver, but in a short period added three additional warehouses (average size 30 000 sq. ft.), located in Chicago, Illinois; Dallas-Fort Worth, Texas; and Williston, South Carolina. While in concept, *repurposedMATERIALS* may be compared to an active waste exchange, the main difference is that the company purchases the unwanted material soon after it is discarded or declared surplus, enabling the seller to receive payment immediately, thus eliminating the need to maintain the inventory at his facility until a buyer is found. This arrangement is preferred by the waste material owner who can free up storage space as soon as the deal is finalized.

9.5.4 NGOs' Efforts

A number of NGOs, mainly in the developing countries, are also contributing to waste minimization efforts. Two examples are included to illustrate an individual's role in waste minimization and pollution prevention:

An enterprising woman in Ghana established a plastic recycling foundation to empower poor women engaged in waste collection. The women go to collect recyclable waste plastics from churches and mosques, bring them to the foundation, which sells them to waste recyclers. A portion of the money earned is used to pay waste collectors, and the other to local public schools to pay for sanitation and hygiene supplies, and water bill (paid directly to the utility supplier). The foundation runs mainly on donations but its goal is to become self-supporting.

Another example is from Pamohi, a remote village in the northeastern part of India in the state of Assam, where a young couple started the Akshar School in 2016 for children of poor people,

(a)

(b)

(c)

Figure 9.5 Discarded materials repurposed for various uses: (a) Bowling alley flooring repurposed for furniture; (b) Gymnasium floor used for flooring in a hotel meeting room; and (c) old ski cables for stair railings in luxury apartments. Left and right sides show the before and after conditions of the material. *Source:* Repurposed Materials.

dropout kids, and child labors. The school does not charge a fee but students are required to collect recyclable clean plastics and bring it to a recycling center at the school in exchange for the day's lesson. The school turns the waste plastics into bricks and plastic beams for use in construction. The children were asked to also bring waste plastics from their homes but parents did not participate and kept dumping and burning plastics outside their homes. The school, that offers free education, then imposed a fee on these families. This instantly changed their mindset and resulted in saving discarded plastics and sending them to the school to avoid fees. The children get a fee waiver if they bring 20 discarded plastic items from their homes and local area each week. The successful innovative project that started from a school in a village is now being established in selected schools in major cities like Delhi and Mumbai in India (Lal 2020).

9.6 Waste Exchange

A waste exchange is an online service to facilitate putting waste materials back into use by matching companies generating specific wastes with companies that use those wastes as input material in their manufacturing process. The term waste exchange is synonymous with materials exchange. Waste exchanges are private- or government-funded organizations that bring together generators and manufacturers of waste materials who can use the waste product of the former as a feedstock or substitute material in their operations. There are two types of waste exchanges: *information exchanges* (passive exchanges) and *material exchanges* (active exchanges). Information exchanges are clearinghouses for information on wastes generated by one manufacturer that may be needed by another as feedstock. Information exchange put generators in touch with potential users for using waste materials back into their manufacturing processes. Material exchanges take actual physical possession of the waste and may initiate or actively participate in the transfer of wastes from the generator to the user. A majority of waste exchanges in the USA deal with hazardous waste. In fact, the first such waste operation was started in 1973 by Paul Palmer, a physical chemist, in California. He named his company Zero Waste Systems that recycled used industrial solvents and deconstructed circuit boards to recover gold and rare earth elements after chemical treatment in a laboratory at his facility. The hazardous waste materials were mainly collected from Silicon Valley, California, recycled, cleaned, and sold to other users. Palmer deserves the credit for being the first to start hazardous waste recycling in a methodical and scientific way long before the USA and other countries felt the need for proper management of hazardous waste. However, the term "zero waste (ZW)" was used as the company moniker and did not imply the elimination of waste to zero or near zero. Later, during the 1990s, he promoted the concept of ZW as it is applied today (Palmer 2004, p. 8). On the other hand, Zero Waste Systems deserves the credit for being the first active waste exchange in its true sense of meaning.

Solvents, organics, acids, and alkalis are the most commonly recycled hazardous materials. Most transactions involve relatively "pure" wastes that can be used directly with minimal processing. Some example entries from a waste exchange catalog are shown below.

> *Paraffin Wax.* Paraffin wax from clean-out of chewing gum base mixers. Fully refined. Potential use: fire logs, crayons, etc. Contains traces of gum base and calcium carbonate. 80 000 lbs. in 50-gallon drums. Quantities continuous. Thereafter 40 000 lbs./quarter.
> *Formaldehyde Surplus.* Formaldehyde solution. Potential Use: embalming fluid. Type 1: Contains 25% formaldehyde with 10% glycerin, 10% alcohols (ethanol, isopropanol, and methanol) and distilled water by wet weight. Type 2: Contains 25% formaldehyde with

25–35% alcohols (ethanol, isopropanol, and methanol) and distilled water by wet weight. 165 000 gallons in 15-gallon drums/plastic carboys in steel drums. One time. Independent analysis (specifications) available.

1,1,1-trichloroethane. 1,1,1-trichloroethane from asphalt extractions. Contains 90% 1,1,1-trichloroethane with 10% asphalt and 1% oil. 220 gallons in drums available. Quantities vary. Thereafter, 220 gallons/year. Sample available.

A slightly different scheme that represents a combination of waste exchange and reclamation exists in the United Kingdom and is known as the *National Industrial Symbiosis Programme* (NISB). Like the waste exchange NISB puts together waste generators with potential users. However, instead of using these materials as input in their manufacturing process as in waste exchange, they are used to produce energy. For example, turning pastry waste into electricity, converting fatty acids into bio-diesel, and so on. It is estimated that the program has boosted the UK economy by as much as €3 billion (European Commission 2010), equivalent to 13.3 billion 2020 US dollars.

9.7 Zero Waste

ZW is total waste elimination and is not the same as "waste diversion" or "zero emissions." ZW goals cannot be attained unless all waste generated from the production and consumption of raw materials, energy, and water, is recirculated into the production process through reuse, recycling, reassembling, repair, resale, redesign, and repurposing. ZW is a visionary concept of waste minimization that aims at eliminating waste altogether and conserving all resources from the waste stream so that there is nothing left of a product and its packaging that will end up in a landfill. Although technologically it may be an attainable goal, but from practical and economic viewpoints, it may not always be feasible; yet all waste generators should aim at getting as close to ZW as practicable. Some of the main challenges in achieving the ZW goal include: short-sighted policies of producers: preference of economic benefits over environmental preservation; careless attitude of consumers; lack of political will; and absence of strong community motivation.

9.7.1 Evolution and Implementation of the Zero Waste Concept

Although the term ZW was first used by Palmer in 1973 in reference to the recycling of industrial chemicals, it was adopted for MSW and other kinds of wastes during the 1990s. Growing interest to design environmentally sustainable communities, such as smart cities, during the early decades of the twenty-first century, led to many municipalities, and local, regional, and national authorities to include ZW in their waste management practice, emphasizing waste diversion and zero CO_2 emission. Since then, the term ZW with different connotations has been incorporated in numerous sustainability policies and waste management practices all over the world. Most of them framed the definition and scope of ZW in the context of their specific needs and preferences, which is not universally applicable. To avoid confusion, the Zero Waste International Alliance (ZWIA) proposed a comprehensive definition that has been universally accepted, defining ZW as:

> Conservation of all resources by means of responsible production, consumption, reuse, and recovery of products, packaging, and materials without burning and with no discharges to land, water, or air that threaten the environment or human health.
>
> *(ZWIA 2018).*

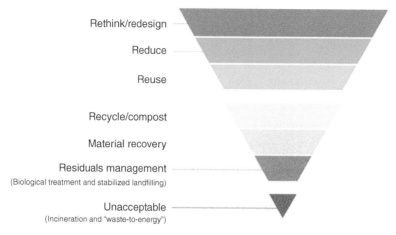

Figure 9.6   ZWIA waste minimization hierarchy. *Source:* ZWIA.

ZW focuses on eliminating waste, which should not be confused with "waste diversion" or "zero emissions." Waste generated from the production and consumption of raw materials, energy, and water, should be recirculated to the production processes through reuse, recycling, reassembling, repair, resell, redesign, and repurposing. According to ZWIA, ZW as an ethical, economical, and eco-efficient goal that offers a road map for people to adopt sustainable behavior and modify their life styles to emulate nature where all discarded materials get used as a resource for others.

ZWI's definition expands the traditional waste management hierarchy (Figure 9.1), giving the highest priority to waste avoidance – the top three rungs of the waste pyramid (Figure 9.6), followed by resource recovery – the next three rungs. ZW does not encourage incineration to generate energy as it leaves behind harmful residues that require disposal on land.

9.7.2   Tool for Measuring ZW Success

Zaman (2015) provides a comprehensive review of the evolution and scope of the ZW concept, observing that the current practice of diverting waste from a landfill, which has been the primary focus of adding ZW in public and private waste management policies, is short-sighted. He pointed out that any ZW program should, in keeping with ZWIA's universally accepted definition, also consider emissions reduction, energy savings, and overall ecological benefits.

ZW requires a shift from a linear economy to a circular economy. Unlike the conventional practice of taking resources from the earth and turning it into products that are discarded at the end of their designed life, ZW products are designed for reuse of their components for making new or similar products repeatedly. Since nature works on the circular economy concept, where everything is recycled and nothing goes waste, ZW attempts to mimic nature. ZW is an evolving concept that is receiving a great deal of attention from researchers not only from environmental and earth science fields but from numerous others in architectural, engineering, social, behavioral, business, and management fields as well. It is a key element in the United Nations' sustainable development goals (SDGs) (UN 2015). One of the major problems in assessing fulfillment of SDGs through the adoption of ZW practices has been lack of a reliable tool to compare savings of resource, water, energy, and emission reduction. A promising measure called the zero waste index (ZWI) has been developed by Zaman and Lehmann (2013) to measure the performance of waste management systems in achieving the ZW goal, with a higher ZW score corresponding to higher level of attainment of ZW goal. ZWI can be used to measure and compare the value of resources recovered from waste streams against the costs of raw materials, energy, water, and greenhouse gas emissions that went into the production and use of the material found in the waste stream. Zaman (2014) used ZWI to rank three major global cities: Adelaide, Australia; San Francisco, USA; and Stockholm, Sweden, all of which consume large amounts of goods and products. The respective ZWI scores were found to be 0.23, 0.51, and 0.17; indicating that about 23, 51 and 17% of resources were recovered and potentially substituted for raw materials. The proposed ZWI has limited applicability as it uses only six of the dozen or so common MSW components and excludes textiles, e-waste, C&D, and hazardous waste. A detailed discussion of ZWI is available in *Zero-Waste: Reconsidering Waste Management for the Future* (Zaman and Ahsan 2020).

9.8 Ship Recycling

Gone are the days when old ships after reaching their end of life (EoL) were abandoned in the coastal and inland waters to rot away. This practice has essentially stopped but their legacy is still around. These locations, known as shipyard graves, still exist in many parts of the world. Some of better-known yards include: the Arthur Kill Boat Yard; Witte Marine Yard, Mallows Bay, and Tugboat Grave Yard, along the US Atlantic Coast; and the Bikini Atoll, Marshall Island in the central Pacific Ocean where 90 naval vessels are lying in its lagoons. Olenya Bay, Kola Peninsula is a large submarine graveyard in Russia. Aral Sea, Uzbekistan, and Bay of Nouadhibou, Mauritania, are some of the other large ship graveyards in the world. Abandoning used ships in the ocean was a common practice world over until about the early1980s; it stopped in most of the developed countries after the enactment of environmental laws.

Globally, about 100 000 commercial ships and 25 000 naval vessels crisscross the oceans. The average number of large ships being scrapped each year is about 500–700, but could be as high as 3000 if vessels of all sizes are included. Ocean-going vessels, containers, vehicle carriers, general cargo carriers – weighing 20 000–45 000 gross tons (GT), are discarded after 25 years; and oil tankers, ore carriers (175 000–250 000 GT) after 35 years of service. Cruise liners retire after about 25–30 years of service. Globally, thousands of ships and marine vessels are being scrapped every year.

Discarded ships command a high market price, around $5 million for a 15 000 LDT (Light deadweight tonnage or Light displacement tonnage; excluding cargo, fuel, water, ballast, passenger, crew, but includes water in the boilers) ship. Recyclable materials include steel scrap, electric cables, pipes, engines, fuel, interior equipment, etc. Of these, steel is the main marketable commodity because scrap steel can be completely recycled without loss of quality. At the 2020 average price of $300/LDT for salvaged steel in South Asia, which is the same as the market price of newly manufactured steel, ship recycling has become a very profitable business in this region. With about 50% of the steel used in Bangladesh generated from ship breaking, recycling also contributes significantly to the circular economy of steel.

9.8.1 Methods of Ship Recycling

Considerable confusion exists in the ship recycling industry because of a lack of uniform terminology resulting in various entities using their own terms. For example, the International Maritime Organization (IMO) uses *Ship Dismantling*; International Labour Organization (ILO) calls it *Ship Breaking*; and Environmental nongovernmental organizations (NGOs) use *Disposal*, and ship owners use *Scrapping* – all of which imply taking apart a ship for recovering useable parts and materials, i.e. recycling.

Ship recycling is accomplished by using one of the four methods: (i) Dry docking, used in some European countries; (ii) Pier breaking or Alongside, in China, Europe, and the USA; (iii) Landing or Slipway, common in Turkey; and (iv) Beaching in Bangladesh, India, and Pakistan. Beaching, by far, is the most common method and accounts for 80% of all ships recycled globally. These methods are explained below:

Alongside. This method involves securing the ship along a wharf or quay in calm waters (mainly in rivers or harbors) where a crane removes the pieces of the dismantled ship from top to bottom until the lower part of the hull can be lifted out in one piece, pulled up a slipway for final cutting in a fully contained dry dock. Mainly used in China, Europe, and the USA.

Beaching. The recycling yards are located on beaches that have a large tidal range and vast mud-flats. The beaching method involves bringing the vessel onto a tidal mudflat, under its own power during high tide. Breaking operations are carried out during low tide while the ship is above the water surface, allowing workers to access the ship to cut it off into pieces that are removed onshore for transport to recycling centers. Common in Bangladesh, India, and Pakistan.

Dry Docking. The ship for recycling is brought into a flooded dock and after pumping the water out, workers dismantle the ship in a fully contained area that allows the use of cranes. Upon completion, the dock is cleaned and flooded again. The main advantage of this method is lower risk of environmental pollution because the work is carried out in an enclosed area. Construction and maintenance of dry docks are costly, so this method is used not only for ship recycling but for other purposes only. Dry-docks are mainly used in Europe.

Landing or Slipway. This method is suitable for areas with little or no tides, and is used in Turkey along the Aegean Sea coast. The ship is brought to the shore, or onto a concrete slipway, which extends into the sea such that the aft (back area) of the ship stays afloat while the front is held above water. Cranes, located on the shore or barges, are used to remove cut-off sections of the ship, which is gradually pulled further on the shore. Temporary quays or jetty are also used for mobilizing heavy lifting or cutting equipment.

9.8.2 Ship Recycling – A Hazardous Occupation

After the legal formalities of ownership, permitting, etc., the ship-breaking operation proceeds through a series of sequential steps. In developing countries, ships at the end of their life are beached at full speed during high tide, following which workers vent out flammable gases in the interior of the ship either by hammering or punching large holes in the hull, taking advantage of seawater during high tide to flush out the fuel tanks. Next, all furnishings and appliances, compressors, generators and other machineries, navigation equipment, piping, wiring, lifesaving equipment, toilets, wooden doors, foam, including asbestos and other toxic chemicals, are stripped out of the ship and sold to recyclers. Afterwards, large sections of steel are cut using gas torches and moved closer to the shore by large winches. Larger steel plates are then cut up into smaller pieces and carried by several men for loading onto trucks and transported to re-rolling mills for recycling. The recycled steel is used domestically in building and road construction. The entire operation can be accomplished in 3–5 months using 200–250 workers.

Among all waste recycling industries, ship recycling is most efficient in the sense that 95% of the materials are recycled routinely and a 98% recycling rate has been achieved in some cases at ship-breaking facilities in the USA and other developed countries. However, ship recycling in developing countries causes the largest number of deaths, diseases, and accidents than any other materials recycling operation. In 2019 alone, at least 26 workers lost their lives when breaking apart the global fleet of ships. The ILO has described shipbreaking as one of the most dangerous occupations, with an extremely high number of deaths, injuries, and work-related diseases (ILO 2019). Every year hundreds of workers die, become disabled from accidents, and suffer from serious diseases caused by exposure to toxic chemicals. The toll is heaviest in Bangladesh, India, and Pakistan in South Asia where thousands of unskilled migrant workers, including children, work to break down the vessels manually. Without any protective gear, they cut wires, pipes, and blast through ship hulls with blowtorches to salvage recyclable materials. Gas explosions, crashing down of massive steel parts and falls from height cause death to numerous workers each year. In addition, exposure to toxic chemicals, such as asbestos, PAHs, PCBs, TBT (tributyltin), and others causes irreversible diseases that add to high mortality. In Bangladesh, at the Chittagong (re-named Chittagram) yard, 44 workers were killed in 2018 and 2019. At the Alang ship-breaking yard in India, 16 workers died in the same period, and at the Gadani yard, Pakistan, 30 workers died from fire burns following two explosions that occurred within two months in November 2016 and January 2017 (NGO Platform, 2020b). In terms of environmental damage, shipbreaking is a highly polluting industry. In South Asia, ships are grounded and broken apart on tidal mudflats without any arrangements to contain pollutants, resulting in an uncontrolled release of toxic oil, sludge, and heavy metals-contaminated debris that destroys the sensitive coastal ecosystems.

Recycling of discarded ships is a complex undertaking and is very different from the recycling of any other waste commodity. Large size, enormous weight, complex design, a mix of metals, plastics, petroleum-derived fuel, lubricants, along with large amounts of asbestos (up to seven tons), and carcinogenic chemicals such as PCBs, PVC, PAHs, Hg, Pb, isocyanates, and sulfuric acid, require adequate control and monitoring of workers' safety and health along with full compliance with environmental and legal regulations. In reality, these critical controls are not observed in developing countries because most of the ship recycling is carried out in an informal sector with practically nonexistent safety controls or inspection, where toxic substances are routinely dumped in coastal water and on land. Lack of proper training and no or limited use of personal protective equipment (PPE), limited access to health service, inadequate housing and sanitary facilities, further exacerbate the plight of the workers. The death rate in the Indian shipbreaking yard at Alang is 2/1000 workers, higher than in the mining sector at 0.34/1000 workers (NGO Shipbreaking Platform 2019). Since the majority of yards have no system to manage the waste properly or, to control pollution, ship recycling inflicts an enormous toll on the environment, local communities, marine ecosystem, flora, and fauna. This results in serious environmental degradation with long-term adverse impacts on human and ecological health. The International Maritime Organization, ILO, and the UNEP's Basel Convention, after long deliberations, have developed guidelines, and established a joint working group to coordinate their activities. Efforts are underway to find solutions to improve health and environmental standards in the ship recycling industry, but regulations had not been enforced as of 2019 (Gourdon 2019).

Hossain (2017) inventoried useable materials in 27 ships brought at the shipbreaking yard in Bangladesh from 2009 to 2016, and found that on an average 91% (range 87.6–94.6%) of useable materials, dominated by steel, were collected from dismantling operations. A study by Demaria (2010) reported that up to 95% of useful materials, bulk of which comprises steel (75–85%), worth 65% of the total market value of all salvaged materials can be recovered from ship dismantling operations at the Alang yard in India. Table 9.3 lists the material composition and market value of the recovered commodities.

Like all other recycling ventures, ship recycling is also market-driven, and fluctuates with the market price and demand for steel. During international trading when ships for renting are in high demand, the number of ships offered for recycling goes down. At the same time, when the price of steel is high the recyclers offer higher price for EoL ships. Low steel price forces closure or reduction in the capacity of recycling yards. Conversely, when the shipping market is depressed, more

Table 9.3 Generalized material content of a recycled ship at Alang, India.

Material	% of ship weight	Value (%)
Steel	78–85	67
Nonferrous metal	1	7
Oil and lubricants	2	0.50
Reconditioned machinery	10–15	25
Furniture and fittings	2	0.50
Waste	5–10	0

Source: Modified after Demaria 2010.

Table 9.4 Average quantity of bulk hazardous waste in various types of merchant ships, Alang shipyard, India.

Ship type waste	Hazardous waste[b] kg/LTD[a]	Bilge water[c] kg/LTD	Total hazardous kg/LTD (%)
General cargo, bulk carrier, and container ships	21.2	2.3	23.4 (2.3)
Chemicals and oil tankers	16.7	4.4	21.1 (2.1)
Refrigerated ships	101.9	14.3	116.2 (11.6)
Passenger ships	28.1	1.4	29.5 (2.9)

[a] LTD is the weight of water in metric tons, displaced by a ship without cargo, fuel, lubricating oil, ballast water, fresh water and feed water, consumable stores, and passengers and crew and their belongings, but including liquids in piping.
[b] Includes asbestos, ceramics, ashes, broken glass, rusted iron scales, paints and coatings, oil contaminated rags, oily sludge, polyurethane, rubber gasket, PVC, and plastic wastes.
[c] Bilge water is a toxic aqueous mixture of seawater, oil, sludge, chemicals, and various other fluids.
Source: Modified after Hiremath et al. 2015.

ships are offered for recycling and recyclers buy EoL ships at relatively lower prices. If at such times steel price also happens to be high, ship recycling becomes more profitable, enabling increased recycling capacity through reopening of closed yards.

Hiremath et al. (2015) investigated ship recycling activities at Alang in India, for a 24-month period between April 2011 and March 2013 in 241 ships that included cargo, containers, oil and chemical tankers, passenger ships, and other types. Although no breakdown of various hazardous chemicals was reported, the study provided information on total quantities of hazardous wastes generated during recycling of the ships and the bilge water for general cargo ships, oil and chemical tankers, refrigerated ships, and passenger carriers. Table 9.4 summarizes hazardous waste found in various types of ships.

9.8.3 Modern Ship Recycling Industry

Ship recycling is an international venture that involves a number of parties including ship owners, brokers, financers, ship flaggers, buyers, and sellers of recycled materials. The industry has been infamous for circumventing international and local laws to accomplish ship breaking and recycling at the least cost. This approach has resulted in a high number of accidents, deaths, and serious illness among the workers engaged in actual ship dismantling and has also led to serious environmental pollution of sensitive ecological areas, particularly in Bangladesh, India, and Pakistan. According to a recent report of the NGO Shipbreaking Platform (2020a), 674 commercial ships and offshore units were sold to ship breaking yards in 2019. These included 469 large tankers, bulkers, floating platforms, cargo- and passenger ships that were broken down on three beaches in Bangladesh, India and Pakistan, which collectively accounted for nearly 90% of the gross tonnage dismantled globally; the remaining 10% took place in Turkey (107 ships), China and EU (29 each), and 40 vessels in rest of the world.

In the USA, most of the shipbreaking operations are currently being carried out in Texas in the Gulf of Mexico by four companies: (i) ESCO Marine, (ii) International Shipbreaking, Ltd., (iii) Maritimes metals, and (iv) All-Star metals. ESCO is the largest shipbreaking company that has dismantled about 500 vessels, followed by International Shipbreaking, Ltd., which has recycled about 100.

International Shipbreaking Ltd., operates three shipbreaking facilities along the Gulf of Mexico in Texas, and Louisiana, the largest one is located at Brownsville, Texas (Case Study 9.1). All facilities strictly comply with environmental regulations to safely handle and dispose of toxic materials, such as hydrocarbons, explosives, leaded paints, Hg, asbestos, PCBs, isocyanates, etc. The Federal

---

Case Study 9.1   EMR'S Interntaional Shipbreaking, Brownsville, Texas, the USA

European Metal Recycling (EMR) is a major metal and marine vessels recycler in the US. EMR, originally known as the Shepperd Group, was established in the United Kingdom in 1940 as a small metal recycling business. The company experienced rapid growth, and during the next 60 years it acquired several companies in Europe and changed its name to EMR in 1994. It began operations in the USA in the early 2000s and established its headquarters in Camden, NJ.

EMR's International Shipbreaking Ltd. operates three facilities in the southern USA along the Gulf of Mexico coast in Texas and Louisiana (EMR, 2021). With its ability to decommission and recycle over 272 155 t of ships, marine vessels, and marine rigs annually, EMR is one of the world's leading sustainable marine recycling company. It is capable of handling a wide variety of vessels, from small tugboats and offshore supply vessels to largest commercial ships and military vessels in the world. It uses state-of-the art equipment for shipbreaking and recycling, complying with national and international regulations and treaties.

International Shipbreaking largest operation, located at Brownsville, Texas, uses the *Alongside* method of ship breaking (Figure B9.1). Nearly 100 vessels belonging to the US Maritime Administration, the US Navy, and commercial shipping companies have been dismantled and recycled at this location in the past 15 years.

EMR carries out shipbreaking operations following best management practices to ensure workers safety; it strives to attain the highest level of environmental protection by continuously monitoring and improving upon its pollution prevention measures for air, land, and water. Before accepting a ship for recycling EMR evaluates the nature of hazardous materials on board that is used to formulate a plan for an environmentally safe handling and disposal of all hazardous materials. The company offers full range of shipbreaking services, listed below, including towing large vessels from hundreds of km offshore.

Figure B9.1 EMR's US ship recycling facility at Brownsville, Texas. Note the clean operations with neatly stacked recyclates stored in secured areas. *Source:* International Shipbreaking Ltd.

- Ships and barge breaking
- Remediation, including safe handling and disposal of hazardous materials and waste
- Recycling of drilling platforms and other marine petroleum production equipment

EMR is also the designated navy vessels recycler of the US Navy, the US Maritime Administration, and the Royal Australian Navy. In October 2020, it received two large ships: the *USS Barry*, and the guided missile frigate, the *USS Howes* for breaking and recycling. Shipbreaking and recycling of large ships are accomplished in less than one year. EMR claims that 98% of the materials removed from the ships is recyclable.

References

EMR (2021). Marine Structures and Vessels. https://us.emrgroup.com/what-we-do/our-specialist-areas/marine-structures-and-vessels.

requirement for the US Navy not to send its vessels for scrapping (recycling) in foreign countries, has given a boost to the modern shipbreaking industry in the USA where hundreds of ships have been recycled during the past 50 years and several 100 are awaiting recycling (CFLUI 2010). EMR Metal Recycling, the owner of International Shipbreaking Ltd., a global multi-national corporation, operates major shipbreaking facilities in the USA; the U.K; Germany, and the Netherlands with a total of 26 docks to service the marine shipping industry's recycling needs, complying with all national and international treaties and regulations.

In contrast with the developed countries where shipbreaking is carried out under strict compliance with environmental laws, the developing countries that account for a substantially greater volume of shipbreaking, have a poor record of worker safety and environmental compliance. A majority of ships are broken on the beaches of South Asia: along the Arabian Sea coast at Alang in India, and Gadani in Pakistan; and along the Bay of Bengal coast at Chittagong in Bangladesh (Figure 9.7), China, Taiwan and other SE Asian countries account for a small percent of shipbreaking business. In terms of the number of ships recycled in 2019 Bangladesh, India, and Pakistan accounted for about 70% of the total of 674 ships recycled worldwide, with Bangladesh and India accounting for 436 (NGO Shipbreaking Platform 2020).

Common features of all three South Asian ship breaking yards are summarized below:

1) All yards are well-connected to major commercial centers, and are located on beaches that have high tidal ranges (e.g. Alang, India: tidal range is about 13 m).
2) All use the beaching method of shipbreaking
3) Most ships brought in for recycling have changed flags so it is very difficult to find and prosecute the original owner for violation of the law.
4) Environmental and workers safety laws are poorly implemented and are generally ignored.
5) None or very basic job site training to workers.

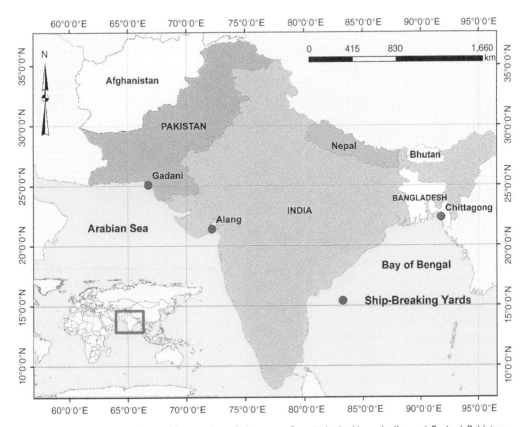

Figure 9.7   South Asia shipbreaking yards at Chittagong, Bangladesh; Alang, India; and Gadani, Pakistan.

6) Lack of adequate housing and medical facilities.
7) The exploitation of cheap labor: between 20 000 to 40 000 people may be working at peak season receiving very low wages.
8) High death rate from accidents and exposure to toxic substances are common.
9) Poverty, chronic unemployment, and lack of education prevent workers to seek legal actions against the yard owners
10) Corruption at various levels of the administration allows offenders to go unpunished.
11) Conditions might change with increasing public awareness of the deplorable conditions and accession to the Hong Kong Convention by India (joined 2019). Bangladesh and Pakistan are likely to join soon.

9.8.4 International Treaties

Ship recycling in developed countries was drastically reduced after the passage of environmental laws during the 1980s and 1990s. But the availability of cheap labor and lax and poorly enforced environmental laws led to a significant increase in ship recycling business in developing countries – the majority in the South Asian region. However, disregard for the worker's safety and health that resulted in a large number of serious accidents and deaths, and callous attitude toward environmental pollution have plagued the industry. These deplorable conditions were first reported in a series of articles in the *Baltimore Sun* in December 1997 by Gary Cohn and Will Englund, who, in April 1998, were awarded the Pulitzer Prize for their reporting (Hossain 2017). Their exposé caught world's attention that led to the development of regulations and guidelines to ensure uniform standards for worker's safety, environmental compliance, and accountability.

A comprehensive set of rules and regulations was adopted at the Hong Kong International Convention for the Safe and Environmentally Sound Recycling of Ships, held in Hong Kong in May 2009. The *Hong Kong Convention* (HKC) was attended by delegates from 63 countries and was fully supported by the international shipping industry. HKC addresses the design, construction, operation, and maintenance of ships to make sure that they can be recycled safely in an environmentally sound manner at the end of their lives. HKC also provides guidelines on how ships should be prepared for their final voyage to a recycling facility, without compromising safety or operational efficiency. Under HKC, ships sent for recycling should have an inventory of all hazardous materials on board. Based on a ship's particular characteristics and inventory of its hazardous materials, owners of ship recycling facilities are required to provide a "Ship Recycling Plan," specifying how each ship will be recycled.

HKC has not been fully enforced yet, because according to the 2009 agreement, the rules will become enforceable 24 months after the following three conditions are met:

1) The treaty must be ratified by 15 countries
2) These countries must represent 40% of the world's merchant shipping by gross tonnage, and
3) The combined maximum annual ship recycling volume (during the preceding 10 years) should not be less than 3% of their combined gross tonnage.

With India's accession to HKC in November 2019, the first requirement has been satisfied. The 15 countries include: Belgium, the Republic of the Congo, Denmark, Estonia, France, Germany, Ghana, India, Japan, Malta, the Netherlands, Norway, Panama, Serbia, and Turkey. The second condition was met in 2019, when nine countries whose combined merchant fleets gross tonnage of 293 173 037 comprised 54.9% of the world's merchant, signed the treaty. But the combined maximum annual ship recycling volume as of the writing of this chapter (June 2020) was about 94%, which is 6% short of the 3% gross tonnage requirement set in 3 above. Thus, all three requirements have not yet been fulfilled, but may be met in the next two years with enforcement likely to follow in 2022.

9.9 Airplane Recycling

Like ship recycling, airplane recycling also aims at the recovery of its components and materials that have value in the secondary product market. With the projected increase in commercial airplane fleet from 25 830 in 2018 to 50 660 in 2038, combined with the high cost of a new passenger airplane (starting at about $90 million), there is a high demand for EoL airplanes' engines, machinery, equipment, and other reusable items. For example, the A380 super jumbo that cost $446 million in 2007, upon retirement after 15 years of commercial passenger service, yielded $45 million worth of useable parts. The US-based Boeing Company and the European multinational Airbus Company are the industry leaders in commercial and defense airplanes manufacturing, commanding 99% of sale. The three competitors, Bombardier Airplane Co. based in Canada, Mitsubishi Heavy Industries in Japan, and Commercial Airplane Corporation China (COMAC), account for <1% of the world's large plane orders. Like the other manufacturers, their aging and retired airplanes also need recycling.

9.9.1 Airplane Recycling Market

Boeing's 737 series of airplane has been its bestselling model among its narrow-bodied airplanes (single isle with three seats on either side). In 2018, 1413 Boeing 737s were in service in the USA, as compared to 521 of Airbus's most popular model A320s. However, after the crash of its two new 737 MAX8 airplanes within six months (in October 2018 and March 2019) of commercial operation, Boeing's order for the new model plummeted from 5011 to 69 airplanes by January 2019.

Airplane EoL recycling comprises four major steps: (i) decontamination, (ii) disassembly of useable parts, (iii) dismantling of the remaining carcass, and (iv) materials recovery and residual disposal. With 12 000 airplanes estimated to reach their EoL by 2035, and the projected air travel to increase two-fold, from about four billion in 2018 to 8.2 billion in 2037 (IATA 2018), the airplane recycling industry is destined for expansion. However, if the dismantling operations are not carried out properly and in an environmentally safe manner, it could harm workers and the ecosystem from hazardous wastes. In addition, strict control and careful monitoring of engines and machineries are essential to guarantee their quality before these secondhand components re-enter the supply chain. Both Boeing and Airbus have moved proactively to ensure safety and quality control in the airplane recycling industry.

9.9.2 Airplane Recycling Standards

The Boeing Company in 2006, established the Airplane Fleet Recycling Association (AFRA) with 10 other founding members drawn from the global aviation industry. In collaboration with members from the supply chain, ARFA developed the *Airplane Disassembly Best Management Practice* in 2009 and an *Airplane Recycling Best Management Practice* in 2012. These two standards of practice comprise the basis for certification of recycling facilities that meet ARFA's standards (AFRA, 2017). The AFRA initiative not only defines minimum standards, but also suggests control technologies that a facility should adopt in order to meet the standards that include: fully protected ground surface, storm-water runoff pathways protection with spill barriers (drains, culverts), oil/water separator, and wastewater and airplane fluid treatment capabilities. The standards also promote sustainable recycling practices, and encourage the reuse of scrap parts in operational airplanes (Boeing 2008).

Airbus launched a pilot project called Process for Advanced Management of End-of-Life of Airplane (PAMELA) in 2005 to study various aspects of airplane recycling. The project demonstrated that an airplane's components can be safely dismantled and recycled for reuse in aviation or other sectors (Ribeiro and de Oliveira Gomes 2015). Prior to PAMELA, the industry had no standardized procedures for airplane dismantling. The project ensured compliance with relevant waste regulations, and encouraged recycling firms to work toward achieving a recycling target of 85%. The success of this project resulted in the establishment of TARMAC (Top Advanced Recycling and Maintenance Airplane Company) Aerosave in 2009. TARMAC Aerosave is a consortium of three companies: (i) Airbus, an international company that designs, manufactures, and sells civil and military aeronautical products worldwide; (ii) Safran, supplier of systems and equipment for aerospace, defense and security, and (iii) SUEZ, an international company specializing in sustainable management of waste and water resources.

TARMAC Aerosave, with three recycling locations in Europe, has emerged as the world leader in airplane recycling due to its innovative use of automated systems. Starting with the removal and sorting of equipment and cabin materials, it uses a gantry and diamond-impregnated cutting wire to cut the fuselage and wings. Using dismantling and recycling techniques in an environmentally safe manner, it claims to have achieved a recovery rate of 92% of the airplane weight in an average time of about five weeks. Since 2007, TARMAC Aerosave has recycled 220 airplanes that represent 75% of all A340s airplanes recycled in the world. Airplane recycling has a significant economic benefit as the cost to store a disused airplane could be as high as $25 000/month, compared to a one-time cost of between $125 000 and $185 000 to tear down a plane and salvaging items that can be reused or sold at a profit. In addition to the monetary value of useable parts, another benefit derived from airplane dismantling and salvaging operations is enabling aerospace engineers to understand how parts erode, decay, or degrade under repeated stress and fatigue over time, enabling them to design more efficient airplanes in the future (TARMAC 2020).

9.9.3 Airplane Recycling

Airplanes, like ships, have a working life of between 20 and 30 years. Between 550 and 750 airplanes were declared out of service every year and sent for dismantling and recycling before COVID-19. The pandemic had the worst economic impact on commercial aviation than 9/11 or the 2008 global economic recession. Out of the global fleet of 28 000 airplanes in 2019, 15 000 were removed from service by January 2020; about 24 000 were brought back into service in 2021. All major world airlines were affected and about 10 permanently retired their older airplanes and earmarked them for recycling (Marcontell et al. 2020).

After reaching their EoL, passenger airplanes are either converted for use in freight transport, and when maintenance and repair costs become prohibitive, they are scrapped for recovery of

(a) (b) (c)

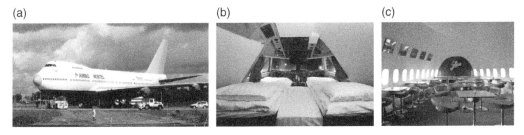

Figure 9.8   A Boeing 747 converted into a hotel, Stockholm Arlanda Airport, Sweden (a), Cockpit-view bedroom (b), and Cafeteria (c). *Source:* Jumbo Stay, Stockholm, Sweden.

engines, machineries, and other items for reuse or recycling. A few end up in museums and in commercial ventures, such as the Jumbo Hostel at the Stockholm Arlanda airport, where a 1976 Boeing 747 has been reconfigured to a 33-room hotel, complete with a conference room and cafeteria (Figure 9.8).

Airplanes, like ships, are complex and very expensive pieces of equipment and a modern wide-body jet airplane costs anywhere from $90 million (base model, Boeing 737-700) to $442 million for luxury model (Boeing 777-9) in 2019 (Statista 2020). Airplanes are made from aluminum, titanium, steel and composites. Composites may consist of carbon fiber, polymers, glass, and other materials that are strong, stiff, lightweight, and corrosion-resistant. Boeing Co., after extensive research determined that the recycled carbon fiber reinforced polymer (CFRP) is safe to replace virgin CFRP, with substantial cost savings–70% less to produce and using up to 95% less energy than virgin CFRP with comparable performance (Carberry 2008). As of 2013, Airbus and Boeing both have been producing planes made from at least 50% composite material. However, increasing the use of CFRPs in airplanes will result in larger volumes of composite waste. It is estimated that globally 34 200 t of CFRPs will be generated annually from EoL airplanes by 2050, requiring more efficient methods for its recycling (Zhang et al. 2020).

The largest Boeing 747-8, wide-bodied, 467-passenger airplane, was put into service in 2012, with the allowable maximum takeoff weight (MTOW) of nearly 448 t that includes 237 000 liters of fuel, weighing 193.3 t (Boeing 2012). The plane consists of a variety of materials: metals, carbon composites, plastics, electronics, entertainment items, furniture, and many more. Table 9.5 provides a list of major components of Boeing jet airplanes.

9.9.4   Composites

Carbon fiber reinforced polymer composites are finding increasing use in making a wide variety of equipment. These are used in air, land, sea, and space vehicles; wind turbines, storage tanks, sports (fishing and golfing equipment; bicycles, racquets, hockey, and ski poles), and pressure vessels for gas and liquid storage. Of the three common types of composites, fiber, glass and polyamide, the fibrous, petroleum-derived CFRPs are extensively used in aviation vehicles and wind turbine blades and other applications. Favorable properties, such as high tensile and compressive strengths, low thermal and electrical conductivity, corrosion resistance, high stiffness, low density, high weight to strength ratio, and flexibility in design, make CFRPs material of choice. Replacing metals with plastics lowers airplanes assembly costs. Composites also save fuel costs and improve the overall efficiency of airplanes.

Table 9.5 Material content of Boeing jet airplanes (data from aviation.
stackexchange.com and other sources).

Material	Percentage of airplane weight		
	747 (1970)	777 (1995)	787 (2009)
Aluminum	81	70	20
Steel	13	11	10
Titanium	4	7	15
Composites	1	11	50
Miscellaneous	1	1	5
Total	100	100	100

Year indicates first commercial flight.

Demand for CFRPs has tripled in just one decade–from a little over 60 000 t in 2010 to about 163 000 t in 2020, and is estimated to reach 190 000 t by the year 2050. However, CFRPs have two disadvantages: high cost, and no biodegradation. These two limitations result in a high volume of composite wastes. It is estimated that if not recycled, 0.42 million t of CFRPs scraps from the manufacturing sector and EoL waste from the aviation sector will accumulate by 2035. Total accumulated quantity will be much greater, about 1.1 million t by 2030 from wind turbines, due to increasing use of wind energy and approximately 20-year life spans of turbine blades.

9.9.4.1 Composites Recycling

CFRP recycling uses high energy to separate carbon fibers from the thermoset matrix, and produces dust and harmful gases besides loss in strength of the recycled fiber. CFRP recycling can be grouped into three methods:

- Mechanical
- Thermal
- Chemical

Mechanical recycling involves multiple steps of pulling, shredding, and grinding to reduce the size of the CFRP waste. Mechanical recycling produces small fibers that retain 50–65% of the tensile strength of the virgin CFRP. This is one of the reasons why mechanically recycled CFRPs cannot be used in applications where high strength is required, but they can be used as fillers in short fiber composites such as sheet molding compounds. The main drawback of the mechanical method is high wear and tear and overall damage to the processing equipment, requiring frequent parts replacement, which increases the cost of mechanical recycling. On the positive side, the mechanical process is nontoxic.

Thermal recycling methods, pyrolysis, and fluidized bed treatment, use high temperatures to break down the matrix to recover the fibers. Pyrolysis is performed in an anaerobic and inert gas atmosphere where CFRPs are heated to high temperature between 400° and 1000 °C to yield long fibers retaining about 50–85% of the tensile strength of the virgin fibers.

Fluidized bed recycling involves shredding CRFPs into small pieces and feeding it into a bed of coarse silica sand (<1 mm in diameter) which is fluidized by a stream of hot air at 450–550 °C temperature and under a pressure of 10–25 kPa. Rapid heating causes thermal decomposition and degradation of the matrix, releasing the fibers by attrition. Gases released from the matrix are subjected to combustion to oxidize the by-products. The recycled fiber length is in the 5–10 mm range, retaining 10–75% of the tensile strength of virgin carbon fibers (Zhang et al. 2020).

Solvolysis is an example of the chemical method and involves the use of solvents to decompose the thermoset matrix to separate the fibers.

Investigations to develop green and cost-efficient composites recycling technologies are underway. Pyrolysis has been commercialized in the United Kingdom and Germany but it is constrained by char formation and loss of mechanical properties in the recycled product. Chemical recycling has shown promise in laboratory studies but its commercialization has not occurred yet (Gopalraj and Kärki 2020).

9.10 Summary

The increasing quantity of wastes being generated all over the world calls for a multi-pronged solution to manage it in an environmentally sound way. Waste minimization, a dynamic process, should be practiced by all waste generators with the ultimate goal of attaining ZW. ZW aims at conservation of all resources used in manufacturing products through the full recovery of materials with no release of any harmful substance into the environment.

Recycling has been practiced since ancient times; human feces and animal excreta, contain rich nutrients for the soil. It also has a high calorific value, more than paper. New methods and technologies for efficient waste minimization and resource recovery are being developed at a rapid pace. Many innovative methods of waste minimization have been developed in the past 20 years, which include microfactories, plant-based 100% recyclable plastics, etc.

The USA affirmed its commitment to control pollution by enacting the Pollution Prevention (P2) Act in 1990 and declaring pollution prevention to be its national policy for the elimination of pollution through recycling, waste treatment, and all other feasible means, requiring disposal to be the last option to manage the waste. Another US law, the Emergency Planning and Community Right-to-Know Act, mandated major industries to include waste minimization and pollution prevention in their corporate plans and submit information on toxic release annually to the EPA. The TRI reports the industry's performance in chemical waste management and pollution prevention, which are made public. Enforcement of this program has cut down pollutant emissions by about 15% in 22 years. *Green manufacturing* and *cleaner production* approaches hold great promise as both aim at waste minimization and pollution elimination.

A large number of commercial and military fleet of ships and other marine vessels, along with airplanes, have been declared non-serviceable, awaiting disposal. Most of the ship recycling is carried out in Asian countries where proper measures for workers' safety and environmental protection are not implemented resulting in deaths, injuries and diseases, and serious marine pollution. The Hong Kong Convention to ensure safe shipbreaking is likely to be implemented by 2025.

Airplane recycling is being done in Europe by TARMAC Aerosave in full compliance with environmental regulations. Useful parts are being sold in the secondary market contributing to resource conservation and sustainability. Large-scale substitution of composites for aluminum in airplane has created challenges in recycling of the growing volume of scrap composites. COVID-19 has produced a major and longest-lasting economic impact in the commercial aviation industry, worse than 9/11 or the 2008 global economic recession, forcing nearly all major airlines to earmark their old airplanes for recycling.

Study Questions

1   What is waste minimization? How is it different from integrated waste management?

2   Historically waste management philosophy has gone through several evolutions. What has prompted the on-going changes? With the latest approach emphasizing pollution prevention and source reduction, have we achieved the best possible practice? Discuss the implications of this evolution.

3   What are the various techniques of waste minimization? Give appropriate examples for each.

4   What is a waste exchange? How is an active waste exchange different from a passive exchange? What is the main difference between waste exchange and materials repurposing? Explain.

5   Among the recyclable plastics, carrying the numbers 1–7, which one is being recycled most and why? What are the main products that can be made from recycled plastic? Which two other plastics are possibly harmful and should be avoided?

6   List the methods that can be used as a source reduction strategy for a facility that manufactures computer chips and uses hundreds of gallons of TCE for cleaning the final product before shipping it to a laptop assembly plant.

7   As an entrepreneur you have obtained financing to build a microfactory to make a useful product from waste. Considering green manufacturing and sustainability, which waste material would you choose? Some factors to consider in making your decision should include: a continuous supply of waste material, its impact on the environment, pollution, GHG emission, potential harmful effects on ecosystems, etc.

8   Discuss the potential impacts of the adoption of the Hong Kong Convention to the ship recycling industry in Bangladesh, India, and Pakistan after these countries agree to follow the regulations of the Convention. How would it protect workers' health and the environment?

9   Airplanes are getting lighter by replacing aluminum with composites. The growing quantities of waste composites would require cost-effective and environmentally sound recycling methods. Research the developments in the composite recycling field and discuss a recycling technology that is now commercially available.

10   What are composites? What properties make CFRPs desirable material for airplanes, space ships, and wind turbines? Why it is difficult to recycle CFRPs?

References

AFRA (Airplane Fleet Recycling Association) (2017). AFRA mission. https://afraassociation.org/about-us/afra-mission (accessed 3 June 2020).

Avantium (2020). Avantium to build FDCA flagship plant at Chemie Park Delfzijl, Netherlands. https://bioplasticsnews.com/wp-content/uploads/2020/01/20200108-Avantium-press-release-site-selection-FDCA-flagship-plant-final.pdf (accessed 13 June 2020).

Becerril-Arreola, R. and Bucklin, R.E. (2021). Beverage bottle capacity, packaging efficiency, and the potential for plastic waste reduction. *Science Reports* 11: 3542. https://doi.org/10.1038/s41598-021-82983-x.

Boeing (2008). Airplane recycling efforts-benefits for Boeing operators. https://www.boeing.com/commercial/aeromagazine/articles/qtr_4_08/article_02_4.html (accessed 3 June 2020).

Boeing (2012). 747-8 airplane characteristics for airport planning, Document D6-58326-3, 126 p. http://www.boeing.com/assets/pdf/commercial/airports/acaps/747_8.pdf (accessed 7 July 2020).

Bogaard, A., Frasera, R., Heaton, T.H.E. et al. (2013). Crop manuring and intensive land management by Europe's first farmers. *Proceedings of National Academy of Sciences* 110 (31): 12589–12594.

Carberry, W; 2008. Airplane recycling efforts benefit Boeing operators. *Aero Quarterly*, p. 7–13. https://www.boeing.com/commercial/aeromagazine/articles/qtr_4_08/pdfs/AERO_Q408_article02.pdf (accessed 16 June 2020).

CFLUI (The Center for Land Use Interpretation) (2010). *American ship breaking*. Spring 2010 Newsletter. http://www.clui.org/newsletter/spring-2010/american-ship-breaking (accessed 24 October 2020).

Christensen, P.R., Scheuermann, A.M., Loeffler, K.E., and Hels, B.A. (2019). Closed-loop recycling of plastics enabled by dynamic covalent diketoenamine bonds. *Nature Chemistry* 11: 442–448.

Demaria, F. (2010). Shipbreaking at Alang-Sosiya (India): an ecological distribution conflict. *Ecological Economic* 70: 250260. https://doi.org/10.1016/j.ecolecon.2010.09.006.

ECE (Economic Commission for Europe (1978). Non-waste technology and production. *Proceedings of an International Seminar*, held at Paris, France (29 November–4 December 1976). UK: Pergamon Press. 680 p.

Egger, M., Sulu-Gambari, F. & Lebreton, L., 2020. First evidence of plastic fallout from the North Pacific Garbage Patch. *Science Reports* **10**, 7495. https://doi.org/10.1038/s41598-020-64465-8 (accessed 12 June 2020).

EPA (1988) Waste Minimization Opportunity Assessment Manual. Cincinnati, OH: Hazardous Waste Engineering Research Laboratory, Report No. *EPA/625/7-88/003*, 25 p. plus appendices.

EPA (2019). Facts and figures about materials, waste and recycling: containers and packaging: product-specific data. https://www.epa.gov/facts-and-figures-about-materials-waste-and-recycling/containers-and-packaging-product-specific-data (accessed 29 May 2020).

EPA (2020). Toxics release inventory (TRI) program: measuring the impact of source reduction. https://www.epa.gov/toxics-release-inventory-tri-program/measuring-impact-source-reduction (accessed 26 February 2020).

EPA (2021). TRI Factsheet for US, Data Source: 2019 Updated Dataset (released June 2021). 2019 TRI Factsheet for US | TRI Explorer | US EPA.

European Commission (2010). *Being Wise with Waste: The EU's Approach to Waste Management*, 16. Luxembourg: Publications Office of the European Union.

Gopalraj, S.K. and Kärki, T. (2020). A review on the recycling of waste carbon fibre/glass fibre-reinforced composites: fibre recovery, properties and life-cycle analysis. *SN Applied Sciences* 2: 433. https://doi.org/10.1007/s42452-020-2195-4.

Gourdon, K. (2019). Ship recycling: an overview. In: *OECD Science, Technology and Industry Policy Papers*, No. 68. Paris: OECD Publishing, 49 p. https://doi.org/10.1787/397de00c-en (accessed 3 June 2019).

Hiremath, A.M., Tilwankar, A.K., and Asolekar, S.R. (2015). Significant steps in ship recycling vis-a-vis wastes generated in a cluster of yards in Alang: a case study. *Journal of Cleaner Production* 87: 520–532.

Hossain, K.A. (2017). Ship recycling practice and annual reusable material output from Bangladesh ship recycling industry. *Journal of Fundamentals of Renewable Energy and Applications* 7: 238. https://doi.org/10.4172/2090-4541.1000238.

IATA (International Air Transport Association) (2018). Remarks of Alexandre de Juniac, President, IATA, at 2018 Global Media Day, Geneva; IATA Press Release, December 12, 2018. https://www.iata.org/en/pressroom/speeches/2018-12-12-01 (accessed 23 July 2020).

ILO (2019). Ship-breaking: a hazardous work. http://www.ilo.org/safework/areasofwork/hazardous-work/WCMS_110335/lang--en/index.htm (accessed 3 June 2019).

Lal, N. (2020). The Indian school where students pay for lessons with plastic waste. *The Guardian*. https://www.theguardian.com/global-development/2020/nov/25/the-indian-school-where-students-pay-for-lessons-with-plastic-waste 1-27-2021 (accessed 27 January 2021).

Marcontell, D., Cooper, T., Martin, C.G., and Reagan, I. (2020). Update: impact of COVID-19 on commercial MRO. Oliver Wyman Co. Global Fleet and MRO Market Forecast 2021-2031 (oliverwyman.com) accessed 12 September 2021.

NGO Shipbreaking Platform (2019). *Where Ships Go to Die*. https://www.shipbreakingplatform.org/spotlight-swiss-focus (accessed 5 June 2020).

NGO Shipbreaking Platform (2020a). *Impact Report 2018–2019*. https://www.shipbreakingplatform.org/wp-content/uploads/2020/06/NGOSBP-Bi-Annual-Report-18-19.pdf (accessed 12 June 2019).

NGO Shipbreaking Platform (2020b). *The Toxic Tide: 2019 Shipbreaking Records*. https://www.shipbreakingplatform.org/spotlight-data-2019 (accessed 13 June 2020).

Palmer, P. (2004). *Getting to Zero Waste*, 290. Sebastopol, California: Purple Sky Press.

Ranson, M., Cox, B., Keenan, C., and Teitelbaum, D. (2015). The impact of pollution prevention on toxic environmental releases from U.S. manufacturing facilities. *Environmental Science & Technology* 49: 12951–12957.

Ribeiro, J. and J. de Oliveira Gomes (2015), Proposed framework for end-of-life airplane recycling. *Procedia CIRP*, Vol. 26, pp. 311–316. https://doi.org/10.1016/j.procir.2014.07.048 accessed 4 June 2020.

Rose, C., Parker, A., Jefferson, B., and Cartmell, E. (2015). The characterization of feces and urine: a review of the literature to inform advanced treatment technology. *Critical Reviews in Environmental Science and Technology* 45 (17): 1827–1879. https://doi.org/10.1080/10643389.2014.1000761.

Sierra (2020). Detox your digs. 105:3, May/June 2020, p. 11.

Statista (2020). https://www.statista.com/statistics/273941/prices-of-boeing-airplane-by-type (accessed 15 June 2020).

TARMAC (2020). TARMAC History. https://www.tarmacaerosave.aero/history (accessed 23 July 2020).

UN (2015). Sustainable Development Goals. https://sustainabledevelopment.un.org/sdgs accessed 27 May 2020.

UNSW (2018). World-first e-waste microfactory launched at UNSW. https://newsroom.unsw.edu.au/news/science-tech/world-first-e-waste-microfactory-launched-unsw (accessed 13 June 2020).

Wetherbee, G., Baldwin, A., and Ranville, J. (2019). It is raining plastic. U.S. Geological Survey Open-File Report 2019–1048, 1 sheet. https://doi.org/10.3133/ofr20191048 (accessed 12 June 2020).

Zaman, A. (2014). Measuring waste management performance using the 'Zero Waste Index': the case of Adelaide, Australia. *Journal of Cleaner Production* 66: 407–419.

Zaman, A.U. (2015). A comprehensive review of the development of zero waste management: lessons learned and guidelines. *Journal of Cleaner Production* 91: 21–25. https://doi.org/10.1016/j.jclepro.2014.12.013 0959-6526/.

Zaman, A. and Ahsan, T. (2020). *Zero-Waste: Reconsidering Waste Management for the Future*, 216. Abingdon, Oxon, U.K.: Taylor & Francis Group.

Zaman, A. and Lehmann, S. (2013). The zero waste index: a performance measurement tool for waste management systems in a 'zero waste city'. *Journal of Cleaner Production* 50: 123–132.

Zhang, J., Chevali, Wang, H., and Wang, C.-H. (2020). Current status of carbon fibre and carbon fibre composites recycling. *Composites Part B: Engineering* 193: https://doi.org/10.1016/j.compositesb.2020.108053.

ZWIA (Zero Waste International Alliance) (2018). Definition of zero waste. http://zwia.org/zero-waste-definition/ (accessed 22 May 2020).

Supplemental Reading

Connett, P.H. (2013). *The Zero Waste Solution: Untrashing the Planet One Community at a Time*, 380. Vermont, U.S.A: Chelsea Green Publishing, White River Junction.

Zaman, A. and Ahsan, T. (2020). *Zero-Waste: Reconsidering Waste Management for the Future*, 216. Abingdon, Oxon, U.K.: Taylor & Francis Group.

Web Resources

https://www.sciencedirect.com/topics/earth-and-planetary-sciences/waste-minimisation/pdf. Collection of articles on waste minimization in various industries, available at Science Direct. Provides good summary of application of waste minimization along with access to full articles.

https://www.waste360.com/. Waste360, with over 90 000 members, provides useful information on solid waste, recycling, organics and sustainable communities and connects industry professionals from all across the globe. Its annual event, the WasteExpo, attracts thousands of participants from all over the world; proceedings of sessions are posted on its website. Provides regular coverage of new development in all solid waste topics on its website.

https://recyclemania.org/. RecycleMania promotes waste minimization and recycling at college campuses in the USA and Canada. It started in a small way in January 2001 as a recycling tournament between the Ohio University and Miami University in Ohio. RecycleMania has continued to grow. Since 2001 over 1000 colleges and universities across the USA and Canada have participated in the annual RecycleMania. In 2020, RecycleMania changed its name to Campus Race to Zero Waste to help colleges and universities find pathways toward ZW (90+% diverted from trash).

Acronyms/Symbols

AI	Artificial intelligence
g	gram
MRO	Maintenance Repair and Overhaul (of aircrafts)
t	Metric ton

10

Pharmaceuticals and Personal Care Products

LEARNING OBJECTIVES

After studying this chapter, you will be able to:

- Define pharmaceuticals and personal care products (PPCPs) and explain their nature and threat to human and ecological health.
- Identify the source, occurrence, and hazards of PPCPs.
- Describe the pathways and fate of PPCPs in the environment.
- Summarize current and future research on PPCPs.

10.1   Introduction

Humans have been using plants, minerals, and animal products for the healing and treatment of diseases since antiquity. Ancient Arab, Chinese, and Indian, used a combination of herbs and minerals, such as arsenolite (As_2O_3), alum $KAl(SO_4)2.12H_2O$, bitumen, cinnabar (HgS), galena (PbS), pearl ($CaCO_3$), potassium nitrate (KNO_3), realgar (As_4S_4), and sodium carbonate (Na_2CO_3), along with chemical elements such as Au, Ag, Cu, Fe, Pb, and Zn, for therapeutic purposes, going as far back as 3000 BCE (Hasan 2021). Naturally occurring chemicals in the form of native elements and minerals, to a large extent, have been replaced by synthetic chemicals in modern medicine, with the exception of the Ayurvedic, Unani, and traditional Chinese medicines, where they constitute the significant composition of therapeutic remedies even now. For the past 150 years, synthetic chemicals have been increasingly used as the main therapeutic ingredient in thousands of prescription and over-the-counter (OTC) or nonprescription medicines in the form of ingestible tablets, capsules, liquids; inhalers, topical preparations; injectable compounds; along with radioisotopes, for treatment of a wide variety of diseases all over the world.

> Personal care products and pharmaceuticals are designed to stimulate a physiological response in humans, plants, and animals. Potential concerns from the environmental presence of these compounds include abnormal physiological processes and reproductive impairment, increased incidences of cancer, the development of antibiotic-resistant bacteria, and the potential increased toxicity of chemical mixtures.
> —*Bradley and Kolpin, US Geological Survey, 2013*

The dramatic onset and rapid propagation of COVID-19, one of the deadliest pandemics of modern time, in the early years of the 2020s, brought in a lightning awareness of vaccines and the

Table 10.1 2020 ranking of the world's top 10 pharmaceutical companies.

Rank	Name, city, country	Prescriptions sold $ (billion)[a]	Top-selling drugs
1	Roche, Basel, Switzerland	48.247	Avastin, Rituxan, Herceptin
2	Novartis, Basel, Switzerland	46.085	Cosentyx, Gilenya, Lucentis
3	Pfizer, New York, NY; USA	43.662	Prevenar 13, Ibrance, Lyrica
4	Merck & Co., Kenilworth, NJ; USA	40.903	Keytruda, Gardasil, Januvia
5	Bristol Myers Squibb, New York, NY; USA	40.689	Revlimid, Eliquis, Opdivo
6	Johnson & Johnson, New Brunswick, NJ; USA	40.083	Stelara, Remicade, Darzalex
7	Sanofi, Paris, France	34.924	Lantus, Dipoxent, Pentacel
8	AbbVie, Chicago, IL; USA	32.351	Humira, Imbruvica, Mavyret
9	GlaxoSmithKline, Bretford, UK	31.288	Triumeq, Shingrix, Advair
10	Takeda	29.247	Entyvio, Vyvanse, Gammagard

[a] Based on 2019 sale.
Source: Data from Christel (2020).

pharmaceutical industry to billions of people in every corner of the world. Global efforts to combat the deadly SARS-CoV-2 virus created an enormous volume of medical waste comprising PPE (at the pandemic peak, 130 billion disposable face masks were used globally every month; Sierra 2021), along with disposable syringes, discarded needles, etc., used in the medical care of over 200 billion infected persons (as of September 2021).

The modern pharmaceutical industry, globally dominated by the USA and Europe, constitutes the major sector of a nation's economy. Table 10.1 shows the 2020 ranking of the world's top 10 pharmaceutical companies (Christel 2020).

The global pharmaceutical industry is projected to witness robust growth due to: (i) concerted global initiatives to assure health security for everyone, (ii) improved life expectancy and greater dependence of the aging population on pharmaceutical products, particularly in developed countries, and (iii) new target age group: greater incidence of diabetics, hypertension, and cardiovascular diseases in the younger population, (iv) discovery of new uses for existing drugs, and (v) projected increase in incidences of epidemics/pandemics, associated with climate change and urbanization.

The use of synthetic chemicals in industrial manufacturing, including pharmaceutical production, mushroomed in the second half of the twentieth century and is on the increase. Based on a detailed analysis of chemical inventories from 19 countries, Wang et al. (2020) estimated that over 350 000 chemicals were in industrial use globally in early 2020 – about 3 times greater than previous estimates.

Besides medicinal use, a large number of new chemicals and related substances are being used in personal care products, such as body washes, makeups, shampoos, fragrances, insect repellents, etc. Many of the active chemical ingredients used in PPCPs are bioaccumulative, persistent, toxic, and can remain in the water, soil, and sediment for a long period of time. Due to the lack of complete understanding of toxicity and potential risks to human and ecological health, the US EPA grouped many of the PPCP chemicals along with pesticides, etc., as contaminants of emerging concern (CEC) in the early 2000s. CECs are also referred to as "forever chemicals" in popular media. The following chemicals are included in EPA's list of CECs (EPA 2008):

- Persistent organic pollutants (POPs) such as polybrominated diphenyl ethers (PBDEs), used in flame retardants.
- Furniture foam, plastics, and other organic contaminants such as per- and polyfluoroalkyl substances (PFAS).
- PPCPs, including a wide suite of prescription drugs (e.g. antibiotics, analgesics, antidepressants, etc.), over-the-counter medications (e.g. ibuprofen), bactericides (e.g. triclosan), sunscreens, synthetic musk, etc.
- Veterinary medicines such as antimicrobials, antibiotics, antifungals, growth promoters, and hormones.
- Endocrine-disrupting chemicals (EDCs), including synthetic estrogens (e.g. 17α-ethynylestradiol), naturally occurring estrogens (e.g. 17β-estradiol, testosterone), and androgens (e.g. trenbolone, a veterinary drug), and others (e.g. organochlorine pesticides, alkylphenols), capable of modulating normal hormonal functions and steroidal synthesis in aquatic organisms.
- Nanomaterials such as carbon nanotubes or nanoscale particulate titanium dioxide, of which little is known about either their environmental fate or effects.

During the decades of 1980 and 1990, chemical analyses of waters in streams and rivers in the United States of America and other European countries revealed that they were contaminated with chemicals, including EDCs, which are common ingredients of PPCPs. The US Geological Survey, in a nationwide study of toxic substances in the nation's streams and rivers, found that nearly all major streams in the country were contaminated with PPCPs. This finding, combined with results obtained from a number of studies in Europe on PPCPs presence in drinking water, brought to fore awareness of this issue and prompted regulatory agencies to consider steps for its control. The EU in 2001 adopted measures that require assessment of risk associated with all medicinal products. The US EPA noted that PPCPs pose a threat to aquatic life forms in particular and the environment in general, but has not yet come up with rules and regulations at the federal level to address this problem. On the other hand, some US states, notably California and Washington, have moved forward to regulate PPCPs.

10.1.1 Definition of PPCPs

The US EPA defines pharmaceuticals and personal care products (PPCPs) as "any product used by individuals for personal health or cosmetic reasons or used by agribusiness to enhance growth or health of livestock." A comprehensive definition was provided by Daughton and Ternes (1999) who defined PPCPs as a "very broad, diverse collection of thousands of chemical substances, including prescription and over-the-counter therapeutic drugs, fragrances, cosmetics, sunscreen agents, diagnostic agents, nutraceuticals, biopharmaceuticals, and many others," and suggested using the acronym PPCPs for such products. Other acronyms, such as PhACs (pharmaceutically active compounds), APIs (active pharmaceutical ingredients), PCPIs (personal care product ingredients), or PPCFPs (pharmaceuticals, personal care, and food products) have been used but did not find much currency in the literature. Another term, pharmaceuticals in the environment (PiE), was introduced in the early 2000s to include the all-encompassing aspects of PPCPs. Daughton (2016) published an exhaustive bibliometric analysis of articles on PPCPs and their impacts on human and ecological health. He used the term PiE to include a broad area of study where a wide range of investigators representing "many different and usually disconnected technical disciplines" contribute "an extremely large body of disparate published literature." In this chapter, we will use PPCPs for the broad range of hazardous substances found in PPCPs that enter the waste stream.

10.1.2 Nature of PPCPs

Unlike other types of wastes, discussed in this book, PPCPs represent a very special class of contaminants. Many are persistent and bioaccumulative and can accumulate in organisms at different trophic levels. PPCPs are formulated and used for their biological activity, targeting certain organ(s) that are influenced by their ionic nature with multiple ionization sites within the molecule. Pharmaceuticals do not represent a homogeneous group of compounds because of variations in their chemical structure, large molecular weight (300–1000), ability to form a salt, polymorphs, etc. (Cunningham 2004). Unlike other chemicals, PPCPs contain ingredients that are ingested or topically applied. Most pharmaceuticals are subject to metabolic transformation; for this reason, the resulting chemical species that are excreted and enter the environment may have very different toxicological, pharmacological, and physicochemical properties than the original ingredients. Therefore, the metabolism of pharmaceutical products used in human and animal (veterinary medicines) therapy must be given due consideration while attempting to ascertain the nature of released compounds for assessing their fate and ecological impacts.

Many pharmaceuticals undergo biotransformation upon entering the human body. The process of metabolism causes absorption of the ingredients; since metabolism is frequently incomplete, the chemical ingredients are excreted by the organism. Most pharmaceuticals or their metabolites used by humans are excreted and end up in urban wastewaters. Table 10.2 shows the excretion rates of some of the common pharmaceutical products.

Due to the very low concentration of PPCPs in water, in the parts per billion (ppb) to parts per trillion (ppt) range, and the wide variation in their chemical characteristics, no single chemical analytical method can be used for their detection and quantitation. Using a combination of methods – high-performance liquid chromatography-tandem mass spectrometry (HPLC-MS/MS), liquid chromatography-Fourier transform mass spectrometry (LC-FTMS), full-scan capillary gas chromatography-mass spectrometry (GC-MS), or liquid chromatography-mass spectrometer (LC-MS) – along with meticulous QA/QC program, enables detection of the majority of PPCPs in drinking water at the desired levels of analytical accuracy (Batt et al. 2017).

Table 10.2 Excretion rates of some common pharmaceuticals.

Pharmaceutical group	Drug name	Percent excreted
Antibiotic	Amoxycillin	60
	Erythromycin	25
β-blocker	Atenolol	90
Lipid regulator	Bezafibrate	50
Antiepileptic	Carbamazepine	3
	Felbamate	40–50
Antihistamine	Cetirizine	50
Anti-inflammatory	Diclofenac	15
Analgesics	Ibuprofen	10

Source: Modified after DEFRA (2007).

Table 10.3   Major PPCPs with example products.

Major drug type	Example products
A. Pharmaceuticals	
Analgesics	Acetaminophen, Aspirin, Paracetamol
Antibiotics	Levofloxacin, Penicillin, Sulfamethoxazole, β-lactam, cephalosporin, quinolone
Anti-inflammatory	Diclofenac, Ibuprofen, Naproxen
Antihypertensives	Losartan, Spirapril HCl, Perindopril erbumine, Nisoldipine
β-Blockers (cardiac drug)	Bisoprolol, Metoprolol, Amlodipine, Captopril
Cycostatics	Methotrexate, Bleomycin, Inforamide, Cyclophosphamide
Lipid regulators	Clofibric acid, Gemfibrozil, Bezafibrate
Hormones	Diethylstilbestrol, Estrone, Estriol, Ethiynloestradiol
Psychiatrics	Carbamazepine, Fluoxetine, Clorazepate
Stimulants	Caffeine, Paraxanthine
B. Personal care products	
Bactericides, disinfectants	Triclosan, triclocarban
Fragrances	Glaxolide, toxalide
Insect repellents	*N,N*-Diethyl-*m*-toluamide (DEET)
Preservatives	Parabens
Sunscreen UV filters	2-Ethyl-hexyl-4-trimethoxycinnamate (EHMC), 4-Methyl-benzylidene-camphor (4-MBC), Octyl-methoxycinnamate (OMC), octyl-triazone (OC)
C. Contrast media	Iopamidol, iopromide, amidotrizoic acid, gadodiamid, gadopentat

10.1.3   What Comprises PPCPs

Based on the purpose and properties, PPCPs represent multiple classes of chemicals and include a broad range of drugs grouped in major types under analgesics, antibiotics, anti-inflammatory drugs, cardiac drugs, lipid regulators, β-blockers, hormones, nutraceuticals (vitamins), psychiatric and cytostatic drugs, and chemicals used for diagnostic contrast; along with personal care products – cosmetics, fragrances, sunscreens, insect repellents, etc. Table 10.3 shows major drug types with common examples.

In addition to PPCPs mentioned in Table 10.3, other substances and their metabolites, such as caffeine, nicotine, dietary supplements, pharmaceuticals used in making illicit drugs (fentanyl, phenobarbital, valium, etc.), and disinfectants are also included in PPCPs. They too have been detected in sewer system effluents and water bodies in the United States, EU, and other countries.

10.2   Concerns for PPCPs

The discovery of altered sex characteristics in fish, frogs, and other animals in the late 1970s, caused by farm chemicals and pharmaceuticals, resulted in a high level of global awareness on contamination of water and its potential impacts on human health (Rahman et al. 2009). A large number of anthropogenic chemicals – most pesticides, many pharmaceuticals, PCBs, PAHs, etc. – in common use, can cause disruption of sex hormones in animals. Such chemicals are referred to as hormone disruptors or EDCs because they adversely affect endocrine glands that secrete the hormones. Toxic pesticides, such as organochlorides, organophosphates, and carbamates have caused disruption of sex hormones in aquatic organisms, resulting in male fish showing female characteristics, leading to reduced fertility of females and sterility in males (Khan and Law 2005).

A large quantity of antibiotics is used to cure various diseases in humans and animals. The main drugs classes include: anti-infectives, such as antibiotics, parasiticides, etc.; biologics, comprising viruses, serums, toxins, etc.; and medicinal feed additives such as vitamins, antioxidants, food enzymes, etc. Pharmaceuticals, such as macrolide, sulfonamide, and tetracycline, as well as anesthetics, antacids, antiparasitic, bronchodilators, growth promoters, nutritional supplements, tranquilizers, etc., are routinely used in animal husbandry. Large-scale use of antibiotics triggers microbial resistance to antibiotics, making them ineffective in killing the microbes, which is counteracted by manufacturing higher potency antibiotics. After repeated exposure, the microbes again develop immunity, making the high-potency antibiotics ineffective. This creates an unending cycle of toxic and pharmaceutically active ingredients entering the hydrologic system, threatening human and ecological health. In the United States alone, each year, 2.8 million people are infected by antibiotic-resistant microbes (ARMs), resulting in over 3500 deaths (CDC 2021).

Besides the use of pharmaceuticals in industrial animal farming, a large amount is also used in fruit and vegetable production. For example, the antibiotic streptomycin is heavily used in fruit growing and also in bee-keeping, which has raised concern about the resistance of pathogens to these antibiotics.

In the United States and other developed countries, large-scale industrial operations to raise livestock, variously known as industrial livestock production, or concentrated feedlot operations (CAFOs), or animal feedlot operations (AFOs), proliferated during the 1980s. According to the US EPA, AFO is an agricultural operation where animals are kept and raised in confined conditions. AFOs are built to congregate animals, feed, manure, urine, dead animals, and production operations on a small land area. Feed is brought to the animals rather than the animals grazing or otherwise seeking feed in pastures, fields, or on rangeland. There were approximately 450 000 AFOs in the United States in 2019.

CAFO is a large AFO, with more than 1000 animal units (an animal unit is defined as an animal equivalent of 1000 lbs. live weight and equates to 1000 heads of beef cattle, 700 dairy cows, 2500 swine weighing more than 55 lbs., 125 000 broiler chickens, or 82 000 egg-laying hens) are confined on site for more than 45 days during the year (USDA 2021). An AFO that discharges manure or wastewater into a natural or man-made ditch, stream, or other waterway is defined as a CAFO, regardless of size. CAFOs are regulated by EPA under the Clean Water Act (see Chapter 3).

Due to the close proximity of hundreds to thousands of animals in small space, and to control and prevent the rapid spread of disease, veterinary pharmaceuticals (VPs) are used in large volumes to maintain and assure animal health for maximum meat production. VPs are delivered to the animals by mixing it with water, feed, or via injection, implant, oral, or topical mode. Antimicrobials, growth-promoting hormones, sedatives, and several other pharmaceuticals are routinely administered to the animals to prevent disease and accelerate their growth.

A large volume of pharmaceuticals is used in industrial livestock production – 11 000 t of antibiotics were used in livestock farms in 2017. AFOs have resulted in heavy demand for VPs that is evidenced in their global sales revenue, which increased from $18.5 bn in 2005 to $24.2 bn in 2015 (Sneeringer et al. 2019). These and other pharmaceutical products, administered to tens of thousands of livestock, are excreted in large volumes through animal urine and feces containing the drugs and their metabolites, which is turned into slurry, temporarily held in ponds, and later

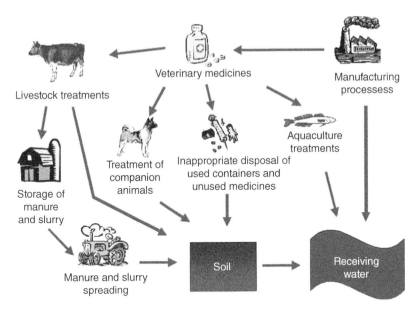

Figure 10.1 Pathways of veterinary pharmaceuticals in the environment. *Source:* USGS (2021). http://toxics.usgs.gov/highlights/vet_meds.html. Retrieved 20 May 2021.

disposed of by spreading on land. The slurry runs off the land and enters surface waters or seeps downward to contaminate groundwater. Surface water contamination affects aquatic life while contaminated groundwater, in many cases, ends up in water supplies with potentially harmful effects to people who draw their drinking water supply from it. One of the reasons given for disposing of animal excreta on the fields is to add nutrients to the soil. However, the presence of harmful chemicals in VPs has the potential to contaminate the soil. The development of ARMs is yet another concern related to the heavy use of antimicrobial drugs in VPs. Figure 10.1 shows the pathways by which VPs find their way in surface and groundwater systems.

Major ecological accidents occur when the holding ponds breach or overflow, releasing the slurry loaded with high amounts of nitrogen, antibiotics, and other harmful chemicals that cause mass fish killings upon entering surface water, such as rivers, streams, and lakes. One such incident, in July 2012, caused by the uncontrolled release of pig manure from a large industrial pig farm in Iroquois County, northern Illinois, caused pollution of over 32 km of the Beaver Creek and killed about 150 000 fish and 20 000 freshwater mussels. Of the 27 fish species, nine were lost forever as they were not detected in the Beaver Creek even two years after the spill; and two of the 18 mussel species that were on the Illinois State's threatened species list, were wiped out (Jackson and Marx 2016).

The use of biosolids – processed dry sewage sludge approved for agricultural applications – in farmlands is yet another issue of concern because they contain PPCPs and their metabolites, in addition to toxic metals. Reports of adverse impacts on wildlife and in a few instances on human health have been reported (Kinney et al. 2008; Lowman et al. 2013).

10.3 Sources of PPCPs in the Environment

The occurrence of PPCPs in water and soil is not a new phenomenon. Ever since PPCPs have been in use, some of them get into the environment through excretion from end users (humans, pets, and cattle) or as direct disposal (flushing in the toilet or tossing in the trash bin). The chemical ingredients may stay unchanged but usually metabolize by oxidation, reduction, hydrolysis, or other reactions into other products, many of which are generally toxic. The fact that PPCPs were not given any attention by environmental regulators was due to their tiny amount – ppb to ppt level – and lack of appropriate analytical technology for its accurate detection. Interest in the study of PPCPs in the environment was initiated in Europe in the late 1980s. Incentives for research on potential health impacts to humans came about because of the small land area of most European countries and release of PPCPs-contaminated sewage treatment plant (STP) effluents into water bodies, next to other water users in neighboring countries.

PPCPs are generated from a number of sources: residential, industrial, and agricultural waste-waters; pharmaceutical production facilities, careless disposal of leftover medications by individu-als and pharmacists; medical waste from hospitals, nursing homes, and clinics; landfills, STPs, application of biosolids to land, illicit drug labs; farm chemicals, sewage discharged from cruise ships, AFOs, aquaculture facilities, and washing and release of personal care products applied topically on the body. Since PPCPs from these sources end up in sewage systems and because wastewater treatment plants (WWTPs) are not designed to remove PPCPs, it stays in the effluent that is discharged into water bodies and is also retained in sewage sludge. Figure 10.2 shows com-mon sources and pathways of PPCPs' entry into the environment.

Enforcement of environmental laws in the majority of Western countries prohibits the release of hazardous and toxic effluents from pharmaceutical manufacturing plants. The situation is different in

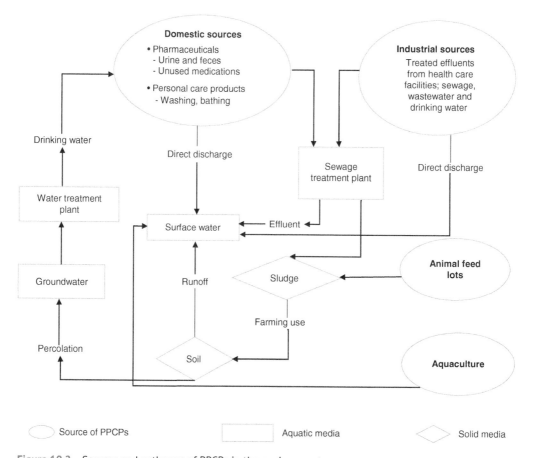

Figure 10.2   Sources and pathways of PPCPs in the environment.

developing countries where due to lax or poor enforcement of environmental laws, large quantities of harmful effluents from pharmaceutical manufacturing plants are carelessly released into nearby land and water bodies. For example, treated effluent from a WWTP that received process water from pharmaceutical production plants located at the Patancheru Industrial Development District, near Hyderabad city, India, was found to be loaded with 23 drugs, all with concentrations of >1 ppb. Exceptionally high level of ciprofloxacin, an active ingredient in the antibiotic, fluoroquinolone, was found to range between 28 000 and 31 000 ppb (Larsson et al. 2007). Extensive pollution of the two nearby streams, Nakkavagu and Peddavagu, killed all aquatic life, rendered agricultural fields infertile, caused health problems and diseases to the village residents, and heavily contaminated the groundwater due to hydraulic connection between the streams and the aquifer (Rao et al. 2001).

PPCPs and their metabolites are found in all three environmental media, namely air, water, and soil (land). But it is the aquatic compartment of the environment, the major receptacle, which has been studied the most. As discussed before, pharmaceuticals and their metabolites used in human and veterinary medicines are only partly absorbed in the body, and a significant fraction is excreted in both metabolized and unmetabolized forms in urine or feces that enter the raw sewage.

Veterinary drugs can directly contaminate soils and water because, unlike human drugs, they do not pass through STPs. Embalming fluids and other chemicals used during the burial of dead bodies can leach from cemeteries to contaminate soil, surface, and groundwater. Disposal of unused or expired medications by flushing in the toilet; waste-containing drugs from manufacturing establishments, and patients' excretion during and after receiving therapy also contribute to PPCPs' entry into the aquatic environment.

10.3.1 PPCPS in Sewage Treatment Plants

News of the discovery of PPCPs in sewage effluents during the 1980s first studied in Europe (Ternes 2004) and later in the United States (Kolpin et al. 2002; Stackelberg et al. 2004), Canada (Metcalfe et al. 2004), and presence of EDCs in the drinking water supply of major cities in the US and EU countries (Khiari 2007), was extensively carried by the popular media and caught the attention of regulators and water supply industries.

The US Geological Survey's Contaminant Biology Program that started in the 1940s had initially focused on the effects of contaminants in fish and wildlife. However, increasing pollution and deterioration of the nation's water quality during the 1960s–1980s led to the establishment of the Toxic Hydrology Program in 1982. These two programs were merged into the Environmental Health mission in 2010. The program investigates contaminant and pathogen sources, transport, exposure, pathways, biological effects, and potential human health consequences. The United States Geological Survey (USGS) in 1999–2000 conducted water sampling at 139 streams near heavily urbanized areas and livestock farms, and detected several PPCPs including coprostanol (fecal steroid), cholesterol (plant and animal steroid), N,N-diethyltoluamide (insect repellant), caffeine (stimulant), triclosan (antimicrobial disinfectant), tri(2-chloroethyl) phosphate (fire retardant), and 4-nonylphenol (nonionic detergent metabolite). However, measured concentrations were found to be low, rarely exceeding drinking water guidelines (Kolpin et al. 2002). This was the first national survey of water resources that highlighted the importance of obtaining data on PPCPs and their metabolites to understand their fate and transport in water bodies and their potential effect on human and ecological health.

During the mid-1970s to mid-1980s, some studies were conducted in the USA and Europe to detect the presence of PPCPs in STP effluents. Garrison et al. (1976) were probably the first in the United States who in 1972 and 1973 analyzed the effluents from STPs located in Cincinnati, Ohio, and identified clofibrate metabolite, caffeine, nicotine, steroids (cholesterol, coprostanol), among other organic compounds in the effluent. Rogers et al. (1986) conducted studies on effluent from the Iona Island STP, Vancouver, Canada and identified two common PPCPs, ibuprofen (analgesic) and naproxen (anti-inflammatory). Detailed investigations on characterizing influents and effluents in the STPs took off in the 1990s in several countries including Brazil, Canada, China, Germany, India, Italy, Spain, the USA, etc., and for the past 20 years, studies on the presence of PPCPs in the environment have received serious consideration due to their potential adverse impacts on human and ecological health.

Conventional STPs that use screening, degritting, primary sedimentation, aeration, and final sedimentation are designed to remove C-, N-, and P-compounds and microorganisms, that regularly arrive at STPs in ppm concentration, but they are generally ineffective in removing PPCPs. Removal of PPCPs in STPs depends on the biological and chemical nature of the pollutants. While some PPCPs, such as parabens can be effectively eliminated in STPs (average removal rate >90%), most PPCPs are only partially removed, and others are not removed at all. Couto et al. (2019) provide an extensive discussion of 45 PPCPs occurring in 30 STPs from all over the world, along with their removal rates.

10.3.2   Occurrence of PPCPs in Drinking Water

The ongoing increase in the world's urban population – from about 34% in 1960 to over 56% in 2020, and projected to reach 68% by 2050 – requires the municipalities/city government to ensure that all essential services provided to the citizens are safe, including drinking water supply and sanitation. Water treatment plants (WTPs) are designed to collect raw water from surface water bodies or groundwater and treat it to the required federal and local specifications before selling it to consumers. In addition, local governments are responsible for the treatment of wastewaters coming from residences and businesses to an acceptable level of purity before discharging it into water bodies. Allowable limits for various contaminants have been set under the Water Pollution Act and Safe Drinking Water Act as discussed in Chapter 3.

A variety of hazardous and environmentally persistent chemicals in PPCPs are not removed in conventional WTPs and enter surface and groundwater, which are the primary sources of drinking water supply in urban areas. The USGS, in collaboration with the US EPA, conducted a nationwide study involving the presence of PPCPs in both the source and treated drinking waters across the United States between 2007 and 2012. Furlong et al. (2017) reported the presence of 118 PPCPs in drinking water samples collected from 25 WTPs. Studies conducted during the past 20 years on the presence of PPCPs in hydrologic systems have concluded that drinking water poses no risk to the urban population, although its severity is yet to be fully investigated.

10.4   Environmental Impacts of PPCPs

Studies carried out so far indicate that owing to the low concentration of PPCPs in the aquatic environment, in the ppt to ppb range, its occurrence in humans is likely to be even lower, and may not be detrimental to health. However, caution needs to be exercised because a full understanding of life-long exposure from ingesting PPCPs-contaminated water is lacking.

10.4.1   PPCPs in Drinking Water and Its Health Impact

PPCPs' occurrence in the urban drinking water supply is influenced by:

• Source of raw (or intake) water – lake, reservoir, stream, or groundwater

- Location of the raw water source – whether near, upstream, or downstream of STP or industrial WWTP
- Type of treatment used for raw water purification.

In general, groundwater is the least contaminated source of raw water, followed by unpolluted streams. Enclosed bodies of water, such as lakes and reservoirs, can accumulate harmful PPCP chemicals over a period of time to pose risks. Raw water intake should be located as far upstream as possible from sources of discharge of contaminated effluents from industries, AFOs, and similar sources.

Water supply companies generally treat raw water by subjecting it to flocculation, bed (or media) filtration, and chlorination; this treatment system has not been found to be effective in removing most PPCPs. Long-term exposure to low doses of individual drugs or a combination of drugs, particularly if their effect is additive, could be harmful. Despite the low concentration, lifelong exposure to PPCPs has the potential to cause serious health problems. In addition, scarcity of water in many regions of the world, including some of the arid and semi-arid areas in the southwest United States, has led to investigating the feasibility of using wastewater for drinking purposes. There is no federal law in the United States to regulate PPCPs in source and finished drinking waters, but the state of California requires monitoring PPCPs in wastewater intended for use as a source of drinking water.

10.4.2 Treatment Technologies for PPCPs' Removal

As discussed before, conventional WWTPs, using the two-step sedimentation (primary) and activated sludge (secondary) treatment process, can remove some biodegradable PPCPs, but cannot remove many other PPCPs. However, coagulation and filtration, if used in combination with chlorination, can remove about 50% of PPCPs. Advanced treatment involving ozonation, UV irradiation, GAC, photocatalysis, reverse osmosis (RO) and nanofiltration, can remove up to 100% of PPCPs (WHO 2012; Yang et al. 2017).

Table 10.4 shows the occurrence of some common PPCPs found in drinking water provided by a water supply company to a large metropolitan area in the Southeastern United States that uses river water as the source.

Table 10.4   Occurrence of common PPCPs in drinking water.

PPCPs	Finished water concentration, ng/L	
	Median	Range
Bisphenol-A	2.7	54.3–0
Clarithromycin	0.1	0.3–0
DEET	11.9	32.2–0.4
Erythromycin	1.5	16.4–0.9
Nonylphenol	19.5	79.8–7.1
TCEP (reducing agent, used as flame retardant)	3.7	26.2–0
Triclosan	1.4	85.3–0
Trimethoprim	1.5	24.3–0

Source: Modified after Padhye et al. (2014).

Conventional drinking WTPs, using coagulation, flocculation, and filtration, is generally ineffective in PPCPs' removal. Chlorination, using free chlorine, was found to be highly effective in removing antibiotics. When combined with ozonation, chlorination can achieve higher removal efficiency by adjusting pH and oxidation dose.

Ozonation can remove many PPCPs, including endocrine disrupters, antiviral and antibacterial compounds, through a chemical transformation but does not achieve mineralization, which is breaking down the constituent chemicals into simple, harmless molecules, like H_2O, O_2, or CO_2. So, despite the removal of these compounds, the toxicity of the transformed compounds and their potential impacts on human health are a matter of concern that needs to be fully investigated.

RO has emerged as an effective and reliable method of pharmaceutical removal from drinking water and is being used for raw water treatment or polishing of drinking water supply. Table 10.5 lists the removal of selected pharmaceuticals in drinking water by various treatment systems.

The ability to detect even the minutest amounts (ppt level) while useful in determining harmful levels of pharmaceuticals in drinking water should be viewed with prudence: There should not be an overemphasis on upgrading the water treatment infrastructure for removing all PPCPs until conclusive data on harmful effects are available. This is because drinking water quality monitoring and treatment plant upgrading are highly capital-intensive undertakings, and given the uncertainty, may not justify the use of limited resources.

10.5 Forensic Applications of PPCPs

Daughton (2001) was one of the first researchers to propose using drugs or their metabolites in sewage as an indicator of the use of an illicit drug in a population, suggesting that wastewater analysis can be used to control illicit drug use in a community. The presence and concentrations of benzoylecgonine or ecgonine methyl ester, for example, can serve as a surrogate for cocaine to determine its use. Similarly, the concentration of morphine in sewage water could be used to determine the presence of several classes of opiates. The idea led to the development of a new field of study called wastewater-based epidemiology (WBE). The first application of wastewater analysis to estimate cocaine use in Italy was carried out by Zuccato et al. (2005). Since then, there has been a rapid increase in studies using WBE to provide objective and near real-time data on the concentration of illicit or abused drugs within the catchment area of a WWTP and the population residing therein. WBE is being used as a complementary method for estimating illicit drug consumption in the population. Temporal and spatial drug consumption estimates derived from WBE are being used by law enforcement and public health agencies for surveillance of suspected drug use locales and in developing drug use policies. WBE has recently (2021) been used to determine the prevalence of COVID-19 in a given population.

10.5.1 PPCPs' Application in Geological Dating

Assigning an age to geological events on a narrow time frame (years–decades) has been a daunting task. An interesting aspect of PPCPs in the environment is related to their potential use as a tracer in hydrological studies. Kummerer (2008) pointed out that some chemicals found in PPCPs persist in the environment and can serve as a possible tracer in the hydrological investigation to determine the human impact on the aquatic environment, and to estimate the age of the groundwater. One of the contrast media, gadolinium-bearing solution, used in magnetic resonance imaging (MRI) for

Table 10.5 Removal of selected pharmaceuticals by various drinking water treatment systems.

Pharmaceuticals	Treatment system	Concertation, ng/L		Removal rate, %
		Raw water	Treated water	
A. Anti-inflammatory drugs				
Ibuprofen	PO, CO, SD, MF, DS	314	0.5	90.2
	CO, FO, SD, MS, OZ, CL	6.6	1.3	80.3
	DS	16.6	8.8	47
Diclofenac	DC, CO, FO, SD, MS,OZ, AC	234	ND	>99
B. Analgesics				
Acetaminophen	PO, CO, SD. MF, DS	75	<0.03	>99
C. Antibiotics				
Sulfamethoxazole	CO, SD, MS	4.4	ND	>99
	MS	0.087	0.37	57.5
Clarithromycin	DC, CO, FO, SD, MS, OZ, AC	48	ND	>99
Erythromycin	DC, CO, FO, SD, MS, OZ, AC	3200	200	99.4
Trimethoprim	DC, CO, FO, SD, MS, OZ, AC	16	ND	>99
D. β-Blockers				
Atenolol	CO, FO, SD, MS, OZ, CL	11	0.4	96.3
	CL, CO, FO, MS	470	380	19.1
E. Cardiac drugs				
Clopidogrel	CL, CO, MF	2	ND	>99
Hydrochlorothiazide	CL, CO, MF	670	74	89
Warfarin	CL, CO, FO, MS	1	0.2	80
F. Hormones				
Estrone	CL, CO, FO, MF	0.3	ND	>99
Estriol	CL, CO, FO, MF	26	ND	>99
Ethinyl estradiol	CL, CO, FO, MF	2.5	—	>99
Tamoxifen	CL, CO, FO, MS	0.1	ND	>99
G. Lipid regulators				
Gemfibrozil	DC, CO, FO, SD, MS, OZ, AC	257	ND	>99
Bezafibrate	CO, FO, SD, MS, OZ, CL	1.9	ND	>99
	MS, DS	0.7	0.5	28.6
H. Psychiatric drugs				
Carbamazepine	CO, SD, MS	1.8	ND	>99
	PO, CO, SD, MF, DS	186	40.4	75.5

AC = activated carbon; CO = coagulation; CL = chlorination; DC = dioxychlorination; DS = disinfection; FO = flocculation; GD = groundwater dilution; MF = filtration in anthracite-sand media; MS = filtration in sand media; OZ = ozonation; PO = preoxidation; SD = sedimentation ND = not detected.
Source: Modified after Couto et al. (2019).

disease diagnosis, and other common PPCP compounds, such as caffeine and clofibrate, could serve as good tracers because of their persistence in the environment.

The presence of persistent and nonbiodegradable PPCP chemicals in contaminated sediment or groundwater could provide information on the age of the geological material. For example, the drug *Vioxx*, a nonsteroidal anti-inflammatory drug was prescribed to 80 million people worldwide for treatment of osteoarthritis and acute/chronic pain conditions. *Vioxx* was approved by the US Food and Drug Administration on 20 May 1999 and was widely used for about five years. On 30 September 2004, the drug manufacturer, Merck, voluntarily withdrew the drug from the market owing to concerns about an increased risk of heart attack and stroke associated with long-term and high-dose use of *Vioxx*. Given this time frame, the presence of *Vioxx* or its metabolites in sediment or groundwater could narrow down their age to within a 5-year time bracket of 1999–2004.

10.6   Research Status and Future Needs

A great deal of valuable studies on PPCPs and their environmental impacts have been conducted during the past 30 years. Currently, there is an impressive array of ongoing research world over focusing on filling the data gaps and generating reliable information and conclusive evidence to answer some of the uncertainties that exist today. This is evident from the comprehensive bibliometric work of Daughton (2016) and Daughton and Scuderi (2019), involving the search of about 30 000 published works on PPCPs, covering a 70-year period, ending 2017. Relatively fewer articles were published before the 1940s, but concerted research began in the late 1980s, and articles dealing with PPCPs have exploded during the past 50 years (Figure 10.3).

It is worth noting that the majority of PPCP articles were published in journals in environmental sciences and environmental toxicology, and only a small number (< 1%) were published in health science journals (medicine and health care).

PPPCs contain chemical ingredients that are designed to maximize their biological activity at low concentrations over a long period of time. These properties highlight any chronic risks associated with the presence of PPCPs in the environment. Future research should address:

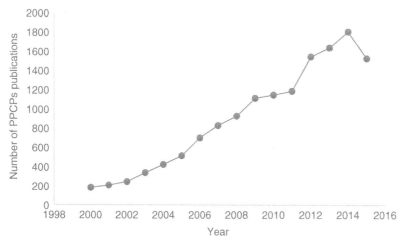

Figure 10.3   Growth of published PPCP articles during the past 15 years. *Source:* Data from Daughton (2016).

- *Innovative treatment methods*: STPs, along with agricultural and animal farms, PPCP production plants, and aquaculture factories, are the main sources of PPCPs' entry into the aquatic environment. Since WWTPs do not completely remove PPCPs, there is a critical need to investigate advanced treatment technologies for cost-effective and more efficient removal of PPCPs.
- *Impacts on human health*: Though it is well known that the presence of PPCPs in the aquatic environment produces detrimental impacts on aquatic life, very little is known about the health impacts on humans. This aspect needs to be studied in full detail.
- *Temporal changes*: Knowledge about the seasonal variability in concentrations of common PPCPs in the aquatic environment is very limited. Further investigations are needed to understand the nature of seasonal variations of PPCPs in various environmental compartments.
  Bioaccumulation in the food chain and wildlife: (1) The full extent of bioaccumulation of PPCPs in aquatic organisms such as algae, crustaceans, and fish and their potential implications for human exposure from the consumption of contaminated fish or shellfish, need detailed studies. (2) Currently, very little is known about the levels of PPCPs in wildlife. Few studies have investigated PPCP residues in fish, birds, and mammals. There is a lack of information on the potential trophic magnification of these compounds or the influence of prenatal exposure on the possible transfer of PPCPs to birds' eggs and other wildlife.
- *PPCPs' fate*: PPCPs' sorption to sediment particles has been found useful in determining the fate of PPCPs in the aquatic environment. Detailed studies on how sediment acts as a sink for these contaminants are required.
  Toxicological effects: (1) Current understanding of toxicological effects from chronic exposure to mixtures of PPCPs at subtherapeutic levels in humans and other organisms need to be advanced. (2) Degradation products and metabolites of EDCs and other drugs under varying environmental conditions, such as temperature, pressure, humidity, UV light, etc., need to be thoroughly investigated because of the possibility of formation of more toxic and/or bioaccumulative compounds than the parent PPCPs.(3) Majority of the PPCPs are designed for humans, mammals, and birds used in agribusiness, targeting specific organs to treat infection or disease, but not for aquatic species. Acute effects from PPCP exposure are relatively well known, but knowledge on chronic effects, especially on fish, is limited.
- *Other*: While studies done in Europe and North America have provided ample information on PPCPs' presence in water bodies, such data are lacking for countries in Africa, Asia, and South America.

10.7 Summary

Humans have relied on plants, minerals, and animal products for the healing and treatment of diseases since ancient times. For the past 150 years, synthetic chemicals have been increasingly used as active chemical ingredients in thousands of medicinal formulations for the treatment of a wide variety of diseases.

PPCPs represent a large group of pharmaceuticals and personal care products used by individuals for personal health or cosmetic reasons, and in agribusiness to prevent disease and enhance livestock production. Major sources of PPCPs in the environment include: STPs, agricultural and animal farms, residences, hospitals, clinics, and drug production facilities. Heavy use of antibiotics has led to the development of antibiotic-resistant microbes. Pharmaceuticals used in animal feedlots have caused major ecological accidents due to the mismanagement of animal excreta.

Many of the active chemical ingredients used in PPCPs are bioaccumulative, persistent, toxic, and can remain in the water, soil, and sediment for an indefinite period of time. A wide variety of hazardous and environmentally persistent chemicals, including PPCPs, are present in urban wastewater that survives conventional STPs to enter surface and groundwater. The presence of PPCPs in urban drinking water supply has been reported from all over the world. Conventional WWTPs are not effective in removing most PPCPs. Advanced treatment involving ozonation, UV irradiation, GAC, RO, and nanofiltration, can remove up to 100% of PPCPs from wastewater.

Wastewater analyses of drugs or their metabolites in sewage have led to the development of a new field of study, called WBE, which is being used as an indicator of illicit drug use in a community and a complementary tool for drug control and enforcement policies. PPCPs' presence in the waters can also be used as tracers in hydrological investigations and for geologic age determination because of their persistence in the environment.

Data gap and research needs include addressing the potential health impacts from PPCPs to humans, wildlife, and levels of trophic magnification. Detailed studies on the toxicity of degradation products of EDCs and other drugs need to be investigated, as well as potential human health problems from consuming PPCP-contaminated fish. There is a need to evaluate environmental contamination from pharmaceutical production facilities in emerging economies, particularly India and China, and enforce measures to control the resulting problems.

Study Questions

1   What are PPCPs? Discuss the main sources and occurrence of PPCPs in the environment.

2   Why are the aquatic life forms most vulnerable to PPCPs? Why are humans not as susceptible?

3   Why can conventional sewage treatment plants (STPs) not remove most of the PPCPs? What advanced methods can be used to remove the majority of PPCPs from STP effluents?

4   Effluents from conventional STPs and animal manure from AFOs are discharged into land and water. Which of the environmental ecosystem (terrestrial or aquatic) is most threatened by PPCPs? Explain why, and discuss its long-term ecological consequences?

5   The public drinking water supply in many US cities contains traces of PPCPs. Why is drinking such water still considered safe?

6   What is wastewater-based epidemiology? Where is it used most? Do you think using this method to identify illicit drug makers or users raises socio-ethical issues? If so, why?

7   List two forensic applications of PPCPs? How can the presence of a particular drug in water be used for narrowing down the age range of geological materials, such as sediment, groundwater, etc.?

8   List some of the data gaps for assessing the ecological and human health effects of PPCPs. Discuss at least two of them in detail.

References

Batt, A.L., Furlong, E.T., Heath, E.M. et al. (2017). The importance of quality control in validating concentrations of contaminants of emerging concern in source and treated drinking water samples. *Science of the Total Environment* 579: 1620–1628. https://doi.org/10.1016/j.scitotenv.2016.02.127.

Bradley, P.M. and Kolpin, D.W. (2013). Managing the effects of endocrine disrupting chemicals. In: *Wastewater-Impacted Streams, Current Perspectives in Contaminant Hydrology and Water Resources Sustainability* (ed. P.M. Bradley), 3–26. IntechOpen https://doi.org/10.5772/54337. https://www.intechopen.com/books/current-perspectives-in-contaminant-hydrology-and-water-resources-sustainability/managing-the-effects-of-endocrine-disrupting-chemicals-in-wastewater-impacted-streams.

CDC (2021). Antibiotic Resistance Threats in the United States, 150 p. www.cdc.gov/DrugResistance/Biggest-Threats.html. http://dx.doi.org/10.15620/cdc:82532 (accessed 14 August 2021).

Christel, M. (2020). Pharm Exec's Top 50 Companies 2020. https://www.pharmexec.com/view/pharm-execs-top-50-companies-2020 (accessed 10 August 2021).

Couto, C.F., Lange, L.C., and Amaral, M.C.S. (2019). Occurrence, fate and removal of pharmaceutically active compounds (PhACs) in water and wastewater treatment plants—a review. *Journal of Water Process Engineering* 32: 100927. https://doi.org/10.1016/j.jwoe.2019.100927.

Cunningham, V.L. (2004). Special characteristics of pharmaceuticals related to environmental fate. In: *Pharmaceuticals in the Environment: Sources, Fate, Effects and Risks*, 2e (ed. K. Kummerer), 13–24. Berlin: Springer.

Daughton, C.G. (2016). Pharmaceuticals and the Environment (PiE): evolution and impact of the published literature revealed by bibliometric analysis. *Science of the Total Environment* 562: 391–426. https://doi.org/10.1016/j.scitotenv.2016.03.109.

Daughton, C.G. (2001). Illicit drugs in municipal sewage: proposed new non-intrusive tool to heighten public awareness of societal use of illicit/abused drugs and their potential for ecological consequences. In: *Pharmaceuticals and Personal Care Products in the Environment: Scientific and Regulatory Issue*, Symposium Series 791 (ed. C.G. Daughton and T.L. Jones-Lepp), 348–364. American Chemical Society.

Daughton, C.G. and Scuderi, M.S.T. (2019). *Pharmaceuticals and Personal Care Products (PPCPs): Relevant Literature*. Las Vegas, NV: U.S. Environmental Protection Agency https://sites.google.com/site/daughton/PPCPs-bibliographic_database.

Daughton, C.G. and Ternes, T.A. (1999). Pharmaceuticals and Personal Care Products in the Environment: Agents of Subtle Change? *Environmental Health Perspectives* 107 (Supplement 6): 907–930.

DEFRA (2007). Desk based review of current knowledge on pharmaceuticals in drinking water and estimation of potential levels. Final Report for Department of Environment, Food and Rural Affairs, *CSA 7184/WT02046/DW170/2/213*. https://dwi.defra.gov.uk/resaerch/reports/dwi70-2-213.pdf (accessed 14 August 2021).

EPA (2008). White paper: aquatic life criteria for contaminants of emerging concern, 86 p.

Furlong, E.T., Batt, A.L., Glassmeyer, S.T. et al. (2017). Nationwide reconnaissance of contaminants of emerging concern in source and treated drinking waters of the United States: pharmaceuticals. *Science of the Total Environment* 579: 1629–1642. https://doi.org/10.1016/j.scitotenv.2016.03.128.

Garrison, A.W., Pope, J.D., and Allen, F.R. (1976). GC/MS analysis of organic pollutants in water. In: *Identification and Analysis of Organic Pollutants in Water* (ed. L.H. Keith), 517–556. Chichester: Wiley.

Hasan, S.E. (2021). Medical geology. In: *Encyclopedia of Geology*, 2e (ed. D. Alderton and S.A. Elias), 684–702. United Kingdom: Academic Press https://doi.org/10.1016/B978-0-12-409548-9.12523-0.

Jackson, D. and Marx, G. (2016). Spills of Pig Waste Kill Hundreds of Thousands of Fish in Illinois. Chicago Tribune. https://www.chicagotribune.com/investigations/ct-pig-farms-pollution-met-20160802-story.html (accessed 20 May 2021).

Khan, M.Z. and Law, F.C.P. (2005). Adverse effects of pesticides and related chemicals on enzyme and hormone systems of fish, amphibians and reptiles: a review. *Proceedings, Pakistan Academy of Sciences* 42 (4): 315–323.

Khiari, D. (2007). Endocrine disruptors, pharmaceuticals and personal care products in drinking water: an overview of AWWARF research to date. *Drinking Water Research 17* (2): 2–7.

Kinney, C.A., Furlong, E.T., Kolpin, D.W. et al. (2008). Bioaccumulation of pharmaceuticals and other anthropogenic waste indicators in earthworms from agricultural soil amended with biosolids or swine manure. *Environmental Science & Technology, vol.* 42: 1863–1870.

Kolpin, D.K., Furlong, E.T., Meyer, M.T. et al. (2002). Pharmaceuticals, hormones, and other organic wastewater contaminants in U.S. streams, 1999–2000: a national reconnaissance. *Environmental Science & Technology* 36 (6): 1202–1211.

Larsson, D.G.J., de Pedro, C., and Paxeus, N. (2007). Effluent from drug manufactures contains extremely high levels of pharmaceuticals. *Journal of Hazardous Materials* 148 (3): 751–755. https://doi.org/10.1016/j.jhazmat.2007.07.008.

Lowman, A., McDonald, M.A., Wing, S., and N; and Muhammad, N. (2013). Land application of treated sewage sludge: community health and environmental justice. *Environmental Health Perspectives* 121: 537–542.

Metcalfe, C., Miao, X.-S., Hua, W. et al. (2004). Pharmaceuticals in the Canadian environment. In: *Pharmaceuticals in the Environment: Sources, Fate, Effects and Risks*, 2e (ed. K. Kummerer), 67–90. Berlin: Springer.

Padhye, P., Yao, H., and Kung, F.T. (2014). Year-long evaluation on the occurrence and fate of pharmaceuticals, personal care products, and endocrine disrupting chemicals in an urban drinking water treatment plant. *Water Research* 51: 266–276. https://doi.org/10.1016/j.watres.2013.10.070.

Rahman, M.F., Yanful, E.K., and Jasim, S.Y. (2009). Endocrine disrupting compounds (EDCs) and pharmaceuticals and personal care products (PPCPs) in the aquatic environment: implications for the drinking water industry and global environmental health. *Journal of Water and Health* 7 (2): 224–243. https://doi.org/10.2166/wh.2009.021.

Rao, V.V.S.G., Dhar, R.L., and Subrahmanyam, K. (2001). Assessment of contaminant migration in groundwater from an industrial development area, Medak district, Andhra Pradesh, India. *Water Air Soil Pollution* 128: 369–389.

Rogers, I.L., Birtwell, I.K., and Kruznyski, G.M. (1986). Organic extractables in municipal wastewater of Vancouver, British Columbia. *Water Pollution Research Journal of Canada, vol.* 21: 187–204.

Sierra (2021). PPE under the sea. *Sierra* 106 (4): 44.

Sneeringer, S., Bowman, M., and Clancy, M. (2019). *The U.S. and EU Animal Pharmaceutical Industries in the Age of Antibiotic Resistance, ERR-264*. U.S. Department of Agriculture, Economic Research Service 69 p.

Stackelberg, P.E., Furlong, E.T., Meyer, M.T. et al. (2004). Persistence of pharmaceutical compounds and other organic wastewater contaminants in a conventional drinking-water-treatment plant. *Science of the Total Environment* 329 (1–3): 99–113. https://doi.org/10.1016/j.scitotenv.2004.03.015.

Ternes, T.A. (2004). Assessment of Technologies for the Removal of Pharmaceuticals and Personal Care Products in Sewage and Drinking Water Facilities to Improve the Indirect Potable Water Reuse, PSEIDON Detailed Report, 58 p.

USDA (2021). Animal Feeding Operations (AFO) and Concentrated Animal Feeding Operations (CAFO). www.nrcs.usda.gov (accessed 10 July 2021).

USGS (2021). Environmental Health – Toxic Substances Hydrology Program: Veterinary Medicines in the Environment. https://toxics.usgs.gov/highlights/vet_meds.html (accessed 10 July 2021).

Wang, Z., Walker, G.W., Muir, D.C.G., and Nagatani-Yoshida, K. (2020). Toward a global understanding of chemical pollution: a first comprehensive analysis of national and regional chemical inventories. *Environmental Science & Technology* 54 (5): 2575–2584. https://doi.org/10.1021/acs.est.9b06379.

WHO (2012). *Pharmaceuticals in Drinking-Water*, 35 p. Geneva, Switzerland: WHO Press 9789241502085_eng.pdf (who.int) (accessed 12 February 2022).

Yang, Y., Ok, Y.S., Kim, K.-H. et al. (2017). Occurrences and removal of pharmaceuticals and personal care products (PPCPs) in drinking water and water/sewage treatment plants: a review. *Science of the Total Environment* 596–597: 303–320. https://doi.org/10.1016/j.scitotenv.2017.04.102.

Zuccato, E., Chiabarndo, C., Castiglioni, S. et al. (2005). Cocaine in surface waters: a new evidence-based tool to monitor community drug abuse. *Environmental Health* 4: 14. https://doi.org/10.118 6/1476-069X-4-14.

Supplementary Reading

Daughton, C.G. (2016). Pharmaceuticals and the environment (PiE): evolution and impact of the published literature revealed by bibliometric analysis. *Science of the Total Environment* 562: 391–426. https://doi.org/10.1016/j.scitotenv.2016.03.109. [An excellent account of history of articles on PPCPs with detailed listing of major articles on the subject].

Ebele, A.J., Abdallah, M.A.-E., and Harrad, S. (2017). Pharmaceuticals and personal care products (PPCPs) in the freshwater aquatic environment. *Emerging Contaminants* 3 (1): 1–17. https://doi.org/10.1016/j.emcon.2016.12.004. [Good discussion of data gap and future research needs for PPCPs].

Kummerer, K. (2008). *Pharmaceuticals in the Environment: Sources, Fate, Effects and Risks*, 3e. Berlin: Springer [A valuable book that offers a comprehensive coverage of all aspects of PPCPs and could serve as a required reading in degree courses].

Petrovic, M. and Barcelo, D. (ed.) (2007). Analysis, fate and removal of pharmaceuticals in the water cycle. In: *Wilson and Wilson's Comprehensive Analytical Chemistry*, vol. 50. Amsterdam: Elsevier 564 p. [The entire volume is devoted to PPCPs: its sources, occurrences, ecotoxicity, risks, fate and removal, treatment technologies, and chemical and biological analytical methods. This is the only publication that has a list of about 150 common drugs with their therapeutic group, chemical formula, structure, molecular weight, and other parameters].

Web Resources

Berkey Co; PPCPs and EDC in Drinking Water – Contaminants of Emerging Concern. A layperson summary of potential environmental and health impacts of PPCPs and EDCs in drinking water and tips for avoiding them. https://theberkey.com/blogs/water-filter/ ppcps-and-edcs-in-drinking-water-contaminants-of-emerging-concern.

Daughton, C. G. and Scuderi, M. S. T. (2017. Pharmaceuticals and Personal Care Products (PPCPs). https://sites.google.com/site/daughton/PPCPs-bibliographic_database (A most comprehensive 1382-page data base, first implemented 19 February 2008, and updated 29 December 2019, listing about 30 000 s on all aspects of PPCPs, published during 1930–2019-an excellent resource for PPCPs research).

Acronyms/Symbols

bn	billion
GAC	Granulated activated charcoal
ng	nanogram, $1 \times 10^{-9} = 1\,ppb$
ppb	parts per billion, 1×10^{-9}
ppt	parts per trillion, 1×10^{-12}
QA/QC	Quality assurance/quality control
STP	Sewage treatment plant
WTP	Water treatment plant (drinking)
WWTP	Wastewater treatment plant

Glossary

A

Abiotic Without life; any system characterized by a lack of living organisms.

Aboveground storage tank (AST) One or more devices, including any connected piping, designed to contain an accumulation of petroleum, of which the volume, including the volume of underground pipes, is 90% or more above the surface of the grade.

Absorption Taking up, incorporation, or assimilation, as of liquids in solids, or of gases in liquids.

Accumulator plants Plants that accumulate high concentrations of certain metals in their systems.

Acid A solution that has a pH value lower than 7.

Activated carbon Finely powdered charcoal, having a very large surface area, used for the treatment of liquid waste.

Active exchange An organization that arranges for the transfer of hazardous waste from a generator to a manufacturer for use as raw material.

Active fault A fault in which the latest movement(s) occurred anytime between the present and the past 10 000 years.

Activity The disintegration of a radionuclide in a particular energy state at a given time per time interval (rate of radiation emission).

Acute exposure A single exposure to a hazardous material for a brief length of time.

Acutely hazardous waste Wastes listed in 40 CFR 261.31, including all P-code wastes, F022-F023 and F026-F028 wastes.

Adsorption Adherence of ions or molecules in solutions to the surface of solids.

Advection Transportation of dissolved contaminants with flowing groundwater.

Aerobic microorganisms Microorganisms that grow in the presence of oxygen.

Agency for Toxic Substances and Disease Registry (ATSDR) A federal agency established under the Comprehensive Environmental Response, Compensation, and Liability Act to perform specific functions concerning the effect of hazardous substances on public health and the environment. Specific functions include health assessments and health studies.

Agreement state A US State that has signed an agreement with the US Nuclear Regulatory Commission authorizing the State to regulate certain uses of radioactive materials within the state.

Introduction to Waste Management: A Textbook, First Edition. Syed E. Hasan.
© 2022 John Wiley & Sons Ltd. Published 2022 by John Wiley & Sons Ltd.

Air sparging A technique to treat contaminated groundwater. Compressed air is injected into the groundwater through specially designed wells. The air moves upward through the groundwater and soil, releasing the contaminant as vapor which may be extracted and treated using a soil vapor extraction system.

Air stripping A treatment system that removes or "strips" volatile organic compounds from contaminated groundwater or surface water by forcing an airstream through the water and causing the volatile compounds to dissipate.

Aliphatic organic compounds Hydrocarbon compounds having an open-chain structure, e.g. methane, ethane, and propane.

Aliquot Definite proportion of a given quantity, e.g. a portion from a large sample.

Alkane An organic compound composed of a straight chain of carbon atoms bound on all sides by hydrogen atoms and not containing any double bonds between carbon atoms, e.g. methane.

Alluvial Sediment formed by water action.

Anaerobic bacteria Microorganisms that grow in the absence of oxygen; some may even be killed by oxygen.

Analytes Chemical elements and compounds of interest that should be determined in a chemical analysis procedure.

Anion An atom or molecule with more electrons than protons. Anions have a net negative charge.

Anisotropism Property of earth materials that result in different values for a parameter depending on the direction of measurement.

Anthropogenic Anything related to human activity (as opposed to natural).

Anthropomorphic effects Effects of human activities.

Aqueous phase Of or pertaining to water.

Aquifer An underground geologic formation composed of materials such as rock, sand, soil, or gravel of high porosity and high permeability that can store and supply groundwater to wells and springs. A groundwater supply is usually considered an aquifer if it contains enough water to supply the water needs of a community.

Aquitard A confining layer of very low porosity and low permeability that prevents the flow of groundwater to and from an adjacent aquifer.

Aromatic compounds Generally refer to aromatic hydrocarbons having characteristic odor and benzene rings structure, e.g. benzene, naphthalene, toluene, etc.

Artesian well A well in a confined aquifer where the groundwater, under high hydrostatic pressure, rises above the top of the aquifer and flows out at the land surface.

Atomize Breaking of molecules of liquids into very fine particles.

Atterberg limits The liquid limit, plastic limit, and shrinkage limit for soil. The water content at which the soil behavior changes from the plastic to the liquid state is the liquid limit; from the semisolid to the plastic state is the plastic limit; and from the semisolid to the solid state is the shrinkage limit.

Autotrophic Microorganisms utilizing inorganic compounds as their sources of nutrients.

B

Background concentrations The level of a chemical that is consistently present in the environment or the vicinity of the site and is naturally present, or is the result of human activities unrelated to discharges or releases from the site.

Base A solution that has a pH value greater than 7.

Benthic Relating to or occurring at the bottom of a body of water.

Benzene A cancer-causing chemical associated with fuels, such as gasoline. Benzene evaporates quickly and dissolves easily in water.

Benzene, Toluene, Ethylbenzene, and Xylene (BTEX) Organic chemicals found in fuels that evaporate quickly and can cause cancer.

Best available technology A general term for the best method currently available to treat/dispose of a hazardous waste.

Bioaccumulate Substances that when taken into the body through contaminated food, water, or air slowly accumulate in body fat or tissues because the substances are slow to break down or excreted.

Biochemical oxygen demand (BOD) A measure of the amount of dissolved oxygen in a unit volume of water that is necessary for decomposition of organic materials. Water is considered polluted if the BOD drops to less than 5 milligrams per liter of water.

Biochemical response Measure of a change in or damage to the blood chemistry of a species as a result of exposure to a contaminant.

Biological air sparging Introduction of air into contaminated groundwater to promote the growth of microorganisms for eventual biodegradation of the hazardous constituents.

Biological degradation As used in the Superfund Program, the process by which biological agents can reduce or eliminate risks posed by a hazardous substance through decomposition into less hazardous.

Bioremediation A technique that uses microbes or plants to clean up contamination. Microbes generally break down the contamination into less harmful components, such as carbon dioxide and water. Bioremediation can be used to clean up contaminated soil or water. Some chemicals, such as gasoline, are easily bioremediated while others, such as pesticides, cannot be effectively treated using bioremediation.

Biostabilization The end point in a series of biochemical decomposition of waste where all elements for growth and survival of the microorganism have been used up and no further transformation of waste constituents can occur.

Bioventing A technique to treat soil contaminated with petroleum or organic chemicals. Air is forced into the soil through specially designed wells. The oxygen enhances the growth of naturally occurring bacteria in soils. The bacteria feed on the contaminants in the soils, chemically breaking down the contaminants into nonhazardous components.

Brittle solid Solids that fail when the applied stress exceeds their elastic limit.

Brownfield site Contaminated property which complicates its redevelopment, reuse, or expansion. The US Environmental Protection Agency's Brownfields Initiative is designed to empower states, communities, and other stakeholders in economic development to work together to prevent, assess, safely clean up, and sustainably reuse brownfields.

C

Caliche A solid, almost impervious, layer of whitish calcium carbonate in a soil profile.

Calorific value See heating value.

Capillary action The rise of water along narrow passages facilitated and caused by surface tension.

Capillary fringe The lower subdivision of the zone of aeration, immediately above the water table, in which the interstices are filled with water under pressure less than that of the atmosphere, being continuous with groundwater below but held above it by surface tension.

Capping Placement of a barrier over the contamination to prevent infiltration of water into the material below the cap. Caps are made of different materials including a geotextile (fabric) cover, soil, clay, sand, gravel, asphalt, or vegetation top layer. Caps are designed specifically for each area and can range from several inches to several feet thick.

Carbon adsorption/carbon filtration A treatment system for contaminated water or air, where the contaminated media is forced through tanks containing activated carbon. Activated carbon adsorbs the contaminants. This treatment is usually combined with other forms of treatment such as air stripping or oil/water separator. Spent carbon must be treated or properly disposed of.

Carboniferous period The Mississippian and Pennsylvanian periods combined, ranging from about 345 to about 280 million years ago.

Carcinogen A substance that causes or induces cancer.

Carcinogenicity Cancer-causing potential of a substance.

Cask A heavily shielded container used for the dry storage or shipment (or both) of radioactive materials such as spent nuclear fuel or other high-level radioactive waste (HLW). Casks are often made from lead, concrete, and/or steel and must meet regulatory requirements.

Cation exchange A reaction in which cations adsorbed on the surface of a solid, such as a clay mineral, are replaced by cations in the surrounding solution.

Cation An atom or molecule with more protons than electrons. Cations have a net positive charge.

Chain-of-custody A required document that contains information on the responsible parties that has the custody of analytical sample or samples during various stages of its sampling, transportation, analyses, and storage.

Characteristic wastes Waste that fails any of the characteristics of hazardous waste that include ignitability, corrosivity, reactivity, and/or toxicity.

Characterization The determination of the physical and chemical and, for radioactive waste, radiological properties of waste, or of other features, to establish the need for further adjustment, treatment or conditioning, or suitability for further handling, processing, storage, or disposal.

Chemical weathering The decomposition of rocks through chemical reactions such as hydration and oxidation.

Chlorinated hydrocarbons Any organic compound that contains chlorine in its chemical structures besides carbon and hydrogen.

Chronic disease Disease in which symptoms develop slowly after exposure, over a long period of time.

Clastic sedimentary rocks Rock composed principally of fragments derived from preexisting rocks or minerals.

Clay Very small mineral particles having a layered structure, formed as a result of chemical alteration of primary rock minerals. Clay particle dimensions are smaller than 0.002 mm (2 microns).

Clean close Removal or decontamination of all contaminated equipment, structures, liners, and soils, including records of sampling protocols, schedules, and the cleanup levels, to be used as standards for assessing whether the desired level of removal or decontamination has been achieved.

Clean Water Act A federal law that controls the discharge of pollutants into surface water in a number of ways, including discharge permits.

Cleanup Efforts to mitigate environmental damages or threats to human health, safety, or welfare from hazardous substances. Include removal of a hazardous substance from the environment, restoration, remediation, and/or other measures to mitigate or avoid further threat to public health, safety and welfare, or the environment. Cleanup is often used interchangeably with terms like corrective actions, remedial action, removal action, or response action.

Clearance levels In the context of radioactive waste management, this refers to a set of values established by the regulatory authority and expressed in terms of activity concentrations and/or total activities, at or below which sources of radiation can be released from regulatory control.

Coagulation A process of using coagulant chemicals and mixing by which colloidal and suspended materials are destabilized and agglomerated into flocs.

Code of Federal Regulations (CFR) A compilation of all final federal regulations in effect in the United States at the time of its publication. It contains the full text of all final regulations, excluding the preamble, promulgated by all federal government agencies. The CFR is updated each year in July. The US EPA's regulations are included in Title 40 of the CFR, commonly referred to as 40 CFR.

Co-disposal (of waste) Household and industrial wastes disposed of in the same landfill.

Collision zone A convergent plate margin where two earth's plates collide.

Colloids A particle-size range of less than 0.005 mm, i.e. smaller than clay size.

Commingling The act of mixing two or more sources of wastes.

Compact A group of two or more US States that have formed alliances to dispose of low-level radioactive waste (LLW).

Compaction The process of increasing the density or unit weight of soil (frequently fill soil) by rolling, tamping, vibrating, or other mechanical means.

Compliance order by consent (COBC) An enforceable agreement to resolve violations of environmental or health laws. COBC is often utilized when the violator agrees to perform a certain task to operate while coming into compliance or conducting remediation and cleanup.

Compliance orders (CO) A unilateral, nonjudicial enforcement tool that establishes a step or series of steps that the violator must undertake in order to abate a violation; also called consent order/decree.

Composite liner A barrier made of synthetic material, such as plastic, used to hold liquid.

Composting The decomposition of yard waste and vegetable scraps into organic material.

Comprehensive Environmental Response, Compensation, and Liability Act (CERCLA) Commonly known as the Superfund law, CERCLA is a federal law passed in 1980 and modified in 1986 by the Superfund Amendments and Reauthorization Act. The Acts created a special tax that goes into a Trust fund, commonly known as the Superfund, to investigate and clean up abandoned or uncontrolled hazardous waste sites.

Compressibility The change, or tendency for change, that occurs in a soil mass when it is subjected to compressive loading.

Concentration The amount of one material dispersed or distributed in a larger amount of another material.

Conceptual site model (CSM) A summary of conditions at a site that identifies the type and location of all potential sources of contamination and how and where people, plants, or animals may be exposed to the contamination.

Cone of depression The lowered surface of the groundwater table resulting from the pumping of water; the maximum lowering or depression of the groundwater table occurs at the center, forming a cone-like feature in three dimensions.

Confined aquifer An aquifer bounded on the top by confining earth materials; water pressure in confined aquifers exceeds atmospheric pressure.

Containment The process of confining a material at the place where it occurs or at the desired location to prevent environmental contamination.

Contaminant level A measure of how much of a contaminant is present.

Contaminant plume Mass of contaminated groundwater.

Contaminant reeducation zone The area at a hazardous waste site that has been set aside for the decontamination of equipment and personnel.

Contaminant Harmful or hazardous matter introduced into the environment.

Contaminated site (CS) A location where hazardous substances, including petroleum products, have been improperly disposed. Many of these sites resulted from disposal methods considered standard practices before we became aware of the problems or hazards they can cause. Contaminated sites often threaten public health or the environment and can cause economic hardship to people and communities.

Contamination Undesirable radiological, chemical, or biological material (with a potentially harmful effect) that is airborne or deposited in (or on the surface of) structures, objects, soil, water, or living organisms.

Convergent plate margins The zone in which adjacent earth's plates either collide with each other or one of the plates sinks beneath the other.

Corrective action Cleanup of hazardous waste contamination at non-Superfund sites.

Corrosivity One of the criteria used to designate a waste as hazardous.

Crud A colloquial term for corrosion and wear products (rust particles, etc.) that become radioactive (i.e. activated) when exposed to radiation.

Curie A unit or measure of radioactivity from a certain element or radionuclide. One Curie equals the amount of radioactivity from one gram of ^{226}Radium. Alternatively, one Curie equals 3.7×10^{10} Becquerel or undergoes 3.7×10^{10} disintegrations per second.

Cytostatic Causing suppression of growth and multiplication of cells.

Cytotoxic Possessing a specific destructive action on certain cells; used in referring to the lysis (disintegration or dissolution) of cells brought about by immune phenomena and to antineoplastic drugs that selectively kill dividing cells.

D

Decommissioning The act of removing from service any facilities that were used to store, process, or stage radioactive materials.

Decon A phase of reactor decommissioning in which structures, systems, and components that contain radioactive contamination are removed from a site and safely disposed of at a commercially operated low-level waste (LLW) disposal facility or decontaminated to a level that permits the site to be released for unrestricted use.

Decontamination In nuclear waste, the act of removing radionuclides from equipment, structures, or other materials that have been in contact with radionuclides.

Deep-well injection Underground disposal of hazardous liquid into deep wells drilled below aquifers.

Dense nonaqueous phase liquid (DNAPL) A contaminant that is insoluble or has low solubility, is heavier than water and sinks to the bottom of an aquifer and potentially through the underlying materials. Examples are solvents such as PERC, and TCE; common dry-cleaning chemicals.

Depleted uranium Uranium with a percentage of ^{235}uranium lower than the 0.7% (by mass) contained in natural uranium. Depleted uranium is the by-product of the uranium enrichment process. Depleted uranium can be blended with highly enriched uranium, such as that from weapons, to make reactor fuel.

Destruction and removal efficiency (DRE) The ratio of the difference in mass of feed rate of POHC and mass emission rate of the same POHC to the mass feed rate of the POHC.

Diffusion The process that causes solutes to move from zones of higher concentration to zones of lower concentrations.

Dioxin Dioxin is a general term that describes a group of hundreds of chemicals that are highly persistent in the environment. The most toxic compound is 2,3,7,8-tetrachlorodibenzo-p-dioxin or TCDD. Dioxin is formed as an unintentional by-product of many industrial processes involving chlorine such as waste incineration, chemical and pesticide manufacturing, and pulp and paper bleaching.

Discharge areas Locations where groundwater flows or is discharged to the surface.

Discontinuities An interruption in the continuity in the rock mass caused by the presence of planes of weakness, such as joints, bedding, and foliation planes, etc.

Disinfectant Chemical agent that can reduce the viability of microorganisms. Treatment aimed at reducing the number of microorganisms to safe levels.

Dispersion Mixing of contaminated groundwater as it moves through a porous medium.

Disposal waste pile An accumulation of noncontainerized and nonflowing solid wastes.

Disposal Intentional burial, deposit, discharge, dumping, placing or release of any waste material into or on any air, land, or water. In the context of radioactive waste management, disposal means the placement of waste in an approved, specified facility (e.g. near-surface or geological repository) or the approved direct discharge of effluents into the environment. Disposal is undertaken without the intention of retrieval.

Divergent plate margins A fracture in the lithosphere where two earth's plates move apart.

Dose A measure of the energy deposited in a medium by ionizing radiation per unit mass. In toxicology, the amount of a chemical per unit body weight administered to an organism.

Due diligence Any procedure or service used by a potential buyer of real estate to ensure that no hazardous waste is present at the property.

E

Earth's plates Rigid thin segments of the earth's lithosphere, which move horizontally along adjoining plates.

Ecology Study of the relationships of living organisms to each other and to their environment.

Economic geology The study and analysis of geologic bodies and materials that can be utilized profitably by man, including fuels, metals, nonmetallic minerals, and water.

Ecosystem A specialized community, including all the component organisms, that form an interacting system; for example, a marsh, a coast, a forest, etc.

Emergency Planning and Community Right-To-Know Act (EPCRA) A federal act established to help local communities to protect public health, safety, and the environment from hazardous chemicals.

Emergency response A response action to situations that may cause immediate and serious harm to people or the environment.

Endogenous phase A phase of bacterial growth in which the microbes use the polysaccharide layer from their cell walls as nutrients.

Endothermic A chemical reaction that is accompanied by absorption of heat (opposite of exothermic).

Engineering evaluation/Cost analysis (EE/CA) An EE/CA is an analysis of removal alternatives for a site, similar to a feasibility study.

Engineering geology Application of the geological sciences to engineering practice, to assure that the geologic factors affecting the location, design, and construction of engineering works are recognized and adequately provided for.

Entomb A method of decommissioning a nuclear power plant, in which radioactive contaminants are encased in a structurally long-lived material, such as concrete.

Environment The physical and biological aspects of a specific area; includes all living things, soil, air, and water.

Environmental audit Assessment of a real estate property or a site for signs of contamination; also called site assessment.

Environmental geology Application of geologic principles and knowledge to problems created by man's occupancy and exploitation of the physical environment.

Environmental impact statement A document prepared by industry or a political entity on the probable environmental impact of its proposals before construction is allowed.

Environmental risk Likelihood, or probability of injury, disease, or death resulting from exposure to a potential environmental hazard.

Environmental site assessment (ESA) An investigation of a property, often funded by a potential buyer or seller of the property, to determine whether or not the property may be contaminated with hazardous substances.

Ethylene dibromide (EDB) One of several lead (Pb) scavengers that were added to leaded gasoline to prevent the buildup of lead deposits in engines; phased out in the 1980s. Lead scavengers are slow to break down and persist in the environment for a long time.

Eukaryotic Refers to higher life forms; eukaryotic cell has a true nucleus.

Evapotranspiration That portion of the precipitation returned to the air through evaporation and transpiration.

Exempt waste In the context of radioactive waste management, it is the waste released from nuclear regulatory control in accordance with clearance levels because the associated radiological hazards are negligible.

Exothermic Chemical reaction that gives off heat.

Exposure (radiation) Absorption of ionizing radiation or the amount of a hazardous substance that has been ingested, inhaled, or contacted the skin.

Ex-situ Treatment Treatment conducted on materials that have been moved from their original location.

Extrusive igneous (or volcanic) rocks Rocks that form from the cooling and crystallization of minerals from magma at or above the Earth's surface.

F

Facultative anaerobes Microbes that can grow in the presence or absence of oxygen.

Fault A fracture or fracture zone in rock or sediment deposits along which there has been displacement of the sides relative to one another.

Fauna Animal life.

Feasibility Study (FS) A study to develop and evaluate options for remedial action using data from the Remedial Investigation.

Federal Insecticide, Fungicide, and Rodenticide Act (FIFRA) A federal law that requires labels on pesticides that provide clear directions for safe use; FIFRA also authorizes EPA to set standards to control how pesticides are used.

Feedstock Raw material used in a manufacturing process.

Ferrous Metals Includes Fe, Cr, Ni, and its alloys.

Final cover Layer of compacted silty clay used to close a landfill after it becomes full.

Fine-grained soils Soil containing particles smaller than 0.074 mm diameter.

Fission The splitting of an atom, which releases a considerable amount of energy (usually in the form of heat).

Flash point The lowest temperature at which a substance gives off enough combustible vapor to produce a momentary flash of fire when a small flame is passed near its surface.

Flexible membrane liner (FML) A liner made of synthetic material used in landfills.

Flocculation The process by which many minute suspended particles are held together in clot-like masses or are loosely aggregated into small lumps or granules.

Flora Plant life.

Flue gas (or exhaust gas) Gases and suspended particles emitted from an industrial stack or chimney.

Fluff An accumulation of nonflowing and nonmagnetic solid hazardous waste.

Folding The process of bending of rocks or sediments.

Foliated metamorphic rocks Metamorphic rocks that exhibit parallel arrangements of minerals giving the appearance of layering, as seen in schist, phyllite, and gneiss.

Foliation planes Planar structures formed by parallel to subparallel alignment of mineral grains or structures in metamorphic rocks.

Fractional distillation Separation of liquids of different boiling points by distillation.

Fracture A crack, joint, fault, or other breaks in rocks.

Fuel cycle The series of steps involved in supplying fuel for nuclear power reactors.

Fuel reprocessing (recycling) The processing of reactor fuel to separate the unused fissionable material from waste material. Reprocessing extracts uranium and plutonium from spent nuclear fuel so they can be used again as reactor fuel.

Fuel rod A long, slender, zirconium metal tube containing pellets of fissionable material, which provide fuel for nuclear reactors. Fuel rods are assembled into bundles called fuel assemblies, which are loaded individually into the reactor core.

G

Gaseous diffusion A process used to increase the concentration of ^{235}U in uranium for use in fuel for nuclear reactors by separating its isotopes (as gases) based on their flight difference in mass.

Gauging devices Devices used to measure, monitor, and control the thickness of sheet metal, textiles, paper napkins, newspaper, plastics, photographic film, and other products as they are manufactured.

Generation (gross) The total amount of electrical energy produced by a power-generating station.

Generation (net) The gross amount of electric energy produced by a generating station, minus the amount used to operate the station.

Generator A person or entity whose act or process produces hazardous and other wastes.

Geochemical cycle Nature's way of causing concentration of chemical elements and compounds at one location or their removal at other locations by the interaction of chemical elements through various paths.

Geological repository An excavated, underground facility that is designed, constructed, and operated for safe and secure disposal and/or retrieval of high-level radioactive waste (HLW). A geological repository uses an engineered barrier system and a portion of the site's natural geology, hydrology, and geochemical nature to contain the radiation.

Geologic structures The attitude and relative positions of the rock masses of an area; the sum total of features resulting from faulting, folding, and igneous intrusion.

Geology The study of the planet earth, the materials of which it is made, the process that act on these materials, the products formed, and the history of the planet and its life forms since its origin.

Geomechanics The study of the mechanical characteristics of rocks and soils.

Geomorphology The science that deals with the general configuration of the earth's surface, specifically, the study of the classification, description, nature, origin, and development of landforms and their relationship to underlying structures, and the history of geological changes as recorded by these surface features.

Geophysics A branch of earth science that deals with the study of the physics of the earth; includes seismology, geomagnetism, volcanology, etc.

Geosynthetics A general term for synthetic fabrics used as liners in landfills and other engineering applications.

Genotoxic A substance that is capable of interacting directly with genetic material, causing DNA damage that can be assayed. The term may refer to carcinogenic, mutagenic, or teratogenic substances.

Gonzales amendment A 1986 amendment to the Safe Drinking Water Act, authorizing the US EPA to designate aquifers that are especially valuable because they are the only source of drinking water in an area.

Gradient A measure of the vertical drop over a given horizontal distance.

Grain size Average diameter of sediments or soil particles.

Grain size distribution Determines the range in size of mineral solids in a soil sample.

Granular activated carbon Finely powdered carbon (usually charcoal) used for the treatment of hazardous waste.

Granular soil Soil made up of grains of nearly the same size and in the range of 2 to 10 mm.

Greenhouse effects The heating of the earth's surface because outgoing long-wavelength terrestrial radiation is absorbed and reemitted by carbon dioxide and water vapor in the lower atmosphere eventually returning to the earth.

Groundwater Water found beneath the earth's surface that fills pores in sand, soil particles, or gravel deposits or rocks, creating a saturated zone.

Groundwater table (GWT) The uppermost surface of the zone of saturation.

Groundwater table aquifer See unconfined aquifer.

H

Half-life (radiological) The time required for half the atoms of a particular radioactive material to decay. Measured half-lives range from millionths of a second to billions of years.

Halogenated Introduction of a halogen, usually chlorine or bromine, into a compound by substitution or addition.

Halophile An organism requiring salt (NaCl) for growth.

Handling The functions associated with the movement of solid waste materials, excluding storage, processing, and ultimate disposal.

Hazard index The sum of the hazard quotients attributed to noncarcinogenic hazardous substances with similar critical endpoints.

Hazardous materials (HAZMAT) HAZMAT are chemicals, combustible liquids, compressed gases, controlled substances, corrosives, explosives, flammable materials, oxidizers, poisons, and radioactive materials.

Hazard ranking system The principal screening tool used by the US EPA to evaluate risks to public health and the environment associated with abandoned or uncontrolled hazardous waste sites. This score is the primary factor in deciding if the site should be on the National Priorities List and, if so, what ranking it should have compared to other sites on the list.

Hazardous substance A broad term that includes all substances that can be harmful to people or the environment. Toxic substances, hazardous materials, and other similar terms are subsets of hazardous substances.

Hazardous waste By-products or waste materials of manufacturing and other processes that have some dangerous properties, generally categorized as corrosive, ignitable, toxic, or reactive, and are potentially harmful to people or the environment.

Head The pressure exerted by a column of water or by an elevated water source.

Heap leach recovery process A method for extracting uranium from ore.

Heating value (or calorific value) The quantity of heat that is produced when the unit mass of a material undergoes complete combustion under certain specified conditions. For solids, it is expressed in terms of calories or joules per kilogram (kcal/kg, kJ/kg, MJ/kg, etc.).

Heavy Metals Metals such as lead, chromium, copper, cobalt, etc., which can be toxic at relatively low concentrations.

Heterotrophic Microorganisms that use organic compounds as nutrients.

High-level radioactive waste (HLW) Highly radioactive materials produced as by-products of fuel reprocessing or of the reactions that occur inside nuclear reactors.

Highly (or high-) enriched uranium Uranium enriched to at least 20% ^{235}U (a higher concentration than exists in natural uranium ore).

Historical geology A branch of geology that deals with the evolution of the earth and its life from its origins to the present.

Hotline The boundary between the contaminant reduction zone and the support zone at a hazardous waste site.

Humus The organic matter of soil, so well decomposed that the original source cannot be identified.

Hydraulic conductivity Permeability coefficient; the numerical value of permeability.

Hydraulic head The height of the free surface of a body of water above a given reference point.

Hydrocarbon Any organic compound (gas, liquid, or solid) consisting wholly of carbon and hydrogen.

Hydrologic cycle The process of evaporation, transpiration, condensation, precipitation, infiltration, runoff, and percolations in which water molecules travel above, below, and on the earth's surface. Also called water cycle.

Hyperthermophiles Microorganisms that can survive in high-temperature environments, generally above 80 °C.

I

Igneous rocks Rocks that have solidified from the cooling of magma (molten earth material).

Ignitable Capable of bursting into flames easily.

Ignitibility The ability of a material to be set afire.

Immobilization The process that causes the conversion of inorganic ions or compounds into organic form.

Incineration The controlled burning of solid, liquid, or gaseous combustible wastes to produce gases and residues containing little or no combustible material.

Incineration/thermal treatment This treatment technique uses heat to remove contaminants from solid, liquid, or gaseous materials. Hazardous organic compounds are converted to ash, carbon dioxide, and water.

Independent spent fuel storage installation (ISFSI) A storage facility designed and constructed for the interim storage of spent nuclear fuel; solid, reactor-related, greater-than-Class-C waste; and other associated radioactive materials.

Index properties Soil properties that indicate its condition and provide an estimate of its engineering behavior.

In-situ recovery (ISR) A common method currently used to extract uranium from ore bodies without physical excavation of the ore. ISR is also known as "solution mining" or *in-situ* leaching.

In-situ treatment In-situ means "in place"; describes any treatment technique that treats the contaminated water or soil in place.

Infiltration The movement of water through the ground surface into the unsaturated zone.

Information exchanges A matchmaking operation based on the idea that one manufacturer's waste may be another manufacturer's raw material.

Innovative treatment technologies Remedies that have been tested, selected, or used for treating hazardous waste or contaminated materials but don't have much information on cost and performance.

Inorganic compounds Chemical compounds that do not contain carbon, usually associated with life processes; for example, metals.

Input material Raw materials used in a manufacturing process to produce the finished product.

Institutional controls (IC) Barriers and other measures placed at a contaminated site to protect people and the environment from exposure to oil and hazardous substances during the cleanup process.

Interim remedial action (IRA) An interim measure to remove or isolate contamination. This action can be taken any time during the process and is usually taken to protect people and the environment from high levels of contamination until the final remedial action can be taken.

International Atomic Energy Agency (IAEA) A United Nations agency established in 1957 to serve as a world center of cooperation in the nuclear field. The agency works with nearly 170 members states and multiple partners worldwide to promote safe, secure, and peaceful nuclear technology.

Intrusive igneous rocks Any igneous rock formed by the solidification of magma below the earth's surface.

Ion exchange Reversible exchange of ions of the same charge between a solution, usually aqueous, and an insoluble solid in contact with it.

Ionizing radiation Radiation that either directly or indirectly displaces electrons from an atom, molecule, or ion.

Irradiate The process of exposing materials to ionizing radiation. If the radiation is a neutron beam, the resulting material can become radioactive.

Irradiation Exposure to ionizing radiation. Irradiation may be intentional, such as in cancer treatments or in sterilizing medical instruments. Irradiation may also be accidental, such as from exposure to an unshielded source. Irradiation does not usually result in radioactive contamination, but damage can occur, depending on the dose received.

Isotope Two or more forms (or atomic configurations) of a given element that have identical atomic numbers and the same or very similar chemical properties but different atomic masses and distinct physical properties. Thus, ^{12}C, ^{13}C, and ^{14}C are isotopes of the element carbon, and the numbers denote the proximate atomic masses. Among their distinct physical properties, some isotopes (known as radioisotopes) are radioactive because their nuclei are unstable and emit radiation as they decay spontaneously toward a more stable nuclear configuration. For example, ^{12}C and ^{13}C are stable but ^{14}C is unstable and radioactive.

J

Joint or several liability A provision in the law that permits the US EPA to recover the cost of cleanup from parties responsible for the waste.

Joints Fractures in rocks along which no observable movement has occurred.

K

Karst features A type of topography that is formed over limestone, dolomite, or gypsum by dissolution, and is characterized by sinkholes, caves, and underground drainage.

Ketones Any of a class of organic compounds containing a carbonyl group attached to two organic groups, e.g. acetone.

Kilowatt (kW) A unit of power equivalent to 1000 watts.

L

Land disposal restrictions Bans land disposal of hazardous waste without pretreatment.

Land farm A general term for the practice of using the soil or the land for simultaneous treatment or disposal of hazardous waste.

Landfill A location for the disposal of wastes on land designed to protect the public and the environment from hazards; sanitary landfills, designed to receive municipal solid waste, are distinguished from hazardous waste landfills that are designed to isolate hazardous substances.

Landfill gas (LFG) Methane and related gases produced by the decomposition of organic constituents in a landfill.

Land treatment Use of soil or land to simultaneously treat and dispose of hazardous waste (synonyms: land-farming, land cultivation, and land application).

Large quantity generator (LQG) Generators that produce more than 1000 kg of nonacutely hazardous waste or over 1 kg of acutely hazardous waste per month.

Latency The time gap between exposure of an individual to a hazardous substance and the clinical manifestation of an adverse effect.

Leachants A solution used to remove solids by dissolution.

Leachate A liquid resulting when water percolates, or trickles through waste materials and becomes contaminated. Leachate may occur at landfills or at contaminated sites.

Leachate management system A provision in the design of a secured landfill to monitor, collect, and remove any leachate that may be produced over a period of time

Liability Under Superfund, a party or parties responsible for the presence of hazardous waste at a site and legally responsible for paying to reduce or eliminate the risk posed by the site.

Light nonaqueous phase liquid (LNAPL) LNAPLs are undissolved chemicals, typically petroleum products, which float on the surface of groundwater.

Light-water reactor A term used to describe reactors using ordinary water as a moderated coolant, including boiling-water reactors (BWRs) and pressurized-water reactors (PWRs), the most common types used in the USA.

Lineation A general term for any linear structures in a rock.

Liner A structure of natural clay or manufactured material, which serves as an impermeable barrier between the clean soil and contaminated material stored around the liner.

Liquid limit See *Atterberg limits*.

Listed wastes A list of various hazardous wastes, included in 40 CFR, part 261.

Lithification The process of conversion of sediments into a sedimentary rock.

Lithology The systematic description of rocks in terms of mineral assemblage and texture.

Lithosphere The outer 100 km of the solid earth.

Low-level radioactive waste (LLW) A general term for a wide range of waste that is contaminated with radioactive material or has become radioactive through exposure to neutron radiation. LLW has a low level of radiation and a short half-life.

M

Macronutrients Chemical elements that are needed in large quantities by humans, animals, and plants to maintain satisfactory growth.

Magma Molten rock, together with any suspended mineral grains and dissolved gases, that forms when temperatures rise and melting occurs in the earth's mantle or crust.

Manifest system A system used to track hazardous waste.

Mantle Zone of earth below the crust and above the core.

Mass density The ratio of the mass to volume of a material.

Mass transfer Movement of material through porous medium along with the flow of groundwater.

Massive Non-foliated rock.

Material exchanges An organization that arranges physical exchange of hazardous waste from a generator to a manufacturer for use as a feedstock; same as *active exchange*.

Maximum contaminant level (MCL) The maximum level of certain contaminants permitted in public drinking water supplies. EPA, under the Safe Drinking Water Act, sets these levels.

Medium-quantity generator (MQG) A generator that produces hazardous waste between 100 and 1000 kg per month.

Megawatt (MW) A unit equals 1000 kilowatts of electricity.

Metamorphic rocks Rocks derived from preexisting rocks by mineralogical, chemical, and/or structural changes, essentially in the solid state, in response to marked changes in temperature, pressure, shearing stress, and chemical environment, generally at depth in earth's crust.

Methanogenesis Process of conversion of organic constituents in a hazardous waste into methane and carbon dioxide by anaerobic bacteria.

Methyl isocyanate A toxic chemical compound, CH_3NCO, having a boiling point of 39.1 °C.

Micronutrients Nutrients (chemical elements) needed by plants and humans in very small quantities to maintain satisfactory growth.

Microorganism Any microbiological entity, cellular or noncellular, capable of replication or of transferring genetic material.

Mill tailings The solid residue from a conventional uranium recovery facility in which U or Th ore is crushed and processed mechanically or chemically to recover the U, Th, or other valuable materials. The "tailings" contain several naturally occurring radioactive elements, including U, Th, Ra, Rn, and Po, as well as heavy metals and other constituents.

Mineralization Conversion of organic constituents in hazardous waste into CO_2 and H_2O by aerobic bacteria.

Mississippian A period of the Paleozoic era (after the Devonian and before the Pennsylvanian) between 345 and 320 million years ago.

Moisture content In geotechnics, it is defined as the ratio of the mass (weight) of water to that of the solids present in the soil or rock. In agronomy, it is the ratio of the mass of water to that of the soil.

Monitoring wells Wells drilled at specific locations where aquifer parameters (depth, flow direction, chemical nature, etc.) can be sampled to determine the types and amounts of contaminants present.

Monofill A landfill that contains only one category of waste, with the bottom covered by a large sheet of plastic to prevent the waste from coming in contact with the outside soil, particularly the groundwater.

Multimedia filter A separation process utilizing layers of different materials of varying pore size and density.

Municipal solid waste Common household and commercial solid waste, abbreviated MSW. It is typically collected by municipalities and transported to the disposal facility.

Mutagenicity The property of causing a permanent genetic change in a cell other than that which occurs during normal genetic recombination.

N

National pollutant discharge elimination system (NPDES) The primary permitting program under the Clean Water Act that regulates all discharges to surface water bodies.

National priorities list (NPL) A list maintained by the US EPA of the worst contaminated hazardous waste sites identified for possible long-term cleanup using money from the Superfund trust fund. EPA is required to update the NPL at least once a year.

Natural uranium Uranium containing the relative concentrations of isotopes found in nature: 0.7% ^{235}U, 99.3% ^{238}U, and a trace amount of ^{234}U by mass.

Net electric generation The gross amount of electric energy produced by a generating station, minus the amount used to operate the station.

Nonacute hazardous waste Any waste that is not classified as acutely hazardous.

Nonaqueous phase liquid (NAPL) Contaminants that remain undiluted as the original bulk liquid and do not readily dissolve in water, e.g. spilled oil.

Nonferrous Metals Includes: Al, Cu, Pb, Zn, Sn, and precious metals Au and Ag.

Nonfoliated metamorphic rocks (Massive) without banding, e.g. marble and quartzite.

Notice of violation (NOV) An NOV is a written "ticket" informing a business or individual that they have failed to comply with a State regulation or statute. NOV is not an order but a notice to a person that a violation of the statutes, regulations, or permit condition has occurred.

Nuclear fuel Fissionable material that has been enriched to a composition that will support a self-sustaining fission chain reaction when used to fuel a nuclear reactor, thereby releasing energy.

Nuclear materials Materials capable of firing off energy by fission or fusion of their atomic nuclei.

Nuclear poison (or neutron poison) In reactor physics, a substance (other than fissionable material) that has a large capacity for absorbing neutrons in the vicinity of the reactor core. This effect may be undesirable in some reactor applications because it may prevent or disrupt the fission chain reaction, thereby affecting normal operation. However, neutron-absorbing materials (commonly known as "poisons") are intentionally inserted into some types of reactors to decrease the reactivity of their initial fresh fuel load for fuel intended to achieve a higher burnup level during the fuel cycle. Adding poisons, such as control rods or boron, is described as adding "negative reactivity" to the reactor.

Nuclear power plant A thermal power plant in which the energy (heat) released by fission of nuclear fuel is used to boil water to produce steam. The steam spins the propeller-like blades of a turbine that turns the generator to produce electricity.

Nuclear reactor The heart of a nuclear power plant, in which nuclear fission may be initiated and controlled in a self-sustaining chain reaction to generate energy or produce useful radiation.

Nuclear waste A subset of radioactive waste that includes unstable by-products during the various stages of the nuclear fuel cycle, and use of the fuel in nuclear reactors, which are regulated by the NRC. (By contrast, "radioactive waste" is a broader term, which includes all wastes that contain radioactivity, regardless of how they are produced. It is not considered "nuclear waste" because it is not produced through the nuclear fuel cycle and is generally not regulated by the NRC).

O

Obligate anaerobes Microbes that grow only in the absence of oxygen.

Offshore The geographic area that lies seaward of the coastline.

Operable unit (OU) A complex contaminated site may be divided into areas, which are grouped together on the basis of risks, for ease of investigation and cleanup. These groups are frequently called operable units.

Optimum moisture content The moisture content at which soil attains maximum dry density.

Organic substrate Food (nutrient) source for microbes.

Organohalogen compound An organic compound that contains one or more halogens (chlorine, bromine, fluorine, and iodine) in its structure, e.g. DDT, chlordane, and other pesticides.

Osmosis The transport of solvent through a semipermeable membrane separating two solutions of different (solute) concentrations. The solvent diffuses from the solution that is diluted to the solution that is concentrated.

Outer core The outer or upper zone of the earth's core, extending from a depth of 2900 km to 5100 km. It is presumed to be liquid because it sharply reduces compressional wave velocities and does not transmit shear waves.

Ozone depletion Reduction in the concentration of natural ozone in the stratosphere (upper atmosphere).

Ozone layer Stratospheric ozone that shields the earth from ultraviolet radiation.

P

Parent material Original rock or sediment from which soil has developed.

Particulate matter (PM) Substances that occur as very fine particles, generally become airborne, causing air pollution.

Parts per billion (ppb) Unit commonly used to express concentrations of contamination; 1 ppb is 1/1 000 000 000 or 1×10^{-9}.

Parts per million (ppm) Unit commonly used to express concentrations of contamination; 1 ppm is 1/1 000 000 or 1×10^{-6}.

Passive exchange Facilitates that exchange information on hazardous materials between the waste generator and potential user.

Perched water table The upper surface of a body of water perched atop an aquiclude that lies above the main water table.

Perchloroethylene (PCE) Perchloroethylene is a man-made chemical used for dry-cleaning clothes, degreasing metal parts, and as an ingredient in the manufacturing of other chemicals. Perchloroethylene is also known as tetrachloroethylene, tetrachloroethene, Perc, Percaline, and Perchlor.

Permafrost Represents permanently frozen ground where the temperature remains below freezing for two or more years.

Permeability A hydrologic characteristic of soils or other porous materials. Permeability is an indication of the relative ability of a fluid to move through the porous material.

Petroleum A broadly defined class of liquid hydrocarbon mixtures, largely of the methane series that includes crude oil, release condensate, unfinished oils, natural gas plant liquids, and refined products, such as kerosene, benzene, gasoline, diesel, paraffin, etc., obtained from the processing of crude oil.

Petrology A branch of geology dealing with the origin, occurrence, classification, structure, and history of rocks.

pH Hydrogen ion concentartion in a liquid; a measure of acidity or alkalinity.

Phase I and II of an environmental site assessment (ESA) Two parts of an investigation of a property, often funded by a potential buyer or seller of the property, that examine whether or not the property may be contaminated with hazardous substances.

Phosgene A deadly gas.

Phreatic zone Zone of saturation in soil or rock; also called the zone of saturation.

Phytoremediation An example of bioremediation where certain plant species are used to clean up the contaminated soil and/or groundwater.

Phytotoxicity Study of the toxic effect of chemicals on plants.

Plasma A highly ionized gas.

Plastic limit See *Atterberg limits*.

Plasticity index The numerical difference between the values of liquid limit and plastic limit.

Plate margin The boundary of two adjacent earth plates.

Pleistocene period An epoch of the Quaternary Period that began 1.6 million years ago and lasted until the start of the Holocene some 10 000 years ago.

Plume A visible or measurable discharge or release of a contaminant as it displaces water or air from a given point of origin. The plume of a contaminant in groundwater is the area of water which, as it moves in the subsurface, carries the contaminant with it. The shape is often like that of a skinny balloon. Naturally physical, chemical, and biological processes diminish the concentration levels as the water carries the contaminant away from the source.

Pollutant Anything that may result in the degradation of environmental quality. Includes dredged spoil, solid waste, incinerator residue, filter backwash, sewage, garbage, sewage sludge, munitions, chemical wastes, biological materials, radioactive materials, heat, wrecked or discarded equipment, rock, sand, dirt, and industrial, municipal, agricultural waste discharge water, etc.

Pollution prevention Reduction or elimination of hazardous waste in a manufacturing process.

Polycyclic aromatic hydrocarbons (PAHs) A group of compounds composed of two or more fused aromatic rings. PAHs are introduced into the environment through the combustion process (i.e. forest fire, automobile exhaust, and fossil fuel power plants).

Polychlorinated biphenyls (PCBs) A group of toxic, persistent chemicals formerly used in electrical transformers and capacitors for insulating purposes and in gas pipeline systems as a lubricant; also used in heat transfer liquids, hydraulic fluids, plasticizers, and caulking materials. They are classified as a possible carcinogen. The sale and new use of PCBs were banned in 1979.

Porosity Percentage of pore spaces in a unit volume of rock or soil.

Potentially responsible party (PRP) An individual or company – such as owners, operators, transporters, or generators of hazardous waste – who may be potentially responsible for, or contributing to, the contamination problems at a Superfund site, and to clean up sites they have contaminated.

Potentiometric surface Elevation of the groundwater table in confined aquifers, usually higher than the regional groundwater table.

Preliminary assessment (PA) The initial step of a site assessment under Superfund which involves record review, designed to distinguish between sites that pose little or no threat to human health and the environment, and sites that require further investigation.

Prion A poorly characterized slow infectious agent. Prions are believed to be the cause of a number of neurodegenerative diseases (e.g. Creutzfeldt–Jakob disease).

Priority substances list (PSL) A list of substances that are toxic or are capable of becoming toxic.

Procaryotic Simple organisms, e.g. bacteria.

Pump and treat A groundwater treatment technique that includes removal of the contaminated groundwater by pumping it to the surface and treating it by various methods, such as by air stripping or carbon adsorption.

Pyrolysis Decomposition of organic material by heat in the absence, or with a limited supply, of oxygen.

Q

Quality assurance/quality control (QA/QC) A system of procedures, checks, audits, and corrective actions used to ensure that fieldwork and laboratory analysis during the investigation and cleanup meet established sampling and analytical standards.

Quality assurance The systematic process of checking to see whether a product or service being developed is meeting specified requirements.

Quality control Involves the tools used to monitor or regulate the process. Quality control is an aspect of quality assurance.

Quaternary period The second period of the Cenozoic era, following the Tertiary period. It began 2.58 million years ago and extends to the present.

R

Radioactive element An element capable of changing spontaneously into another element by the emission of charged particles from the nuclei of its atoms.

Radioactive materials Any material which spontaneously emits radiation.

Radioactive waste Material that contains, or is contaminated with, radionuclides at concentrations or activities greater than clearance levels and for which no use is foreseen.

Radioactivity The property possessed by some elements (such as U) of spontaneously emitting energy in the form of radiation as a result of the decay (or disintegration) of an unstable atom. Radioactivity is also the term used to describe the rate at which radioactive materials emit radiation. Radioactivity is measured in units of becquerels (Bq) or disintegrations per second.

Radiography The use of sealed sources of ionizing radiation for nondestructive examination of the structure of materials.

Radioisotope (radionuclide) An unstable isotope of an element that decays or disintegrates spontaneously, thereby emitting radiation. About 5000 natural and artificial radioisotopes have been identified.

Radionuclide A nuclide (i.e. an atom of specified atomic number and mass number) that exhibits properties of spontaneous disintegration, liberating energy, generally resulting in the formation of new nuclides. This process is accompanied by the emission of one or more types of radiation, such as α- and β-particles and γ-rays.

Radiopharmaceutical A pharmaceutical drug that emits radiation and is used in diagnostic or therapeutic medical procedures. Radioisotopes that have short half-lives are generally preferred to minimize the radiation dose to the patient and the risk of prolonged exposure.

Radiotherapy The use of ionizing radiation to treat disease.

Radon emanation The process by which radium decays into radon, a radioactive gas. As a gas, radon is transported into the environment quicker than other radionuclides. Thus, it appears as if it is emanating.

Reactivity One of the criteria used by the US EPA to characterize a waste as hazardous.

Reactor core The central portion of a nuclear reactor, which contains the fuel assemblies, water, and control mechanisms, as well as the supporting structure. The reactor core is where fission takes place.

Recalcitrant Chemicals with a structure that is not analogous to any naturally occurring substance and will not biodegrade.

Record of Decision (ROD) A document that explains which cleanup alternative(s) will be used at a site or is used to justify no further action. ROD is based on the information and technical analysis generated during the remedial investigation/feasibility study and consideration of public comments and community concerns.

Recycling Converting waste into a reusable material or returning materials to an earlier stage in a cyclic process. Recycling is distinct from reuse.

Redox reactions A chemical reaction involving reduction and oxidation.

Rem A unit of radiation dose.

Rem (roentgen equivalent man) Radiation dose (rads) that will cause the same amount of biological injury as one rad of X rays or γ rays.

Remediation Process of cleaning up contaminated water, soil, or rock.

Remedial action (RA) The actual construction or implementation of the selected cleanup plan.

Remedial design (RD) The phase of a remediation project where engineering plans, technical drawings, and specifications are developed for the selected cleanup plan.

Remedial investigation/feasibility study (RI/FS) Two different but related studies. Remedial Investigation gathers the data necessary to determine the type and extent of contamination at a site. The Feasibility Study establishes the criteria for cleaning up a site and identifies and screens possible cleanup alternatives. The Feasibility Study also analyzes the technologies and costs of the alternatives.

Removal action An emergency or short-term action to respond to threats to public health, welfare, and/or the environment from hazardous waste. These actions are limited in scope and cost. Removal actions are divided into emergency, time-critical, or non-time critical.

Repository A nuclear facility where radioactive waste is emplaced for disposal with the possibility of future retrieval.

Residence time The time that elapses between the entry of a substance into a furnace or incinerator and the exit of exhaust gases or burnout residue from the furnace or incinerator.

Resource Conservation and Recovery Act (RCRA) A US federal law that established a regulatory system to track hazardous waste from the time of its generation to disposal.

Reverse osmosis (RO) The process that causes the flow of solvent from a concentrated solution to a dilute solution.

Risk The probability that a hazard will cause harm in combination with the severity of that harm.

Risk assessment A study to determine risks posed by the site if no cleanup action was taken and what cleanup levels need to be established to protect human health and the environment. Risks to both human and ecological health are evaluated.

Risk management The process of making decisions about whether an environmental risk is high enough to present a significant public health concern and about the appropriate means for controlling the risk based on political, social, economic, and engineering information.

Rock cycle The cyclic movement of rock material, in the course of which rock is created, destroyed, and altered through the operation of internal and external earth processes.

Rock mass Rock in place, includes rock outcrops and rock formations in the subsurface.

Room-and-pillar method A common method of underground mining in which void spaces, called *rooms*, created by extraction of geologic materials are supported by columns of the same materials, called *pillars*.

Runoff In waste management, represents the fraction of precipitation, leachate, or other liquid that flows over the land surface or a hazardous waste facility.

Run-on The portion of rainfall, leachate, or other liquid that flows into a hazardous waste facility.

S

SAFSTOR A long-term storage condition to permanently shut-down nuclear power plant. During SAGSTOR, radioactive contamination decreases substantially, making subsequent decontamination and demolition easier and reducing the amount of low-level waste (LLW) requiring disposal.

Sand A detrital particle smaller than a granule and larger than a silt grain, having a diameter in the range of 0.074 to 4.75 mm.

Sanitary landfilling An engineered method of disposing of solid waste on land in a manner that protects the environment; done by spreading the waste in thin layers, compacting it to the smallest practical volume, covering it with soil at the end of each working day, constructing barriers to infiltration, and evacuating the gases produced.

Saturated zone The zone below the water table where the pore spaces in geological materials are full of water.

Scavenging Manual sorting of solid waste at landfills or dumpsites, and removal of usable material.

Screening A physical method of hazardous waste treatment to separate suspended solids from liquid waste.

Sealed source Radioactive material that is permanently encapsulated or closely bound in a solid form to prevent its release under the most severe conditions likely to be encountered in normal use and handling.

Secure landfill A landfill with multiple barrier systems designed to contain the waste and with provision to monitor, collect, and remove leachate and landfill gases.

Segregation The systematic separation of solid waste into designated categories.

Sedimentary rocks Layered rocks resulting from the consolidation of sediment.

Sedimentation Separation of solids from the liquid by gravity.

Shutdown A decrease in the rate of fission (and heat or energy production) in a rector (usually by insertion of control rods into the core).

Silt A detrital particle finer than sand and coarser than clay, commonly in the size range of 0.002 to 0.074 mm.

Sinkholes Circular depressions in a karst area; its drainage is subterranean; size could range from meters to tens of meters, and it is commonly funnel-shaped in profile.

Sludge Accumulated solids that separate from liquids such as water or wastewater during processing. Distinct from sediments, which are deposits on the bottom of streams or other bodies of water.

Small-quantity generator (SQG) Any entity generating less than 100 kg of nonacutely hazardous waste or <1 kg of acutely hazardous waste per month.

Soil horizon A layer of soil that is distinguishable from adjacent layers by characteristic physical properties such as structure, color, or texture, or by chemical composition, including the content of organic matter or degree of acidity or alkalinity.

Soil profile A vertical section through a soil mass that displays its component horizons.

Soil taxonomy Soil classification.

Soil texture Relates to the size of mineral grains making up the soil solids, e.g. sand, silt, and clay.

Soil vapor extraction (SVE) A treatment technique that extracts vapors from subsurface sediments or soils by removing air through special extraction wells. This system may be combined with air sparging.

Soil washing A treatment technique to remove contamination from sediments. The contaminated materials are excavated and screened to remove large cobbles, debris, and gravel. The remaining material is washed using a detergent or solvent and the wash liquid is also treated. Very small soil particles, called fines, may not be easily treated in this manner and may require other treatment or disposal methods.

Sole source aquifer An aquifer designated as such under Section 1424(e) of the Safe Drinking Water Act.

Solidification/fixation A technique that involves physically mixing contaminated soils with cementing agents, creating a solidified mass that immobilizes the contamination and prevents exposure.

Sorption Process of using a sorption agent (sorbent) that attracts, takes up, and holds hazardous waste for removal.

Source reduction Good operating practices, technology changes, material or product changes to reduce the amount of waste.

Specific gravity The ratio of the weight of a given volume of a substance to the weight of an equal volume of water.

Spent fuel pool An underwater storage and cooling facility for spent (depleted) fuel assemblies that have been removed from a nuclear power reactor.

Spent (depleted or used) nuclear fuel Nuclear reactor fuel that has been used to the extent that it can no longer effectively sustain a chain reaction.

Strength The ability of a material to withstand differential stress, measured in units of stress.

Sterilization A reduction in microorganisms of more than 10^6 (more than 99.9999%) of its original population.

Storage Placement of waste in a suitable location or facility where isolation, environmental and health protection, and human control (e.g. monitoring for radioactivity, limitation of access) are provided. This is done with the intention that the waste will be subsequently retrieved for treatment and conditioning and/or disposal (or clearance of radioactive waste).

Strict aerobes Microorganisms that must have oxygen to survive.

Stripping In hazardous waste treatment, it is the transfer of dissolved organic compounds present in a liquid into a vapor stream or gas flow.

Subduction zone The linear zone along which a plate of lithosphere sinks into the asthenosphere.

Superfund Common name for the Comprehensive Environmental Response Compensation and Liability Act.

Superfund trust fund A public trust fund created with the passage of the Comprehensive Environmental Response, Compensation, and Liability Act (CERCLA) in 1980 to be used to pay for the cleanup of abandoned hazardous waste sites.

Surface water Bodies of water that are above ground, such as rivers, lakes, and streams. It could also include wetland areas where water may be present intermittently according to the season. It can also mean the snowmelt or rain which is flowing on the ground surface.

Surface impoundments Lined ponds storing hazardous waste.

Surface tension The force that holds water in pores against the force of gravity.

T

TDS facility Any facility that is involved in the treatment, disposal, or storage of hazardous waste.

Tectonic cycle A natural cycle responsible for the development of large-scale features of the earth, such as mountains, oceans, and continents; also responsible for the occurrence of earthquakes and volcanic activities.

Teletherapy Treatment in which the source of the therapeutic radiation is at a distance from the body. Because teletherapy is often used to treat malignant tumors deep within the body by bombarding them with a high-energy beam of gamma rays (from a radioisotope such as ^{60}cobalt) projected from outside the body, it is often called "external beam radiotherapy."

Telemedicine Rapid access to shared and remote medical expertise by means of telecommunications and information technologies, no matter where the patient or relevant information is located. Telehealth is a method of source reduction – it can reduce the need for clinical visits and reduce the transportation (carbon footprint) as well as the wastes produced from clinical activities.

Tetrachloroethylene (PERC or PCE) Tetrachloroethylene is a manufactured chemical that is widely used for dry cleaning of fabrics and for metal-degreasing. It is also used to make other chemicals and is used in some consumer products. Other names for tetrachloroethylene include perchloroethylene, PCE, and tetrachloroethene.

Texture (i) The overall appearance that a rock has because of the size, shape, and arrangement of its constituent mineral grains. (ii) The grain size of soil solids.

Thermoplastic materials Materials that do not undergo any change in their inherent properties upon heating.

Throughput Raw materials processed in a given time.

Toxicity The ability of a material to produce injury or disease to living organisms upon exposure, ingestion, inhalation, or assimilation.

Toxic Substances Control Act (TSCA) Enacted in 1976, this law requires the testing, regulating, and screening of all chemicals produced or imported in the USA for possible toxic effects. Any existing chemical that poses health and environmental hazards is tracked and reported under this law.

Toxicology Study of the effects of poisons in living organisms.

Transform fault plate margin A fracture in the lithosphere along which two plates slide past each other, e.g. the San Andreas Fault.

Transpiration A part of the hydrologic cycle in which water vapor passes out of living organisms through a membrane or pores.

Transuranic A term usually referring to radionuclides (or elements) with the number of protons greater than that of uranium. These radionuclides are synthetic and not found in nature.

Transuranic waste Material contaminated with transuranic elements – artificially made radioactive elements, such as Np, Pu, Am, etc. – that have atomic numbers higher than uranium in the periodic table of elements. Transuranic waste is primarily produced from recycling spent fuel or using Pu to fabricate nuclear weapons.

Treatment Any method, technique, or process for altering the biological, chemical, or physical characteristics of waste to reduce the hazards it presents and facilitate, or reduce the costs of disposal.

Treatment technologies The process applied to hazardous waste or contaminated materials to permanently alter their condition through chemical, biological, or physical means, and reduce or eliminate the danger to people and the environment.

Trichloroethylene (TCE) A nonflammable, colorless liquid with a somewhat sweet odor and a sweet, burning taste. It is used mainly as a solvent to remove grease from metal parts, but it is also an ingredient in adhesives, paint removers, typewriter correction fluids, and spot removers.

U

Unconfined aquifer An aquifer not bound by confining earth materials whose upper surface is exposed to air and water pressure is the same as the atmospheric pressure.

Unconfined compressive strength A common measure of the strength of geologic and other materials (synonyms: uniaxial compressive strength; strength).

Unconsolidated Sediment that is loosely arranged or unstratified, or whose particles are not cemented together.

Unconsolidated aquifers Uncemented and generally loose geologic materials, such as sand and gravel, which are capable of providing groundwater supply.

Uncontrolled site Generally, an abandoned hazardous waste site; also, un- or poorly-engineered MSW dumping sites.

Underground Storage Tank An underground tank storing hazardous substances or petroleum products.

Underground source of drinking water (USDW) Any aquifer or its portion that supplies or may supply water to any public water supply system, or for human consumption, or contains less than 10 000 mg/L of total dissolved solids.

Underground storage tank system (UST) Underground storage tank system means one or more stationary devices, including any connected underground pipes, designed to contain an accumulation of petroleum, of which the volume, including the volume of underground pipes, is 10% or more below the ground surface.

Uniformly graded In geotechnical engineering, the term refers to a soil that has a narrow range in the grain size of its solids, e.g. dune sand.

Universal hydrologic equation An empirical relationship between precipitation, runoff, infiltration, and evapotranspiration.

Upland Part of the landscape that is above the bottomland.

V

Vapor pressure The pressure exerted at any temperature by vapor existing in equilibrium with its liquid or solid phases.

Viscosity The property of a substance to offer internal resistance to flow; its internal friction.

Volatilization Vaporization.

W

Waste exchange Matchmaking operation based on the idea that one manufacturer's waste may be another manufacturer's feedstock (related terms: *active exchange*; *passive exchange*)

Waste generator Any person, organization or facility engaged in activities that generate waste.

Waste management All activities, administrative and operational, involved in the handling, treatment, conditioning, storage and disposal of waste, including transportation.

Waste package The product of waste conditioning, which includes the waste form, waste container(s) and any internal barriers (e.g. absorbing materials or liners), prepared in accordance with requirements for handling, transportation, storage, and/or disposal.

Waste pile A noncontainerized accumulation of nonflowing solid hazardous waste.

Waste (radioactive) Radioactive materials at the end of their useful life or in a product that is no longer useful and requires proper disposal (see high-level waste, low-level waste, and spent nuclear fuel).

Well graded In geotechnics, it means a soil that shows a wide range in the grain size of its solids, e.g. glacial till.

Whistleblower/bounty provision The US EPA's provision to pay a reward for information leading to a criminal conviction.

Wipe sampling A procedure that involves taking samples by wiping the contaminated material and chemically and/or physically examining the "wipe" for the presence of hazardous substances.

Workability The relative ease with which an earth material lends itself to handling during excavation and construction.

Index

Geologic Time Scale

Era	Period	Epoch	Interval started (my*)	Interval duration (my)	Percent of time
Cenozoic		Anthropocene	1950 CE		
	Quaternary	Holocene	0.0118	0.0118	0.0002
		Pleistocene	1.6	1.599	0.035
	Neogene	Pliocene	5.3	3.7	0.08
		Miocene	23.7	18.4	0.4
		Oligocene	36.6	12.9	0.28
	Paleogene	Eocene	57.8	21.2	0.46
		Paleocene	66.4	8.6	0.19
Mesozoic	Cretaceous		144	77.6	1.69
	Jurassic	Age of reptiles	208	64	1.39
	Triassic		245	37	0.80
Paleozoic	Permian	Age of	286	41	0.89
	Carboniferous	amphibians	360	74	1.61
	Devonian	Age of fish	408	48	1.04
	Silurian		436	30	0.65
Ordovician		Age of	505	76	1.65
	Cambrian	invertebrates	570	65	1.41
Proterozoic	First multicellular life appears		2500	1730	37.61
Archean	First unicellular life appears		3800	1300	28.26
Hadean	Earth forms		4600	800	17.39

*= million years

Introduction to Waste Management: A Textbook, First Edition. Syed E. Hasan.
© 2022 John Wiley & Sons Ltd. Published 2022 by John Wiley & Sons Ltd.

Common Units and Conversion Factors

To convert	To	Multiply by
acres	hectare	0.405
	sq ft	43 560
acre-feet	gallons	325 900
	cub m	1233.5
barrels of oil	cubic feet	5.61
	gallons (US)	42
bars	lbs/sq in. (psi)	14.504
	kPa	100
BTU	calories	252
BTU/h	watts	0.2931
BTU/lb	cal/kg	0.556
Celsius	Fahrenheit	$1.8^{o}C+32$
cm/s	ft/d	2835
	m/d	864
cub m	cub ft	35.315
cub m/s	cub ft/s	353.107
cub km	cub miles	0.240
cub miles	cub km	4.167
cub ft	cub m	0.028
cub ft	gallons	7.48
cub ft	liters	28.32
cub ft/s	cub m/s	0.003
cub m	acre-feet	0.000811
cub yd	cub m	0.7646
Fahrenheit	Celsius	$0.555\ (^{o}F\text{-}32)$
ft	m	0.3048
ft of water	cub in of Hg	0.883

Introduction to Waste Management: A Textbook, First Edition. Syed E. Hasan.
© 2022 John Wiley & Sons Ltd. Published 2022 by John Wiley & Sons Ltd.

(Continued)

To convert	To	Multiply by
	psi	0.4335
ft/d	cm/s	0.000353
ft/mile	m/km	0.188
gallons (US)	liters	3.785
gallons (Imperial)	liters	4.546
gallons of water	lbs of water	8.345
gallons/min	L/s	0.063
grains/gallon	ppm	17.12
gal/d/sq ft	cm/s	0.0000472
gram (g)	oz	0.035
hectare	sq ft	107
	acres	2.469
inch of water	psi	0.0361
kg	lb	2.205
kg/sq cm	psi	14.22
kg/cub m	lb/cub ft	0.0624
knots	miles/h	1.151
m	ft	3.281
	yd	1.024
	km	0.001
m/d	cm/s	0.00116
m/km	ft/mi	5.283
mile	km	1.609
oz	g	28.350
oz (fluid)	liter	0.0296
lb	kg	0.454
lb/cub yd	lb/cub ft	0.037
	kg/cub m	0.593
lb/cub ft	kg/cub m	16.018
ppm	%	0.0001
	ppb	1000
ppb	ppm	0.001
%	ppm	10 000
sq m	sq ft	10.753
	sq yd	1.196
sq mile	sq km	2.589
yd	m	0.914
ton (short, US)	metric ton	0.9072

Conversion Factors for Hydraulic Conductivity

gallon/d/sq ft	cm/s	4.72 x 10^{-5}		
	m/d	.00408		
	ft/d	0.134		
ft/day	gallon/d/sq ft	7.48		
	m/d	0.305		
	cm/s	3.53 x 10^{-4}		
cm/s	m/d	864		
	ft/d	2835		
	gallon/d/sq ft	21 200		
m/day	cm/s	0.00116		
	gallon/d/sq ft	24.5	ft/d	3.28

Trace Concentration Equivalents

1 ppm = mg/kg, μg/g, ng/mg, mg/μL, μg/mL, ng/L,1000 ppb, 0.00001%
1 ppb = μg/kg, ng/g, μg/L, ng/mL, 0.001 ppm, 1000 ppt
1 ppt = ng/kg, ng/L, 0.000001 ppm, 0.001ppb

United Nations' classification of countries based on income (as of July 2021)

High-income countries	Upper-middle-income countries	Lower-middle-income countries	Low-income countries
Australia	Albania	Algeria	Afghanistan
Austria	Argentina	Angola	Burkina Faso
Bahamas	Armenia	Bangladesh	Burundi
Bahrain	Azerbaijan	Belize	Central African
Barbados	Belarus	Benin	Republic
Belgium	Bosnia and	Bhutan	Chad
Brunei	Herzegovina	Bolivia	Congo Democratic
Canada	Botswana	Cabo Verde	Republic of
Chile	Brazil	Cambodia	Eritrea
Croatia	Bulgaria	Cameroon	Ethiopia
Cyprus	China	Comoros	Gambia
Czechia	Colombia	Congo	Guinea
Denmark	Costa Rica	Côte d'Ivoire	Guinea-Bissau
Estonia	Cuba	Djibouti	Korea Democratic
Finland	Dominican	Egypt	People's Republic
France	Republic	El Salvador	Liberia
Germany	Ecuador	Eswatini	Madagascar
Greece	Equatorial	Ghana	Malawi
Hong Kong	Guinea	Haiti	Mali
Hungary	Fiji	Honduras	Mozambique
Iceland	Gabon	India	Niger
Ireland	Georgia	Indonesia	Rwanda
Israel	Guatemala	Iran Islamic Republic of	Sierra Leone
Italy	Guyana	Kenya	Somalia
Japan	Iraq	Kiribati	South Sudan
Kuwait	Jamaica	Kyrgyzstan	Sudan
Latvia	Jordan	Lao People's Democratic	Syrian Arab Republic
Lithuania	Kazakhstan	Republic	Togo
Luxembourg	Lebanon	Lesotho	Uganda

Introduction to Waste Management: A Textbook, First Edition. Syed E. Hasan.
© 2022 John Wiley & Sons Ltd. Published 2022 by John Wiley & Sons Ltd.

(Continued)

High-income countries	Upper-middle-income countries	Lower-middle-income countries	Low-income countries
Malta	Libya	Mauritania	Yemen
Netherlands	Malaysia	Mongolia	
New Zealand	Maldives	Morocco	
Norway	Mauritius	Myanmar	
Oman	Mexico	Nepal	
Poland	Montenegro	Nicaragua	
Portugal	Namibia	Nigeria	
Qatar	North	Pakistan	
Republic of Korea	Macedonia	Papua New Guinea	
Saudi Arabia	Panama	Philippines	
Singapore	Paraguay	Samoa	
Slovakia	Peru Republic of	Sao Tome and Principe	
Slovenia	Moldova	Senegal	
Spain	Romania	Solomon Islands	
Sweden	Russian	Sri Lanka	
Switzerland	Federation	State of Palestine	
Taiwan	Serbia	Tajikistan	
Trinidad and	South Africa	Timor-Leste	
Tobago United	Suriname	Tunisia	
Arab Emirates	Thailand	Ukraine	
United Kingdom	Turkey	United Republic of	
United States	Turkmenistan	Tanzania	
Uruguay		Uzbekistan	
		Vanuatu	
		Viet Nam	
		Zambia	
		Zimbabwe	

High income countries: Per capita gross national income (GNI) > $12695; Upper-middle income countries: GNI $12695-4096; Lower-middle income countries: GNI $4095-1046; Low-income countries: GNI < $1046 (World Bank).
Source: https://www.un.org/development/desa/dpad/wp-content/uploads/sites/45/WESP2022_ANNEX.pdf. Accessed 7 June 2022